THE

Natural Health

FIRST-AID
GUIDE

◆

THE EDITORS OF *NATURAL HEALTH* MAGAZINE

Thomas H. Rawls, Editor
Dan Seamens, Senior Editor
Bill Thomson, Senior Editor
Laurel Vukovich, Assistant Editor

◆

PANEL OF MEDICAL ADVISERS

David Eagle, O.M.D.   Jennifer Jacobs, M.D.
Holly Eagle, O.M.D.   Shari Lieberman, Ph.D., R.D.
Michael Reed Gach   Joseph Pizzorno, N.D.
Christopher Hobbs   Andrew Weil, M.D.

◆

THE
Natural Health
FIRST-AID GUIDE

◆

The definitive handbook
of natural remedies
for treating minor emergencies

◆

MARK MAYELL
and the Editors of
Natural Health Magazine

POCKET BOOKS
New York London Toronto Sydney Tokyo Singapore

The author of this book is not a physician, and the ideas, procedures, and suggestions in this book are intended to supplement, not replace, the medical advice of trained professionals. All matters regarding your health require medical supervision. Consult your physician before adopting the medical suggestions in this book as well as about any condition that may require diagnosis or medical attention.

The author and publisher disclaim any liability arising directly or indirectly from the use of this book.

POCKET BOOKS, a division of Simon & Schuster Inc.
1230 Avenue of the Americas, New York, NY 10020

Library of Congress Cataloging-in-Publication Data

Mayell, Mark.
    The *Natural Health* first-aid guide : the definitive handbook of
  natural remedies for treating minor emergencies / Mark Mayell and
  the editors of *Natural Health* magazine.
      p. cm.
    ISBN 0-671-79272-5
    1. Wounds and injuries—Alternative treatment. I. Natural
  health. II. Title.
  RC86.7.M39 1994
  616.02′52—dc20   93-11906
                                                                       CIP

First Pocket Books hardcover printing April 1994

10 9 8 7 6 5 4 3 2 1

Printed in the U.S.A.

Acknowledgments

The editors of *Natural Health* thank our dedicated panel of advisers for the immense help they offered during the writing of this book. The comments and suggestions of David Eagle, O.M.D., Holly Eagle, O.M.D., Michael Reed Gach, Christopher Hobbs, Jennifer Jacobs, M.D., Shari Lieberman, Ph.D., R.D., Joseph Pizzorno, N.D., and Andrew Weil, M.D., added much practical wisdom and medical knowledge to the final book. Others who read the manuscript and offered comments on it or helped us in various ways during the compilation of this book include Bob Felt, L. Larry McKinley, D.D.S., Barbara Tosti, Mark Blumenthal, Anthony Capobianco, D.O., Dana Ullman, Gene Bruce, Meera Helwig, Paul Gaylon, and Rudy Shur.

We'd also like to thank the seventy-five or so readers of *Natural Health* who responded to our query in the magazine for first-aid remedies that work (or should work but don't!). We received thoughtful letters from readers throughout the country and even from overseas. The overwhelmingly positive response and the outpouring of unique and useful first-aid suggestions inspired confidence in our assumption that natural first aid is a worthwhile topic for a book.

Finally, we thank literary agent Nat Sobel, and at Pocket Books editor Claire Zion and assistant editor Angela Kyle, for their guidance, enthusiasm, and support. Without their help, and the assistance of the other talented publishing professionals at Pocket Books, this book would still be an idea only.

Preface

Since 1971, the editors and writers of *Natural Health* magazine have been exploring the many facets of natural healing. We have interviewed or talked with thousands of people, both medical practitioners and laypeople, who have used the techniques of natural health to cure disease and promote longevity. Throughout this journey of social- and self-discovery, *Natural Health* has sought to relay to readers the best tools and techniques for helping the body heal itself. At the core of this search is a conviction widely shared by followers of natural methods of healing: the body has an innate wisdom capable of healing it, and by learning about the body and taking responsibility for its health, most people can be their own physician.

Much of what we've learned we've tried to summarize in the following pages, resulting in a book that we hope fills a significant gap in the literature on natural health. We believe that never before has anyone included such a variety of natural healing techniques in a first-aid book. (Indeed, the only similar books on the market are a few homeopathic guides to treating common emergencies.) In addition to being a unique guide to natural first aid, this book is similar to conventional books on first aid since it covers the basic, common sense steps that you need to know to treat—and to prevent—common medical emergencies. This book also goes beyond treatment and prevention, however, by providing readers with suggestions for natural remedies that can help the person recover from his or her injuries.

Section One describes the various therapies in the practice of natural health, including herbalism, homeopathy, acupressure, aromatherapy, nutrition, and folk healing. It also covers *Natural Health*'s top forty natural first-aid remedies. Readers can refer to these summaries if they need more background information on a technique or remedy described in Section Two of the book.

Section Two presents an alphabetically organized discussion of medical emergencies. Chapter 3 covers life-threatening accidents, including choking, shock, neck and spinal injuries, and unconsciousness. Chapters 4–22 cover loosely categorized emergencies: allergic reactions, bites and stings, bleeding, and so forth. For quick reference, on the first page of each chapter is a list of what the chapter covers and related injuries or emergencies that are dealt with in other chapters.

Section Three offers an extensive list of resources for contacting natural health practitioners or for finding more information about the tools, techniques, and remedies presented. We also review the commercially available natural first-aid kits.

Every effort has been made to check and verify the information included here. Nevertheless readers must take personal responsibility for how they use this information. The tools and techniques of natural medicine in general are safe and nontoxic. Yet individuals vary widely in how they respond to medicines. Medical emergencies by definition come on suddenly and require immediate action. Some can become life-threatening in a matter of minutes. There is no substitute for appropriate professional medical care when a serious emergency requires it. We have taken care to alert readers to signs or symptoms that call for such action, but no book, including this one, can cover all situations and possibilities.

A wise man once said, "The practice of medicine is a thinker's art, the practice of surgery a plumber's." Admittedly, injuries, accidents, and other medical emergencies sometimes require the services of a well-trained medical plumber. But even in first aid, there is much that the thoughtful, caring, and informed layperson can do to prevent a medical catastrophe and to jump-start the body's healing actions.

The Editors of *Natural Health*
Brookline, Massachusetts
Spring 1993

Contents

ACKNOWLEDGMENTS   **v**

PREFACE   **vii**

SECTION ONE

PREPARING FOR AN EMERGENCY

1 Introduction to Natural First Aid   **3**

The tools of natural healing: herbs and herbalism,
homeopathy and flower essences, acupressure and massage,
aromatherapy and essential oils, nutrition and
supplements, and traditional folk remedies
Emergency response guidelines

2 The Natural First-Aid Kit   **28**

Putting together the natural first-aid kit
Natural first-aid remedies: the top forty
The first-aid herbs
Homeopathic first-aid remedies
The flower essence first-aid remedy
The essential oil first-aid remedies
The first-aid vitamins and supplements
Food and household first-aid items
Actions of natural remedies

SECTION TWO
FIRST AID FOR EMERGENCIES

3 Basic Emergency Care   75

Assessing the emergency
Unconsciousness
Neck and spinal injuries
The ABCs: airway, breathing, and circulation
How to do rescue breathing
How to do chest compressions and cardiopulmonary
  resuscitation (CPR)
Shock
Choking
The recovery position
Transporting an injured person
Natural first-aid remedies for basic emergencies

4 Allergic Reactions   99

The many routes to reaction: pollen, dust, mold spores,
  animal dander, insect venom, drugs and vaccines,
  household products, foods
Acute reactions: the worst-case scenario
Basic first aid for mild allergic reactions
Recovery and prevention

5 Bites and Stings   115

Animal and human bites
Snakebites
Spider, scorpion, and tick bites
Bee, wasp, and ant stings
Stings from the sea
Mosquitoes, flies, fleas, and kissing bugs
Recovering from toxic bites and stings

6 Bleeding   164

Deep wounds
Minor cuts and scrapes
Nosebleeds
Bleeding under the nails
Bleeding from the rectum
Internal bleeding
Recovering from bleeding episodes

7   Bone Injuries   **185**

When bones fracture
When bones dislocate
Natural first-aid remedies for bone injuries
Recovery from bone injuries
Preventing bone injuries

8   Breathing Problems   **204**

Asthma attack
Croup and epiglottitis
Hyperventilation, panic attack, and breath-holding

9   Burns   **226**

Sunburn
Chemical burns
Electric shock
Lightning strike
Home or hospital?
Basic first aid for burns
Natural first-aid remedies for burns
Recovering from burns
Preventing burns

10   Contusions   **246**

When a bruise is more than a bruise
Black eye
Crushed fingers and toes
Natural first-aid remedies for contusions
Prevention and recovery

11   Convulsions and Seizures   **262**

Epilepsy
High fever (febrile) convulsions
Prevention and recovery

12   Dental Emergencies   **279**

Toothache
Teething
Loose, cracked, knocked-out, and extracted tooth
Mouth infections and abscesses
Preventing and recovering from dental emergencies

13 Dizziness and Fainting   299

Dizziness
Fainting
Natural remedies for benign dizziness and fainting
Prevention and recovery

14 Drowning   318

Rescuing a drowning person
The basic first-aid steps for drowning
Natural first-aid remedies

15 Exposure to Altitude and Cold   333

High-altitude sickness
Frostnip and frostbite
Hypothermia

16 Eye and Ear Emergencies   359

Foreign bodies in the eye
Snow blindness and frozen cornea
Chemical and thermal burns of the eyes
Acute glaucoma
Preventing and recovering from eye emergencies
Insects and other foreign bodies in the ears
Ruptured eardrum
Acute ear infections
Preventing and recovering from ear emergencies

17 Heat Illness   385

When the body overheats
Heat cramps
Heat exhaustion
Heatstroke
Recovering from heat illness
Preventing heat illness

18 High Fever   403

The mechanism of fever
Basic first aid for a high fever
Natural first-aid fever remedies

19 Muscle and Joint Injuries   **426**

Cramps
Strains, ruptures, and sprains

20 Poisoning   **443**

Chemicals and other toxic substances
Food poisoning
Recovery from acute poisoning

21 Skin Emergencies   **465**

Eruptions from poison ivy, oak, and sumac
Local skin infections
Splinters and fishhook removal
Recovering from skin emergencies

22 Travel Problems   **493**

Motion sickness
Jet lag

SECTION THREE

RESOURCES

ORGANIZATIONS, BOOKS, AND PRODUCTS   **507**

NATURAL FIRST-AID KITS   **519**

NATURAL FIRST-AID VIDEOS   **522**

INDEX   **525**

ABOUT THE ADVISORY PANEL   **541**

ABOUT THE AUTHORS: MARK MAYELL AND THE
   EDITORS OF *NATURAL HEALTH* MAGAZINE   **543**

EMERGENCY PHONE NUMBERS   **545**

PREPARING
FOR
AN
EMERGENCY

ONE

Introduction to Natural First Aid

THIS CHAPTER COVERS:

◆ *the tools of natural healing*
  • herbs and herbalism
  • homeopathic and flower essence remedies
  • acupressure and massage
  • aromatherapy and essential oils
  • nutrition and supplements
  • traditional folk remedies

◆ *Emergency response guidelines*

Accidents happen. As a matter of fact, in modern industrial societies such as the United States, they happen frequently. Accidents cause far more deaths and serious injuries to children and young adults than all diseases put together. Public health officials say that, on average, each year in the United States approximately:

◆ one in three people suffer a nonfatal injury
◆ 20 million people suffer an injury in their home
◆ 10 million people suffer an injury from a car accident
◆ 50,000 children become permanently disabled from accidental injuries
◆ 20 million children, one in four of all children, are injured badly enough to need medical treatment
◆ 140,000 people die from accidents and injuries, including about 45,000 from car accidents

According to federal Consumer Product Safety Commission statistics, many of these accidents and deaths are from common household—and usually safe—objects such as high chairs, garage-door openers, bathtubs, bicycles, sleds, cribs, toys, toothpicks,

3

baseballs, mouthwash, and water beds. The list of everyday objects and activities that can and do cause harm is almost endless.

Clearly, even the most alert, deliberate, and risk-averse among us is likely to get hurt occasionally. If your personality, on the other hand, runs more to the oblivious, wild, and bungee-jumping side of things, then you're likely to injure yourself quite frequently. Moreover, most people spend much of their lives in the company of coworkers, children, teammates, and others, who sometimes injure themselves and require help.

For selfish as well as social reasons, knowing basic first-aid techniques makes sense. Becoming more aware of first aid is like buckling your seat belt when driving. It's an expression of respect for the human body, an affirmation of life over death.

◆ The Tools of Natural Healing

According to a study published with considerable fanfare in early 1993, Americans are increasingly disenchanted with modern medicine. The study, based on the results of a survey of 1,539 Americans, was conducted by researchers at Boston's Beth Israel Hospital and summarized in the *New England Journal of Medicine*. The researchers found that today's health consumers are almost as likely to turn to acupuncturists, chiropractors, and other practitioners of natural medicine for relief from common ailments as people are to turn to internists and other practitioners of conventional medicine. The poll revealed that one in three of the survey respondents had consulted with an alternative practitioner such as an herbalist, homeopath, or dietary counselor within the past year.

According to David M. Eisenberg, M.D., one of the report's coauthors, the study "forces those of us in the conventional medical community to look at whether or not [the practices of natural medicine] are effective and whether they save money." Though the survey probably didn't surprise Eisenberg, whose 1985 book, *Encounters with Qi,* documented his firsthand experiences exploring Chinese medicine, it apparently did surprise most doctors. Why? Because patients by and large don't tell their conventional doctors about the natural practitioners they visit.

These natural practitioners run the gamut from doctors of ayurveda (the traditional medicine of India) to zone reflexologists (who practice a specialized form of massage). A short list of natural medical practices would include herbalism, chiropractic, therapeutic massage, folk medicine, biofeedback, self-hypnosis, homeopathy, spiritual healing, and orthomolecular medicine. Even such a short list represents an extremely diverse group of practices, but at the risk of oversimplifying, there are a few elements that most of these practices share and that tend to distinguish them from conventional medicine. These elements include:

Holism. The theory is that the whole is greater than the sum of the parts, and the parts cannot be reduced to isolated substances. In medical practice it means treat the patient, not just the disease or injury. It also means treat the underlying condition, not just the symptom.

Traditional wisdom combined with scientific/clinical evidence. *Traditional* is a problematic word. Physicians often refer to what they practice as "traditional medicine." In this book our preferred shorthand for Western, analytic, science-dominated medical practice is *conventional medicine. Traditional* we reserve to describe systems of medicine, such as that still practiced in much of China today, that are based at least in part on the handing down of accumulated wisdom from a variety of sources, including folk remedies and anecdotal evidence.

An alternative philosophy. Despite its gains, natural medicine still stands well outside many social and cultural norms in the United States. It offers a challenging and contrary view of healing (in essence, "nature heals, the doctor nurses") and the human body (in essence, "mind/body/spirit as energy field and holy being" rather than "body as machine") when compared with widely accepted Western beliefs. In the near future "alternative medicine" may truly be what is already a more popular descriptive term in Great Britain: *complementary medicine.* That is, a cooperative and inclusive effort at combining the best tools, techniques, and perspectives of Eastern and Western, modern and traditional, intuitive and analytic approaches.

A preventive and wellness-oriented approach. Practitioners of natural medicine in general place a much higher degree of emphasis on boosting immunity, preventing disease, and actively maintaining wellness than the more cure-oriented, crisis-management practitioners of conventional medicine. Natural healers readily recommend changes in lifestyle habits, diet, and attitudes to assist the healing process. Practitioners of modern medicine are more likely to focus on the role of germs, parasites, and viruses in causing disease and the importance of genetic factors than are natural healers.

Natural products and techniques. The emphasis among alternative practitioners is on looking to plants for herbs, the human hand for massage, nutrients from foods, and other substances found in nature to act as therapeutic partners with the body. That is, the healing tools and techniques are not so much "agents" that work on the body as aids that support and encourage the body's inherent wisdom and power to heal itself.

Of course, all of these characteristics are not shared by all methods of natural or alternative medicine. Nor are all holistic practitioners paragons of concerned and enlightened practice. There are any number of money-obsessed and symptom-treating chiropractors out there, as well as herbalists mechanically using herbs in much the same way most doctors use synthetic drugs. Yet as the recent survey shows, there are enough natural practitioners of medicine who exhibit at least some of these characteristics, which most patients consider to be useful in a healer, to begin to seriously erode the support shown for modern medicine in this country.

STORMING THE STRONGHOLD OF CONVENTIONAL MEDICINE

The principal methods of natural medicine that are used in this book include herbalism, homeopathy and flower remedies, aromatherapy and essential oils, acupressure and massage, nutrition and supplements, and folk remedies. We do not mean to slight practitioners or patients of such practices as chiropractic and acupuncture. This book primarily focuses on techniques of self-care. It describes what the individual can do immediately, with a few readily available remedies and tools, when an accident or emergency happens. In the sections on recovery from injuries and acute illnesses, it often recommends practices, such as chiropractic and acupuncture, that require a consultation with a medical professional.

Before taking a brief look at the tools of natural medicine that make up the bulk of the recommendations in this book, let's address head-on a reservation many people will bring to a book on "natural first aid." Aren't crisis intervention and emergency medicine the unassailable strong suits of conventional medicine? Don't emergencies by definition require just what conventional medicine best delivers: potent drugs and dramatic, often invasive interventions? Well, yes and no to both questions.

Yes, many persons with serious injuries benefit from oxygen tents and intravenous blood transfusions and other high-tech measures. When appropriate, though, the quick and simple first-aid steps the average person can provide may be absolutely essential to make sure that the seriously injured person even makes it to the hospital alive. In other words, it is not necessarily an either/or proposition. The provider of first aid must use what is readily available, and that is more often than not the kinds of remedies and common household items mentioned prominently throughout this book.

In addition, for each emergency medical condition in this book the reader is provided a summary of the basic first-aid steps that anyone should do, regardless of distinctions between "conventional" and "natural." (Such distinctions are often more blurred than one would think. Is applying pressure to arterial bleeding a natural self-care step or a conventional medical technique? Do such distinctions really matter?) Using the tools and techniques of natural medicine does not rule out using conventional techniques, and vice versa.

Yes as well, many synthetic drugs are fast- and dramatic-acting when compared to the more subtle effects of most homeopathic remedies, for instance. But other natural remedies, including some herbs and most essential oils, can be quite potent and provoke almost immediate biochemical reactions in the body. Keep in mind that active compounds in more than one-quarter of today's prescription drugs were originally derived from wild plants.

And finally, no, we should not leave totally unchallenged the belief that all high-tech emergency interventions are necessarily quick, 100 percent effective, or even necessary. Though this is not the place to answer the following questions, they are worth posing: To what extent does conventional emergency medicine suffer from the same potential excesses as does conventional medicine in general? That is, to what extent do the tools and technology themselves determine treatment and sometimes cause more problems than they cure? In the book *Emergency Room Diary*, Theodore Isaac Rubin, M.D., relates the following example:

"Two of us, Lazo and me, were desperately trying to get a marble out of a four-year-old girl's nose with all kinds of probes and forceps . . . [when Aiken] walks over to our case, gently takes forceps and nasal speculum out of our hands, and closes the kid's free nostril with his index finger and shouts, 'Blow!' The kid blows and out comes the marble. . . . I've learned a lesson though, several in fact: Use common sense! Don't complicate matters with fancy procedures! Keep an open mind! Keep loose, flexible!"

Would a close examination of the tools and techniques in widespread use in today's emergency rooms yield similar examples of "fancy procedures" taking precedence over common sense? Perhaps not. But perhaps, too, there is no reason to be defensive about the idea of natural first aid, no reason to turn exclusively to modern medicine for safe, simple, side-effect-free treatments for bites and stings, cuts, burns, and other common injuries.

Let many flowers bloom, as the Chinese say.

HERBS AND HERBALISM

Plants are perhaps the most widely used tool in natural medicine. The tradition of herbalism, using leaves, roots, seeds, and other parts of a plant as medicine, goes back tens of thousands of years. The first herbalist was some unknown early hominid who may have bound a wound with the leaf of some healing plant and noticed a positive effect. Not only are the exact origins of herbalism lost in the early pages of history, but some researchers believe herbalism may even predate humans.

Scientists have recently begun to study the field of zoopharmacognosy—how animals use certain plants medicinally. Field researchers have determined, for instance, that the woolly spider monkey of Brazil's rain forest uses at least a dozen different plants much as humans use herbs: to prevent certain diseases and to regulate bodily functions. For example, female woolly spider monkeys during mating season seek out a section of the forest that contains certain types of legumes. One of these plants has been found to increase the monkeys' sex drive because the legume contains a steroid that promotes bodily production of the hormone progesterone.

In cultures around the world, herbalists have long been using plant remedies for a variety of medicinal effects on the body. Various herbs have been found to relieve pain, stop or induce vomiting, reduce inflammation, decrease or increase the flow of urine, lower a fever, stimulate the bowels, soothe nerves, promote relaxation and sleep, and invigorate and strengthen ("tonify") the whole body.

Herbalism is both a science and an art. Unique healing plants grow throughout the world. Any single plant, moreover, varies in its makeup depending upon dozens of factors ranging from quality of soil to weather to harvesting and preparation techniques. Though many scientific studies have been performed on thousands of herbs and their chemical constituents for hundreds of years, much is still unknown in terms of how and why herbs help heal.

One of the current disagreements in the field relates to whether a more effective remedy is one that uses the whole herb or a partial extract. A whole-plant remedy as well as a partial extract may be from just the roots or leaves; either may be administered as a tea, compress, salve, and so forth. The distinction is whether all of the potentially hundreds of chemical compounds found in the plant are left intact, or whether certain compounds, presumably more active than others, are extracted from the whole plant or delivered in a standardized dose.

Many traditional and home-remedy-type herbalists favor using the whole plant. They argue that humanity's knowledge of how plants affect the body is incomplete, and leaving some parts of the herb out may result in potentially beneficial effects being missed. Moreover, some herbalists say, a plant's overall "energy," whether it is "warming" or "cooling" as the traditional herbalists of China, India, and elsewhere describe it, can be as important to healing as any single active ingredient.

Herbal companies have developed standardized commercial extracts only within the past decade or so. Herbalists who favor standardized extracts contend that research has clearly identified important active constituents in certain plants, and that the only way to make herbal prescribing and treatment more consistent is to develop such partial herbal remedies. One of the commercial appeals of standardized extracts is that although whole herbs or natural plant components cannot be patented, new herbal formulations and extraction and purifying processes can be.

"Whole vs. partial" is an interesting philosophical and practical debate within the field of herbal medicine. For the purposes of this book, however, it is not necessary for our recommendations to be limited to one side of the disagreement. In some ways the extracts are easier to use than whole preparations; for people who are new to herbs they're often a good choice. As you gain more confidence and knowledge about herbs and how to use them, decide for yourself what types of preparations you prefer.

Herbs are generally safe and nontoxic, but should be used with knowledge and caution. Christopher Hobbs, a fourth-generation herbalist and founder of the Institute for Natural Products Research in Capitola, California, says, "Although the charge is often made that herbalists say that all herbs are safe, no responsible herbalist would ever make such a claim. Herbs are often very safe, usually much safer than synthetic drugs, both for the person taking them and on our environment and energy resources. But herbs are complex mixtures of chemical compounds that can heal, change different body processes, and sometimes cause side effects, especially when overused or used unconsciously."

Paul Bergner, a widely published herbal writer and the editor of *Medical Herbalism,* a newsletter for practicing herbalists, agrees. He identifies three misconceptions about the limits of herbal self-care: that herbs have no side effects or contraindications at all; that an herb can "cure" a specific illness, especially a serious one; and that you can take advantage of herbs' benefits without study on your part or consultation with an expert. He also notes, "Many herbs that are safe for regular use may pose risks during pregnancy."

Herbs for medical emergencies are for the most part used in ways that minimize risks. The use is frequently onetime or limited in duration, rather than ongoing over a period of time. Another factor is that for wounds and skin injuries, herbs are typically applied topically, a more gentle route of administration compared to taking an herb (or any drug) orally. Nevertheless, herbs should be respected for their powers and treated as the medicines they are.

HOMEOPATHY AND FLOWER ESSENCES

The name *homeopathy* provides an immediate clue to the nature of this distinctive brand of medicine. *Homeopathy* is from the Greek words *homoio,* meaning "like, the same, similar" and *pathos,* for suffering or disease. The term was coined almost two hundred years ago by the German physician Samuel Hahnemann (1755–1843) to distinguish his new theory and practice from allopathy (from the Greek *allos,* "other"). Hahnemann discovered that certain diseases can be cured by giving minute doses of drugs that in a healthy person would produce symptoms like those of the disease. He called this idea that "like cures like" the law of similars. It is fundamentally opposed to the theory and practice of allopathy (which provides the philosophical foundation for conventional medicine). Allopathy posits that the best treatment of disease is by using drugs that produce effects different from or opposite to those produced by the disease.

Hahnemann was in part reacting to what he recognized as harmful medical practices of the time, which included bloodletting and prescribing large doses of extremely toxic substances such as mercury to treat illness. He abandoned this type of medicine and began to experiment with minute doses of herbs, minerals, and other substances, recording closely the symptoms and subjective feelings that these substances would provoke in a healthy person. He called these experiments "provings." Many thousands of provings were soon being collected into gigantic reference works called *materia medica*. These books summarized the dozens and dozens of symptoms associated with each of hundreds (later thousands) of homeopathic remedies. Practicing homeopaths use these references to match an individual's feelings and symptoms with the single best remedy that would help promote his or her healing.

Hahnemann maintained that the presence of small amounts of a homeopathic remedy in the body will stimulate the body's ability to fight off the disease. From his perspective, symptoms are as much a part of healing as they are of disease. To suppress symptoms is only to drive the disease deeper within the body, where it will soon manifest in a more serious condition.

Hahnemann believed that the body needed only a tiny push in the right direction to marshal its inherent healing powers. He also wanted to avoid the obvious problem of harmful toxic side effects from taking the drugs common at the time. Through experiment he found that extremely dilute solutions were effective at boosting the healing process, yet did not cause unwanted side effects. Moreover, the more dilute the remedy, the more powerfully it worked on the body to promote the symptoms of disease. The remedies increase in potency, however, only when they are produced in a specific manner, which involves shaking and succussing successive dilutions.

Homeopaths use vanishingly small amounts of a variety of substances, primarily plants such as arnica but also animal products such as snake and bee venom, and minerals. Conventional medical scientists contend that the minute amounts of these active substances left in diluted homeopathic remedies cannot possibly have any physical effect on the body. Homeopaths respond with two arguments, which may seem to be but are not necessarily mutually exclusive.

One, homeopaths say that allopathic medicine should not be amazed at the power of minute doses. Recent research confirms that tiny amounts of substances can often trigger physical and biochemical processes. For instance:

◆ Certain essential trace vitamins and minerals are absorbed and utilized by the body in infinitesimal quantities, yet their presence (or the lack of them) determines health or illness. For instance, a single atom of zinc set in the center of an enzyme molecule is brought into contact with 600,000 of its target molecules (carbonic acid) in a single second. Nutrition authority Rudolph Ballentine, M.D., points out in *Diet & Nutrition: A Holistic Approach,* "Our ability to rid ourselves of carbon dioxide through the exhaled air is then utterly dependent on the presence of these critically located atoms of zinc. Yet the total amount of this mineral in the body is so little that it was, up until a few years ago, considered to be of no significance!"

♦ A single milligram of acetylcholine, a nerve-impulse transmitter, dissolved in 500,000 gallons of blood can lower the blood pressure of a cat. Even smaller amounts will affect the beat of a frog's heart.

♦ The body manufactures only 50–100 millionths of a gram of thyroid hormone each day, resulting in a concentration of free thyroid hormone in the normal blood of one part per 10,000 million parts of blood plasma. Yet if this infinitesimal amount of thyroid is missing, the body experiences faulty metabolism and other health problems.

♦ Test-tube dilutions of up to 1:100,000,000 of pure penicillin will inhibit the development of certain microorganisms.

The second countering argument proposed by homeopaths represents in many ways a far more radical divergence from conventional medical theory. That is, homeopaths say that homeopathy is not strictly a biochemically based medicine. It is also a type of spiritual or energy medicine. Because some of the diluted remedies are so dilute that not even a single molecule of the original substance is left, homeopaths realize that the remedy acts through something other than a purely physical process. Medical historian Paul Starr notes, "Hahnemann and his followers saw disease fundamentally as a matter of spirit; what occurred inside the body did not follow physical laws."

Homeopathic educator Dana Ullman, author of *Homeopathy: Medicine for the 21st Century* and other books in the field, has described the mysterious, nonphysical nature of homeopathic remedies as "the essence of the substance, its resonance, its energy, its pattern." He notes that this essence may interact with the same "life force" that has been identified by practitioners of traditional Oriental medicine. Even so, homeopaths admit that the complete reason why infinitesimal-dose remedies work is not yet fully understood.

A number of scientific studies have tested homeopathic treatments. Some of the research, using double-blind and placebo-controlled methods, has supported homeopathic claims. Other research, most famously the 1988 study published in the respected British scientific journal *Nature* and then quickly rebutted by the magazine's own set of specially chosen "quack-busting" investigators, has yielded less than conclusive results.

Homeopathy flourished in the United States throughout the nineteenth century. By the early twentieth century there were twenty-two homeopathic medical schools, 15 percent of medical doctors were homeopathic physicians, and the remedies were available at over a thousand homeopathic pharmacies. Various factors led to homeopathy's decline in the United States—critics of homeopathy point to the development of stronger, more effective drugs, while proponents of homeopathy say that market forces and unfair competitive practices of a "modern medicine trust" were primarily to blame. Within the past two decades homeopathy's fortunes have reversed. Homeopathy in Europe maintained a much stronger position throughout the early twentieth century and remains a popular medical practice.

Homeopathic remedies come in either single or combination form (multiple single remedies combined to make a "cold and flu" remedy, for instance). These are available primarily as small tablets or pellets, but also with certain remedies as ointments, lotions, and tinctures. Remedies are widely available in health and natural foods stores and in some pharmacies. See "Chapter 2: The Natural First-Aid Kit" for a discussion of how to buy and use homeopathic remedies.

Since 1938 the U.S. Food and Drug Administration (FDA) has regulated homeopathic remedies listed in the official reference work, the multivolume *Homeopathic Pharmacopeia of the United States*. In general the FDA has taken the position that homeopathic remedies are safe and nontoxic. Until recently, homeopathic remedies were technically prescription drugs, though the FDA put little effort into enforcing a prescription-only policy. In the mideighties the FDA did become more concerned about some homeopathic remedies being marketed for serious illnesses such as cancer and heart disease. So in 1988 it issued new labeling and packaging guidelines that said, in effect, that those homeopathic remedies that were marketed for self-limiting conditions such as headache and the common cold can be sold as over-the-counter medicines available without a prescription. The FDA emphasizes that it has not tested homeopathic remedies for effectiveness.

Homeopath Jennifer Jacobs, M.D., says that combination remedies are best used as a stopgap measure for people who don't have access to the appropriate single remedy. "I don't use combination remedies in my practice and in general I don't recommend them. I think that combination remedies represent an untested, shotgun approach to healing. We really don't know how all of these combinations of single remedies work together."

On the other hand, Jacobs adds, "Many people claim to have been helped by combination homeopathic remedies, and through their use the benefits of homeopathic treatment have become available to a large segment of the population. These medicines are safe and have not been found to have any unpleasant side effects."

Boston-area homeopath Richard Moskowitz, M.D., has a similar mixed view on single versus combination remedies. He says, "How effective are the combination remedies? For some people, they are very effective indeed. I have always had patients who swore by this or that teething combination or cold remedy. Many have become justly popular in a short time, and I know of many instances in which they've saved my patients or their friends a visit to the doctor and considerable expense. . . . Nor can it be held against the combination remedies that they don't always work. Single remedies don't work all the time either, even in hands far more skilled than mine. . . . [But] falling ill and recovering from illness are concerted responses of the organism as a whole and cannot simply be programmed or manipulated through temporary relief of a symptom or technological control of an abnormality. This is the best reason for studying and using single remedies, which are distinctive and recognizable totalities that can match and therefore help us understand and work with the unique individuality of living patients."

There are an estimated 1,500 M.D.'s in the United States who treat patients at least in part with homeopathic remedies. A few states, including Connecticut, Arizona, and Nevada, license physicians to practice homeopathy, and a number of homeopathic professional organizations certify practitioners. There are, in addition, many thousands of people who practice some homeopathy but who are licensed as naturopaths, dentists, acupuncturists, and other types of medical practitioners. Levels of training in homeopathy vary. Discuss a homeopath's background, training, and experience with him or her before developing a therapeutic relationship.

Flower essences. Flower essences are homeopathically dilute liquid remedies made from wildflower blossoms. They were first developed into a healing system by the British homeopath Edward Bach. A physician and pathologist, Bach had a successful London medical practice in the 1920s but soured on what he felt was the impersonal, mechanical approach of conventional medicine. He realized, as he later wrote, that "disease will never be cured or eradicated by present materialistic methods, for the simple reason that disease in its origin is not material."

After sinking into a deep depression, in the spring of 1930 at the age of forty-four he set off for the Welsh hills to see if nature held any answers to his dilemma. A lover of nature, he soon began to explore the healing secrets of wildflower blossoms. After much study Bach found he was able to discover the special relationship between a plant's subtle life energies and certain human emotions. Bach said that wildflowers, when picked at special points in their blooming cycle and lovingly prepared, contained healing qualities. Over the next six years of life, until his death at age fifty, he formulated the standard repertory of thirty-eight Bach Flower Remedies, now known worldwide.

Bach's healing system used the essences from European wildflowers such as honeysuckle, holly, and wild rose. (Only a few of his remedies were not from European flowers; Rock Water is potentized spring water, and Cerato is from a Himalayan plant.) Bach chose wildflowers that are nonpoisonous. He disagreed with the common practice among formulators of conventional and homeopathic medicines of using toxic metals, plants, and other substances to make healing drugs.

Chiropractors, homeopaths, and other natural health practitioners who use flower essences say that the remedies are used to heal the body indirectly. The essences address not specific physical illnesses but moods, attitudes, and emotions such as fear, anxiety, and restlessness. As in homeopathy, flower essence practice is a form of subtle energy medicine. The remedies work on a vibrational rather than biochemical basis. The flowers are prescribed to act as a gentle catalyst, promoting health from within. As medical researchers continue to explore the new field of psychoneuroimmunology, flower essence practitioners contend that the links between emotions, biochemistry, and the physical condition of the body will become more evident.

Since Bach's death in 1936, his followers have marketed his original thirty-eight flower essences through the Bach Flowers Remedy company of Great Britain, which has trademarked the term Flower Remedy. *Flower essence* has become the generic description. Within the past two decades, flower essence practitioners around the world have expanded on Bach's findings and developed new flower essences. These are sold both as single-flower and combination-flower remedies. In the United States, for instance, Deva Flower Remedies, produced by Natural Labs Corp. of Sedona, Arizona, is a line of thirty-two combination flower essences with such names as Doubt/Lost Faith and Depression/Gloom. Pegasus Products in Boulder, Colorado, and Flower Essence Services of Nevada City, California, offer between them an expanding assortment of hundreds of flower essences.

For regulatory purposes the FDA considers Bach Remedies and other flower essences over-the-counter homeopathic drugs. Flower essences are included in the *Homeopathic Pharmacopeia of the United States*.

Flower essence formulators say that the best remedies are made when flower blossoms are picked in peak form. A common technique is to put the blossoms in a bowl of spring water and expose them to sunlight. This extracts the essence, which is then usually poured into brandy to dilute and preserve it. These flower essence "mother tinctures" may then be further diluted when taken.

Flower essences are typically liquid preparations meant to be taken in small doses of three to four drops, repeated about three times over fifteen to thirty minutes. There are some flower essence first-aid creams. As are all homeopathic-strength remedies, first-aid flower essences are completely nontoxic. If they don't have any positive effects, they will at least cause no ill effects. Using flower essences will not interfere with other forms of healing, including herbs, conventional medicine, and homeopathy.

ACUPRESSURE AND MASSAGE

Acupressure and massage are ancient forms of healing bodywork. The terms cover a variety of practices that use the fingers, hands, and elbows to touch, rub, and stimulate a partner's or one's own body. Though humans have no doubt been using for tens of thousands of years the technique of holding an injured body part, the origins of a systematic approach to healing bodywork go back about five thousand years to traditional Chinese practitioners.

Both *acupressure* and *massage* are generic terms for a wide variety of bodywork practices that differ in how the practitioner touches, strokes, and moves the body. Acupressure encompasses:

- shiatsu, a Japanese form of rhythmically applied pressure
- do-in, an Oriental self-care practice that includes movement, stretching, and invigorating self-massage techniques
- tui na, a Chinese form of massage designed to release muscle tension
- acu-yoga, an ancient Asian healing practice that combines yoga poses, stretching, breathing, and meditation, using the whole body to stimulate acupressure points

Some of the most popular forms of Western massage, such as Swedish and sports massage, use basic strokes on all parts of the body to increase blood circulation, lower muscle lactic-acid levels, and reduce overall bodily tension. Most forms of acupressure, and Eastern-based massage practices such as reflexology, take an approach to the body that is dramatically different from that of Western medical practitioners. Acupressurists press and stimulate key energy points on the body to affect the flow of vital energy within the person. This in turn stimulates the body's ability to heal itself.

The location of the key points are based on the Eastern conception of the body as an energy vessel. From the point of view of the traditional healers of China, India, and Japan, the body contains more than a dozen specific channels, or meridians, that direct the flow of energy. The meridians are the same on both sides of the body (see illustration #1). Most of the meridians are named for the organ systems that the channels are associated with, such as the gall bladder meridian and the kidney meridian. From the Oriental perspective, the meridian system is not merely hidden, blood-vessel-like channels; it is an intricate set of relationships and communications between organs, systems, and senses.

The life energy that is said to flow in these channels is called *qi* (or *chi*) by the Chinese, *ki* by the Japanese, and *prana* by the people of India. The life energy runs smoothly and harmoniously in the body of a person who is active and healthy, but is said to be blocked or deficient in a person who suffers from an illness or injury.

Practitioners of traditional Oriental medicine have developed a number of techniques to stimulate or balance the flow of energy. The energy model is the basis of acupuncture, in which slim needles are inserted into the skin at special points, and moxibustion, in which heat is applied to the skin. Since acupressure practitioners press on the body's vital energy points primarily with the fingers and hands, acupressure is the simplest and

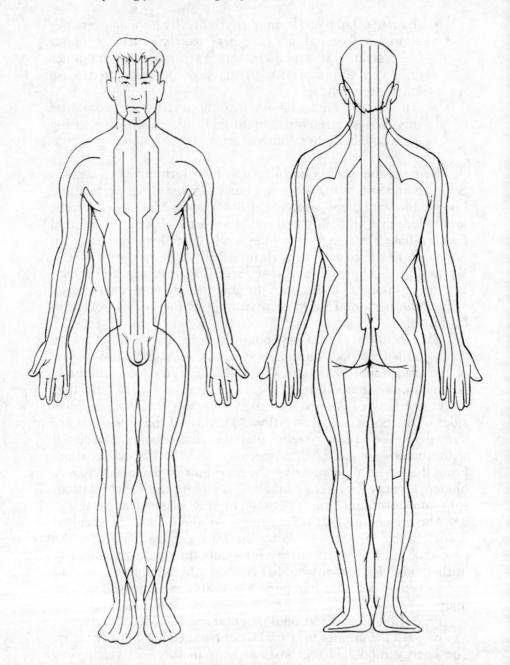

Illustration #1:

The traditional healers of the Orient have identified more than a dozen
channels, or meridians, that direct the flow of vital energy throughout
the body.

easiest-to-use method for harmonizing the body's life energies and balancing the flow of *qi*. Acupressure techniques are also the most practical for first-aid and self-care techniques. Though acupressure may be used in conjunction with herbs, acupuncture, exercise, and breathing techniques, it is powerful enough to boost the body's healing efforts on its own.

Among the most prominent popularizers of self-care acupressure in the United States are Michael Reed Gach, founder of the Acupressure Institute in Berkeley, California, and author of *Acupressure's Potent Points* and numerous books on the topic (and a member of the advisory panel for this book), and Cathryn Bauer, author of *Acupressure for Everybody* and other books on acupressure for common ailments.

Though acupuncture practitioners need to know the location of hundreds of energy points on the body, for first-aid purposes you need to know the location of only two dozen or so of the most common. These points can come in handy after a trauma by affecting the bodily systems that help control such functions as breathing, circulation, and consciousness.

Forms of acupressure differ according to how much pressure is applied to which points and for how long. In general, here are the basic steps for applying the acupressure treatments recommended in this book.

Create a healing environment for the technique. This is often difficult during an emergency, when treatment must be done on the spot. But it helps the injured person begin to recover and increases the healing effects of acupressure. The person doing the acupressure should wash his or her hands and briskly rub them together to warm them. Both the injured person and the person doing the acupressure should try to relax, get in a comfortable position, and concentrate on the breath.

Apply pressure to the appropriate point or points for two to three minutes. Most people prefer to apply pressure using the tip of the middle finger or the thumb (fingernails should be trimmed), but you can also use other fingers, your knuckles, or the palm or side of your hand. Use firm, deep, but not painful pressure. Apply it in a steady, stationary manner, at an angle of ninety degrees to the skin. Get over the point with your body and use your body weight to gradually penetrate to deeper levels of the skin. Gach recommends that the pressure be firm enough to "hurt good—something between pleasant, firm pressure and outright pain." He says you should use a firmer, deeper touch on areas of the body such as the shoulders and back than on the more sensitive areas of the body such as the face and abdomen. When the treatment is over, release the pressure gradually.

Acupressure in general is safe and has no side effects. There are, however, some restrictions. You shouldn't press directly on injured, burned, or infected areas. Avoid touching an area with a malignant tumor or a contagious skin condition. You also shouldn't apply hard pressure to a recently formed scar. Always stop or use less pressure if the treatment is causing severe pain or is aggravating the injury. Consult with a knowledgeable practitioner or a medical professional before performing acupressure on a pregnant woman, a seriously ill person, or anyone with an acute contagious condition.

AROMATHERAPY AND ESSENTIAL OILS

Aromatherapists use essential oils derived from the leaves, barks, roots, flowers, resins, or seeds of plants to address physical and psychological health problems. Typically the oils are inhaled for respiratory and nervous problems or applied topically or added to a bath for skin and muscle problems. (Essential oils are rarely taken internally, and then only with caution and under the instruction of someone knowledgeable about essential oils.) Thus, in some ways the term *aromatherapy* is a misnomer, since it implies that the only effect that essential oils have on the body comes through their being inhaled, or smelled, through the nose.

A number of ancient civilizations used aromatic plants, gums, and oils in their cooking, cosmetics, or spiritual practices. The extent to which they used essential oils for medical purposes is unclear. The Babylonians, Chinese, and Egyptians learned how to distill plants to obtain essential oils. One four-thousand-year-old Egyptian papyrus mentions "fine oils and choice perfumes." The Egyptians even used the aromatic gums and oils of cedar and myrrh in the mummification process to stop decay. The Greeks and Romans continued the use of essential oils, often adding aromatics to their baths. Among these civilizations there is better evidence for medical applications of essential oils, including their use on battlefields to heal wounds.

Essential oils' popularity has risen and fallen in the past two millennia depending upon factors that include technology, trade, and the philosophy of medicine. The great Arab physician Avicenna (980–1037) refined the distillation process and produced essential oils of high purity. Another medical pioneer, the Swiss physician Paracelsus (1493–1541), also explored the healing powers of essential oils. The use of essential oils in Europe increased after the Crusades. Along with herbs, essential oils were an integral part of Western medicine until the advent of scientific chemistry and the development of synthetic drugs in the nineteenth and twentieth centuries. Though the medicinal use of essential oils declined, they continued to be used in cooking and cosmetics.

Despite the long history of essential oils, the word *aromatherapy* is relatively new. The French cosmetic chemist Dr. René-Maurice Gattefossé coined the term in the late 1920s. He became fascinated with the healing potential of essential oils after he burned his hand and on impulse plunged it into a container of Lavender oil. The hand healed quickly and without blistering. The French led the rebirth of interest in aromatherapy and it remains popular in France, Great Britain, and Italy today, with over a thousand medical practitioners using essential oils in France alone.

The proponents of aromatherapy say that certain essential oils applied to the skin can play a useful role in healing wounds, for instance by promoting the formation of scar tissue, killing bacteria and viruses, and increasing circulation to an area of the body. Essential oils are also used medicinally by being inhaled. The body's sense of smell has been shown to have close connections to mood, emotions, and even sexual desire. These connections have long been recognized and exploited by the perfume industry, a major producer and buyer of essential oils until the advent of synthetic fragrances around 1930.

Researchers at Columbia University's Howard Hughes Medical Institute recently confirmed that nerve cells located high in the nose reach into a part of the brain associated with emotion and memory. Scientists at the Memorial Sloan-Kettering Cancer Center, the Fragrance Research Fund in New York, and elsewhere are trying to determine whether it is possible to use fragrances to send messages directly to the brain. Large cosmetic companies aren't waiting for the scientific data to catch up with what they know. Estée Lauder has introduced Sensory Therapy oil for bathing, and gels for massage with such names as Sleep Time and Energy Boost.

Some aromatherapists prefer to explain how essential oils work by referring to the "vital energy" of the whole plant. Aromatherapists and scientists with a more analytic and reductionistic approach focus on essential oils' chemical constituents and how they affect the body. These chemical constituents can be extremely numerous and complex. Scientists have isolated some 160 components of the essential oil of Lavender and don't think they've found them all. Certainly at this point the components and mechanisms by which essential oils act on the body are only partially understood.

Among the recent pioneers of aromatherapy is Dr. Jean Valnet, a French medical doctor and former army surgeon who used essential oils during World War II to treat severe burns and other battle injuries. He has written extensively since the 1960s on the medical applications of essential oils and is the author of the popular book on the topic *The Practice of Aromatherapy*. Another popularizer in the United States is the British aromatherapist Robert Tisserand, author of *The Art of Aromatherapy*. Though the practice of aromatherapy remains greater in Europe than in the United States, interest here is growing, and many natural foods stores carry lines of essential oils.

Essential oils are not greasy and fatty like vegetable oils. Rather they're volatile, quickly evaporating from the skin. Oils may be thin or thick, clear or colored. Some seven hundred plants have been used to make essential oils, though most aromatherapists use only one hundred or so of these. A dozen essential oils can cover almost all first-aid problems you're likely to face. (See "Chapter 2: The Natural First-Aid Kit" for guidelines on how to use essential oils.)

Properly used, essential oils have no side effects. In general, however, essential oils are extremely potent, more so than most of the other natural remedies used in this book. Essential oils should be kept out of the reach of children. Essential oils are used in minute amounts for healing purposes. Measurement is by the drop, and most essential oils are diluted before being applied to the body. Topically some can cause allergic reactions and photosensitivity, so it is a good idea to patch-test on the skin before applying to large areas of the body. Certain oils should be avoided if you're pregnant, have a seizure disorder, or have high blood pressure.

Some of the stronger oils may counteract homeopathic remedies. Check with your medical practitioner if you want to use oils in conjunction with homeopathic remedies. On the other hand, practitioners say that aromatherapy is compatible with flower essences such as the Bach Remedies.

NUTRITION AND SUPPLEMENTS

The origins of therapeutic nutrition—preventing or treating disease through diet and supplements—go back to at least the ancient Egyptians. Some of their writings from circa 1500 B.C. refer to dietary cures for various diseases. The great Greek physician Hippocrates (c. 460–377 B.C.) is not only the "father of medicine" but the "father of practical nutrition." One of his most famous sayings, "Let thy food be thy medicine," neatly summarizes the movement's emphasis on diet in controlling disease.

One of the earliest scientific inquiries into the role of nutrients was performed in 1753 by the Scottish physician Dr. James Lind. He discovered that citrus fruit could prevent scurvy, though the active ingredient (ascorbic acid, or vitamin C) was not identified until early in the twentieth century. Another pioneering finding, in the early 1800s, was the discovery of dietary calcium's importance to bone growth. "Nutritional factors" were named *vitamines* in 1911 by Casimir Funk, and recent years have seen an explosion of scientific study on the effects of vitamins, minerals, and other nutrients on physiological processes. Seminal figures such as Abram Hoffer and Linus Pauling have confirmed various important health benefits of nutrition, not only in the prevention of disease but for treatment: vitamin A/beta carotene to treat diseased skin, vitamin D for some cancers, magnesium for certain types of heart pain, fish oils for arthritis, and more. Within the past decade research has exploded to the point that today there are more important scientific discoveries on nutrition and disease in a single year than there were in any entire century up to the current one.

The federal government has established recommended daily allowances (RDAs) for most of the currently known vitamins and minerals. The RDAs are average levels meant to prevent overt nutritional disease, not necessarily to maximize health. With a few exceptions essential nutrients are not manufactured in the body and must be obtained from foods or supplements. Many nutritionists and dietary counselors contend that most Americans routinely do not obtain sufficient nutrients from diet alone and would benefit greatly from supplementation. In addition, studies have shown that illness and injury can substantially increase the body's need for certain nutrients.

So-called natural vitamins and supplements have some minor but noteworthy differences from conventional brands. A few vitamins, such as vitamin E, differ slightly in their natural form compared to when they are synthetically produced. The research is not complete but there's some indication that the natural form may present advantages in terms of factors like bioavailability, the rate at which the nutrient enters the bloodstream and is circulated to specific organs. In most cases, however, supplement producers use the same synthetically derived compounds for the principal ingredient of natural and conventional tablets. Supplements may differ significantly, however, in the other ingredients that make up a vitamin or mineral tablet, such as the binding and preserving agents. Natural supplements in general have no artificial colors, flavors, or sweeteners, and no chemical binders or preservatives. In some cases natural supplements are strictly vegetarian, by substituting for the animal-based gelatin used to make capsules, for instance.

With minor exceptions (such as potassium tablets larger than 99 mg), vitamins, minerals, and other micronutrients don't require a doctor's prescription to buy. They are widely available over the counter in drugstores, health and natural foods stores, and by mail order.

Taking large doses of some vitamins (particularly the fat-soluble ones, such as vitamins A and D) over extended periods of time can cause adverse health effects. Some large doses of supplements should also be avoided by pregnant women, infants, and people with certain illnesses. The supplement levels recommended in this book are safe and nontoxic for most people. Some of the recommendations, however, may present some risk to certain individuals. For instance, the common recommendation to take two to five grams per day of vitamin C for its wound-healing and other benefits should not be followed by pregnant women, since vitamin C at that level may induce a miscarriage. It is best always to check with a knowledgeable practitioner if you have a special health condition or are unsure about the safety of a supplement program.

Some natural vitamins and supplements are quite large. You can crush them into a powder and ingest, or add the powder to your favorite drink, to make them easier to take.

TRADITIONAL FOLK REMEDIES

Folk remedies for common ailments such as cuts, burns, bites, and stings come from a variety of sources. They come from your grandmother, from old herbal reference books, from "friends of a friend," from a culture's myth and folklore. Folk medicine is made up of tried-and-true, though mostly untested by scientific methods, remedies employing plants and foods and virtually any substance likely to be found in peoples' kitchens, gardens, and yards. Folk remedies tend to vary from culture to culture, depending upon local plants, culinary traditions, and other factors.

That traditional folk remedies work, at least some of the time, is affirmed in part by their longevity. Modern medical practitioners are likely to dismiss them out of hand as "snake oil." Therein lies a tale.

A popular nineteenth-century folk medicine, since the turn of the century snake oil has become synonymous with bogus health claims for traditional substances. Recent research into the health benefits of certain fatty acids, such as the omega-3s found in fish oil, inspired one physician, Dr. Richard Kunin, to take a fresh look at snake oil. According to his letter to the *Western Journal of Medicine*, in the late 1980s he tested snake oils and found they were indeed high in omega-3s. Some snake oils were even higher in the health-boosting fatty acids than the cold-blooded fish often recommended even by conventional physicians to help control inflammatory disorders and cardiovascular disease. In other words, snake oil peddlers were probably right in claiming their product could help cure arthritis.

"It is not unusual that an ancient remedy or a folk medicine turns out to have some merit," Kunin concluded. "What is unusual is that this particular therapy, snake oil, has long been our favorite symbol of quackery. I find it humbling that the science of today invests the quackery of yesterday with new credibility."

Some other notable examples of new scientific research that validates a traditional folk remedy include willow as a pain reliever, sugar as a wound healer, gold for arthritis, garlic for heart problems, sunlight for jaundice, onions for asthma, and meat tenderizer as a sting remedy. Oranges, lemons, and limes were merely a folk cure for scurvy until vitamin C was identified in 1928. Lest we seem to overstate the case, many folk remedies do not now, and may never have, an identifiable, nonplacebo, physiological effect on the body. That they may nevertheless work cannot be completely denied.

As herbalist James Green has written, folkloric medicine "is at once the most ancient of sciences and the most advanced, for it embraces all healing science known to us. Folkloric medicine is forever now in the making. There are no experts in folkloric herbalism; there are myriads of participants, and we are forever students. We are all contributors and we are all heirs to its wisdom and its practicalities."

Many of the folk remedy suggestions included in this book came from longtime readers of *Natural Health*. Others have filtered into our national treasury of folk remedies from various sources or been suggested by natural healers who've used them successfully. As with the other remedies suggested in this book, we don't recommend that anyone forgo basic medical care to rely exclusively on folk medicine.

◆ Emergency Response Guidelines

Medical emergencies can be frightening and upsetting for the victim. All too often, the first-aid giver is frightened and upset as well. An agitated state breeds confusion, hurry, and possibly treatment mistakes that worsen the victim's condition. That's one of the reasons why proper preparation is crucial for effective emergency response. A person who is prepared, who has at hand a good first-aid kit and guide, and who has posted emergency numbers next to phones (or better yet entered them into the phone's speed-dialing memory) has a better chance of staying calm and providing effective care than the ill-prepared person faced with an emergency. Parents should also instruct children on the following elements of quick and safe emergency response.

Remain calm and respond promptly. In other words, don't panic but don't stop to ponder your life goals either. Move quickly and efficiently.

If necessary, call for emergency help as soon as possible. There are no hard and fast rules for when to rush immediately to the phone and when to administer immediate first aid. When you're alone, you have to rely on your common sense. If a person has arterial bleeding or is not breathing, for instance, it is best to offer immediate care. When the immediate threat to life is over, call as quickly as possible. Except to call for help, don't leave the person alone.

Quickly assess the situation and prioritize your first-aid actions. Among your first considerations should be whether you and the victim face an ongoing and immediate danger, from a fire, toxic fumes, or moving traffic, for instance. First aid should always be administered in a way that doesn't endanger the caregiver. Becoming another victim won't help the person with an injury.

In assessing the person's injuries, first do whatever is necessary to keep the person alive. When examining the person, assume the worst. That is, it is always safest to act as if the person has more severe injuries than is immediately visible. Check the person's vital signs immediately to determine whether the person is in need of immediate cardiopulmonary resuscitation (CPR). Also check for signs of severe bleeding, shock, acute poisoning, broken bones, or exposure injury. Look for emergency medical information on a tag or bracelet.

Do no harm. Your goal is to treat the injury or illness without doing anything that could conceivably make the condition even worse. In general you should never:

- move a person with potentially serious injuries, use force to move body parts, or move body parts without supporting them in some way
- give food or water unless you're sure it is safe and necessary (never administer anything orally to an unconscious person)
- do anything that would potentially block his or her airway, such as putting a pillow under an unconscious person's head or laying him flat on his back (unless to do CPR)

Treat the person as well as the symptom or condition. There is not just a broken arm lying on the ground before you, there is a person with a broken arm. Attend to the needs and fears of the individual. In other words, don't emulate those robo-docs notorious for walking up to a patient's bed and considering only the chart not the person. Especially if you're offering first aid to a stranger, if possible identify yourself to the person. Obtain his or her permission to perform first aid while keeping in mind he or she may be confused and unable to make rational decisions. Tell him or her what you intend to do, and don't unnecessarily violate the person's sense of privacy or modesty.

Keep these basic guidelines in mind when you administer first aid and the outcome is likely to be as successful as humanly possible.

TWO

The Natural First-Aid Kit

THIS CHAPTER COVERS:

- ◆ *putting together the natural first-aid kit*
- ◆ *natural first-aid remedies: the top forty*
- ◆ *the first-aid herbs*
- ◆ *homeopathic first-aid remedies*
- ◆ *the flower essence first-aid remedy*
- ◆ *the essential oil first-aid remedies*
- ◆ *the first-aid vitamins and supplements*
- ◆ *food and household first-aid items*
- ◆ *actions of natural remedies*

SEE "SECTION THREE: RESOURCES" FOR:

- ◆ *review of commercially available natural first-aid kits*

The natural first-aid kit that is best for you and your family will depend upon several factors. Do you prefer using herbs to homeopathic remedies? What other natural remedies are you comfortable with? Will you be using the kit mainly around the home or while you are hiking and camping? How close are you to the nearest medical professional? How much (or little) medical training do you have?

Since the answers to such questions vary markedly, it's clear that there is no single perfect natural first-aid kit. Rather there are as many variations on the theme as there are individual users. Some people may prefer buying one of the half dozen or so natural first-aid kits on the market today. They come in all sizes and shapes, with most specializing in either homeopathic or herbal remedies (see "Resources" for a review of the most popular ones). Many people will prefer to put together a personalized kit, one that may contain not only herbs and homeopathic remedies but essential oils, vitamins, enzyme supplements, and other natural products. In this chapter we'll take a look at the materials and medicines that can most profitably be included in any natural first-aid kit. These are also the first-aid tools that we most frequently refer to throughout this book.

◆ Putting Together the Natural First-Aid Kit

Some of the elements of the natural first-aid kit are the same as you would find in a conventional kit. Soap, dressings, and bandages are needed to clean and cover wounds, cloth and safety pins to immobilize a limb, and so forth. Here are the basics:

DRESSINGS AND BANDAGES

elastic (Ace) bandages, 2–3 inches wide: for wrapping sprains, to apply pressure to large, bleeding wounds

sterile gauze pads, various sizes (approximately 2×2, 3×3, and 4×4 inches): to cover cuts, scrapes, and abrasions

sterile alcohol-saturated pads: to clean skin wounds

roll of adhesive waterproof tape, ½ inch wide: to hold dressings

commercial bandages (Band-Aids), various sizes: to protect minor cuts and scrapes

butterfly bandages: to pull the edges of a cut together

large triangular cloth, approximately $40 \times 40 \times 55$: to make a sling, secure splints to a broken ankle

eye pad: to cover injured eye

instant cold pack: to prevent swelling of soft-tissue injuries

INSTRUMENTS

scissors: for cutting dressings and bandages

tweezers: for removing splinters, ticks, and foreign objects

thermometer: for measuring high fever

safety pins: for securing slings and splints

eyewash cup: for irrigating eye

MISCELLANEOUS

mild soap: for washing out minor cuts and scrapes

flashlight

matches

cotton swabs

insect sting kit: a necessity for anyone who experiences allergic
reactions to stings

snake kit with venom extractor: important if you live near or will
be hiking in snake country

◆ Natural First-Aid Remedies: The Top Forty

The following list of natural remedies includes thirteen herbs,
nine homeopathic remedies, one flower remedy, six essential oils,
four vitamins/supplements, and seven foods or household items.
These are the most basic and essential natural first-aid remedies.

HERBS

aloe	ipecac
calendula	pau d'arco
chamomile	plantain
comfrey	slippery elm
echinacea	witch hazel
ephedra	yarrow
goldenseal	

HOMEOPATHIC REMEDIES

Aconite	*Hypericum*
Apis	*Ledum*
Arnica	*Rhus tox*
Arsenicum	*Ruta*
Calendula	

FLOWER ESSENCE

Rescue Remedy

ESSENTIAL OILS

Chamomile	Lavender
Clove	Peppermint
Eucalyptus	Tea Tree

NUTRITION AND SUPPLEMENTS

bromelain	vitamin C
papain	vitamin E

FOODS AND HOUSEHOLD ITEMS

activated charcoal	garlic and onions
baking soda	hydrogen peroxide
cold water	vinegar

First, a note about distinguishing among herbs, homeopathic medicines, and essential oils. As you notice from the above lists, some plants play an important role in different branches of natural medicine, and it's necessary to distinguish how the plant has been prepared for its use as a remedy. For instance, both herbalists and homeopaths use calendula (a form of the common marigold plant) to make tablets, tinctures, lotions, ointments, and other types of preparations. There is also an essential oil of calendula used by herbalists and aromatherapists. The level of active chemical constituents and the potency of these preparations vary dramatically. The essential oil is the most concentrated form in terms of chemical constituents, and in general essential oils need to be diluted before they can safely be applied to the skin. Some homeopathic preparations, on the other hand, may not have even a single molecule of calendula, though their potency is high for other reasons. Thus, when we say "apply calendula to a cut," it's necessary to be clear as to what type of preparation we're talking about. The convention we'll follow will be to:

- refer to herbal remedies using lowercase letters in a roman typeface: calendula tincture, calendula ointment
- refer to homeopathic remedies using an initial capital and italics: *Calendula* ointment
- and refer to the medicines in the form of essential oils and the one flower essence (Rescue Remedy) using an initial cap and roman typeface (Calendula oil)

The first time we mention a plant we'll provide the Latin name for the genus and species, to avoid the confusion that sometimes arises from the multitude of common names. For instance comfrey (Latin: *Symphytum officinale*) is sometimes called boneset, a name shared by a different plant *(Eupatorium perfoliatum).* Consumers should be aware of this potential for misidentification of plants when they purchase remedies at natural foods stores or Oriental pharmacies.

Also note that unless stated otherwise, the dosage recommendations for herbs and supplements in this book are for adults. Children's dosages are usually one-half, one-third, or even less, depending on the child's size.

◆ The First-Aid Herbs

Some herbs are as easy to use as aspirin: open the jar and pop a pill. In many cases though, a somewhat different form will help speed the herb's healing ingredients to where they're most needed. Here's a rundown of the most common ways herbs are prepared and used.

Fresh or dried plant. This is the herb in its most natural, unprocessed forms. The fresh herb is the recently picked leaves, stems, flowers, roots, or bark of a plant. These begin to dry immediately upon being picked so most fresh herbs are obtained from growing your own or wildcrafting it (picking it in the wild), rather than purchasing it at the natural foods stores. Herbal manufacturers pick the fresh herb and dry it. They then lightly pulverize or powder it and package it in bottles or plastic bags. Herbs lose potency over time. Look for a fresh smell and taste, and natural, not-washed-out colors.

Tea. Start with about one-half to one ounce, or one teaspoon, of dried herb or three teaspoons of fresh herb per cup of water. Pour boiling water over and steep for five minutes or so before straining. Only the herb's water-soluble elements will be present.

Infusion. Prepare a tea but steep it longer, for ten to twenty minutes, so it becomes considerably darker and more potent. Like a tea it may be bitter and need to be sweetened for drinking. An infusion has a limited shelf life in the refrigerator, so most people make only as much as they need at the moment. Teas and infusions are appropriate for herbs in which the upper parts of the plant, the flowers and leaves, contain the active ingredients.

Decoction. This is essentially an infusion that is boiled instead of steeped. A decoction is used for herbs that are hard and woody, in which the roots and barks harbor the main healing chemicals. Prepare as you would an infusion, cutting the herb into small pieces or grinding it into a powder, and adding to boiling water. But instead of turning off the heat and steeping the herb for ten to twenty minutes, cover the pot and keep the water boiling at a simmer. Strain while still hot. Making a decoction helps to break down the tougher cell walls of barks and roots and allows the transfer of the active chemicals. Unfortunately, the high heat does tend to destroy some of the herb's volatile oils.

Tincture. You make a tincture by steeping herbs in an alcohol/water mixture for several weeks. This is a more involved process, obviously, and most people prefer to buy ready-made tinctures at the natural foods store. The use of alcohol allows you to extract more of the plant's active ingredients and preserves the solution so that it has a longer shelf life. Most herbal books provide directions for making a tincture at home (see "Resources").

Lotion. Herbal companies make lotions by mixing a water extract with vegetable glycerin. This stiffens the preparation without making it oily.

Salves and ointments. These are semisolid fatty preparations that liquefy on contact with the skin. The distinction is minor: some herbalists consider a salve to be a stiff ointment. They're both easy to apply and are used in similar manners. You can make your own salves by adding essential oils or herbal concentrates to beeswax, and your own ointments by adding one teaspoon of herbal tincture for each ounce of natural skin lotion.

Liniment. This is a mixture of alcohol, or in some cases vinegar, with herbal oils. The active herbs are often ones like cayenne, camphor, peppermint, and eucalyptus, which work to increase circulation and remove pain from muscles and ligaments.

Fluid, solid, and concentrated-solid extracts. These are concentrated tincture products. Solid extracts are made by evaporating the tincture to obtain a gummy residue, which is dried and then used to make tablets or capsules. Standardized extracts, in which most (though not all) of the active ingredients of the whole plant are included in specific percentages, have become widely available in recent years.

Tablets, capsules, and lozenges. These are all pill-sized, dry concentrates. A tablet is simply the powdered herb and a base compressed into a pill, sometimes with added binders and stabilizers. A capsule is a gelatin container filled with the herb in the form of a powder, juice, or oil. And a lozenge is the powdered herb or oil combined with sugar and mucilage or gum into pills that are meant to be sucked.

Essential oils. Some plants can be steam-distilled or cold-pressed to yield pure essential oils, aromatic concentrates of most of the important chemical constituents (see below for more information on essential oils).

HOW TO APPLY HERBS EXTERNALLY

Almost all of the basic herb forms—fresh or dried herb, tea, infusion, decoction, essential oil—can be applied to the body to promote wound healing, treat a burn or skin irritation, reduce inflammation, and more. Here are the most commonly used applications.

Poultice. This is simple and basic: apply the herb itself, fresh or dried, directly to the skin. To use the dried herb, make a paste by adding hot water and mixing. Fresh leaves or flowers are usually crushed or bruised first and then applied to the skin. Some people prefer putting the paste or leaves between two thin layers of gauze, and taping that to the injured area.

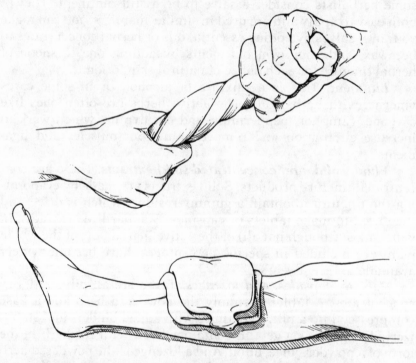

Illustration #2:

To make a compress, soak a cloth in a hot herbal solution and wring it slightly before applying it to the skin. A hot-water bottle or heating pad over the cloth helps to keep it warm.

Compress. Soak sterile gauze or a clean cotton cloth in an infusion or decoction, wring slightly, and apply to the skin. A compress should be applied hot. You can leave it uncovered, or place a hot-water bottle or heating pad over the cloth to keep it warm (see illustration #2). Replace the compress when it cools. Another type of compress can be made by putting fresh or dried herbs in a fabric bag, dipping it into boiling water, and applying the bag directly to the skin (or to a cloth on top of the skin, if the bag is too hot). You can also simmer roots or woody herbs for a few minutes, remove them from the water, place them in a thin cloth bag, and apply to the skin.

Bath. To relieve sunburn and skin irritations, for instance, you may want to apply an herbal solution to the whole body. An herbal bath is the answer. Add two cups of an infusion or decoction to the bathwater, or a few drops of an essential oil. You can also put either the fresh or dried herb in a muslin or gauze bag and suspend it from the tub's tap as water fills the bath.

FINDING HERBAL PRODUCTS

Most natural foods stores carry a wide variety of fresh or dried herbs, tablets, tinctures, oils, combination products, lotions, and the like. You can also purchase herbs at Oriental pharmacies or order them through the mail (see "Resources"). Many herbs are appropriate for inclusion in an herb garden or can be wildcrafted. If you do wildcraft, it is essential to be absolutely sure of the identity of any herb you intend to use for healing purposes. There are a number of excellent herbal books with color plates that make identification easier (see "Resources"). You should also consider the environmental consequences of wildcrafting plants.

For each of the following herbs, we'll provide some historical background, discuss the plant's chemical constituents and how they affect the body, and alert readers to the most common injuries and conditions the plants are used for.

Aloe. A cactuslike member of the lily family, the gel from the aloe plant (*Aloe vera* and over three hundred other species) has been used to treat burns, wounds, and skin irritations for thousands of years. Ancient Egyptian and Greek herbalists knew of its benefits as a topical healer, and Alexander the Great's troops once even seized an island full of aloe plants to assure a supply of the gel for treating wounds. Diverse cultures around the world have incorporated aloe into their medical practices. Today aloe is widely grown in Africa, the Mediterranean, and other arid regions.

The semisolid, transparent gel obtained from the innermost layers of the plant's fleshy leaves contains a number of therapeutically active compounds including glycosides (a sugar derivative), polysaccharides (complex carbohydrate molecules), resinous material, and volatile oil. Other compounds that may account for aloe's healing, softening, and moisturizing effects on skin include vitamins C and E and the mineral zinc.

A more outer layer of the aloe leaf has long been used as the source for aloe latex (juice). Traditional herbalists recommend liquid or dried latex preparations, taken internally, for a number of conditions. For instance, aloe latex remedies act as a powerful laxative to stimulate the bowels (though a number of modern herbalists say there are better, less irritating herbal laxatives). For first-aid purposes, the most useful part of the plant is the gel, applied externally.

A landmark study in 1935 on third-degree X-ray burns first confirmed aloe's benefits as a burn treatment. Subsequent scientific studies done over the past fifty years support its ability to boost cell regeneration, speed the healing of burns and wounds, and prevent infection. Most dramatically, a recent animal study reported in the medical journal *Plastic and Reconstructive Surgery* showed that aloe-treated burns healed in an average of thirty days while untreated burns took fifty.

Most natural practitioners agree that fresh aloe gel is best. An aloe plant requires little more than occasional watering to grow, so it's an easy houseplant to keep around. To use it, break a few inches off one of the older, lower leaves of the aloe plant, slice the leaf lengthwise, squeeze its gel onto the injury, and allow it to dry. It can be reapplied frequently. Fresh aloe is safe to use on broken skin and can also be applied after healing begins. Allergic reactions are uncommon, but discontinue use if one does occur.

Natural bodycare companies market a wide variety of "medicinal" aloe products, including lotions, creams, juices, and gels, and a slew of aloe-containing bodycare products such as shampoos and hand lotions. For healing purposes, fresh is best, but otherwise look for juice or gel products whose labels proclaim 96–100 percent pure aloe. Most of the scientific studies that have confirmed aloe's wound-healing properties have used the fresh gel. Bottled and "stabilized" aloe that is produced by harsh solvent-extraction methods may contain little of the healing ingredients of fresh aloe. Also look for aloe products that haven't been preserved with alcohol, which will neutralize aloe's skin-healing properties. Try to find concentrates or gels without mineral oil, paraffin waxes, or coloring. Check ingredient listings carefully.

Calendula. An ancient herb that originated in Egypt, calendula *(Calendula officinalis)* is a member of the huge botanical family that includes dandelions and daisies. It has long been bred for its colorful flowers, and most people know it today as the popular annual garden plant the European marigold. Europeans have cultivated calendula in their gardens since about the twelfth century, and its bright orange or yellow flowers can now be found in habitats around the world. It is one of the most versatile and widely used first-aid herbs, popular among herbalists, homeopaths, and aromatherapists.

Nineteenth-century American herbalists used calendula, with one doctor in 1886 even proclaiming that a calendula compress worked to heal bullet wounds. Today's natural healers are more likely to use calendula for small cuts and abrasions, inflammation, skin irritations, bruises, strains and sprains, minor burns and scalds, and hemorrhoids. Calendula stimulates blood circulation and can ease cramps. It is also used as a mouthwash and to fight gum infections.

Calendula's chemical constituents include flavonoids, carotenes, saponin, resin, and volatile oil. Studies have linked some of these to specific biochemical actions. For instance, the volatile oils stimulate blood circulation and cause sweating. One effect is to make skin eruptions come out faster and rashes to disappear. Certain constituents and the high resin content of the tincture gives the herb its strong local anti-inflammatory effect. Calendula is also astringent and promotes blood clotting. It's thus a good herb to stop bleeding. It fights bacterial, viral, and even fungal infections such as athlete's foot.

A calendula tincture or concentrated extract is more effective for external use than a compress made from an infusion, since the tincture and extract include the healing resinous compounds. Calendula is frequently combined with other herbs to produce all-purpose healing salves. One popular combination is with goldenseal and myrrh (also high in resin) to make an antiseptic and antifungal lotion.

Chamomile. Natural health practitioners use the flowers from two types of chamomile: the annual German variety *(Matricaria recutita)* and Roman chamomile *(Anthemis nobilis)*. Though botanists make a clear distinction between the two, most herbalists consider their healing properties to be similar. The traditional herbalists of ancient Greece, Egypt, and India prescribed chamomile tea to treat anxiety, insomnia, and digestive problems. Chamomile is still taken internally for these problems and has also long enjoyed widespread use externally to spur wound healing.

Herbal companies process chamomile's yellow flowers to produce a distinctive blue oil containing a number of active ingredients that are anti-inflammatory, analgesic, and antiseptic. Chamomile has many constituents in common with another healing herb, yarrow, including azulene. The blue color of the oil is from azulene, a powerful anti-inflammatory substance. Studies have shown that azulene is highly effective at reducing fever, encouraging the healing of wounds, and inactivating toxins produced by bacteria. Researchers have proven that applying chamomile to burns reduces the time it takes them to heal. Chamomile seems to improve tissue regeneration and stimulate the immune-boosting activity of white blood cells.

Researchers have also established that taking chamomile internally does have a depressive effect on the central nervous system, confirming its reputation as a gentle sedative.

Chamomile is also the source for a popular essential oil used to induce relaxation, and to treat burns, minor wounds, and muscle aches (see section on essential oils for more information).

In general chamomile products are minimally toxic and are gentle enough for use on children. There's a minor risk of allergic reaction, especially if you're allergic to ragweed.

Natural foods stores carry a variety of chamomile preparations. You can also brew a strong tea and apply it as a poultice, compress, or herbal wash to cuts and scrapes, sore muscles, rashes, and burns.

Comfrey. The early Greeks crushed the roots and leaves of comfrey and applied it to wounds, and the herb remains a major element of any natural first-aid kit today. Comfrey's nicknames—boneset, knitbone, bruisewort—give an indication of its other traditional uses, to help heal broken bones and contusions. A hardy perennial with small purple flowers, comfrey is easy to grow and adapts to various climates.

Chemical analysis of the plant shows that it contains tannins, alkaloids, proteins, and allantoin, a potent wound-healing agent. Allantoin, which is found in higher concentrations in the roots than the leaves or stems, both promotes cell regeneration and helps relieve inflammation. It is easily absorbed through the skin and reaches deep tissue, where it particularly promotes the activity of osteoblast cells to produce bones, and fibroblasts to produce connective tissue. Bodycare companies are now using allantoin for its skin-soothing properties in some over-the-counter skin creams and other cosmetic products. Note that many herbalists believe that comfrey's ability to spark the growth of new cells is not due solely to allantoin, and that other compounds in the whole herb may enhance the action of allantoin, soothe mucous membranes, and offer other benefits.

A fan of herbal healing from Valley Stream, New York, says, "I have been using comfrey salve for bruises, sprains, insect bites, and a variety of skin conditions and I'm always surprised at the rapid improvement from just one or two applications."

Although comfrey's principal use has been as a topical wound healer, in the past some herbalists have prescribed oral doses as well. Taking comfrey internally, however, is currently controversial. The FDA considers comfrey of "undefined safety" for internal use, and Canadian officials have banned the herb. The dispute centers around certain of comfrey's chemicals, the pyrrolizidine alkaloids, which may be toxic to the liver. Scientists have tied pyrrolizidine alkaloids to liver cancer on the basis of a study in which animals were fed extremely large amounts of the herb. Another study on internal consumption, however, suggested that the risk of cancer posed by drinking one cup of comfrey tea was less than the risk posed by drinking a saccharin-sweetened soft drink.

Many herbalists believe that most people can safely take limited oral doses of comfrey (pregnant women, however, should not take it). But until further research settles the debate, the prudent person will avoid taking comfrey internally or will shop around for pyrrolizidine-free comfrey, which is now being offered by a number of herbal companies. Comfrey is widely considered safe and nontoxic applied externally.

Though you can find comfrey root in fresh, dried, and powdered forms, by itself comfrey is a somewhat uncommon product on natural pharmacy shelves. Herbal companies usually combine comfrey with other herbs. For instance, the Swiss herbal manufacturer Bioforce markets a Comfrey Complex liquid, which includes comfrey, witch hazel, St.-John's-wort, arnica, and other herbs in a 1.7-ounce bottle. Salves and ointments containing comfrey are also popular, such as WiseWays Herbals' All-Heal Salve with comfrey, calendula, echinacea, plantain, and other herbs.

The liquids and ointments can be applied directly to the skin, or you can make a comfrey poultice by mixing three tablespoons of fresh grated or powdered root with three ounces of hot water and stirring it into a paste. Apply while still warm directly to the skin and cover with sterile gauze or clean cloth. Secure with a bandage and leave the poultice on for a few hours or overnight. After removing, massage the area with a comfrey ointment.

Echinacea. This herb *(Echinacea angustifolia, E. purpurea)* was the classic snakebite and insect-sting remedy among the Sioux and other Native American tribes of the Plains. It was also one of their primary healing herbs for a variety of injuries and illnesses. Herbalists today use it widely both for external injuries and for any condition that requires internal detoxifying and blood cleansing. Studies have shown that it fights bacterial and viral infections and boosts the immune system.

The plant is a perennial that is native to the prairies of midwestern North America. Preparations using the dried root became some of the most popular patent medicines in the late nineteenth century. Taking their cue from Native Americans, pioneers and citizens of the frontier used lotions or poultices for a variety of injuries, bites, and stings. One enthusiastic promoter volunteered to allow himself to be bitten by a rattlesnake to demonstrate echinacea's antisnakebite powers. By the beginning of the twentieth century echinacea approached the status of panacea, being used for everything from toothache to mumps.

A critical backlash was inevitable, and it was ushered in by articles such as the *Journal of the American Medical Association*'s "Echinacea Considered Valueless" in 1909. The advent of antibiotics in the 1930s and 1940s further diminished popular use in the United States. Echinacea did remain common, however, in Europe. German scientists have studied it closely over the past forty years, and today there are more than two hundred echinacea-based pharmaceutical preparations sold in Germany. Echinacea was "rediscovered" by American herbalists over the past twenty years and now is on the verge of reclaiming its previous position at the top of the herbal repertoire.

Herbalists today prescribe echinacea to relieve the itching of bites, stings, poison oak and ivy, and hives, to lower fever, to cleanse cuts and wounds, to alleviate the pain of teething, to soothe boils and skin infections, to calm allergic reactions, to reduce inflammation, and to help prevent the side effects of vaccination. Herbalist Lesley Tierra, author of *The Herbs of Life*, says, "I always carry echinacea tincture in my purse for first aid and emergencies."

Scientific studies have proven echinacea does have many powerful healing and immune-boosting properties. The plant contains a broad range of chemical compounds with potential medicinal effects. Important constituents include polysaccharides such as inulin, flavonoids such as rutoside and quercetin, the compound echinacoside, resins, and fatty acids. Studies have found that, singly or in combination, these compounds have a number of positive actions on the body. Echinacea has been found to stimulate the body's immune system, enhance the body's ability to counter bacterial and viral infections, and promote the body's power to regenerate healthy cells and maintain the structure of connective tissue. One large recent study of almost five thousand patients found that an echinacea salve had an 85 percent success rate in treating wounds, burns, and inflammatory skin conditions. Echinacea may also act as a local anesthetic (you can feel this action as a tingling on the tongue when taking potent, fresh echinacea concentrates or tinctures). Finally, some researchers think that echinacea's legendary effectiveness in treating snakebites is due to the herb's ability to inhibit the enzyme hyaluronidase, a compound found in certain venoms that breaks down connective tissue when injected into the snake's victim.

Echinacea is available in various forms, including fresh, dried, freeze-dried, or in a concentrate or tincture. There is no known level of toxicity associated with taking echinacea, and it can be taken internally and applied externally in relatively large quantities. For instance, many herbalists suggest that patients with infections take two to three droppersful of the tincture three times daily as a general immune stimulant. For acute conditions, patients may take a dropperful of tincture every half hour. "It's not toxic, and you need a high dose to quickly activate the immune system," says herbalist Christopher Hobbs, author of *Echinacea: The Immune Herb!*

For external use, take a cotton pad and saturate it with echinacea tincture. Tape it on the wound, or blend fresh echinacea and apply as a poultice. Change the poultice often.

Ephedra. With a history of use that goes back at least five millennia, this branching shrub is one of the world's oldest medicines. In China herbalists have been prescribing a species *(Ephedra sinica)*, which they call *ma huang*, to relieve congested breathing since around 3000 B.C. Other species of ephedra are found in arid regions around the world, including one in North America *(E. vulgaris)* that was used by the Mormons as a substitute for coffee and thus became known as Mormon tea.

The stems and branches of ephedra contain the alkaloid ephedrine. Researchers first extracted this strong central nervous system stimulant over a century ago, although it wasn't until 1924 that a Chinese scientist demonstrated ephedrine's pharmacological effects. A few years later the German firm Merck synthesized it. Ephedrine was used medically for the next twenty years or so, until pharmaceutical companies switched to using a chemically similar compound, pseudoephedrine.

Doctors said that pseudoephedrine was preferable to ephedrine because it caused fewer side effects. On the other hand, some herbalists today contend that the whole plant is safer than either ephedrine or pseudoephedrine. Pseudoephedrine remains a major ingredient in Sudafed and other over-the-counter cold and allergy products.

The active constituents of ephedra make it an effective natural bronchial decongestant. (The Chinese species contains more ephedrine than the North American species, which may have little or no ephedrine.) Ephedrine quickly dilates bronchial tubes while stimulating the heart. In more ways than the name, it is similar to another stimulant, epinephrine, the adrenal hormone also known as adrenaline. Though both are readily absorbed orally, epinephrine is more potent and faster acting.

Ephedra can play a role in treating bronchial asthma, hay fever, and the common cold. As a first-aid remedy it is sometimes used for allergic reactions that cause a feeling of constriction in the chest and difficulty breathing.

Ephedra's stimulating effects are stronger than caffeine's. The FDA considers it an herb of "undefined safety," and it is on the U.S. Olympic Committee's list of banned substances. Potential side effects include increased blood pressure and heart palpitations. Herbalists warn that it shouldn't be taken by patients with heart disease or high blood pressure. If used steadily for a long period of time, ephedra may weaken the adrenal gland and the digestive system.

A typical dose for the tincture would be one-quarter to one-half teaspoon, and for a 10 percent alkaloid-content extract 125–250 mg, up to three times daily.

Goldenseal. The distinctive yellow root of this plant (*Hydrastis canadensis*) lends it its name and accounts for much of its popularity as a healing herb. Goldenseal is a small perennial with delicate, light green flowers that is native to eastern North America. Native Americans dyed their clothes with it and took advantage of its antiseptic properties to heal wounds. Like echinacea it became a popular ingredient of patent medicines and tonics in late-nineteenth-century America. Until 1936, it was even listed in the official U.S. Pharmacopoeia as an astringent and antiseptic. Modern antibiotics and other trends in medicine, however, over-shadowed it in the twentieth century.

Today goldenseal is one of the most widely used herbs, with both external and internal applications. Topically it is used for its anti-inflammatory, antibiotic, and antiseptic actions. Herbalists prescribe it for hemorrhoids and various skin infections or sores, including ringworm, athlete's foot, and itching. It combines well with other herbs such as witch hazel and is an ingredient in eye lotions and eardrops. Patients take it internally for excessive menstrual flow and after-birth bleeding. It is also widely used to heal infections of mucous membranes and for colds, digestive ailments, and food allergies.

The active constituents of goldenseal include tannin, volatile oil, resin, and the alkaloids hydrastine and berberine. Many of the scientific studies done on goldenseal have concentrated on berber-ine. Researchers say that berberine does kill a broad spectrum of bacteria, and it reduces fever. It activates macrophages, cells in the body that boost the immune system. Berberine apparently also calms the uterus, confirming its usefulness for menstrual problems. The tannin in goldenseal may be responsible for a healing effect on the lining of the gastrointestinal system.

The FDA considers goldenseal of "undefined safety." Most herbalists consider it safe, though they recommend against using it if you have high blood pressure or are pregnant. Like ephedra and some other herbs, it shouldn't be taken in large amounts every day for weeks or months.

Goldenseal's popularity has caused overforaging in some areas, with the result that it has become more rare and thus a relatively expensive herb. There's also more potential for adulter-ation and mislabeling. Check labels and sources before buying.

Ipecac. The dried roots of this tropical South American shrub *(Cephaelis ipecacuanha)* contain the alkaloid emetine, a substance that induces vomiting. Conventional pharmaceutical companies worldwide market inexpensive, sweet-tasting syrup of ipecac made with tiny amounts of emetine, and the medicine has saved many lives by quickly emptying the stomach of poison victims. (Strong acids and some other poisons should not be vomited; see Chapter 20 on poisoning for details.)

Native Brazilians have long used ipecac, though not exclu-sively to induce vomiting. In some preparations the herb can be an expectorant. That is, it brings up phlegm and mucus from the lungs, thus relieving bronchitis. Early colonists brought ipecac back to Portugal in the sixteenth century, and a few European herbalists still consider it the herb of choice for bronchitis. Some formulations of ipecac can be highly toxic, however, and its main use in the United States is as an emetic, a substance that induces vomiting.

Ipecac irritates stomach walls and increases the secretion of gastric enzymes. This stimulates the "vomiting center" in the medulla of the brain, and within about twenty minutes in most cases, the victim throws up. One or two doses of the syrup preparations are safe even if not vomited. Some pharmaceutical companies, however, also sell concentrated fluid extracts of ipecac. These are much more toxic than the syrup preparations and need to be diluted before taking. Stick to concentrated sugar solutions.

Homeopaths use extremely dilute preparations of ipecac to treat persistent and extreme nausea and some types of bleeding.

Pau d'arco. Also known as lapacho and taheebo *(Tabebuia avellanedae, T. impetiginosa)*, this herb is produced from the inner bark of a tree native to Brazil. Indian tribes of the Amazon region have used medicinal preparations of pau d'arco for centuries to heal wounds and treat snakebite. It is widely used in South America, and within the past decade it has become popular among herbalists in the United States and Europe as an antibacterial, antiviral, and anti-inflammatory agent.

The chemical constituent of pau d'arco that has most attracted the attention of researchers is a quinone called lapachol. It was first isolated in 1882 and synthesized in 1927. Various researchers have studied it since, including the National Cancer Institute in the late 1960s. Scientists there were interested in pau d'arco's potential anticancer properties. That line of inquiry was abandoned because of the potential toxicity of lapachol. Proponents of the herb claim that toxicity of the whole-bark preparation is lower, possibly without sacrificing effectiveness. Many herbal studies do show better results with a whole extract compared to a refined or individual chemical constituent.

Pau d'arco is available as the dried, shredded bark, in capsules, and liquid standardized extract. Look for pau d'arco products labeled as one of the two Tabebuia species, since other species may not have the same healing properties. The tea and extract can be taken orally or applied topically for bites and stings, infections, and inflammation.

Plantain. Americans can thank early European settlers for this common weed with important wound-healing powers. Plantain is common along roadsides and in uncultivated places of Europe. It spreads so quickly that after it arrived from the Old World, Native Americans called the plant "white man's footprint." Homeowners who don't know of plantain's medicinal uses (and some who do) spend much time and money trying to eradicate it from their lawns. One of the two main types of plantain, "broadleaf plantain" *(Plantago major)*, with its flat leaves and seed-covered spikelike stems, may be the chief weed keeping ChemLawn in business. The other plantain, known as ribwort *(Plantago lanceolata)*, has thinner leaves and seeds concentrated at the top of stems. Both plantains can be used internally (for coughs, bronchitis, and diarrhea) and externally (to heal wounds).

Plantain was mentioned by Shakespeare as a panacea, and many contemporary herbalists are equally enthusiastic. Herbalist Lesley Tierra terms plantain a "seemingly miraculous poultice for stopping the pain of bee stings, spider and snake bites, and other insect wounds." Herbalists use it as well for chronic skin problems, burns, cuts and scrapes, and hemorrhoids. A reader from Grafton, Massachusetts, says, "I constantly marvel at the humble plantain for its ability to stop bleeding and heal wounds, burns, and even ulcers of the skin. A carpenter friend who's always hurting his hands prefers plantain leaves to any over-the-counter remedy."

This herb is traditionally used fresh, in the form of crushed or chewed-up leaves applied to wounds to stop bleeding and promote healing. Recent studies have confirmed that certain of its chemical constituents, particularly the compound aucubin, promote coagulation of blood and healing of wounds. Aucubin also appears to be antibiotic. In addition to aucubin, plantain contains mucilages, flavonoids, and tannins, which give it astringent and antiseptic capabilities. The mucilages have the special property of expanding into a spongy mass in the presence of liquid. They thus act to coat tissue with a slimy substance that soothes and heals, and they bind damaged tissue as they dry. Other plants that are also high in mucilages, such as comfrey and slippery-elm bark, are also known for their ability to heal wounds and relieve pain and irritation.

Plantain's leaves also contain allantoin, the constituent in comfrey that studies indicate heals wounds, promotes cell regeneration, and helps relieve inflammation. "Plantain is safer than comfrey and a good substitute for that herb," says herbalist Christopher Hobbs.

Though most herbalists assert that the fresh leaves provide

the best healing action, plantain is also available from herbal companies in dried and tincture forms. It is a common constituent in some healing salves and ointments.

Slippery elm. The inner bark of this tree *(Ulmus rubra, U. fulva)* has been the basis for both a food and various medicines for thousands of years. The ancient Greeks made a slippery-elm paste to help heal broken bones (an application that has yet to be verified by modern science). The herb became extremely popular in eighteenth- and nineteenth-century America as a cough and cold remedy and was also used to soothe and heal minor skin injuries and irritations. To apply to wounds, herbalists ground the bark, mixed it with water, and spread the resulting spongy paste over the injury as a bandage.

Some people also mixed the ground bark with water or milk to make a nutritious food. Folk healers contend that the slippery-elm gruel was especially helpful to eat while recovering from illness because it is easily assimilated. Subsequent analysis found that slippery elm is a good source of nutrients, including calcium.

While slippery-elm lozenges to remedy cough and colds are still available, other medicinal and food uses of the bark have almost died out. Partly that is because the tree itself was once on the verge of dying out, as whole groves were ravaged by Dutch elm disease. It doesn't help, of course, that the stripping of the bark necessary to make slippery-elm products often kills the tree.

Medical researchers trace many of slippery elm's healing powers to its mucilages. Even the FDA calls it an "excellent demulcent," or soothing agent. Just like the mucilages in plantain, those in slippery elm coat and then bind damaged tissue as they dry. The effect is to soothe and heal skin disorders, rashes, and wounds. Mucilages coat and heal tissue of the digestive tract, too, which is why it is popular as a digestive tonic and even to treat food poisoning. Slippery elm also contains tannins, which when used on the skin tend to stop bleeding.

The highest quality slippery-elm products are made from the fine inner bark, a more potent healer than the coarser outer bark. To apply it externally, mix slippery-elm powder with boiling water to make paste. A small minority of people experience allergic reactions to slippery elm, so test first on a patch of skin.

Witch hazel. One of the most commonly used medical herbs in the United States, witch hazel *(Hamamelis virginiana)* is sometimes recommended as an astringent or liniment even by medical doctors. Conventional pharmacies sell over a million gallons of distilled witch hazel a year. Witch hazel is also a component in many cosmetics, and in some over-the-counter remedies such as Preparation H cleansing pads.

Witch hazel is derived from a North American shrub or small tree. Some Native Americans included dried witch hazel leaves in their medicine kits to make into a tea. This would be drunk for relief of colds and sore throats or applied to the skin to stop minor bleeding or soothe insect bites. Distilled extracts made from the bark are still used today by some people for hemorrhoids, varicose veins, and bruises. The bark's action is thought to be due to tannins and an astringent compound, hamamelitanin, that constricts blood vessels and stops bleeding.

Bottled "witch hazel water" and some distilled commercial products sold in pharmacies have few of the chemical tannins of the fresh plant that provide most of witch hazel's astringent powers. These products may, however, have other active ingredients that still allow them to be effective healers. Rather than using these products, herbalists recommend that you make a decoction from the powdered bark (available in natural foods stores). Alternatively, use one of the tincture preparations available from herbal manufacturers and sold in natural foods stores. Even these preparations are pretty mild. You can apply them directly to the skin, for a cut like a shaving nick, or to gauze and cover the wound.

Yarrow. This herb's Latin name *(Achillea millefolium)* indicates its legendary use by Achilles during the Trojan War to stem bleeding on his fellow soldiers. Yarrow's traditional use as a wound healer by the Chinese and others has garnered it some descriptive nicknames: nosebleed, bloodwort, and soldier's woundwort (*wort* means "plant" in Old English). When the Europeans introduced it to the New World, Native Americans quickly adopted it, rolling up leaves, for instance, to insert into the nose to stop a nosebleed. Many modern herbalists continue to use it as a first-aid remedy. "Yarrow is the best herb for external bleeding," says herbalist Christopher Hobbs.

Indeed studies have shown that the leaves, stems, and flower-tops of yarrow contain volatile oils and tannins that may account for its power as an astringent and antiseptic, and the blood-coagulating chemicals achilletin and achilleine. In addition to using yarrow externally on burns, cuts, bruises, and hemorrhoids, herbalists also prescribe it internally to relieve cramps, control menstrual bleeding, and reduce fevers.

Yarrow is available in a tincture that can be applied directly to gauze to cover a clean wound. If you have fresh leaves and flowertops, you can dry them and make a powder, which can be sprinkled right on minor cuts and scrapes. Powdered yarrow products are also available at natural foods stores. In a small minority of people yarrow may cause a rash.

◆ Homeopathic First-Aid Remedies

Laypeople have been using homeopathic remedies to treat everyday emergencies at home for close to two centuries. Homeopathic medicines can almost always complement conventional first-aid steps and sometimes are all that is needed.

Homeopathic preparations include powders, tablets, tinctures, and an array of lotions, ointments, creams, and sprays. Production processes are similar to those for herbs, with a few subtle differences. Homeopathic manufacturers start by steeping a substance (for example, bees to make *Apis*) in alcohol and straining the liquid to obtain a pure or 100 percent "mother tincture." This mother tincture is usually then diluted by mixing it with more alcohol and succussing, or shaking, the remedy. To make tablets, the homeopathic manufacturer pours a dilution of the mother tincture onto sugar granules, which absorb the medication as the alcohol evaporates. The tablets are tiny compared to herbal tablets, but they're taken orally in much the same way. A homeopathic tincture is an alcoholic solution and may in turn be used to make creams or lotions that, like herbal preparations, are applied to the skin.

It is in the devising of *potency* that homeopathic medicine differs most radically from herbalism. When you buy homeopathic remedies, you'll notice they are available in different strengths. For instance, the label may say *"Apis* 6X" or *"Apis* 30X." The 6X and 30X refer to the number of times the mother tincture has been diluted to produce the remedy.

Dilutions are either decimal (and noted as 1X, 2X, etc.) or centesimal (1C, 2C, etc.) in scale. A 1X remedy is one that was made by adding one part pure mother tincture and nine parts alcohol (and then succussing the solution). It is thus a 10 percent solution. To make a 2X (or 1C) remedy, homeopathic manufacturers add one part of a 10 percent solution to nine parts alcohol. The resulting solution is now one part mother tincture and ninety-nine parts dilution, or a 1 percent solution. The process is continued so that, for instance, a 6X (or 3C) remedy is essentially a one-part-in-a-million dilution, and a 12X (or 6C) remedy is a one-part-in-a-trillion dilution.

A few dilutions or "potencies" are more commonly used than others. Most natural foods stores carry lines of homeopathic products that are labeled as either 6X, 12X, 24X, or 30X, or 6C, 12C, or 30C. Homeopaths consider these to be relatively "low potencies" that are best for self-care purposes. The "higher potency" remedies such as 400X and 200C (up to and beyond 2,000,000X!) are usually reserved for use by professional homeopaths, since these remedies are thought to be more powerful and deeper acting than lower potencies.

The designation of "low" and "high" potency is initially confusing to some people, since "high" potencies are those that are more dilute. This seems counter to common sense. After all, the higher potencies are more dilute and by conventional standards have less of the "active ingredient." Potencies beyond 24X are likely not to have even a single molecule of the mother tincture substance (such dilutions are beyond the Avogadro limit). Basic homeopathic theory, however, contends that each dilution gains in healing potency from the shaking of the remedy's molecules. Homeopaths prefer that these higher potencies be used by laypeople only after being recommended by a homeopathic physician.

Homeopaths say that it is best to use the minimum, lowest-potency dose necessary to provoke the healing response. According to homeopath Jennifer Jacobs, M.D., "In general you don't want to take a 30X remedy more than once or twice a day. The 6X or 12X potency is best for those remedies used more frequently, like once or twice an hour, and usually if the condition is severe and acute, you want to give the remedy more frequently. So the 6X or 12X potencies are usually the best for most first-aid situations."

Homeopathic creams, ointments, and sprays are much less dilute. For instance, most *Calendula* creams are 1X, a 10 percent active ingredient product. Some ointments may be labeled without the X or C. For instance, Standard Homeopathic Co. makes *"Hypericum 2%"* and *"Apis Mellifica 2%"* ointments.

To take advantage of homeopathy's benefits, it is usually necessary to consider carefully the "totality" of the patient's symptoms and condition. Before prescribing a remedy, professional homeopaths will usually ask a dozen or more questions about the person's condition. Is the patient thirsty? What does his tongue look like? Is his discomfort made worse by cold air? Is the pain throbbing or stinging? The homeopath then tries to match the answers to these questions with the individual remedy, chosen from an extensive sourcebook called a *materia medica*, that is appropriate for the greatest number of the symptoms.

For the most part injuries don't require such detailed observation. Still, there are a few medicines that could be appropriate for each type of injury. There is no single "bee sting remedy." Rather, one will work slightly better under certain circumstances, such as when the sting feels hot, and another would be appropriate if the sting were piercing or cold and numb. The following nine homeopathic remedies cover a broad spectrum of injuries and conditions that can be treated with first-aid measures. In this section and throughout the book, homeotherapeutic suggestions will include not only the name of a common remedy for a condition, but also what the average patient's typical symptoms and characteristics are when such a remedy is appropriate. The symptoms and patient characteristics are to help you decide whether the suggested remedy is the best one to take in each instance.

Homeopaths recommend that homeopathic remedies be ingested at least fifteen minutes before or after eating or drinking anything, and that the remedies not be touched (put them right from a piece of clean paper or the tube cap into your mouth). Homeopaths also say that certain substances act to counter the effects of a homeopathic remedy and thus should be avoided while using homeopathy. These antidoting substances include camphor, coffee, and synthetic drugs. In practice, however, many homeopathic physicians do use allopathic drugs along with homeopathic remedies for some acute conditions.

Aconite. This remedy is derived from the whole fresh aconite (*Aconitum napellus*), or monkshood, plant as it comes into flower. Like a number of other sources of homeopathic remedies, aconite is extremely poisonous until it is diluted. (A related species from Nepal is thought to be the most powerful plant poison in the world; even *smelling* it can cause serious poisoning.) Homeopaths use *Aconite* to relieve states of acute emotional upset, especially those that come on suddenly from extreme anxiety, intense fear or pain, and shocking or violent situations. It is one of a number of remedies that can help alleviate shock. It is used whenever symptoms come on violently and suddenly (obviously the case with most injuries). Homeopaths also recommend it to treat the aftereffects of surgical operation, for a foreign body in the eye, and for the early stages of inflammation or fever.

The patient who is fearful and restless is often helped by *Aconite.* Usually the victim cannot bear to be touched and has pain that is followed by numbness and tingling sensations. He or she may also experience sudden nausea and vomiting.

Apis. To prepare this remedy, homeopathic manufacturers

soak honey bees *(Apis mellifica)* in an alcohol mixture for ten days. The resulting tincture is then diluted. Some "mother tinctures," however, are prepared from bee venom rather than whole bees.

Not surprisingly given its origin, *Apis* relieves the type of symptoms associated with bee stings: marked, rapid, and reddish swelling of the skin. The face gets flushed and there is often puffy swelling around the mouth, face, and eyes. Excessive swelling, however, may be anywhere on the body. The skin becomes exquisitely sensitive to touch. The pain is stinging and burning rather than cool and numb, and symptoms are made worse by applying heat and better by cold.

Thus homeopaths recommend *Apis* for most conditions associated with hot, red swelling, including insect stings and bites, sunburn, skin irritations, hives (urticaria), burns, early stages of boils, and frostbite.

Arnica. This remedy comes from the whole fresh arnica plant *(Arnica montana,* also known as leopard's-bane) or dried flowers or root. Arnica grows high in the mountains of Europe. Legend has it that peasants observed that if a sheep or goat fell down a hill and hurt itself, it would nibble the leaves of this plant.

Arnica's main function is to counter the immediate effects of a fall or a blow from a blunt object. It is often the first medicine given after an injury, with a cream, ointment, or spray being applied locally and tablets taken internally. The topical applications help to reduce bruising, swelling, and local tenderness. *Arnica* ointment speeds the absorption of blood under skin. Internally, *Arnica* works like *Aconite* to calm someone who is in a dazed or shocked state. It dispels the feelings of shock and distress that usually accompany accidents and injuries. The victim may feel hot around the head and face, but cold at the extremities.

Arnica is the premier homeopathic contusion remedy, readily used for bruises, black eye, and concussion. It is also commonly used for muscle pains, sore and aching muscles, and sports injuries. Sprains, dislocated joints, fractures, and any internal bleeding caused by injury may benefit by treatment with *Arnica.* Homeopathic M.D.'s also use it before and after surgery and childbirth to prevent bruising and speed recovery.

For severe injuries homeopaths may recommend taking *Arnica* every one-half to every three hours during the first two to three days. If the swelling and bruising go down, it may be appropriate to switch to *Rhus tox.*

Arnica lotions, ointments, and tinctures are not used on broken skin, which they may irritate.

Arsenicum. Like *Aconite,* the source of this remedy is extremely toxic: arsenic trioxide, a compound of the poisonous chemical element arsenic that's known as an effective killer of insects and rodents. In microdilute dosages the homeopathic remedy *Arsenicum* is used to treat skin rash (especially when it comes on suddenly and is improved by heat), hay fever and asthma (especially if either is brought on by anxiety), and vomiting, diarrhea, or stomach upsets (especially those from food poisoning). The typical *Arsenicum* patient is anxious, restless, and fearful.

Calendula. Homeopaths use this remedy for many of the same purposes that herbalists do. *Calendula* promotes the healing of wounds, burns, and skin irritations, helps stop bleeding, and inhibits infection. It is widely used for minor cuts and shallow scrapes, sunburn, and diaper rash. "*Calendula* ointment is mild yet protects and heals most sores in a day or two. It's good stuff. Inexpensive, too," notes a reader from Garden Grove, California.

Calendula is available in a variety of homeopathic preparations. The ointment is usually 1X strength (10 percent calendula extract) and comes in a one-ounce tube. It is usually used for skin irritations, burns, and minor scrapes, but not cuts. Homeopaths often dilute the tincture one part tincture to three to four parts water to prevent stinging. There are also lotions (a nonalcoholic, glycerine-and-water solution that's great for minor burns), oil (use like the ointment), and even "calendulated" soap bars.

Hypericum. Homeopaths refer to this remedy as "*Arnica* for the nerves." It comes from the whole fresh St.-John's-wort plant (*Hypericum perforatum*). Herbal preparations of the plant's leaves and flowers have been used since antiquity as a wound healer, perhaps initially because of the bloodlike appearance of a reddish oil the plant exudes. Many herbalists still recommend St.-John's-wort for its wound-healing properties.

Homeopaths focus on *Hypericum*'s ability to relieve pain and trauma related to nerves and the central nervous system. They have found that the remedy is best for an injury that causes the type of shooting pain that seems to ascend the length of a nerve. Wounds to an area of many nerve endings, such as the ends of the fingers and toes, will be improved by *Hypericum.*

If you catch your fingers or toes in a door or drop a heavy object on them, *Hypericum* is your remedy. Also turn to it to speed the healing of jagged cuts, and to relieve the pain from dental surgery, toothaches, injuries to the tailbone or coccyx after a fall, and some burns.

Tincture, lotion, and spray preparations for applying this remedy to the skin are widely available from homeopathic manufacturers. The spray is typically a 10 percent extract of *Hypericum* in a 50 percent alcohol solution. It smells like alcohol and evaporates quickly off the skin.

Ledum. This remedy is prepared from the leaves and twigs of wild rosemary *(Ledum palustre)*, a small evergreen shrub sometimes cultivated as an ornamental. Although the plant is toxic, herbalists in the past have used it to treat rheumatism and arthritis, and to induce abortion.

Homeopaths use dilute preparations of *Ledum* to treat puncture wounds from various sharp objects, including nails, needles, bites by insects (especially mosquitoes), and small animals. It is also used to relieve stiff joints, sprained ankles, black eyes, and severe or persisting bruises.

Notice that some of *Ledum*'s uses overlap with the remedy *Apis*. One of the most important ways to distinguish between them is that *Ledum* is more appropriate if the site of the injury is cold and numb, or swollen and relieved by cold. *Apis* is more appropriate if the injured body part feels hot.

Ledum is available in tincture and tablet forms.

Rhus tox. The source of this remedy, the leaves of the poison ivy *(Rhus toxicodendron)* plant, clearly indicate its main use: to alleviate the rash and joint stiffness you get from touching poison ivy. Homeopaths say that *Rhus tox* acts not only on skin but on muscles, ligaments, and tendons.

Homeopaths prescribe *Rhus tox* to treat skin that is red, swollen, or blistered. It relieves poison ivy, hives (also known as urticaria), burns, itchy rashes such as eczema, and high temperatures. It is also used to treat the pain and swelling that affects joints, ligaments, and tendons, including some sprains and tendinitis, and muscle injuries from overexertion or lifting heavy objects.

Rhus tox is a prominent sports-injury medicine. Homeopaths call it the "rusty gate" remedy: it works best for the person who feels stiff and sore at first but better and better as he or she moves the affected areas and gets loose. It is sometimes used after *Arnica*, when for instance a joint injury becomes hot and swollen.

It is available in both internal and external applications.

Ruta. "The herb of grace," rue *(Ruta graveolens)* is a strong-scented flowering plant that originated in the Mediterranean. Its yellow flowers and bitter-tasting leaves are no longer used by herbalists, but homeopathic preparations are used as treatments for injuries to the periosteum, the tough connective tissue that covers bones. The most common of such injuries is probably bruised shinbone. Homeopaths also use the remedy for bruised kneecap or elbow, sprained wrists and ankles, torn tendons, stretched ligaments, and tennis elbow. The candidate for *Ruta* is made worse from cold or by lying down.

◆ The Flower Essence First-Aid Remedy

One of the most popular formulations developed by the flower-essence pioneer Edward Bach is Rescue Remedy. As formulated by Bach in the 1930s, this is a combination remedy of five flower essences: Rock Rose (to relieve terror and panic); Clematis (out-of-body feeling); Impatiens (mental stress and tension); Cherry Plum (desperation); and Star of Bethlehem (shock). Bach combined these essences to counter fear, anxiety, shock, and panic, the emotional partners of accidents, emergencies, and traumatic injury. Rescue Remedy has become a widely recommended natural first-aid remedy. It won't stop bleeding or set a fracture, but many people say that it plays a valuable emotional and psychological role during an emergency.

An Albuquerque, New Mexico, mother of two young children says, "I've had plenty of occasions to use Rescue Remedy, both the drops and the cream, for temper tantrums, bruises, scraped knees, hay fever, and more. I've even heard that nurses in neonatal intensive care units use it on premature babies. Rescue Remedy is amazing stuff, both for emotional and physical pain. I hope folks will give it a try."

Rescue Remedy is made by the Bach Flowers Remedy company of Great Britain. Other flower-essence companies produce similar first-aid combination products. For instance, the Deva Flower Remedies line includes a product called First Aid Remedy. It is made from the same five flower essences as Rescue Remedy. For convenience's sake, in most cases we'll refer to the first-aid flower essence as Rescue Remedy, since most practitioners and consumers know it by that name.

Rescue Remedy. This is the chief flower remedy for all types of emergencies, but especially any that might cause panic, shock, or hysteria. Proponents recommend it to help alleviate distress while an injured party awaits medical attention, to calm a patient before visiting the dentist, and to help a person cope effectively in times of stress. It may complement medical attention but should never supplant it.

Rescue Remedy is a liquid formula that is 27 percent alcohol. It comes in a tiny, amber, 7.5-ml (quarter-ounce) bottle with a fine glass dropper top. The First Aid Remedy from Natural Labs is more economical and comes in a one-ounce bottle. Bach also makes a Rescue Remedy cream packaged in a 27-gram tube, for topical application (though not to a burn).

The standard dosage recommendation for acute conditions is three to four drops of the liquid concentrate placed directly from the bottle under the tongue. You can also dilute the remedy by putting four drops in a quarter of a glass of water, tea, or juice, to be sipped every three to five minutes. When an accident victim is unconscious, some people administer it by rubbing a few drops into the lips, behind the ears, or on the wrists, or soaking a cotton cloth in a pint of water with five to six drops of Rescue Remedy and applying it as a compress.

◆ The Essential Oil First-Aid Remedies

Essential oils are aromatic concentrates of plants, trees, and flowers. Most are derived by steam distillation, though a few (from the rinds of citrus fruits, for instance) are cold-pressed. Natural foods stores may carry several dozen types, in tiny, amber glass vials with twist-off dropper tops. Some of the more exotic ones, such as Rose, are quite expensive, since it can take hundreds of pounds of petals to make a single ounce of oil. The typical unit of measurement for self-care is the drop.

Some essential oils are never taken internally, while others shouldn't be used even externally if you're pregnant. Keep them out of the reach of children. The following six essential oils are relatively mild, nontoxic, and moderately priced. All are widely available at natural foods stores.

Though there are exceptions, in general essential oils are so highly concentrated that they should not be applied directly to the skin without diluting them first. If you do apply them "neat" (without diluting), it's a good idea to first patch-test on the skin.

One of the most common ways to dilute essential oils for external application is to add them to a natural vegetable "carrier" oil, such as safflower, wheat-germ, or olive oil. As a general guideline, add two drops of essential oil per tablespoon of carrier oil.

To use in a bath, add six to eight drops of essential oil to a full tub of warm water (hot water will quickly evaporate the oils) and stroke the water a few times to disperse.

The easiest way to inhale the aroma of an essential oil is to sprinkle six to eight drops on a tissue or cotton cloth and hold it up to your nose while breathing deeply. Keep your eyes closed to prevent the oil from irritating them. You can also add three or four drops to a sink full of hot water, cover your head with a towel, lean over, and breathe in deeply. Vaporizers put a fine scent of essential oil into the air over an extended period of time. Most are electric- or candle-powered clay bowls to which you add eight to ten drops of essential oil and a small amount of water. The heat gently evaporates the oil and fills an entire room with a healing mist.

To apply as a spray, put eight to ten drops of an essential oil in a spray bottle or plant mister and fill with water. This can be used to spray the skin directly, or like a vaporizer to add a fine mist to the air in a room.

To apply as a compress, put three to four drops of essential oil in hot or cold water (depending on the ailment), soak a cotton cloth in the solution, wring it slightly, and apply to the injured area.

Chamomile. Like the herb (see above), the essential oil may be steam-distilled from either German or Roman varieties. Its main constituent, the effective anti-inflammatory substance azulene, is found in somewhat higher concentrations in German chamomile. The essential oil is also renowned for its antiseptic and antibacterial properties. It is used to treat skin irritations, burns, minor wounds and cuts, muscle aches and cramps, hay fever, sprains and strains, sunburn, and acne. It is mild enough to be used to alleviate teething pain in young children.

Clove. The flower buds of this tropical evergreen tree *(Eugenia caryophyllata* or *Syzygium aromaticum)* yield a potent essential oil that is the major first-aid remedy for dental emergencies. Clove is one of most aromatic healing herbs, with its distinctive taste now flavoring everything from Life Savers to cigarettes.

Clove trees are widely cultivated in tropical areas, particularly around the Indian Ocean, in the West Indies, and Brazil. Dried and powdered, the herb is a fine spice widely used in cooking. Medicinal use of the plant goes back at least to ancient China, whose herbalists have been prescribing it for thousands of years for indigestion and skin infections. The Arabs introduced it into ancient Egypt, and Europeans have used it since well before the Middle Ages. Rubbing the oil on gums to relieve toothache was a favorite remedy of the "eclectic" herbalists prominent in this country in the nineteenth century.

Nearly 20 percent of clove's active constituents are essential oils, the main element of which is the compound eugenol. This colorless, aromatic liquid is the source of the plant's natural antiseptic and anesthetic properties. The essential oil of Clove is strong enough that surgeons have used it to sterilize their instruments. Eugenol has also been shown to stimulate secretion of saliva and help eliminate intestinal gases.

Some dentists still use Clove as an oral anesthetic and to disinfect root canals. It is an ingredient in over-the-counter toothache-pain remedies as well as mouthwash products such as Lavoris. For temporary relief of toothaches, dip a cotton swab in the oil and rub the painful tooth and surrounding gum. This is not a cure: you still need to see a dentist.

Herbalists and other practitioners of natural medicine also use the essential oil externally to disinfect minor wounds and scrapes, reduce warts, and alleviate skin problems such as scabies and insect bites. Taken internally (diluted two drops per cup of water), Clove can control vomiting and nausea. Its smell repels insects.

Undiluted essential oil of Clove is potentially toxic in large doses. It can also sting the gums, and many people dilute it before using it on a toothache. Always dilute it for use on the skin, and avoid taking it during pregnancy.

Eucalyptus. The unique properties of this Australian tree gave the Blue Mountains of New South Wales their name. The leaves of the eucalyptus *(Eucalyptus globulus)* species exude a gum that, as it is evaporated by the summer sun, creates a blue haze. This natural fog not only colors the local mountain range but protects the eucalyptus trees from insects and blight. The chemicals in Eucalyptus thought to be responsible for these effects are cineole and pinene.

Australians have been distilling a strong-smelling essential oil from eucalyptus leaves for over two hundred years. The tree is now grown in other temperate countries, including Spain, Portugal, and China, but Australia remains the principal source. Eucalyptus is one of the least costly essential oils.

The essential oil of Eucalyptus has noted antibacterial and antiviral effects. It also helps relieve pain and inflammation. Practitioners use it to promote the healing of wounds, reduce muscle spasms, and loosen mucus to treat asthma and bronchitis. It also combats sunburn, blisters, and sprains and repels insects.

Aromatherapists apply Eucalyptus through inhalers or vaporizers, in the bath, or by massage. High concentrations or doses of

Eucalyptus can irritate the kidneys when taken internally, or the skin when used externally. Follow recommended dosages.

Lavender. The leaves and exquisite blue flowers of the lavender shrub *(Lavandula officinalis)* are the source for this mild and multipurpose essential oil. The Romans added lavender to their bathwater, and herbal preparations of lavender have been used since ancient times for skin complaints and for scent in perfumes, soaps, and cosmetics. Lavender is grown mostly in the sunny regions around the Mediterranean. The true wild lavender is now more prized for its oil than the hybrid lavandin *(Lavandula x intermedia)* that colors southern France in the summer.

Lavender's constituents include a highly fragrant volatile oil and much tannin. The oil is widely used in cosmetics and perfumes. Aromatherapists and other practitioners of natural medicine recommend the essential oil be inhaled or applied to the skin. There's also a homeopathic tincture that is used internally and externally.

Inhaled through the nose, Lavender's fresh, flowery aroma stimulates a region of the brain in a way that has a sedating effect on the central nervous system. It is thus a mild soporific that can help induce sleep, alleviate stress, and overcome the anxiety and psychological shock of injuries. Aromatherapists also recommend it to treat headaches. Topically, the oil is a wound healer, promoting cell rejuvenation and stimulating the immune system. It also has some analgesic, antiseptic, and anti-inflammatory effects. (Its name, from the Latin *lavare,* "to wash," reflects a use that continues in some parts of the world: to wash and disinfect hospital and sickrooms.) Lavender is mild enough to be applied full strength to treat various types of wounds, cuts, scrapes, and burns as well as sprains, insect bites and stings, athlete's foot, muscular aches and pains, and earache. Lavender is recommended for use by children.

Peppermint. Manufacturers worldwide use the essential oil from this familiar garden perennial *(Mentha piperita)* primarily as a flavoring agent in foods, candies, chewing gum, and toothpastes. Though its use as a remedy goes back two centuries, today less than 1 percent of Peppermint oil is used medicinally. This is unfortunate, because the oil has significant antiseptic, anti-inflammatory, and astringent powers.

Although herbalists in ancient Egypt and China first started using some mint species thousands of years ago, peppermint is a relative newcomer to the medical scene. Peppermint apparently began to be cultivated and used in England around the beginning of the eighteenth century. It was being grown commercially in western Massachusetts by the end of the eighteenth century, and being distilled into oil by 1812. The plant is native to Europe and is still grown there and in the United States primarily for its essential oil. The annual crop in the United States is worth around $100 million.

Peppermint-leaf tea has long been popular as a digestive remedy, and some herbalists still prescribe it for indigestion, nausea, diarrhea, and cramps. The essential oil is used internally for shock, asthma, travel sickness, fainting, and nausea, and externally for a range of conditions including itchy skin, hemorrhoids, toothaches, muscle aches, and insect bites. The oil is also a good insect repellent.

The oil is produced by steam distillation of the leaves. A high percentage of its constituents is the alcohol menthol, and it also contains azulenes and tannins. Studies of the oil indicate it has antimicrobial and antiviral activities and is antispasmodic.

Peppermint oil may irritate some people's skin if applied undiluted or in high doses.

Tea Tree. In 1770, a botanist accompanying British sailor James Cook's exploration of Australia's east coast became intrigued with an unusual tree. Cook's crew made tea from the aromatic leaves of the tree *(Melaleuca alternifolia)*, later identified as a member of the myrtle family. The name *tea tree* stuck, and back in England the botanist, Joseph Banks, did the first in a continuing line of investigations into the leaves' many healing properties. Today the essential oil of the tea tree plant is recognized as one of the premier natural first-aid remedies, useful for treating burns, cuts, scrapes, bites, stings, and various skin irritations.

If Cook's crew had asked Australia's Aborigines about it, we might know the plant as "wound tree" today, because the Aborigines had long used the plant to cleanse and heal wounds. Researchers in Australia confirmed Tea Tree's powers as a disinfectant, and by the 1930s it was a widely respected medicine in that country. Tea tree growers were exempted from serving in the military during World War II until a steady supply of the oil was assured for inclusion in first-aid kits. Commercial production of Tea Tree is still centered in New South Wales, the only place in the world where the tree grows naturally. The pale yellow oil is quickly becoming known worldwide for its antibiotic, antiseptic, and antiviral powers.

Scientists have identified some forty-eight organic compounds in Tea Tree oil. Although all may play some role in making the oil a powerful germicide and fungicide, two with obvious medicinal activity are the chemicals terpinen 4-ol and cineole. Australian product regulations require that Tea Tree must have at least 30 percent terpinen 4-ol. According to Cynthia Olsen, author of *Australian Tea Tree Oil Guide,* "The higher the better, since this compound contains healing properties." Olsen notes that some hospitals in Switzerland use Tea Tree oil to control infections.

Studies have shown that Tea Tree is effective against a range of bacterial, viral, and fungal conditions, including athlete's foot, nail infections, and mouth sores. It's also an effective insect repellent. "Tea Tree oil is my favorite home remedy," says a reader from Salmon, Idaho. "I've been using it for years with excellent results, for everything from the common cold to bug bites. My husband swears by it for athlete's foot, and I couldn't imagine raising kids without Tea Tree oil. I send the kids for the Tea Tree whenever they have a bump, scratch, scrape, cut, or rash, and the problem is fixed."

Some producers dilute their Tea Tree oil with other oils, or the oil from other varieties of tea tree. The studies that have demonstrated healing effects have used pure oil of *Melaleuca alternifolia,* so look for oil products that are 100 percent *Melaleuca alternifolia.* Some companies make a therapeutic tea tree cream for sunburn and skin irritations. Look for those with at least 5 percent Tea Tree oil. Natural bodycare companies also use the oil as an ingredient in shampoos, soaps, toothpastes, deodorants, massage oils, and a variety of other products.

Tea Tree is nonallergenic and nontoxic. It is safely applied directly to the skin without being diluted (avoid getting it in the eyes, though). You can put a few drops in some hot water and inhale it to relieve nasal congestion, but it is not otherwise taken internally. It is often sold in 10-ml dropper-topped bottles.

◆ The First-Aid Vitamins and Supplements

A number of vitamins and enzyme supplement products have some surprising uses as topical remedies or internal medicines to promote healing, reduce swelling, and relieve pain.

Bromelain. A naturally occurring enzyme derived from the pineapple plant, bromelain has become a popular sports-injury medicine since being introduced in the mid-1950s. Japan and Hawaii are leading suppliers of commercial bromelain, as well as the sites of much of the research into its applications. Bromelain is also widely used to assist in the digestion of protein, to relieve painful menstruation, and to treat arthritis.

A number of studies support its use as a first-aid remedy to relieve swelling and promote wound healing. Surgeons who studied 146 boxers found that about 80 percent of those who took bromelain experienced complete clearing of their bruises within four days, while almost 90 percent of those who didn't receive bromelain took seven to fourteen days for their bruises to clear. One hypothesis is that bromelain helps break down fibrin, a blood protein involved in both the clotting and inflammation processes. It thus prevents fibrin from forming a wall around the area of inflammation, from blocking blood and lymph vessels, and from causing swelling. The result is better tissue drainage and reduced localized pain and swelling.

"I've done a fair amount of work with bromelain for all kinds of contusions, injuries, and surgery," says Joseph Pizzorno, N.D. "I recommend taking 125 to 400 milligrams three times daily, thirty minutes before or ninety minutes after a meal. Taking it between meals is crucial, since if you take it at meals, it will be used to digest the food."

Bromelain is nontoxic even at high doses. It is available in 100-mg tablets from a number of natural supplement manufacturers.

Papain. Like bromelain this is a naturally occurring enzyme, obtained not from the pineapple but from the milky juice of unripe papayas. The active ingredient in meat tenderizers such as Adolph's, papain softens meat by breaking down muscle tissue. This same action gives papain its first-aid powers: applied topically in a paste, it breaks down the large protein molecules of insect venom, deactivating the poison before it gets circulated throughout your body.

Papain is available either in a commercial meat tenderizer or as papaya tablets from natural supplement manufacturers. To make a paste, crush five or six tablets with a wooden spoon in a coffee cup, or even better, use a mortar and pestle. Add a drop or two of water at a time to the powder (it is easy to put too much water in and end up with a tea instead of a paste) until you obtain a sticky consistency. Brush the paste on the skin with your finger.

Vitamin C. Scientists have known for two centuries that some element in citrus fruits is essential for human health. In 1928 they identified that element as ascorbic (from *antiscurvy*) acid or vitamin C, a substance that strengthens the walls of blood vessels, helps the body resist infection, and protects other vitamins from oxidation. Vitamin C also plays a crucial role in the healing of wounds and broken bones, in part because it is vital to the formation of collagen, a fibrous tissue found throughout the body. Studies indicate that high levels of C (2–5 g per day) can dramatically speed recovery from injury or surgery. Vitamin C is also crucial to immune system function and has been shown to reduce the symptoms of asthma, allergy, and food sensitivity.

Adequate vitamin C intake will form healthy collagen tissue in the skin and thus protect blood vessels from the effects of trauma and bruising. It can also help prevent nosebleeds. Vitamin C is thought to play a role in wound healing though this has not been widely studied by scientists. The high acidity of a vitamin C paste used topically may help to kill viruses that cause warts and other skin problems. Topical applications may also help relieve pain, reduce inflammation, and lessen the risk of infection.

Some amount of the vitamin is found in many foods, with the highest level in green leafy vegetables, broccoli, brussels sprouts, cauliflower, potatoes, strawberries, and grapefruit. Supplements are inexpensive and widely available.

Vitamin C is nontoxic. If you take approximately two to five grams or more per day, you may develop diarrhea or loose stools. Many practitioners of natural medicine call this a person's "bowel tolerance" and recommend that C be taken up to the point that it doesn't cause any overt symptoms. You can determine your bowel tolerance by taking one gram of C per day for three or four days, noting the condition of your stools, and then increasing your daily dose to two grams and so on up to five grams if the stools say normal. Pregnant women should not take over one to two grams of vitamin C daily, since megadoses may induce miscarriage.

Vitamin C can be applied topically to a sting or minor burn by crushing tablets with a few drops of water to form a paste, or crushing 1,000 mg of C into a powder and dissolving it in one cup of tepid water. This yields a 1–3 percent solution. Apply it with a spray bottle or plant mister. In some people topical applications may irritate the skin and should be discontinued.

Vitamin E. First isolated in 1936, vitamin E is a powerful antioxidant that plays a crucial role in promoting overall health. Antioxidants protect the body against the effects of free radicals, reactive and unstable atoms or molecules (from chemicals, smoke, fatty foods, and other sources) that are damaging to living cells. Antioxidant nutrients such as vitamins A, C, and E can combine with and neutralize free radicals without themselves becoming unstable, thus defending the body against harmful effects that may range from cancer to aging.

Vitamin E is used by most of the tissues of the body. It protects vitamins A and C from destruction and aids the formation of red blood cells, muscles, and other tissues. There is less reliable evidence for claims that the vitamin promotes virility or protects against heart disease.

Vitamin E oil applied to the skin seems to boost the healing of burns and prevent scars from forming. Definitive studies are lacking, but many alternative practitioners have seen positive results among their patients from using E on burns. Vitamin E oil can also be applied to nipples that are sore and cracked from breast-feeding, and to canker sores. Studies suggest that when taken internally, 400–800 IU daily of vitamin E can help eliminate exercise cramps and nighttime leg cramps, perhaps by aiding the release of sugar in muscles.

"I've found that vitamin E oil is an extraordinary natural first-aid tool," says a reader from Glenville, New York. "I've used it on diaper rashes, cuts and bruises, mosquito bites, and burns— all the major skin problems a child faces. Not once was I disappointed with the speed of recovery. Now I keep a bottle in practically every room of the house. It is amazing how much we need to use it and how good it really is."

The highest levels of vitamin E are found in vegetable oils, including safflower, wheat-germ, and corn. The best food sources are dark green leafy vegetables, whole grains, and legumes. Meat and dairy products usually have low amounts. Vitamin E supplements most commonly are oil-filled capsules, which can be broken open for topical use. Some natural foods stores also carry bottled vitamin E, which is more economical than capsules for using on large areas of sunburned skin, for instance.

◆ Food and Household First-Aid Items

The following seven remedies are inexpensive, widely available, and have multiple uses in any first-aid kit.

Activated charcoal. Pharmaceutical companies process pure carbon in a special way to make activated charcoal, an important antipoison first-aid remedy. A French pharmacist first demonstrated its potential in 1831 when he shocked a group of medical colleagues by gulping down some charcoal along with a hefty dose of strychnine. Charcoal saved his life and has since saved tens of thousands more.

Look at particles of activated charcoal under a microscope and you'll notice many small chambers and cavities that add up to an extensive surface area. These are perfect for catching and trapping the large molecules of most toxic substances, which is why charcoal is also used in air and water filters. Charcoal works by *adsorption:* it collects substances in a condensed form on a surface, as distinct from *absorption,* which is to take in and incorporate or assimilate a substance. Activated charcoal adsorbs poisons and drugs in the stomach and intestines and then is excreted along with them by the body. It further prevents toxins from being absorbed into the bloodstream by coating intestinal walls.

Although activated charcoal adsorbs a variety of poisons and drugs, it doesn't work for all toxic substances. It should be used as a poison remedy only after checking with a poison control center. It is also a useful remedy for making into a paste and applying externally to insect bites and stings.

In recent years researchers have also demonstrated a number of nonemergency uses for activated charcoal taken internally. Studies show that it may lower blood cholesterol levels, reduce uric-acid levels and thus treat gout, relieve gas pains, and reduce flatulence.

Activated charcoal is available over the counter at natural foods stores and pharmacies. It comes in a powder, liquid, and capsules (Charcoal Plus, Charcocaps). The capsules can be broken open to use the powder for making a paste.

Baking soda. Otherwise known as bicarbonate of soda or sodium bicarbonate, baking soda is a popular home remedy for indigestion and heartburn that, like activated charcoal and papain, can be made into a versatile paste for external application. Baking soda is an alkali that readily dissolves in water and neutralizes acid. Alka-Seltzer and a number of other commercial products contain baking soda as an ingredient. It is a safe and inexpensive antacid, though high in sodium (500 mg per half a teaspoon). Baking soda is also somewhat of a detoxifier, preventing the absorption of certain drugs (tetracycline) and acting as a tonic for short-term relief of nicotine withdrawal.

Applied to the skin in the form of a paste, baking soda similarly works to neutralize an acidic environment and detoxify. Doctors sometimes use it to reduce pain when they give an injection of a local anesthetic. Many people use a baking soda paste to treat bee stings and insect bites, poison ivy, canker sores, sunburn, and rashes and skin irritations (it's too strong, however, for use on infants; treating a diaper rash with it could lead to too much being absorbed by the skin and cause an acid-base imbalance in the blood). Sprinkled in a warm bath, it can relieve sore muscles.

It is widely available as a powder in supermarkets. To make a paste, dissolve three parts baking soda in one part water. In a bath, add one-half cup to tepid water.

Cold water. Medical practitioners of all persuasions are increasingly applying cold, usually in the form of cold water, as the first treatment for burns, bruises, muscle spasms, strains and sprains, insect stings, and more. It is appropriate both for external skin conditions and internal injuries in which blood vessels are ruptured. Traumas from accidents and sports injuries often cause local swelling as blood leaks into surrounding tissue. Swelling that goes unchecked can restrict movement and impair healing. Cold constricts blood vessels and thus controls swelling. It also acts as a natural painkiller by relieving the pressure on sensitive nerves and blocking the transmission of pain sensations to the brain.

Cold is best applied immediately after an injury occurs. After the first day or so, swelling is usually under control and cold is then replaced by heat, to dilate blood vessels and increase circulation of healing nutrients to the injury.

Apply cold by holding an injury under cold running water, crushing up ice to make an ice pack (ice should never be applied directly to the skin), or using commercial hot/cold packs. Cold is safe in most cases, though it needs to be used wisely. Applied incorrectly, it can cut off circulation and cause frostbite. People suffering from impaired circulation or diabetes should be especially careful when using cold applications.

Garlic and onions. These are two popular members of the allium family, which includes some 450 plants and has a history of medicinal use that goes back at least six thousand years. Along with leek, shallot, and chives, garlic *(Allium sativum)* and onion *(Allium cepa)* figure in a seemingly endless array of folk remedies for everything from insect bites to fever as well as a lengthening list of scientifically validated treatments for conditions including heart disease. Garlic's medicinal value was known by the ancient Chinese, Egyptians, and Greeks. The Russian army used garlic at the front lines during the two World Wars to dress wounds, until it was supplanted by penicillin.

The allium plants are thought to have originated in Central Asia, but they survive in a variety of climates. Today they are grown throughout the world, with China and Spain leading producers. The Japanese are one of the few cultures that avoid garlic, perhaps out of antipathy for the South Koreans, who love it.

Garlic and onions are not roots but bulbs that form on the stem of the plant. Scientists have discovered over two hundred different compounds in garlic. Most garlic researchers believe that the principal medicinal ingredients are the same sulfur compounds as those responsible for garlic's characteristic smell. The odor is released when garlic is crushed or chopped and its chemical constituent allicin starts to break down into diallyl disulfide. The pungent smell may in part be a protective action by the plant, discouraging bacteria and pests from preying on it. This same protective action may be the source for much of alliums' medicinal properties. Allium plants also contain protein, vitamins A, B complex, and C, and various trace minerals.

Garlic research has become a minor industry in the past two decades, with over seven hundred scientific studies completed. The evidence indicates that garlic is one of the best natural antibiotics and antiseptics. Its antibacterial properties were clinically observed as long ago as 1858, in a study done by Louis Pasteur. More recently, studies have found that fresh garlic extract is an effective broad-range antibiotic. For instance, it is more effective than common antibiotics such as penicillin and tetracycline in killing diverse bacteria, including those that cause food poisoning and skin viruses. It works well to contain bacteria when an infection first appears or is chronic, and it doesn't create bacterial resistance. It is less effective, however, than the "single bullet" synthetic antibiotics against certain bacteria and acute infections. Scientists attribute garlic's antibacterial effects to its sulfides. These work like the sulfa drugs to wipe out sulfur-containing biological catalysts in bacteria.

Garlic's medicinal value goes well beyond its effect on bacteria. A Japanese study showed garlic juice can trap toxic lead and mercury in the body and remove it. Researchers suggest it works by helping the liver to neutralize poisons. Garlic is also an effective antioxidant. Its antifungal activity has prompted people to use it to combat skin infections such as athlete's foot and ringworm. It is used to treat hemorrhoids and as an antidote to altitude sickness. A Chinese study suggests it may reduce the risk of stomach cancer. Its popularity in Mediterranean countries that have relatively low rates of heart disease has led researchers to explore its effects on the circulatory system. There's growing evidence that it can prevent heart attacks by lowering both cholesterol levels and blood pressure.

Onions share most of garlic's powers against heart disease and may even outshine garlic in one respect: German researchers have identified several substances in onions that they believe can prevent an asthma attack. In one animal study the onion medicine prevented attacks for up to twelve hours. The researchers speculate that in a few years there may be an onion-based asthma drug.

A number of folk remedies for insect bites and stings call for topical applications of onions. Scientists suggest that the sulfur compounds in onions block extra oxygen from being introduced to the cells. This in turn affects the body's production of prostaglandins, hormonelike substances that govern blood pressure, the inflammation response, and other bodily processes.

The garlic industry sells $100 million worth of products to U.S. consumers each year. Fresh garlic, garlic juice, and liquid garlic extracts such as Kyolic have high levels of allicin, as do "allicin-stabilized" tablets such as Garlicin. Most scientists believe that as allicin decays over time, it loses its medicinal values. Though some also believe that if there is no smell, there is no therapeutic value (a scientist writing in *The Lancet* stated unequivocally that "totally odorless garlic preparations are ineffective"), there is solid evidence that "odor-free" and "odor-controlled" products release allicin during digestion and do have significant health effects.

Applying garlic to the skin may cause an allergic reaction in a small percentage of people.

Hydrogen peroxide. Known to chemists as H_2O_2, hydrogen peroxide is found widely in nature (in rainwater, for instance); industry (added to the linings of nonrefrigerated beverage containers to prevent bacterial decay and used in cosmetics to bleach hair); and in the human body (it serves to regulate temperature, hormone activities, and immune response). Medical practitioners use it to disinfect wounds and, to a more limited extent, to treat canker sores, gingivitis, and shingles. A small number of radical "oxygen therapists" are even administering it internally, a practice that has generated considerable controversy.

To kill germs and bacteria on a fresh wound, practitioners use a 3 percent solution. It is a colorless, syrupy liquid whose antibacterial properties are visible (it foams up on the skin) but not otherwise remarkable or long-lasting. The foaming is oxygen at work. Hydrogen peroxide reacts with catalase, an enzyme found in most cells, and releases oxygen in the form of bubbles. The wound is cleaned as dirt and germs are carried to the surface.

Make sure you use a 3 percent solution, not "food grade" hydrogen peroxide, a more caustic 35 percent solution. While some proponents of oxygen therapy recommend taking hydrogen peroxide orally (or intravenously) for AIDS or chronic fatigue syndrome, internal use is possibly dangerous and should be considered only under the supervision of an experienced practitioner.

Hydrogen peroxide is sometimes combined with aloe gel for use on wounds. Others make a paste with H_2O_2 and baking soda for gum infections and inflammation. There's even a specially formulated toothpaste that produces hydrogen peroxide during brushing. The 3 percent solution is widely sold in pharmacies.

Vinegar. A pungent-smelling liquid that contains the sour, colorless substance acetic acid, vinegar has traditionally been used to preserve food, cleanse household items, and promote health. The Japanese add it to sushi rice to kill bacteria that might cause food poisoning, as well as to prevent the rice from spoiling. A traditional Vermont folk remedy is to take two teaspoons of apple-cider vinegar in water, to maintain a healthy acid/alkali balance in the blood and urine.

Vinegar is made by fermenting dilute alcoholic liquids that have been derived from sugarcane, molasses, fruit, or grain. Vinegar has a long history of use in folk medicine, taken internally to treat fatigue, headache, high blood pressure, sore throat, obesity, and yeast infections. Topically it is a powerful antiseptic and astringent applied to relieve jellyfish stings, nosebleed, sunburn, swimmer's ear, and more.

Vinegar's high acidity explains some of its effects. Japanese scientists have also speculated that the more than two dozen amino and organic acids in natural vinegar prevent toxic fat peroxides from forming in the body. This may be partly responsible for vinegar's ability to counter the effects of lactic acid buildup in the blood, a physical process that tends to increase in the summer and lead to fatigue, irritability, and stiff and sore muscles.

Highly processed and distilled vinegar may have few of its helpful amino acids left, so for medicinal purposes use high-quality natural products. Traditionally brewed brown-rice vinegar from Japan is widely available in natural foods stores. Also look for naturally brewed white-wine and apple-cider vinegars without added colorings.

◆ Actions of Natural Remedies

Here's a summary of the major effects for the top forty natural first-aid remedies.

ANALGESICS AND ANESTHETICS
to relieve pain and reduce nerve excitability

chamomile	Lavender
echinacea	Eucalyptus
Arnica	Clove

ANTIBIOTICS AND ANTIBACTERIALS
to inhibit growth of or kill bacteria

echinacea	Eucalyptus
goldenseal	Chamomile
pau d'arco	garlic and onion
yarrow	hydrogen peroxide

ANTIFUNGALS
to inhibit growth of or kill fungi

calendula	Tea Tree
echinacea	Clove
goldenseal	garlic and onion
Lavender	

ANTI-INFLAMMATORIES
to prevent or reduce swelling

calendula	*Rhus tox*
chamomile	Lavender
echinacea	Eucalyptus
comfrey	Peppermint
goldenseal	Chamomile
pau d'arco	bromelain
Apis	baking soda
Arnica	garlic and onion

ANTIOXIDANTS
to neutralize free radicals in the body

vitamin E	garlic and onions
vitamin C	

ANTISEPTICS
internally or externally, to prevent breakdown of organic tissues or inhibit growth of microorganisms

calendula	Lavender
chamomile	Eucalyptus
echinacea	Peppermint
plantain	Tea Tree
goldenseal	Chamomile
Hypericum	Clove
Calendula	

ANTISPASMODICS
to prevent muscular spasm, cramps, asthma

calendula	Eucalyptus
chamomile	Chamomile
Rhus tox	vitamin E

ANTIVIRALS
to inhibit growth of or kill viruses

echinacea	Tea Tree
pau d'arco	garlic
Eucalyptus	

ASTRINGENTS
to cause hardening and contraction of tissue and stop discharge and bleeding

calendula	yarrow
plantain	witch hazel
goldenseal	vinegar

BLOOD PURIFIERS AND DETOXIFIERS
to treat conditions of toxicity such as poisoning and venomous stings

echinacea	papain
pau d'arco	activated charcoal
plantain	baking soda
Arsenicum	garlic

DECONGESTANTS
to relieve bronchial spasm and open breathing tubes

ephedra   Chamomile
Peppermint   onion

DEMULCENTS
to reduce irritation of and soothe, soften, and protect mucous membranes

comfrey   goldenseal
slippery elm   Eucalyptus
plantain

DIGESTIVE DETOXIFIERS
to eliminate poisons in the stomach and intestines

activated charcoal

EMETICS
to induce vomiting

ipecac

IMMUNE BOOSTERS
to assist white-blood-cell activity

chamomile   vitamin C
echinacea   vitamin E
goldenseal

NERVINES/SEDATIVES
to calm nervous tension and induce sleep

chamomile   Lavender
Aconite   Chamomile
Arsenicum   Rescue Remedy
Hypericum

STIMULANTS
to excite the central nervous system, increase pulse, and restore circulation

ephedra

WOUND HEALERS
to stop bleeding, prevent swelling, and boost the immune system

calendula

echinacea

plantain

comfrey

chamomile

goldenseal

yarrow

aloe

slippery elm

Arnica

Hypericum

Ledum

Calendula

Lavender

Chamomile

FIRST
AID
FOR
EMERGENCIES

THREE

Basic Emergency Care

THIS CHAPTER COVERS:

◆ *assessing the emergency*
◆ *unconsciousness*
◆ *neck and spinal injuries*
◆ *the ABCs: airway, breathing, and circulation*
◆ *how to do rescue breathing*
◆ *how to do chest compressions and cardiopulmonary resuscitation (CPR)*
◆ *shock*
◆ *choking*
◆ *the recovery position*
◆ *transporting an injured person*

SEE "CHAPTER 4: ALLERGIC REACTIONS" FOR:

◆ *acute allergic reaction (anaphylactic shock)*

SEE "CHAPTER 6: BLEEDING" FOR:

◆ *deep wounds*

Before turning to allergies, bites and stings, and a host of common, often minor emergencies, it is necessary to learn some of the basic first-aid tools needed to respond to major emergencies. Many people will never need to provide first aid in a life-threatening situation, such as a heart attack, stroke, choking, or shock. If you're with someone who is faced with one of these medical emergencies, the basic techniques outlined in this chapter will help you deal successfully with the problem.

◆ Assessing the Emergency

Common sense and sound judgment are prerequisites for success-fully administering first aid. The provider of first aid needs to stay calm and rationally assess the situation. Ready-fire-aim is a ter-rible strategy for providing first aid. In a worst-case scenario, it can lead to greater injuries than not providing first aid.

In any emergency, first stop for at least a moment to take stock of the situation. If your three-year-old son gets a minor paper cut on his finger, obviously an evaluation can be made quickly. With more serious emergencies, such as car accidents, fires, and electrical hazards, with possibly two or more injured people, a quick and accurate assessment of the situation is essen-tial. You need to consider:

◆ Does the situation present an ongoing danger to the victims or to you and other rescuers? If so, you need to address these dangers first, to prevent further injuries. This may require you to leave the scene and go for help or to try to move the injured person. It may also require you first to remove the danger, for instance by putting out a fire, setting flares around an automobile accident, or cutting off a source of electricity.

◆ Can you determine exactly what happened? Calling (or sending someone else to call) for help is often the most important single act of first aid. This step is all the more valuable if you are able to give medical or emergency personnel a brief newspaper-type report on the situation: who, what, where, how, why, when? The emergency re-sponse and the need for specialized equipment can be tailored to meet the demands of the situation if the neces-sary background information can be relayed early.

◆ What are the treatment priorities? The answer to this question may depend upon such factors as how serious a person's injury is, if others are also injured, whether you are alone in providing first aid or others can assist, and whether emergency help, a doctor or other medical profes-sional is nearby.

Some of these questions can be answered by observation, while others may require talking to the victims. Time is a major factor. In cases of severe shock, heavy bleeding, choking, and others, you may have only a matter of minutes before a person can die from his or her injuries. Keep in mind the emergency response guidelines summarized in Chapter 1: remain calm, use common sense, and do no harm.

A rescuer's top treatment priority when confronted with an injured person requiring first aid is to assess his or her vital signs. The first questions are:

- ♦ Is the person conscious?
- ♦ Has he or she suffered a neck or spinal injury?
- ♦ Are his or her lungs, heart, and circulatory systems providing the body with oxygenated blood?

The answers to these questions will let you know whether you are dealing with a major or minor emergency.

♦ Unconsciousness

An unconscious person may be either completely unresponsive to outside stimuli or drowsy and slipping in and out of consciousness. There are any number of potential causes of unconsciousness, ranging from a simple and relatively benign fainting episode due to being in an overheated, ill-ventilated room to a potentially deadly major heart attack. Unconsciousness that lasts for an extended period of time is coma. In states of unconsciousness, something is interrupting the flow of oxygenated blood to the brain.

Until the brain starts to get the energy, in the form of oxygen, it needs to function, the unconscious body is in a precarious state. If the person vomits, she won't know to turn the head to one side. If the person gets something stuck in her throat, she won't know to cough (much less perform the Heimlich maneuver on herself). The person may also have suffered other serious injuries from the trauma that initiated the unconsciousness. It is best to assume the worst when you come upon an unconscious person and treat the condition as a major medical emergency.

BASIC FIRST AID FOR UNCONSCIOUSNESS

First, determine whether the person is indeed unconscious. In most cases the person's state of consciousness is evident. If you're not sure and the person is on the ground and still, tap the person's chest or gently shake him or her and say clearly, "Are you okay?" Don't shake the person forcefully, since this could conceivably cause injury, especially if the person has suffered a neck or spinal injury. Also, don't throw water in his or her face, slap the person, or take other violent steps to revive the person.

If the person does not quickly regain consciousness from tapping or gentle shaking, call emergency medical personnel right away. Evaluate the person's condition by checking for obvious causes of unconsciousness. If the person is bleeding severely, for instance, provide first aid for bleeding.

Never give an unconscious person anything to eat or drink or a drug to take orally. Administering anything orally to an unconscious person presents a serious choking risk. In general it's not a good idea to give the person anything to eat or drink when he or she is revived, either. It is possible the person could lose consciousness again. Also, recent food or drink may interfere with necessary emergency treatment steps to be taken in the immediate future in the hospital. If possible, consult with a medical professional before giving any food or drink to a recently revived person.

Check and monitor the unconscious person's ABCs: airway, breathing, and circulation (see below). Check frequently, since the person could stop breathing at any moment.

Check for a neck or spinal injury (see below). If such an injury can be ruled out, put the person in the recovery position (see below). If you do suspect a neck or spinal injury, don't move the person except to open his airway or to restore breathing or circulation.

Stay with the person and keep him or her warm until medical help arrives.

If the person regains consciousness and is breathing, question him about his condition while continuing to check and monitor his airway, breathing, and circulation (see below). Further first-aid steps depend on the injury or illness.

(See "Chapter 13: Dizziness and Fainting" for heat faint.)

◆ Neck and Spinal Injuries

One of the essential steps to avoid causing further harm while providing first aid is to check whether the person has suffered a neck or spinal injury. The spine's intricate set of interlocking bones, tendons, muscles, and nerves is easily damaged by a fall or hard force, as in a diving accident or auto wreck. It is possible after a neck or spinal injury for the vertebrae to be twisted in such a way that movement of the body causes further injury, possibly to the sheath of nerves running up the spinal cord to the brain. The wrong type of rescue movement done by an untrained but well-meaning bystander can lead to a first-aid nightmare—a paralyzing injury that could have been prevented.

If the injured person is conscious, ask about such symptoms of neck and spinal injuries as pain in the neck or back, numbness or tingling in an arm or leg, and loss of movement in a limb. The person may also show signs of shock, such as cold and clammy skin.

If the person is unconscious, without moving him or her, look for signs of trauma to the neck, head, or back. Consider the entire injury scene. Was the person injured by a severe force, such as getting hit by a moving vehicle or falling down stairs? If so, a neck or spinal injury may have resulted.

BASIC FIRST AID FOR NECK AND SPINAL EMERGENCIES

If you suspect a neck or spinal injury, or if you are not sure, call emergency medical personnel immediately.

Leave the person in the position he or she is in. Move the person only if you have to for safety reasons, or to turn him or her over to perform rescue breathing or chest compressions (see below). If you must move the person, always move the body as a unit, with the head and neck stabilized, avoiding any twisting of the head, neck, or trunk.

Check and monitor his or her ABCs: airway, breathing, and circulation. If you must open the airway (because the person is vomiting, for instance) turn the person onto one side while moving the body as a unit and supporting the head and neck. If you have to perform rescue breathing, turn the person over with the same amount of caution. Lift the person's chin to open the airway but don't tilt the head back.

If the person is unconscious, hold his or her head between your hands while waiting for help to arrive. This is to prevent sudden movements upon reviving. If the person is conscious, try to dissuade him or her from moving. Use stiff objects and padding to immobilize the person's head, neck, and spine. Don't move the person into the shock position (lying on the back with the feet elevated), but try to keep him or her warm and prevent shock nevertheless.

Treat any obvious severe injuries such as bleeding, if possible without moving the body.

◆ The ABCs: Airway, Breathing, and Circulation

The next crucial and immediate assessment to make on an injured person also relates to how severe of an emergency you face. Is the illness or trauma so severe that it has caused the person's lungs or heart (or both) to stop functioning? Is there a deep wound or internal injury that is causing severe bleeding? Find out by checking the ABCs: airway, breathing, and circulation. Whatever other first aid you offer won't be worthwhile if you can't help the person maintain an open airway, the transfer of oxygen from air to blood, and sufficient supplies of oxygenated blood to organs and tissues.

Airway. Determine whether the person is breathing. Can you feel or hear the air being exhaled by putting your ear up close to the person's mouth and nose, or your ear against his or her chest? Is the chest rising and falling as well? In some cases a person's chest will be moving but the person won't be breathing, so make sure you feel or hear the breath as well as see the chest rising and falling.

Breathing. If the person is not breathing, you need to open the airway and perform rescue breathing as quickly as possible (see "How to Do Rescue Breathing," below).

Circulation. If the person is breathing, check his or her circulation. To find the person's pulse on the neck, put your fingertips on the person's Adam's apple and then slide them down into the depression between the throat and the muscle on the side of the neck. For five to ten seconds use your fingertips (not your thumb, which could cause you to take your own pulse) to feel whether blood is moving through the carotid artery (see illustration #3). If the person has a pulse, check for severe bleeding anywhere on the body and take steps to control it (see "Deep Wounds" in "Chapter 6: Bleeding").

If the injured person is less than a year old, check the pulse by feeling for the brachial artery in the upper arm rather than the carotid artery in the neck. Use your index and middle finger to feel for the pulse on the inside of the arm between the elbow and the shoulder.

If the person has no pulse and is not breathing, it is necessary to perform rescue breathing and chest compressions, the combination of which is known as cardiopulmonary resuscitation.

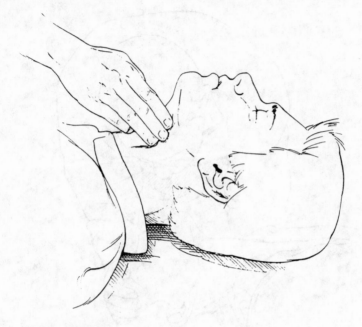

Illustration #3:

Take a neck pulse by putting your fingertips in the depression between the throat and the muscle on the side of the neck for five to ten seconds.

◆ How to Do Rescue Breathing

Rescue breathing is also known as artificial respiration and mouth-to-mouth resuscitation. Make sure the person is not breathing before attempting to perform it.

Put the injured person on her back on the floor, or an even, firm surface. If she needs to be rolled over, do so while supporting her head and neck. Kneel down beside her, between her chest and head.

Open her airway. If she has not suffered a neck or spinal injury, put one hand beneath her neck and the other on her forehead. Simultaneously lift the neck and tilt the head backward (see illustration #4). Pull upward on the jaw to open the mouth. Check in the mouth for anything that might block the breath. A person's airway can be blocked not only by an object that gets stuck in the windpipe (see "Choking" section below), but by bodily fluids such as blood and vomit. If necessary, clear the

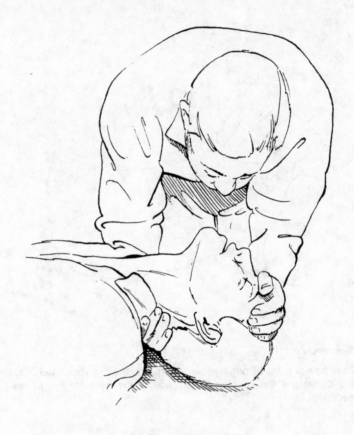

Illustration #4:

Open an injured person's airway by putting one hand beneath the neck and the other on the forehead, and then simultaneously lifting the neck and tilting the head backward.

mouth of an object with a finger sweep (see "Choking") or of fluid by turning the head to one side.

At this point again check to see whether the person is breathing. In some instances opening the airway and clearing the mouth are enough to induce breathing. If the person has resumed breathing, check her pulse for circulation. Take steps to restore circulation if necessary, or put the person in the recovery position.

If the person is still not breathing, keep her head tilted back while pinching her nostrils shut with the thumb and index finger of one hand. Take a deep breath and place your mouth tightly

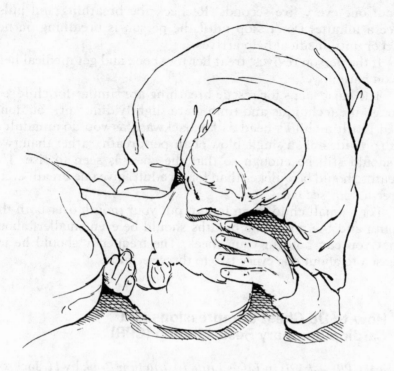

Illustration #5:

To do rescue breathing, keep the person's head tilted back, while pinching the nostrils shut with the thumb and index finger of one hand. Take a deep breath, place your mouth tightly around the person's mouth, and blow with enough force to cause the person's chest to rise.

around the person's mouth (see illustration #5). Blow into her mouth two times in quick succession. You may feel some resistance, but do it hard enough to cause her chest to rise. If the chest doesn't rise, it's either because you haven't blown forcefully enough or something is blocking the victim's airway. If the latter is the problem, see the section on first aid for an unconscious choking person.

When the person's chest is expanded, stop blowing and take your mouth away. The injured person's chest should fall. Keep her head tilted back and look, listen, and feel for breathing for about five to ten seconds. Then check the person's circulation.

If the person is not breathing and has no pulse, begin CPR. If she has a pulse, but is still not breathing, continue to perform rescue breathing. Give breaths at a rate of twelve per minute, about one every five seconds. Recheck the breathing and pulse once a minute. Don't stop until the person is breathing on her own or until medical help arrives.

If the person revives, treat her for shock and get medical help if you haven't yet.

The basic steps for rescue breathing are similar for children, though the technique and timing are slightly different. You don't need to tilt a child's head as far backward as you do an adult's. Also provide only a single blow of air per breath, rather than two. It should still be enough so that the chest is seen to rise. The breaths should be quicker than for an adult: give one breath every three to four seconds.

For a small child or an infant, put your mouth over both the mouth and the nose. The breaths should be even smaller, about what you can hold in your cheek. The frequency should be increased to about one every two to three seconds.

◆ How to Do Chest Compressions and Cardiopulmonary Resuscitation (CPR)

"Learn CPR"—#120 in *Life's Little Instruction Book* by H. Jackson Brown, Jr.

Rescue breathing by itself can save someone who is not breathing but still has circulation. In dire emergencies, however, a person may be unconscious, not breathing, and have no pulse. In such cases, don't assume the person is dead. If he has lost consciousness, breathing, and circulation within the past five to six minutes (and in some cases, such as near-drowning in cold water, longer), he may still be revived and his life saved. Only CPR can do that.

Ideally CPR should be performed only by someone who has taken a course in it from a trained professional or from organizations like the American Red Cross. If chest compressions are done incorrectly, it is possible they can cause internal injuries to the victim.

First, here are the basic guidelines for how to do chest compressions.

If the person without circulation is an adult or a child over age eight: Position your hands by finding the notch at the lower tip of the breastbone in the center of the chest. Place your middle finger in the notch and your index finger next to it and above it, toward the neck. Place the heel of your other hand next to and above your index finger, the fingers pointing across the chest. On top of this hand place the heal of the other hand. Keeping the fingers off the chest, the shoulders over the hands, and the arms locked straight, press down forcefully on the injured person's chest (see illustration #6). Compress the chest one and a half to two inches. Use a smooth, downward pressure. Don't rock. Release the compression by lifting up with your body weight, rather than by removing or shifting the hands. A sequence for adults and children over age eight is fifteen compressions at a rate of eighty to one hundred per minute.

If the person without circulation is a child age one to eight: Find the same spot in the middle of the chest but use only the heel of one hand to make compressions. With each compression depress the chest approximately one to one and a half inches. A sequence is five compressions at a rate of eighty to one hundred per minute.

If the person without circulation is an infant under one year old: Draw an imaginary line across the baby's chest from one

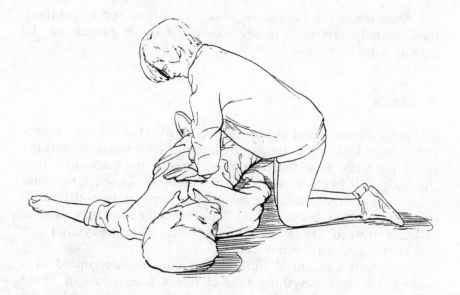

Illustration #6:

Use a smooth, downward pressure to do chest compressions on an adult. Your hands should be on top of each other and positioned in the center of the person's chest. Keep your arms straight, with your shoulders over your hands, and compress the chest one and one-half to two inches.

nipple to the other. Put your index finger and middle finger in the middle of the infant's breastbone about one finger-width below this line. Use these two fingers to give chest compressions, depressing the chest about one-half to one inch. One sequence is five chest compressions at a rate of one hundred per minute.

Here's the proper sequence for combining rescue breaths with chest compressions to perform CPR. Assume in the following scenario that the person is unconscious, has no neck or spinal injury, is not breathing, and has no pulse.

Check for consciousness and neck or spinal injuries. Put the person on his back and check for breathing. Open the airway and check for breathing again. Check circulation.

- If the person is an adult or a child over age eight, do fifteen chest compressions and then two rescue breaths for four cycles. Recheck the pulse after each four cycles.
- If the person is a child under age eight, do five chest compressions and one rescue breath for ten cycles. Recheck the pulse after each ten cycles.

Stop when the person regains respiration and circulation, medical help arrives, you are exhausted or in danger, or the person is obviously dead.

◆ Shock

The body's tissues and organs need a constant supply of oxygen-rich blood and other fluids to function. Whenever something interferes with these fluid supplies, there is the possibility that the body will begin to shut down. The brain, heart, lungs, and other major organs receive insufficient oxygen to continue to function. As they cease to function, the body goes into what is called a state of shock. Shock is a severe emergency that can quickly lead to death if not treated.

The body's essential fluid supply can be interrupted in a number of ways. Anything that causes a severe loss of blood volume can cause shock. For instance, a deep wound, a perforated ulcer, or extensive internal bleeding can cause a dangerous loss of circulating blood. The supply of other essential fluids can be disrupted by a severe burn or anything that causes dehydration, including exposure to extremes of heat or cold or long-term diarrhea. Shock can also result from a trauma or condition that limits the rate of blood flow, including a drug overdose, poisoning, or a heart problem. If the heart stops its usually efficient pumping, blood pressure falls and insufficient amounts of blood are reoxygenated in the lungs.

Another way that shock can occur is from a trauma that dramatically increases the diameter of blood vessels. Even though no blood has been lost from the body, and the heart is pumping, the body experiences a seeming loss of blood. The most common causes of this type of shock are severe allergic reactions (see anaphylactic shock in "Chapter 4: Allergic Reactions") and body-wide, systemic infections (septic shock). Those with diabetes can suffer from another type of shock, from lowered levels of sugar in the blood. This type of diabetic emergency is known as insulin shock.

When the body goes into shock for whatever reason, the brain tries to compensate for the lack of sufficient blood. It sends signals to the skin to constrict blood vessels, to the heart to increase heart rate, and to the lungs to breathe faster. The person thus develops such symptoms as pale, cold, and clammy skin, a bluish tinge to lips and fingernails, rapid heartbeat but weak pulse, and quick, shallow breathing. As the condition worsens, other symptoms may include dizziness, confusion, nausea, vomiting, dilated pupils, intense thirst, and unconsciousness. (Though the person is thirsty, don't give someone in shock any liquids until the shock has been treated successfully, since he or she may lose consciousness at any moment.)

In the hospital, doctors can hook a shock victim up to special monitors that report on blood pressure and heart rate. Intravenous blood transfusions are often necessary to restore normal blood circulation. Diagnostic tests are employed to determine whether organs such as the kidneys have experienced permanent damage.

BASIC TREATMENT OF SHOCK

Shock needs to be treated immediately to prevent it from rapidly deteriorating into a life-threatening situation.

Call emergency medical personnel immediately. Do this no matter what the cause of the shock. Check to see if the person is wearing or carrying medical alert information.

Check the ABCs: airway, breathing, and circulation. Maintain an open airway. If the person vomits, turn the head to the side. Do rescue breathing or chest compressions if necessary. If the person is unconscious or nauseous, don't give him anything to be taken orally. Loosen any tight clothing to improve circulation.

Put the person in the shock position. Keep the person warm and lying flat on his or her back. (If the person is unconscious, put him or her facedown in the recovery position (see below), because of the danger of choking.) Unless the person is having difficulty breathing or has serious injuries to the head, neck, or chest, elevate the feet about ten inches, putting whatever is handy under the feet, and lower legs (see illustration #7). Don't put any pillows under the head, which can interfere with an open airway.

Give first aid for the underlying cause of shock as quickly as possible. Examine the person for signs of internal bleeding, dehydration, poisoning, and other causes of shock and treat appropriately.

Keep the person warm and comfortable while waiting for medical assistance. Unless the person is overheated, cover him or her with a coat or blanket, though don't apply direct heat. Unless medical help is hours away, don't give the person anything to eat or drink. Continue to monitor the ABCs until help arrives.

The basic steps for treating insulin shock are similar to those for other types of shock. Any further steps would depend upon how certain you or the victim can be of the diagnosis. Diabetics have a problem processing sugar in the blood, so it is also possible that the condition is not insulin shock, from too little sugar, but diabetic coma, from too much sugar. A person suffering from insulin shock usually has cold and clammy skin, a person suffering from diabetic shock a flushed face and dry skin. Diabetic shock is also characterized by an odor of acetone on the breath

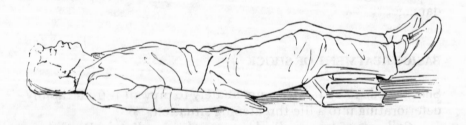

Illustration #7:

Put an injured person in the shock position by placing him on his back and elevating his feet about ten inches. Support the lower legs with books or other objects.

and spasmodic breathing. Certain other symptoms, such as mental confusion, are shared by insulin and diabetic shock, so an inexperienced person may not easily distinguish the two emergencies. Diabetics are trained to treat themselves in emergencies and can almost always self-diagnose the condition.

Treatment beyond basic first aid varies by 180 degrees for diabetic emergencies. A person suffering from diabetic shock needs an injection of insulin. A person suffering from insulin shock needs sugar, usually given orally in solution or as fruit juice, or as sugar placed under the tongue. The wrong diagnosis and the wrong treatment may worsen the person's condition (particularly if you mistakenly give insulin to a person suffering from insulin shock; giving some sugar to a person suffering from diabetic coma won't ruinously worsen the condition). In this instance as in most others, take steps beyond basic first aid only when you are sure they will cause no harm, the situation is serious, and medical help is not available in the near future.

◆ Choking

If you swallow something that completely or partially blocks your windpipe, your body responds by sudden spasms of the lungs and throat. This coughing, choking action will often cause the object to be ejected from the airway. If an object is wedged tightly enough in the trachea, however, your body's natural expelling response won't be enough. Air supply to the lungs gets cut off and oxygen content of the blood falls quickly. After as few as ten to fifteen seconds, you black out. Brain death follows within four to six minutes unless emergency action successfully dislodges the object.

Among adults, the most common cause of choking is swallowing an unchewed piece of meat. Talking and laughing while eating, drinking large amounts of alcohol, eating too fast, and wearing dentures, all can interfere with proper swallowing. Among infants, choking may result from virtually any object that fits in the mouth and is about the diameter of the windpipe, including pennies, buttons, and marbles. Pieces of balloons or plastic wrap can also be inhaled and block the windpipe. Foods that children frequently choke on include grapes, hot dogs, chewing gum, and hard candies.

Choking symptoms vary depending upon the degree of blockage. In some cases what appears to be a choking episode is not one at all. Some heart attacks, allergic reactions, and breathing problems can resemble choking. What usually distinguishes these emergencies from choking is that the person is able to talk at least weakly. If the windpipe is completely blocked, talking is not possible. Also, most choking accidents among adults happen during a meal.

You should not intervene and perform first aid for choking steps unless someone is choking from complete or acute partial blockage. If the person has minor blockage of the windpipe, he will be able to cough forcefully. In such cases watch and wait. If the condition worsens, act immediately. But unless the person is turning blue, he's getting enough air. In most cases his own efforts will dislodge the object.

The main first-aid method for choking, the Heimlich maneuver, presents a small risk of injury. If you position your hands incorrectly on the choking person's chest, it is possible to fracture some ribs and cause internal injuries. So perform the Heimlich only when you really have to.

When the person's windpipe is totally blocked, she won't be able to talk, cough, or breathe. She may be grabbing her throat with her hands in the universal sign of choking. Her skin may start to turn pale or blue, especially around the face. She may experience convulsions or loss of consciousness. In cases of acute partial blockage, she may be gagging, breathing with obvious difficulty, or coughing feebly. When these symptoms are present, perform the following basic first-aid steps.

BASIC FIRST AID FOR CHOKING

Since there is a slight risk of injury, if you are unsure how serious the blockage is and the person is conscious, ask the choking person whether he needs help. If he indicates he needs help or can't respond verbally, perform the Heimlich maneuver.

Developed in recent decades by the U.S. surgeon H. J. Heimlich, the Heimlich maneuver is a series of sharp thrusts to the chest that can pop an object out of the windpipe. The technique elevates the diaphragm, the curtain of muscles and tendons between the chest and abdominal cavities. When done correctly, this causes up to a fourfold increase in air pressure inside the chest cavity, compared to a normal exhale, and an artificial cough that presses residual air in the lungs against the object, expelling it from the trachea.

The following series of instructions vary slightly according to the age, size, and condition of the person who is choking.

Perform the following steps if an adult or a child over the age of one is choking. Move to behind a choking person who is standing or sitting. Wrap both of your arms around the person's waist slightly below the rib cage and above the navel. Clench one of your hands into a fist and place it with the thumb side in against the middle of the choking person's abdomen. It should be situated between the navel and the lower tip of the breastbone. Grip the wrist of the fisted hand with your other hand. Keeping your elbows out, use your hands to press with a quick, upward thrust into person's abdominal wall. Each sharp thrust creates a forceful rush of air out of the lungs and is intended to dislodge the blocking object. Do as many thrusts as is necessary to clear the windpipe.

In some instances performing the Heimlich maneuver causes the person to vomit. If so, position the person's head so that the vomit drains from the mouth and doesn't cause its own blockage of the airway.

If the blockage had been complete, even if the object was dislodged in the first few attempts, it is a good idea for the choking person to be checked by a medical professional. It is possible that a piece of the object entered the lungs or that the Heimlich maneuver itself caused an internal injury.

Perform the following steps if the choking person loses consciousness. If you haven't dislodged the object and the person loses consciousness, you need to begin to combine the Heimlich maneuver with the ABCs: checking airway, breathing, and circulation. Lie the person down on her back on a firm, level spot. Open the airway and check for breathing. If the person is not breathing give four rescue breaths.

If the chest is not rising because of an airway obstruction, straddle the person's thighs. Place the heel of one of your hands against the middle of the person's abdomen, just above the navel. Cover this hand with the other, with the fingers of both hands pointing toward the person's head. Give six to ten quick upward thrusts. Each thrust is a separate attempt to clear the windpipe.

Open the person's mouth to check to see whether the object has been dislodged. Do this with a finger sweep. Start by grasping the person's tongue and lower jaw with one hand, lifting and pulling slightly to open the mouth and pull the tongue out of the back of the throat. Use the index finger of the other hand to reach down the inside of the cheek to the base of the tongue. If the object has been dislodged, hook the finger behind the object and remove it with a sweeping motion. Don't, however, pinch, push, or poke an object in the throat. This may force it farther down.

Check the person's breathing once again. If he or she is not breathing, give another set of four rescue breaths. Repeat the cycle of six to ten abdominal thrusts, a finger sweep, and rescue breathing until the object is dislodged and breathing is restored, or until help arrives.

Perform the following steps if an obese or pregnant person is choking. Move behind a choking person who is conscious and standing or sitting. Wrap your arms around the person's chest, though in a higher position than for a nonobese, nonpregnant adult. Place the thumb side of your fist on the middle of the breastbone—not on the ribs or the lower tip of the breastbone. Grab your fist with the other hand and do a series of quick backward and upward thrusts. Each thrust is a separate attempt to dislodge the object.

If this doesn't work and the obese or pregnant person loses consciousness, lie him or her down on the back and kneel alongside. Place the heel of your other hand over the first hand. Keeping your fingers off the chest, do a series of quick upward thrusts. Check the person's mouth, do a finger sweep, and check his or her breathing. If the object failed to dislodge and the person is not breathing, give two rescue breaths. Repeat the cycle of two full breaths, chest thrusts, and finger sweeps until the person's airway is cleared.

Perform the following steps if a newborn to one-year-old baby is choking. An infant with complete blockage will not be able to cough or cry. In this case give a series of sharp slaps to the infant's back. (This back-slap technique is no longer recommended for use on anyone but infants, since when it is performed on adults, there is a danger that it can cause the obstructing object to become more tightly lodged in the windpipe.)

Place the infant facedown across your lap or forearm. Support the infant's head with one hand by holding her jaw between your index finger and thumb, allowing the head to hang slightly lower than the rest of her body. Give the infant four sharp blows between her shoulder blades with the heel of your other hand. Each blow is a separate attempt to dislodge whatever is choking her.

Then turn the child over onto her back and do chest thrusts. Place your index finger and middle finger on the baby's breastbone, slightly below the line of the nipples. Give four quick upward thrusts, pressing about one-half to one inch deep. Do a finger sweep. Continue the cycle of four back blows and four chest thrusts until the object is dislodged or the infant loses consciousness.

If the infant is unconscious, put her on her back, open her airway, check her breathing, and if necessary, give two rescue breaths. Continue the cycle of four back blows, four chest thrusts, a finger sweep, and two rescue breaths until the infant starts to breathe or medical help arrives.

Perform the following steps if you are choking and alone. It is possible to use your own fists to perform the Heimlich maneuver on yourself. Tuck your fist into your abdomen and give four quick, upward thrusts. You can also apply upward thrusts by leaning your abdomen across the back of a chair, a railing, or some other firm, hard object and pressing it with forceful pushes.

Prevent choking episodes by making it a habit to chew thoroughly, especially if you're a steak-and-brew eater. Children should be taught not to talk, play, or run when eating. Parents of infants need to keep small objects out of childrens' reach. When young children begin to eat solid foods, some common items that are about the same diameter as a child's windpipe, such as grapes and hot dogs, should be cut up into smaller than normal pieces before being served.

◆ The Recovery Position

When a person is unconscious but breathing, the safest bodily position in most cases is lying on the stomach with the head turned to one side. This "recovery position" improves circulation to the brain and keeps the airway open. The person breathes easily and is prevented from inhaling fluids, such as blood or vomit, or choking on the tongue.

Under certain circumstances you should not automatically move a person into the recovery position. Extreme care needs to be exercised when moving a person who has suffered:

- ◆ a neck or spinal injury
- ◆ severe trauma
- ◆ broken bones

In such cases any movements should be kept to an absolute minimum. The risk is that moving the body can aggravate the injury or in some cases even cause the person to become paralyzed. Of course, if the person's current position or location presents an imminent danger (the person's in the middle of railroad tracks and a train is approaching), you have to move him or her (see the section below on transporting the injured). When there is no imminent danger (and usually there isn't), a person who has potentially suffered a neck or spinal injury should be kept still until emergency personnel arrive.

To put a person in the recovery position, place him facedown on firm and level ground. If he is lying on his back, turn him over by tucking one arm under the buttocks, putting the other across the chest, and crossing the ankles. Kneeling at his side, grab the hips with one hand and pull him toward you while supporting the head with the other hand. When he is lying on his stomach, turn the head to one side. Position the upper arm and the upper leg, on the same side that the face is turned toward, at right angles to the body. Also bend the same arm and leg at right angles at the elbow and the knee. Place the hand flat on the ground and pointing away from the feet. On the other side of the body, make sure the leg is straight, in line with the body, and the arm is lying beside the trunk.

Tilt the person's head back slightly to make sure his airway is open. Loosen his clothing, particularly at the neck, and stay with him until emergency personnel arrive or he safely recovers.

◆ Transporting an Injured Person

Whether to move an injured person is an important first-aid decision. If the person has suffered a severe injury or an injury to the neck or spine, it is always preferable to let professional emergency personnel do the moving. Sometimes that is not possible. For instance, the accident may occur in a remote rural or wilderness area. Or the life of the injured person and the life of the rescuer may be in danger because of a burning building, an electrical hazard, or the risk of explosion. In such cases, as well as those when the person's injuries are obviously minor, transporting the person can be done in a number of ways.

If you are alone on a rescue, you can do the drag transport, a walking assist, or a one-person back carry.

Drag transport. This is the preferable one-person transport in instances when you absolutely must move a person with a neck or spinal injury. It is also useful when the injured person is too large to lift and too injured to walk. Always drag an injured person by pulling the body lengthwise, not sideways. If you have to go only a few feet, position the person on his or her back. (This is preferable to a stomach drag, though if you have difficulty turning the person or time is extremely short, you can use the stomach drag.) Grab the person at the shoulders or grab his clothing at the shoulders, cradling his head between your arms. Pull slowly, walking backward and keeping your back as straight as possible to prevent injuring yourself.

If you need to go some distance with a drag, it may be easier to put the person on a coat or blanket and pull that. Position the coat or blanket in line with the person and drag her onto it. You may need to pull it under the lower part of the body.

Walking assist. This is useful if the injured person is conscious and has not had a heart attack or suffered a severe trauma. With the injured person sitting, kneel down next to him and place your arm around his back at waist level. Put his arm over your shoulder and grasp the wrist of this arm. Help him to his feet and lend support while walking.

One-person back carry. This is used for a person who is lighter than you and not severely injured. Have the person get behind you. Bend at the waist and have the injured person put her chest to your back. Bring her arms over your shoulders, grasp both of her wrists, and walk as best you can.

When more than one person is available to help move an injured person, you can use a seat carry, a hammock carry, or a real or makeshift stretcher.

Seat carry. Use this carry if the injured person is conscious and capable of cooperating to some extent. Don't use it if the person has a possible neck or spine injury. The two rescuers should face each other and with one arm grasp each other's wrists with an interlocking grip to form a seat. The other arms go behind each other's back to form the back of the seat. Bend low to allow the injured person to sit on the "arm seat." The injured person should put his arms around the necks of the two rescuers.

Hammock carry. The idea here is to support each part of the body while carrying a person lying on her back. You need at least three people. If a fourth is available, position him at the injured person's head to keep the head and neck steady. Two rescuers get on one side of the injured person, the other rescuer in the middle position on the opposite side. The rescuers place their hands under the person, positioning their hands from the neck to the knees. The rescuers should try to lift and move in unison so as not to twist or bend the injured person.

Stretcher. This is obviously the ideal way to transport an injured person. The injured person should be lifted as described above and placed stomach up on the stretcher. When a stretcher is unavailable, it is possible to fashion one from a board, shutter, tabletop, or other firm surface. Bandages, belts, and the like can be used to secure the person to the stretcher. The rescuers should carry the person's body as level as possible to prevent her from sliding off or rolling from side to side.

◆ Natural First-Aid Remedies for Basic Emergencies

Though you don't want to give a person who is unconscious, not breathing, or in shock anything to be taken orally, there are still a few natural remedies and techniques to consider. The following should not supplant or interfere with the execution of any of the basic steps for restoring the ABCs or treating choking or shock. You can use these natural remedies along with the basic steps to help revive someone who is not breathing, is in shock, or has no pulse.

(See "Chapter 4: Allergic Reactions" for natural remedies for anaphylactic shock.)

Give the person a dose of homeopathic **Arnica.** Crush five or six *Arnica* tablets into a powder and put it in the person's mouth, on the tongue or gums, and let it dissolve by itself, homeopath Jennifer Jacobs, M.D., suggests. *Arnica* is the homeopathic remedy for most forms of shock, especially if it results from physical trauma. Give a 6X dose every five minutes until the person recovers normal breathing and heart rate.

Apply acupressure massage to the first-aid revival point. This useful point is located two-thirds of the way up from the upper lip to the nose (see illustration #8). Apply constant pressure with the thumb to help restore normal bodily function. If more than one person is able to help treat, you can massage the injured person's hands, fingers, feet, and toes to help stimulate circulation.

In cases of partial choking and spasms in the throat, apply firm acupressure to points on the neck and back. Acupressure authority Michael Reed Gach also recommends a point on the front of the chest, in the hollow below the collarbone next to the breastbone. He says, "This point is excellent for spasms in the throat and choking. As you manipulate it, the person can breathe up into the pressure to help relieve choking."

Administer a first-aid flower remedy such as **Rescue Remedy.**

Illustration #8:

The acupressure point on the upper lip is a useful first-aid revival point.
It's located two-thirds of the way up from the upper lip to the nose.

Flower remedy practitioners say that Rescue Remedy is often helpful during emergencies that cause shock. Place three to four drops of the liquid concentrate directly from the bottle under the tongue. You can also dilute the remedy by putting four drops in one-quarter glass of water, tea, or juice. This should be sipped every three to five minutes. When an accident victim is unconscious, administer it by rubbing a few drops into the lips, behind the ears, or on the wrists. You can also soak a cotton cloth in a pint of water with five to six drops of Rescue Remedy and apply it as a compress.

If you have an extensive flower essence collection, try the single remedy Rock Rose for emergencies involving shock.

Help revive an unconscious person by holding consciousness-reviving herbs or essential oils under the nose. "You can mix Rosemary oil with essential oil of Camphor to make a powerful herbal smelling salt, or just use Rosemary oil itself. It's quite stimulating and all you have to do is wave it under the nose to gently arouse consciousness," herbalist Christopher Hobbs says.

In addition to Rosemary *(Rosmarinus officinalis)* and Camphor *(Cinnamomum camphora)*, aromatherapists recommend the essential oil of Peppermint for its uplifting and stimulating effects and its ability to help restore brain and heart function. You can either open a bottle of Peppermint oil and hold it under the person's nose, or put four to five drops of the oil on a clean cotton cloth or handkerchief and hold it up to the person's nose to be inhaled.

The conventional consciousness-reviving substance is smelling salts. These are usually an aromatic mixture of carbonate of ammonium with some fragrant scent. Rosemary and other essential oils provide effective plant-based alternatives to revive an unconscious person. "You generally want to rouse an unconscious person," Hobbs says, "because bodily functions are depressed during unconsciousness and it's not a particularly desirable state."

FOUR

Allergic Reactions

THIS CHAPTER COVERS:

◆ *mild allergic reactions from pollen, dust, mold spores, animal dander, insect venom, drugs and vaccines, household products, foods*
◆ *acute allergic reactions (anaphylactic shock)*

SEE "CHAPTER 5: BITES AND STINGS" FOR:

◆ *nonallergic insect stings*

SEE "CHAPTER 8: BREATHING PROBLEMS" FOR:

◆ *asthma attack*

SEE "CHAPTER 21: SKIN EMERGENCIES" FOR:

◆ *allergic reactions to poison ivy, oak, and sumac*

The average American is exposed to more than fifty thousand chemicals each day, through food and drink, bodycare products and cosmetics, and air. For some 30–40 million Americans, these chemical encounters, along with a host of other factors ranging from emotions to exercise, are not benign. They trigger allergic reactions, for which modern medicine offers neither vaccine nor reliable cure.

Allergies are a malfunction primarily of the immune system. Why a person's immune system becomes overly sensitive to normally harmless substances is not clearly understood. The mechanics of the malfunction are pretty straightforward though. Let's say you have a ragweed allergy. The plant releases a pollen grain that floats through the air until you inhale it. The pollen settles on the mucous membrane inside your nose. Your body misreads the chemical message encoded in the pollen grain's cell wall, perceiving the pollen to be a much more serious disease threat than it is. This sets off a chain reaction of biochemical events. The body decides to combat the pollen by kicking the immune system into action. It begins to create antibodies in the blood to attack the invading, reaction-causing "antigen." These immunoglobulin E, or IgE, antibodies attach to special "mast" cells in the blood. The mast cells release histamine and other chemicals against the antigen. It's these chemicals that cause runny nose, swelling, itching, and other symptoms of allergic reaction.

For some people, however, an allergic reaction can become so acute as to be life-threatening. Their body's immune system wildly overreacts, most commonly to certain drugs taken intravenously (penicillin and other antibiotics, and some vaccines), bee venom, and rarely, to foods such as shellfish or peanuts. The antibodies cause the mast cells to release massive amounts of powerful chemicals, including histamine, which contract the smooth muscles of the throat and lungs and dilate blood vessels throughout the body. Vital bodily functions go on red alert as blood pressure plummets and the lungs, brain, and heart are deprived of oxygenated blood. Breathing becomes difficult because of swelling of the vocal cords or severe restriction and congestion of the bronchial tubes. If not treated, death can occur in a matter of minutes.

Such a total body reaction to an allergen is known as anaphylactic shock, from the Greek *ana* meaning "excessive" and *phylaxis* for "protection." If you or one of your family are one of the unlucky few who are subject to these dangerous malfunctions of the immune system, it's crucial that you learn how to prevent reactions as well as treat them should they occur. Though anaphylactic shock accounts for about two thousand deaths per year in the United States, acute reactions are rarely life-threatening if treated.

◆ The Many Routes to Reaction

Allergic reactions can be caused by a variety of substances and conditions, including:

Pollen. This is the most common allergen, affecting some 20–25 million Americans. The pollen comes primarily from certain grasses and the yellow and green flowers of the ragweed plant and reaches its highest concentrations in the air from about June to

August. The early spring can also present problems for people with hay fever who live in areas where pollen from oaks and other trees is abundant. Pollen causes allergic rhinitis or hay fever, characterized by runny nose, sneezing, and watering eyes.

Dust. It's not the dust itself that causes allergic reactions in some people but the feces of a microscopic mite that lives on the particle, which is usually a fleck of shedded skin (dander) from a human or animal. Dust mites, which like spiders are arachnids, also populate mattresses, curtains, sofas, and the like. Inhaling their pollen-sized droppings leads to bouts of sneezing, coughing, and itching.

Mold spores. These can grow outdoors, on grass and dead leaves (especially from July to October), or indoors on everything from foods to furniture. Infrequently cleaned air conditioners and humidifiers are a common household source.

Animal dander. Some 2 million American families have members who are allergic to cats. The offending substance is not the dander but a protein called Fel d1 (for *Felis domesticus 1*) from cat saliva, which the cat leaves on its fur and skin during preening. Homes that are full of cat hair and dander cause reactions in 25 percent of allergy sufferers. Cats recently passed dogs as the most numerous pet in the United States, and since surveys have found that upward of 70 percent of cat owners sleep with their pet, the potential for reactions is large and increasing.

Insect venom. The venom from a bite or sting by bees, wasps, spiders, snakes, or sea creatures is a potent mix of proteins and enzymes that causes allergic reactions of varying severity in some people.

Drugs and vaccines. Most people are aware that drugs such as penicillin can cause an allergic reaction, but various other drugs ranging from aspirin to zidovudine are also known to cause reactions. A drug (or vaccine) that is injected into the bloodstream is more likely to cause an allergic reaction than one taken orally. A drug reaction may not appear immediately, however, and lesser reactions can sometimes take days to manifest themselves.

Even fewer people are aware that allergic reactions are among the potential side effects of routine vaccinations given to virtually all American infants today. Allergic reactions that do occur are usually immediate, taking the form of local symptoms such as rashes and swelling. More severe body-wide reactions may cause fever, convulsions, or worse. The reaction may even result in deleterious, delayed effects, such as encephalitis and brain damage, due to the disruption of normal nerve development, accord-

ing to Harris Coulter, Ph.D., a prominent critic of routine vaccinations.

Some of the vaccines that present the greatest danger of
allergic reaction include pertussis (whooping cough), tetanus,
injectable "killed" (Salk) polio, Hib *(Hemophilus influenzae b)*, and
pneumococcal pneumonia. The most controversial routine vaccination is the pertussis, due to the frequency of reactions including
fever, retardation, and death. A study done at UCLA in 1978–79
found that 40 percent of pertussis vaccinees experienced local
inflammation, while a British study put the risk of serious neurological damage at 1:110,000. Coulter and other foes of vaccination
say that the frequency of serious neurological damage is actually
much higher.

Household products. These include everything from cleansers
to off-gassing building materials to bodycare products and cosmetics, such as antiperspirants, hair dyes, deodorant soaps, and
colognes. The drummer for the rock band Toto recently died from
a heart attack caused by an allergic reaction to pesticides he was
spraying in his backyard. Even metals, such as the nickel used in
most costume jewelry, have been known to cause allergic reactions in some people. One estimate is that one in seven young
women is allergic to nickel.

Foods. The most frequently cited allergy-provoking foods include milk and other dairy products, eggs, wheat, soy, corn, and
spices. Some people are allergic to shellfish and nuts (especially
peanuts), which seem to be more likely than other foods to cause
acute reactions and deaths. Peanut-based additives used in processed foods are particularly worrisome.

Doctors at Johns Hopkins recently reviewed the cases of
thirteen children who experienced acute allergic reactions to
foods. (Six of the reactions were fatal.) The doctors found that
although the children knew what they were allergic to, their
reactions were caused by hidden ingredients in seemingly harmless foods such as cupcakes.

Less acute food reactions can also be hard to identify, since it
may be hours between when you eat a food and when the body's
chain reaction kicks in. Reactions to food are also complicated by
the fact that the offending substance may come from a food
combination, or the reaction may be triggered only when a certain
food is eaten under stress.

Some allergists say that it is necessary to make a clear
distinction between a food allergy (which provokes an immunological response in the body) and a food sensitivity (which in-

volves a distinct physiological response). For instance, a common food sensitivity that causes various levels of physical reaction in a number of people is from monosodium glutamate or MSG, the flavor enhancer that may be referred to on labels only as "natural flavors" or "hydrolyzed vegetable protein."

Many authorities also believe that foods get blamed for more allergic reactions than they deserve and that many people who think they are reacting to a food are in fact reacting to some other allergen. One survey found that seven of ten people believe they have at least one food allergy, while some clinicians put the number who actually do have one at less than one in ten.

Allergies to foods have been tied to increased susceptibility to asthma and heart disease.

◆ Acute Reactions: The Worst-Case Scenario

When an acute allergic reaction does happen, it usually happens quickly, often within a few minutes of getting stung or being injected with a drug. Acute reactions almost always appear within a half hour and may last for hours. The chief symptom to watch for is difficulty in breathing, particularly as a result of a sudden swelling of the tongue or tissues of the throat. "Swelling of the respiratory tract is where an allergic reaction crosses the line to hospital emergency room material," notes Holly Eagle, O.M.D.

Breathing difficulty may be accompanied by:

- ◆ bronchial spasms or chest tightness
- ◆ severe swelling at the site of a bite, and in another part of the body, such as the eyes, lips, or tongue
- ◆ severe itching or hives
- ◆ nausea and vomiting
- ◆ possible bluish tinge to skin
- ◆ dizziness and fainting

The person may experience weakness, coughing, stomach cramps, anxiety, a severe headache, cool or moist skin, swollen and teary eyes, and thirst. Look for a pulse that is weak but fast. Sometimes the breathing is all right but there are other symptoms of shock, such as blue skin or severe nausea. Ask the person if he or she has had prior allergic reactions, and if so, how severe they were.

Keep in mind that difficult breathing may also indicate an asthma attack (in which case it's usually accompanied by wheezing) or a heart attack (usually accompanied by chest pain). An allergic reaction can often be identified by a local skin reaction.

If an individual has been exposed to an agent that is known to cause him or her to react acutely, get medical help without even waiting for symptoms to appear. It's also a good idea to get emergency care if the person has been stung many times by bees.

If you can definitely confirm an acute allergic reaction that seems to be life-threatening (the person is having trouble breathing and is turning blue), proceed with the following basic emergency steps.

BASIC FIRST AID FOR ACUTE ALLERGIC REACTIONS

Acute allergic reactions are serious medical emergencies that call for professional treatment as soon as possible. Nevertheless there are various steps that the layperson can take to prevent the situation from worsening.

Summon emergency help as soon as possible if you identify the symptoms of a sudden and severe allergic reaction. If more than one person is on the scene, have one call for help while another takes emergency steps.

While waiting for emergency personnel to arrive, do what's necessary to keep the person alive. The first concern should be the ABCs: maintain an open airway and restore breathing and circulation (see "Chapter 3: Basic Emergency Care"). Keep the person comfortable and quiet, preferably lying down.

Try to identify what the reaction is from and prevent further contact or ingestion. For instance, if the reaction is from the sting of a honeybee or certain wasps, the stinger and its accompanying venom sac may still be in the skin. The venom sac can continue to contract and deposit venom in the body for hours or even days if it isn't removed.

Don't attempt to squeeze a stinger out, since this will also cause more venom to empty into the person. Rather, first remove the venom sac by gently scraping across the sting site with a sharp object such as a knife blade or a credit card. Usually that will remove both stinger and sac. If that doesn't bring out the stinger along with the venom sac, then it's safe to use tweezers to pull at the stinger. (See "Chapter 5: Bites and Stings" for further treatment of bee and insect stings.)

If the person has had previous severe allergic reactions and has with them or nearby a special prescription-only first-aid kit, get it and, with permission, follow directions.

The Ana-kit and others contain a syringe or an EpiPen spring-loaded injector with epinephrine, the adrenal hormone also known as adrenaline (trademarked as Adrenalin), which stimulates the heart and dilates bronchial tubes. The kit will contain explicit instructions for its use.

The kit will also contain an inhaler of adrenaline, a liquid antihistamine, and a constricting band. The latter should be used with caution and, again, only if the person's life seems to be at stake—applied improperly it can restrict arterial flow and permanently damage the limb. The purpose is to slow the flow of blood from the sting site to the rest of body. It should also be used only if the sting just occurred and it is somewhere on a leg or arm.

Lacking a kit with a constricting band, you can fashion one from a piece of cloth or cord. Tie it two to five inches above the sting, between the sting and the rest of the body. It should be loose enough that you can slip a finger under the band. Make sure that you can find a pulse below the band. Also, loosen it every three to five minutes for about thirty seconds, until medical assistance comes.

Check to see whether the person has emergency allergy-relief medication. This step may be necessary if it's clear that the person is experiencing an acute allergic reaction and is having difficulty breathing and a sting kit with epinephrine is not available. For instance, the person may have an anti-asthmatic epinephrine inhaler such as Primatene Mist, or an antihistamine tablet such as Benadryl. The former would be much more effective in an emergency, of course, since it takes some time for a pill to get into the bloodstream and an acute allergic reaction needs an immediate response. (You can speed the absorption of a pill by crushing it into a powder or by letting it dissolve under the tongue.) Don't give anything orally, however, to an unconscious person, and it's always best to give any drug only with the advice of a physician.

If you haven't yet called for medical help, do it now. Once you've rescued the person from the threat of immediate death, you can take the next steps to comfort him or her, prevent further damage, and control the condition. Continue to check breathing and pulse. Take steps necessary to prevent shock (see Chapter 3).

NATURAL REMEDIES FOR ACUTE ALLERGIC REACTIONS

It's necessary to emphasize that acute allergic reactions are major emergencies that call for no-holds-barred medical responses. There are, however, a number of natural remedies that can either open up airways or help relieve symptoms associated with the shock and trauma of breathing difficulty. These remedies should not supplant professional medical attention. But they can be of potential help, for instance, after taking the basic first-aid steps and summoning emergency medical help.

Administer a tincture or liquid concentrate of the herb ephedra. Herbalist Christopher Hobbs says that he recommends people who have acute allergic reactions to stings keep ephedra tincture on hand. "For an allergic reaction that may affect breathing," he says, "take a dropperful or two internally right away. It's a safe amount—there are higher levels of ephedra in some herbal stimulant products sold in natural foods stores. I've seen the tincture work in as quickly as a few minutes to free breathing during an allergic reaction."

Ephedra, which works rapidly to open airways and dry out mucous membranes, would work even better than an antihistamine pill, such as Benadryl mentioned above, if a more powerful epinephrine-based bronchodilator was not available. The Chinese have used a species of ephedra (*Ephedra sinica*, which they call *ma huang*) for thousands of years to clear up breathing problems associated with asthma and hay fever. Among ephedra's active ingredients are the stimulants ephedrine and pseudoephedrine, which like epinephrine open bronchial passages and increase blood pressure. Chinese ephedra has higher levels of ephredrine than Western species (such as *E. nevadensis*, sometimes known as Mormon tea, and *E. viridis*) and is thus better at restoring clear breathing.

Naturopathic doctor Joseph Pizzorno, a coauthor of *Encyclopedia of Natural Medicine*, emphasizes that "it is worthwhile to take ephedra immediately for anaphylactic shock, but the person should be on the way to the hospital emergency room at the first sign of any respiratory restriction."

Take the common homeopathic remedy Apis for anaphylactic shock with local swelling. Homeopath Jennifer Jacobs, M.D., says that she's used *Apis* in conjunction with conventional steps to treat an acute reaction by administering it while waiting for medical attention or while on the way to the hospital. *Apis* would be used if the person has swelling of the tongue or a sensation of throat and lung constriction that impedes breathing.

Try the combination-flower remedy Rescue Remedy. This popular Bach flower remedy "has a general calming effect on psyche and body," says Holly Eagle. "I give it to both the person having the reaction and the first-aid giver. It really helps calm both the physical and mental hysteria that often occur during emergencies."

WHAT TO EXPECT AT THE HOSPITAL

A doctor will treat an acute allergic reaction by immediately injecting epinephrine. He or she may also administer cortisonelike drugs intravenously, and oxygen via an inhaler. If epinephrine fails to act quickly and the patient is unable to breathe, an emergency tracheotomy is a life-saving last resort.

Epinephrine is a powerful drug whose side effects typically include a hyper feeling, a significant increase in blood pressure, rapid heartbeat, sleeplessness, and shakiness. (To a lesser degree ephedra shares these potential side effects; it may also cause a few others such as subsequent nosebleeds.) But the body rapidly metabolizes the hormone (injections are sometimes given every fifteen minutes) and short-term reactions are almost always inconsequential given the immediate necessity of saving the patient's life.

After the acute phase, the doctor may prescribe a variety of drugs, including Caladryl (a calamine/Benadryl lotion) or an antihistamine to reduce itching, and one of the cortisonelike steroid drugs, such as prednisone, to reduce swelling.

Antihistamines work by blocking the action of histamine that's been released by sensitized tissue cells. The antihistamine diphenhydramine (Benadryl, Nytol) also has a sedating effect. Among its potential side effects are (yet another) allergic reaction, drowsiness, double vision, and reduced white blood cell count. The newer antihistamine Seldane does not induce drowsiness, though a recent study indicates it presents a major heart-attack risk for certain people.

Cortisonelike steroids reduce inflammation and suppress other effects of allergic reactions. They're available in a variety of forms, including oral and nasal spray, and tablet. Their safety for long-term use is controversial, with some doctors maintaining that side effects are minor if dosages are kept low enough and others contending that the drugs may disrupt endocrine balance, retard normal growth among children, and lead to such serious illnesses as osteoporosis later in life.

After the acute emergency is over, allergists may also suggest a long-term program in which they actually inject the patient with the allergy-causing substance, such as insect venom, cat saliva, or pollen. The idea is to gradually increase the levels and eventually desensitize the patient. Such immunotherapy may take a number of years, with shots required on a weekly basis at first, tapering to monthly. If successful, it allows the person to come in contact with the reaction-causing agent without facing a life-threatening situation. The program is usually more effective for treating allergies to pollen than dust mites or cats.

◆ Basic First Aid for Mild Allergic Reactions

Mild allergic reactions are usually accompanied by such symptoms as hives, blisters, an upset stomach, and swelling at the sting site that may last for several hours. The most important factor distinguishing mild from acute reactions is that with mild reactions the person does not experience swollen airways or breathing difficulties. Authorities disagree on whether a mild reaction calls for an immediate trip to the nearest hospital emergency room. Most medical authorities do say that *all* minor reactions require professional treatment. Others contend that if you closely monitor the person's condition and the reaction is limited to local swelling, itching, and hives that goes down within a few hours, it's not crucial to see a doctor immediately though you should notify him or her of the episode.

The initial steps for treating mild allergic reactions are similar to those for serious ones.

Keep the person calm. Panic will only tend to aggravate or worsen the reaction.

Identify the allergen and prevent further contact.

Watch the person closely for any worsening of the condition. Breathing difficulty is a sign that the reaction is becoming acute.

If the reaction is from an insect sting, wash the area with soap and water and apply cold compresses on and above the sting area. The cold will help stop the absorption and spread of venom. See Chapter 5 for more information on routine care for stings.

NATURAL REMEDIES FOR MILD ALLERGIC REACTIONS

A number of natural remedies, taken orally or applied to the skin, can help alleviate symptoms of mild allergic reactions, such as pain, itching, and inflammation. There are also important self-care steps to recover from a reaction and to prevent further ones.

Take a hefty dose of vitamin C with bioflavonoids. Most alternative practitioners recommend taking three to seven grams of C to take advantage of its potential antiallergy effects. Naturopath Joseph Pizzorno recommends two grams per hour to bowel tolerance. Pregnant women should not take over 500 mg per day of vitamin C.

Many vitamin C products come with bioflavonoids. Taking bioflavonoids as part of the whole vitamin C complex will enhance your body's ability to absorb the C. A number of vitamin manufacturers offer bioflavonoid-only products as well, in combination and singly. Nutritionist Shari Lieberman recommends taking 500–5,000 mg of bioflavonoids along with an equivalent amount of vitamin C as an "optimum daily allowance." Like vitamin C, bioflavonoids are nontoxic. You can also try taking 500–1,000 mg of either hesperidin or quercetin to quell a mild allergic reaction.

A number of studies suggest that large doses of vitamin C have anti-inflammatory and antiallergic properties, perhaps by preventing the antibody-antigen bonding. Bioflavonoids such as hesperidin, quercetin, and rutin are vitaminlike nutrients occurring naturally with vitamin C, most prominently in the peel of citrus fruits. Scientists think that the bioflavonoids line the mast cells implicated in the allergic process, making it harder for them to explode and release histamine and other chemicals into the blood. Researchers have also found that bioflavonoids have antibiotic and anti-inflammatory effects.

Take natural enzymes that have been shown to reduce inflammation. Pizzorno says that enzyme products from animals can be especially effective in preventing the swelling often associated with an allergic reaction. He recommends pancreatin, a preparation made from enzymes isolated from fresh hog pancreas. Naturopaths most often use pancreatin to treat digestive problems but are increasingly prescribing it for inflammatory and autoimmune diseases such as arthritis and athletic injuries. "Pancreatin can quickly start to break down chemicals in the body that cause inflammation," Pizzorno says. He says that for an allergic reaction the person should take six tablets immediately of a full-strength pancreatic extract (8–10X USP), not those diluted with salt or lactose.

Take the herb stinging nettles for its hay-fever-relieving and antiallergy effects. Nettles (*Urtica dioica*) are available in natural foods stores in a variety of capsule and liquid forms, including powdered, freeze-dried, and concentrated drops. (Nettles are also the basis for the homeopathic remedy *Urtica,* which is often used to combat the swelling and inflammation associated with mild allergic response.) Follow dosage recommendations on the label.

Researchers at the National College of Naturopathic Medicine in Portland, Oregon, recently demonstrated that capsules of freeze-dried stinging nettles can relieve the symptoms of hay fever. The study found that 58 percent of the subjects who took 300 mg capsules an average of three times a day for hay fever rated it at least moderately effective in relieving their symptoms.

To relieve the symptoms of a skin reaction to nickel or other metals, apply calendula or chamomile ointment or cream. Dab some of the remedy directly onto the site of redness and swelling.

For an allergy that causes a widespread skin rash, take a special reaction-relieving bath. The above remedies, calendula and chamomile, can also be applied to the entire body by bathing in them. Brew a strong pot of chamomile or calendula tea, and pour three to four cups of it in your bath. Both of these remedies help to reduce rashes and skin reactions. Epsom salts (one-quarter to one-half cup) or colloidal oatmeal (one to two cups) also work well in a bath to reduce itchy, sore, and sensitive skin.

Epsom salts is a white, crystalline product (purified magnesium sulfate) named after the town in England where it was first identified some five hundred years ago. Epsom salts has been a popular folk remedy ever since, primarily applied externally for skin rashes and aching muscles. It is widely available in pharmacies.

Colloidal oatmeal is finely ground powdered oatmeal. It turns into a slippery mass when mixed with water. Added to a bath, it disperses throughout the water and forms a thin gel that coats your skin, holding moisture in and providing relief from itching. Oatmeal-type cereals are too coarsely ground to bind with water and have this soothing effect. Either grind your own oats down to a flourlike powder, or look for the popular commercial colloidal oatmeal product Aveeno in your local pharmacy.

Apply a home-remedy paste to a local reaction from a sting. Three handy pastes are those made by mixing warm water with baking soda, meat tenderizer or other papain-based product, or activated charcoal. Dab the paste on the sting area and cover with gauze or plastic to keep it wet.

- ◆ To make a baking soda paste, dissolve three parts baking soda to one part warm water.
- ◆ To make a papain paste, use meat tenderizer powder or

smash up five to six papaya tablets and dissolve in a few drops of warm water.

♦ To make a charcoal paste, open two or three charcoal capsules and mix the powder with a few drops of warm water.

These are the classic home remedies for insect stings. They can not only reduce pain and swelling but help neutralize some of the toxins in insect venom.

Meat tenderizers such as Adolph's work because the enzyme papain, from the milky juice of unripe papayas, breaks down muscle tissue. This same action also breaks down the large protein molecules of insect venom, deactivating the poison before it gets circulated throughout your body. If you don't have any meat tenderizer around, you can get the same benefit from a paste made from one of the many papain products available in natural foods stores. Vitamin and supplement companies sell natural papaya enzyme in tablet form as a digestive aid.

Activated charcoal is a widely recognized poison antidote that works by adsorbing toxins. That is, it draws them out and collects them in a condensed form on the skin.

Press on the acupressure point located between the thumb and index finger in the webbing of the hand. Acupressure authority Michael Reed Gach says that this is the strongest point to relieve local pain, swelling, and redness such as from hay fever, hives, or a sting. To find it, bring the thumb and index finger together and notice the highest spot on the muscle in the webbing (see illustration #9). Angle pressure underneath the bone that attaches to the index finger, by pressing with the thumb on the outer part of hand and the index finger on the inner. Squeeze firmly for two to three minutes.

Apply a few drops of essential oil of Lavender to a tissue or your wrist and take a whiff every few minutes. When inhaled, the highly fragrant volatile oil found in Lavender stimulates a region of the brain in a way that has a sedating effect on the central nervous system and may help relieve the symptoms of a mild hay fever attack.

♦ Recovery and Prevention

The dire nature of acute allergic reactions makes preventing them of utmost importance. If you've experienced acute reactions, have a doctor prescribe an emergency treatment kit. You should also consider a medical-alert identification card or bracelet.

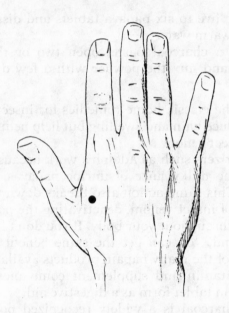

Illustration #9:

The acupressure point in the webbing of the hand between the thumb and index finger can be manipulated to help relieve pain and swelling.

Learning how to avoid the cause of even minor reactions is also well worth the effort. It's usually possible to get tested to find out what's causing your reactions. Allergists inject small amounts of a suspected allergen under the skin and watch for redness, itching, and swelling.

If you're allergic to pollen, you might consider getting a HEPA (high-efficiency particulate-arresting) air filter, or even a less expensive portable room air purifier, for your home.

To control dust mites, either encase upholstery, pillows, and the like in plastic or get rid of them in favor of a more easily cleaned, metal-and-solid-wood decor. You can also devote more time to washing sheets, curtains, and so forth in hot water to kill mites, and vacuuming exhaustively with a special HEPA or water-filter vacuum cleaner.

Animal dander is difficult to remove, so if you experience allergic reactions to pets, it is best not to let any in your home. If you're allergic to your own pet and can't bear to part with it, at least keep it out of the bedroom. There are some indications that washing a cat once a month may after six to ten months cause it to stop producing Fel d1.

If you're allergic to bee stings, learn how to recognize bees' nests and don't wear clothing that attracts them (see Chapter 5).

If you have allergic reactions to cosmetics, try only one new product at a time to help identify reactions. Also patch-test it by applying a dab to your forearm and covering it with a bandage. Repeat for three or four days, then wait two days. Reformulated products, or even ones you've used for years, may cause reactions and need to be discontinued.

Consider forgoing the pertussis vaccine for your child in favor of homeopathic and other natural treatments for whooping cough, should the child come down with it. Before getting any vaccination, take extra levels of antioxidant and immune-boosting vitamins and nutrients for three to four days prior to and after the shot. A typical daily program might be two to five grams of vitamin C plus bioflavonoids in mixed doses or to bowel tolerance, 400–800 IU of vitamin E, 15,000–25,000 IU of vitamin A in the form of beta carotene, 50–100 mg of vitamin B complex, 25–50 mg of B_6, and 25–50 mg of zinc. Specific homeopathic remedies, depending upon the vaccine, can also help to prevent allergic reactions. David Eagle, O.M.D., also recommends including in the program the herbal product milk thistle *(Silybum marianum).* The seeds of the milk thistle plant are used to make silymarin, a standardized extract of a complex compound. "Silymarin is a strong anti-irritant and antioxidant," Eagle says.

Allergies to nickel are often triggered by ear-piercing with a nickel-plated needle, so a much better alternative is piercing with stainless steel. If you suspect a nickel allergy but aren't sure, test for it by taping a nickel to your forearm on a hot day (sweat tends to dissolve nickel) and watching for a local reaction. If you're allergic, you'll have to protect your skin from nickel by wearing it only over clothes or avoiding it altogether. Nickel is common in many alloys including stainless steel and some silver, gold, and platinum products. It is used to make earrings, watchbands, snaps, buckles, and zippers. Brass and copper are nickel-free.

Try to identify foods that cause reactions, keeping in mind that foods are often blamed for reactions that are really due to chemicals, stress, or other factors. Blood tests such as the radioallergosorbent test (RAST) or special elimination diets and fasts can help pinpoint possible food allergens. The usual dietary approach is to stop eating a suspected food for a week to see if symptoms disappear. "This is only rarely successful," notes naturopath Ross Trattler in *Better Health Through Natural Healing,* "since most people respond to several unsuspected foods. The better approach is to fast for five days and then add foods individually to the diet to test for reaction . . . [or eat] only one food item for several days to test for negative reactions. Many reactions take five days to settle down and three to five days to begin again, so you can see this can be a very difficult procedure. It is, however, the best procedure to diagnose food allergy accurately."

All of the above are somewhat reactive steps. A better long-term solution to frequent allergic reactions is to take positive steps to insure the healthy functioning of the immune system.

The best place to start is in infancy, by making sure that babies are breast-fed. Studies have shown that breast-fed babies suffer from fewer allergies and immune-system problems later in life. Also, help prevent food allergies by gradually introducing solids (fresh vegetables, fruits, and grains) into the diet of an infant during the second six months of life.

Among the nutrients that scientists have identified as being central to proper immune-system health are vitamin C, zinc, and beta carotene. Taking two to five grams of C plus bioflavonoids in mixed doses daily (or to bowel tolerance) and 25–50 mg daily of zinc, in conjunction with other vitamins and minerals, can boost the immune system and the body's wound-healing powers, as can high levels of beta carotene, from supplementation or plenty of dark leafy green, or orange, vegetables. Along with vitamin E, these nutrients are also good antioxidants, which help the body break down and digest the toxins that are sometimes caused by— or result from—allergic reactions. Herbs such as echinacea, ginseng, and the healing mushrooms shiitake and reishi can also provide important immune-system support.

FIVE

Bites and Stings

THIS CHAPTER COVERS BITES AND STINGS FROM:

- *animals and humans*
- *snakes, including rattlesnake, copperhead, cotton-mouth, and coral snakes*
- *spiders, scorpions, and ticks*
- *bees, wasps, and ants*
- *sea creatures, including jellyfish, Portuguese man-of-wars, coral, sea anemones, and sea urchins*
- *mosquitoes, flies, fleas, and kissing bugs*

Bites and stings are especially common during the summer, when bees, mosquitoes, and sea creatures do most of the damage. There are a number of general recommendations that apply to almost all bites or all stings, as well as some suggestions for specific animal bites.

◆ Animal and Human Bites

With dogs and cats now numbering over 100 million in the United States, and wild animals such as raccoons increasingly prevalent in urban and suburban areas, bites are on the increase. Indeed, some health authorities are already characterizing the 2–3 million bites inflicted on Americans each year (mostly from dogs) as an epidemic.

Animal bites are similar to wounds in which the flesh is torn or punctured, with the added likelihood of infection. That's because the mouths of humans and animals harbor a large flotilla of bacteria and viruses, including at times those that cause rabies, tetanus, and cat scratch fever. Human bites that break skin may be even more worrisome and infection-prone than animal bites because people seem to be more susceptible to human bacteria.

RABIES

The most feared result of a bite or scratch from any warm-blooded animal is rabies. If you get bitten and decide to forgo vaccination, and rabies symptoms (headache, malaise, muscle spasms, intense thirst) do appear some ten weeks or so later, you have a few days to get your will in order, as the disease is almost inevitably fatal. Rabies is also a painful way to die. "I have seen agony in death only once," medical essayist Lewis Thomas says, "in a patient with rabies; he remained acutely aware of every stage in the process of his own disintegration over a twenty-four-hour period, right up to his final moment." Fortunately, rabies has become more rare in the United States in recent years (only seven people have died from it since 1980), and various steps can be taken to prevent it both before and after a bite.

While human rabies cases are on the decrease, rabies among wild animals is on the rise. Americans are now more likely to contract rabies from a wild animal than from a cat or dog. One study indicated that in 1986 skunks and raccoons accounted for about two-thirds of all animal cases of rabies, with the rest being found mainly among squirrels, foxes, and bats. Rabies among dogs accounted for less than 2 percent of the total cases.

If you're bitten by an animal, there are two ways to tell whether it is rabid. One is to capture it (with *extreme caution*) and have it observed for ten days for such signs as nervousness, excitability, and drooling or foaming at the mouth. It's also possible for a lab technician to identify rabies by examining the brain of a killed animal.

If the animal can't be caught, it's not always necessary to get vaccinated against rabies. Some cities and areas of the United States, including the state of Hawaii, have not reported a single case in years. Rabies rates among wild animal populations vary dramatically by region of the country. For instance, rabies among raccoons has been spreading northward from Florida since the late 1940s, reaching the mid-Atlantic states by 1980. The first rabid raccoons in Massachusetts were found in 1992, and they're expected to soon reach the northern New England states. The risk of contracting rabies from dog and cat bites is low in many instances, though they remain the reason most people undergo treatment. Consult with public health officials and professional health providers before deciding to be treated after a bite. The time between a bite and the first appearance of symptoms is at least ten days, long enough to begin antirabies therapy should that be your choice.

Scientists recently developed a new rabies vaccine that has fewer side effects, involves fewer injections (five shots in the buttocks or arm compared to the old regime of twenty-one excruciating shots in the stomach), and produces better immunity than the earlier vaccine. Still, rabies vaccine does pose a health threat to the individual and it shouldn't be administered indiscriminately. About twenty thousand Americans undergo the treatment annually.

The chief steps for preventing rabies are observing wildlife at a distance, having pets vaccinated against the disease, and immediately and thoroughly washing any animal bite.

TETANUS

Tetanus is caused by certain bacteria that live primarily in soil and in the feces of animals and humans. The bacteria enter the skin through a wound and get sealed off from the air. In the absence of oxygen they then multiply and produce a toxin in the body that attacks the nerves, muscles, and the spinal cord, leading to stiffness in the jaw and neck ("lockjaw"), spasms, and possibly death. Medical treatment is intensive, requiring hospitalization for several weeks, muscle relaxants, antibiotics, artificial respiration, and intravenous feeding.

Infant vaccination by tetanus toxoid injection is widespread in the United States, and since the midseventies there have been fewer than one hundred reported cases annually, mostly affecting the elderly. Preventive vaccination is highly effective, though there are risks. The overall rate of toxic and allergic reactions after repeated exposures may be as high as 3–13 percent. Swelling and abscesses at the injection site are the most common problems; more rarely there can be fever, abdominal pain, and weakness. Vaccination lasts for only five to ten years. Unimmunized individuals can be injected with another form of the vaccine, tetanus immune globulin, within seventy-two hours after an injury to prevent infection.

Since the bacteria are most commonly found in soil, the bites that should routinely require a tetanus shot are those from farm animals, which may harbor tetanus bacteria in their gut. It's also advisable to get a tetanus shot for puncture wounds, in which the skin is pierced by a sharp object and the wound is deep but usually not wide. A tetanus shot is especially important for puncture wounds that have gone untreated for hours, and bites that are deep and dirty, with jagged edges. Scratches from a pet that has been walking in manure-fertilized soil may also present a tetanus risk. Quick and thorough cleaning (see below), especially of shallow wounds, helps prevent tetanus.

CAT SCRATCH FEVER

Young cats that spend a lot of time outdoors sometimes catch a virus that has no apparent effect on them but can cause the systemic illness known as cat scratch fever among infected humans. Cats can transfer the virus by biting or scratching, or even licking an open wound on a human. The disease is most common in fall and winter and usually begins with a slight swelling over the scratch area. An ulcer may form that is slow to heal, and a low-grade fever may go on for months. The only symptoms in some cases are swollen lymph nodes, loss of appetite, and weakness. It usually runs a relatively mild course over a month or two.

Doctors are mostly mystified about how to treat it. Antibodies are ineffective, and the usual recommendation is limited to bed rest during the worst of the disease, and warm, moist soaks on the lymph glands. As is often the case, the best treatment is prevention, in this case by immediately and thoroughly washing any scratch with a topical antiseptic cleansing agent such as alcohol, or any of the herbal preparations described in the section on natural remedies for bites.

BASIC FIRST AID FOR TREATING ANIMAL BITES

It's a good idea to have a health professional treat all but the most minor animal bites, because of the likelihood of infection. How serious a bite is depends on such factors as bite location, its depth, and risk of infection. Immediate medical attention is called for if:

- ◆ a human bite breaks skin
- ◆ the bite is from a wild animal
- ◆ the bite is on the face or neck, which can result in disfigure-

ment, or the hands, where infection is more likely and can be hard to treat
♦ the bite victim is a child who suffers from allergic reactions
♦ the bite causes severe pressure to be applied to the body part, even if the skin remains unbroken (as when a large dog latches onto the arm of a child wearing a heavy coat), resulting in tingling sensations or immediate bluish discoloration near the injury site, since blood vessels or nerves may have been crushed

Puncture wounds also present special worries, since dirt and bacteria can be pushed deep under the skin. Even thorough cleansing may not remove the bacteria, which can thrive and easily infect surrounding tissue. Prevent infection by allowing a puncture wound to bleed (unless the bleeding is severe) so that dirt and bacteria are washed from the wound. You can even press the area around the wound to encourage bleeding. In addition to the basic treatment steps listed below, soak a puncture wound in warm water infused with a dropperful of an antiseptic such as echinacea tincture, or a few drops of the homeopathic remedy *Ledum,* for fifteen minutes twice a day for three days. Lightly bandage the wound and watch closely for signs of infection. In general, seek medical attention for all puncture wounds, especially if they're deep, in a joint, or on the abdomen, chest, neck, or head.

For the routine treatment of bites that result in tears or lacerations you should:

Control any bleeding. Use direct pressure, elevation, or pressure point control (see "Chapter 6: Bleeding"). If the bite is not bleeding, don't try to close the wound, which would trap bacteria and cause infection.

Check for an allergic reaction. Watch for such signs as severe swelling or itching at the site of the bite, dizziness, nausea, or difficulty breathing. These are indications that you need to get medical help as soon as possible.

Rinse the bite to remove any animal saliva from the wound. Hold it under running water for a minute. Thoroughly clean it with a mild soap, then put it under running water for another five minutes.

Dry the bite by patting gently with a clean cloth. Do not put any medications or ointments on an animal bite, since these may act to seal the wound and prevent drainage.

Cover with a sterile bandage or gauze, or clean cloth. While seeking medical attention, you can help reduce any pain by elevating the bitten limb and applying a cold compress if there's swelling. Calm and reassure the victim, make him or her comfortable, and watch for signs of shock.

If the wound is under control, try to catch and confine the animal, alive if possible, to be observed or tested for rabies. This should be done only if it can be accomplished without exposing anyone to the risk of another bite. Most states require that all animal and human bites be reported to local police or health authorities.

WHAT TO EXPECT AT THE HOSPITAL

After cleaning and disinfecting the bite, emergency personnel will close serious wounds with stitches or special bandages. For a puncture wound a physician may recommend antibiotic treatment for a week or longer. If there's a danger of rabies or tetanus, discuss the options with your health practitioner. Keep in mind that some physicians will suggest a tetanus shot even for wounds that may not require it.

Whether treated by a doctor or at home, after being bitten you should watch for signs of infection, such as increased pain, redness, swelling, discharge, and fever.

NATURAL REMEDIES FOR ANIMAL BITES

A number of natural remedies can play a role in helping bite wounds to heal. Here are some that work well on relatively minor bites.

Rinse and wash a bite using a solution with antibacterial or astringent properties. Four of the most effective natural solutions include hydrogen peroxide, tincture of echinacea, tincture of calendula, and Lavender or Tea Tree oil.

◆ Hydrogen peroxide is a good wash that doesn't sting, and it irrigates well in larger quantities. Andrew Weil, M.D., says hydrogen peroxide is especially effective for treating puncture bites. "Try to open the wound up and get the peroxide in so it foams up," he notes.
◆ Tincture of echinacea can be diluted 5:1 with water. After first aid has been administered, give the victim a dropperful of tincture of echinacea internally every hour for three hours.

◆ Tincture of calendula can also be diluted 5:1 with water. "Calendula is a good all-around disinfectant," says Jennifer Jacobs, M.D.

◆ Essential oil of Lavender or Tea Tree can be used by adding three to four drops to a half cup of warm water (shake well) during the initial wash. You can also put a drop or two right on the wound, or onto the gauze bandage after washing. "Oils get into the bloodstream relatively quickly," says herbalist Christopher Hobbs.

Cover a clean bite with a goldenseal-root powder pack. Mix some dried goldenseal root with either water or aloe and apply it to the cleaned bite. Naturopath Joseph Pizzorno recommends this herbal antibacterial treatment "because it breathes and thus is preferable to a greasy preparation."

Goldenseal-root powder is widely available in capsule form, and some herbal companies sell loose goldenseal-root powder.

Use homeopathic remedies to help boost the body's ability to heal a bite wound. Take a 6X or 12X potency homeopathic remedy immediately after the injury and every four to six hours for the next day or two.

There are a number of remedies that can be taken orally or applied topically.

◆ *Ledum* is the most commonly recommended homeopathic remedy for puncture wounds, particularly when the bite area is red, swollen, and cold or numb to the touch. You can also use *Ledum* lotion to wash a puncture wound, and a few drops of *Ledum* in warm water to soak it.

◆ *Apis* is particularly recommended if the pain associated with a bite is stinging and hot and the bite is soothed by applying cold. *Apis* is available in ointment form, but it's not a good idea to put an ointment on a puncture wound, since it can close it off and encourage infection.

◆ *Hypericum* is used if the wound is accompanied by sharp, shooting pain. You can also apply a homeopathic preparation of *Hypericum* externally to a bite site. *Hypericum* is available commercially in spray and tincture forms. Apply it directly to the bite site at the time of injury, and again every two to three hours for the first day. Dilute *Hypericum* tincture 5:1 in water before applying.

Apply fresh plantain leaves. If you're out in the field with no other bandage available, a poultice of plantain leaves can help healing. Crush or chew up the leaves into a slippery mass and apply moist to the injury. Plantain is a common weed throughout the United States (see illustration #10).

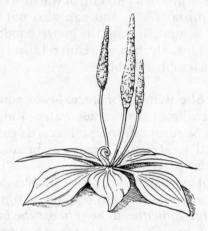

Illustration #10:

Plantain is a common weed throughout the U.S. Its leaves can be crushed or chewed and applied to minor bites and other skin wounds.

RECOVERING FROM ANIMAL BITES

Nutrients that can help the body recover from an animal or human bite include extra vitamin C to reduce infection and repair collagen and connective tissue, vitamin A in the form of beta carotene and vitamin E to aid the immune system and assist healing of the skin, B complex to produce antibodies, and garlic for its natural antibiotic properties.

Take some acidophilus if the wound is serious enough to require antibiotics. Acidophilus has become the generic term for various types of naturally occurring live bacteria that are increasingly popular as dietary supplements. Technically acidophilus is the strain *Lactobacillus acidophilus*, though products sold as acidophilus may also contain *L. bulgaricus* and other strains of lactic bacteria. Why take live bacteria at all? Certain bacteria are essential to the healthy functioning of the gastrointestinal system, where they play a role in food digestion and the production of B vitamins.

Anyone who is taking oral doses of antibiotics may benefit by supplementing the diet with acidophilus. Antibiotics kill not only disease-causing bacteria but the "friendly" microorganisms that your intestines need to function properly. When beneficial intestinal flora are missing, harmful bacteria and microorganisms, including fungi such as *Candida albicans* (a cause of yeast infections), more easily move in and take over. Supplementing the diet with acidophilus helps repopulate the intestines with beneficial bacteria and prevents the establishment of harmful bacterial colonies.

Food producers use acidophilus and other strains of lactic bacteria to ferment milk into such products as yogurt and kefir. Fermented dairy products, however, are unlikely to have high enough levels of live bacteria to replenish intestines that have been depleted of healthful bacteria by ongoing antibiotic use. Much higher concentrations of acidophilus are available in the form of tablets, powders, capsules, and liquids sold in most natural foods stores. Look for acidophilus products that have labels providing information on how many live or "viable" bacteria each capsule or teaspoon provides. Acidophilus capsules may provide 2 billion or more friendly organisms while some liquids provide up to 5 billion per tablespoon. Also look for products with labels that provide an expiration date with a guarantee of product viability until that date, storage instructions, and a listing of additional ingredients. Many acidophilus products need to be kept refrigerated.

Hobbs says, "To replenish intestinal flora you should take doses of acidophilus that provide at least ten billion organisms per day." Nutritionist Shari Lieberman recommends that people who are suffering from any of the conditions associated with depleted intestinal flora take one to two teaspoons of powder or liquid daily during recovery, then one-half to one teaspoon per day for another week or longer to fully repopulate the gut. Acidophilus is safe (though expensive) to take indefinitely. A high-fiber, whole-foods diet can complement acidophilus's positive effect on intestinal flora.

In addition to echinacea, the herbs goldenseal and pau d'arco have wound-healing properties that can help you to recover from a bite.

If you're weak after a bite, says Hobbs, strengthen your immune system by taking the Chinese herbs astragalus and ligustrum or the healing mushrooms reishi and shiitake. Hobbs recommends these "deep immune activators" because of their track record in traditional Chinese medicine and because research has indicated that their chemical constituents (saponins and complex polysaccharides) play an important role in healthy immune function.

Astragalus *(Astragalus membranaceus)* is one of the most famous traditional Chinese herbs, used by healers to strengthen (or "tonify") the body's overall vitality and support the spleen. Make a decoction from six to nine grams of the dried root, or purchase astragalus in concentrated-extract form at your local natural foods store and take according to label instructions.

Ligustrum *(Ligustrum lucidum)*, also known as Chinese privet, is a fruit-bearing evergreen shrub. It grows widely in China, where traditional herbalists dry and powder the fruits for use in products to tonify the liver and kidney. Steven Foster and Yue Chongxi, experts on traditional Chinese herbalism, note in *Herbal Emissaries: Bringing Chinese Herbs to the West,* "Like astragalus *(huang-qi)*, the fruits of Chinese privet, or *nu-zhen-zi,* have been the subject of recent studies both in China and the United States for enhancing white blood cell counts after chemotherapy or radiotherapy treatments, primarily for cancer. . . . Extracts of the fruit seem to enhance immunological function."

Ligustrum is an ingredient in a number of herbal combination products sold in the United States. A typical dose is five to ten grams of powder, extract, or concentrate.

Shiitake *(Lentinus edodes)* is a dark, flavorful mushroom that has been prized by the Chinese for thousands of years for its medicinal properties, especially for treating systemic conditions related to aging and sexual dysfunction. Over one hundred scientific studies, conducted primarily by Japanese researchers since the 1930s, indicate that shiitake extracts can lower blood cholesterol levels, shrink tumors, and combat viruses and bacteria. Scientists say that the polysaccharide lentinan found in shiitake helps stimulate the immune system.

Until recently, most shiitake were imported dried from the Orient and were thus expensive to purchase at natural foods stores. A number of American producers are now growing and selling less costly fresh and dried shiitake, and shiitake concentrates are available from a number of herbal companies. Take according to label directions. Add whole, fresh or dried shiitake to a soup with green leafy vegetables, or use them in a stew, stir-fry, or any other dish that calls for mushrooms.

Reishi *(Ganoderma lucidum)* is another medicinal mushroom that is fast approaching shiitake's popularity in the United States for its overall immune-boosting properties. It's a harder, more bitter and woodlike mushroom than shiitake and thus isn't used as a food. Within the past few years, however, reishi has become available in a variety of forms. Natural foods stores sell dried, powdered reishi in tablets and capsules (take two 100 mg capsules or tablets daily). Reishi is also available in other forms, including a granulated extract used to make a tea (drink two cups per day).

Dr. Andrew Weil, a botanical researcher and physician who has been studying medicinal mushrooms for over fifteen years, says, "That Western medicine has never looked to mushrooms as sources of new treatments for illness is irrationally strange. Mushrooms have unique and highly varied chemistries, producing an array of novel compounds not found elsewhere in nature. Many of these compounds show bioactivity in animals. . . . Most of the medicinal mushrooms of the Orient may have antiviral and anti-tumor properties as a result of [these compounds'] ability to stimulate cells that affect immune responses." In addition to shiitake and reishi, he says that consumers should seek out some of the new mushroom varieties just beginning to appear in natural foods stores, including:

- ◆ enokidake *(Flammulina velutipes)*, a gourmet food mushroom that grows wild in North America; Weil says that it has a polysaccharide that may be more of an immune booster when taken orally than lentinan
- ◆ maitake *(Grifola frondosa)*, also known as "hen of the woods" in the United States, a delicious edible mushroom that may have better and more extensive therapeutic properties than any other species
- ◆ zhu ling *(Polyporus umbellatus*, or *Grifola umbellata)*, a popular Chinese medicinal mushroom that grows only rarely in North America; it is an ingredient in a number of prepared Chinese herbal medicines

PREVENTING ANIMAL BITES

Preventing animal bites begins by teaching young children to approach or pet strange dogs with care, and wild animals not at all. Three out of four dog bites are unprovoked. Large dogs inflict the worst bites, and German shepherds are the dog most likely to bite. In cities and suburbs dogs should be leashed, and if they're high-strung, kept away from children entirely. Young children shouldn't be left alone with animals. Never interfere with animals that are feeding, mating, or fighting.

Have any pets you own immunized against rabies; cats, too, which have been responsible for more rabies cases than dogs in eight out of the last ten years, according to the federal Centers for Disease Control.

Never allow a cat or dog to lick a human's open wound.

Any wild animal that allows itself to be petted may be sick or rabid and thus the last animal you want to pet. When camping, don't keep food in your tent.

◆ Snakebites

Snakes bite over fifty thousand Americans each year, though all but a thousand or so of these bites are inflicted by nonvenomous species, according to the American Association of Poison Control Centers. States with higher-than-average bite rates include Florida, Georgia, Texas, and California.

Nonvenomous bites can be treated as are other bites. They're often relatively minor, due to the small teeth and jaws of most snakes. Bites from any of the four types of venomous snakes of North America, on the other hand, are sometimes anything but minor, and on occasion (a dozen times a year in the United States), they can be deadly.

Venomous snakes can be divided into two families:

- ◆ Pit vipers. These include copperheads, the cottonmouth (or water moccasin), and rattlesnakes.
- ◆ Elapids. These include cobras (not represented in the United States) and the coral snake, which have eastern and western varieties in the United States.

The pit vipers, which are responsible for more than nine out of ten of the venomous bites in the United States, may be eighteen inches to eight feet long. They have a number of physical markings that distinguish them from other snakes:

- ◆ vertical, slitlike eyes
- ◆ a triangular head distinct from the rest of the body
- ◆ pits between the nostrils and eyes
- ◆ long, slightly curved fangs that fold back when not biting

Copperheads. Copperheads live mainly in wild meadows and wooded mountains in the Northeast and the central United States, and swamps in the Southeast. They grow up to four feet long and have dark brown crossbands on the body and (not surprisingly) a copper-colored head. They are the least poisonous of the pit vipers.

Cottonmouths. These are semiaquatic snakes that inhabit lakes and swamps of the Southeast. Cottonmouths have a thick, olive-brown body up to four feet long and get their name from a distinctive white lining on the inside of the mouth. They're the most aggressive of the venomous snakes of North America, sometimes attacking unprovoked.

Rattlesnakes. There are over a dozen species of rattlesnakes in the United States, ranging in size from the eighteen-inch pygmy to the eight-foot Eastern diamondback. Only some have diamond-shaped markings on their bodies, but they all have rattles at the end of the tail.

Coral snakes. Coral snakes are one to four feet long, have round pupils, and have shorter, less visible fangs. They're found primarily in the Southeast, in open woods and sometimes suburban areas. They're most easily identified by the distinctive alternating bands of color, usually thick rings of red and black separated by thinner rings of yellow or white. If a snake has red bands bordered by narrow white or yellow ones, it's a coral. A saying goes, "Red on yellow will kill a fellow; red on black won't hurt Jack." Coral snakes also always have a black snout.

In contrast to pit vipers and coral snakes, all nonvenomous snakes have round pupils and no fangs, pits, or rattles. A bite from

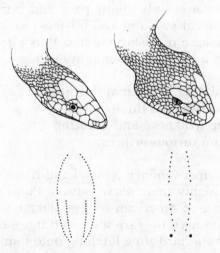

Illustration #11:

You can distinguish poisonous from nonpoisonous snakes by the shape of the snake's head and eyes as well as its bite pattern. Venomous snakes have triangular heads, slitlike pupils, and long fangs, which make distinctive punctures in a bite wound, at the end of each row of teeth.

a nonvenomous snake may show two rows of tiny, shallow punctures, while a venomous bite will usually have one or two distinctive fang punctures at the end of the rows (see illustration #11).

There are also two venomous lizards to be wary of if you live in the Southwest: the Gila monster and Mexican bearded lizard. These prehistoric-looking creatures can grow over a foot in length and administer a painful bite, made worse by their propensity to hang on and chew. Fortunately they are shy animals, and bites on humans are exceedingly rare.

THE EFFECTS OF SNAKE VENOM

When a pit viper sinks its fangs into you and squirts through them a shot of its venom, it's preparing to eat you. These snakes don't chew much—they swallow their prey whole. You'll be spared that particular fate, but the venom circulating in your blood won't know you're not a field mouse beginning a one-way journey down the snake's gullet. Think of the snake venom as liquid teeth. It's a mix of enzymes and other proteins that begins to digest tissues it encounters. In your body, it can cause extensive local tissue damage by destroying muscle and fat, making small blood vessels leak, and disrupting normal blood clotting.

The bite may cause only slight pain and burning at first, followed by rapid local swelling and blisters. Snake venom can also trigger the release of histamine and thus affect breathing. Other symptoms of a pit viper bite might include:

◆ swelling and discoloration at the bite site
◆ dizziness, nausea, and thirst
◆ intense pain, weakness, and sweating
◆ bleeding from various orifices

In general, pit viper venom is a blood-and-tissue poison, while coral venom is a highly toxic nerve poison. Coral venom is the most potent of those of American snakes, though not often fatal because coral snakes need to grasp their victim to sink their fangs, and they often have a hard time latching onto human skin. As a result coral snakes tend to inject relatively small amounts of their venom when they do bite people.

The bite at first may be painless, showing only a little swelling. That's followed by a slight tingling sensation and local muscle spasms, and then a few hours later euphoria (all too briefly), nausea, and blurred vision and slurred speech. In the worst bites, which are rare, there's paralysis of the limbs and finally death by asphyxiation. The only effective therapy for a coral bite is anti-venom.

HOW SEVERE IS THE BITE?

It's sometimes difficult to diagnose venomous snakebites. Quick swelling and discoloration at the bite site can hide telltale fang marks, and the symptoms can resemble allergic reactions and other illnesses. Plus the effect of a poisonous snakebite varies considerably, depending upon such factors as:

+ size, age, and species of snake
+ time of year and length of time since the snake's last meal, which will affect how much venom it has built up in its venom glands
+ health, age, and weight of victims (most at risk are small children, pregnant women, the elderly, and the ill)
+ number, location, and depth of bite, all of which affect the amount of venom injected (20–30 percent of bites by venomous snakes are "dry," that is, no venom is injected, and in another 20–30 percent an insignificant amount gets injected)

Venomous bites to the head or neck are especially dangerous because swelling can constrict air passages and cause suffocation. Bites on the trunk or arms are also serious, since venom gets circulated more quickly than from bites to the legs. A bite directly into a blood vessel can put a person into shock almost immediately.

BASIC FIRST AID FOR SNAKEBITE

The first steps to take when bitten by a snake are to back off to prevent another bite, and to identify the snake if you can. If you're not sure whether it is venomous, assume that it is. If you can do so safely, capture the snake for positive identification at the hospital.

If you're positive the bite is from a nonpoisonous snake, treat it as you would any other animal bite: rinse, clean with soap and water, apply bandage or clean cloth, and seek medical attention. (See basic treatment under "Human and Animal Bites.")

A bite from a poisonous snake is a more serious medical emergency. There's some truth to the saying that the only tool you need to treat a snakebite is car keys. Calling for professional medical assistance as soon as possible is important. Time is important to the victim, and the hospital may need time to obtain or prepare antivenom. In the meantime a number of steps can help assure a positive outcome for the victim.

Remove constrictive items. Even if the bite is not near an extremity, remove from the victim any jewelry such as rings or bracelets, since swelling may come on quickly.

Monitor the ABCs: airway, breathing, and circulation (see "Chapter 3: Basic Emergency Care"). Control any bleeding, and watch for allergic reaction or shock. If it's possible to remove any venom, it should be done quickly, before it begins to circulate. Often it's not possible, so the first-aid focus is on slowing the circulation of the venom.

If possible and safe, remove venom. Removing venom can be tricky. The most direct method of using a razor or knife to make tiny (parallel, not crossed) incisions over the fang marks of a pit viper bite, and applying suction, is difficult to do right without experience or training. Though it used to be commonly recommended in first-aid books, so many poorly performed "cut and sucks" led to infections, severed nerves and arteries, and other major injuries, that the current thinking is that it's usually likely only to make things worse for the victim. It's no longer recommended except in extreme cases, when medical help is hours away, a positive identification of a large poisonous snake has been made, the victim is young or elderly, and the first-aid giver can perform it precisely and calmly.

There is now a better and more effective tool in any case, known as a venom extractor. These syringe and suction cup devices can create a vacuum on the skin's surface strong enough to pull as much as 25–35 percent of the venom out. They should be used within five minutes of the bite to be effective. A venom extractor should be part of your first-aid kit if you're going camping or hiking in snake country. Mail-order first-aid and camping-equipment companies often sell them (see "Resources").

Apply a constricting band when necessary. A constricting band is called for when venom can't be removed, the bite is on an arm or leg, and the person must walk for at least thirty minutes for help. Apply a constricting band *(not a tourniquet!)* above the bite to slow the circulation of venom. A constricting band should be used only for pit viper bites, not coral snakebites, and should be used with caution. Tying it too tightly can restrict blood flow and permanently damage the limb.

Tie a piece of cloth or cord two to five inches above the bite, between the bite and the rest of the body. An elastic bandage works well if you have one. The band should be loose enough that you can slip a finger under the band. Make sure that you can find a pulse below the band. Also, loosen it every three to five minutes for about thirty seconds, until medical assistance comes.

If swelling goes beyond the band, leave it in place and put another above it. When it is time to remove a constricting band, unwrap it slowly.

Take other steps to slow the circulation of venom. These include:

- Keep the victim as still as possible. This is crucial. Don't let him or her exercise or even walk unless necessary.
- Keep the victim calm, since nervousness, panic, and emotional agitation can speed heart rate and increase blood flow.
- Don't apply ice or a tourniquet. These are also techniques that used to be recommended but are no longer considered effective at slowing the spread of venom. Using them may make some snakebites worse by causing frostbite or tissue damage, leading to the need to amputate the limb.
- Wash the bite with soap and water and cover with sterile gauze or a clean cloth.
- Immobilize and splint a bitten extremity, then keep it at or below heart level.

You should have several hours before the worst effects are felt from the bite of any North American snake. Antivenom is most effective if it's given within twelve hours of a bite, but it can be given as many as twenty-four hours afterward and still be effective. With medical treatment the survival rate for venomous snakebites in the United States approaches 100 percent. Without it, it is less than 90 percent.

Don't allow the victim to eat any food, drink any alcohol, or take any prescription medications. These actions could interfere with subsequent emergency treatment.

WHAT TO EXPECT AT THE HOSPITAL

Treatment at the hospital will depend on the severity of the bite and the age and health of the victim. Administering antivenom is not automatic, since many individuals are highly sensitive to it. The only way that antivenom should be administered is by slow intravenous drip. Injecting it into the bite area, or failing to test for possible allergic reaction, may be even more dangerous than the snakebite itself.

The immediate concerns will be to maintain an open airway and keep the patient immobile. The patient may be given oxygen as doctors clean the bite, remove any embedded teeth, and dress the wound. Severe bites may require calcium gluconate for muscle spasms, sedatives for convulsions, blood transfusions, and analgesics for pain. Doctors may recommend a tetanus shot and a long-term program for antibiotics. Most people who are bitten by poisonous snakes are hospitalized.

NATURAL REMEDIES FOR SNAKEBITE

Snakebites used to be more common, and lacking antivenom, traditional societies such as Native American cultures developed numerous herbal and folk remedies. Some of these still make sense to use, in conjunction with the basic steps of immobilizing the victim and seeking medical help.

Take echinacea, internally and externally. Echinacea is available fresh, dried, in a tincture, or freeze-dried. Herbalist Christopher Hobbs recommends taking two to three droppersful of the tincture internally immediately after a snakebite, with another dropperful every hour afterward for up to twelve hours. "It's not toxic, and you need a high dose to quickly activate the immune system," he says.

For external use, take a cotton pad, saturate it with echinacea tincture, and tape it on the bite. You can cover the pad with a piece of plastic wrap and then light cotton cloth to prevent the pad from drying too quickly. Change the pad often. You can also blend fresh echinacea and apply it as a poultice.

Echinacea is the classic snakebite remedy among Native Americans of the Plains. It was widely used for snakebite, as well as a variety of other injuries and conditions, by nineteenth-century Americans and Europeans. One early promoter even volunteered to allow himself to be bitten by a rattlesnake to demonstrate the herb's antisnakebite powers. Echinacea fell in popularity in the 1930s in the United States (it remained popular in Europe), but recent scientific research has confirmed many of its healing powers, and it is now enjoying a major American comeback.

Studies have shown not only that echinacea promotes wound healing and boosts the immune system, but that it can help heal snakebites. The plant contains substances that prevent the enzyme hyaluronidase, found in certain venoms and bacteria, from encouraging infection. According to Michael Murray, N.D., author of *The Healing Power of Herbs*, "Snake venom contains hyaluronidase, 'the spreading factor,' which breaks down ground substance [the thick, gel-like material in which the cell fiber and blood capillaries of cartilage, bone, and connective tissue are embedded] and allows the venom to penetrate into the bloodstream. Echinacea contains compounds that have demonstrated potent inhibition of hyaluronidase. This characteristic might account for much of echinacea's reputed effect as a snakebite antivenom."

Take high doses of vitamin C. Take two grams immediately after the bite, then two to five grams with mixed bioflavonoids daily in mixed doses or to bowel tolerance for the next three to four days. This has been used successfully in some life-threatening situations, for C's antiallergy and antihistamine effects.

Take the homeopathic remedy **Arnica**. This should be taken internally and is good for pain, swelling, and bruising. Homeopaths also have a seldom-used remedy specifically for snakebite: *Crotalus horridus*, made from rattlesnake venom. Check with a homeopathic practitioner for dosage and use. See the section on bee stings later in this chapter for further homeopathic treatment recommendations.

In the field, use plantain as the fresh herb of choice. Freshly crushed or chewed-up leaves have anti-inflammatory, antitoxic, and antibacterial effects. You can get capsules of plantain at natural foods stores, but Hobbs notes that one of the primary active ingredients, aucubin, breaks down easily.

Take pau d'arco. This is the traditional snakebite remedy used by the native Indians of Brazil. For external use, take a cotton pad, saturate it with pau d'arco tincture or extract, and tape it on the bite. You can also make a strong decoction (using one teaspoon per cup of water) and apply the decoction locally as a compress. Supplement topical treatment with repeated oral doses of pau d'arco capsules, extract, or tea.

For long-term treatment of snakebite, apply daily poultices using such healing herbs as echinacea, comfrey, or calendula.

Apply the herb itself, fresh (crush or bruise first) or dried, directly to the skin. An easy way to use the dried herb is to make a paste by adding hot water and mixing. Some people prefer putting the paste or leaves between two thin layers of gauze and taping that to the injured area.

You can also soak the bite wound twice daily in a solution of echinacea or one of the other disinfectants mentioned in natural treatments for animal bites.

There's a plethora of herbs whose names indicate their presumed benefit: rattlesnake master, downy rattlesnake plantain, Virginia snakeroot, rattlesnake root, snakeweed, etc. How all these plants came to be snakebite remedies is unclear, though the reasons may relate to the doctrine of signatures (a plant's physical appearance provides clues to its effect on the body; for instance, a plant with ear-shaped leaves will cure an earache), or traditional healers having seen wild animals use the plants after suffering a bite. Some of these herbs have been proven to have antifever or blood-purifying properties, though their usefulness as snakebite remedies is limited.

Bioelectric authority Robert Becker, M.D., reports a unique snakebite treatment apparently gaining popularity among some river-going Native South Americans. When bitten by a venomous snake, they administer a considerable electric shock to the bite site by touching it with the wire disconnected from the spark plug of one of their boats' outboard motors, while the starter rope is pulled. The toxic effects of the snakebite are said to be neutralized by the resulting twenty-thousand-volt pulse, possibly by the disordering of the complex molecules of the toxin. According to Becker, "The success rate of this low-tech technique is amazingly high, with what would once have been fatal bites now apparently survivable." This is potentially an interesting line of research, but currently it's dangerous and unproven and not recommended.

PREVENTING SNAKEBITES

Preventing snakebites begins with learning about the venomous varieties, if any, in your area or the area you're hiking or camping in, especially in the Southwest and Southeast where most bites occur.

Since snakes are cold-blooded, they hibernate during winter and don't pose a threat then as long as you don't wander into a den. Most bites occur in the early summer when they emerge from hibernation ready for a big meal. When it's cold, they like to sun themselves on rocks. Otherwise they may be found in swamps, under ledges, in caves or hollow logs, in abandoned buildings, and elsewhere. It's always a good idea to check where you step, sit, or reach in snake country.

Most bites occur on the legs. Knee-high leather boots and long pants provide the best protection. Snakes are nocturnal hunters, so stay in camp at night. Hiking alone presents extra risks, not only if you are bitten by a snake but if you fall and break a bone, for instance. Take a friend. Even with a friend, when in snake country carry a snakebite kit and be familiar with its use.

Snakes are shy and as eager as you to avoid contact. Try not to startle or corner one. Stay on clear paths while hiking, and if you do see one in your path, stop and make a wide detour.

Finally, don't handle snakes unless you know what you're doing. Don't even handle the decapitated head of a recently killed snake. A primitive response mechanism allows a severed snake head to still strike and kill.

For tips on recovering from a snakebite, see the section on recovery following the discussion of stings.

◆ Spider, Scorpion, and Tick Bites

There's something about four pairs of legs and a divided body that instills terror in many people. How else to explain the almost universal loathing that many people feel for members of the arachnid order, including spiders, scorpions, mites, and ticks? Like bites from any other animal, arachnid bites call for treatment, but most spiders pose less risk to humans than people assume.

SPIDERS

Spiders are predators and every once in a while, if they're seriously provoked, they'll prey on a human. Like bees, they inject venom into their victims, but through a bite rather than a sting. Of the thousands of species of spiders in the United States, only a dozen or so can bite with enough power to cause even mild symptoms in a person. Of these, two types of spiders (black widows and brown recluses) pose a potentially serious poisoning risk, and one type (the tarantula) poses a moderate risk. A bite from even these rarely kills a human.

If you do get bitten by a spider powerful enough to cause a reaction, usually after ten minutes or so a local swelling with two punctures in the middle will appear on the skin. Spider bites can cause harm in three ways: from an allergic reaction, from the venom, and from infection by bacteria in the spider's saliva. So the basic treatment protocol is to watch for allergic reactions (see Chapter 4 for symptoms), neutralize the poisons, and cleanse the wound.

Many people who think they've been bitten by a spider have actually been bitten by ticks or fleas. A spider bite is usually somewhat more tender and longer lasting than a flea or mosquito bite. If you see a spider bite you, try to identify, capture, or kill it so that if a serious reaction does occur, a doctor will be able to identify the culprit and treat the injury accordingly.

Black widows. Black widows have a hollow fang at the end of each jaw connected to a venom sac. The venom is more potent (though less voluminous) than that of a cobra, containing chemicals that paralyze the spider's prey. In humans the venom acts as a neurotoxin, affecting the nervous system. The female black window is larger than the male and more dangerous, even to its mate, which it eats after mating (unless he hotfoots it out of the web quickly enough). The male is too small to have a harmful bite.

Female black widows have a shiny black, bulbous body about the size of a thumbnail (not including the legs). They have a reddish hourglass marking on their underside.

There are at least five species of black widows in the United States. They're common only in some urban areas of the Southwest. Though the bites are generally serious enough to warrant emergency medical attention, one estimate is that fewer than one in a hundred bites are fatal.

Most black widow bites at first are painless and invisible or feel like a pinprick. Depending on the spider, there may be only relatively minor local symptoms of redness, swelling, and sharp pain around the bite that last for a few hours. If the bite is more serious, body-wide symptoms may develop within ten to sixty minutes after the bite. Often, about fifteen minutes after a serious bite, the victim starts to feel jumpy. Over the next hour intense pain and muscle cramping develop in the bite area and then spread quickly throughout the body. The victim may also experience headache, dizziness, nausea, swelling of the face, and chest pains. In the most severe bites, the victim starts to sweat profusely and the body's temperature and blood pressure go up. The muscles of the stomach and abdomen go rigid, the chest tightens, extremities swell, and the victim has difficulty breathing. The person's speech may be slurred, and he or she may exhibit symptoms of shock: cold, clammy skin, a weak pulse, and shortness of breath. Symptoms may last twenty-four hours, though the worst effects usually pass within the first two to three hours.

In the rare cases that a bite is fatal, the victim is usually either young, elderly, or suffering from high blood pressure.

See "Basic First Aid for Spider Bites" for initial treatment of bites from the black widow and the other most venomous spiders.

Treatment at a hospital may include antivenom, although often that's reserved for people with severe bites, children, and others at high risk. Antivenom should be tested on the skin first to avoid allergic reactions. Doctors may also inject calcium gluconate or methocarbamol, a muscle relaxant, and administer drugs to ease the pain. A tetanus shot may be called for, since secondary complications, such as tetanus bacteria, may be more deadly than the spider's venom.

Brown recluses. In some ways the less well-known brown recluse poses more of a threat to humans than do black widows. There are more of them than black widows, and both sexes bite. Brown recluses also tend to hunt some distance from their webs, unlike black widows. The venom from the brown recluse is more actively toxic than the black widow's, too. It not only harms the nerves but destroys blood and tissue as well, leading to gangrenous ulcers and systemic poisoning. Still, it's rarely fatal.

Also known as violin spiders and fiddlebacks, brown recluses are rather flat spiders, one-half to five-eighths inches long, with a characteristic violin-shaped figure on their top front. They've spread throughout the United States but prefer hot, arid environments and like the black widows are most common in the Southwest.

Typically they venture out at night to hunt insects and may crawl into bedding or clothing. Indoors they're most often found in clothes closets, on or near the floor, and in boxes or piles of paper.

Brown recluse bites may cause a sharp stinging pain, though more frequently the victim feels only a mild pinching at first. Pain, local swelling, and a rash follow within the next one to four hours. Serious bites are characterized by pain that intensifies over the next six to eight hours. After the first day the victim may suffer joint pain, chills, fever, and nausea. Soon a large purple blister forms that gets darker over the next one to three days and may continue to grow for weeks. Eventually it turns into a scab that falls off and leaves a deep ulcer, indicative of irreversible tissue damage around the bite area. Children may get anemia from destruction of red blood cells. Total recovery time may be months.

At the hospital the victim may be given antivenom and antibiotics. Some doctors may recommend excision, antihistamines, and cortisonelike steroid injections; some studies suggest these are not useful. Victims of the worst bites may need a skin graft to repair the ulcer.

Tarantulas. Tarantulas are dark brown to black, hairy, and slow moving. They're the largest spiders in the United States, typically two and a half inches long but up to five inches long among the oldest (they may live up to twenty years).

Though they look more fearsome than black widows and brown recluses, they pose less of a health threat. Often their bite is mild, inflicting no more of an injury than a routine bee sting. One study found no recorded deaths or serious reactions in Arizona, where tarantulas are more common than anywhere else in the United States. Some brave souls even keep them as pets.

Tarantulas burrow in the ground to build their nest and tend to stay close to it except when mating. It's during mating season they're most likely to venture into a house and startle a homeowner.

A tarantula bite usually causes only slight pain at the time of the bite, or a pinprick sensation, with mild pain over the next fifteen to thirty minutes. In the worst cases a painful wound may develop that takes weeks to heal.

SCORPIONS

These arachnids look like small lobsters, three-quarters to three inches long. They have eight legs, a set of pincers up front, and a stinger at the end of a flexible tail that curves up over the body. Like their cousins the spiders, they have poor vision and rely instead on their sense of feel. They'll try to sting any moving object that touches them.

Scorpions are nocturnal creatures who nest by burrowing in sand. They may also be found in fallen trees or under rocks and logs. Since they hibernate during the winter, most bites occur between May and October, when they're liable to be found hiding in a person's shoes or boots, for instance. There are a number of species but the most lethal variety is found primarily in Arizona and southern California.

When a scorpion bites, most people feel only a beelike sting or prickling sensation. The victim suffers some local swelling and a few hours of mild pain. More severe bites lead to intense, burning pain at the area of the bite, which becomes exceedingly sensitive to touch. The venom may cause prolonged overstimulation of the nervous system, making the victim appear restless. Headaches, nausea, stomach pain and abdominal cramps, fever, dizziness, and muscle twitching may also occur. Children may have trouble breathing. Without treatment the end result can be shock, convulsions, and coma.

Serious bites may be treated at the hospital with intravenous medications to relieve muscle pain and spasm. The patient will be told to rest for at least twelve hours.

TICKS

Ticks are tiny arachnids that attach themselves to a host, sink a harpoonlike barb under the skin, embed their heads, and start to suck blood. Unlike bloodsucking insects such as the mosquito that eat and run in a few seconds, ticks are veritable blood gourmands. They dig in for a blood meal that may take days to complete, at the end of which they've bloated to two or three times their initial size.

Because ticks are relatively slow feeders, they can acquire, from mice, squirrels, deer, rats, and other animals, dozens of types of bacteria. When a tick subsequently attaches to a human for a meal, it can pass on these pathogens and cause a wider variety of diseases than perhaps any other pest is capable of spreading. The diseases ticks most commonly cause include Rocky Mountain spotted fever, tick paralysis, and Lyme disease.

Adding to their obnoxiousness are the facts that ticks are long-lived and occur in every part of the United States, especially in overgrown suburban areas and places where there is woodsy underbrush or tall grass. They have few natural enemies and can be so small they're hard to spot until gorged with blood. They're most common in the hot summer months.

Rocky Mountain spotted fever. Rocky Mountain spotted fever is caused by ticks that carry the pathogen *Rickettsia rickettsii*.

Animals such as chipmunks, squirrels, opossums, raccoons, skunks, and some mice are most likely to serve as the transfer agent for ticks with *Rickettsia* to infect humans. The name of the fever is misleading: people in the southeastern and south central United States are more likely to contract the disease than those who live in the Rocky Mountain states, though cases have been reported in all states. Currently about a thousand Americans come down with the condition each year.

The first symptoms usually appear about a week after a tick bite. The person suffers severe headaches and intense itching, followed a few days later by a rash that often appears on the wrists and ankles and a high fever. In rare cases the victim dies within two weeks or so. Hospitalization and intense antibiotic treatment can usually control the disease.

Tick paralysis. Tick paralysis, which is caused by a neurotoxin injected from the wood tick or the dog tick, is most common in the United States in the northwestern and the southeastern states. Symptoms start after the tick has been feeding on the person (in most cases a child) for a week or so. The person loses strength and coordination first in the legs and then, within a day or two, in the upper parts of the body. If the condition is not diagnosed, breathing can be depressed and the person can die. Hospitalization may be required during the acute phase.

Ticks are usually found under hair on the head. If the tick is found, the person's condition visibly improves within hours of removing it. The person can expect to make a full recovery in most cases within a week.

Lyme disease. Lyme disease has existed in Europe for a century or longer and is found worldwide. Scientists trace its spread to the United States back to the Massachusetts island of Nantucket, where it was known as "Nantucket fever" in the early 1970s. An outbreak in 1975 among some children living in the wooded area around Old Lyme, Connecticut, led researchers to link the disease to a specific bacterium carried by ticks. Under the new name of Lyme disease it has now spread to at least forty states, though Connecticut still has the highest incidence. More than nine thousand cases were reported nationwide in 1992.

The ticks responsible are especially tiny ones, such as the northern deer tick *(Ixodes dammini)*. The immature "nymph" ticks that are responsible for about four of every five cases of Lyme disease are even smaller, about the size of a pinhead. Larvae molt into nymphs in the spring, so May and June are the most dangerous months for contacting Lyme disease. The immature ticks wait patiently in low vegetation for a host to wander by, in the east often the white-footed field mouse, and in the West lizards and jackrabbits. After these wild animals provide a few days of blood meals (and the Lyme-causing bacteria *Borrelia burgdorferi*), the ticks fall off again. It is dogs and cats that often carry the ticks into the presence of humans.

The first sign of a bite is often a raised red rash that sometimes has a bull's-eye look, with a red outer ring. It could be faded or relatively dramatic. Sometimes this symptom appears quickly after a bite, but in other cases it may take weeks to appear. Some one in four cases lack this symptom altogether, however, so if you know you've been bitten by a potential carrier, you should get a blood test for the pathogen. Often the rash will then disappear for a number of weeks. Subsequent stages of the disease may exhibit flulike symptoms and then serious, arthriticlike pain, headaches, and possibly strokes or brain tumors. Treatment, with tetracycline and other antibiotics, is more effective early than when the disease has reached later stages.

The coming and going of symptoms is one reason Lyme disease can be hard to diagnose. According to a recent study published in the *Journal of the American Medical Association,* less than 25 percent of patients who were referred to the Lyme Disease Clinic at the New England Medical Center in Boston over a four-year period were found to actually have the disease. The standardized blood test for Lyme is notoriously unreliable; about half of the patients in the *JAMA* study who did not have Lyme disease had tested positive for it in laboratory blood samples. Researchers say that a new, more specific blood test for Lyme disease may become available in the near future.

How to Remove Ticks

Ticks will often stroll around on your skin for a while before finding a spot suitable for their endless meal. If you spot one that has not yet attached, brush it off into a toilet and flush. Frequent brushing with a fine-toothed comb can help catch unattached ticks that settle on dogs and cats.

There are conflicting opinions on the best way to remove ticks once they have attached themselves. Many authorities recommend first covering a tick with gasoline, petroleum jelly, or nail-polish remover to suffocate it before removing it with tweezers. Some experts also suggest applying the tip of a hot match to get the tick to loosen its grip. Even an early-1980s edition of *The American Medical Association Family Medical Guide* recommends these home remedies. These methods "have not been shown to be effective," however, according to *The Wellness Encyclopedia*, edited by two dozen M.D.'s and professors at the University of California, Berkeley, School of Public Health. They say such methods "may actually increase your chance of becoming infected . . . [by causing] the tick to respond by secreting more of the infected organism."

The Berkeley professors agree with the authors of the authoritative *Common-Sense Pest Control* about the best way to remove a tick. Gently grasp the tick with blunt, curved tweezers, as close to the head as possible without crushing or squeezing the tick, which could inject the tick's bacteria-laden body fluids into the wound and lead to infection. Use a slow, steady, upward pressure (don't twist) to withdraw the tick. Take your time and try to get the body, head, and mouthpart as a whole. If the head or mouthpart is left embedded, you need to remove them with tweezers. If you can't get all of the tick out, see a health professional.

Don't touch or remove a tick with bare fingers. Its pathogens can penetrate even unbroken skin and expose you to disease. If you don't have tweezers, protect your hands with a leaf, tissue, or gloves. If you do a lot of hiking or gardening in overgrown areas, consider purchasing special "tick tweezers" available in some sporting goods stores. A kit with tweezers, magnifier, and tick storage bag is available from REI of Seattle, Washington (see "Resources").

If you suspect a removed tick may be a carrier of Lyme, save it for identification by dropping it in a vial of rubbing alcohol.

The bite itself is not as worrisome as the tick's ability to infect you with diseases. Usually the only treatment that is necessary is to clean the bite area with soap and water, and apply an antiseptic such as a few drops of tincture of echinacea or calendula, or Tea Tree oil. If an inflammation or rash develops, check with your health professional.

Prevent ticks from attaching to your body by checking frequently around your hair, ankles, and arms if you've been hiking through grass or in overgrown areas. Also, use an insect repellent on your skin, clothing, and shoes (see discussion of repellents under the section on mosquitoes). Tuck in socks and clothing at ankles and wrists so skin is not exposed to ticks. Wearing light-colored clothing helps you to see ticks better when they do climb aboard.

BASIC FIRST AID FOR SPIDER BITES

Basic first aid for a bite from a black widow or one of the other most venomous spiders starts with checking the ABCs and watching for an allergic reaction. Keep the bite lower than the level of the victim's heart and clean the bite wound with alcohol or soap and water. Then apply ice or cold packs or compresses to the bite area to slow the circulation of the venom. Remove rings or constricting items from the victim since the bitten area may swell. Never cut and suction a spider bite. Keep the victim quiet and don't allow him or her to drink alcohol. Watch for signs of shock.

If a bite from one of the more lethal varieties occurs in the wilderness and you have to walk more than thirty minutes for help, you may want to apply a constricting band. Tie a cloth strip around the limb two to five inches above the bite site (though not on a joint). It should be snug but not so tight that you can't feel a pulse below it. It should be removed after thirty minutes. If symptoms of shock set in, cover the victim with a blanket and keep an eye on breathing and pulse while waiting for emergency help to arrive.

Bites from less venomous species of spiders usually result in only local pain, redness, and swelling. You should see a doctor or go to a hospital emergency room if:

- ◆ you experience significant local pain or generalized muscle pain
- ◆ you experience nausea, convulsions, or other signs of a body-wide reaction
- ◆ the bite is from the black widow, brown recluse, or scorpion
- ◆ the victim is a child who has hay fever, allergies, asthma, or allergic reactions
- ◆ the bite site shows signs of infection, such as increased pain, redness, swelling, and discharge

NATURAL REMEDIES FOR SPIDER BITES

Spider bites call for many of the same natural remedies used to treat snakebites. In addition to those mentioned above:

Apply Hypericum *tincture and vitamin E oil directly on the bite.* This works well if the bite is not from one of the dangerous spiders.

Apply a comfrey poultice to the bite. Mix three tablespoons of fresh-grated or powdered root with three ounces of hot water and stir it into a paste. Apply while still warm directly to the skin and cover with sterile gauze or clean cloth (or put the paste between two thin layers of gauze). Secure with a bandage and leave the poultice on for a few hours or overnight.

Herbalist and licensed acupuncturist Lesley Tierra of Santa Cruz, California, notes in *The Herbs of Life* that "a comfrey poultice is the most effective remedy I have ever found to get rid of spider bites. It also takes away itching and pain." Andrew Weil, M.D., author of *Natural Health, Natural Medicine*, adds that a comfrey poultice can also help stimulate the regrowth of injured tissue after a brown recluse bite.

Apply a few drops of pure Tea Tree oil to the bite site. Look for oil products that are 100 percent *Melaleuca alternifolia*. The oil is nontoxic and can be applied directly to the skin without being diluted (avoid getting it in the eyes, though).

In *Australian Tea Tree Oil Guide,* author Cynthia Olsen relates the experience of an Australian resident who was bitten by the deadly funnelweb spider. He used repeated doses of Tea Tree oil applied to the bite as he was taken to the hospital and found it eased the pain and led to complete recovery. The essential oil from the leaves of the tea tree is a powerful wound healer and germicide.

Cut a clove of garlic and rub it on the bite before the toxin begins to spread. Alternative-medicine researcher Stephen Fulder says that garlic is especially helpful for toxic bites for which no antidotes exist, such as those from South American scorpions. In *Garlic: Nature's Original Remedy,* he says that he has seen it effectively relieve scorpion bites, probably due to the sulfur components in garlic neutralizing the toxins. He adds that garlic is less helpful for bites from mosquitoes and fleas, "since the pain they cause is almost entirely due to inflammation."

Give the homeopathic remedy **Ledum** ***every one to three hours until the victim improves.*** This is especially called for if there's coldness or numbness and swelling of the hands or feet. *Apis* is indicated if the bite causes marked redness and rapid swelling, a hot, burning sensation in which the pain is made worse by heat and touch, or if hives develop.

Press on the acupressure point located at the outer edge of the elbow crease. Bend the arm and note where it forms a crease at the elbow. Put your thumb at the point at the end of the crease, away from the body, and press slowly into the joint. This point helps alleviate the redness and swelling of bites and stings.

Use black ointment to draw out the toxins associated with a tick bite. Apply the remedy directly to the site of the bite.

Holly Eagle, a natural health practitioner and O.M.D. (Oriental Medical Doctor), highly recommends this product, available in slightly different forms from leading herbal producers. Most black ointment formulations contain herbs such as comfrey root, plantain, and goldenseal root along with other ingredients such as activated charcoal, juniper or pine tar or gum, and beeswax or olive oil. Eagle says, "The one we've found works best is the black ointment made by Nature's Way. It has incredible capacity for drawing toxins out of the body."

The FDA recently disallowed herbal companies from making any health claims for black ointment, so labels can no longer tell consumers what it is used for. In addition to tick bites, black ointment can help relieve minor skin irritations and boils.

See recovery suggestions under stings.

PREVENTING SPIDER BITES

In many parts of the country the most venomous spiders are rare. Still it's useful to review some of the basic steps to avoid bites.

Recognize spider habitat and steer clear. Some of the favorite habitats of the black widow and brown recluse include piles of wood and other debris, under stones and in rock ledges, the underside of seats in outdoor toilets, and in barns, outdoor sheds, and the like. When found in the home, webs of the black widow and brown recluse are usually close to the floor in dark, quiet corners, such as rarely used closets, not along the ceiling or near windows.

If you're cleaning up a woodpile, wear long-sleeved pants and shirts. When camping, shake out shoes and clothing in the morning and bedding at night.

Control your indoor spider population. The best way to do this is to limit their food supply of insects by installing or repairing screens. If you live in the Southwest, keep clothes off the floor (or shake them out before donning) and vacuum baseboards and bedrooms. You can also remove potentially dangerous spiders by placing a container over them and slipping a piece of cardboard over the opening, trapping them inside. You can sweep a tarantula into a large garbage bag to be released outdoors.

For many people it is hard to resist the urge to kill any and all spiders they see. But most spiders pose no threat to people.

Even the most venomous spiders are not aggressive and will run from humans when they can. When they do bite, it's usually from being squeezed against a body inside clothing. Even then they don't always bite. "Indeed, many of them must be forced by extreme means to bite when their venom is required for experiment," according to Willis J. Gertsch, author of *American Spiders*.

And although spiders are uniformly venomous, they're generally beneficial to humanity. Spiders feed on insects and can help control such pests as gypsy moths. Like bees, they play a valuable role in the earth's ecology and don't deserve eradication.

Find ticks before they become a problem. Most ticks that latch onto humans have gotten there courtesy of dogs and cats, so it's imperative for pet owners to search and groom their animals closely for ticks on a regular basis. Ticks can also be picked up on humans' legs when hiking through wild fields with tall grass. Some species may even be found on lawns in northern rural/suburban areas where deer are abundant, and lawns in parts of Florida, where the brown dog tick likes the hot, dry environment.

◆ Bee, Wasp, and Ant Stings

For most people, getting stung by a bee represents only a temporary annoyance. For others, the consequences are more long-lasting and there's good reason to be concerned. A few people can even experience a serious allergic reaction that is potentially life-threatening (see "Chapter 4: Allergic Reactions"). Bee stings cause more than fifty deaths per year in the United States from the severe allergic reaction known as anaphylactic shock. This compares to only a dozen or so deaths from snakebite, and the bee sting figure may be even higher since many "unexplained deaths" could be from insect bites. Children, too, often respond to insect stings more intensely than do adults, due to children's lower body weight, which concentrates the effect of venom.

The principal stinging insects to watch out for are the Hymenoptera order, including bees, wasps (yellow jackets, hornets, and paper wasps), and ants. Encounter any of these insects in a way that surprises or antagonizes them, and the result may be a sting. The venom they inject into your body is typically a complex organic substance with a variety of chemical components, primarily proteins and enzymes, capable of affecting any number of tissues and organs.

LOCAL AND BODY-WIDE REACTIONS

Your reaction to a sting depends on the type and number of stings, and your individual sensitivity to them. Another factor is the part of the body where the sting occurs. For instance, body areas such as the scalp with a lot of blood vessels will cause the venom to spread rapidly, and a sting on the throat or mouth represents a threat from swelling that can cut off breathing. The four most typical sting cases are:

You're stung once or twice and the toxic effects of the venom are basically limited to the local area of the sting. There's aching, redness, and local pain and swelling that, with some simple treatments, goes away within a few hours or so.

You receive multiple stings after being attacked by a swarm of bees. Bee venom is potent stuff (one hundred to two hundred stings can be fatal), and the venom from a dozen or more stings will cause local and systemic symptoms such as rapid onset of swelling, headache, muscle cramps, and fever.

You receive a single sting that causes local pain and swelling as well as symptoms of a mild allergic reaction. The allergic reaction may be characterized by hives, severe itching, flushing, nausea, and dizziness. Perhaps one in twenty-five persons will have some type of allergic reaction to bee stings.

You receive one or more stings that cause a potentially severe allergic reaction. The sting victim will have the same pain, redness, and local swelling that most people experience, but it may be accompanied by swelling in other parts of the body, breathing problems, chest constriction, abdominal cramps, and if untreated, shock, unconsciousness, and death. Approximately one in 250 people who get stung face such a dire outcome. (See Chapter 4 for more information on the symptoms and treatment of allergic reactions.)

None of the above cases should be treated lightly. Even the first situation, the simple sting with no allergic reaction, calls for first-aid attention. For instance, if it's a bee sting and the stinger is left in, venom can continue to enter the body and aggravate symptoms for days. In most cases of multiple stings or allergic reactions, it's best to do what you can but also summon emergency medical help.

If the victim has had a previous allergic reaction, or any of the acute symptoms appear, get medical help immediately.

Severe local swelling in itself may not indicate an allergic reaction. Swelling often looks worse when it happens on the face or hands, especially when the victim is a child, because of the relatively small size of children's fingers and cheeks.

The symptoms of a mild allergic reaction may not show up right away. Thus, any time a child is stung, you should watch him or her closely for an hour or so to make sure there's no allergic reaction. If you're unsure, or if a child has pronounced local swelling that doesn't go down within several hours, it's best to see a health professional.

Though stings need to be taken seriously, it's important to try to stay calm and relaxed. Young children especially may be frightened by the sudden pain of a sting. According to Louis J. Casarett, Ph.D., and John Doull, M.D., Ph.D., editors of *Toxicology: The Basic Science of Poisons,* "The emotional impact of [a sting] is often more severe than the actual hazard from the venom. The application of 'mind over matter' in this relationship may prove lifesaving."

HOW TO REMOVE A BEE'S STINGER

The first thing to do for simple insect stings is to check for a stinger and, if there is one, remove it as quickly as possible. Honeybees and certain wasps have barbed stingers and thus can sting only once. When they try to pull the stinger out of your skin, they disembowel themselves, leaving not only their stinger but abdominal muscles and the venom sac attached. This is bad for the insect, since it will soon die, and for you, since the venom sac can continue to contract and deposit venom in your body for hours or even days if it isn't removed. Most wasps, including hornets and yellow jackets, and bumblebees retain their stinger and can sting repeatedly. A honeybee's venom is as potent as a rattlesnake's (though not so plentiful), so it's important to remove the sac as soon as possible.

Don't attempt to squeeze a stinger out, since this will also cause more venom to empty into the victim. Rather, first remove the venom sac by gently scraping across the sting site with a credit card, knife blade, or a (long) fingernail. Usually that will remove both stinger and sac. If that doesn't bring out the stinger along with the venom sac, then it's safe to use tweezers to pull out the stinger.

It's possible to suck the venom out of a sting wound with the Sting-x-tractor made by Tec Laboratories of Albany, Oregon (see "Resources"). The Sting-x-tractor is a small plastic suction device that is placed over the sting immediately after it occurs. The Sting-x-tractor creates a partial vacuum at the surface of the skin that draws the venom out of the bite canal. The sharp edge of the handle can be used to scrape out stingers. The Sting-x-tractor can also help reduce the effects of bites from insects such as mosquitoes and fleas.

BASIC FIRST AID FOR STINGS

After dealing with the stinger, you want to cleanse the area and reduce the pain. Wash the sting site with soap and water or an antiseptic to remove some of the venom from the skin's surface. Then apply cold compresses to the area to keep the problem localized. Have the victim rest while you apply treatments for pain, swelling, and itching.

The treatments doctors will typically recommend include aspirin or acetaminophen taken orally for pain, calamine lotions on the sting for itching, and oral antihistamines such as Benadryl or cortisonelike steroid lotions to control inflammation. Aspirin and acetaminophen are effective analgesics, though some people experience side effects such as gastric upset. Calamine is an over-the-counter preparation of zinc and ferric oxides. Caladryl cream or lotion are Parke-Davis products that combine calamine, the antihistamine Benadryl, and other ingredients. Caladryl shouldn't be used near the eyes or other mucous membranes. Prescription-only antihistamines and cortisonelike steroids are relatively strong drugs for minor inflammations and are often unnecessary.

NATURAL FIRST-AID REMEDIES FOR STINGS

There are a number of effective alternatives to drugs for treating stings. Among the best are the following:

Apply a paste made by mixing warm water and papain to the sting site. Smash up five to six tablets of papain in a few drops of warm water to make a paste and cover the sting area. Don't wash the area first with hydrogen peroxide, since this inactivates the papain.

Vitamin and supplement companies sell papain, a natural enzyme derived from the papaya plant, in tablet form as a digestive aid. If you don't have any papain tablets, use a common papain-based meat tenderizer, such as Adolph's. Mix meat tenderizer with warm water and apply to the sting site.

Meat tenderizers' active ingredient is papain because the enzyme breaks down muscle tissue, thus softening meat. This same enzyme action also breaks down the large protein molecules of insect venom, deactivating the poison before it gets circulated throughout your body.

Apply echinacea tincture to the sting and take it internally. A few drops of the tincture is sufficient to cover the bite. Also take an oral dose of one to two dropperfuls of the tincture or two or three capsules or tablets. Studies have shown that echinacea helps reduce allergic reactions and other immunological disturbances.

Apply a paste made by mixing warm water with powdered activated charcoal to the sting site. Empty two or three capsules into a container and add a small amount of warm water to make a paste. Dab the paste on the sting site with a utensil, or use your finger (the powder creates a black mess but is easily scrubbed off with a towel). Cover the charcoal paste with gauze or plastic to keep it wet.

Activated charcoal is a widely recognized poison antidote that is usually taken internally. In the stomach and intestines, it adsorbs toxins. That is, it catches and traps the poison's molecules and escorts them out the rectum. When made into a paste and applied to the skin, activated charcoal acts like a wick to draw out insect venom molecules and collect them on the skin.

Bentonite clay can be mixed and applied in a similar manner to relieve a sting. Bentonite takes it name from an area in Montana (near Fort Benton, named after Sen. Thomas Hart Benton, granduncle of the painter by the same name) famous for its porous clay produced by the decomposition of volcanic ash. A Montana native says, "I recently put on my sweatpants and they had a bee inside. I got stung on the thigh. I immediately reconstituted dry bentonite clay and put it on the sting. Instantly the pain was gone." Most natural foods stores sell bentonite clay.

Cut an onion in half and place the cut side on the sting for approximately ten minutes, or apply onion juice. Like papayas, onions also contain a sting-healing enzyme, in this case one that breaks down prostaglandins. "I've seen this work well several times," says Oriental Medical Doctor David Eagle.

Some other common kitchen products that have worked for many people to relieve bee stings include applications of:

♦ vinegar

- witch hazel
- honey
- lemon or lime juice

Apply a wet, cold-milk compress. Chill some milk by adding ice cubes, dip in a cotton cloth, wring slightly, and apply to the sting for five to ten minutes.

Cold helps constrict blood vessels and limit inflammation, and perhaps because of its fats and oils milk seems to be more soothing than water. Skin-test yourself for milk before applying it externally if you're lactose intolerant.

Apply a compress of Swedish Bitters. Pour some Swedish Bitters on a piece of cotton cloth, place it on the sting, cover it with a piece of plastic wrap and then another piece of cloth, and secure with a cloth bandage.

This is an increasingly popular European home remedy for stings. Swedish Bitters is an herbal elixir usually taken internally as a general tonic and digestive aid. It contains eleven herbs, including angelica, rhubarb, myrrh, aloe, and saffron, whose varied chemical constituents have anti-inflammatory and pain-relieving properties. It's also possible that, as herbalists and Swedish Bitters users Barbara and Peter Theiss note in *The Family Herbal*, "the principle of synergy applies, that is, that the whole is greater than the sum of its individual parts, which means that the final elixir has a far greater effect than does the taking of each substance separately."

Take the homeopathic remedy Apis or Ledum. *Apis*, made from whole honeybees or their venom, and *Ledum* are the most widely used homeopathic remedies for insect stings. Either can be taken orally or applied directly to the sting. Externally, dab a few drops of *Apis* or *Ledum* tincture on a piece of sterile gauze or clean cotton and apply to the sting site.

Employ your skill at self-diagnosis to determine which will work better. *Apis* is indicated if the bite causes marked redness and rapid swelling, a hot, burning sensation in which the pain is made worse by heat and touch or if hives develop. *Ledum* is indicated if the sting area feels cold or numb and is improved by applying cold.

"My eighteen-month-old son recently turned over a piece of scrap lumber and was bitten by several fire ants," says a mother from Atlantic Beach, Florida. "I've been bitten by them and know that the pain and itching is intense. My son's hand began to swell and turn red, and he was, of course, crying desperately. I administered two tablets of *Apis* 6X and watched the swelling literally go down before my eyes. He was playing again in five minutes."

You can also take *Apis* for three to four days at the beginning of spring if you're allergic to bee stings. A number of people who have tried this report that it worked almost like a vaccination to palliate the effects of later stings.

Help overcome the shock and trauma of a sting with the combination flower remedy Rescue Remedy. Add three to four drops of Rescue Remedy to a small glass of water and have the victim sip it slowly. If no water is available, put three to four drops directly on the tongue. Repeat every half hour until the patient is calm.

Though not a replacement for further treatments, this is a good one for right after the injury.

Spread a few drops of essential oil of Lavender over the sting site. Aromatherapists agree that Lavender is the best choice for bites and stings. You can also use cooling Peppermint oil on a sting that has become hard, red, and swollen the day after the sting.

Apply a warm-water and baking-soda paste to the sting site. To make a baking-soda paste, dissolve three parts baking soda to one part warm water. You can also dissolve a tablespoon of baking soda in a cup of water and soak a cotton cloth in the solution. Apply to the sting site for fifteen to twenty minutes.

Also known as bicarbonate of soda, baking soda is an alkali that readily dissolves in water and neutralizes acid. Applied to the skin, it acts to reduce pain and swelling, help draw out toxins, and neutralize some of the inflammatory agents in the toxin. It is even used by some doctors to reduce pain when they give an injection of a local anesthetic.

This is one of the few home remedies included in conventional first-aid books. Some people have found that baking soda doesn't do much for a sting, while others swear by it. A Florida woman who likes it says, "Last week my ten-year-old son was enjoying a water balloon fight in the yard when he was stung by a bee. My daughter remembered the home remedy of making a paste of baking soda and water. No more tears and back to summer fun." If it works for you, it's an easy, inexpensive home remedy.

Turn to one of the many sting products available from the natural pharmacy. There is a wide array of effective products to choose from for insect bites and stings.

- ◆ Homeopathic companies offer specially formulated salves to be applied on insect bites and stings, such as Hyland's

Apis Mellifica 2% and Boericke & Tafel's SssstingStop Soothing Gel. The Hyland product is a single-remedy ointment that comes in a one-ounce jar. The SssstingStop is a three-remedy gel in a witch hazel base, with the active ingredients of *Echinacea, Ledum,* and *Urtica* (nettles) each in a 1X (10 percent) concentration. It's a good remedy not only for stings but mosquito bites, hives, and hot, itchy skin. It is packaged in a one-ounce tube. Natra-Bio (Botanical Laboratories) markets a four-remedy Insect Bites homeopathic medicine that's taken internally. Ointments or sprays containing *Arnica, Calendula,* or *Hypericum* can be applied directly to stings to reduce pain and itching.

♦ After Bite made by Tender Corp. of Littleton, New Hampshire, is an ammonium hydroxide product that comes in a penlike 14-ml tube. It provides relief from bee and jellyfish stings as well as bites from mosquitoes, fire ants, and black flies.

♦ There are also more general-purpose herbal products that can offer relief from the symptoms of a sting, such as WiseWays Herbals' All-Heal Salve (with extracts of comfrey, echinacea, plantain, and other healing herbs) and Breezy Balms' Oak Away, an anti-itch spray that's primarily used to combat poison ivy and oak.

If you get stung out in the wilderness, make nature your pharmacy. Here are a couple of effective treatments to turn to in the wild:

♦ Put a mudpack over the injury. Mix a clay-containing soil with water to make a mud paste. Spread some on the sting site, cover with a bandage or handkerchief, and allow to dry.

♦ Thoroughly crush or chew up some plantain leaves and apply them moist to the sting. According to herbal author Steve Foster, coauthor of the Peterson Field Guide *Eastern/ Central Medicinal Plants,* "If nature ever supplied a ready-made Band-Aid, it is the ribbed leaf of plantain." He says that tannins and other constituents in plantain have been shown to fight inflammation.

Hobbs agrees that plantain is the best herb for insect bites and stings. He says, "As soon as you're stung, chew some up and apply it to the sting. Or you can mash the leaves and blend them with a little water to make a juicy mass. Just slapping a fresh leaf on the sting won't work—the chewing or blending releases plantain's natural mucilage, allowing the preparation to effectively stick to the site and release anti-inflammatory substances into the sting. If you want, cover it with a clean cloth or bandage, and change the dressing every half hour or so.

"This is the quickest-acting herb you've ever seen. It relieves pain, itching, redness, and swelling," Hobbs says.

Plantain is a common weed throughout much of the United States. It has broad, oval leaves. Its distinctive green spike gives it one of its nicknames: rat's-tail plantain.

Hobbs's secondary choices for herbs to combat bites and stings: comfrey and yellow dock.

HOW TO PREVENT INSECT STINGS

The following relatively simple suggestions are especially important if you've ever had an allergic reaction to an insect sting.

Learn about the dangerous insect's habitat and how to recognize its nests, and stay away. Bees nest in hives, hollow trees, and on buildings, while different types of wasps may prefer rock crevices, nests attached to structures, or underground nests. Yellow jackets, for instance, lodge mostly in the ground, sometimes in rotting tree stumps. Ants nest in the ground, often under stones, though fire ants build moundlike nests in open grassy fields. Disturbing a nest is likely to provoke aggressive behavior, particularly among yellow jackets, which release a chemical signal that causes an attack by the swarm. Bees are also especially touchy on cloudy days, after a rain when pollen is scarce, and when they're making a beeline for their hive.

If you have to remove a yellow jacket nest near your home, it's usually best to get professional help, preferably from someone aware of more environmentally benign nest-removal techniques, such as trapping and vacuuming.

Don't make yourself a target. During the time of the year when bees are common, wear plain, light-colored, long-sleeved clothing. Stinging insects' vision is less than hawklike, so don't wear flowery prints that they may mistake for the real thing. Insects are also attracted by shiny jewelry and scents from perfume, hairspray, after-shave, and lotions. As anyone can attest who's ever had a picnic disrupted by bees, sweet, syrupy foods also attract Hymenoptera. If you walk through a field of clover, make sure you have shoes on.

Don't encourage yellow jackets to nest near your home. More people are stung by yellow jackets than any other insect, often at parks and other public places where yellow jackets congregate around open garbage. They're fast and sometimes aggressive and can sting repeatedly. Keep your household garbage covered and don't leave pet food or other sources of sugar and protein outside and uncovered.

Don't aggravate stinging insects that do approach you. Swatting at stinging insects only makes them mad, so try to restrain the urge. If you do kill one, its smashed venom sac may give off a chemical that attracts an avenging horde. Also, a freshly killed hornet may still be able to sting. A better idea when buzzed is to stay still or move away slowly. If an unprovoked yellow jacket lands on you, it's probably only to inspect a smell. Let it alone and it almost assuredly will not sting. If you want to brush it away, do so slowly and gently.

If you accidently disturb a nest and are attacked by a swarm, lie down and cover your head or run for indoors, woods (they find it hard to follow a person dodging among trees), or water (jump in).

If you do get stung, leave the immediate area. The scent at the sting site attracts other stingers to join in.

Don't rely on repellents to deter stinging insects. Even insect repellents that contain the potent synthetic chemical known by the nickname deet (for diethyl-m-toluamide) are not effective against stinging insects such as bees. Natural and herbal repellents are much less toxic than deet, but are also unlikely to have any effect on stinging insects.

If you've had severe allergic reactions to stings, consider a desensitization treatment. This involves a number of injections of small doses of venom for months or years, which is not particularly pleasant but is generally effective.

One final thought about bees and wasps. As painful and frightening as stings can be, it's important to remember that Hymenopterans are basically peaceable, social creatures that inhabit an important niche in the planet's ecology. Bees are valuable pollinators, and even yellow jackets can help control caterpillars and other insects than can become pests. By taking some simple precautions against getting stung, you can learn to live with, if not love, these common insects.

◆ Stings from the Sea

Jellyfish, Portuguese man-of-wars, and sea anemones have tentacles trailing off their main body that contain stinging cells. In some cases the tentacles may be sixty feet long or even detached from the fish. When you come in contact with the stinging cells, they attach themselves to your skin and release a venom into your body. You may feel intense pain and develop rashlike symptoms on the skin. As with insect stings, there is the possibility of an allergic reaction, characterized by difficulty breathing, nausea, and possible shock.

Your three immediate priorities are:

Rinse the skin. Often the easiest liquid to use is seawater; don't use freshwater, which can make it worse. Also, don't rub the skin. Other effective rinses include alcohol in whatever form is handy (wine or liquor work fine, or rubbing alcohol), vinegar, and ammonia. You can also shave the skin, using shaving cream, a baking soda paste, a flour-and-seawater paste, or a sand-and-seawater paste. Scrape any of these off with a razor, credit card, or knife.

Neutralize the stinging cells. A papain-based product works well (for more information, see the earlier section on natural remedies for stings). An old folk remedy calls for dousing the sting site with urine. This may sound like an appalling idea to some, but urine does have a history of medical applications in a number of cultures, including India. Unless you have an infection of the ureter, the urine will be sterile and at the least won't do any harm.

See the section on insect stings for more remedies.

Remove any tentacles attached to the skin. Tentacles still on the skin should not be touched with bare hands, as that will just cause more stings. Wrap your hands with cloth or put on gloves before touching the tentacles, or use tweezers.

For a coral sting, remove any stinging cells with a cloth, towel, or tweezers, wash with soap and water, and apply calamine lotion or rubbing alcohol.

For sea urchin stings, scrub with soap and water to remove spines, or use a sterilized needle or tweezers, and apply hot compresses or immerse the site into hot water, being careful not to get burned if the part is numb.

Take the homeopathic remedy Apis *after a jellyfish sting.* Apis is perfect for the burning pain.

◆ Mosquitoes, Flies, Fleas, and Kissing Bugs

Like the eight-legged ticks, a number of insects (three pairs of legs) are capable of inflicting bloodsucking bites that range in severity from annoying to life-threatening.

Mosquitoes. Scientists estimate that there are some 100 trillion mosquitoes in the world, and on some summer nights it seems as if half of them are in your backyard. These slender, long-legged flying insects may be responsible for more bites on humans than all other insects combined. That is especially remarkable when you consider that only female mosquitoes are bloodsuckers.

The female needs blood to nourish her eggs. She gets it by landing on a person, cow, bird, or even caterpillar and sinking her long, syringelike nose into one of the victim's tiny blood vessels. Her sharp proboscis has two tubes, one for injecting saliva into the victim that thins the blood in the area of the bite and prevents coagulation, the other for drawing out her blood meal. The bite presents the possibility of serious disease (malaria, yellow fever, viral encephalitis) from injected pathogens, as well as allergic reaction from proteins in the saliva. Most frequently, the only result is minor local itching, redness, and swelling.

Conventional treatment for mosquito bites usually includes washing the bite area thoroughly with soap and water to disinfect it, applying an antiseptic, using a cold compress to reduce swelling and itching, and then applying a calamine or antihistamine lotion for redness and itching.

A number of steps can help prevent mosquito bites. The female mosquito lays her eggs in still or slow-moving water, where the larvae develop for weeks or months, depending on the species, before taking to the air. Female mosquitoes prefer ponds and marshes but are not averse to laying their eggs around houses, where they often find still water in watering cans, birdbaths, gutters, plastic wading pools, saucers for feeding a pet, and the like. As little as a tablespoon of water may be enough to provide the spawning place for two hundred larvae. Most mosquitoes are likely to have been born near where you're bitten, so if they're abundant in your backyard, drain what water has accumulated and look for ways to prevent still water from pooling.

Mosquitoes are attracted by sweat, dark clothing, warmth, and scents. They're also attracted by outdoor lighting and elevated levels of carbon dioxide, which is common when people congregate outside.

Most repellents that are effective at warding off mosquitoes and other small flying insects (not bees) contain deet, a chemical strong enough to dissolve paint. Since deet is readily absorbed through the skin, its safety is questionable at best. According to a consumer bulletin issued by the Environmental Protection Agency, some people may have reactions to deet ranging from headaches and mood changes to convulsions and unconsciousness. Even less is known about deet's potential to cause long-term health problems such as cancer or birth defects.

If you do choose to use a deet-based repellent, avoid products with high concentrations of deet, since they pose more of a health risk. Also don't put it on broken skin or near the eyes and lips. Be especially wary of using a deet product on children for an extended period of time. Consider putting it on your clothes rather than skin.

Smoke is an effective repellent, though also a direct health threat to anyone inhaling it.

Fortunately there are a number of safer alternatives to either deet or smoke. A variety of natural insect repellents (Green Ban, Natrapel, Bug-Off, Bygone Bugs) for topical application are available at natural foods stores. Most of these products use the oil of the herbs citronella, pennyroyal, eucalyptus, or rosemary as the active ingredients. Citronella is the most popular of these, and studies have confirmed that it does have repellent properties. An informal test of these products by *Natural Health*, in which a group of brave volunteers kept track of mosquito "landings" and "bites" on their repellent-treated arms, found that the natural repellents do prevent many bites, though not to the absolute extent that deet does. The natural repellents also tend to wear off quicker than deet and thus require more frequent reapplication.

You can make your own natural repellent with oil of Citronella. Some people apply the oil full-strength directly to the skin, but it's better to dilute three or four drops in an ounce of vegetable oil, to avoid a possible skin reaction. Two other popular topical repellents from the home remedy chest include brewer's yeast and garlic. The latter not only repels insects but, according to a recent Russian study, it wards off ticks.

There's some evidence that by eating certain foods and nutrients you can prevent insect bites. Diet can change the (hopefully) subtle odor your skin gives off in such a way that insects are no longer interested in you as a snack object. The most common supplements are dietary thiamin (vitamin B_1) and zinc. Nutritionists recommend 60–100 mg of thiamin and 25–50 mg of zinc daily to take advantage of this potential benefit. "It is best to take extra thiamin in the form of a vitamin B complex preparation, so that you don't throw other B vitamins out of whack," notes Shari Lieberman.

Other nutrients that, if consumed in sufficient quantity, may turn off mosquitoes include brewer's yeast and garlic (these may also protect pets if added to their diet).

Aerial spraying to kill adult mosquitoes is the proverbial chain saw cutting butter: it harms all wildlife (as well as civilized human life). Any public control program is best aimed at the larval population and should probably stop short of total eradication, since mosquitoes are an important link in the food chain for many birds, fish, and amphibians.

Flies. The flies most known for their bloodsucking bites are horseflies, greenhead flies, black flies, and midges and gnats (no-see-ums). The horseflies and greenheads, most active in the early spring and summer, are the largest, capable of inflicting painful bites that may bleed quite a bit and even cause dizziness, weakness, and wheezing.

Blackflies and their cousins the humpbacked flies breed near quick-rushing streams, mostly in Northern woods during the summer. Like bees, they're swarming insects and are capable of killing a large animal that can't escape their ferocious bites. Their saliva contains an anesthetic, so the bite may at first be painless, though it quickly develops into a red, itchy wheal that may take weeks to heal. Severe attacks can cause blackfly fever, the symptoms of which include headache and fever.

Gnats present an extra level of annoyance because they're small enough to get through screens and become indoor pests. They're most common along the Eastern-seaboard states, especially at dusk and dawn. Bites can cause considerable swelling, especially in children. Gnats like to bite children's eyelids, which can almost close up from the swelling.

Fleas. There are several types of bloodsucking fleas, but the most common in the United States is the cat flea, which occurs on both cats and dogs. They can carry or transmit various pathogens, including the bacterium responsible for bubonic plague. They also secrete saliva during feeding to prevent clotting and cause reactions ranging from small bumps to acute allergies. The reaction to a bite may be immediate or delayed.

Fleas lay eggs on a host animal or in its bedding. Fleas like warm temperatures and high humidity, so are worse in late summer and fall. The adult males and females seek a blood meal by jumping (fleas have no wings) onto whatever potential host happens by. Their best vertical leap is about eighteen inches, so human feet and ankles are primary targets. The fleas then crawl upon the skin, biting and sucking blood as they go. Thus the bites may appear in a line or cluster.

Some of the most common treatments include ice, camphor, or calamine lotion applied to the bite. Some people undergo desensitization treatment.

Once they've invaded your home, fleas are hard to get rid of. The adults can go months without a blood meal, and the eggs can last up to two years before hatching. Prevention is thus crucial:

◆ Use a fine-toothed metal flea comb on your pet regularly.
◆ Vacuum frequently and thoroughly.
◆ Use washable pet bedding and a single pet sleeping area that can be cleaned regularly.
◆ Give your pet an occasional herbal bath by adding four to six drops of Eucalyptus or Pennyroyal oils to the bathwater.

Chemical powders and sprays, and flea collars, use pesticide fumes to kill fleas, though the fumes are also toxic to both pets and people. Try to limit their use to serious infestation.

Kissing bugs. The kissing bug, also known as the conenose, and its cousin the bedbug, are sneaky bloodsuckers that usually attack at night. The relatively large (up to one inch long) kissing bugs are most common in suburban areas of the South and Southwest, where victims of their bite awake in the morning to find a mosquitolike wheal (the bite itself is painless). Some people are hypersensitive to the bites and develop symptoms similar to allergic reactions to stings. Authorities even think that kissing bug bites cause a number of deaths during sleep that are mistakenly attributed to other causes.

Kissing bug bites should be washed as soon as possible with soap and water. Some of the most serious consequences come from scratching the bite and infecting it with feces the insect left behind.

Since kissing bugs are attracted to lights at night and often enter when a door next to a light is opened and closed, in areas of high risk, door lights should be used sparingly. Screens should be intact and window openings fully caulked. If they've gotten into the house, you should check your bedding before sleeping and use a mosquito net over the bed until the bugs can be eliminated. Raccoons, opossums, and pack rats are common carriers, so they shouldn't be allowed to nest near your home.

NATURAL REMEDIES FOR BITING INSECTS

Many of the most common natural remedies are similar to those for spider bites and bee stings. Among some of the more popular treatments:

Apply a few drops of pure Tea Tree oil to the bite site. Look for oil products that are 100 percent *Melaleuca alternifolia,* or a therapeutic tea tree cream with at least 5 percent Tea Tree oil. The oil is nontoxic and can be applied directly to the skin without being diluted (avoid getting it in the eyes, though).

This essential oil from the leaves of a unique Australian tree is a powerful natural first-aid remedy for all types of bites and stings. The colorless to pale yellow oil has potent antibiotic and antiseptic powers. It even doubles as an insect repellent.

Apply calendula ointment or tincture directly on a mosquito bite for swelling. This works well when the bite is large enough to bother a person.

Dab on any of a number of potential pain-relieving and anti-inflammatory remedies, including:

- ◆ fresh aloe (break open a leaf of the plant, or use a 96–100 percent pure aloe gel product)
- ◆ vitamin E oil (from a bottle, or break open a few supplement capsules)
- ◆ lemon juice, from a fresh lemon
- ◆ vinegar, preferably a high-quality natural vinegar such as brown rice, white wine, or apple cider
- ◆ vitamin C, in a paste made from crushing three or four tablets in a few drops of warm water
- ◆ fresh plantain leaves, chewed, or crushed or mashed with a little water
- ◆ bromelain, made into a paste by mixing five or six crushed-up tablets with a few drops of water

Other topical treatments that can help relieve minor insect bites such as those from fleas include activated charcoal, papain, baking soda, and *Apis* tincture. See the section on natural remedies for stings for directions on how to prepare and use.

◆ Recovering from Toxic Bites and Stings

Snake and spider bites, and bee and jellyfish stings, offer a one-two punch to the body. They cause an external local injury that may be accompanied by pain, itching, and swelling. They also introduce a toxin into the blood and lymph systems that affects internal organs and can cause the formation of harmful free radicals in the body. Natural remedies can counter this one-two by promoting healing of the skin, decreasing inflammation, helping the body cleanse residual toxins from the blood, boosting the immune system, and acting as free-radical-gobbling antioxidants.

Take large doses of echinacea to promote general cellular immunity and stimulate infection-fighting white blood cells. "Echinacea is the fastest-acting blood purifier," notes Hobbs. He recommends taking either one dropperful of the tincture or two capsules or tablets orally as a protective dose two or three times a day. You can take this amount of echinacea until the symptoms are gone for up to ten days. Hobbs says that when taking echinacea for the first time, you should start by taking about half the above dosage to make sure you don't have a sensitivity to it.

Apply vitamin E oil to the sting site. Vitamin E offers antioxidant and immunity-boosting effects. Apply it from a bottle or by breaking open a capsule and rubbing it onto the skin twice a day. You can also take 400–800 IU of vitamin E daily.

Increase your intake of vitamin C. Apply vitamin C topically in a dilution or spray and take at least two grams internally daily until fully recovered from the sting. To use vitamin C externally, crush 1,000 mg of C into a powder and dissolve it in one cup of tepid water to make a 1–3 percent solution. Use a clean plant mister to spray this on the sting site every two to four hours.

A high level of C can have anti-inflammatory effects and boost the liver's ability to filter out whatever doesn't belong in the bloodstream.

Spread aloe gel on the bite or sting site twice a day. Aloe can help heal the local skin wound. Most natural practitioners agree that fresh aloe is best, and it's an easy houseplant to keep around. To use it, break a few inches off one of the older, lower leaves of the aloe plant, slice it lengthwise, squeeze its gel onto the sting site, and allow it to dry. Allergic reactions are uncommon, but discontinue use if one does occur. Aloe should not be taken internally.

Take chlorophyll supplements. Concentrated sources of chlorophyll include the algae-based green foods spirulina, chlorella, and blue-green algae, and products made from the young grasses of wheat, barley, and alfalfa. Studies have shown that chlorophyll helps the body in a number of ways, for instance by boosting the immune system and detoxifying blood. Chlorophyll concentrates come in tablets, powders, and liquid. Follow label directions for dosage.

Take an acidophilus supplement. Lieberman notes that this is especially important if you're taking antibiotics during the recovery period, to help reestablish the proper balance of friendly bacteria in the gut and protect the liver from toxins.

Take shiitake or reishi mushroom supplements, or incorporate fresh or dried shiitake into a daily meal. These healing mushrooms are expensive but worth the cost for their overall detoxifying powers. Follow label directions for dosage.

Lieberman adds that an insurance level of recommended vitamins and minerals, plus a trace-mineral supplement, should act as a baseline for the recovery period.

An insurance level of supplements includes the eleven vitamins, four minerals, and three trace elements for which the federal government has determined there are recommended dietary allowances (RDAs). Many supplement companies offer insurance-level, "one-a-day" formulas, though in most cases the pills or capsules are meant to be taken up to six times per day. Such supplementation often exceeds the RDAs, thus providing greater protection against marginal nutrient deficiencies.

SIX

Bleeding

THIS CHAPTER COVERS:

- ◆ *deep wounds*
- ◆ *minor cuts and scrapes*
- ◆ *nosebleed*
- ◆ *bleeding under the nails*
- ◆ *bleeding from the rectum*
- ◆ *internal bleeding*

SEE "CHAPTER 5: BITES AND STINGS" FOR:

- ◆ *puncture wounds*

SEE "CHAPTER 10: CONTUSIONS" FOR:

- ◆ *bruises*

"First aid. How to stop heavy bleeding. Pressure points . . . To close gaping wounds, use needle and thread. To help blood clot, apply cobwebs to the wound. Cobwebs! I don't believe it."
    "They're organic," I said, "and as sterile as most bandages."
—FROM *LONGSHOT* BY DICK FRANCIS

Bleeding, which results from ruptured blood vessels, can be caused by injuries ranging from small cuts on the surface of the skin to severe internal organ damage. Most of the common types of everyday bleeding, such as minor cuts and scrapes and nosebleeds, can be safely treated at home. Deep wounds that bleed severely and internal bleeding are major medical emergencies that require professional treatment as well as first aid.

Blood vessels are either arteries, which carry oxygen-rich blood from the heart to the rest of the body, or veins, which carry used blood back to the heart. When an artery is cut, the blood is bright red and spurts with the pulse and the beat of the heart. Unless arterial bleeding is controlled quickly, the victim can bleed to death within minutes. Blood from a broken vein is darker red and flows more slowly and evenly from the wound. This, too, may present a life-threatening situation if the flow is great enough.

◆ Deep Wounds

Given enough time, the body will mobilize its energies to stop bleeding. Nearby blood vessels contract, and specialized clotting cells begin to stick to the inside walls of the ruptured vessels, and to each other, to close the veins off. With a severe cut, however, such as when you push a hand through a pane of glass or fall on a sharp object, these mechanisms are too slow. The body needs your help, in the form of calm but quick first aid.

First, reassure the victim. Fear and anxiety can raise blood pressure and increase the rate of blood loss. Some cuts look worse than they are. For instance, even relatively minor scalp wounds can bleed profusely because of the many vessels supplying blood to the brain. Tell the victim that the bleeding will soon be under control.

Next, wash your hands to prevent germs from getting into the cut during treatment. Then apply firm, direct pressure to the wound, preferably by covering it with sterile gauze and pressing with your hands. If sterile gauze is not available, a clean cloth is second-best, and your bare hand is all right as a last resort (the danger here is that if have any open wounds, there's the possibility of transmission of disease, including AIDS, through the blood). If the wound is gaping, try to press the edges together. If there are no broken bones and it can be done without causing pain, elevate the bleeding body part above the level of the heart while continuing to apply pressure.

If there's an embedded or protruding object, leave it for emergency room personnel to remove. Neither pull it out nor bandage it in such a way that puts pressure on it and forces it deeper. Also, don't clean a deep wound, either before or after bleeding has been controlled, as this can cause more bleeding. Tourniquets are dangerous unless done correctly and best left to the professionals.

Direct pressure buys time for the wound, allowing blood a chance to clot. Keep the pressure on until the bleeding has stopped, which will usually happen within fifteen minutes. Press harder and use both hands if the bleeding persists after about ten minutes. If the dressing gets soaked through with blood, don't remove it, which would disrupt the clotting. Rather, add another one on top and keep the pressure on. If the bleeding has slowed after 15 minutes but not quite stopped, or you need your hands to deal with other injuries, apply a pressure bandage.

Pressure bandage. This will hold a dressing over a wound while continuing to apply slight pressure. Using a roller bandage or a long strip of cloth, wrap it around the wound, making overlapping turns. Split the end of the bandage into two strips and tie a knot over the wound, checking to make sure it's not too tight. If you can't detect a pulse farther down the arm or leg, or the limb is turning blue, the bandage is too tight and needs to be loosened.

If the wound is still bleeding profusely after fifteen minutes, you may need to use pressure point control in addition to direct pressure. Meanwhile, make sure you've taken steps to get medical help and prevent shock.

Pressure point control. This is pressure applied directly on an artery to stop major bleeding in an arm or leg. Like using a tourniquet or constricting band, pressing on an artery to stop bleeding is risky, since it stops all the blood flow to a limb. It's only called for if pressing on the cut itself and raising the limb have not stopped serious bleeding, and it should be used only in conjunction with these two techniques. It should be discontinued as soon as the bleeding stops. There are at least twenty-two such pressure points (eleven on each side of the body). The two most commonly used pairs are the arms and legs (see illustration #12).

The pressure point for the arm is halfway between the elbow and armpit, between the biceps and triceps on the inside of the arm. Feel for the pulse of the brachial artery, then press with four fingers so that the blood vessel is pushed against the underlying bone. Pressing on the brachial artery here should stop or significantly slow the bleeding below it almost immediately.

Control extreme bleeding of the feet or legs by pressing on the femoral artery on the thigh at the groin crease, where the leg bends. The victim should be lying down. Find the pulse and press on the point with the heel of your hand, so that the artery is compressed against the pelvic bone. This can be difficult to do, or require considerable pressure, when the victim is very muscular.

A puncture wound, such as from stepping on a nail, doesn't usually bleed a lot externally, though it may bleed profusely internally and it does present a higher risk for tetanus infection. Unlike most other cuts, you shouldn't immediately stop external bleeding from a puncture wound. Bleeding allows some of the

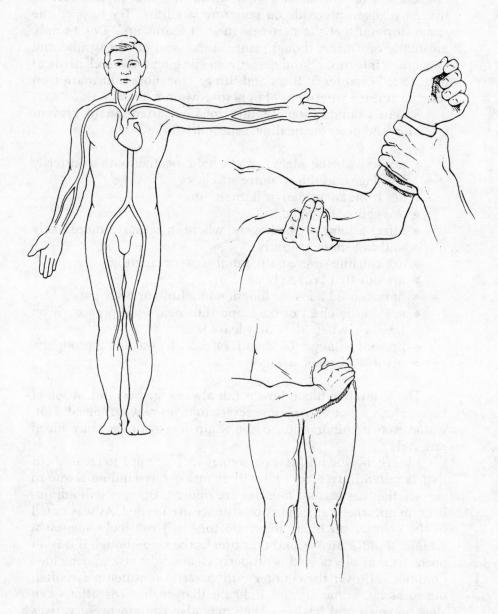

Illustration #12:

You can press firmly on pressure points in the upper arm and the groin
to stop arterial bleeding in an arm or leg.

trapped dirt and bacteria to wash out. Rinse a puncture wound under cold running water and soak the injury in or apply to it an antiseptic solution. Andrew Weil, M.D., says that he has success using hydrogen peroxide on puncture wounds. "Try to open the wound up and get the peroxide in so it foams up." Don't apply antibiotic ointment, though, since it can seal off the wound and encourage infection. Bandage with sterile gauze and seek medical help. (See "Chapter 5: Bites and Stings" for more information on tetanus and the treatment of puncture wounds.)

Severe wounds often require medical attention to prevent infection and promote healing, especially if they:

- are so wide the edges can't be held together with a butterfly bandage and thus require stitches
- are from an animal or human bite
- are gaping or jagged
- affect a joint or the fingers, where infection is more likely and can spread rapidly
- are causing severe pain, numbness, or tingling
- are due to a broken bone
- have caused a loss of function in a limb or body part
- are on the chest or back and thus near vital organs, or on the face, where they may leave scars
- present a danger of tetanus or can't be washed thoroughly
- involve a broken artery

The volume of blood flow is not always the best indication of how serious a wound is. Some severe injuries may not bleed a lot, while even a minor one, to the scalp for instance, may bleed profusely.

Emergency or hospital personnel will attempt to clean a cut that is potentially dirty and will examine surrounding tissue to see whether nerves and muscles are injured. Doctors will administer an anesthetic if surgery or stitches are needed. As was noted in the chapter on bites, many doctors will routinely suggest a tetanus shot for any wound that breaks the skin, though if it is an open cut that bleeds and is properly cleaned the risk may be low. Commercial, over-the-counter antibacterial ointments are often unnecessary. Some studies indicate that such medications can slow down wound healing. They may also contain preservatives that can cause allergic reactions.

◆ Minor Cuts and Scrapes

Minor cuts usually have clean edges, as from a paper or knife slice, while scrapes and abrasions are rough and patchlike. Both can bleed and get infected, though simple home treatments will promote quick and effective healing. A scrape that's extensive, such as the whole length of the arm, with lots of dirt in it, requires medical attention.

Since the bleeding is usually limited with minor cuts and scraps, it is best to first clean these wounds, even if you can't see any dirt inside. For a minor cut or scrape, rinse it under a gentle stream of cold running water and then wash with a mild soap and a clean washcloth. If there's visible dirt or debris, use sterile gauze to wipe it out, working from the inside of the wound toward the edges. If you can't get it clean, you'll have to seek medical help. Blot it dry with sterile gauze or clean cloth, and apply an antibiotic ointment (see natural remedies, below). Don't use iodine or Mercurochrome, which can sting and irritate tissues.

Whether to dress and bandage minor cuts and scrapes is controversial. Some medical authorities say that it's a good idea to cover all wounds, even minor cuts and scrapes, to keep them clean and dry, and that scabs can slow cell repair. Others contend that leaving small wounds exposed to the air allows them to heal faster, if they can be kept clean and dry. For active children who are always getting dirty, a bandage may be more necessary than for an adult. If you do put a bandage on a child's small cut, a small amount of antibacterial ointment or herbal salve can help prevent the bandage from sticking to the wound. Don't leave a bandage on too long. The covered wound can become warm and moist, an environment that can encourage the spread of bacteria. If you allow a scab to form, leave it alone until the wound is healed underneath and the scab falls off naturally.

Sterile gauze is the best dressing, held in place with surgical tape or a bandage. Commercial bandages such as Band-Aids that have nonsticking gauze pads and tiny holes in the tape to allow the skin to breathe also work well for minor cuts and scrapes. Don't use fluffy cotton on an open wound. Apply a bandage that extends at least one inch beyond the edge of the wound. Make sure that a bandage is not applied in a way that cuts off circulation. Loosen it if it causes a tingling sensation or turns the local area blue.

A special type of hourglass-shaped bandage known as a butterfly helps to pull together the sides of a cut that is slightly open but has smooth edges. Make a butterfly by cutting a shallow V into the center on opposite sides of adhesive tape or a bandage. Apply the butterfly to one side of the cut, pull the skin together, and apply the bandage to the other side of the cut, closing the edges. You may need to use two or more for longer cuts.

NATURAL REMEDIES FOR BLEEDING FROM CUTS AND SCRAPES

Natural remedies can help stop bleeding, both by constricting blood vessels and promoting coagulation, and prevent infection through their antibacterial properties. Use any of the following after cleaning a small cut or scrape with mild soap and water.

Apply a tincture, poultice, or compress using any of a number of herbs that are powerful styptics and wound healers. Many herbalists often turn first to yarrow, shepherd's purse, witch hazel, plantain, and calendula.

+ Yarrow is available in a tincture that can be applied directly to gauze to cover a wound. If you have fresh leaves, you can dry them and make a powder that can be sprinkled right on minor cuts and scrapes. You can also buy the dried herb and powder it or obtain powdered yarrow products at well-stocked natural foods stores.

   One of the common names for yarrow is actually nose-bleed. Its Latin name, *Achillea millefolium,* comes from its legendary use by Achilles to stem bleeding on soldiers wounded during the Trojan War. It's also been used by Chinese, Native American, and other traditional herbalists to stop bleeding. Indeed studies have shown that the plant contains chemicals that promote blood coagulation and that it also has strong antibacterial powers. "This is the best herb for external bleeding," claims herbalist Christopher Hobbs, "and a great natural styptic even for shaving cuts."

   Oriental Medical Doctor David Eagle warns that yarrow can stop bleeding so fast that it is possible to seal in dirt and cause an infection if you haven't been careful to wash the injury thoroughly first.

+ Shepherd's purse *(Capsella bursa-pastoris),* as a dried herb, tincture, or concentrated drops, can be used to make a poultice that is applied externally to stop the bleeding of a cut or scrape.

Though it is less widely used than yarrow or witch hazel, shepherd's purse is an effective herb to stop bleeding, both internal and external. A plant of the mustard family, it's been used since ancient times and was especially popular in the Middle Ages. The name is from its distinctive, purse-shaped seed pods. Shepherd's purse contains tyramines and other chemicals that promote blood coagulation and constrict blood vessels. It also has compounds (choline and acetylcholine) that reduce blood pressure. Shepherd's purse is traditionally taken in tea form for internal bleeding and menstrual bleeding.

♦ Witch hazel *(Hamamelis virginiani)* can be applied directly to the skin, for a cut such as a shaving nick, or to gauze to cover the wound.

This is one of the most commonly used herbs in the United States, since it's sometimes recommended as a liniment by doctors and is widely sold in pharmacies. The distilled, commercial form, however, has few of the chemical tannins of the fresh plant that may provide most of its astringent, blood-vessel-constricting powers. Herbalists recommend rather one of the tincture preparations available from herbal manufacturers and sold in natural food stores. "Witch hazel is pretty mild," notes Hobbs.

♦ Plantain. This herb is traditionally used fresh, in the form of thoroughly crushed or chewed-up leaves applied moist to wounds to stop bleeding. Though the fresh herb is apparently stronger, there are plantain herbal products that can be applied in tincture or powder form to a cut or scrape.

Among plantain's constituents are tannins and other chemicals that promote coagulation of blood and healing of wounds. Plantain is an extremely common weed found in yards and suburban areas across the country.

♦ Calendula. Various commercial preparations are excellent wound-healing agents. An outdoorswoman says, "I was camping with friends in Canada when I slashed open the pad of my finger with a utility knife. The gash was deep and should have had stitches, or at the very least a butterfly bandage. I had calendula ointment with me so I put it on the cut and bandaged it up. I continued to use the calendula every time I rebandaged it, and a week later the cut was almost completely healed over with only a faint scar line. I believe the calendula kept the cut from getting infected and caused it to heal evenly and quickly."

To aid healing and prevent infection in superficial cuts and scrapes, apply other natural remedies directly to the wound:

◆ usnea (*Usnea barbata* and other species of *Usnea*)
◆ echinacea tincture diluted 5:1 in water
◆ 3 percent hydrogen peroxide; let it foam up before wiping it off
◆ *Hypericum* or *Calendula* lotion or tincture (homeopathic preparations for external use)
◆ oil of Lavender or Eucalyptus, diluted 5:1 in water and sprinkled on sterile gauze
◆ lemon juice

The above all have varying degrees of antibacterial effects, though the usnea, echinacea, and calendula tinctures, and hydrogen peroxide, are more potent than the others. After thoroughly cleaning the wound with mild soap and water, apply the remedy directly to the skin or dab it on some sterile gauze and bandage in place.

Herbalist Christopher Hobbs is enthusiastic about usnea. He says, "This 'herbal antibiotic' is a famous European remedy, but it grows all over the U.S. Usnea are species of tree lichens; they are the most common source of antibiotic and antifungal lichen acids, particularly usnic acid. They have widespread potential for medicinal application. I've seen usnea tincture stop a bacterial infection on the hand in one day." Usnea tincture and concentrated herbal drops are available in natural foods stores.

Commercial *Hypericum* or *Calendula* lotions can be applied directly to the skin. Tinctures should be diluted 5:1 in water. Spray three or four times a day directly on cuts and abrasions that are not covered by a bandage. Or soak sterile gauze or a cotton pad in dilute *Hypericum* or *Calendula* tincture and place over the injury before securing with a bandage. Deep and painful cuts may be helped by taking oral doses of *Hypericum* as well.

A resident of Norristown, Pennsylvania, says, "I routinely use *Hypericum* tincture to heal wounds from the bottom up and prevent infection. Once it worked spectacularly when I ran my thumb into a large wooden splinter when using a shovel. There was no throbbing as long as I kept the bandage wet with *Hypericum*. Two hours after the injury I was able to resume gardening, and there was new skin in the trough of the wound by the next day."

Sprinkle the powder of the Chinese herbal formula *Yunnan Paiyao* on a wound to stop bleeding. This is a potent remedy for stopping even intense bleeding from a deep cut. To apply externally, break open one or more capsules, sprinkle the powder on the wound, and apply pressure until the bleeding stops.

Produced in China, the remedy's name means Yunnan white medicine. (Yunnan province is the main source of the principal ingredient; the product is also sometimes known as Yun Nan Bai Yao or simply Bai Yao.) Viet Cong soldiers routinely carried tiny bottles of powdered Yunnan Paiyao to apply to their wounds while awaiting emergency help. It is used both internally and externally to stop bleeding and to "disperse blood stagnation," as practitioners of traditional Chinese medicine term it. It can alleviate the pain and reduce the swelling associated with cuts, bruises, and sprains.

A dramatic example of its use on cuts is provided by the following story, related by a young woman. "I was camping in New Mexico when I accidentally sliced the tip of my finger with a sharp blade. The cut was almost to the bone and it was bleeding profusely. I figured we were soon to be packing up and heading for the nearest emergency room for stitches. My mother went to her first-aid kit and handed me a capsule of Yunnan Paiyao. I opened the capsule and worked a few pinches of the powder into the wound. There was no increased pain or sting. Then I covered the cut with sterile gauze and a bandage. Exactly seven days later I was playing collegiate field hockey and there was barely a trace of the cut."

Yunnan Paiyao is also an effective internal remedy. Oriental Medical Doctor Holly Eagle says, "I've seen Yunnan Paiyao, taken internally, help to decrease heavy menstrual bleeding. The standard dose in such cases is two caps four times per day, until the bleeding calms down. Some women may need to take it for a day or two while others will take a couple of caps and the bleeding will stop.

"I've also given it to patients who were going in for surgery and were expected to bleed quite a lot. The surgeons have later told me that they were surprised by how little bleeding there was during the operation. Yunnan Paiyao can help stop the bleeding from ulcers, too, but in such cases it's possible to abuse the remedy since you haven't dealt with the condition's cause and you're not providing a good long-term solution."

Yunnan Paiyao is made primarily from the dried root of the pseudoginseng (*Panax pseudoginseng* or *P. notoginseng*) plant.

Pseudoginseng is called *sanqi* or *tienchi* by the Chinese, which translates roughly as "three seven (leaves) ginseng." Most of the research on pseudoginseng has been conducted in China, Japan, and Hong Kong. According to Chun-Han Zhu, author of the *Clinical Handbook of Chinese Prepared Medicines*, scientific studies have demonstrated that a number of the plant's chemical constituents have coagulant or other properties that can stop bleeding. Zhu notes that animal studies have found that Yunnan Paiyao powder can cut actual bleeding time in half. According to organic chemist Dr. James Ma of Chinese University in Hong Kong, the herb's effect on the body is distinct from anything that is found in Western medicine.

Yunnan Paiyao is produced in China by the Yunnan Paiyao Factory. In the United States as a powder it is one of the most widely available prepared Chinese medicines. (The liquid form, which works well as a bruise remedy, is harder to find.) Most Oriental pharmacies carry the powder, or you can mail-order it from suppliers of traditional Chinese medicines (see "Resources"). It comes in a blister pack of sixteen capsules along with a single red pill of a more potent herb used to prevent shock after an extreme trauma, such as a gunshot wound.

Yunnan Paiyao should not be taken internally by pregnant women.

Take an appropriate internal homeopathic remedy. If the injury was caused by a fall or blow, take *Arnica* orally. (*Arnica* ointments and creams shouldn't be applied to broken skin, as they can cause irritation.) *Phosphorus* is good for all kinds of bleeding, especially for small wounds that bleed a lot. For deep or puncture wounds, *Ledum* is effective. For severe bleeding, or if the person is going into shock, try *Aconite*.

Apply acupressure on one of two special bleeding-control points. Acupressurist Michael Reed Gach says that two major acupressure points can be pressed to help control bleeding anywhere on the body. He notes, however, that acupressure is not a substitute for direct pressure on a wound to stop bleeding. Rather, it can complement direct pressure and help prevent further bleeding when bleeding has stopped.

To find the best point for bleeding on the upper part of the body, bend the arm and note where it forms a crease at the elbow. Put your thumb at the point at the end of the crease, away from the body, and then press slowly into the joint. This point also helps to alleviate the redness and swelling of bites and stings (see Chapter 5).

For bleeding on the lower part of body, find the point four finger-widths below the kneecap, one finger-width toward the outside of the shinbone, on a muscle that pops out as you flex your toes up and down. Press on it firmly with your index finger to help control bleeding.

Gather some spider webbing, roll it in a ball, and apply it to the cut. This is a traditional wilderness first-aid technique that's been known to stop bleeding when more conventional remedies are not at hand.

◆ Nosebleeds

Those who in quarrels interpose
Must often wipe a bloody nose.
—FROM "THE MASTIFFS" BY JOHN GAY

Nosebleeds are among the most common minor bleeding emergencies parents face, since more than half of all children between the age of six and ten have at least one such episode. Simple nosebleeds may be caused by hitting the nose against something hard. Aggravated mucous membranes on the inside of the nose also cause nosebleeds; repeated blowing, scratching, nasal sprays, upper-respiratory-tract infection, and extremely dry air are all culprits.

Nosebleeds occur when tiny blood vessels close to the surface of the inside of the nose rupture. Most nosebleeds, especially among children, are from bleeding in the front of the nose. They're usually not serious and can readily be controlled at home by following the basic steps outlined below. Elderly people, particularly those with high blood pressure, may get bleeding in the back of the nose, which is especially worrisome because the blood can easily flow into the throat, causing nausea or choking.

If possible, you want blood from the nose to flow out of the nostrils rather than back into the throat, so putting the head back or lying down to stop a nosebleed are not such good ideas. Rather, have the victim sit, lean forward, and put his or her head down, leaving the mouth open for free breathing. Try not to allow the victim to swallow blood. Also calm the person to keep their blood pressure down and prevent the bleeding from getting worse. Encourage the person to breathe through the nose because inhaled air will dry the blood and aid coagulation.

The nosebleed victim should first give one vigorous blow of the nostrils, to clear mucus (or clots that are keeping vessels open) that may hamper clotting. Then firmly but gently squeeze the sides of the nose together, between thumb and index finger or the two thumbs, below the cartilage. Also place a cold compress on the top of the nose to further constrict blood vessels. Apply the pressure and cold for six to eight minutes, without interruption, since taking the pressure off can interrupt clotting. If it is still bleeding, hold it for another six to eight minutes. Reassure the victim. The amount of blood flow from some nosebleeds can scare small children in particular, and anxiety can raise blood pressure and make it worse.

Most nosebleeds will stop within fifteen minutes. After it has stopped, have the victim rest for half an hour or so. The victim shouldn't blow the nose or touch it. A serious nosebleed may require you to refrain from vigorous exercise for a day or two. It may be up to a week before the scab comes off and the nose is totally healed.

Seek medical attention for a nosebleed if:

- the bleeding is coming from the back of the nose or hasn't stopped after thirty minutes of pressure and cold
- the bleeding is from a severe impact and is accompanied by such other symptoms as dizziness or nausea
- the nose is clearly crooked and you suspect it is broken
- a child has recurrent unexplained nosebleeds
- the victim is elderly, taking blood thinners (including aspirin), or has high blood pressure

If you haven't been able to stop a nosebleed with direct pressure, usually a doctor will try pressure first and then a medicated compress, petroleum-impregnated gauze, or a silver nitrate solution to stem the bleeding. Doctors can also cauterize blood vessels electrically.

NATURAL NOSEBLEED REMEDIES

Here are some treatment suggestions that can complement the basic steps of putting the head down and applying direct pressure to the nose to stop a nosebleed.

Pack the nose with gauze soaked in a solution that promotes blood clotting. Packing the nose or putting any kind of compress inside the nostrils is usually a job best left to health professionals. If bleeding is persistent and from the front of the nose, though, and medical help is unavailable, you can use sterile gauze that's been soaked in a solution than can promote clotting, such as yarrow, shepherd's purse, witch hazel, or vinegar. Naturopath Joseph Pizzorno especially recommends a pack soaked with tincture of geranium *(Geranium maculatum)*, for its styptic properties, and bayberry *(Myrica cerifera)*, for its astringency. The gauze should be gently inserted into each nostril, with a little left protruding to allow for easy removal. It should be left in for an hour or so. Wetting it first before removal can loosen it and lessen the risk of starting the bleeding all over again.

Take oral doses of the homeopathic remedies Ferrum phos or Arnica. *Ferrum phos* will help stem profuse bleeding, while *Arnica* is especially good for nosebleed due to an injury or a blow to the nose. Homeopaths emphasize that long-term or constitutional treatment is necessary for recurring nosebleeds.

Apply steady acupressure to the point two-thirds of the way up the upper lip to the nose. The conventional recommendation to put a washcloth between the gum and upper lip may work in part by stimulating this acupressure point, notes Gach. Press on it firmly with the tip of the index finger while keeping direct pressure on the nose.

Try one of the many folk remedies for nosebleed. Here are two popular ones:

- ◆ Take advantage of the astringent properties of vinegar. One common folk remedy to stop a nosebleed is to snuff up vinegar and water, and another is to wash the temple, nose, and neck with vinegar. In fact scientists have found there's an element of truth to some vinegar applications: the acid in vinegar gently cauterizes blood vessels.
- ◆ Apply a cold compress to the back of the neck. It's unclear how this works, but apparently it has helped many people control nosebleeds.

RECOVERING FROM AND PREVENTING NOSEBLEEDS

Try eating plenty of dark green, leafy vegetables, and citrus fruits. These are high in vitamin C and bioflavonoids (such as rutin), which help the body form collagen, necessary to create a moist, protective lining for the sinus and nose. They also contain vitamin K, which promotes coagulation.

A pleasant aromatherapy technique for recovering from a nosebleed is to gently inhale essence of Cypress or Lemon, either by adding a few drops of essential oil to a vaporizer or to a clean cloth that's held under the nose for a few minutes.

Recurrent nosebleeds call for more than first-aid treatment.

Treat or address the underlying health problem that is causing nosebleeds. Nosebleeds that don't stem from an injury may result from high blood pressure, nasal tumors, certain infectious diseases, or other health problems. Treating these conditions—for example, controlling blood pressure with a low-fat, low-cholesterol diet—is preferable to continually dealing with nosebleeds.

Discourage the practices and conditions that lead to nosebleeds. For instance, continual nose-picking can cause nosebleeds, especially among children. If the inside of the nose is dry and itchy, you can apply a thin layer of vitamin E oil directly from a capsule, comfrey ointment, aloe gel, or nonpetroleum jelly to moisten nasal membranes.

If nosebleeds are due to overly dry air, sometimes common in electrically heated homes during the winter, consider using a vaporizer or a humidifier. Low humidity also causes some people to get nosebleeds in airplane cabins. These can be prevented by moistening the nasal membranes with oil or gel before boarding.

Smoking dries nasal passages and can cause nosebleeds.

◆ Bleeding Under the Nails

Catching a finger in a car door or dropping a heavy object on a toe may cause bleeding under the nail, a sensitive area with many nerve endings. The injury is similar to a bruise except that the blood is pooled under a nail instead of under the skin. It's often more painful than a bruise, though, because unlike the skin, the nail can't stretch and swell. Consult with a medical professional whenever a finger injury causes severe pain or results in impaired movement or marked deformity.

To treat extensive, painful bleeding under a nail, many health professionals use special equipment that looks like a small hand drill to make a hole in the nail and relieve the pressure. A doctor may also x-ray the finger first and offer local anesthesia.

Though many people will prefer to go to a doctor for treatment, it is possible to treat the condition safely at home. First check to make sure the finger or toe is not broken and can be moved. Then straighten a paper clip, grasp it using pliers or heavy gloves, and heat it over a flame until the tip is red-hot. Hold the hot tip to the discolored area of the nail and press down slightly.

If the tip is hot enough it will quickly burn a small hole through the nail. Pull the tip out and allow the trapped blood to flow out through the hole. The procedure should be relatively painless except for a sensation of pressure. Bandage the fingertip after the blood drains to prevent infection.

◆ Bleeding from the Rectum

This usually calls for a trip to your health professional. It could be due to a slight tear in the lower part of the digestive tract (from constipation or a foreign object), hemorrhoids, or possibly an illness such as cancer. Dark blood, the color of coffee grounds, is often more of a cause for alarm than bright red blood, since darker blood indicates bleeding from deeper inside the body (see "Internal Bleeding").

Minor surface bleeding, such as from hemorrhoids, can often be controlled by natural remedies:

Apply a cotton ball soaked in witch hazel to the hemorrhoids. A witch hazel tincture or concentrated herbal drops are preferable to the common witch hazel liniments containing methyl or wood alcohol that are found in conventional pharmacies. Chill the witch hazel in the refrigerator for extra coolness. Witch hazel will shrink blood vessels and stop minor bleeding. You can also apply twenty to thirty drops of witch hazel tincture directly to the hemorrhoids.

Apply calendula lotion. Put it on a cotton swab or your finger and apply it to sore tissue around and in the rectum before a bowel movement. It will lubricate the elimination and make it less likely to aggravate swollen blood vessels.

Insert a homeopathic suppository. "One that we use a lot clinically," says Pizzorno, "is the Boericke & Tafel product Alpha Hemorrhoids, which is a homeopathic product combining 3X- to 6X-strength *Horse Chestnut, Witch Hazel, Nux Vomica,* and *Sulphur.* Patients report that it works well to relieve rectal pain and itching."

Take advantage of the antihemorrhoidal powers of the herb stoneroot (Collinsonia canadensis). Herbalist Christopher Hobbs suggests taking two 375-mg capsules of stoneroot twice a day with a full glass of water between meals. Stoneroot extract or tincture can also be applied externally to the swollen veins.

"This is the premier hemorrhoid herb," says Hobbs. "It will strengthen the structure and function of veins and act as an astringent. It's pretty miraculous for hemorrhoids."

European horse chestnut *(Aesculus hippocastanum)* is another popular herb that's been used to make preparations to relieve hemorrhoids. Like stoneroot, it contains saponins, tannins, and other astringent compounds that strengthen and tone veins. Studies indicate it is also anti-inflammatory. The glycoside esculoside found in European horse chestnut has been found to shrink hemorrhoids. Commercial horse chestnut salves for external application to hemorrhoids are widely available in Europe and are gradually becoming available in the United States. A number of U.S. herbal companies do offer the powder or concentrated drops made from the seeds, which can be mixed with calendula lotion, for instance, for external application (horse chestnut can be toxic if taken internally).

Try a favorite folk remedy from Russia. Heat up a brick and put some raw garlic on it. Place the brick in the bottom of a sturdy bucket, remove your pants, and have a seat. The fumes from the smoldering garlic pieces are said to offer surprising relief from hemorrhoids. If this seems like a lot of work, try a simpler garlic folk remedy: insert a bruised clove into the rectum as a suppository. Garlic's proven wound-healing effects may speed relief.

Eat the right foods to prevent hemorrhoids. Hemorrhoids are often the result of constipation from stools that are dry and hard, the result of a diet high in overprocessed and overrefined foods. Adding some fiber in the form of bran to the diet and drinking more fluids will tend to soften stools. An even better long-term strategy is to eat more high-fiber foods such as whole grains, leafy green vegetables, and fresh fruit. Hemorrhoids can be difficult to cure, even surgically, so preventing them is well worth the effort.

◆ Internal Bleeding

Minor internal bleeding shows up as a bruise (see "Chapter 10: Contusions") that in most instances can easily be treated at home. A much more serious condition that requires immediate medical attention, sometimes by surgery in a hospital, is any type of extensive internal bleeding that results from a hard fall, crush injury, accident, or some other severe trauma to the body. Suspect internal bleeding in such cases, and when there's a fracture or considerable external injuries. Internal bleeding can also result from illnesses (such as when a peptic ulcer bursts and causes gastrointestinal bleeding) and certain drugs.

Internal bleeding can result from the rupture of an artery, vein, capillary, or any combination of these. It may or may not be accompanied by external bleeding, and it's possible for a person to bleed to death internally without shedding a drop through the skin. Of particular concern is any internal bleeding into the chest, abdominal, or pelvic cavities. Internal organs, particularly the hollow ones such as the bladder, can bleed seriously from being ruptured. A serious blow to the head can cause internal bleeding in which pooled blood dangerously—even fatally—presses on the brain.

The symptoms of internal bleeding don't always appear right away and can be difficult to spot. Not noticing them quickly enough can be life-threatening. Be especially concerned if the victim coughs up blood that is bright red and frothy. Also be concerned about any evidence of blood in vomit, urine, or stools:

- Vomit that is a dark, coffee-grounds color is a sign of internal bleeding that has been going on for some time. If the injury is more recent, vomit will usually take on a brighter red color.
- Urine may look dark or bloody, depending upon how recent the internal bleeding was.
- Stools may be almost black or bright red, also depending upon when the injury occurred.

Other symptoms of internal bleeding to watch for include:

- shocklike symptoms: paleness, cold clammy skin, light-headedness, weakness, decreasing alertness
- a distended, swollen, or rigid abdomen
- abdominal pain or tenderness
- restlessness, apprehension, or mental confusion
- an irregular pulse, or one that's very fast or slow
- early onset of profound shock

BASIC FIRST AID FOR INTERNAL BLEEDING

If you suspect internal bleeding, call for emergency help as soon as possible. If more than one person is at the scene, send someone for help while you:

Attend to the ABCs: airway, breathing, and circulation. (See "Chapter 3: Basic Emergency Care.")

Keep the victim still and treat him or her for shock. Don't put a person in the shock position if you suspect head, neck, or back injuries (see Chapter 3). If the person vomits and there's been no spinal injury, turn her on her side so she doesn't choke on it.

Look for other injuries, such as broken bones, to treat.

Loosen the victim's clothing and calm and reassure him or her. Don't give the person anything to eat or drink.

Continue to check the person's breathing and pulse.

Treatment of internal bleeding may require special training and equipment, blood transfusions to restore proper blood volume, anesthesia, and so forth.

NATURAL REMEDIES FOR INTERNAL BLEEDING

Though there are a number of herbs that have traditionally been used by Native Americans and other societies for serious internal injuries, internal bleeding is a major medical emergency that today calls for the conventional treatment outlined above. What follows are some natural treatments for internal bleeding that could be used in conjunction with *(not in place of)* the basic steps.

Take an appropriate homeopathic remedy. Jennifer Jacobs, a homeopath and M.D., says that the three principal remedies to consider are:

- ◆ *Arnica.* This is a popular homeopathic remedy for internal hemorrhaging after a trauma. The person may have a feeble or irregular pulse.
- ◆ *Veratrum.* This remedy, made from false hellebore roots, helps when the patient is on the verge of collapse or in a state of shock. The person's face is often sweating or turning blue. It works especially well to heal intestinal hemorrhaging.
- ◆ *Aconite.* Use this for internal bleeding after an injury if the person shows signs of fear and restlessness.

You can use 6X or 12X potency remedies every two to five minutes for up to ten doses after a serious trauma.

Take oral doses of an astringent herb to help stop internal bleeding. Christopher Hobbs recommends taking one-half teaspoon of shepherd's purse tincture every fifteen minutes until the bleeding stops (but not more than three teaspoons).

Hobbs notes that just as this herb is good for external bleeding, it also works well for internal bleeding, especially to slow bleeding after giving birth. "I've seen two teaspoons taken over two hours stop severe menstrual bleeding," he says. Although it is generally a nontoxic herb, if you take such large doses of the tincture, you should watch for possible side effects such as heart palpitations.

Other astringent, wound-healing herbs such as yarrow, plantain, stinging nettles, and witch hazel may also help in the recovery phase, taken in tincture form. Follow dose directions on labels.

◆ Recovering from Bleeding Episodes

A number of foods and vitamins can help you to recover from serious bleeding, whether external or internal.

- ◆ Vitamin K is the vitamin most clearly tied to proper blood clotting. Physicians sometimes give patients vitamin K injections after a severe bleeding episode. Foods that are rich in the vitamin or promote its production include alfalfa sprouts, dark green leafy vegetables, soybeans, and lactobacillus-containing yogurt. Avoid aspirin and antibiotics, which work against K.
- ◆ Vitamin C and zinc are essential for wound healing and tissue repair. Clinical nutritionist Shari Lieberman recommends taking daily 25–50 mg zinc and two to five grams in mixed doses of vitamin C plus bioflavonoids (or to bowel tolerance).
- ◆ Bioflavonoids, including rutin, are good for healing capillaries (usually the case with nosebleeds) and are also valuable antioxidants.
- ◆ Vitamins B_{12} and folic acid and iron help build blood and prevent anemia and are especially important if you're feeling faint or tired from blood loss. Taking them in combination works better than just taking iron, notes Lieberman.

  Iron supplements should be used with caution. Though a scientific consensus has not yet been formed, recent studies have linked high intake of dietary iron with an increased risk of heart disease. (Some data indicate that the heme iron found in meat presents more of a risk than

the nonheme iron from whole grains and vegetables.)
Check with a knowledgeable health professional before
taking iron supplements.

Iron supplement overdose by children is a common
cause of accidental poisoning.

◆ Chlorophyll supplements (the algae-based green foods spirulina, chlorella, and blue-green algae, and products made
from the young grasses of wheat, barley, and alfalfa) are
high in vitamins and minerals and are excellent builders
of red blood cells. Chlorophyll supplements come in tablets, powders, and liquid concentrates. Follow label directions for dosage.

In addition to making sure you're getting the right nutrients,
you may want to avoid substances that tend to thin the blood,
such as the drugs aspirin, heparin, and warfarin (Coumadin), fish
oils, and garlic in large amounts over a period of time.

You can encourage scar tissue of a cut or scrape to heal by
applying comfrey ointment or a plantain preparation. Both of
these herbs contain the compound allantoin, which studies have
shown prevents scars from forming and softens those that do
form. Vitamin E oil applied to the scar every day can also soften
scar tissue.

SEVEN

Bone Injuries

THIS CHAPTER COVERS:

♦ *fractures*
♦ *dislocations*

SEE "CHAPTER 19: MUSCLE AND JOINT INJURIES" FOR:

♦ *sprains*

The average person has 206 bones to provide structure to the body and protect internal organs, among other functions. Healthy bones are made up of a thin exterior layer of blood vessels and nerves, a hard, dense latticework of mostly calcium and phosphorus, and a core of spongy marrow tissue that produces red and white blood cells. Though usually sturdy and weight-bearing, when put under enough pressure bones can split, break, or dislocate from each other.

♦ When Bones Fracture

A fracture is the same as a break and may range in severity from a slight chip to an injury in which the bone ends protrude from the skin. The most common fractures occur to bones in the wrists, hands, and feet, and the upper arm/collarbone, due to falls, accidents, and other traumas. Less frequently bones fracture from "fatigue," after prolonged and repeated stress. It's also possible for weakened bones to break spontaneously, such as from advanced osteoporosis (often the hip) or bone cancer. Fractures are more likely to happen later in life, since bones are more resilient in children and get brittle with age.

The simplest fractures are closed ones (beneath the skin) in which the bone splinters slightly or the bone ends are not widely separated. Even these, however, are painful because of the nerves in bones, and the likelihood of damage to surrounding muscles and blood vessels. Open fractures, in which bones protrude or a wound extends down to the fracture, are usually more serious because of severe bleeding and the possibility of infection.

Fractures call for immediate emergency treatment by medical professionals. Delaying treatment can allow bones to rejoin out of alignment. There's also the possibility that damage to neighboring tissue may be serious, or that the broken bone may pose a threat to a nearby internal organ, such as the risk of lung puncture from a broken rib.

In some cases a fracture will be unmistakable: the victim will feel or hear the bone snap, there will be a grating sensation of bone ends rubbing together, and he or she will feel severe pain. In other cases the break won't be as obvious, but the victim may notice:

◆ immediate swelling and bruising
◆ pain and tenderness at the injury site, particularly when the body part is touched or moved
◆ difficulty in moving the injured body part, or it moves abnormally or unnaturally
◆ the injured part looks unnatural, especially when compared to the shape or length of its counterpart on the other side of the body

Many of these symptoms may be missing for minor fractures, which sometimes are misdiagnosed as sprains. Swelling that doesn't go down within a few days should probably be x-rayed.

BASIC FIRST AID FOR FRACTURES

First-aid treatment for a fracture depends on how severe the break is. With the most severe open break, the immediate concern should be to check the ABCs, clear clothing from the wound, and stop the bleeding. The possibility of other wounds should be quickly considered, especially if the victim is unconscious, there's paralysis in the arms or legs, or there's evidence of head, neck, or spinal injuries.

With open fractures, never push back a protruding bone end, wash the wound, or insert anything into it. Rather, gently apply pressure to stop bleeding, cover the wound (including the protruding bone) with sterile dressing or clean bandage, and immobilize it as you would for a closed break. As with all fractures, move the victim as little as possible and don't allow the person to eat or drink (which may delay treatment under general anesthesia at the hospital). Watch for the possibility of shock and call for emergency help as soon as possible.

Basic steps for closed fractures are simpler because there's no external bleeding or possibility of infection. The principal treatment is contained in the old adage of "splint 'em where they lie." That is, never attempt to straighten or set a fracture. Leave that to the doctor. The first-aid concern is to immobilize the break so that the area suffers no further damage. In general, don't move the victim or try to test the fractured part for loss of function. Try to keep the victim still. Don't allow him or her to sit up or change position, unless the injured area is first immobilized, and don't move a person with an injured hip, pelvis, or upper leg unless absolutely necessary. With broken extremities such as ankles and wrists, it's usually all right to gently put the hand or foot in as natural a position as possible before splinting or immobilizing. Finally, elevate a broken extremity after it has been splinted to reduce swelling.

Victims with serious fractures shouldn't be jammed into the backseat of a car to be taken to a hospital, since this may aggravate the injury. It's better to wait for an ambulance so that the person can be moved while lying down.

HOW TO IMMOBILIZE BONES AND JOINTS

The three basic tools necessary to immobilize fractured or dislocated bones are a stiff object, some padding, and something ropelike to use to tie the stiff object and padding to the injured body part. The stiff object can be a household item such as a board, broomstick, umbrella, or a rolled newspaper or magazine. In the wilderness, branches may be handy. If no stiff objects are available, it's sometimes possible to use just padding, in the form of a pillow, blanket, towels, or clothing. Otherwise the padding goes between the stiff object and the skin. Ties can be anything from strips of cloth to ropes, neckties, or belts.

A splint is applied to prevent the injured body part from moving, which could cause extreme pain and make the injury worse.

Some general splinting guidelines:

- ◆ Splint an injury in the position you found it.
- ◆ Always care for wounds before applying a splint.
- ◆ Tie a splint above or below an injury or a joint, not right over it. Ideally a splint should extend beyond both the joint above and the joint below the break.
- ◆ Don't tie a splint so tightly that it interferes with circulation. Make sure fingers or toes are not swelling, turning blue, or developing numbness or a tingling sensation. Check for circulation after fastening, and loosen knots if blood flow is being cut off.

Lower arm/wrist splint. Place the injured arm at a right angle across the victim's chest, with the palm in and the thumb up. Using two stiff objects and padding, put a splint on each side of the arm from the elbow to beyond the wrist. Tie these in place on both sides of the break. The lower arm can be supported with a sling (see below).

Finger and toe splint. Place cotton between the injured digit and the one next to it, and tape the two digits together.

Foot/ankle splint. Have the victim lie down and remove the shoe from the injured leg. This splint can be done without a board, by placing a pillow or other thick padding under the foot so that it extends from the calf to beyond the heel, and the edges of the padding meet on top of the leg. Tie it around the shin and around the foot. Tuck in the ends of the padding at the heel. The toes should be exposed.

Upper-arm/collarbone/shoulder splint. After placing some padding in the armpit, gently put the lower part of the injured arm at a right angle across the victim's chest. Put padding and a stiff object on the outside of the upper arm, and tie in place above and below the break. Support the lower arm with an arm sling and a chest tie.

Arm sling. A sling will help immobilize a splinted arm or shoulder. It's possible to improvise a sling from odd-shaped cloth, or even a shirt or sweater, but the ideal material would be a $40'' \times 40'' \times 55''$ right triangle. You can approximate that by taking a piece of square cloth about a yard long on each side and cutting or folding on the diagonal. Put the victim's arm at a right angle across his or her chest. Slide the material under the injured arm with the right angle corner of the sling just past the elbow of the injured arm. The longest side should be parallel with the victim's body and extend just beyond the edge of the hand. Bring the top point of the sling over the uninjured shoulder and the bottom point up and over the injured shoulder. Elevate the lower arm so that the fingers are three to four inches higher than the elbow. Tie the two points together behind the neck, off to one side so that the knot doesn't press into the back of the neck. Finally, fold the point at the elbow over the front of the sling and attach it with a pin. The fingers should be exposed.

Improvise a sling from a shirt or sweater by tying the sleeves around the victim's neck.

Chest tie. It's often helpful to further immobilize the arm and prevent it from swinging away from the body by wrapping a narrow cloth around the chest, over the injured upper arm but under the uninjured arm. Tie it on the side away from the injury.

WHAT TO EXPECT AT THE HOSPITAL

Conventional medical treatment of a fracture or dislocation will usually begin with an X ray. The patient will then be anesthetized while the doctor sets the break. Some fractures may require a physician to insert metal screws or plates to hold the bones together. Afterward the bone must be kept still long enough to allow the body to heal it. Thus, the injury will again be immobilized, with a long-term splint or plastic or resin casts.

Some breaks, such as to the ribs, don't require a cast, while others need more drastic measures than a cast to be immobilized. For instance, when the femur, the longest and heaviest bone in the body, breaks, the strong muscles in the upper leg often prevent the two broken ends from staying together. The patient must be put in traction to pull on the opposite parts of the bone and allow them to realign.

Anytime a body part is kept still for weeks or months at a time, muscles atrophy and joints stiffen. Thus, rehabilitation after immobilization is an essential part of medical treatment. Full movement and strength will return more quickly if, even while a cast is still on, the patient moves and exercises the broken limb, stimulating blood flow and healing.

◆ When Bones Dislocate

Bones are held together at joints by ligaments and other connective tissues. To some extent they're also held together by the shape of the bones, as in the case of the ball-and-socket connections at the shoulder and the hip. When there's a hard blow or a sudden twisting force applied to the joint site, such as from a sports injury, fall, or other accident, the bones can separate, or dislocate, causing the joint to no longer function. Dislocations can also result from severe cases of rheumatoid arthritis. A joint that has been weakened by previous dislocations may become dislocated without the person falling or experiencing some other obvious injury.

A dislocation usually stretches or tears the ligaments and may damage the joint capsule, the membrane that encases the joint. The accident ruptures local blood vessels as well, leading to internal bleeding, bruising, and swelling. The pressure on nearby nerves from the swelling causes marked pain.

About half of all dislocations are to the very maneuverable joint at the shoulder, usually as a result of a strong backward force on an elevated arm. Other common sites of dislocations are:

- the fingers, usually the first joint of the finger, often from being struck and bent back by a thrown ball, and toes
- the elbow, from a hard fall on the arm, or a forceful yank upon the arm of a child
- the jaw, sometimes during dental work, or as a result of a punch or other trauma to the open mouth
- the kneecap, usually from a hiking accident in which the knee gets twisted while scrambling down a mountain

Dislocations to the hip are rare, as it's a stable joint that requires extreme force to separate.

When you suspect a dislocation, keep in mind that it's often difficult to distinguish from a fracture, or even from a strain and sprain. Also, a blow that's hard enough to cause a dislocation may also have broken a bone, so there may be signs of this injury as well. Symptoms of a simple dislocation include:

- marked swelling
- deformity or an unnatural shape at the joint, or a longer or shorter look on the injured limb
- severe pain around the joint, especially on trying to move the injured part
- discoloration of the skin around the joint
- tenderness to the touch
- rigidity and loss of function or movement of the injured part

With a shoulder dislocation, the victim will often hold the injured arm out from the body and won't be able to place the hand of the injured arm on the uninjured shoulder.

Like fractures, dislocations are serious injuries that call for professional treatment. Although it is sometimes possible (and, less frequently, advisable) for a layperson to manipulate dislocated bones back into place (this is called "reducing" the dislocation), in almost all cases this is a job for trained professionals. The wrong type of pulling on or moving of a dislocated body part can further injure connective tissues, blood vessels, and nerves. If the dislocation is complicated by a fracture, any attempt to reduce may be even more damaging to tissues.

BASIC FIRST AID FOR DISLOCATIONS

Here are some general guidelines for treating dislocations:

- ◆ Don't try to straighten the injured part.
- ◆ Immobilize the joint with a splint or sling, changing the original position as little as possible.
- ◆ Apply cold compresses to the area around the dislocation.
- ◆ If a knee or ankle is dislocated, elevate it to help reduce swelling.
- ◆ Put the victim in a comfortable position and reassure him or her.
- ◆ Get emergency help.
- ◆ Watch for signs of shock.

Serious dislocations may require the victim to be put under general anesthesia for reduction, so it's best not to let him or her eat or drink after the injury. Treatment at the hospital will include X rays to determine the extent of the damage. Doctors reduce most dislocations by skillfully manipulating the injured parts to replace the bones in their proper positions. Some dislocations are particularly difficult to reduce. For instance, the thumb, because of its complicated anatomy, is hard to set with manipulation and may require surgery. The injured joint is usually then immobilized and splinted for two to three weeks to allow tissues to heal, and physiotherapy may be recommended after that.

The first dislocation often results in a chronically weak joint susceptible to further dislocations. Surgeons may be able to tighten ligaments or reconstruct the joint socket.

WHEN TO SELF-TREAT A DISLOCATION

There are only a few instances when an untrained person should weigh the risks of reducing a dislocation. One is when an uncomplicated shoulder, finger, or toe dislocation has just happened within the past few minutes in the wilderness and professional care will not be available for a number of hours. Quick and effective treatment can save the victim much pain and discomfort. Another instance is when a severe dislocation is causing a bone to press on nerves and blood vessels in such a way that the injured arm or limb has no pulse and is turning blue, in which case delay may threaten the entire limb.

According to first-aid expert Paul G. Gill, M.D., author of *Simon & Schuster's Pocket Guide to Wilderness Medicine*, one of the best techniques for reducing a simple shoulder dislocation that occurs in the wilderness is to have the victim lie on his or her stomach on a ledge or other flat surface with the dislocated arm hanging freely over the edge. Tie ten to fifteen pounds of weight to the wrist, wait ten minutes, and the shoulder bones will often move back together.

To reduce a finger dislocation in the wilderness, have the victim hold the injured hand out with the palm down. If you're right-handed, take a firm hold of the outer part of the dislocated finger with your right hand, and with the other grasp the base of the dislocated bone. Give a strong, direct pull with your right hand, while pushing the base back into the joint with the thumb of the left hand. Don't attempt to reduce a dislocated thumb, since its anatomy is more complicated than that of the other fingers and minor surgery may be needed to set it.

To reduce a dislocated toe, pull on it firmly while bending it backward. After reducing a dislocated finger or toe, splint it to the digit next to it.

If you can't reduce a dislocation after the first attempt, don't try again since you'll probably just further injure the joint. Rather, immobilize the injury and get medical help as soon as possible. Even if you successfully reduce a dislocation, the victim should see a doctor as soon as possible.

◆ Natural First-Aid Remedies for Bone Injuries

It's necessary to emphasize that natural remedies for use at the time of a bone injury are primarily for treating symptoms such as pain, swelling, and shock rather than the fracture or dislocation itself, which is best treated by a physician. Natural remedies, foods and supplements, and bodywork can play a much greater role, however, to help you recover from bone injuries and prevent further ones.

To relieve pain and prevent shock, take the homeopathic remedy **Arnica** ***or Bach Flower Rescue Remedy internally at the time of the injury.*** Take an immediate oral dose of 6X or 12X *Arnica*. You can follow up by taking *Arnica* each half hour after the injury for three hours, and then every three hours during the next two to three days. If the injury is a dislocation or a closed break, you can also apply *Arnica* tincture or salve externally to the area around the injury, to reduce swelling and bruising.

To take Rescue Remedy, add three to four drops of the liquid to a small glass of water and have the victim sip it slowly. If no water is available, put three to four drops of undiluted Rescue Remedy directly on the tongue. Repeat every half hour until the patient is calm.

Using either of these is highly recommended at the time of a severe injury such as a broken bone. They will help to minimize the local pain and alleviate some of the fear and shock commonly experienced along with a break or dislocation.

Help stimulate the healing of minor dislocations and closed fractures and their local tissue damage with herbal preparations made from comfrey. Natural pharmacies carry a number of salves and ointments that contain comfrey. These can be rubbed right into the skin over a bone injury. A comfrey poultice or compress is more difficult to make and use than a commercial salve, but it may be stronger acting. Mix three tablespoons of powdered root with three ounces of hot water. Stir into a paste. Apply the warm mixture directly to the skin and cover with sterile gauze or clean cloth. Secure with a bandage and leave the application on for a few hours or overnight. After removing, massage the area with a comfrey ointment.

Naturopath Joseph Pizzorno suggests that, if comfrey grows in your area, you find some fresh leaves. Put a comfrey leaf on a cutting board and roll it with a rolling pin from the tip to stem. You'll get a thick jelly that can be rubbed directly onto unbroken skin. "You can even take comfrey-leaf capsules (the active ingredient is destroyed in a tea) internally for a short time," says Pizzorno. "Look for pyrrolizidine-free varieties."

Herbalist Christopher Hobbs recommends applying a comfrey salve in the acute phase right after a bone injury. When the break is not a serious one and can be immobilized with a remov-able cast, comfrey can also be applied over the break on a daily basis.

Comfrey is sometimes known as knitbone. In past centuries it was used to make a paste that would be wrapped around broken bones and left to harden into a plaster cast. It's been replaced by plastic and resins for this mechanical function, but is often still recommended by herbalists for external use on dislocations and (nonopen) fractures. For good reason: comfrey contains the chem-ical allantoin, which scientists have shown helps tissue cells throughout the body regenerate. Allantoin is easily absorbed through the skin and reaches deep tissue, where it particularly promotes the activity of osteoblast cells to produce bones, and fibroblasts to produce connective tissue.

Despite its name, the herb known as boneset *(Eupatorium perfoliatum)* does not mend broken bones, though it may be an effective fever remedy. The name comes from its being a tradi-tional remedy for "breakbone fever," in which the muscle pain was so great it felt as if the bones were on the point of breaking.

Beginning a couple of days after a bone injury, take the homeopathic remedy Symphytum **for a broken or dislocated bone.** *Symphytum* is prepared from comfrey, the herb that's long been used to help heal bone injuries. Take *Symphytum* 30C daily for three to four weeks while recuperating from a bone injury. According to homeopath Jennifer Jacobs, M.D., "Taking *Symphy-tum* on a daily basis for weeks will help bones to heal. I've seen it work very well in cases where's there's an old fracture that won't heal. After several weeks taking *Symphytum*, they're healed."

Apply healing magnets to the area of the bone injury. Practi-tioners of biomagnetism recommend that for self-care, apply medical magnets near the source of pain, directly to the skin, and keep them on for a week longer.

An increasing number of scientists in the United States, Russia, and the Orient are now studying biomagnetism, the effect of extremely weak magnetic fields on the human body. Healing with magnets is already popular in some European countries and in Japan, where drugstores carry a variety of products such as elasticized cloth bandages with tiny magnets sewn in, and Band-Aid-type magnet-containing strips.

In the United States, the FDA considers such devices "nonap-proved" for medical use. Nevertheless, a number of enterprising mail-order companies (see "Resources") now offer biomagnetic products to American consumers. The strength of biomagnets is identified in gauss, the unit used for measuring magnetic fields; biomagnets typically range from four hundred to three thousand gauss. Iron magnets are bulky, so modern biomagnets are made from complex alloys that may include nickel, copper, cobalt, or rare-earth metals such as cerium, and coverings of gold or ceramic. These healing magnets retain their magnetism much longer than iron and are thus reusable. They're typically flat and pea-sized. In addition to bandages, other items are also available including magnetic bracelets, necklaces, and shoe inserts.

Though biomagnetism as a diagnostic device (magnetic resonance imaging, or MRI, for instance) is well-known and highly developed in the West, most of the research on the healing effects of weak magnetic fields has been done in Japan. Studies have demonstrated that elecromagnetic fields can affect enzyme reaction, wound healing, tumor growth, blood leukocyte count, stress response, and other functions in the body. Perhaps the most dramatic effect, however, relates to healing bones.

Applying minute amounts of electrical stimulation is now an accepted practice among orthopedic surgeons to encourage the union of fractures that have failed to heal in the expected time period. This new technique was inspired by the pioneering research of Robert O. Becker, M.D., author of *The Body Electric* and the nation's foremost authority on the healing effects (as well as the hazards) of electromagnetic fields. Becker notes in his most recent book, *Cross Currents*, "The FDA's approval in 1978 of several types of electrical and electromagnetic devices for stimulating the healing of human bone fractures that have failed to heal has played a major role in gaining acceptance for electrotherapeutics in general. More than 100,000 patients have been treated in this country and abroad with these devices."

Oriental Medical Doctor Holly Eagle notes, "There are hospitals where the doctors are now putting small magnets under the cast, packed in around bone injuries, to restore the proper magnetic field that was disrupted by the fracture. I've seen dramatic results with broken ribs from simply using magnets near the break."

◆ Recovery from Bone Injuries

"There are very specific recommendations for nutrients that can help the body recover from a bone injury," says Shari Lieberman, Ph.D., a certified nutrition consultant and registered dietitian. "Bone building requires virtually all of the vitamins and minerals, plus the trace minerals, such as silicon and boron, that are sometimes missing from the average American diet."

The principal bone-repair nutrients include the following:

◆ Vitamins A (25,000 IU daily in the form of beta carotene), C (two to five grams in mixed doses or to bowel tolerance), D (400–600 mg), and E (400–800 IU), all help repair tissue, while vitamin D is also crucial for proper calcium absorption. Daily exposure to the sun can provide necessary D, as this is one of the vitamins the body manufactures. Dietary sources of D are limited to fatty fish, liver, and egg yolks, foods that unfortunately are high in both fat and cholesterol.

◆ The minerals calcium and magnesium (in a 2:1 ratio, such as 1,500 mg calcium and 750 mg magnesium), manganese (15–30 mg), and zinc (25–50 mg) are crucial in balanced formulations. Calcium has received most of the attention lately, due at least in part to promotion by the dairy industry, but other minerals and proper intake levels are necessary to form strong bones. For instance, magnesium is intimately connected with calcium, and taking too much of one or the other can play havoc with not only the bones but nerves, muscles, and the heart. On the other hand, too much phosphorus can have a negative, demineralizing effect on bones, by impairing their absorption of calcium as well as causing them to lose calcium to the blood. A zinc deficiency may delay healing, while proper levels help build bones.

Reliable dietary sources of calcium include leafy green vegetables, tofu, sea vegetables, and dairy foods. Foods rich in magnesium include fish, leafy green vegetables, whole grains, nuts, and beans. Foods to avoid for their calcium-draining effects are those high in phosphorus, such as colas and some highly processed foods. Lentils, oatmeal, cowpeas, and oysters are good sources of zinc.

◆ Trace minerals play an important role. Chief among these is silicon, which has only recently begun to gain scientific recognition for its role in the formation of bones, cartilage, and connective tissue. Studies have shown that animals fed silicon-deficient diets develop bone and skeletal abnormalities that are corrected by silicon supplementation. The highest levels of silicon in the body are found in connective tissue, bones, teeth, and nails. The most common dietary sources include whole-grain breads and cereals, vegetables, cooked dried beans and peas, and seafoods. Some researchers believe that the overprocessing of industrialized nations' food supplies has led to a general deficiency of the trace mineral. The federal government's position is that though "there is substantial evidence" to establish that a number of trace elements including silicon are essential, "there are no data from which a human requirement could be established and thus no provisional (dietary) allowance can be set."

Though toxic if inhaled (as silica dust, a byproduct of semiconductor production), no adverse effects have been reported from consuming silicon supplements.

According to Lieberman, "After a bone injury, you should be taking an insurance-level multivitamin, plus extra calcium, magnesium, and the trace minerals silicon [2 mg daily] and boron [2 mg]."

An insurance level of supplements includes the eleven vitamins, four minerals, and three trace elements for which the federal government has determined there are recommended dietary allowances (RDAs). Many supplement companies offer insurance-level, "one-a-day" formulas, though in most cases the pills or capsules are meant to be taken up to six times per day. Such supplementation often exceeds the RDAs, thus providing greater protection against marginal nutrient deficiencies.

Some special herbs, foods, and supplements that are especially high in the bone-building vitamins and minerals include the following:

◆ Field horsetail *(Equisetum arvense)* is a traditional European remedy for wounds, joint pain, and broken-bone repair. It is one of the best herbal sources for silicon and other trace minerals. Research is scanty in the United States, but there are some studies in Europe that have indicated fracture victims heal more quickly when they consume horsetail.

Make a horsetail tea by simmering two teaspoons of the dried herb for ten minutes in a cup of water. Let steep for another five minutes, strain, and drink.

Horsetail extracts, powders, and tinctures are available from a number of herb companies. The product that's most widely recommended by herbalists is an extract called Alta Sil·X Silica, developed in the early 1970s by Richard Barmakian, a naturopath and homeopath, and produced by Alta Health Products in Pasadena, California. It's produced from pesticide-free horsetail herb in a way that maximizes the levels of usable silica in the finished product. Suggested use is one to three 500-mg tablets daily with meals.

According to Hobbs, "I've seen a lot of success with Alta Sil·X, for speeding up broken bones and nails, as well as healing sinews and tendons. This is a classic product for bone injuries."

Certain of horsetail's chemical constituents suggest that it shouldn't be used extensively for long periods (though these chemicals are usually removed by heating or cooking), nor should it be taken at all by children or pregnant women. Check with a reputable herbalist before taking it on a medical basis.

◆ Stinging nettles is both a healing herb as well as a favorite "superfood" among many herbalists, notes Hobbs. Nettles are rich in such minerals as calcium, magnesium, iron, and potassium. It's an excellent nutritional boost for healing bones, muscle strains, and tendon injuries. Grow or wild-craft the young shoots and cook them up as a tasty green, or sprinkle dried nettles on salads, soups, and vegetables. The herb is also widely available in natural foods stores in capsule form. Take 300 mg daily.

◆ Sea vegetables such as kelp, nori, and wakame are renowned for their complete and balanced range of vitamins, minerals, and trace minerals. If you're new to them, one of the easiest way to incorporate them into your diet is as a condiment. For instance, nori comes in thin sheets that can be toasted by briefly holding over a gas flame, then crushed up and sprinkled in soups and salads.

◆ Herbal alfalfa-leaf extracts and concentrates are rich in chlorophyll (which promotes the assimilation of other nutrients), vitamins (especially beta carotene and vitamin E), minerals, and trace minerals.

◆ Essential fatty acids may help bones heal. According to nutritionist Lieberman, "After a bone injury you're more prone to arthritis, and the essential fatty acids will prevent that. They work in a similar fashion to the cortisonelike steroids to prevent inflammation in joints, though without the side effects." Some EFAs may also play a role in mineral deposition in bones.

Your body manufactures most of the fat it needs to function properly. Other fats—those termed the essential fatty acid (EFAs)—must be obtained through the diet. Two of the most important EFAs are the omega-3s and omega-6s. Two specific omega-3s that are desirable for human health are eicosapentaenoic acid (EPA) and docosahexaenoic acid (DHA). The most important omega-6 so far discovered is gamma linolenic acid (GLA).

Why is this alphabet soup so important? Various essential fatty acids play crucial roles in the body. Though scientists began to identify the effects of EFAs only within the past decade or so, it is now known that EFAs thin the blood and inhibit clotting, improve cholesterol profiles, and strengthen cell membranes. Perhaps the EFAs' most striking physical action, however, is their natural anti-inflammatory effect on the body. The EFAs are now being used therapeutically to help treat or prevent diseases including arthritis, heart disease, cancer, allergies, and asthma.

Food sources of the EFAs are somewhat limited. The highest concentrations can be found in:

The fat of cold-water fish including salmon, cod, mackerel, sardines, bluefish, herring, and tuna. These fish are naturally high in the omega-3s. Vitamin companies make fish oil supplements from the fats of these fish.

The seeds of certain plants including rape (Brassica napus), ***flax*** (Linum usitatissimum), ***and hemp (marijuana:*** Cannabis sativa). Although you'd have to eat a lot of seeds to get much useful EFA from these plants, you can get higher amounts by drinking (or eating capsules of) the oils pressed from these seeds. (The oil made from rape seeds is called canola oil.) Because EFAs are chemically fragile and light- and heat-sensitive, reliable oil sources should be dated for freshness, sold in opaque containers, and kept refrigerated.

Hemp oil is new to the natural foods market. Currently it is pressed from sterilized seeds imported from Canada. The seeds and the oil have no psychoactive property and are completely legal products in the United States (see "Resources" for the address of the producer).

The plants evening primrose (Oenothera biennis), ***borage*** (Borago officinalis), ***and black currant*** (Ribes nigrum). Oils made from these three plants are among the highest known sources of the omega-6 GLA.

Natural foods stores sell a variety of EFA products in bottles and capsules of oils from these fish, seeds, and plants. Lieberman says, "To a certain extent the omega-3s and omega-6s overlap. Both tend to enhance the body's ability to reduce inflammation and improve cholesterol profiles. Which one is best for an individual is often a matter of trial and error. Some studies have shown that the best results are achieved by using the omega-3s and omega-6s together."

Beyond dietary recommendations, there are a number of other long-term treatments for bone injuries.

◆ In addition to the homeopathic remedy *Symphytum*, homeopathic *Phosphorus*, taken daily, has been known to help heal bones.

◆ Massage and bodywork should play a major role in the recovery from bone injuries. Massage can stimulate circulation, remove swelling, disperse blood from sites of internal bleeding, and prevent or relieve adhesions (fibrous tissue joining bodily parts that are normally separate). A bodyworker skilled in working with bone injuries can also help prevent poor realignment of bones, atrophy of surrounding muscles, and loss of tension in ligaments.

Some types of bodywork can begin immediately after an injury. According to Holly Eagle, "I think it's important to begin right away to massage the opposite side of the body from where the injury was. What happens with one limb is neurologically close to what's going on with the other." Light kneading and palm-rub-type massage can also be applied near the area of fracture or dislocation. Other techniques that involve extending, bending, and rotating the injured limb are done after the bones have healed.

Performed improperly, however, massage may be harmful, so it's best to develop a program in conjunction with a knowledgeable bodyworker and your health professional. The ten-thousand-member American Massage Therapy Association in Evanston, Illinois, can direct you to bodyworkers in your area (see "Resources").

Acupressure author Michael Reed Gach says that traditional Chinese medicine identifies a specific point related to bones. It is located close to the spine on the upper back, at the level of the upper inside tip of each shoulder blade. Press on this point firmly with the thumb for two minutes three times a day to help heal broken or dislocated bones.

◆ Another alternative worth exploring is a consultation with a holistically inclined osteopath. Doctors of osteopathy, D.O.'s, hold a degree equivalent to an M.D. but are much more highly trained than conventional physicians in the benefits and techniques of soft-tissue manipulation. According to osteopath Anthony Capobianco of Glen Cove, New York, "It is a general misconception that administering first aid and applying a cast are all that need to be done for a bone injury. A fracture is not only a break in a bone but a massive soft tissue injury. The tremendous force of the injury often disrupts the harmony of function and movement in related fluids and tissue. This damage to the body's finely tuned and balanced homeostatic mechanism is often ignored, in part because it may not even be apparent until after the visible effects of the injury have passed.

"Traditional osteopathy can tremendously assist nature's healing of a bone injury. Osteopaths use palpatory diagnosis and manipulative treatment to address the straining of tissue and the blockage of circulation that follows the trauma. We work local and distant to the fracture or dislocation to reduce pain, limitation of motion, swelling, or malfunction of related parts. This speeds up healing by restoring and enhancing arterial blood flow into, and venous and lymphatic drainage out of, the area, thus accelerating repair and minimizing disability."

The American Ostopathic Association in Chicago can help you located a nearby osteopath (see "Resources").

♦ Naturopaths are trained in physical therapy and can often help patients recover more quickly from bone injuries, notes Joe Pizzorno, N.D. For instance, one tool they use is therapeutic ultrasound, the same high-frequency sound vibrations used by obstetricians to view fetuses in utero. At higher levels than is used diagnostically, ultrasound speeds the healing of bones and tendons by heating up the injured area, increasing blood and lymph circulation, and removing adhesions. "Ultrasound should not be used near the eyes, over malignancies, or over a recent bone break," Pizzorno notes.

♦ Preventing Bone Injuries

Most serious bone injuries are due to sports injuries and accidents that may not be easily prevented. It is a good idea, though, to limit the possibilities for falls and accidents around the home and workplace by identifying and improving unsafe conditions, such as inadequate lighting, slippery floors, and objects left lying about.

An equally important and effective way to prevent bone injuries is to develop hard, sturdy bones that resist breaking. This is an enterprise that should be begun early in life, since bone mass is usually gained up to the age of thirty-five or so and slowly lost after that age. The diet and everyday habits that develop a strong musculoskeletal system also benefit the body's overall health and thus are well worth making a lifetime commitment to.

One of the best ways to prevent weak bones is to engage in plenty of weight-bearing activity or exercise, such as walking, running, tennis, and most sports except swimming. The saying "use them or lose them" applies to bones—people who are so inactive that they never put any stress on their bones risk becoming wormlike.

Stretching exercises are also important to bone health, since they reduce the possibility of extreme cramping or contraction of connecting muscles, which in rare cases can put bones under such pressure they fracture.

Full-spectrum light, such as sunlight, is important for strong bones. Sunlight reacts with certain chemicals in the skin to form vitamin D, a hormonelike substance that helps regulate blood levels of calcium. A lack of vitamin D can lead to bone problems, including rickets. On the other hand, too much D, whether from dietary sources or exposure to sun, is toxic. Fifteen minutes of sun per day is enough to manufacture sufficient vitamin D for most people.

Eating the right foods can make or break bones, to use an appropriate cliché. A diet for healthy bones should include lots of whole grains, dark green leafy vegetables, legumes, and fruits and nuts. Vegetarians may have stronger bones than meat eaters, according to a study, "Incidence of Osteroporosis in Vegetarians and Omnivores," published by the *American Journal of Clinical Nutrition* in 1972. Researchers suggest that, compared to average American meat eaters, vegetarians tend to consume more calcium, fewer processed foods, and less protein and fat.

Two foods sometimes touted as the best for bones, milk and red meat, may in excess actually have a negative effect on bone health. Both of these foods have poor calcium/phosphorus ratios and relatively high protein levels. When the body metabolizes protein, acid levels in the bloodstream increase, causing the bones to secrete more calcium, an alkalizing substance, to neutralize the acid.

Beyond improper diet, some of the risk factors for poor bone health include:

- ◆ alcoholism
- ◆ excess aluminum intake, such as from regular consumption of buffered aspirin, aluminum-containing antacids (Mylanta, Maalox), or aluminum-based baking powders, or from regular use of aluminum-containing antiperspirants or aluminum cookware
- ◆ smoking
- ◆ caffeine
- ◆ cortisonelike steroid drugs, such as prednisone
- ◆ emotional stress and tension

Most people break or dislocate bones at least once in their lives, but by staying active and eating healthful foods you can lower your risk considerably and recover that much faster when you do have a bone injury.

EIGHT

Breathing Problems

THIS CHAPTER COVERS:

- *asthma attack*
- *croup and epiglottitis*
- *hyperventilation, panic attack, and breath-holding*

SEE "CHAPTER 3: BASIC EMERGENCY CARE" FOR:

- *rescue breathing*
- *choking*

Full, deep breathing requires the coordinated activity of brain, lungs, various muscles, the central nervous system, and myriad other parts of the body. Illness or injury that constricts the airways or clogs the lungs, or an object stuck in the windpipe, can interfere with the usually automatic act of breathing. Such breathing problems are among the most serious emergencies most people face. When the body's supply of air is cut off, cells start to die and organs cease to function. Deprived of oxygen for as few as three to four minutes, the brain suffers irreversible damage. Quick and effective steps and remedies for restoring free breathing are thus essential first-aid tools.

◆ Asthma Attack

Both the number and the severity of asthma cases are increasing worldwide. In the United States, the age-adjusted prevalence rate of asthma increased 38 percent from 1980 to 1990, according to the federal Centers for Disease Control. Almost half of all pediatricians are today treating more asthmatic children than they were five to ten years ago. Approximately one in every twenty-five

Americans, an estimated 10–12 million people, suffer asthma attacks. The age-adjusted death rate in the United States, after declining in 1970s, increased 46 percent during the 1980s. Asthma now causes some five thousand deaths annually.

The reason for this rapid rise in asthma is unclear. Is it increased air pollution? Too many pets? An overprocessed food supply? Airtight homes and office buildings? Whatever the reason, asthma is a serious respiratory disorder, especially if it comes on in adulthood. It is more often "managed" than cured and at times calls for emergency measures.

Hippocrates coined the word *asthma* to describe the panting and breathlessness he saw among some of his fellow Greeks twenty-four centuries ago. It occurs because of a narrowing of the trachea, or windpipe, the bronchi (the major tubes from the trachea to the lungs), or the bronchioles, the smaller airways of the lungs. This narrowing can be due to:

- constriction or spasms of the smooth muscles that wrap the exterior of these tubes
- a swelling of the mucous membranes that line the tubes' interior
- excess mucus secreted by the mucous glands inside the bronchial walls, which plugs up the bronchial airway

The main effect of narrowed airways is difficulty breathing, especially on the exhale. The degree of airway obstruction can vary, as can its duration. The typical asthma symptoms of coughing and wheezing may be mild or severe and may be experienced daily or infrequently. Symptoms that come on suddenly are said to constitute an asthma attack, which may end within minutes or may last for hours or even days. A severe, prolonged attack can threaten a person's life.

A variety of conditions or substances may bring on an asthma attack, including the following:

- Allergies can not only trigger individual episodes but lead to chronic asthma. This is because when an allergen or pollutant overstimulates the lungs, the body responds by activating the immune system, causing various physical reactions including swelling of airways. After a number of attacks, the airways no longer routinely return to normal. In effect they're in a constant state of inflammation. This damages bronchial walls and creates scar tissue. Eventually, the situation is so severe that an allergen is no longer needed to trigger an attack: asthma has become the normal state of the lungs.

Many asthma specialists think allergies are responsible for the majority of asthma cases among people up to the age of forty, while for older people other factors are more important. (Not all people with allergies suffer from asthma attacks, though.) Pollen, mold, and house dust are common triggers of allergic asthma.

◆ Exercise and other activities can cause the asthmatic to inhale large amounts of cool, dry air. This can aggravate the airways and thus trigger wheezing and coughing in some people. (On the other hand, the right type of exercise can help relieve asthma by working to increase lung capacity.)

◆ Infections, especially viral respiratory-tract and sinus infections, can cause attacks by increasing the "reactivity" of the airways.

◆ Stress, strong emotions, and mental tension or strain can bring on an attack, but only if you already have hyperactive airways.

◆ Hormonal changes can play a role. Though the reason why is unclear, asthmatic women sometimes experience more frequent attacks just before menstruation.

◆ Cold weather and sudden lungfuls of cold air can induce an attack.

◆ Aspirin and other drugs can trigger asthma attacks. For unknown reasons, one in five asthmatics is sensitive to aspirin. About two dozen other drugs, including acetaminophen, oral contraceptives, penicillin, and ibuprofen (Advil, Motrin, Nuprin) can also trigger asthma symptoms.

◆ Airborne irritants, including smoke from cigarettes or wood-burning stoves, aerosol sprays, strong odors, and toxic household or workplace chemicals, can aggravate asthma.

SYMPTOMS

The most common symptoms of asthma attack are:

◆ a hard, tight cough
◆ wheezing, shortness of breath, or difficulty in exhaling

♦ chest tightness or a choking sensation
♦ mucus production
♦ nervousness, tenseness, or fright

The victim may also have nasal congestion, nausea, a slight fever, sweat on the forehead, and a rapid heartbeat. At the end of an attack the victim may cough hard enough to bring up sticky mucus, thus clearing the air passageways and freeing the breath.

During an acute attack, breathing is so restricted that it becomes almost inaudible. Even coughing becomes difficult. The victim may start to panic from the choking sensation or try vigorously to pull up the shoulders and the chin in an attempt to expand the chest and gulp down more air. Pulse may increase to over 120 beats per minute. Starved of oxygen, the skin, lips, and nails take on a bluish tinge. When such symptoms occur, the victim may be near respiratory failure and collapse. Emergency medical care should be summoned at once.

It's also important to seek medical attention for less acute asthma attacks, especially if:

♦ It's the first such episode.
♦ There's pronounced wheezing or difficulty breathing, particularly if the victim is a pregnant woman or an infant.
♦ Medication fails to improve symptoms.
♦ There's a severe respiratory infection.
♦ The victim seems confused or lethargic.

BASIC FIRST AID FOR ASTHMA

The basic steps for an acute asthma attack are similar to those for an acute allergic reaction: maintain an open airway and restore breathing and circulation (see "Chapter 3: Basic Emergency Care"). Send for emergency help as soon as possible while frequently checking the victim's breathing and pulse rate.

If the victim has been prescribed medication for an attack, administer the drugs according to the instructions on the container. It's best to give any drugs, however, only with a doctor's consent.

Keep the victim sitting in a comfortable position and try to calm him or her. If an attack subsides within thirty minutes, it's nevertheless a good idea to report the attack to the victim's doctor or health practitioners. If symptoms return, call a health professional.

WHAT TO EXPECT AT THE HOSPITAL

When you take a person who's experiencing an acute attack to the hospital, the physician will ask a series of questions and listen to the heart and lungs. The procedures and drugs used will vary according to the type and severity of the attack.

If the breathing problem is severe, the physician may administer epinephrine (adrenaline), by injection or inhaler, as well as oxygen. Epinephrine increases the heartbeat and relaxes the smooth muscles in the wall of the bronchi. Its potential side effects range from allergic reaction to headache, shakiness, and restlessness. Epinephrine inhalers such as Primatene Mist are sometimes prescribed to manage asthma attacks, but these drugs are falling out of favor because of the side effects, including on occasion sudden death from excessive use.

Three classes of drugs are now more commonly used than epinephrine for treatment of asthma: the beta-boosting bronchodilators, xanthine preparations, and cortisonelike steroids.

Beta-boosting bronchodilators include such potent drugs as terbutaline (Brethaire, Bricanyl) and albuterol (Proventil, Ventolin), available in both pill and aerosol form. These drugs reliably dilate the bronchi without causing the heart to beat too rapidly. They also have potentially significant side effects such as increased blood pressure, headaches, insomnia, and muscle cramps. They're also relatively short-lived and thus easily misused.

Xanthine preparations such as theophylline (Bronkodyl, Theolair) are used both for prompt relief of acute asthma and to control chronic, recurrent asthma. Theophylline comes in capsule or tablet form, as well as in combination with other drugs such as ephedrine or sedatives such as phenobarbital. Theophylline inhibits a certain enzyme and thus relaxes the muscles and blood vessels of the lungs. These drugs are also central nervous system stimulants. Caffeine is a member of the theophylline family. The risks of theophylline use include stomach irritation, nervousness, personality change, headache, dizziness, nausea, allergic reactions, and gastrointestinal bleeding. Children may develop learning difficulties while taking theophylline. An increasing number of doctors are now reluctant to prescribe theophylline products routinely because of the seriousness of their side effects.

Cortisonelike steroids (prednisone, Beclovent), as tablets, oral solutions, and inhalers, won't relieve acute asthma but are increasingly popular for long-term management. Though doctors don't known exactly how these drugs work, they have an anti-inflammatory effect. The ratio of their benefits to risks remains a controversial topic. Some doctors think they represent a great advance in asthma therapy, especially if the dose is kept low. Others are unconvinced, pointing to the possibility of functional dependence and a long list of potential side effects, including disruption of endocrine balance, retarding or damaging normal growth and development among children, glaucoma, osteoporosis, immune suppression, and serious mental and emotional disturbances.

Another anti-inflammatory drug, cromolyn (Intal inhaler), is a relatively safe asthma medication that seems to work better for children than adults.

It should be stressed that none of the above treatment drugs "cure" asthma. They alleviate symptoms by relaxing bronchial muscles, for instance, but do not directly address the specific allergies or other factors that trigger an asthma attack. Nor, obviously, do they strengthen and balance the body's constitution in a way that can help prevent further attacks.

NATURAL FIRST-AID REMEDIES FOR ASTHMA ATTACK

Like an acute allergic reaction, an acute asthma attack is a serious emergency that calls for medical attention. By recognizing the earliest symptoms, however, and responding with appropriate treatments, a more severe attack can often be prevented. Try some of the following strategies at the onset of an attack:

Use the Chinese herb ephedra (ma huang) to help relieve bronchial spasms. If you have raw ephedra, available at Oriental markets and some natural foods stores, just chew on the stems, suggests Joseph Pizzorno, N.D., coauthor of *Encyclopedia of Natural Medicine*. You can also brew an ephedra tea. Put the stems in a pot with a quart of water, bring it to a boil, lower the heat, steep for twenty minutes, and strain. Its peak effects will be felt some one to five hours later. A tincture or standardized liquid extract is much faster acting and better to halt an acute attack. Take one-quarter to one-half teaspoon or follow label directions.

As noted in Chapter 4 on allergic reactions, the Chinese have been using a species of ephedra they call *ma huang (Ephedra sinica)* for thousands of years to treat asthma. It contains the adrenalinelike substance ephedrine and thus can be especially effective during a crisis. (North American species of ephedra such

as *E. nevadensis*—Mormon tea—and *E. viridis* contain little or no
ephedrine.) *Ma huang* works by stimulating the sympathetic nervous system and thus relieving the bronchial muscle spasms that
can help cause the underlying asthmatic state.

Continued prolonged use of ephedra for asthma is not recommended since it can weaken the adrenal glands and lead to
nervousness, insomnia, and other side effects in sensitive individuals. There's some evidence, though, that people have a higher
tolerance for the natural form of ephedra, compared to pure
synthetic ephedrine. Pizzorno notes that many naturopaths use
ephedra in combination with herbs such as licorice and nutrients
such as vitamin C and zinc that support adrenal function.

**Use the herbs lobelia and cayenne to help gain control of a
mild asthma attack.** Andrew Weil, M.D., author of *Natural Health,
Natural Medicine,* recommends a lobelia-cayenne preparation as
one way to manage an asthma attack. Make it by mixing three
parts tincture of lobelia with one part tincture of capsicum (cayenne pepper). Weil says take twenty drops of the mixture in water
at the start of an asthma attack, and repeat every thirty minutes
for a total of three or four doses.

Herbalist Christopher Hobbs notes that you can also take
lobelia by itself, ten to fifteen drops every half hour as tincture.
He cautions against overuse, though, since it can cause nausea.

**Try the homeopathic remedy Arsenicum, especially for dry,
wheezing asthma that comes on about midnight accompanied by
anxiety and restlessness.** This is the most commonly relied upon
homeopathic remedy for asthma. Two other major homeopathic
asthma remedies are *Ipecac* (for profuse mucus that can't be
coughed up, gagging, or long spasms of coughing that may end in
vomiting) and *Spongia* (especially if there's loud wheezing).

Homeopaths who treat asthma emphasize that, although
these and dozens of other asthma remedies can provide some
symptomatic relief, asthma really needs to be addressed at the
constitutional level. "Asthma should be treated chronically over a
long period of time," says homeopath Jennifer Jacobs, M.D. Homeopaths may attempt to reduce the severity of allergen-caused
attacks by prescribing homeopathically dilute allergens such as
Cat's Hair 6X.

Do pursed-lip breathing at the first sign of an attack. Breathe
in deeply through the nose, exhaling through the mouth with the
lips shaped as if to blow up a balloon. This helps expel the buildup
of stale air in the lungs that accompanies some attacks. It also
helps relax the body and prevent a cycle of panic and respiratory
distress.

***Massage either or both of the two major sets of acupressure
points for relief of congested breathing, coughing, and chest
tension.*** The two pairs of points to try are:

- ◆ the lung points, located in the upper chest, about two
  inches below the shoulder end of the collarbones
- ◆ a set of points on the back, one finger-width below the
  upper tip of the shoulder blade, between the spine and the
  scapula

Acupressurist Michael Reed Gach suggests closing your eyes
while feeling for the lung points, which tend to knot up when you
have breathing problems. Maintain firm pressure with the thumbs
while breathing deeply for two minutes.

To massage the points on your back, bring your hand over the
opposite shoulder, curve the fingers, and press the point while
taking five deep breaths. Switch sides and press on the opposite
point for five breaths.

"These are the strongest points to free the lungs," says Gach.
"Ideally you can lie down on tennis balls placed at the back
points, while using thumbs or fingers on the upper chest points,
and apply pressure on both sets of points."

***If a child is having difficulty breathing, give a series of light
chops with a cupped hand to the back.*** Have him or her bend over
with head below waist and pound lightly. This may help the
victim cough up mucus that is blocking the windpipe and obstructing the breath.

Drink a caffeinated beverage or a warm liquid, such as soup.
The caffeine found in coffee, tea, and some soft drinks is a central
nervous system stimulant and bronchodilator. Herbs other than
coffee and tea that contain caffeine include kola, cocoa, and maté.
Though not a substitute for medical attention nor a long-term
solution, one or two strong cups of coffee or tea can help with the
occasional attack. (Some studies even indicate caffeine may prevent asthma attacks.) There are about 100–120 mg of caffeine in
an average drip-brewed cup of coffee, 40 mg in a cup of tea, and
40–50 mg in twelve ounces of caffeinated cola drinks. Warm
liquids in general soothe the bronchial tubes, while cold liquids
can trigger attacks in some people. So if you're drinking a cola or
some other caffeinated soft drink to alleviate a mild attack, it
shouldn't be served with ice.

Give a placebo. Tell the person you're administering something he or she knows works, dissolved in a liquid, for instance.
Recent studies have proven that in many cases of asthma, psycho-

emotional factors play an important role. Researchers who have conducted double-blind trials have found that giving a placebo may stop an asthma attack in as many as three out of five cases.

NATURAL REMEDIES FOR LONG-TERM TREATMENT OF ASTHMA

The following suggestions may complement or in some cases replace conventional drug management of asthma.

Take a nutritional supplement with extra vitamin B$_6$ and magnesium. Nutritionists agree that 500–750 mg of magnesium daily is a safe dose (the RDA is 350 mg). An effective therapeutic dose of B$_6$ is in the 50–150 mg range (the RDA is 2 mg).

Studies have shown that B$_6$ may reduce the incidence and severity of childhood asthma attacks, and that a magnesium deficiency may play a role in some types of asthma. High doses of magnesium may even stop an asthmatic episode while it's happening. (Among its other effects, magnesium helps muscles relax.) According to a study published in the February 27, 1987, issue of the *Journal of the American Medical Association,* "Magnesium sulfate (Epsom salts) given intravenously was able to treat asthma attacks quickly and effectively in ten humans tested."

Include other vitamins and minerals in an asthma prevention and treatment program. The principal ones to try are:

◆ two to five grams daily of vitamin C with bioflavonoids in mixed doses, or to bowel tolerance, which has been shown to reduce sensitivity to toxins in the air, prevent bronchial spasms, and act as an antihistamine
◆ 25,000 IU daily of vitamin A in the form of beta carotene, to repair tissue and stimulate immunity
◆ 50–150 mg daily of vitamin B complex, to stimulate immunity
◆ 400 IU daily of vitamin E, to destroy free radicals

Supplement your diet as well with high levels of the omega-3s and omega-6s, the desirable essential fatty acids that have a natural anti-inflammatory effect. Sources of beneficial EFAs include:

◆ fatty, cold-water fish such as salmon, cod, mackerel, sardines, bluefish, herring, and tuna, and oil supplements made from these fish

- canola, flaxseed, and hemp oil
- evening primrose, borage, and black-currant oil

Dietary recommendations for breathing problems are similar to those for allergies, notes registered dietitian Shari Lieberman. In addition to the above nutrients, she recommends an "insurance level" of the eleven vitamins, four minerals, and three trace elements for which the federal government has determined there are recommended dietary allowances (RDAs). Most supplement companies offer insurance-level, "one-a-day" formulas, though in most cases the pills or capsules are meant to be taken up to six times per day. Such supplementation often exceeds the RDAs, thus providing greater protection against marginal nutrient deficiencies.

Take an antiasthma herb to improve breathing and lung function. Here are three favorites among herbalists:

- Ginkgo *(Ginkgo biloba)* is an ancient Chinese herb that's been used for thousands of years to treat asthma, allergies, and coughs. Practitioners of traditional Chinese medicine spray a tea made from the leaves into the throat for asthma, notes herbalist Christopher Hobbs, author of *Ginkgo: Elixir of Youth.*

    Scientists have isolated an active ingredient, ginkgolide B, that interferes with a substance in the body known as platelet activation factor (PAF). PAF causes several kinds of cells in the body to secrete chemicals that create inflammation. PAF can thus constrict bronchial tubes and play a role in asthma attack. Studies have shown that subjects who took ginkgo have experienced a significant inhibited response to the allergens.

    Herbal ginkgo preparations are widely available. A typical dosage is 40 mg three times per day of a standardized extract containing 24 percent ginkgo heterosides.
- Coltsfoot *(Tussilago farfara)* is not fast-acting enough for acute attacks, though it has been used as a cough and congestion remedy by Chinese and Indian ayurvedic healers for thousands of years and today remains a popular cough remedy in Europe. Research indicates that the leaves contain substances that can soothe inflamed mucous membranes and suppress asthma attacks. It's usually taken as an infusion or tincture. The herb is potentially toxic in large doses, and the FDA has it on the list of herbs of

"undefined safety." Thus it should be used only for short periods of time, preferably under the guidance of a knowledgeable practitioner. Pregnant women should not use it.

♦ Mullein *(Verbascum thapsus)* is another traditional respiratory remedy. It contains mucilage, a substance that soothes the throat by becoming slippery as it absorbs water. Dried leaves or flowers can be brewed into a tea, or it can be taken as a tincture. (Do not use mullein oil, which is intended for use as ear drops.)

Relax, using a yoga exercise, biofeedback technique, guided imagery, or whatever appeals to you. Even for asthma attacks that are not triggered by an emotional factor, anxiety can be a major contributor that makes an attack worse. Learning how you can best relax is important, to use both during an attack as well as on a regular basis to help prevent one.

♦ The most basic yoga position for relaxation is the appropriately named corpse pose, in which you lie on your back with feet slightly apart and arms about six inches from your side, palms up. Close your eyes and allow all the muscles of the body to relax and sink into the floor. Breathe deeply using the abdomen. Starting with the feet and moving up to the scalp, relax each individual part of the body, releasing tension through the out-breath. As you tell your ankles to relax, your calf muscles, your thighs, you may be surprised to feel tension released that you haven't consciously noticed. When all parts of the body are relaxed, clear your mind by focusing on the breath and the rise and fall of the abdomen. Ten minutes of the corpse pose can be tremendously relaxing.

♦ Biofeedback works especially well for people whose asthma attacks are related to stress. The training is done with any of a number of devices that monitor subtle bodily functions, such as changes in brain waves, hand temperature, or electrical skin resistance. The subject learns how to stay in an "awake and aware" state, during which he or she can recognize and control feelings of tension. Usually it takes about ten weekly hour-long sessions to learn biofeedback. Eventually the subject can dispense with the machine and still consciously induce a relaxation response. (See "Resources" for how to find a biofeedback practitioner in your area.)

♦ Guided imagery techniques produce beneficial results for some people. For instance, asthma sufferers can imagine that their bronchial tubes are opening, relaxing, and widening in a way that allows the free and easy passage of air into and out of the lungs.

Place a few drops of essential oil of Eucalyptus on a tissue or clean cloth and inhale deeply. This is a popular aromatherapy treatment for clearing air passages. Eucalyptus has a regenerative effect on lung cells and promotes the uptake of oxygen from the lungs into the bloodstream.

Eat more of the foods that may have a healing effect on the lungs and the respiratory system, including:

♦ fatty, cold-water fish and other sources of beneficial EFAs
♦ black beans, black pepper, and garlic
♦ onions, which contain a compound that has been found to relieve asthma attacks

Lieberman also notes that cutting down on (non-omega-3 or - 6) fats and oils will help prevent inflammation in general.

PREVENTING ASTHMA

Long-term control should be married to preventive steps to be most effective:

Find out what triggers your asthma, and learn how to avoid it. Asthma's close association with allergies points to the importance of reducing exposure to high concentrations of pollutants, dust mites, pet dander, and the like. Not all asthma sufferers respond to specific allergens, but many do. Thus, if you have pets, move them outdoors, take steps to control dust mites (see Chapter 4 on allergic reactions), remove toxic household pesticides and cleaning products, and so forth. It should go without saying that asthma sufferers shouldn't smoke, and they should also try to avoid secondhand smoke, including that from a wood stove or a fireplace.

Asthma sufferers are also much more likely than the average person to have a food sensitivity, so you should try to become aware of how particular foods might affect our condition and then avoid them. Common problem foods include dairy, eggs, nuts, and seafood.

Food additives may also trigger an attack, especially sulfite compounds such as those found in beer, wine, shrimp, and dried fruits. (The government recently banned spraying sulfites on salads, which restaurants did to retard browning.) Many drugs also contain sulfites. Monosodium glutamate (MSG), found in some processed foods and still often used in Chinese restaurants, also triggers asthma.

Exercise in a way that benefits your condition rather than aggravates it. People who have "exercise-induced" asthma should not stop exercising, but rather take some simple steps to prevent an attack. For instance, they should warm up beforehand and keep a slower pace while exercising, breathing through the nose to prevent cold air from rushing in over the back of the throat. Also, sports that allow frequent moments of rest, such as baseball, doubles tennis, and bicycling are often tolerated better than ones that require constant prolonged movement. Walking is a good asthma exercise, as is swimming, which has the added benefit of exposing the asthmatic to a high-humidity environment that keeps the mouth from drying out. Also, one study showed that asthmatics who took 500 mg of vitamin C about ninety minutes before exercise had fewer bronchial spasms.

"I would recommend using a bronchodilator inhaler immediately before beginning exercise," adds Andrew Weil, M.D.

Learn how to breathe deeply using the abdomen. Many asthma victims breathe inefficiently, using the upper chest to draw in rapid, shallow breaths. Demonstrate to yourself full, deep, abdomen breathing by first lying on your back. Put one hand on your upper chest and the other on your stomach. Inhale through the nose, checking to make sure the hand on the stomach is rising and the one on the chest is not. Exhale slowly through pursed lips, pushing the abdomen down with the hand on the stomach. Practice this abdominal breathing so that you can do it while sitting, standing, walking, and eventually as your normal way of breathing.

Sing or play a wind instrument. These are excellent activities for asthmatics, as they strengthen abdominal muscles and help develop proper breathing.

Regularly practice a few basic yoga exercises that can relax the muscles used for breathing and open the airways. One of the best is the yogic posture or "asana" known as the cobra. Lie on your stomach with your forehead on the floor, palms down under the shoulders. Inhale deeply as you slowly use your back muscles to raise first your head and then your chest off the floor.

Straighten your arms as you tilt your head back as far as possible within your comfort zone (see illustration #13). Exhale as you slowly reverse the motion and come back to a prone position. Rest for a few breaths and then repeat.

 If poor movement, posture, or body use is interfering with healthy breathing patterns, consult any of a number of alternative practitioners who can help. Many people routinely carry the head too far forward on the spine, tilt or cock the neck to one side (a common problem among those who spend hours on the phone each day), or cave the shoulders in over the chest. Such habits can adversely affect breathing by contracting the rib cage and restricting air intake. Consider consulting with a specialist who focuses on proper body structure and the mechanics of movement and breathing. These include:

- ◆ osteopaths, who manipulate the muscles, bones, and joints (craniosacral osteopaths focus on the head and neck) to restore the body's natural ability to heal itself
- ◆ Rolfers, who practice a form of deep massage therapy that attempts to reorganize the body's structure by manipulating the fascia, the web of connective tissue around muscles and bones
- ◆ Feldenkrais practitioners, who have developed a bodywork and exercise system that seeks to reprogram the brain to allow more fluid and effective patterns of action, movement, and awareness

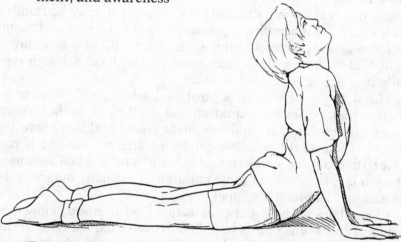

Illustration #13:

The yoga pose known as the cobra can help open the airways and relax the muscles used for breathing.

♦ Alexander Technique trainers, who help students become more aware of ways they can improve how they use their bodies to make routine movements

♦ chiropractors, who manipulate the spine and adjust the body's joints to align its parts and allow the free flow of vital energy

Any of these practitioners can help you change your breathing patterns for the better. See "Resources" for addresses of membership associations.

Avoid sudden inhalations of cold air. To prevent cold air from inducing an attack, use a scarf around or over the mouth in the winter months. Also try to acclimate to weather changes for a few minutes, such as by standing in the foyer of a building after coming in from extreme cold.

If you're a new mother, breast-feed your newborn for six months or longer. Breast-feeding won't affect asthma in the mother, but studies have shown that it plays a major role in preventing the child from developing asthma later in his or her life.

♦ Croup and Epiglottitis

If you've ever been awakened in the middle of a fall or spring night by the sound of your child's barklike cough and found the young one was having difficulty breathing, you may be familiar with croup. This condition primarily affects infants and young children aged two to six, often as the aftermath of a sore throat, mild cold, or laryngitis. It may develop over days, although typically it strikes at night.

Croup may be due to a viral or bacterial infection, or an allergy, that causes inflammation and swelling of the larynx and upper air passages. It tends to affect young children more frequently than adults because childrens' airways are much narrower than adults' and often clog with mucus when inflamed. Though common among some children, it's usually outgrown by adolescence as breathing tubes enlarge.

The characteristic noise associated with croup, known as stridor, results when air is breathed in over inflamed vocal cords. In addition to having difficulty breathing (particularly on the in-breath) and a loud, hacking cough, the child may be hoarse and restless.

BASIC FIRST AID FOR CROUP

Croup can usually be treated at home. It's important to remain calm and reassure the child, who may experience anxiety when he finds that he's having difficulty breathing. It may be tempting to put a spoon or some such object in the child's mouth to make breathing easier, but don't, it won't. Rather, encourage opening of the airways by humidifying the air. Cool, moist air is preferable to warm, moist air, but either will do. For instance:

Set up a cool-mist vaporizer, if you have one, or a humidifier in the child's room. You can improvise a tent of sheets and blankets over the bed to keep the humidity high near the child. Make sure the child doesn't, however, become chilled. Run the vaporizer or humidifier for several nights.

Bring the child into the bathroom, close the door, and turn on the hot water in the shower. Hold the child in your lap, not in the shower, while the room steams up. After ten to fifteen minutes the child's breathing should be more normal.

Expose the child to a draft of cool air. For instance, if it's a cool but not cold night, open a window in the child's bedroom and let in some fresh air. Or position the child in front of an open refrigerator and encourage a series of slow, deep breaths for a few minutes. Again, don't chill the victim.

Place a warm, wet washcloth over the child's mouth and nose. This provides instant humidity but should be explained to the child first, since it's often frightening to have something placed over one's face at a time when it's difficult to breathe.

If none of these methods has worked to ease breathing after twenty minutes or so, put the child in the car and set off for the emergency room. Leave the car window down, giving the cool-air treatment one last shot at easing the child's breathing. If the attack ends on the way to the hospital, you can turn around and go back home since the child no longer requires emergency medical treatment.

WHEN TO CALL A MEDICAL PROFESSIONAL

Though croup is rarely serious, it's important to be aware of symptoms that indicate a worsening condition. These include:

- extreme difficulty in breathing or symptoms of suffocation such as gasping

- ◆ a bluish tinge to the lips or skin, or extreme paleness
- ◆ a sudden high fever of 103° F or higher
- ◆ the child sits upright with his or her chin jutting forward and begins to drool

These symptoms may be signs of epiglottitis, a severe breathing-impaired condition that represents a major emegency. The epiglottis is a lidlike piece of tissue at the back of the throat that closes off the windpipe during swallowing. When a bacterial infection causes it to swell, it can completely block the victim's airway. Drooling, from not being able to swallow saliva, and the absence of a cough, are signs of epiglottitis rather than croup. Epiglottitis is most common among three- to six-year-olds.

If you suspect epiglottitis, get medical help as soon as possible. In the meantime keep the child upright in a sitting position.

At the hospital, practitioners will confirm the diagnosis of either croup or epiglottitis. Croup may be treated with nothing more than a cool-air vaporizer and perhaps a sedative. More severe cases and epiglottitis may require a throat X ray, intravenous antibiotics, and oxygen.

NATURAL REMEDIES FOR CROUP

Some natural remedies work well along with the cool, moist air that is the best treatment for croup. For instance:

Administer a homeopathic remedy to help counter croup. *Aconite* and *Spongia* are the two remedies homeopaths use most often for relieving croup.

- ◆ *Aconite* is usually prescribed for symptoms of a dry, loud cough and restlessness, the exact conditions at the onset of croup. Homeopath Jennifer Jacobs, M.D., says that *Aconite* is appropriate "particularly when a child wakes up in the middle of the night, there's a lot of fear and anxiety, and it comes on suddenly." The authors of *Homeopathic Medicine at Home*, Maesimund Panos, M.D., and Jane Heimlich, note that a 6X or 12X potency dose of *Aconite* at the onset of croup is often all that is needed to treat the condition, though a second dose of *Aconite* can be given an hour or so later if needed.
- ◆ *Spongia* is the remedy to turn to after *Aconite* if breathing becomes labored.

Add ten to fifteen drops of the essential oil of Eucalyptus to the humidifier or vaporizer. Eucalyptus is an excellent essential oil for the relief of breathing problems. It helps to alleviate coughing and eases the production of phlegm.

Make a cup of soothing catnip, chamomile, or savory tea. These traditional cough remedies are gentle enough for use any-time by children.

See also the acupressure suggestions under asthma for help with relieving breathing difficulties.

RECOVERY AND PREVENTION

The following vitamins and minerals will help a child recuperate from croup or epiglottitis.

- ◆ 500 mg vitamin C four times daily, to boost the immune system and control infection
- ◆ zinc lozenges, to promote immune function
- ◆ vitmin A in the form of beta carotene, 2,000 IU daily, to heal mucous membranes
- ◆ vitamin E, 50 mg daily, to destroy free radicals

◆ Hyperventilation, Panic Attack, and Breath-Holding

Children sometimes purposely alter their consciousness by breathing rapidly and shallowly and then holding their breath to the point of blacking out. Other kids, usually in the "terrible-two-plus" age, defy parents by holding their breath, sometimes to the point of fainting. Adults, on the other hand, may suffer from hyperventilation or "overbreathing" as an unintended conse-quence of an anxiety or panic attack. Though it doesn't usually result in fainting or unconsciousness, it can be scary and upset-ting.

During a hyperventilation episode, the victim paradoxically feels out of breath while breathing more and more rapidly. Some doctors refer to it as "overbreathing," as the victim is breathing too often but too shallowly. In addition to extreme anxiety or panic, overbreathing may also be caused by a drug reaction, an illness such as asthma, or an injury to the head.

Rapid, shallow breathing causes carbon dioxide levels in the blood to fall quickly. This leads to changes in the body's internal chemistry that reinforce the hyperventilation episode. The blood becomes more alkaline, muscles tighten in the throat and chest, and nerves are excited. The victim feels even more worried or panicked, leading to increased hyperventilation. Fortunately, a number of steps can be taken to break this vicious cycle.

Hyperventilation may be accompanied by:

- tightness in the throat
- pounding heart
- sweaty palms
- tingling or numbness in the hands, arms, and legs, or around the mouth
- lightheadedness
- cramping of the hands

Most attacks end even with no treatment after about twenty to thirty minutes, though some may last hours. People who suffer from them often experience repeat attacks.

Hyperventilation is often only one of the symptoms of a panic attack, which may also include palpitations, rapid heartbeat, chest pain, muscle spasms, dizziness, and fainting. Note that these symptoms can mimic a heart attack. A panic disorder is often related to a phobia about a specific situation or object, such as heights, crowds, or spiders.

Modern medicine offers a plethora of drugs for treating (perhaps more accurately, numbing) anxiety, including potent and habit-forming tranquilizers and antidepressants. Any benefit is mostly temporary, though in some cases drugs are an effective stopgap measure that buys time for more long-term stress-management approaches. A more sophisticated approach is taken for phobias, involving gradual desensitization.

Breath-holding by children is often preceded by hysterical crying. Most episodes are harmless and don't last long. Some can lead to fainting or convulsion like twitching that may be mistaken for an epilepsy attack. The latter, however, usually comes on without warning, not at the end of a fit. Once children reach age four they usually stop.

During the episode the child is often beyond reason. Afterward the parent should to try to identify the issues, often relating to self-identity, family love, and security, that cause the behavior and come to terms with the child on them.

BASIC FIRST AID FOR HYPERVENTILATION

The most popular remedy for an overbreathing episode is a low-tech but tried-and-true one: place a paper bag (but never a plastic bag) loosely over the victim's nose and mouth. The victim breathes into it, then rebreathes the same carbon-dioxide-rich air just expelled. Breathing in and out of one's cupped hands also works for some people. Usually doing this for three to five minutes wil cause carbon dioxide levels to rise in the blood. This in turn signals the part of the brain that controls respiration to order slower, deeper inhalations. Soon respiratory muscles begin to relax and breathing returns to normal.

If anxiety has triggered the hyperventilation, it's important to calm and reassure the victim in order to break the cycle of anxiety causing hyperventilation causing more anxiety. Encourage the victim to breathe or exhale more slowly and even try to hold his or her breath after inhaling. Have the victim sit and try to relax. It may help to distract the victim from his or her symptoms by talking.

The special deep-breathing technique described above for asthma attacks can also help during a hyperventilation episode. "Patients can learn to control their breathing and thereby relax the involuntary nervous system," Weil notes. For a panic attack he recommends a simple yogic breathing exercise that is a "natural tranquilizer of the nervous system" (see the section on recovery from near-drowning in Chapter 14 for a description). It may also work to have the victim hold his or her breath as long as possible between in- and out-breaths.

NATURAL REMEDIES FOR HYPERVENTILATION

In addition to the paper bag treatment, you might also try the following remedies for hyperventilation. If none of these tactics works within twenty to thirty minutes, contact your health care provider. A healer may also be helpful in determining the underlying causes of hyperventilation or anxiety attacks.

Administer the homeopathic remedy* Aconite *for shock or fear, or* Arsenicum *for anxiety. These can be taken every five minutes for four or five doses. Homeopaths stress that chronic attacks require constitutional treatment that will help victims improve their breathing and reduce stress.

Press on the acupressure point in the middle of the breast-bone, three thumb-widths up from base of bone, at the level of the heart. Position the fingertips of either hand on the point and press firmly. Suggest that the person close his or her eyes and concentrate on taking slow, deep breaths for at least two minutes. Gach notes that in the Orient this point is known as "sea of tranquillity" and is pressed to help relieve anxiety, chest tension, fear, hysteria, and other emotional imbalances.

For mild anxiety drink a warm cup of calming herbal tea. The most immediately calming herb, according to herbalist Christopher Hobbs, is California poppy. For relief faster than a tea will bring, put a half a teaspoon of the extract or tincture in warm water and drink every twenty to thirty minutes. Valerian and chamomile are also calming herbs, though milder than California poppy.

Inhale the aroma from the essential oil of Lavender. The aromatic volatile oil obtained from Lavender plants is widely used in cosmetics and perfumes. Aromatherapists have found that when inhaled through the nose, Lavender stimulates a region of the brain in a way that has a sedating effect on the central nervous system. It thus helps reverse the effects of sudden stress and anxiety, including out-of-control breathing. Simply sprinkle four drops of Lavender on a tissue and inhale deeply.

The East Indian ylang-ylang (pronounced *ee-lan ee-lan*) tree *(Cananga odorata var. genuina)* is the source for an essential oil that is less common than Lavender but potentially as effective for treating abnormally fast breathing. The essential oil of Ylang-ylang yields an intense scent that reduces blood pressure, inhibits adrenaline, and calms nerves. Sprinkle a few drops onto a tissue and inhale.

Take the combination flower remedy Rescue Remedy orally, or Rock Rose, one of its components. To take Rescue Remedy, add three to four drops of the liquid to a small glass of water and have the victim sip it slowly. If no water is available, put three to four drops of undiluted Rescue Remedy directly on the tongue. Repeat every half hour until the patient is calm.

These work well for terror and panic.

For a child who is holding his breath, after he recovers consciousness give the homeopathic remedy Chamomilla every five minutes for up to half an hour. *Chamomilla* is a remedy commonly prescribed for children that can also be used to calm a colicky infant. It can help whenever a child is crying angrily or throwing a screaming tantrum or is otherwise inconsolable and extremely irritable.

Provide extra potassium and magnesium for a child recovering from a breath-holding attack. Many common fresh foods are high in potassium, including winter squash, bananas, cantaloupes, lentils, and split peas. Foods high in magnesium include kidney beans and soybeans. Most fresh fruit juices and fresh vegetable broths are high in electrolyte-replacing minerals, as are sports drinks such as Gatorade. You can buy potassium supplements at natural foods stores, but the tab size is limited by law to 99 mg (higher dosages are available by prescription only), about what you get in one inch of banana.

"Taking these minerals right away can help normalize an electrolyte imbalance in the blood induced by hyperventilation," notes naturopath Joseph Pizzorno.

PREVENTING HYPERVENTILATION

There are a number of positive steps most victims of hyperventilation can take to prevent attacks.

Learn better breathing habits. This one is crucial for sufferers of hyperventilation. Overbreathers tend to breathe too rapidly (fifteen to twenty times per minute) even when not having an attack. Proper breathing, from the diaphragm, should result in a normal respiration rate of eight to twelve breaths per minute. A technique that some people find helpful is to breathe with the idea that you are "smelling the world" rather than just sucking in air.

Take positive steps to reduce tension. It's important to identify and avoid situations that trigger episodes, or better yet learn to deal with them in a constructive way. Many people with panic disorders have benefited by learning meditation techniques and safe methods for emotional release.

The body's ability to deal with stress is also adversely affected by unhealthful habits such as poor diet and lack of exercise.

Avoid stimulants. Drugs such as caffeine and nicotine are potential hyperventilation triggers for some people.

Breathing is a major physical function that the human body accomplishes some twenty thousand times per day, each time bringing life-giving energy in the form of oxygen to the lungs and the blood, and eventually to all the body's tissues. When breathing doesn't work well, the whole body operates at less than its optimum. Taking the time and making the effort to alleviate the breathing problems associated with asthma attacks, croup, and hyperventilation is well worth it.

NINE

Burns

THIS CHAPTER COVERS:

◆ *sunburn*
◆ *chemical burns*
◆ *electric shock*
◆ *lightning strike*

SEE "CHAPTER 16: EYE AND EAR EMERGENCIES" FOR:

◆ *chemical and thermal burns to the eyes*

SEE "CHAPTER 17: HEAT ILLNESS" FOR:

◆ *heatstroke*

Burns result from contact with such heat sources as open fires, hot liquids, the sun, chemicals (internally or externally), electricity, or radiation. Burns are among the most frequently encountered emergencies. Not surprisingly, there are also a wide variety of natural first-aid measures and home remedies for burns. While some of these (such as applying butter to a burn) were never good ideas and have been discredited, many other natural treatments have begun to gain acceptance even among conventional health practitioners.

KNOW YOUR BURNS

Burns are classified as first-, second-, or third-degree by the severity of their damage to living tissue and by how many layers of skin are affected. Treatment is also affected by the size of the burn, the burn's location on the body, as well as the burning agent.

◆ First-degree burns, from minor accidents such as briefly touching a hot object or staying in the sun too long, affect only the epidermis, the top layer of skin. The area turns pink or red and there's pain and mild swelling though no blisters. In general, first-degree burns will heal in three to four days.

◆ Second-degree burns, such as from a deep sunburn or spilling boiling water on the skin, damage the two upper layers, the dermis and epidermis, of the skin. They are very painful and cause swelling that lasts several days, blistering, and often scar formation. Most such burns will take a week or longer to heal.

◆ Third-degree burns, such as from prolonged exposure to a hot substance or from a serious electrical shock, injure all skin layers, including the subcutaneous tissue, usually with extensive damage to muscles and other tissues as well. These burns can lead to severe loss of fluids and electrolytes, shock, and death. Unlike first- and second-degree burns, third-degree burns destroy the bodily cells that help to continually form new skin, so healing must happen not from under the skin upward but from the outer edges of burned skin inward. The burn areas may be oozing, raw, or either charred or whitish in appearance. Ironically, the victim may feel little or no pain, since the nerve cells that transmit pain messages to the brain are often destroyed as well. Third-degree burns often take months to heal.

In addition to determining how severe a burn is, it is important to determine how extensive it is. Any second-degree burn that covers more than 10 percent of the body should be considered severe, as well as a third-degree burn that covers more than 2 percent of the body. Two easy methods to determine the size of a burn are the rule of nines and the handprint measure:

◆ The rule of nines breaks the body's surface into sections, with the head, the right arm, and the left arm representing 9 percent each of the body's total surface area. The chest, the back, the right leg, and the left leg each represent 18 percent of the body, with the groin area the remaining one percent.

◆ The handprint measure allows one to calculate the size of a burn by using the hand, including palm and fingers, to represent roughly one percent of the body's surface area.

Finally, burns that affect the eyes, fingers, genital/anal areas, or face are potentially more serious than those inflicted on other parts of the body.

◆ Sunburn

Some amount of sunlight is healthful and beneficial. After all, the skin uses it to produce most of the vitamin D the body needs. Without vitamin D, a number of the body's systems start to go awry, including the bones' ability to absorb calcium from the blood. Too much sunlight, on the other hand, can cause both the familiar painful, red skin and a toxic condition in the body from an excess of vitamin D.

Ultraviolet light is the part of the sun's spectrum that is potentially most damaging to skin. Scientists distinguish two types: ultraviolet "A" (UVA) and "B" (UVB). The shorter UVB rays are strongest between ten A.M. and two P.M. and cause most cases of sunburn. Longer UVA rays predominate in early morning and late afternoon. Though less frequently the main cause of a burn, they can burn and can cause photosensitivity reactions as well. Most ultraviolet rays can penetrate light clouds and even light-weight clothing.

Don't take sunburn lightly. Left untreated it can result in a blistering second-degree burn. Various factors can combine to cause a bad sunburn even on a cloudy day, including the following:

- ◆ People with delicate skin, light-colored hair, and blue eyes burn more easily than do darker-skinned people. Dermatologists say that fair-skinned people can damage their skin even while slowly getting tan.
- ◆ High altitudes allow for greater exposure to burning rays. At six thousand feet the skin burns twice as fast as at sea level.
- ◆ Photosensitizing agents can increase sunburning. These include some prescription drugs (tetracycline and certain oral contraceptives, antihistamines, and tranquilizers); food additives (including saccharine); some sunscreens; and skin contact with certain plants and essential oils (including Lemon and Bergamot).

Some of the photosensitizing agents can not only make sunburn worse, they may cause a type of allergic reaction known as photoallergy.

The most direct way to prevent sunburn is of course to limit your exposure during midday hours of highest levels of harmful ultraviolet. You should also wear protective clothing, including a broad-brimmed hat. Sunscreens are effective, depending upon their sun-protective factor (SPF) rating. If you have fair skin and burn easily, choose one with a rating of 12 or above. If you sometimes tan lightly, you can use 6–12, while if you burn infrequently or almost never (even black skin can burn sometimes), try a sunscreen rated 2–6.

Sunblocks such as zinc oxide block almost all of the sun's rays and are good for highly exposed areas such as the lips, nose, and neck. If you're caught out in the wilderness without a screen or block, try charcoal or wood ashes. Ideally sunscreens should be applied a half hour or so before exposure to sunlight, to allow for full skin penetration. They should also be reapplied after swimming. Allergic reactions are more common with PABA-based brands.

Natural sunscreens use some of the same UVA- and UVB-blocking chemicals that conventional sunscreens use. That's because the FDA has listed twenty-one active ingredients, including para-aminobenzoic acid (PABA), from which sunscreen manufacturers must choose to call their product a sunscreen. Some of these chemicals can cause allergic reactions in some people. What distinguishes natural sunscreens? "We don't use mineral oil, petrolatum, paraffin wax, PABA, artificial coloring, or animal by-products . . . and we don't do any animal testing," Jeffrey Light, owner of Jason Natural Products of Culver City, California, told *Natural Health*.

In addition to aloe and the other treatments listed under "Natural First-Aid Remedies for Burns," here are a few that work especially well for sunburn:

Apply chamomile cream that's been mixed with five or six drops of Peppermint oil. Herbalist Christopher Hobbs notes that this has an immediate cooling and anti-inflammatory effect.

Apply vinegar to the burn. Vinegar is a popular home remedy for sunburn. "I've found that nothing is better for sunburn than plain old pure cider vinegar," says a woman from Fairport, New York. "Splash it on to take advantage of its cooling effects."

Apply cool compresses soaked in whole milk. Exactly why this folk remedy seems to soothe a sunburn is a mystery, though many people swear it's an effective treatment.

Apply used black or green tea bags to skin. This works well if the burn is limited to a small area of the body. The tannic acid from black or green tea helps reduce redness and swelling.

Chemical Burns

Chemical burns may be limited to a small skin injury, or they may be so extensive as to cause a bodywide reaction. Lye, strong acids and alkalies, and harsh detergents and cleansers are the most common agents, though exposure is more frequent in industrial settings than in the home. Chemical burns can also develop immediately or over time. Symptoms might include:

◆ a rash or blisters on the skin
◆ local pain despite little evidence of skin damage
◆ headaches or dizziness
◆ difficulty breathing

Before treating it's best to try to identify the product. If it's a household product and the container is available, read the label for instructions and call a poison hot line for advice. Don't try to neutralize a substance without such professional advice.

The first step is to prevent further contamination. If the chemical is dry, brush it off with a towel, not your bare hands. Next, remove contaminated clothing and jewelry from the victim, then flush the burn area with cold running water, for ten minutes or longer. Apply cool, wet compresses to skin and cover with loose, dry, sterile dressings. Call for medical help while checking the ABCs and watching for symptoms of shock.

If a chemical is causing a burn to the eye, place it under cold running water in such a way that the runoff doesn't enter the other eye. Try not to rub the eye. Close the lid, cover with a bandage, and get medical help (see "Chapter 16: Eye and Ear Emergencies" for more information on treating chemical and thermal burns to the eyes).

◆ Electric Shock

The body is a good conductor of electricity. When it comes into direct contact with household current, or high-voltage lines, electricity surges through tissues, breaking down skin and baking internal organs. It is possible for an electric burn to look minor but for it to have caused serious internal injuries. In the worst cases it will damage the heart, stop breathing, or cause death. Symptoms include:

- ◆ a sensation that may range from tingling to a severe jolt
- ◆ skin burns where electricity entered and left body
- ◆ muscular pain, headache, and loss of consciousness

The severity of an electric shock depends on the strength of the current, how long the victim is exposed to it, whether he or she is in contact with any insulation, and the path the electricity takes through the body. A brief shock from household current, for instance, will usually cause only skin burns. If the victim was taking a bath, though, the high conductivity of water would make the shock much more severe. Any shock in which the victim freezes to the current is serious, as well.

If a victim is in contact with a live current, the best action is to shut it off as quickly as possible. Pull a plug (just turning off an appliance may not be enough) or throw a main power switch. Touching the person directly will allow the current to flow into your body.

Even coming close to someone who is in contact with a live high-voltage line can be dangerous, since the current could arc as far as twenty feet and possibly just claim another victim. Unfortunately, the safest way to rescue a person touching a high-voltage line is time-consuming: call the power company to have the power turned off. In almost all such emergencies, death will have been instantaneous in any case. If you're in a car near a downed power line, stay put till the power is turned off, taking care not to touch anything metallic in the car.

If a household current can't easily be shut off, safely try to push or pull the victim from the current. Standing on some type of insulation (a thick book works well), use a dry piece of heavy wood (not metal), such as a board or chair, to move the victim off the current. It's also possible to loop a length of rope around the victim and pull him or her off.

Call for medical help, check the ABCs, and take steps to prevent or treat shock.

In addition to the treatments listed under "Natural First-Aid Remedies for Burns," here's one that is specific for electric shock or burn:

Take the homeopathic remedy **Phosphorus.** Take a 6X or 12X potency dose immediately. If necessary, follow up by taking another dose every thirty minutes for up to six doses after the shock.

◆ Lightning Strike

A thousand or so Americans are hit by lightning every year; about three hundred of them do not live to tell about the experience. Some of the fatalities result when a lightning bolt directly strikes a person, while others result from an indirect hit (lightning splashing off a nearby tree) or current carried through the ground from a nearby strike. Sadly, many of the fatalities, especially from the indirect hits, could probably have been avoided if proper emergency steps, including CPR, had been adminstered.

Many people wonder why more victims don't die when struck by lightning. After all, a lightning bolt typically generates 100 million volts, sometimes even up to 2 billion volts, of electrical potential. Fortunately, the duration of the event is one-thousandth of a second or so, usually resulting in the electricity's passing around the outside of the body rather than through it. Thus, internal organs can escape the damage that longer but lesser shocks inflict.

Which is not to say that getting hit by lightning is nothing but a momentary annoyance. Being surrounded by that much electricity for even a fraction of a second is enough to blast the clothes and shoes right off your body. Belt buckles or jewelry that are not blasted off may be red-hot and inflict serious burns. A lightning strike can momentarily stop your heart, paralyze your breathing, and even change your personality. Victims may also experience temporary blindness, deafness, and confusion. Even if you're not hit directly by lightning, the blast of exploding, super-heated air from a nearby strike can break bones and inflict other injuries.

Immediate and prolonged CPR (see "Chapter 3: Basic Emergency Care") is the principal first-aid response to revive a victim of lightning strike. Often the heart will begin to beat again soon after a strike. The brain may take longer to kick in, and until it does, the victim needs mouth-to-mouth resuscitation to prevent death from a second cardiac arrest.

Some common sense precautions can usually prevent strikes. Lightning tends to strike the tallest object in an area (the Empire State Building gets hit thousands of times every year), so you want to avoid becoming that tallest object. Don't be caught out in the open, for instance, carrying an umbrella, swinging a golf club, or waving a fishing rod. Getting under a tall tree is not a good idea either, since lightning can strike the tree and jump to persons next to the tree or carry through the ground and hit people nearby. It's better to find a low area with a thick growth of small trees. A hardtop car is pretty safe, since if it's struck, the electricity will pass through the metal frame. Inside a home, with windows and doors closed, is also safe, though you should avoid contact with metal objects, the telephone, and plumbing. Being out in the water, such as in a small aluminum boat, is anything but safe. Get to shore or pull into the protective shadow of a larger boat. Don't assume that a lightning risk has passed because a thunderstorm has moved off: lightning can strike in a wide area around storms.

◆ Home or Hospital?

Knowing the source, severity, size, and location of a burn will help to determine whether to try to self-treat it at home or go immediately to a doctor or the hospital emergency room. The most important general guidelines to keep in mind are:

- ◆ Most first- and second-degree burns of limited size can be safely treated at home.
- ◆ Extensive second-degree burns (that cover over 10 percent of an adult's body or 5 percent of a child's) and all third-degree burns require medical attention in addition to first-aid care.
- ◆ Since it is difficult to judge the severity of a burn that results from swallowing or inhaling scalding water or steam, if there is significant pain or symptoms of shock, see a doctor immediately.
- ◆ Because a child's skin is more sensitive to heat than an adult's, a child can be burned more seriously and at lower temperatures. Thus, if pain from a first- or second-degree burn persists for more than two days, get a doctor's advice.

♦ Most chemical and electrical burns call for a doctor's attention, since the extent and severity of such burns are difficult to judge visually.

♦ If a burn becomes increasingly painful two days or more after the accident, if it discharges pus, if the victim is having difficulty moving his or her joints, or if high fever develops, seek medical care.

If you do go to a hospital emergency room for a relatively minor first- or second-degree burn, expect to have the burn cleaned and dressed. You may also be offered over-the-counter anesthetic sprays or a "preventive" prescription for antibiotics. These can cause allergic reactions and lower resistance, and you may want to consider safer natural alternatives such as those listed below under "Natural First-Aid Remedies for Burns."

Extensive third-degree burns may require hospitalization and fluid-replacement therapy, pain medication, special antiburn products such as Silvadene cream or the Biobrane bandage (a synthetic membrane dressing with pores that direct fluid up and into an absorbent gauze layer), and possibly skin grafts. Some recent developments for extensive burns include artificial skin and cloned skin. To clone skin, doctors remove a small section of a burn victim's healthy skin, nurture it in a special laboratory culture, and graft it back onto the burn site. Cloned skin replaces only the outer layers of skin, so even more serious burns may require artificial skin.

Conventional doctors may not be aware of nutritional supplements for hospitalized burn victims, even though recent scientific research has established that certain nutrients promote the healing of burns. Probably the best known special nutritional formula used in hospitals for serious burns is produced by the Shriners Burn Institute in Cincinnati. The formula is made from whey protein, fish oils, and other nutrients and is high in protein (needed for tissue repair), zinc, the vitamins A, C, and E, and omega-3 fatty acids. If you are ever hospitalized for a burn, you may need to educate your doctor on the importance of nutritional supplements to your recovery.

♦ Basic First Aid for Burns

The three most important first-aid objectives for burn treatment are to remove the victim from the heat source, prevent or treat shock, and decrease the temperature of the burned area.

Remove the victim from the heat source. In the vast majority of cases the burn victim has taken the precaution of moving away from the heat source, by covering up after being sunburned or dropping the hot pan, for instance. Two special cases to keep in mind are contact with a live current, and third-degree burns that are so severe the victim might not be experiencing the pain that would cause him or her to pull away from the hot object.

Prevent or treat shock. Before proceeding to treat the burn itself, check for serious injury and make sure that breathing and circulation are restored if necessary and shock is prevented or treated (see Chapter 3). Try to estimate the severity and size of the burn and call an ambulance if necessary.

Decrease the temperature of the burned area. The next priority is to lower the temperature of the burn, since skin can continue to burn even after it has been removed from a heat source. Thus, there is the possibility of a first-degree burn unnecessarily becoming a second-degree burn, and so forth. To prevent this from happening:

◆ Remove clothes that are soaked with chemicals or scalding water.
◆ Remove any heat-retaining jewelry, and if second-degree burns are a possibility, remove all rings and bracelets even from unburned parts, since swelling may come on quickly.
◆ For chemical burns, use large amounts of running water to flush chemicals away from the skin.

Cooling a burn with water (or other drinkable cold liquid) is one of the most important steps for treating the vast majority of burns. For first- and second-degree burns that cover a small area of unbroken skin, run cold but not freezing water over the area. If you're at a sink, fill the basin and immerse the burn in the cold water for as long as it takes for the pain to subside. If water is limited, wrap the burned area with clean, wet cloths and apply water at frequent intervals. Cold water and cold compresses can stop the burn and relieve the pain by helping to close damaged blood vessels below the skin surface and preventing further swelling and fluid loss. These steps can be especially effective if applied in the first thirty seconds after the burn.

Apply cold water for as long as it's necessary to stop the pain, or until the area no longer feels hot. This may be ten minutes or longer. Cooling-water therapy is a simple, helpful treatment for burns that's often not used as effectively as it should be.

If skin is blistered or broken, use ice encased in a plastic bag instead of water. Take care not to leave ice directly on skin long enough to cause frostbite.

Two other important steps to take after attempting to reduce the temperature of a burn include:

- ◆ For major burns, have the victim drink fluids to prevent becoming dehydrated.
- ◆ Elevate arms or legs that have suffered second-degree or worse burns to prevent swelling.

The most common cautions about burn treatment include:

- ◆ Don't apply butter, grease, or other fats to a burn, as they impede healing and can increase the chance of infection.
- ◆ Protect burns from exposure to the sun.
- ◆ Cold-water treatments should not be used for third-degree burns larger than the size of a silver dollar because of the danger of causing shock or hypothermia. Also, do not immerse the whole body in ice water.
- ◆ It's best not to break open blisters because of the increased chance of infection. If a blister does break open, allow the fluid to drain and leave the loose skin in place before applying gauze.
- ◆ In general first-degree burns heal best when left uncovered by any type of dressing or bandage—but kept clean. On the other hand, it is usually best to cover second-degree burns, especially if they are likely to rub against clothing, and all third-degree burns. Use a bandage or clean, dry, nonfluffy cloth to prevent infection.

◆ Natural First-Aid Remedies for Burns

After you've taken care of the three most basic first-aid steps, it is time to turn to some natural and home remedies that can relieve pain and help prevent infection. Although severe burns require professional care, even they respond to home treatment measures. According to naturopath Ross Trattler in *Better Health Through Natural Healing*, "There are a vast number of home remedies or first aid for burns. Of this large variety, however, several stand out as the most effective. They are simple, readily available, and reliable. Most have slowly graduated from the 'folk remedy' status to at least the fringe of standard orthodox practice."

Trattler's "most effective" list includes "hydrotherapy" (using water to heal), such as the above-described cold-water techniques, and the vitamins E and C, both applied externally and taken internally. Other natural healers successfully use herbs (particularly aloe and comfrey) and other ingredients in poultices, compresses, and teas; homeopathic remedies; bath soaks; massage; and vitamins and minerals to help promote the healing of burns. Let's look at the consensus favorites.

Spread on soothing fresh aloe. Most natural practitioners agree that fresh aloe is best. Aloe requires little more than occasional watering to grow, so it's an easy houseplant to keep around (see illustration #14). To use it, first clean and cool the burn with water. Break a few inches off one of the older, lower leaves of the aloe plant, slice it lengthwise, squeeze its gel onto the burn, and allow it to dry. It is especially effective to use as soon as possible on first- or second-degree burns. Reapply four to six times a day.

"This remedy is inexpensive and always available, and the plant actually benefits from having its older leaves cut off," notes an aloe user in Ames, Iowa.

Fresh aloe is safe to use on broken skin and can also be applied after healing begins. Allergic reactions are uncommon, but discontinue use if one does occur. Aloe gel should not be taken internally for a burn. (Some herbalists recommend aloe tablets or capsules, prepared from the plant's latex rather than its gel, taken orally for other conditions, such as constipation.)

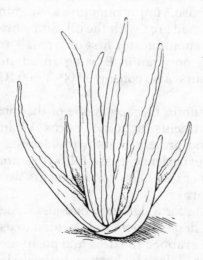

Illustration #14:

The leaves of the aloe plant contain a gel that can soothe the pain and redness of minor burns.

Though some bottled aloe products may not contain the healing ingredients of fresh aloe, others do and can be effective. Look for juices or gels of 96–100 percent pure aloe, without mineral oil, paraffin waxes, or coloring, and that haven't been "stabilized" or preserved with alcohol, which will neutralize aloe's skin-healing properties. Richard Israel, author of *The Natural Pharmacy Product Guide*, recommends Naturade Aloe Vera 80, which is 96 pecent aloe gel and also contains the herb comfrey. According to Israel, "This is a fine product to keep in mind when you want to soothe a painful sunburn or treat other minor wounds." Another good product is Burn Gel from Aerobic Life Products, which contains aloe as well as other herbs.

Naturopathic doctor Joseph Pizzorno, coauthor of the *Encyclopedia of Natural Medicine*, has a cool tip: "Keep your bottle of aloe gel or juice in the refrigerator. Or, put some in an ice tray and make aloe cubes. When you get a burn, apply the gel cold or frozen to combine the best of two first-aid treatments."

A succulent member of the lily family, aloe has been used to treat burns and wounds for thousands of years. Scientific studies done over the past fifty years support its power to speed the healing of burns and help prevent infection. Most dramatically, a recent animal study reported in the medical journal *Plastic and Reconstructive Surgery* showed that aloe-treated burns healed in an average of thirty days while untreated burns took fifty.

Apply vitamin E to the burn. Vitamin E oil is available in capsules or bottles at drugstores, supermarkets, and natural foods stores. For a small burn, simply puncture a vitamin E capsule and gently cover the burned area with the oil. Some brands of vitamin E may sting so you should test it first on a small area. To apply to a larger area, spray on vitamin E using an oil atomizer. Repeat every one to four hours. Also consume 800–1,600 IU of the vitamin daily.

This topical vitamin therapy is one of the most popular and effective home treatments for minor burns. Vitamin E can help promote healing and prevent scars from forming even for third-degree burns. The experience of the following woman from New York City is typical of the many endorsements we've heard about vitamin E oil for burns:

"I was preparing for a date and had just ironed a blouse and put my iron on the floor to cool off. I decided to ask a question of my tarot cards, so I grabbed the deck and positioned myself cross-legged on the floor. I leaned back a little and my bare back attached itself to the edge of the still-hot iron. For the first time in my life, I actually saw stars! There was a huge, long burn on my back and some of the skin had come off. It was painful, but I was determined to go out on my date. I took a small bottle of vitamin E and began to rub the oil all over the burn. The pain quickly subsided. I applied more vitamin E oil that night and every day for the next couple of days.

"I was sure I was going to have a long, vertical scar, but instead at the end of three days the burn was completely healed and my skin was once again smooth. Anytime I burn myself now, I apply 20,000 or more units of bottled vitamin E oil. I always keep a bottle in my medicine cabinet. It's much more handy than trying to use the oil from capsules, since you need quite a bit to get the full benefits."

Vitamin E oil can be combined with other substances, too. For instance, you can squeeze some aloe from a leaf and mix it with vitamin E out of a capsule.

Apply vitamin C to the burn. External applications of vitamin C can help to reduce pain and swelling and the chance of infection. To use vitamin C externally, crush 1,000 mg of C into powder and dissolve it in one cup of tepid water to make a 1–3 percent solution. Use a clean plant mister to spray this on the burn every two to four hours. It is especially effective between vitamin E applications. Also, take one gram of vitamin C internally every hour for the first two to three hours after a bad burn, and then two to five grams or to bowel tolerance daily in mixed doses until the burn is healed.

Apply a calendula-based poultice, ointment, or cream. "This is the number one herbal burn remedy," according to herbalist Christopher Hobbs. He also highly recommends:

- chamomile, in the form of the cream product Chamocare, chamomile essential oil mixed with a cream, or as an ointment or salve
- ginger, as an essential oil sprinkled on gauze or cotton and applied, or even better as a fresh poultice made by grating fresh ginger and packing it into cheesecloth until wet and juicy.
- St.-John's-wort oil, applied right on a burn during the acute phase, or onto a sunburn.
- a plantain or comfrey poultice or compress

To make a comfrey poultice, clean the burn and then wrap some dried, powdered root (available in most natural foods stores) in thin gauze and apply to the skin. Comfrey can also be applied directly to the skin (apply some vitamin E oil first to make it easier to remove the comfrey) and covered with a clean, damp cloth, or made into a paste and applied to the skin. These types of poultice present more of a risk of causing a skin rash on some people, although such reactions are rare.

To make a compress, first make an infusion (steep like a tea) or decoction (boil and strain) from the fresh herb. Then soak a clean cloth of linen, cotton, or gauze in the infusion or decoction and apply it to the burn.

Apply the traditional Chinese burn ointment known as Jing Wan Hong. For minor burns, after cleaning the area apply Jing Wan Hong directly to the burn, or apply to sterile gauze that is put over the burn and secured with a bandage. It's not necessary to reapply.

This is one of the more popular topical treatments in China, widely available at drugstores there. It is used for first- and second-degree burns caused by the sun, steam, hot water, electricity, and chemicals. The name translates roughly as "capital city many red color," referring to the red of fire and inflamed skin. Jing Wan Hong is a prepared medicine containing eight Chinese herbs, including species of lobelia and angelica. The ointment reduces the immediate pain of a burn, prevents infection, and speeds recovery. It's a thin, brownish, medicinal-smelling ointment, slightly greasy to the touch.

Jing Wan Hong is the generic name. In the U.S. it's often available as Ching Wan Hung, made by the Tianjin Drug Manufactory of China. They produce it in tubes of 30 and 500 grams (approximately one ounce and one pound, respectively). It's available at some well-stocked natural foods pharmacies and in Oriental pharmacies, or from mail-order suppliers of Oriental herbal products (see "Resources").

Take the popular homeopathic burn remedy Cantharis. Prepared from a type of Spanish fly whose bite causes burning pain, *Cantharis* is thus used to relieve that very symptom. Take it internally immediately after the burn and again every half an hour until the acute pain is gone. Other homeopathic remedies to take internally to help heal burns include:

- *Phosphorus* for electrical burns
- *Urtica urens* for first- or second-degree burns that sting and itch
- *Aconite* or *Arnica* for the most severe burns, to prevent and treat shock and fright

For external applications, *Calendula* or *Hypericum* sprays or lotions are especially effective for sunburn and painful first-degree burns, says homeopath Jennifer Jacobs, M.D. To make a spray, dilute one-half teaspoon of homeopathic tincture of *Calendula* or *Hypericum* in a cup of water and pour the solution in a clean spray bottle or atomizer. Prepared sprays of *Calendula* and *Hypericum* are widely available from homeopathic manufacturers. Applied to a burn, either of these remedies relieves pain and prevents infection.

Jacobs emphasizes that homeopathic remedies can and should be combined with other first-aid measures for burns.

Take a whole-body soak in the tub. For minor burns that cover a large part of the body, such as most sunburns, there are two "whole-body soaks" that can offer some immediate benefits:

- Fill your tub with tepid water, add colloidal oatmeal bath soak, and soak for thirty minutes or so. Colloidal oatmeal is available as the product Aveeno from most drugstores. It is oatmeal that has been milled to a fine powder; don't use breakfast oatmeal because the flakes are too large to dissolve in water and do any good. When dissolved in water, oatmeal thinly coats the skin to relieve itchiness and act as a protective barrier against further irritation.
- Dissolve one-half cup of baking soda in warm bathwater, let the water cool to a comfortable temperature, and soak for thirty minutes or so.

Take advantage of the healing potential contained in a few drops of the essential oil of Lavender. For small, minor burns, apply a few drops of Lavender right onto the affected area or put five to seven drops on a cool, dry compress and cover the burn. Secure at the edges only with adhesive tape, and repeat as needed. If the burn is still not healed after twenty-four hours, dilute six drops of Lavender in one teaspoon of carrier oil or lotion and apply the mix to the affected area. Repeat two or three times per day until healed. For larger burns such as sunburn, dilute Lavender in a carrier oil, or mix with aloe gel, and spread over the skin.

Lavender's almost immediate soothing effect on a burn was what inspired the French cosmetic chemist Dr. René-Maurice Gattefossé to devote his life to exploring the healing potential of essential oils. After burning his hand, he plunged it, on impulse, into a container of Lavender oil. The hand healed quickly and without blistering. Gattefossé went on to coin the term *aroma-*

therapy in the late 1920s and pioneer a new branch of natural medicine.

"Every home should have a bottle of Lavender, if no other oil, because it is so effective in the treatment of burns and scalds," according to Valerie Ann Worwood, author of *The Complete Book of Essential Oils and Aromatherapy.* Lavender's constituents include a highly fragrant volatile oil that is widely used in cosmetics and perfumes. Alternative medical practitioners recommend the essential oil for its wound-healing properties. It promotes cell rejuvenation and relieves pain and swelling. It is mild enough to be applied full-strength even to broken skin.

Herbalist Christopher Hobbs also recommends essential oil of Peppermint for its cooling effect on burns. Peppermint has more potential as a skin irritant than Lavender when applied directly to a burn, so try only small amounts neat (undiluted) or dilute with carrier oil.

Tea Tree oil or cream is also soothing when applied to a burn. A reader from Dover, New Hampshire, says, "I have tried everything for burns, which I get frequently from cooking, and nothing worked until I tried Tea Tree. I once burned two fingers and put Tea Tree on one and nothing on the other. On the finger with the Tea Tree, the pain disappeared in minutes, the burn didn't blister, and the skin dried to form a thin scab that peeled off within a week. The other finger hurt for days, blistered, and took a week longer to heal."

Massage the acupressure point at the outside of the crease of the elbow. Acupressure expert Michael Reed Gach says that to locate this point, bend the arm and note where it forms a crease. Put the thumb on a point at the outer end of the crease and press slowly into the joint for a few minutes. Applying pressure at this point helps to relieve skin conditions involving pain, redness, and inflammation. Acupressure practitioners caution not to manipulate points on a burn, though other points around it are fine.

Try a time-tested folk remedy to relieve the pain of a burn. Here are a few suggestions that may work for you:

- Keep the burn immersed in cool, very salty water until the pain is gone. "Kosher salt works best," says acupuncturist Leah Fineberg of Santa Fe, New Mexico.
- Moisten strips of the brown sea vegetable kelp in cool water and apply them to the burn. Bacteria grow relatively readily on sea vegetables so don't use this method where skin is broken, and don't leave strips of kelp on for more than a few hours.

Herbalist Jeanne Rose, author of *Jeanne Rose's Modern Herbal* and other books, has this related suggestion. Mix a handful of kelp, one-half cup of baking soda, and two tablespoons of sea salt into a tepid bath to soothe a sunburn.

Brown sea plants such as kelp have been known for their medicinal value since at least 3000 B.C., when a Chinese physician wrote about them. Modern research has confirmed some of the healing powers of certain sea plants. Scientists have focused on a thick, sticky substance known as mucilage and the gelatinous material alginate found in brown sea plants. Kelp has mucilage ducts along its surface to coat its exterior and prevent drying out between tides. Alginates have been widely used by the cosmetic and food industries for decades as emulsifiers and stabilizers, to control gelling. Alginate fibers have also recently begun to be used in surgical gauze and bandages, due to their ability to stop bleeding (see Chapter 6). Researchers have found that when they spray a thin layer of alginate gel over a burn, moisture loss is prevented and the burn heals more quickly.

A Massachusetts woman who has used strips of seaweed to relieve burns suffered while cooking says, "Kelp almost immediately relieves pain and soothes burned skin."

Kelp is widely available in natural foods stores. It's packaged dried, in strips.

◆ Apply honey or propolis to the burn. These are popular home remedies to relieve minor burns. Propolis is a resinous substance that bees accumulate from the plants they visit. The bees use it along with beeswax to make their hives. Supplement producers gather it from hives to make a tincture. Like honey, it has some antibacterial and antimicrobial properties. Honey is slightly acidic and is able to absorb water, thus helping to dry damaged tissue and protect the skin from infection.

Honey and propolis, however, may pose a risk for some people when used topically. Nutritionist Shari Lieberman cautions that "some honey can have a lot of bacteria. And propolis, though excellent to take internally to support healing from a burn, has been known to cause allergic reactions when used externally." If you do want to use honey or propolis, it thus makes sense to do a skin test first, and to reserve them for only minor first-degree burns.

◆ Recovering from Burns

A person recovering from a serious burn needs to consume higher levels both of macronutrients such as calories and protein and micronutrients such as vitamins and minerals. The following supplements and herbs are those most commonly included in nutritional programs designed to help heal tissue damaged by a burn:

- ◆ 400–800 IU of vitamin E
- ◆ 50–100 mg of vitamin B complex
- ◆ 25–50 mg of zinc
- ◆ 15,000–25,000 IU vitamin A in the form of beta carotene
- ◆ branch-chain amino acids in addition to a protein supplement
- ◆ 5,000–25,000 IU of vitamin A in the form of an emulsion for easier assimilation
- ◆ two–five grams of vitamin C plus bioflavonoids, or to bowel tolerance
- ◆ 250–500 mg magnesium
- ◆ 200 mcg of selenium

Lieberman says, "I've found that people with bad burns are susceptible to candida infections, so I recommend that while recovering from a burn you take garlic supplements and acidophilus, and herbs like echinacea or pau d'arco, for their antifungal properties. You should also increase your consumption of the omega-3 essential fatty acids, found in cold-water fish, fish oils, and a few vegetarian sources like flaxseed oil. These can act to decrease inflammation."

Herbs can be taken internally in tea, tablet, or tincture form to help prevent infection and promote the healing of burns. In addition to garlic, echinacea, and pau d'arco, try St.-John's-wort and yarrow. A plantain poultice boosts recovery and cell regeneration, notes Hobbs. He also highly recommends nettles internally, and chlorophyll-rich products such as spirulina and blue-green algae.

Acidophilus has become the generic term for various types of naturally occurring live bacteria that are increasingly popular as dietary supplements. It is available in the form of tablets, powders, capsules, and liquids sold in most natural foods stores. Look for acidophilus products that have labels providing information on how many live or "viable" bacteria each capsule or teaspoon provides, an expiration date with a guarantee of product viability until that date, and a listing of additional ingredients. Take doses of acidophilus that provide approximately 10 billion organisms per day.

◆ Preventing Burns

Most burns that occur in the home are preventable with a little forethought. Neglecting such safeguards can result in an injury with lifelong consequences.

- ◆ Install smoke detectors and make sure they're functional.
- ◆ Keep hot liquids and caustic chemicals out of the reach of small children.
- ◆ Closely and constantly supervise any open flames, whether from the stove, a candle, or the fireplace.
- ◆ Don't leave space heaters on all night, and don't use kerosene heaters indoors.
- ◆ Keep household tap water at 120–130°.
- ◆ Have your home's furnace checked annually.
- ◆ Never store rags, paint thinner, or anything combustible near a furnace or other heat source.
- ◆ Place small fire extinguishers in the kitchen, basement, and workshop. Make sure you, your children, and baby-sitters know how to use them. You should have all of your extinguishers inspected and recharged annually.
- ◆ Know your escape routes in case of fire.

TEN

Contusions

THIS CHAPTER COVERS:

♦ *bruise*
♦ *black eye*
♦ *crushed fingers and toes*

SEE "CHAPTER 6: BLEEDING" FOR:

♦ *internal bleeding*
♦ *bleeding under the fingernail*

Most bruises and other types of contusions result from the sudden impact of a blunt object on the skin. Though the skin is not torn and there's no external bleeding, blood vessels and tiny capillaries under the skin are broken. The blood leaks out into the surrounding tissue, causing the familiar black-and-blue markings. Doctors refer to this internal pool of blood as a hematoma. Normally the bleeding is limited by the body's clotting mechanism. Local blood vessels contract, platelets pour into the area, and strands of protein in blood serum mat together. Depending upon the extent of the injury and the body's response, the bleeding stops within minutes or hours.

The pool of red blood cells looks blue through the skin, but as white blood cells congregate to begin the healing and as other biochemical reactions occur, the bruise may go through the spectrum of colors, from red to yellow to green. Bruises sometimes appear darker on the face and hands than on the thighs, due to differences in levels in the skin of collagen, a fibrous protein.

♦ When a Bruise Is More Than a Bruise

The most common types of bruises, from walking into the edge of a table, slipping on ice, and getting hit by a ball or other moving object, can almost always be safely and effectively treated at home. There are, however, some instances in which a bruise needs to be taken more seriously and may need to be evaluated by a health professional.

- An extensive bruise may indicate there are serious underlying injuries, such as a fracture or a damaged internal organ. For instance, a black eye is sometimes accompanied by an injury to the eye itself, and an extensive bruise on the head may be a sign of a skull fracture. Sometimes such serious injuries are immediately apparent, but not always.
- In rare cases of massive bruising, such as when you fall off a ladder onto your buttocks, the area of internal bleeding may actually become infected and cause an abscess to form.
- Bruises that don't result from an obvious trauma may be an early symptom of a serious illness such as anemia, leukemia, or other cancer.
- People taking certain medications need to monitor bruises closely. Blood-thinning or anticoagulant drugs (warfarin, Coumadin) or substances can sometimes allow internal bleeding to go unchecked. Aspirin is one of the most common blood thinners, and certain anti-inflammatory drugs, antidepressants, and asthma medicines can inhibit clotting. Fish oils can thin the blood and increase the risk of bruising. Likewise, people suffering from certain diseases including hemophilia, alcoholism, and drug abuse should closely monitor bruises.
- Bruising too easily may be a sign that the victim is suffering from malnutrition or certain nutritional deficiencies, including low intake of vitamins C or K.
- Children's skin is softer than adults. Children are also active, often reckless, and not yet fully coordinated, so it's not unusual for a child to routinely sport various minor bruises on his or her legs and arms. Extensive bruising, however, especially on the abdomen, may be a sign of something more serious, including child abuse or a potential visual or balance disorder.
- If a bruise doesn't start to improve or increases in size after twenty-four hours, there may be a problem requiring professional medical attention.

If you incur a huge bruise, get a moderate to severe black eye, suspect internal bleeding or a broken bone, experience numbness or a tingling feeling in the area, or bruise easily or for no obvious reason, seek the advice of a medical professional. Such cases may call for a complete physical exam in which the blood is tested for anemia or clotting disorders, and the eyes, ears, and nervous system are examined for possible problems. In rare cases a physician may treat a massive bruise with oral antibiotics and, if it becomes infected, may recommend surgical drainage.

BASIC FIRST AID FOR CONTUSIONS

The majority of bruises are not serious, and you can treat them easily at home. The most important steps, in the correct order of application, are:

If the bruise is on an arm or leg, elevate the injury. By raising the bruise above the level of your heart, you help to reduce the flow of blood, and thus swelling, to the injured area. (Never move a victim's arm or legs if you suspect a spinal injury.)

Apply cold treatments. This step is the most crucial of the four. If you only do one step, do this one.

In recent years medical practitioners of all types have increasingly recognized the benefits of applying cold treatments to a bruise. Physicians now even have a scientific name for healing applications of cold: *cryotherapy*. Studies have shown that not only contusions but burns, stings, sprains, strains, and other muscle injuries heal more quickly when you apply cold treatments as soon as possible after the injury occurs. Cold treatments numb the area and prevent nerves from sending pain messages to the brain. They are thus an effective painkiller. Cold treatments also constrict local blood vessels, stemming internal bleeding, and reduce the release of histamines, thus further limiting inflammation. By keeping swelling in check, cold treatments overcome a major impediment to quick healing, since inflammation tends to restrict movement in the injured area and allows muscles and joints to become stiff.

Apply a cold treatment to a contusion as soon as possible after the injury occurs. Depending upon the severity of the bruise, one fifteen-to-twenty-minute application may suffice, or you may want to reapply the cold treatment for five to ten minutes every hour for the first day.

You can safely apply a variety of cold treatments to a contusion. If the bruise is to an extremity, you can comfortably hold it under cold running water. Or make an ice pack by putting some crushed ice in a plastic bag and wrapping it in a towel or cloth. (Never put ice directly on the skin, as it may cause frostbite.) A bag of frozen corn from the freezer makes a handy instant ice pack and is less messy than slapping a cold steak on a black eye. A number of manufacturers produce flexible cold packs that are cooled in a freezer and are reusable. In the wilderness you may want to carry instant cold compresses that are activated by breaking open chemical packets inside a plastic covering. These last fifteen to twenty minutes and are used only once.

Be careful not to overdo cold treatments. You want the area to become slightly numb and reddish, but not white, a sign of too severely restricted circulation. Cold treatments also shouldn't be used on victims who have impaired circulation or diabetes.

Rest the injured area for a day or longer. This further limits blood flow to the injured area and helps restrict swelling.

After the first sixteen to twenty-four hours, apply heat in some form. After the injury that causes a bruise, it will take up to a day or so before the characteristic black-and-blue color develops. This is an indication that it is appropriate to switch from cold treatments to heat treatments. Heat is more appropriate than cold after the bruise has turned color because the swelling and inflammation will have peaked. (Applying heat too soon can promote swelling and thus interfere with healing.) When the swelling has stopped, you want to restore blood flow and circulation to the area. Heat promotes healing by dilating blood vessels and bringing fresh blood to the site, thus increasing the release of oxygen from blood into tissues. Heat also relaxes muscles and lowers the sensitivity of nerves. Some studies also indicate that heat activates the immune system and stimulates antibodies.

Heat can be in the form of hot wet compresses, a hot-water bottle or heating pad, or warming liniments. Make a hot wet compress by soaking a cotton towel in hot water or soaking a towel and then heating it in a microwave; wring slightly before applying. Cover the compress with a piece of plastic and a dry towel to retain heat.

To use a hot-water bottle, fill it halfway with hot or boiling water. Lay it flat to put the cap on so that it doesn't hold a lot of air. Cover it with a towel if it is too hot for the skin. A child's skin is more sensitive to heat than an adult's, so be careful with children.

Over-the-counter warming liniments include mentholated creams such as Ben-Gay. Don't use these in conjunction with a heating pad, since doing so could result in a burn. Heat treatments in general need to be closely monitored to prevent injuries.

Avoid taking aspirin or ibuprofen (Advil, Motrin) for the pain of bruises, since these drugs can slow blood clotting.

◆ Black Eye

Any injury to the nose or trauma around the eye socket can develop into a black eye. This type of contusion can look worse than a bruise on any other part of the body because there are lots of tiny blood vessels around the eye. A punch to the eye or other injury causes blood to leak into surrounding tissue, and within twelve hours or less, you have a shiner.

Seek medical help if any vision problem accompanies a black eye. A severe bruise around the eye may need to be x-rayed to rule out fractures of the orbital bones. You may need to see an ophthalmologist for examination of the eyeball and vision testing to make sure the eye itself has not been seriously injured. Treatment at an emergency room or doctor's office is otherwise limited to cold compresses, analgesics (not aspirin), an eye patch, and possibly antibiotics.

A simple black eye is easily treated at home with any of the following remedies.

Immediately after the injury, apply cold treatments to the cheek and around the eye, but not to the eyeball itself. You can use cold compresses or whatever is handy in the refrigerator, such as a pack of frozen vegetables or a clean can of fruit juice. If you use ice, wrap it in a towel, since applying it directly to the skin can cause frostbite.

Crush plantain leaves and apply them to the area around the eye. Mash or chew it up and apply to the bruise. Cover it with a clean cloth or bandage, and change the dressing every half hour or so.

Tannins and other constituents in plantain fight inflammation. Plantain is a common broadleaf "weed" almost everywhere in the United States.

Use light acupressure to help relieve a black eye. Michael Reed Gach, author of *Acupressure's Potent Points*, recommends first applying prolonged finger pressure, for two to three minutes at a time, to two points on the back of the head just below the base of the skull. The points are in the hollow between the two large neck muscles, two to three inches apart depending on the size of the person's head.

A good point to press for a throbbing black eye is located between the thumb and index finger in the webbing of the hand.

To find it, bring the thumb and index finger together and notice the highest spot on the muscle in the webbing. Angle pressure underneath the bone that attaches to the index finger, by pressing with the thumb on the outer part of hand and the index finger on the inner. Squeeze firmly for two to three minutes.

Take the homeopathic remedy **Ledum** *for black eyes.* It's available as a tincture, tablet, or pellet from homeopathic companies.

◆ Crushed Fingers and Toes

Crushed digits usually result from catching your fingers in a door as it closes, hitting your fingers while hammering, or dropping a heavy object onto a finger or toe. Sometimes crushed fingertips cause blood to accumulate under the nail, which is exceptionally painful because unlike skin the nail cannot expand to release the internal pressure. This is one of the few cases where external draining may be helpful, by relieving pain and possibly saving the nail (see "Chapter 6: Bleeding" for how to relieve bleeding under a nail). If the trauma was great enough you may need an X ray to rule out broken bones. Otherwise try the following:

Take the homeopathic remedy **Hypericum.** Homeopaths view *Hypericum* as *"Arnica* for nerves." It works especially well to help heal injuries to parts of the body, such as the hands and feet, that contain an abundance of nerve endings. It is available in many forms for both external application and internal use.

Soak the injured digit in an herbal arnica solution. Arnica is a premier bruise-relieving herb (see below). Dilute one tablespoon of arnica tincture into a pint of cold water or chilled, distilled witch hazel, a mild astringent. Soak the injured digit in the dilution for fifteen minutes. Then wrap the finger or toe in cloth that has been soaked in the solution.

◆ Natural First-Aid Remedies for Contusions

A wide variety of natural remedies can complement elevation, cold, rest, and heat in the treatment of contusions. The most prominent of the bruise remedies, popular among both herbalists and homeopaths, is the herb arnica. Both herbalists and homeopaths make prominent use of external arnica preparations, while homeopaths also use arnica (greatly diluted) as an internal remedy. Other herbs, including comfrey, aid the resorption of blood from the bruised tissues, while nutrients such as vitamin K are essential for proper blood clotting.

Apply an herbal arnica tincture compress externally to the bruise. Herbal tinctures of arnica are more widely available than either the whole fresh plant or dried flowers. Dilute the tincture before applying to the skin by mixing approximately one tablespoon of tincture per pint of cold water. You can also mix arnica with distilled witch hazel or St.-John's-wort (the plant source for the homeopathic remedy *Hypericum*). Soak a cotton towel or cloth in the dilution and apply as a compress to the bruise three to four times per day.

The Germans refer to arnica as "fall-kraut." Legend has it that it was first used by mountain peasants who noticed that a sheep that fell down a hillside and injured itself would nibble arnica leaves. European herbalists have long prescribed arnica to alleviate the effects of shock and trauma, especially the bruising that comes from a fall or being hit by a blunt object. It can also help heal concussion, sprains, and muscle ache. Recent research has determined that certain of arnica's chemical compounds (such as the lactone helenalin) have anti-inflammatory and pain-relieving properties.

Herbalist Christopher Hobbs says, "I was recently needled next to my eye by an acupuncturist and the area turned black within an hour. I rubbed a few drops of an arnica oil on it right away and soon thereafter applied heat. Within six hours of the bruise forming it was seventy percent better." Hobbs warns that you need to be careful when using arnica tincture around the eye because the tincture's alcohol can be irritating should it get into the eye itself. Alternatively, use an oil of arnica (sometimes labeled "arnicated oil"), which is available at some natural food stores.

A small minority of individuals may experience an allergic reaction to arnica, so test it first on a small patch of skin. Also, don't apply it to broken skin, which increases the chance of irritation, or take it internally. (Homeopathically diluted *Arnica* can be take orally.)

Use a homeopathic preparation of Arnica both externally and internally. Spread some of the ointment or lotion on a bruise site as soon as possible after an injury. Dilute a tincture in water as you would for an herbal preparation, and apply with a cold compress. A typical oral dose of *Arnica* for a minor bruise would be two to five tablets of 6X or 12X potency at the time of the injury and the same dose once daily for two to three days. For more severe contusions, supplement the first-day dose by taking two to three more tablets every three to four hours for the next two to three days.

Manufacturers of homeopathic remedies use the herb arnica to make both ointments, lotions, and tinctures for external application and pills for internal consumption. Homeopathic *Arnica* for external application is usually prepared in the form of a 1X dilution. (The same warning applies as for the herbal preparation: don't use *Arnica* tincture on broken skin; the alcohol in the base material may be irritating to a cut or abrasion.) Because oral homeopathic remedies are much more highly diluted, taking *Arnica* tablets or pellets orally is perfectly safe. You can use external and internal doses of *Arnica* by themselves or in conjunction with each other.

For parents of young children, *Arnica* is the most widely used homeopathic first-aid remedy. Bruises and many forms of muscle injuries respond well to homeopathic *Arnica*, which reduces swelling and pain and helps the victim regain strength and composure.

Take oral or topical doses of one of the other homeopathic preparations for certain types of contusions. Homeopath and M.D. Jennifer Jacobs notes that *Arnica* is the homeopathic remedy of choice for most bruises, but if symptoms persist or the condition changes, another remedy may be more appropriate. She recommends using *Arnica* first and then:

- Take the "rusty gate" remedy, *Rhus tox*, if there is swelling, bruising, and inflammation of the soft tissue around an injured joint, and it feels better after you've moved it and warmed it up.
- Take *Ledum* for severe bruises that persist a long time, feel cold and numb, or feel better after applying cold treatments.
- Take *Ruta* for a bruise to the shinbone, kneecap, or elbow. These types of bruises often injure the sensitive bone covering known as the periosteum. Homeopaths have found that *Ruta* is the remedy with the most direct effect on the periosteum.

Apply a comfrey poultice. A comfrey poultice is more difficult to make and use than a commercial salve but may be more effective. Mix three tablespoons of powdered root with three ounces of hot water. Stir into a paste. Apply while still warm directly to the skin and cover with sterile gauze or clean cloth. Secure with a bandage and leave the poultice on for a few hours or overnight. After removing, massage the area with a comfrey ointment.

A more simple approach is to sprinkle some of the powdered root directly on the bruise and cover with a moist towel or cotton cloth.

Natural pharmacies carry a number of salves and ointments that contain comfrey, often in combination with other wound-healing herbs. Rub these right into the skin over a bruise. Oriental Medical Doctor David Eagle cautions people not to use fresh or dried comfrey leaves for a black eye. He says, "Comfrey poultices are great for bruises and contusions, but the tiny hairs on the leaves can irritate the eye, so plantain is better for a black eye." A comfrey-root powder preparation is free of potentially irritating hairs, notes Hobbs.

Sometimes known as bruisewort, comfrey has been used for thousands of years for its wound-healing properties. It is one of the best herbs for helping bones to heal, and herbalists also sprinkle the powdered root on burns, bites, and bruises to relieve pain and swelling. Comfrey contains the chemical allantoin, which studies have shown promotes the growth of new cells and reduces inflammation. For many years conventional drug companies have been using allantoin in some skin creams because of its moisturizing and cell proliferating properties. It is easily absorbed through the skin and penetrates deeply, where it particularly promotes the activity of cells that produce connective tissue.

Apply a few drops of essential oil to a cold compress to stimulate the body's ability to heal the bruise. Use the essential oil of either Lavender or Chamomile, two popular first-aid oils. To make an essential oil cold compress, sprinkle four to six drops of oil in about two cups of cold water. Stir vigorously. Soak a small cotton towel or cloth by placing it on top of the water, wring it slightly, and put it over the bruise. Leave it in place until it warms to body temperature and reapply. You can also make a massage oil by combining approximately fifteen drops of any of the above oils with one ounce of a carrier oil such as vegetable oil or a lotion; apply resulting combination to the bruise. Essential oils shouldn't be used around the eyes.

Lavender helps heal burns, sprains, insect stings, and minor cuts and scrapes. It's also widely used for bruises and sore, aching muscles. Like comfrey, it helps cells to regenerate and reduces inflammation. It also has some local analgesic properties. It's mild enough for children and everyday use.

Chamomile is another healing essential oil of low toxicity and broad healing powers. Scientists have traced some of Chamomile's healing effects to its constituent azulene, a powerful anti-inflammatory substance.

If you have other essential oils available, try Marjoram, Rosemary, or Geranium, all of which aromatherapists recommend for bruises.

To help recover from a severe bruise, take bromelain. Joseph Pizzorno, N.D., coauthor of *Encyclopedia of Natural Medicine*, recommends taking 125–400 mg of bromelain three times daily, one-half hour before or one and one-half hours after a meal (to make sure it isn't used to digest the food). Bromelain is available in 100-mg tablets from a number of supplement manufacturers.

Bromelain is a natural enzyme derived from the pineapple plant. In addition to assisting digestion, bromelain is now being used after surgical operations, traumas, and sports injuries to reduce inflammation and speed tissue repair. According to one clinical study of boxers, those who used bromelain found that their bruises disappeared much faster than those who didn't use it.

Press on two acupressure points in the lower back that can help reduce bruising anywhere on the body. The Chinese call these the "sea of vitality" points. They manipulate them to fortify the kidneys because easy bruising results when these organs are depleted. The two points are located between the second and third lumbar vertebrae, on each side of the spine, two to four finger widths away from the spine at waist level. Acupressure teacher Michael Reed Gach recommends treating a partner by applying pressure with the thumbs in a slow, rhythmic manner for two to five minutes. To self-treat, use the backs of your hands to rub the lower back for a minute as you breath deeply.

Gach notes that you can also treat a bruise anywhere on the body by pressing lightly above and below it at various depths "to attract a pulse," a sign of increased circulation of blood and energy.

Apply some of the Chinese bruise-relieving liniment Zheng Gu Shui. This combination of eight herbs and other substances translates as "bone-correcting water." According to Holly and David Eagle, who frequently use prepared Chinese medicines in their clinical practice, Zheng Gu Shui is among the most popular of a huge array of external "bone medicines" produced by Chinese herbal companies. The bone medicines are used to promote the healing of fractures as well as eliminate bruising, control bleeding, and reduce swelling. Oriental Medical Doctor Holly Eagle says, "Most of the bone medicines have blood-vitalizing herbs in them that seep in and move circulation. They're great for relieving any bruise or crush wound that's not open."

David Eagle adds, "Zheng Gu Shui works a lot like Ben-Gay. There are a few cautions, though. You shouldn't apply it to the skin and then cover it with a dressing or an elasticized bandage. It's volatile enough to cause blistering when covered. You also don't want to put it near the eyes. And in general the bruising and contusion medicines employ relatively strong herbs that shouldn't be used if you're pregnant."

Two other popular Chinese prepared medicines for bruises are:

◆ Yunnan Paiyao. The principal ingredient in this remedy is the dried root of the pseudoginseng plant. Yunnan Paiyao is widely used by practitioners of traditional Chinese medicine to stop external bleeding, "disperse blood stagnation," and reduce the pain and swelling of bruises and other soft-tissue injuries. Take one or two capsules for minor internal bleeding such as bruises.

"Yunnan Paiyao also comes as a liquid," says Holly Eagle, "and for bruises it works well to spread the liquid over the area."

◆ Qi Li San (roughly, "seven pinches powder"). Qi Li San contains myrrh and a number of other herbs that work to decrease swelling, promote blood circulation, and relieve pain. For external contusions, sports injuries, and sprains, wait until at least twenty-four hours after the injury to use it, since it has a warming effect and cold treatments are preferable in the immediate aftermath of soft-tissue injuries. Make a paste from the powder and apply it to the injury. Cover with a sterile dressing and bandage and reapply the paste once a day.

Zheng Gu Shui is produced by the Tulin Drug Manufactory in Kwangsi, China. It comes in 50- and 100-ml bottles. Yunnan Paiyao is produced in China by the Yunnan Paiyao Factory. In the United States the powder form, which comes in a blister pack of sixteen capsules, is one of the most widely available prepared Chinese medicines. The liquid is somewhat harder to find. Qi Li San is produced by the Tung Jen Tang pharmacy of Beijing in 1.5-gram vials of powder. Most Oriental pharmacies carry these prepared medicines, or you can mail-order them from suppliers of traditional Chinese medicines (see "Resources").

Apply a ginger poultice to the bruise. Grate some ginger and lightly steam to heat. Wrap the ginger in thin gauze or apply directly to the skin. Keep heat over the poultice with a hot-water bottle. "I've found that this is one of the best ways to disperse stagnant blood, as the Chinese say," notes Hobbs.

Apply a warming herbal liniment to promote healing of the bruise. Warming liniments should be used only after a bruise has turned a dark color. Rub them into the skin to dilate local blood vessels and increase circulation. Many practitioners of sports medicine contend that warming liniments are better for bruises than for strained muscles or sprains, because liniments tend to warm surface areas (where bruises occur) more effectively than the deeper tissues affected by more serious injuries.

One of the most popular warming liniments available at most natural foods stores is Tiger Balm, an ointment combination of camphor and menthol.

Camphor is derived from the wood of the camphor tree of the Far East. Camphor's medical properties have been known for at least a thousand years. Folk herbalists have used it to relieve fainting fits and convulsions (it's an ingredient in most smelling salts) and increase circulation to muscles and skin (rubbed on the body). Camphor is found in many conventional over-the-counter heating liniments, such as Vicks VapoRub.

Menthol is a white, crystalline alcohol that is the major chemical component of the essential oil of Peppermint and other mints. Like camphor, menthol has long been recognized as a local stimulant when applied to the skin. Menthol is also found in conventional over-the-counter preparations such as Ben-Gay. Menthol may cause allergic reactions in some people.

Tiger Balm has been used worldwide for over a hundred years to reduce swelling, relieve pain, and increase circulation to bruises, sprains, and strains. Tiger Balm is imported from Singapore and is packaged in .63-ounce jars.

Another popular bruise-relieving balm, also from the Orient, is White Flower Analgesic Balm, a combination of wintergreen, menthol, camphor, and oils of Lavender, Eucalyptus, and Peppermint. This minty-smelling liquid comes in a tiny .08-ounce bottle.

"A great all-purpose oil I use," says Hobbs, "is the Chinese medicine Wan Hua. It has a heating energy similar to ginger. You rub it right on a bruise and it is really effective. It's not as heating as Tiger Balm, but is good for dispersing blood stagnation and relieving sore muscles, too." Wan Hua is sold as Die Da Wan Hua You ("myriad flowers impact trauma oil") by the United Pharmaceutical Manufactory in Guangzhou, China. It is a combination of ginseng, aloe, and seven other herbs and comes in a 15-ml bottle.

Apply a castor-oil pack to the bruise. To make a castor-oil pack, dampen a cotton cloth with castor oil. Bake the cloth in a 350° oven for ten to fifteen minutes. Apply the cloth to the bruise, cover with a piece of plastic, apply a heating pad or hot-water bottle on top of the plastic, and cover the whole thing with a towel for a half hour or so. Since this is a heated application, it is appropriate only after you've had the bruise for at least twenty-four hours.

According to Holly Eagle, "If you use castor-oil packs for a week or so, you may develop what looks like a heat rash but is actually from the opening up of small blood vessels. At that point I tell people to back off on the packs until the area starts to heal again."

Castor oil comes from the castor-oil plant *(Ricinus communis)* and has been a popular (perhaps more accurately, widely taken but unpopular, because of its nasty taste) constipation medicine since ancient times. As a laxative, it's effective but overly strong. Externally, it's an emollient that some people use to relieve ringworm, soften corns, and help heal bruises.

Try one of the many folk remedies people use for bruises. Although it is unclear exactly *why* any of the following remedies would help clear up bruising, these have worked for many people and may help you.

♦ Apply a slice of raw onion to the bruise until the swelling goes down. A woman from Mims, Florida, confirms, "This is one of the easiest and most effective treatments I have used for severe bruises. It pulls the inflammation and hurt out and prevents discoloration."

♦ Pulp or crush a cabbage leaf and bind the juice and leafy mass over the bruise.

♦ Apply several sprigs of crushed parsley leaf directly to the bruise. This is an old Romanian Gypsy remedy.

♦ Make a clay poultice to put on the bruise and reduce swelling. Mix white or yellow clay with water to make a thick paste. Apply it to the bruise site and cover with a wet towel or cotton cloth.

♦ Grate a chunk of turnip and apply the mash to the bruise.

- ◆ Crush chive leaves or roots and apply the juice to the bruise. This is a traditional Chinese folk cure.
- ◆ Rub in some hydrogen peroxide gel or apply a spray of the 3 percent solution twice a day.
- ◆ Apply the inner side of a banana skin to a bruise.

◆ Prevention and Recovery

Preventing contusions in everyday life is mostly a case of paying more attention to where you're going and what you're doing. More easily said than done, for many. A lot of bruises, too, arise from sports injuries that many participants accept as part of the game. A less direct but potentially more effective antibruising route is to boost the body's ability to resist bruising and recover from it when it does happen.

The nutrients that play the most crucial role in limiting and healing bruises are:

Vitamin K. This is the vitamin most clearly tied to proper blood clotting—its name comes from the Danish word *koagulation*. Easy bruising is one of the symptoms of a vitamin K deficiency. According to nutritionist Shari Lieberman, "Vitamin K is readily bioavailable from foods, particularly dark green leafy vegetables." Other foods that are rich in the vitamin or promote its production in the body include alfalfa sprouts, soybeans, oats, green tea, and lactobacillus-containing yogurt. Some vitamin companies do market vitamin K in 100 mcg tablets, but they're not commonly found in natural foods stores. Other supplements that are high in K include green food concentrates and alfalfa tablets (follow dosage levels on the label). Aspirin and prolonged antibiotic therapy work against K.

Vitamin C plus bioflavonoids. One of the symptoms of scurvy from a vitamin C deficiency is tiny bruises below the skin. Vitamin C plays a part in the formation of collagen, a fibrous protein found in connective tissue, bone, and the walls of blood vessels. Collagen helps hold the body's cells together. Without it, tissues start to fall apart. Blood vessels become weak and fragile, making it much easier for blood to leak into the surrounding tissues and cause bruises. Researchers at Duke University Medical Center have confirmed that people who lack adequate C in the diet tend to bruise more easily.

The bioflavonoids are also important for wound healing, tissue repair, and bleeding control. They were discovered by Albert

Szent-Györgyi, the late Hungarian researcher who also discovered vitamin C. Szent-Györgyi noticed that a subject given pure vitamin C continued to suffer from bleeding gums, while an "impure" C preparation (containing bioflavonoids) stopped the bleeding. Subsequent research has confirmed that bioflavonoids help protect and strengthen tiny capillaries. Quercetin and other bioflavonoids also have anti-inflammatory properties and like C are valuable antioxidants.

To help recover from a serious bruise, take two to five grams of C daily, plus 300–1,000 mg daily of bioflavonoids. An optimal ongoing daily dose might be 500–3,000 mg of C and 500 mg of bioflavonoids.

Two herbs high in bioflavonoids are ginkgo and hawthorn *(Crataegus oxyacantha)*. According to Hobbs, "The standardized or liquid extract forms of these herbs are the best to assure a good portion of the bioflavonoids." Follow label directions for dosages.

Hobbs also recommends fruit peels as an excellent source of bioflavonoids, particularly from citrus. "The white portion of the peel of lemons, oranges, and tangerines is called the rag. It's high in bioflavonoids like hesperidin and rutin. You can eat small amounts of the rag or use it to brew a tea. The peels of apples, grapes, and pears are also good, though the fruit should be organically grown."

Antioxidants. Extra antioxidants can help to neutralize free radicals and thus reduce swelling and speed recovery. Free radicals are molecular marauders generated in the body by physical trauma such as bruising, among other causes. Free radicals lack an electron, and in their search for the stability an additional electron will provide, they attack other cells. This causes damage to muscle and other tissue in the body. Antioxidants combine with and neutralize the free radicals before the harm is done.

Effective antioxidants include vitamin C with bioflavonoids (take two to five grams daily in mixed doses, or to bowel tolerance), vitamin E (400–800 IU), beta carotene (from green leafy or orange vegetables, or 25,000 IU from supplements), and the herbs garlic (use in your cooking, or one of the allicin-stabilized tablets available in natural foods stores) and ginkgo (follow dosage recommendations on package labels).

B complex, especially folic acid and B₁₂. Many of the B vitamins play an important role in skin health and tissue repair. Lieberman recommends as an optimal daily dose 50–300 mg of B complex (most supplement formulas will contain, for instance, 50 mg of all the B vitamins measured in mg) and 25–300 mcg for folic acid and B_{12}.

Beta carotene. This precursor for vitamin A promotes rapid tissue healing and acts as an antioxidant. Prominent dietary sources are green leafy or orange vegetables. In supplement form take approximately 25,000 IU daily.

The minerals iron, calcium, copper, magnesium, silica, and zinc. All of these have been tied to bodily processes related to healing from contusions, such as the formation of blood and blood vessel cells (iron, copper, magnesium), fighting free radicals (iron, copper, magnesium), blood clotting (calcium), and tissue growth and repair (magnesium, silica, zinc).

Lieberman recommends as a daily optimal dose 15–30 mg iron, 1,000–1,500 mg calcium, 0.5–2 mg copper, 500–750 mg magnesium, 50–75 mg silicon, and 25–50 mg zinc. Some persons should limit their intake of certain minerals, including iron and copper. Check with a qualified nutritionist.

Many of the B complex vitamins and the minerals are most prominent in natural, whole foods, especially leafy green vegetables, sea vegetables, whole grains, beans, and legumes. The refining process by which whole-wheat bread is transformed into white bread, brown rice into white rice, and so forth removes many of the B vitamins and trace minerals. (In some instances fortification puts these nutrients back in.)

Chlorophyll supplements (the microalgae-based green foods spirulina, chlorella, and blue-green algae, and products made from the young grasses of wheat, barley, and alfalfa) provide many of the above nutrients. They may also provide other compounds not yet identified as vitamins or minerals that are possibly in minute doses necessary to health. Concentrated sources of chlorophyll are balanced whole-food supplements that allow the body to digest and assimilate nutrients easily. In addition, chlorophyll is an excellent builder of red blood cells. Chlorophyll supplements come in tablets, powders, and liquid concentrates. Follow label directions for dosage.

Of course, the same daily habits—a low-fat, high-fiber diet, regular exercise, control of stress—that are best for the overall health of mind and body also provide the groundwork for the prevention and treatment of contusions.

ELEVEN

Convulsions and Seizures

THIS CHAPTER COVERS:

◆ *epilepsy*
◆ *high fever (febrile) convulsions*

SEE "CHAPTER 18: HIGH FEVER" FOR:

◆ *reducing a fever*

Anyone who has witnessed a person in the throes of a convulsion is not likely to forget it. The victim loses consciousness, falls to the floor, and shakes or twitches in the arms, legs, or body for a minute or longer. Upon awakening, he or she is confused and disoriented and has no memory of the seizure itself.

Such a scene is repeated thousands of times a day throughout the United States. Approximately one child in twenty can expect to suffer at least one convulsion before age sixteen, usually as a consequence of a high fever, poisoning, or an injury. Epilepsy, a serious neurological disease characterized by recurrent seizures, affects over 2 million Americans.

Medical authorities have only a partial understanding of what happens inside the body before and during a seizure. Many seizures are thought to result from an imbalance in the body's bioelectrical system that causes an unusual electrical discharge that affects the nervous system and the brain. Typically a group of nerve cells in one part of the brain suddenly becomes electrically unstable. This creates a strong electrical charge that spreads like a storm over surrounding cells, disrupting their normal function. The electrical disturbance may affect all or part of the brain and result in a seizure. The seizure may be characterized by uncontrollable jerking and twitching of various parts of the body, unconsciousness, an episode of blank staring or unresponsiveness, distorted perceptions, or other changes in the person's state of consciousness.

Medical authorities distinguish between primary seizures, in which the underlying cause is unknown, and secondary ones, clearly resulting from an illness, injury, or poisoning. It is often much more difficult to determine the cause of seizures that unexpectedly start to strike an adult than those that strike a child. For instance, poisoning is frequently suspected whenever a child who has never before had a seizure (and is not feverish) experiences multiple ones. Nevertheless, there are also many childhood seizure cases in which no underlying cause can be found. Frequently, children stop experiencing seizures by the time they reach puberty.

◆ Epilepsy

About 1 percent of the U.S. population suffers from some form of epilepsy (now also known as seizure disorder). Three out of every four cases arise before age eighteen, with the ratio of male to female epileptics being about equal. Famous epileptics include Alexander the Great, Julius Caesar, Fyodor Dostoyevsky, and Vincent van Gogh.

A person who has suffered a single seizure is not necessarily epileptic, since seizures must be chronic and recurring to be considered epileptic in origin. Doctors can find no organic cause of epilepsy in about two-thirds of all cases. If epilepsy strikes an adult, though, it is more likely to have resulted from an identifiable disase or injury, such as a brain tumor, head injury, or meningitis. Heredity probably plays a relatively minor role, accounting for epilepsy among an estimated 2–5 percent of children of epileptics.

One of the most common and readily identified causes of seizures among children up to the age of five to six years is high fever. Seizures associated with fever are called febrile convulsions. Other agents that can either cause seizures or aggravate a convulsive disorder include:

- ◆ medical conditions, including infections that affect the nervous system (particularly meningitis and encephalitis), high blood pressure, heart disease, stroke, brain diseases or tumors, congenital brain damage, and heat illness
- ◆ nutritional deficiencies, including overall malnutrition and

lack of sufficient levels of certain nutrients including the amino acid taurine, the minerals calcium, magnesium, manganese (during pregnancy), phosphorus, and zinc, and the vitamins folic acid, B_6, A, and D

◆ poisoning from toxic agents or metals including aluminum, lead, and mercury, and allergic reactions to chemicals

◆ accident or injury, especially to the brain or head (such injuries can result from cerebral trauma at birth or violently shaking a young child), electric shock, venomous bites and stings, and choking

◆ drug or alcohol overdose, or withdrawal

◆ certain drugs and vaccinations, including the phenothiazine class of tranquilizer drugs, amphetamines, antihistamines, oral contraceptives, tricyclic antidepressants, theophylline, and vaccinations for pertussis, measles, mumps, and Hib meningitis

◆ certain health products, including fennel oil, the antiaging drug Gerovital H3, oil of evening primrose, gamma-linolenic acid (GLA), camphor, and the artificial sweetener aspartame (NutraSweet, Equal)

◆ sensory triggers, including strobe lights, a flickering television, or loud sounds

◆ poor diet, including hypoglycemia, constipation, and overhydration

Many of the above factors can be controlled. Seizure experts contend that up to 50 percent of all cases may be preventable.

TYPES OF SEIZURES

Seizures take on a wide variety of forms. Indeed, there are as many types of seizures as there are individuals who experience them. Seizures vary in duration, severity, type of bodily movements, and sensations felt by the victim. They range from a short episode of blank staring to prolonged muscular contractions. The three basic types of epileptic seizures are:

Grand mal (tonic-clonic). This is the most common form of severe epileptic seizure, usually lasting one to three minutes. It may begin with the person experiencing an almost euphoric feeling, the so-called "aura" that novelist Fyodor Dostoyevsky described so eloquently. Usually the person suddenly falls to the floor unconscious and then makes violent convulsive movements of the head, arms, and legs. There may be a loss of bladder or bowel control, or temporary cessation of breathing. During a grand mal seizure, the person won't be able to respond to questions or commands. After the movements stop, the person awakens in a confused state, without being able to remember the episode. Sometimes the victim has a headache. Unless physically hurt during the attack, he or she usually won't feel any other pain. Often the victim will want to sleep for several hours after the attack.

Petit mal (absence seizures). A person having this type of seizure does not fall down or experience major convulsions. Rather, he or she has a sudden, momentary lapse of consciousness, characterized by blank staring or a vacant expression, that lasts up to about thirty seconds. There may be minor twitching of the face or jerking of the hand. The person snaps out of it spontaneously and goes on with what he or she was doing without realizing there has been a seizure. Children in the two-to-twelve age range experience these more often than do adults. Sometimes these episodes happen many times during a day. If a parent or teacher does not recognize them, they can lead to a serious learning difficulty. In nine out of ten cases children will stop experiencing petit mal seizures by the time they are twenty years old.

Partial seizures. These involve electrical discharges in only certain areas of the brain. The person may experience the blank stare and mental confusion of a petit mal seizure or the random movements and twitching of a grand mal seizure. He may suddenly alter his behavior or have sensory hallucinations affecting smell, taste, or sight. Although on occasion it can go on for hours, the seizure usually lasts a minute or two. When it is over, the person is often confused and retains no memory of the attack.

Children will sometimes throw a fit during which they hold their breath to the point of falling unconscious. This is not considered a true seizure (see "Chapter 8: Breathing Problems"), nor are trembling movements from night terrors or hysteria.

BASIC FIRST AID FOR SEIZURES

If you're out in the ocean when a hurricane is about to hit, you batten down the hatches and ride it out. Seizures are natural storms that sweep over the brain and body, and like real storms, they, too, are impossible to fight while they're occurring. As with a hurricane, you can take some preventive steps such as clearing the decks of objects that might injure the victim, but otherwise must observe and wait.

For someone who is having a seizure that involves only a brief period of blank staring or minor shaking of limbs, there is little that needs to be done. Often all that you should do is watch the person and stay with her until she regains full consciousness. You shouldn't touch her unless it is to protect her from a dangerous situation, such as walking into a road or falling down stairs. In that case gently guide her away. Offer help in getting her home if she needs it upon coming out of the episode.

First-aid steps for a grand mal seizure are also simple.

Have the person lie on the floor. Often you'll come upon a person who is already on the floor convulsing. If he has not yet fallen, or if he feels a seizure coming on, have him lie down on his side or ease him onto the floor. A prone position protects the person from being injured by a fall at the onset of the seizure. Don't have him lie down on a bed, however, since he may be injured falling off of it. Lying on his side helps keep his airway open.

Stay with the victim and help protect him from self-inflicted injury by clearing the surrounding area of anything that presents a potential danger. This includes sharp objects and hard furniture. Don't move a victim unless he's in the middle of a road, for instance, or near something dangerous that can't be moved, such as stairs. A victim who has fallen may have suffered a head or neck injury, so if necessary, take steps to protect against aggravating these if you need to move the person (see "Chapter 3: Basic Emergency Care").

Remove glasses and loosen any tight clothing on the person. Loosen a necktie or other article worn around the neck.

Put something soft but flat, such as a folded towel, under the head. This protects the back of the head from banging on the floor. A pillow is not recommended, however, since it elevates the head and adds an unwanted kink to the airway.

Don't try to hold or restrain seizure victims, or force them to snap out of it. Once a seizure has begun the person cannot control it by a conscious force of will. Slapping a seizure victim or throwing water in the face will do no good and may actually harm the person.

Don't put anything between the person's teeth. Some first-aid books advise that, if a seizure victim's mouth is already open, you can put a soft object such as a folded handkerchief between the victim's side teeth to keep the person from biting or swallowing his or her tongue. The Epilepsy Foundation of America and other medical authorities, however, have stopped recommending this. They now advise that nothing ever be put or forced between the teeth (especially your fingers, which could get severely bitten). The current thinking is that putting something between the teeth rarely does any good. It sometimes causes injuries such as broken teeth and has the potential to do severe harm should it cause the object or the person's tongue to block the airway. It's also not true that a person experiencing a seizure can swallow his or her tongue. Swallowing an object and choking on it is much more dangerous than biting a tongue. A bitten tongue heals quickly in any case.

Don't try to do rescue breathing or CPR on a convulsing person, and don't try to give him or her anything orally until the seizure stops. During a seizure a person could choke on pills or a liquid forced into the mouth. Don't offer the victim anything to eat or drink until he is fully conscious.

Observe the person closely. Once you've taken the above steps, you may be able to play an important diagnostic role by observing the victim. Time the seizure to help indicate its severity. Try to note whether the victim's complexion is becoming pale or blue, if muscle contractions are evident on both sides of the body, and if other symptoms are present. Particularly if this is the victim's first seizure, your observations may help to pinpoint the type and cause. They may also determine subsequent first-aid steps.

When the person has stopped convulsing, check the ABCs: airway, breathing, and circulation. (See Chapter 3.) Only in rare cases will a seizure victim have stopped breathing and need rescue breathing to be revived. If the person appears to have suffered a spinal injury, support his neck and head with the help of others and gently roll him onto his side if he's not already in that position. If there is no spinal injury, put him in the recovery position (see Chapter 3) or turn the head to one side, keeping it low, to drain any saliva or vomit from the airway. If the convulsion resulted from a dangerously high fever, take steps to reduce it (see "Chapter 18: High Fever").

Check for a medical alert tag. The tag will have instructions on what further steps to take.

Don't leave the victim until he or she fully regains consciousness or has medical help. If another person is available, he or she should call for medical help, if appropriate. Victims of a grand mal seizure will usually be somewhat disoriented upon regaining consciousness. It may take them a moment to begin to remember general information, though they'll have no memory at all of the actual seizure. Stay with the seizure victim and reassure him or her as mental clarity returns, which may take an hour or so. It may be helpful to ask about the person's history of seizures and prescribed medications. Often persons who have just had a grand mal seizure will be extremely tired and may drop into a deep sleep. Let them rest or stay calm. Offer help in getting them to a medical practitioner if they seem confused or unable to get to one on their own, or better yet have them taken by ambulance to a hospital.

WHEN TO CALL FOR HELP

Even parents who are sure that they've just witnessed a simple, naturally ending (or "self-limiting") febrile seizure in their child should report the episode to their health care provider to rule out potentially serious underlying causes. So should victims of grand mal seizures. On the other hand, victims of epilepsy who have had a petit mal seizure may not need to see a doctor after each attack. Here are some general guidelines for determining whether medical attention is warranted following a seizure.

Call for emergency help if:

- the seizure lasts longer than three to five minutes
- the victim does not regain consciousness between seizure episodes or soon after convulsions have stopped
- one seizure is followed by another within an hour
- the victim experiences a seizure in water
- the victim is having trouble breathing or seems very ill or injured
- the victim is pregnant

Though not necessarily an emergency, you should still notify a medical practitioner if the seizure victim:

- is an infant
- has never had a seizure before
- has diabetes or high blood pressure
- seems weak and feverish after the seizure has stopped

WHAT MEDICAL PERSONNEL WILL DO

If a person is experiencing an ongoing convulsion when emergency technicians arrive on the scene, they may inject phenobarbital or some other barbiturate to stop the seizure. A health care practitioner's next order of business will be to determine its cause. Is it the result of an organic disease, a neurological defect, or poisoning? The search for answers begins with an extensive physical exam and a detailed questionnaire. Doctors also employ various diagnostic tests, such as a CAT scan, a spinal tap (to check for meningitis or encephalitis), and an electroencephalogram (EEG, to monitor brain-wave activity).

Treatment will depend on what is found. If the cause is a small tumor, it can be surgically removed. If it is epilepsy, the conventional treatment of choice for frequent, severe convulsions is prolonged use of any of a dozen or so anticonvulsant drugs, depending on the type of seizure. Dilantin is the most commonly prescribed drug for grand mal seizure, Zarontin for petit mal. Sometimes more than one drug is needed. These drugs don't cure epilepsy, though for slightly more than half of all subjects they can eliminte seizures completely. In about two out of three cases, drug therapy will be lifelong (unless alternatives are explored).

The drawback to anticonvulsants is that they affect the user's mood and energy level. Doctors must finely tune dosages to prevent seizures or reduce their severity, as well as to minimize side effects such as birth defects, drowsiness, dizziness, slurred speech, and liver toxicity.

In rare cases a doctor may recommend anticonvulsant drugs for someone who has had only one seizure. If so, get a second (and third) opinion. The anticonvulsants are strong drugs that should not be prescribed cavalierly. The patient's complete case history should be analyzed to determine whether the drug should be prescribed, notes naturopath Ross Trattler. In his book *Better Health Through Natural Healing,* he relates a medical horror story about a patient who experienced one seizure and was placed on Dilantin for life. It turned out the man was spraying pesticides for three days before the seizure, a fact not elicited by the prescribing doctor.

◆ High Fever (Febrile) Convulsions

Scientists are unsure why children are more likely than adults to experience convulsions during a high fever. Some researchers suggest it is because of infants' more immature nervous systems. Febrile convulsions are most common in infants between the ages of one and three and do not occur in children older than six. The seizures usually occur on the first day of the fever, while the body temperature is rising rapidly and has reached 104° or higher. They tend to affect the whole body, rather than just one side.

Febrile seizures are classified as simple or complex. Simple ones typically last for two to three minutes or less and occur only once during the illness. Sometimes the child's arms and legs may twitch for only a few seconds, or she may urinate or defecate. The child shows no evidence of neurological problems either before or after the seizure. Afterward she typically falls asleep and is fine upon wakening.

Since complex febrile seizures tend to last longer (fifteen minutes or more) and repeat themselves, they present greater risks. Often there's a history of epilepsy in the family. The child may suffer neurological abnormalities afterward.

Consider the possibility of a more serious underlying cause if a child's seizure doesn't fit the febrile model or if a seizure occurs in absence of a fever.

Simple febrile seizures may be frightening for a parent to observe but should not cause undue alarm. They're somewhat common and don't cause brain damage (though *severe, repeating* seizures can cause brain damage) or otherwise pose a serious health threat. Neither do they lead to epilepsy later in life (though a complex febrile convulsion is on some occasions the initial convulsion of an epileptic child). One study of 1,706 children with febrile convulsions showed that the seizures did not lead to a single death or motor defect.

Whenever a child suffers a seizure, it is a good idea to arrange for an evaluation with a medical professional. For a simple febrile convulsion, it's not necessary for the consultation to be immediate. A complex febrile seizure or a seizure from any other cause should be treated as an immediate emergency.

Professional medical evaluation of a simple febrile seizure will include an attempt to determine the underlying cause. The cause is often merely an upper-respiratory-tract infection. Doctors may order a spinal tap to check the infant's spinal fluid for evidence of a neurological disease such as meningitis. Parents can help the diagnosis by offering a precise description of the events up to and including the seizure. For instance, did the seizure start with several minutes of blank staring? Was it accompanied by vomiting or anything else that might suggest poisoning?

If a child having a complex febrile seizure is brought to the hospital, doctors will take steps to keep the child's airway open. They may administer oxygen and draw blood for analysis. The child may be given a shot of phenobarbital, acetaminophen or a tranquilizer up the rectum, or other drugs to stop the convulsions and control the fever. Children under six months old will usually be admitted to the hospital for observation.

Children who suffer from frequent, severe seizures are usually put on anticonvulsants, though safer measures should be explored first. In some cases doctors will recommend that an infant be given daily doses of phenobarbital or other anticonvulsant drugs, for at least two seizure-free years, even after a single simple febrile seizure. Such recommendations are controversial since anticonvulsants cause so many health problems—one estimate is that 40 percent of children taking anticonvulsants suffer from at least one adverse effect. The vast majority of children who have a febrile seizure will never have another one, whether they take drugs or not. "Some say the medication is given to the child to treat the parent," note Phylis Austin, Agatha Thrash, M.D., and Calvin Thash, M.D., the authors of *Natural Healthcare for Your Child*.

TREATING SIMPLE FEBRILE CONVULSIONS AT HOME

Simple febrile seizures should be treated similarly to other seizures, described above. Parents should stay with the child and prevent her from hurting herself in case she loses consciousness and falls. Clear the area of dangerous objects and loosen any constrictive clothing. Children aged one to six should be put on their stomach with the head turned to one side to prevent them from choking if they vomit.

If the child is less than a year old, you can hold him in your lap. Turn him on his side so that his head is facing down to keep his airway open. You can also grasp the child's chin and gently pull away from the chest to extend the neck and keep his airway open. When the seizure is over, place the child on his stomach with the head turned to the side. In most cases he'll fall asleep and be fine upon wakening.

Most episodes are over quickly and painlessly. Afterward parents should take steps to reduce the fever (don't give aspirin or put the child in a bath) and monitor the child's temperature (see Chapter 18 for natural fever-reducing techniques). Naturopath Joseph Pizzorno notes that many children are dehydrated after a febrile seizure episode. To replace lost fluids and electrolytes, he recommends Oral Rehydration Solution (see "What to Drink" in "Chapter 17: Heat Illness").

Parents may find it useful to know the child's temperature immediately before the seizure. One child may experience febrile convulsions at 104° and another at 106°. Knowing your child's point can alert you to when to reduce the child's temperature when he again has a fever.

Following are a few natural remedies to accompany the basic first-aid steps for a simple febrile convulsion.

At the first sign of a seizure, administer the homeopathic remedy Belladonna. Most febrile convulsions will be over before any remedy can be given, but if you have *Belladonna* handy, crush some pellets into a powder and touch it to the child's inner cheek. (Don't give an unconscious person anything to swallow.) Administer *Belladonna* every minute for up to three minutes, or until the seizure ends.

During the seizure, press on the acupressure point on the upper lip. This first-aid revival point is located two-thirds of the way to the base of the nose. Press on it in an upward motion with the end of the thumb. You might also try pressing on the point where the heart meridian ends, at the base of the fingernail of the pinky.

Administer homeopathic Aconite or a first-aid flower essence such as Rescue Remedy—not to the child but to the parents. To take Rescue Remedy, add three to four drops of the liquid to a small glass of water and sip it slowly. If no water is available, put three to four drops of undiluted Rescue Remedy directly on the tongue. Repeat every half hour until calm.

These remedies are to prevent the parents from becoming so upset that they instill fear and panic in the child.

◆ Prevention and Recovery

Since seizure episodes usually last only a minute or two, there are a limited number of natural remedies for use during the emergency. While the victim is convulsing, your focus should be on the conventional steps of clearing the area and preventing injury. Remedies, natural and otherwise, are primarily for prevention, long-term treatment, and recovery. Steps can also be taken to help the person recover from contusions, exhaustion, and other consequences of a seizure.

Researchers have identified a number of factors, including emotional stress, nutrients, overall diet, and physical activity, that may play a role in seizure disorders. Though no one is claiming a cure for epilepsy, some alternative practitioners have reported marked improvement among their seizure patients who have been treated with natural healing methods.

Before discussing alternative approaches to seizures, a warning from Andrew Weil, M.D., an internationally known expert on topics relating to alternative medicine and mind-active drugs: "I always caution seizure patients about the dangers of stopping anticonvulsant drugs. Even normal people will have seizures if you put them on these drugs for a time, then cut them off. A person should never stop taking antiepileptic drugs suddenly. Always cut the dose gradually and not until you begin using other measures to reduce the chance of seizures. If a seizure occurs, go back to the prescribed dose." Weil says that he's seen a few patients eliminate anticonvulsant drugs totally, although a more realistic goal is to reduce them to a level the person can live with and still enjoy normal alertness.

Nutritional supplements may be as effective as some pharmaceutical drugs in preventing seizures or reducing their frequency and severity. The principal antiseizure nutrients, in approximate order of the depth of scientific research that supports seizure-reducing effects, are:

Taurine. One of the more obscure amino acids, taurine in the body is concentrated in the brain, where it plays a central role in regulating the nervous system and coordinating electrical activity. Taurine is intimately connected with the minerals sodium, potassium, calcium, magnesium, and zinc, all of which also affect brain metabolism. Its main therapeutic use (at dosages of about 1,500 mg per day) is in epilepsy management.

You can find taurine supplements in some natural foods stores, but most practitioners say that taurine should be prescribed by a physician or knowledgeable nutritionist. High levels may cause depression or other adverse effects. Fish proteins are high in taurine.

Magnesium and calcium. Magnesium helps keep cells electrically stable and, with calcium, regulates the body's energy levels and maintains normal nerve transmission. Researchers have established that a magnesium deficiency can cause muscle tremors and convulsive seizures, and that epileptics have lower blood levels of magnesium than normal subjects. The mineral has been used to treat convulsions in pregnant women. For his seizure patients, Weil recommends 1,000 mg of magnesium and calcium at bedtime and 500 mg of each twelve hours later. He notes that citrates, gluconates, and chelated forms are best. Herbalist Christopher Hobbs suggests ample amounts of seaweeds for their good mineral balance. (The brown seaweed kelp shouldn't be taken in excess, Hobbs notes, because its high concentrations of iodine can (rarely) lead to health problems.)

Vitamin B₆. This is an important vitamin for healthy bioelectric functioning of the central nervous system. Vitamin B_6 also plays a role in the metabolism of the neurotransmitters norepinephrine and acetylcholine, which may inhibit certain types of seizures. In addition B_6 helps maintain a proper balance of sodium, potassium, and magnesium. Researchers found that a B_6 deficiency in certain baby formulas can cause infantile epilepsy, which can then be reversed by supplying B_6 (yet another argument in favor of breast milk, which also provides other nutrients, such as taurine, that may be missing in infant formula).

Daily supplementary doses up to about 50 mg are widely considered to be safe. Ongoing daily dosages of B_6 in the 200–500 mg range may be toxic for some people and should be taken only with professional supervision. Dietary sources include bananas, chicken, salmon, sunflower seeds, wheat germ, and whole grains.

Pizzorno notes that it is also important to eliminate pyridoxine (B_6) antagonists, substances such as alcohol and oral contraceptives that prevent the body from maintaining high levels of the vitamin.

Folic acid. Some nutritional therapists are successfully giving epileptics daily doses of 400–800 mcg of this important B vitamin to improve mood and to offset the adverse side effects of anticonvulsants such as Dilantin. This is a safe level of supplementation for anyone. Leafy green vegetables are the best dietary source of folic acid.

Vitamin E. Studies indicate that some epileptic children have abnormally low blood levels of E and experience fewer severe seizures when administered the vitamin. Some 400–800 IU daily may improve circulation and immunity, among other benefits.

Lecithin. A fatty acid sold as a supplement and used as a food additive, lecithin is an important natural source of choline, which many nutritional scientists consider one of the B complex vitamins. Choline and the neurotransmitter acetylcholine play a number of roles in the healthy functioning of cells, nerves, and the brain. Studies have found that some people who are deficient in acetylcholine suffer from certain neurologic disorders, such as Parkinson's disease and tardive dyskinesia, that are characterized by convulsionlike muscular movements. Victims of such conditions have improved by taking choline supplements.

Egg yolks, lentils, soybeans, brown rice, and cauliflower are rich in lecithin. Pure choline has the potential side effect of causing depression in some people who take it at high levels (more than 3 grams per day), so dietitians recommend that consumers stick with natural sources or lecithin granules rather than pure choline supplements in tablet or liquid form. Daily consumption of 500–1,000 mg of lecithin is safe. Therapeutic doses of choline to control neurological diseases are much higher, up to twelve to sixteen grams per day, and such programs should be devised only with the supervision of a knowledgeable practitioner.

Vitamin A. Beta carotene protects brain function and is an important antioxidant. Therapeutic doses average 25,000 IU daily.

Vitamin C plus bioflavonoids. The usual dose is two to five grams daily, or to bowel tolerance, to protect the adrenal gland and help cope with emotional stress.

Anyone considering taking high dosages of vitamins or minerals as part of a therapeutic approach to a seizure condition should consult with a knowledgeable practitioner. High levels of some nutrients can cause deficiencies in other nutrients or have other adverse side effects.

Overall dietary recommendations for seizure disorders are controversial. Conventional medicine actually recognizes a dietary treatment for epilepsy: a high-fat diet that uses a specially formulated synthetic oil product as a major source of calories. Protein and carbohydrate intake is limited. A number of studies have shown that such a diet can reduce seizures. Nutritionist Shari Lieberman and other alternative practitioners contend that the diet's side effects, including diarrhea, and more importantly the long-term health problems associated with high-fat diets in general, argue for a different approach. Lieberman says, "A better seizure-prevention program would include well-balanced but smaller meals at regular intervals, like five times per day, with a baseline of an insurance-level multivitamin and mineral supplement."

An insurance level of supplements includes the eleven vitamins, four minerals, and three trace elements for which the federal government has determined there are recommended dietary allowances (RDAs). Many supplement companies offer insurance-level, "one-a-day" formulas, though in most cases the pills or capsules are meant to be taken up to six times per day. Such supplementation often exceeds the RDAs, thus providing greater protection against marginal nutrient deficiencies.

Diet may affect seizure activity in other ways. For instance, researchers have found that a seizure victim's blood sugar levels fall just before an attack. A number of nutritional practitioners report anecdotal evidence that food allergies and constipation can increase the chance of a seizure in some people.

Studies such as "Nutritional Aspects of Epilepsy," published in 1983 in the *International Clinical Nutrition Review*, have helped solidify the role of nutrients in controlling convulsive disorders. There's less evidence for effective herbal therapies, though there are interesting possibilities. For instance, research in India and China points to possible antiepilepsy effects of garlic and a black-pepper extract. Hobbs says that skullcap *(Scutellaria laterifolia)* extract or tincture (not capsules, which he says may be adulterated) taken long-term is the best known antiseizure herb. According to Hobbs, "I know several people who have had some success just taking herbal antispasmodics over a period of time. Some have been able to reduce the amount of anticonvulsant drugs they were taking."

Other herbs that relax the nerves or have antispasmodic properties include valerian, passionflower, catnip, and California poppy. A popular formula for an antispasmodic tea combines black cohosh, chamomile, skullcap, and valerian. Drink two to three cups at the first sign of an attack. Herbs such as oatstraw and alfalfa that are high in healthful minerals may also play a role in preventing seizures.

Acupuncture, the ancient Chinese medical system of inserting needles into the body's energy points, shows promise as a treatment for epilepsy. Studies by veterinary acupuncturists indicate that the technique may prevent convulsions even in difficult-to-treat cases of epilepsy with no known cause. Bioelectric authority Robert O. Becker, M.D., author of *The Body Electric*, suggests that acupuncture's ability to affect epilepsy is due to the fact that tiny needles inserted into the skin cause minute changes in electrical currents in the body, an effect he has confirmed in his studies. He even theorizes that the preconvulsion aura some epileptics feel is a conscious perception of a change in the electrical potential of nerve cells in the brain. Becker cautions against the use of electro-acupuncture, a new technique marrying bioelectric therapy with acupuncture. He says that the levels of current and voltage electro-acupuncturists use may be dangerously high.

Michael Reed Gach and other acupressure practitioners recommend massage of a number of points to help recover from a seizure. These include:

♦ the points on the back of the jawbone, in the indentation behind the earlobes, to relax facial tensions
♦ the points on the sole of each foot, at the base of the ball between the two pads, to stimulate the kidneys and rejuvenate the spirit

Aromatherapists recommend inhaling the aroma from the essential oil of Lavender or Chamomile at the first indication of a convulsion. Put a few drops on a cotton cloth and hold under the nose for a few breaths, keeping the eyes closed to avoid irritating them. Some essential oils, including Camphor and Sage, should be avoided by anyone with a seizure disorder.

Though long-term constitutional care is more common, homeopaths use the following remedies for after a seizure:

♦ *Aconite*, for a seizure brought on from fright or fever
♦ *Belladonna*, if the person is red-faced with dilated pupils

A number of natural therapists have had positive results treating childhood seizures by manipulating the bones and joints of the head, neck, and spine. Contact a knowledgeable osteopath, craniosacral osteopath, or chiropractor about the possibilities (see "Resources").

Among the recommendations Weil makes to his seizure patients is that they use biofeedback to learn to produce slower alpha- and theta-rhythm brain waves. Other mind/body treatments, including relaxation techniques, behavior therapy, and psychological counseling have also been used as effective adjuncts to conventional medical therapy for epilepsy. Two pioneers in the mind/body approach to epilepsy are psychologist Donna Andrews and neurologist Joel Reiter, who treat and study epilepsy at their clinic in Santa Rosa, California (see "Resources"). They have published research showing that over 80 percent of their patients, who combine mind/body techniques with anticonvulsant medication, are able to completely control their seizures (compared to an approximately 60 percent success rate for drugs alone).

Weil suggests that persons with seizure disorders may benefit from learning the following simple yogic breathing exercise. Sitting with your back straight, place the tip of your tongue against the ridge of tissue just behind your upper front teeth. Keep it there during the entire exercise. To inhale, close the mouth and draw air in quietly through the nose to a mental count of four. Hold your breath for a count of seven. Now exhale completely through the mouth and around the tongue, making a whoosh sound and silently counting to eight. If the tongue position seems awkward, try pursing your lips slightly. Inhale again and repeat the cycle three more times for a total of four breaths.

Weil notes that the exhalation should always take twice as long as the inhalation, so the ratio of 4:7:8 is important. According to yoga theory, the position of the tongue on the ridge of the mouth is a factor in completing an energy circuit in the body.

Certain lifestyle adjustments may help prevent seizures. Since emotional stress, financial worries, and overexcitement may lead to seizures, people who are at risk for seizures should try to lead a balanced, steady life. Family love and support are crucial. You also want to avoid stimulants such as caffeine and refined sugar, which can increase the excitability of the brain.

Regular physical activity may help to reduce the frequency of seizures, though excessive fatigue should be avoided.

People who suffer from frequent seizures may want to carry a card or wear a tag that informs others about the condition. Epileptics may also want to alert close coworkers, a sensible practice that would probably be more widespread if epileptics were not too frequently, and unfairly, discriminated against because of their illness.

TWELVE

Dental Emergencies

THIS CHAPTER COVERS:

♦ *toothache*
♦ *teething*
♦ *loose, cracked, knocked-out, and extracted tooth*
♦ *mouth infections and abscesses*

The enamel layer that covers a healthy human tooth is the hardest substance in the body. Like other hard objects, however, teeth are subject to the forces of erosion and trauma. The most common form of tooth erosion is decay, due to an acid that forms on the teeth from festering food particles and bacteria. The acid can eventually eat a hole (a cavity, or caries) into the tooth that can be painful if deep enough to affect the nerves in the tooth's root.

Trauma comes in the usual forms: a blow suffered during a sporting event or auto accident, biting down hard on an object that is harder than the tooth, or a punch to the mouth. Injuries such as these can loosen teeth, crack them, or even cause them to be knocked out of their socket entirely. Since teeth are living structures that contain blood vessels and nerves, such injuries can be painful and permanent. Teeth and gums can also be injured by infections that occur in the mouth. Whatever the source of the injury, proper first-aid steps can help you to avoid the worst consequences of dental emergencies.

♦ Toothache

The direct cause of most toothaches is a cavity that has been ignored for too long. When a cavity is not cleaned and filled in its early stages, it can progress beneath the tooth's surface enamel layer to the dentin, the hard substance that surrounds the tooth's inner core, or pulp. Tiny canals in the dentin allow bacteria to get into the pulp, which houses the tooth's nerves and blood vessels. As white blood cells flood the pulp to fight the bacteria, blood vessels swell and apply pressure to the tooth's nerves. You feel this pressure as a toothache.

The initial symptoms of such a toothache are usually sensitivity to heat, cold, or sweets, and mild pain. This is enough reason to contact your dentist. The pain gradually worsens (and may become persistent enough to prevent you from sleeping) until the cavity is treated, or the nerves are killed by the bacteria (in which case an abscess may form). Dental treatment is more difficult, and drastic, when you wait until symptoms reach these final stages.

Somewhat less common causes of toothaches include:

◆ temporomandibular joint (TMJ) syndrome, poor bite, or other problems with the jaw joint
◆ inflammations or infections of the gums or the tissue around the root of the tooth
◆ dental traumas such as a fractured tooth

Schedule an appointment with your dentist whenever a toothache develops. You should be seen within twelve hours if the toothache is accompanied by a fever or swelling of the face or gums. Until the appointment, if you have a mild toothache, physicians and dentists are likely to suggest merely taking an analgesic such as aspirin or acetaminophen. The dentist treats the cavity by drilling and filling it. If the cavity is too deep, the dentist may have to put in a temporary filling and schedule you for a root canal. Extractions are rarely necessary for these conditions.

BASIC FIRST AID FOR TOOTHACHES

Basic first-aid steps for a toothache can help to relieve some of the pain. Such steps, however, do not substitute for professional dental treatment.

Remove food that is trapped in the cavity. Pry gently with a toothpick, floss, or rinse the mouth with warm, salty water.

Apply cold to deaden nerves and relieve pain. Put an ice cube in the mouth to suck on, or wrap ice in a cloth and apply it to the tooth or to the exterior of the cheek. Apply cold for fifteen minutes or so three to four times per day.

If the cold seems to be making the pain worse, try a warm, wet compress or facial pack (not a heating pad, which can heat the area too thoroughly and worsen an infection). Alternating periods of cold and warmth may also help, particularly if the pain is throbbing and there is visible swelling of the cheeks. Try twelve minutes of cold and then twelve minutes of warmth for a few cycles.

Some toothaches may also be helped by gently massaging the area around the cheek and gums. You can also try putting a wad of gauze between the tooth and the inside of the cheek, which may help relieve a toothache by lessening pressure on the tooth.

Eat soft foods like yogurt. The pressure of chewing often aggravates a toothache.

NATURAL FIRST-AID REMEDIES FOR TOOTHACHES

The following steps can be used along with the basic treatments during the period before you get to the dentist.

Apply the essential oil of Clove to relieve constant toothache pain. It's usually best to dilute Clove oil, since it lessens the sting and may only marginally affect the pain-relieving effects. Try diluting it with equal parts olive or other vegetable oil, or brandy. If that's still too strong, mix fifteen to twenty drops of Clove per teaspoon of oil. The easiest way to apply it to a toothache is to dip a cotton swab or cotton ball in the oil mixture and rub the painful tooth and surrounding gum.

Clove oil is the most common and time-tested of the natural toothache remedies, but undiluted it is potentially toxic in large doses or taken continually for longer than a week or so. Avoid taking it during pregnancy. It can also be irritating to the skin or gums. Most people find that it stings for ten to fifteen seconds (or more) when applied undiluted to the gums.

The essential oil of Clove is produced from the dried flower buds of a tropical evergreen tree widely cultivated around the Indian Ocean and in the West Indies. With its distinctive taste and smell, Clove oil is a popular flavoring and spice in the food industry. Herbalists have also been using the potent essential oil for thousands of years, primarily for relieving tooth pain. One of the principal active ingredients in the essential oil is the compound eugenol, which is still used by some dentists as a pain reliever and oral disinfectant. A number of over-the-counter toothache remedies, such as Numzident, contain eugenol. Clove oil is an all-purpose dental remedy, effective for relieving the pain not only of toothaches but canker sores, teething, and tooth and gum abscesses.

Other essential oils that have a topical analgesic effect similar to Clove oil's include Peppermint, Cinnamon, and Eucalyptus. The Chinese essential oil product White Flower Analgesic Balm, which is mostly Wintergreen and Eucalyptus oils, can also be used on a toothache. Like Clove, these oils may irritate or sting on application, so test with a small amount and dilute if necessary. These oils are also potentially toxic if consumed in large amounts, so use only in small doses and not during pregnancy.

Apply a healing herbal poultice or compress. Topical herbal applications are more difficult than mouthwashes to make and apply, but offer the advantage of longer direct contact with the site of pain. One common method is to make a tea from a heaping teaspoon of the dried herb. Put the moist herb inside a piece of cheesecloth, strain out the liquid, and apply as a poultice to the toothache. You can also make a tea, dip a clean cotton cloth into it, wring slightly, and apply the cloth to the tooth or the cheek. Redip and reapply frequently. Alternatively, use a cloth dipped into a solution made by adding ten to fifteen drops herbal concentrate or tincture to half a glass of warm water. Use any of the following herbs:

- yarrow
- chamomile
- comfrey
- aloe
- osha
- ginger
- echinacea

Echinacea was a favorite toothache herb of various Native American tribes: the Crow people chewed the fresh root, the Cheyenne put the juice of the root in the mouth, and the Oglala Dakota took it internally for toothache. Some herbalists recommend mixing echinacea with myrrh for added effect. Herbalist Christopher Hobbs—author of *Echinacea: The Immune Herb!*—recommends applying drops of tincture right on the tooth every fifteen minutes until the pain is relieved. "Echinacea also activates the immune system and initiates the healing response," he notes.

Take an appropriate homeopathic remedy. "I've had quite a bit of experience with dental problems using homeopathy," says homeopath and M.D. Jennifer Jacobs. Here's what she recommends:

- *Belladonna.* Use this remedy for rapid onset of throbbing pain with dry mouth, especially when the gums are red and swollen.
- *Chamomilla.* Try this for severe or unbearable pain that is worse at night or is made worse by cold air, or by warm food and drink.
- *Coffea.* Homeopaths recommend this when a toothache is made worse by heat and hot food or relieved by applying cold in the form of ice water held in the mouth. (Swallow the water when it warms up and take another mouthful of ice water to help relieve the pain of a toothache.)
- *Magnesia phos.* This remedy, made from magnesium phosphate, works well for a piercing pain that seems to be shooting along the length of a tooth's nerve. The pain is relieved by heat and warmth.

A number of homeopathic companies also offer combination remedies, such as NatraBio's Teeth & Gums tincture.

Apply acupressure to the end of the index finger on each side of the fingernail. Squeeze the index finger on the hand that corresponds to the side of the mouth affected. Give rapid, circular massage to the end of the index finger for a minute or so to help relieve a toothache. "The point in the middle of the webbing between the thumb and index finger, which is on the same meridian, also works well to relieve a toothache or teething pain," acupressure authority Michael Reed Gach says.

He adds, "Another effective area to press for a toothache is on the arm, one-third of the way down from the tip of the shoulder to the elbow. Find the sore spot on the side or back of the upper arm and rub firmly, pressing with the fingers against the upper arm bone."

Try one of the traditional folk remedies widely used for toothaches. Many of the following have been used as toothache remedies for centuries.

- Apply a few grains, or drops of concentrate, of cayenne pepper to the toothache. Even more so than Clove oil, cayenne will sting initially but will then dull the pain. Obtained from various types of hot chili peppers, cayenne contains the compound capsaicin. Capsaicin seems to reduce pain and inflammation by blocking the activity of substance P in the body, a compound needed for transmitting pain impulses.

Putting any kind of cayenne preparation in the mouth is not for the timid, Hobbs notes. "Cayenne will kill pain, but it's so hot most people will find it extremely unpleasant. You have to be in bad pain, or be a fan of extra spicy foods, to use cayenne for a toothache. You can lessen the hotness somewhat by adding myrrh or even Peppermint oil to a cayenne preparation."

◆ Peel a clove of garlic and place it on the tooth for an hour or so.

◆ Dip a cotton swab or ball in lime juice and apply to the tooth.

◆ Apply wet cold packs to the feet and surround them by a wool blanket. "I've seen this work pretty well for a toothache," says Joseph Pizzorno, N.D., "perhaps because it draws blood and irritation away from the head."

◆ Dilute 3 percent hydrogen peroxide in a 1:4 ratio with slightly salty water and use as a mouthwash to rinse the tooth and gums.

◆ Crush three fresh star fruits to make a juice and drink twice a day. This is a Chinese folk remedy to relieve toothache and canker sores.

One folk remedy should be skipped. Crushing an aspirin tablet and holding the powder to the gums is not a good idea. Topically applied aspirin can burn sensitive gum tissues.

◆ Teething

An infant cutting her first teeth may appear to be in the throes of torture. She'll drool, cry, squirm, and stay awake at night. Parents of such apparently inconsolable children often wonder if they, the parents, don't suffer as much during the search for effective ways to soothe the wild one. Fortunately some of the same natural health remedies and techniques that relieve an adult's toothache can help soothe a child who is teething. These steps can also help an adult who is suffering from the teething pain that may occur when wisdom teeth come in.

Children teethe at varying rates. On occasion a child is born with a tooth or two showing, while other children may not cut their first tooth until age two. Usually infants begin to get their lower front teeth first, around six to seven months. The back teeth, the first and second molars, are usually cut between the ages of one and two. These are more likely than the front teeth to cause teething pain. The rest of the set of twenty infant teeth come in over the next year or so. Around age six to seven the infant teeth will start falling out and being replaced by the permanent teeth.

Many children grow their infant teeth without much pain or fuss. Mild symptoms of teething are red and swollen gums, drooling, and cheeks on the affected side that may be tender, hot, or flushed. Often the child will attempt to relieve the teething pain by biting or chewing on something, whether fingers, toys, or foods. When the teething pain is more severe, the child may have trouble eating or going to sleep.

Teething is sometimes used by parents as a catch-all diagnosis. Observe the child's symptoms closely to make sure he is teething and not suffering from a fever, ear infection, or other more serious condition that calls for professional evaluation. (See "Chapter 16: Eye and Ear Emergencies" for treatment of ear infections, and "Chapter 18: High Fever" for how best to lower a fever.)

NATURAL FIRST-AID REMEDIES FOR TEETHING

The simplest ways to help relieve a child's teething pains are to gently rub the gums (many parents first apply a drop or two of alcohol, or any herbal tincture that is alcohol-based) and offer a cool drink from a cup. Here are some other quick and effective steps that may help.

Offer the child cold foods to eat or suck on. Parents have reported success using raw carrot sticks, yogurt (after the child reaches nine to ten months old), frozen bagels, and the like. Be careful not to give an infant something like crackers that could break into chunky pieces and present a choking hazard.

Give the baby a chilled teething ring or toy. Keep one in the refrigerator if your child is in the teething age.

Apply a few drops of a pain-relieving herbal tincture. Herbalist Christopher Hobbs says, "I prefer using alcoholic tinctures to essential oils for teething because the latter can be a little harsh." He suggests using a tincture of

- ◆ catnip *(Nepeta cataria)* and echinacea mixed equally
- ◆ chamomile
- ◆ valerian

"Apply two to three drops directly to the gums where the teeth are coming up," he says. "The valerian tincture seems not only to relieve the local pain but to have an overall calming, sedative effect, perhaps due to the herb's essential oil penetrating and getting into the bloodstream.

"You can also make a sweetened chamomile and catnip tea for the baby to drink, but the tinctures are stronger and work faster, of course."

Use diluted preparations of the essential oils of Clove or Tea Tree to reduce pain and swelling and prevent infection. Mix one drop of Clove or Tea Tree oil for each of three to five drops of olive oil, put a little on a cotton swab or your finger, and lightly massage it into the baby's gums. This dilution should reduce Clove's tendency to sting. You can also put ten to fifteen drops of Clove oil or Tea Tree oil in half a cup of warm water, mix well, saturate a cloth, and apply the solution to the gums with the cloth.

Administer a homeopathic remedy to the infant. According to one homeopathic practitioner, "The treatment of teething children has probably convinced more people of the efficacy of homeopathy than anything else." Homeopathic remedies are easy for children to swallow and can be given up to three times daily. Here are the principal choices:

♦ *Chamomilla.* This is the first homeopathic remedy to consider. It is most likely to help when the child is extremely irritable, impatient, and capricious (she asks for something, but when you give it to her, she throws it away). The pain is worse in the evening and at night, and the baby may have difficulty sleeping. She is made better by being picked up and carried. Green stools are common with the *Chamomilla* child.

♦ *Belladonna.* Try this remedy if the baby is feverish, and irritable though not quite so much as the *Chamomilla* baby. Homeopath Jacobs says, "I usually won't give *Belladonna* to a teething baby unless he or she has a high fever with a flushed face."

♦ *Calcarea phos.* Use this remedy, made from calcium phosphate, if the child is whining and complaining, though not striking out as the *Chamomilla* child may. *Calcarea phos* is usually best for the child who is late in teething; often he or she is thin and sweaty.

Almost all homeopathic manufacturers who make combination remedies have one for teething, usually using two or more of the above remedies. For instance, Hyland's Teething tablets, made by Standard Homeopathic Co., contain a mixture of *Calcarea phos* 3X, *Chamomilla* 3X, *Coffea* 3X, and *Belladonna* 3X. Other common teething products include Boericke & Tafel's Alpha TC for Teething and Colic, Nova's Teething, and Medicine From Nature's Teething.

Try Walnut, the best flower remedy for teething. Flower essence practitioners recommend Walnut whenever a person is going through a difficult stage in life. Walnut seems to be able to help such people, including teething infants, adjust to normal activity. Rub a few drops of Walnut flower essence directly into the gums.

◆ Loose, Cracked, Knocked-Out, and Extracted Tooth

Each year some 2 million Americans have accidents serious enough to knock a tooth completely from its socket. Most of these accidents happen during a sporting activity or result from an auto accident. Even greater numbers of people suffer from minor accidents that result in loosened or cracked teeth. Grinding the teeth or biting into hard objects can also injure teeth. Prompt first aid is essential for such injuries to the teeth and gums.

A tooth that is merely loosened by an impact to the mouth area is the easiest to treat. Leave it in place. Gently bite down to keep it in place but avoid chewing on it or putting any twisting pressure on it. Consult with your dentist immediately. If the loose tooth has been knocked crooked, a dentist can usually manipulate it back into place. In some instances an oral surgeon may need to immobilize the tooth to allow time for the ligament tissues to reattach and grow strong and firm in the socket.

If you crack a filling, crown, or denture, it is usually best to leave it in place if it doesn't readily come out. For extra safety, use a narrow strip of electrical tape to secure a denture that is broken but not loose (put the tape on the tongue side of the denture after drying it). When dental work breaks and falls out, save it. Do not attempt to replace it. (The danger of replacing a broken dental work is that it will fall into the mouth again and cause you to choke on it.) Rinse your mouth with warm salt water and apply a few drops of Clove oil to the exposed tooth area.

Contact your dentist immediately to have the broken dental work reattached.

If a tooth cracks or fractures, examine it for bleeding. If it is not bleeding, the pulp has not been ruptured. If you are experiencing only mild pain, chances are the pulp has not been affected. A fracture that goes into the pulp will usually cause excruciating pain. Cracked enamel or dentin is a less serious emergency than damaged pulp, but nevertheless you should consult with your dentist as soon as possible. As with broken dental work, leave a cracked tooth in place unless it readily falls out. Avoid further use of the tooth until it can be repaired.

When a crack extends into the pulp, the tooth should be treated in the same manner as a tooth that has been knocked out (see below). A pulp crack is a major dental emergency that calls for dental treatment within forty-eight hours. If not treated by then, the tooth will die.

WHAT TO DO WHEN A TOOTH IS KNOCKED OUT

When a tooth is knocked out, ligaments, the tough tissues that hold tooth to socket, snap. When a hard force breaks a tooth's ligament, part of the ligament stays attached to the root of the tooth and part remains in the tooth socket. Anything that further injures the ligament left on the tooth, such as allowing the ligament to dry out or scraping it off the tooth to "clean" the root, prevents the tooth from being successfully reimplanted. An adult tooth that is knocked out of its socket can usually be saved if you act quickly enough. If the ligament can be restored to its blood-rich environment within fifteen to thirty minutes, there's a 90 percent chance that the tooth will reattach to the socket.

If a tooth gets knocked out and it doesn't fall out of your mouth, there is no need even to take it out of the mouth. Grasp the tooth by the crown and place it back in the socket. Cover it with a piece of sterile gauze, apply gentle compression, and go immediately to your dentist or hospital emergency room (hospitals keep dentists on call).

If a tooth gets knocked out of your mouth, you need to gently and very briefly rinse it off before replacing it in the socket. Again, grasp the tooth only by the sides or crown, never the root. Don't clean, scrape, or sterilize the tooth. When it is back in its socket, cover it with sterile gauze, apply gentle compression, and seek emergency treatment.

In cases where it is not possible to immediately replace the tooth in its socket, gently rinse the tooth under water. Then put the tooth in a clean, plastic container filled with cold, whole milk, and cover. Milk is chemically an almost ideal solution for this purpose. If milk is not available, use water. If the tooth can't be transported submerged in liquid, wrap it in sterile gauze or clean cloth that has been soaked in milk or water. Don't transport the tooth in dry gauze or cloth, since doing so can dry out the ligament. Seek emergency treatment as soon as possible.

A baby tooth that has been knocked out doesn't call for such emergency steps, since another tooth will eventually grow into the socket. If adult teeth are years away or you have some other concern, don't replace the tooth in an infant's mouth since it could fall out again and be swallowed. Put the tooth in milk and get it and the baby to the dentist as quickly as possible.

Apply cold compresses to the tooth or cheeks to help relieve some of the pain associated with a knocked-out tooth. A sterile gauze pad and direct pressure created by biting down will help control any bleeding. The injured person shouldn't eat or drink anything until emergency treatment is completed.

NATURAL REMEDIES FOR TOOTH TRAUMAS

Here are some natural remedies to use after trauma to a tooth. Some of these may also work well for before and after having a tooth pulled or filled, or any other dental treatment or surgery.

Apply gentle pressure to the point in the web of the hand between the thumb and index finger. Manipulating this point can calm nerves and help relieve pain. Do it to the hand that's on the same side as the dental problem.

To help stop gums or other mouth tissues from bleeding, apply a cool, used green or black tea bag to the injury. The tannins in green and black tea have an astringent effect that will constrict blood vessels and inhibit bleeding. Green or black tea bags can also be placed over a loose tooth to tighten it in place. (The tannins in these teas may also prevent tooth decay and gum disease.) Many people find that cool, moist chamomile tea bags have a soothing effect when applied to gum and mouth tissues, perhaps because of chamomile's anti-inflammatory and wound-healing properties.

Chew a leaf. "The best remedy I've found," herbalist Christopher Hobbs says, "is to chew up a green leaf of yarrow or plantain and keep it close to the area of bleeding. Yarrow in particular is an incredible styptic for stopping bleeding of the gums almost instantly. Yarrow also has some antibacterial effects. I used yarrow in this way a couple of years ago when I had some wisdom teeth pulled and it worked incredibly well. Plantain works in a similar way though it has more soothing and anti-inflammatory effects."

Take oral doses of the Bach flower remedy Rescue Remedy to calm a person who has had a tooth knocked out. Place three to four drops of the liquid concentrate directly from the bottle under the tongue. You can also dilute Rescue Remedy by putting four drops in one-quarter glass of water, tea, or juice. This should be sipped every three to five minutes.

Traumas severe enough to knock out a tooth may be emotionally frightening. Rescue Remedy or one of the other first-aid flower remedies can help relieve the fear, anxiety, shock, and panic that may accompany a dental emergency.

Take oral doses of the homeopathic remedy Arnica. A reader in Atlantic Beach, Florida, says, "I once had two identical dental surgeries two weeks apart. The first time I took an entire bottle of acetaminophen over four days to get comfortable. That experience prompted me to look into homeopathic remedies. Before the next procedure, I took two *Arnica* 6X tablets before the surgery, then two more immediately after. I never had a discomfort."

"Arnica is usually all that's needed," says Jennifer Jacobs, M.D. She says that other homeopathic remedies that sometimes help following a tooth trauma include:

- *Hypericum*. This remedy helps reduce nerve pain.
- *Aconite*. Use this before a visit to the dentist to calm the person and alleviate fears.
- *Ledum*. This "puncture injury" remedy works well to reduce pain after an anesthesia injection.
- *Belladonna*. This is a good remedy for throbbing pain accompanied by a dry mouth.
- *Apis*. Think bee stings. If tooth pain is stinging and burning, reach for the *Apis*.

Tighten up a loose tooth using myrrh or oak bark. Like green and black tea, these two herbs are astringent. They're effective not only for loose teeth but for any type of gum ailment, including sore and receding gums. Apply as a powder or tincture, suggests Hobbs. "Put some drops in your mouth, or directly on the loose tooth. Unlike echinacea or Clove oil, myrrh and oak bark are not numbing, but they are good astringents. Myrrh is rather pleasant tasting and oak bark is not bad either," Hobbs says.

Astringent herbs can also be applied to the teeth and gums as a strong tea. Dissolve ten to fifteen drops concentrate or tincture of myrrh in half a glass of warm water. Three or four times a day swirl the herbal liquid around or hold it in your mouth for thirty seconds or so. Then either swallow or spit out.

To speed recovery from extractions and other serious dental operations, take bromelain. Take 250–500 mg three times a day between meals for three days prior to the dental procedure.

A natural enzyme derived from the pineapple plant, bromelain has anti-inflammatory and wound-healing properties. Tooth extractions can bruise the gums, cheeks, and mouth. Bromelain and other oral remedies to reduce bruising (see "Chapter 10: Contusions") can prevent the side effects of the procedure from causing pain for days afterward. Bromelain is available in 100-mg tablets from a number of supplement manufacturers.

◆ Mouth Infections and Abscesses

The wet, warm environment of the mouth is one of the body's most favorable breeding grounds for bacteria. If bacteria are allowed to proliferate, an infection or abscess (a swollen, inflamed area in body tissues, in which pus gathers) may develop in various places in the mouth. Bacteria from a cavity can get through the pulp and into the socket of a tooth to form an abscess there. Abscesses also typically form in the gums, usually from food particles that get trapped between the teeth and the gums. Infections sometimes develop in the gums as they part to allow a wisdom tooth to emerge.

Another common mouth problem is canker sores, painful ulcers that form on the inner surface of the cheeks. Why some people get more canker sores than others is a mystery to dental researchers. Some of the instigating agents are food allergies, stress, physical trauma, and poor dental hygiene.

Bacterial infections and abscesses are often painless at first. An infected tooth may be tender to the touch or painful to chew on. As the infection or abscess grows, the person experiences more persistent pain and swelling in the jaw or along the gum line.

Like infections elsewhere on the body, dental infections can spread if not successfully treated. A tooth infection can spread to the face and neck, possibly leading to swelling that can impair breathing. If enough bacteria get into the bloodstream, the person may become feverish or even develop a type of blood poisoning known as septic shock. This potentially life-threatening condition is a major medical emergency that requires hospitalization and high doses of antibiotics.

An infected tooth is usually the result of a cavity that needs to be treated by a dentist. The conventional treatment is to drain pus and disinfect the tooth, then either fill the tooth or extract it. Antibiotics are often prescribed as well. Gum infections are also treated mechanically, by scaling or surgery.

Basic first aid for dental infections and abscesses is similar to that for toothaches. Apply warm compresses, eat only soft foods, floss, rinse the mouth with warm salt water or herbal mouthwashes, and use Clove oil to help relieve the pain. Don't substitute these steps, however, for visits to a dentist.

NATURAL FIRST-AID REMEDIES FOR MOUTH INFECTIONS AND ABSCESSES

The following natural remedies can complement dental treatment of infections by increasing circulation to mouth tissues and supplying additional antibiotic power.

Combine the healing powers of echinacea and myrrh to relieve mouth and gum infections. Naturopath Joe Pizzorno says that the pioneering naturopath John Bastyr developed an excellent formula. Mix tincture of echinacea with myrrh gum powder to make a paste. Apply the paste locally to the infection. "Try to keep the saliva from washing it away," says Pizzorno, "but there's no problem swallowing it. I've used this a lot, and it works great."

Echinacea and myrrh, as well as the herbs cayenne and goldenseal, can also be applied in an herbal compress or poultice, singly or in combination. Make a tea, dip a clean cotton cloth into it, wring slightly, and apply the cloth to the tooth or the gums. Redip and reapply frequently. Alternatively, use a cloth dipped into a solution made by adding ten to fifteen drops herbal concentrate or tincture to half a glass of warm water.

A well-traveled woman from Greendell, New Jersey, champions myrrh and goldenseal. She tells us, "I was in a remote province of India a few years back when my gums became irritated and started to bleed. I reached for my hebal kit and combined my myrrh mouthwash and powder from goldenseal tablets to make a pumice. I applied this to my gums twice a day, and within three days my gums were normal."

Another application method is to apply drops of herbal concentrate or tincture directly to teeth or gums. Echinacea is also available as a salve or cream.

Apply propolis tincture. Herbalist Christopher Hobbs says, "For mouth and cold sores, I've found that the best thing by far is propolis tincture. It works like a charm even on inflamed gums. You don't want to put a lot in your mouth, since it can create a yellow film that will stick to your teeth. Rather put a few drops right where the inflamed gum is and let it sit. I've seen propolis tincture get rid of many mouth sores and abscesses over the years, especially more superficial ones like cold sores."

Propolis is a resinous substance that bees collect from plants to use in the construction of the beehive. A few studies have confirmed antibacterial effects when bee propolis is applied to wounds. Bee propolis products are widely available in natural foods stores. Manufacturers claim propolis taken internally can increase energy and boost athletic performance, though scientific studies have for the most part failed to confirm such properties. Some propolis products contain pollen and may cause allergic reactions in certain individuals.

Choose from a number of potential gum healers in your herbal and essential oil kit. If you don't have echinacea and myrrh, try one or more of the following topical applications. Any of these can be applied several times a day to help heal an infection or abscess:

- ◆ Aloe gel from a freshly broken leaf, or a product containing at least 96 percent pure aloe, can be soothing.
- ◆ Tea Tree oil is a powerful natural disinfectant.
- ◆ Calendula in gel form is a mild and widely available herbal analgesic and antibiotic. An effective, although rather bitter-tasting, herbal mouthwash can be made by putting two full droppers of tincture of calendula in half a glass of water.
- ◆ Black ointment is a tarlike topical ointment available in slightly different forms from leading herbal producers. Typically it contains herbs such as comfrey root, plantain, and goldenseal root and other ingredients such as activated charcoal, pine or juniper tar, pine gum, beeswax, and lanolin.
- ◆ Garlic can be helpful if you wrap a raw garlic clove or garlic powder in cheesecloth or a layer of sterile gauze and apply it between cheek and gum. Some people use topical

applications of fresh-grated garlic or garlic oil, though these can sting.

◆ Plantain is a favorite remedy for mouth infections that herbalist Christopher Hobbs says he has used on a lot of people. "Thoroughly chew, mash, or blend up some fresh plantain leaves," he says. "Mix in five to six drops of echinacea tincture and a capsuleful of vitamin E. Then take a small, two-inch-square piece of gauze and roll up the herbal mixture into a little cigarette-shaped wad. Place the gauze between the gum and cheek so that it sits on the abscess or sore like an internal poultice. You can leave it on for hours or even overnight. Plantain's antibacterial and anti-inflammatory powers are so remarkable I've seen people who've used this poultice avoid having a tooth pulled."

◆ Astragalus is a popular Chinese medicinal plant that also grows in the United States. Holly Eagle, an Oriental Medical Doctor, notes, "It is often hard to reverse the growth of a mouth ulcer, but we've found that putting some astragalus in a tincture of other gum-healing herbs like myrrh or echinacea can help promote the development of healthy tissue."

Let a homeopathic remedy boost your healing powers. Take any of the following homeopathic remedies for dental infections or abscesses:

◆ *Belladonna.* Take this at the first hint of an abscess or gum boil, particularly one at the base of the cheek that is throbbing, hot, red, and swollen.

◆ *Hepar sulph.* Use this remedy, made from calcium sulfide, if the abscess is extremely sensitive to touch and to cold air and causes a sharp, splinterlike pain.

◆ *Silica.* Made from flint, *Silica* will help relieve a slow-developing abscess at the root of a tooth, especially one that is sensitive to cold water.

◆ *Mercurius.* Try this remedy, made from mercury, if the person has a foul odor and a metallic taste in the mouth, and excessive saliva. The affected tooth usually feels loose.

Apply some of the prepared Chinese medicine known as Watermelon Frost formula. Practitioners of traditional Chinese medicine say that this remedy is excellent applied topically to relieve toothaches as well as the pain of mouth sores and ulcers. The main ingredient is made by a special process that involves sealing small pieces of whole watermelon in clay jars. Eventually small crystals of "watermelon frost" form on the outside of the jars. These crystals are scraped off, powdered, and combined with seven other herbs to make a sweet-tasting compound formula that is used both internally and externally.

Watermelon Frost is called Fu Fang Xi Gua Shuang (or simply Xi Gua Shuang) by the producer, the Kweilin Drug Manufactory of Kwangsi, China. It is sold as a powder in 2-gram vials, six vials to a box. To make a paste, mix the powder from one vial with water. Watermelon Frost is also available as a lozenge (let it slowly dissolve in the mouth) or liquid spray. It is available in Oriental pharmacies or by mail order from distributors of Chinese herbs (see "Resources").

Nip canker sores early on with any of the following natural treatments:

- ◆ Dissolve one-half teaspoon baking soda in half a cup of warm water and use as a mouthwash.
- ◆ Apply a wet tea bag to the sore for temporary pain relief.
- ◆ Mix one tablespoon of 3 percent hydrogen peroxide in half a cup of warm water and use as a mouthwash.
- ◆ Once the sore has started to heal, gently apply some vitamin E oil to the area.
- ◆ Soak a cotton swab or cloth in castor oil and apply it to the sore. This is a favorite remedy of followers of the late psychic Edgar Cayce.
- ◆ Mix five drops each of homeopathic *Hypericum* and *Calendula* mother tincture in half a cup warm water and use as a mouthwash.

Take an acidophilus supplement every day if you're taking high doses of antibiotics to treat an abscess or infection. Hobbs says, "To replenish intestinal flora you should take doses of acidophilus that provide at least ten billion organisms per day." Nutritionist Shari Lieberman recommends that people with depleted intestinal flora take one to two teaspoons of powder or liquid daily during recovery, then one-half to one teaspoon per day for another week or longer to fully repopulate the gut.

Acidophilus has become the generic term for various types of naturally occurring live bacteria that are increasingly popular as dietary supplements. Anyone who is taking oral doses of antibiotics may benefit by supplementing the diet with acidophilus.

Antibiotics kill not only disease-causing bacteria but the "friendly" microorganisms that your intestines need to function properly. When beneficial intestinal flora are missing, harmful bacteria and microorganisms, including fungi such as *Candida albicans* (a cause of yeast infections), more easily move in and take over. Supplementing the diet with acidophilus helps repopulate the intestines with beneficial bacteria and prevent the establishment of harmful bacterial colonies. A high-fiber, whole-foods diet can complement acidophilus's positive effect on intestinal flora.

Acidophilus is available in the form of tablets, powders, capsules, and liquids sold in most natural foods stores. Look for acidophilus products that have labels providing information on how many live or "viable" bacteria each capsule or teaspoon provides, an expiration date with a guarantee of product viability until that date, and a listing of additional ingredients.

◆ Preventing and Recovering from Dental Emergencies

A full set of teeth for an adult comprises thirty-two teeth. Because of poor dietary and dental habits, injuries, and routine removal of wisdom teeth, most adults are chewing away with only twenty-four. The average senior citizen has a mere fourteen teeth. Moreover, dentists estimate that some form of gum disease afflicts one in two people aged eighteen or older.

Protect yourself from the two main sources of mouth trauma: sports injuries and automobile accidents. Anyone who plays a contact sport should protect his or her teeth by wearing appropriate equipment, such as a helmet, face mask, and mouthpiece. In an auto, wearing a seat belt can save not only your life but your looks: authorities estimate that seat belts could prevent one in four of the fifty thousand facial injuries, many to the teeth and jaw, sustained in auto accidents each year.

Don't use your teeth to do anything but chew food. Leave stunts like opening beer bottles with the teeth to stuntmen and bottle openers.

Eat more of the foods that promote strong teeth and gums and fewer of those that weaken them. A healthful diet is probably the single most important influence on teeth, especially for young people. Whole, natural, and fresh foods high in nutrients can build strong teeth and bones, while overprocessed and highly sweetened and refined foods increase the likelihood of cavities and gum disease.

- Foods that promote healthy teeth include leafy green vegetables and others high in fiber and calcium. Crunchy foods such as apples, carrots, and celery that need to be chewed well not only exercise the jaw muscles and increase circulation to the teeth and gums, they have a cleansing effect on the tooth surfaces. Dental researchers have also identified a number of foods that, eaten after a meal, may help prevent tooth decay by preventing tooth-eroding acids from forming in the mouth. These tooth-saving foods include peanuts, cashews, and other nuts; tea (rich in decay-preventing fluoride); sunflower and other seeds; and cheese, olives, dill pickles, and blackstrap molasses.
- Avoid fatty, sticky, and acid-producing foods. Such foods can affect your mouth and saliva in a way that increases the risk of tooth decay and enamel erosion. Raisins and dried fruits are more healthful snacks than candy or potato chips, but since dried fruits easily stick to the teeth, it's a good idea to brush your teeth soon after eating them. Acid-producing foods and drinks include citrus fruits and juices, and colas. Aspirin and some chewable forms of vitamin C tablets are acidic, so you should avoid leaving them in your mouth for longer than it takes to swallow them.

If you suffer from bleeding gums, loose teeth, or other signs of a poor diet, consider improving your eating habits and starting a program of nutritional supplements. All of the nutrients critical to bone health are also essential for teeth. Among the supplements to consider taking every day are:

- vitamin A, 25,000 IU in the form of beta carotene
- niacin, 50–100 mg (one study indicated daily niacin can prevent canker sores)
- vitamin C, two to five grams to bowel tolerance (critical for gum health and making the matrix of bone)
- vitamin D, 400–600 mg
- the minerals calcium and magnesium in a 2:1 ratio, such as 1,500 mg calcium and 750 mg magnesium
- manganese, 15–30 mg, and zinc, 25–50 mg, in balanced mineral formulations
- the trace minerals silicon, 2 mg, and boron, 2 mg

You might also consider daily gum massages with vitamin E oil, and taking 400–800 IU of E internally.

Lieberman notes that coenzyme Q10 (coQ10) has demonstrated excellent results in clinical trials on periodontal disease. CoQ10 is a natural, vitaminlike nutrient that may help the body's cells use oxygen. "The studies have been positive in showing a speedup of healing time, reduced pockets, and improvements in other factors associated with gum disease," she says. Natural foods stores carry a variety of coQ10 supplements in tablet form. Take 30–50 mg of coQ10 each day to help reverse periodontal disease.

Most people think only of calcium for teeth and bones, but this is a mistake. Calcium is important but its role has been overemphasized because of an expensive (and often misleading) promotional campaign sponsored by the dairy industry. See the recommendations under the recovery and prevention sections in "Chapter 7: Bone Injuries" for the other herbs, foods, and supplements that are especially high in the bone-building vitamins and minerals.

Floss your teeth regularly and brush them with a natural toothpaste or other healthful product. Natural toothpastes such as those made by Tom's of Maine, Weleda, and Nature's Gate contain none of the potential carcinogens (including synthetic colors and sodium saccharin) that conventional toothpastes use. Other safe and effective substances to brush the teeth with include baking soda (many people use equal parts baking soda and sea salt) and papain powder.

Rinse your mouth occasionally with a healing solution. Try:

- five drops of Tea Tree oil added to one-third cup of warm water
- one tablespoon of 3 percent hydrogen peroxide in eight ounces water

Get regular dental checkups. Dentists can often spot tooth and gum problems before they become critical. Dentists who are savvy about nutrition (and increasing numbers are) are also often the first health professional to notice nutritional deficiencies in a patient. Loose teeth, root canals, or gum disease, for instance, may be an indication of bone loss and thus an early sign of osteoporosis.

THIRTEEN

Dizziness and Fainting

THIS CHAPTER COVERS:

◆ *mild vertigo*
◆ *postural hypotension (low blood pressure)*
◆ *emotional shock and nervous exhaustion*
◆ *stifling atmosphere/heat faint*

SEE "CHAPTER 3: BASIC EMERGENCY CARE" FOR:

◆ *unconsciousness*
◆ *shock*

SEE "CHAPTER 8: BREATHING PROBLEMS" FOR:

◆ *hyperventilation, panic attack, and breath-holding*

SEE "CHAPTER 17: HEAT ILLNESS" FOR:

◆ *heat exhaustion*

SEE "CHAPTER 22: TRAVEL PROBLEMS" FOR:

◆ *motion sickness*

The classic conditions for causing a simple or benign faint are lack of a sufficient oxygen supply coupled with a bodily condition that prevents efficient delivery of available oxygen to the brain. For instance, soldiers forced to stand at attention for a number of hours in hot, poorly ventilated rooms will often faint. At the other end of the spectrum from a benign faint is unconsciousness associated with life-threatening conditions such as heart attack and diabetic coma. These call for immediate professional emergency help (see "Chapter 3: Basic Emergency Care" for details).

Like fainting, dizziness is a relatively common condition that in its mildest form is usually easily treated and prevented, but that can also serve as a warning light about more serious underlying problems.

◆ Dizziness

A general term for a variety of sensations, dizziness is primarily a symptom rather than a condition. Most forms of dizziness are characterized by a feeling of some kind of movement that isn't really there. For instance, when standing still, the person may feel as if he or she is swaying, whirling, reeling, or falling. Or the person may perceive the environment as moving and not be able to orient his or her body in relation to surrounding objects. In its simplest form dizziness may be experienced as a brief moment of light-headedness, while a victim of severe dizziness, also known as vertigo, may suffer for hours from a hallucination that he, or the room he is in, is spinning about. (A common misconception is that vertigo is acrophobia, or a fear of heights; *height vertigo* is a misleading term at times used to describe the feeling of faintness some people experience when they look down from a high place.) Dizziness is often accompanied by other symptoms such as nausea, a lack of depth perception, and sweating. On occasion it ends in a faint.

Any inner-ear condition may cause dizziness because the delicate organs of the ear play a central role in maintaining the body's sense of balance. Deep in the ear are three loop-shaped, tubular structures set at right angles to each other. These tiny loops, known as the semicircular canals, serve as the body's gyroscope. Special hairlike nerve cells in the semicircular canals receive information on the position of the head relative to gravity, as well as on how fast and in which direction the head and body are moving. Nerves relay this data to the cerebellum of the brain, which automatically coordinates thousands of minute muscle movements of the eyes and limbs in a way that allows a person to maintain balance.

A malfunction in this delicate sensory system that controls balance may result in dizziness. For instance, there may be an infection of the inner ear or a lack of oxygen being supplied to the part of the brain in control of balance. It is also possible for confusing sensory input and constant motion to cause the inner ear to send conflicting information to the brain. This is what happens in most cases of motion sickness (see "Chapter 22: Travel Problems").

CAUSES OF DIZZINESS

Dizziness may be caused by something as simple as motion sickness or the accumulation of wax in the inner ear, or by something as serious as brain disease. Probably the most common causes are injuries or infections that affect the inner ear, side effects from use of tobacco, drugs, or alcohol, and postural hypotension. Some other causes and factors to consider are:

Age. Dizziness is more common among older people, perhaps due to vascular changes such as hardening of the arteries of the brain. Dizziness from postural hypotension and sudden movements of the head are more common among the elderly.

Diseases. Those that may cause dizziness include Ménière's syndrome, heat illness, hyperventilation, hypothermia, poisoning, shock, cardiovascular disorders, drug and chemical toxicity, severe eyestrain, and high or low blood pressure.

Injuries and operations. Dizziness is common after injuries to the head (especially concussions), neck, spine, and ears, and after surgery on the brain and inner ear. Excessive bleeding may cause dizziness.

Allergic and toxic reactions. Dizziness may result from a bite or sting or from chemical exposure.

Fright or shock. A startling experience such as the sight of blood can briefly slow the heart and lower blood pressure enough to cause dizziness.

Diet. Dizziness among overweight people may be related to a high-fat, high-cholesterol diet. Marathon runners and other athletes sometimes experience dizziness from drinking only water during extended exertion and thereby depleting electrolyte levels in the blood.

Poor alignment of the jaw or the cervical spine. Dentists have traced some cases of vertigo to temporomandibular joint (TMJ) syndrome. Chiropractors contend that dizziness can be one of the symptoms of a blockage in vital energy flowing through the vertebrae.

One of the more easily treated causes of dizziness (and more rarely fainting) is postural hypotension, resulting from standing up suddenly after a period of sitting or lying. An estimated 6 percent of healthy elderly people suffer from this condition.

Hypotension is low blood pressure, the lesser known cousin of hypertension, or high blood pressure. Chronic hypotension is usually of no medical concern and may even confer some health benefits. In contrast with chronic hypotension, postural hypotension is a fleeting condition that happens only briefly with most people. When you sit or lie down, your blood vessels expand slightly. Stand up quickly and they must contract to maintain the same arterial blood pressure in the new position. The nervous system normally accomplishes this change quickly and automatically. With postural hypotension, however, the reaction occurs a little too slowly. Your blood pressure falls and the flow of blood to the brain is temporarily reduced. The lack of oxygen causes a spell of dizziness.

There's usually no need to be overly concerned about occasional dizziness from postural hypotension. In the remedies section you'll find a number of simple and effective techniques to prevent dizziness from postural hypotension, and it's possible to alleviate the condition itself over time. Often the cause is as simple as chronic anxiety or a long period of convalescence spent in bed. In rare cases, however, it may indicate a more severe problem such as hardening of the arteries, diabetes, or undernourishment. It is also a potential side effect of certain drugs, including marijuana and some of those prescribed for high blood pressure, heart disease, and depression. If your postural hypotension is causing frequent fainting spells, you should discuss it with your medical practitioner.

One of the most significant aspects of a dizziness episode is whether it represents a recurring problem. An isolated episode may be related to some other passing condition. Dizziness that occurs repeatedly needs to be monitored more closely to determine the underlying cause.

You may need to see a medical practitioner if the dizziness:

♦ does not pass quickly, is severe, or recurs
♦ is followed by unconsciousness

A complete medical exam and the use of diagnostic tools such as a CAT scan or magnetic resonance imaging (MRI) may identify an underlying condition.

BASIC FIRST AID FOR DIZZINESS

The immediate strategy for combating a spell of dizziness is threefold:

Reduce sensory input. If you can, go into a darkened room, slowly seat yourself or lie down, and close your eyes. If you're in a public place and this isn't possible, try focusing on your fist in front of your face or some nearby, nonmoving object.

Place your head below the rest of your body. If possible, lie down on a bed and prop your lower body and feet up slightly, allowing the blood to flow more easily to the brain. Some people with persistent dizziness have found that by repeating this slant-board effect over a period of time, they can open up the circulation to the head enough to prevent dizziness.

Keep your head still. The goal is to reorient yourself to a stable environment.

◆ Fainting

When the brain is being deprived of an adequate supply of oxygenated blood, the body quickly begins to lose strength and vigor. The person's skin turns pale and his hands get cold and clammy. He may yawn repeatedly in an attempt to take in more oxygen. Often he seems restless or anxious. If oxygen levels in the blood continue to fall, he gets light-headed, disoriented, or drowsy. His vision blurs and then finally he keels over unconscious.

Though some cases of fainting are characterized by only a partial loss of consciousness, usually the victim appears to be asleep. Unlike a sleeping person though, a fainting victim is difficult to arouse until something is done to reoxygenate the brain. A victim of fainting loses consciousness only briefly, usually for a minute or less. Typically he lies down, more blood gets to the brain, and he awakens, perhaps a little confused but otherwise all right. If the lack of oxygen is due to a serious injury or illness, however, the unconsciousness may be complete and last indefinitely, in which case the victim is said to be in a coma.

CAUSES OF FAINTING

Like dizziness, fainting can result from a variety of conditions and circumstances, including most of the same ones that cause dizziness. The least worrisome causes are those that lead to a simple or benign faint, such as from:

Sudden, intense pain, fear, or emotion. In some people an unpleasant emotional shock, such as news of the death of a loved one or the sight of an injured person covered with blood, can cause a quick fall in blood pressure and a slowing of the heart, leading to a fainting episode.

An overall weakened state of health, sometimes coupled with nervous exhaustion. A lack or loss of bodily strength, which may result from factors ranging from malnutrition to low blood sugar to extreme, unrelieved anxiety, can lead to fatigue, weakness, and even fainting.

Staying in a room with a lack of circulating oxygen. For instance, oxygen levels may be low from the room's being over-crowded, unventilated, and full of cigarette smoke.

Standing for a long time without moving. This causes blood to accumulate in the legs and reduces the blood available to the brain. Fainting may also result from something as simple as an overly tight collar.

Of much greater long-term medical concern are any episodes of fainting or unconsciousness that result from a serious illness or accident that interrupts the flow of blood to the brain. These include:

◆ accidents, including choking, drug overdose, electrical in-jury, bites or stings, chemical exposure, head or spinal injury, and poisoning
◆ exposure leading to heat illness or hypothermia
◆ medical conditions that can partially impair brain circu-lation, including allergy and migraine
◆ medical conditions that cause a sudden and total interrup-tion of blood flow to the brain, such as stroke, heart attack, pulmonary embolism, medical shock (distinguished from emotional shock), seizure, internal bleeding, and diabetic or insulin coma

Fainting, like dizziness, is not a disease per se but rather a symptom. When confronted with it, your first concern is to deter-mine the seriousness of the underlying cause. With a benign faint from hearing bad news, the cause may be obvious. Otherwise you may need to consider the victim's age and health history, and observe him or her for:

Color of skin and face. Does the victim appear to be red and flushed (indicating he or she may have fainted from, for instance, sunstroke or stroke, or be suffering from carbon monoxide poisoning)? Pale and white (shock, hemorrhage, insulin coma, heart attack)? Or blue (respiratory obstruction)?

Breath. Is the victim's rate of breathing rapid and shallow (medical shock) or gasping and labored (choking, heart disease)? The breath's odor may also provide clues to alcohol overdose or diabetic coma (a spoiled-fruit- or nail-polish-remover-like smell).

Pulse. Is it slow, weak, or strong? A victim's pulse is often full in an early state of bleeding, thin and rapid in states of shock, and irregular or faint after severe injury.

Pupils. These may be dilated, pinpoint, or unequal in size (the latter an indication of possible stroke).

Visible injuries. Bleeding from the ears is a sign of skull fracture, for instance. Also look for signs of bites or stings, or nearby chemicals or poisons.

If you're not sure of the cause of a fainting or unconsciousness episode, it is always safest to assume a serious illness or injury and to call for emergency help while attending to the ABCs (airway, breathing, and circulation) and preventing shock. See the discussion of unconsciousness in Chapter 3.

Call for emergency help as soon as possible if:

- the victim does not regain consciousness within five minutes
- you suspect a serious medical condition such as a heart attack, stroke, or diabetic coma
- the victim is elderly

Meanwhile treat for the major condition.

BASIC FIRST AID FOR BENIGN FAINTING

When circumstances make it clear that someone has suffered a simple, benign faint, for instance from being in a closed space, first-aid steps are in line with the body's natural instincts.

Have the person lie down. If your brain is not getting enough oxygen, your body shuts down those functions (consciousness and balance) that keep you upright. Flat on your back, more blood starts to get to the brain, and you regain consciousness. Of course, it is much safer to start this process consciously at the first sign of fainting than to risk injury in a fall. If you can't lie all the way down, sit and lower your head so that it falls between the knees. This won't work quite as well, since blood is more likely to have pooled in your legs than your abdomen, but it will still help.

While the person is lying on his or her back, prop the legs six to twelve inches higher than the body to allow gravity to take blood back to the head. Don't put a pillow under the head, which not only slows the flow of blood to the head but increases the possibility of choking.

Loosen a tie or tight collar. You want to prevent any clothing from interfering with breathing and circulation.

Take gentle steps to help the person revive. Wipe the forehead with a cool compress, or take any of the steps offered below in the natural treatments section. Don't, however, slap the victim, throw water in his face, or shake him. Keep crowds away to allow the victim fresh air.

Make sure the person's airway stays open until medical help arrives. When you're unconscious, you face a danger of choking since you can't clear your throat, so a fainting victim who vomits or doesn't revive within a few minutes should be put in the recovery position (see Chapter 3).

When the victim regains consciousness, keep him or her lying down for a few more minutes to prevent another faint upon standing. Offer small sips of water or one of the other natural remedies listed below.

◆ Natural Remedies for Benign Dizziness and Fainting

A number of natural remedies are available for the simplest forms of dizziness and fainting, such as those that result from mild vertigo, postural hypotension, emotional shock, and a stifling atmosphere. The following can be used to revive someone who has fainted or to prevent a dizziness or fainting episode from worsening. Never administer an oral remedy to an unconscious person.

Press on the acupressure point widely used to help anchor a spinning world. "The best point for all types of dizziness," says acupressure authority Michael Reed Gach, "is the point two-thirds of the way up from the upper lip to the nose. Manipulating it helps to stabilize the person's energy and sense of balance." Press on the point with the end of your thumb using slightly upward pressure.

Inhale the scent of an essential oil that can restore brain and heart function and stimulate the mind and senses.

"You can mix Rosemary oil with essential oil of Camphor to make a powerful herbal smelling salt, or just use Rosemary oil itself. It's quite stimulating and all you have to do is wave it under the nose to gently arouse consciousness. Once the person is awake, keep them warm and give them some ginger tea to stimulate circulation," herbalist Christopher Hobbs says.

In addition to Rosemary and Camphor, aromatherapists recommend the essential oil of Peppermint for its uplifting and stimulating effects and its ability to help restore brain and heart function. You can either open a bottle of Peppermint oil and hold it under the person's nose, or put four to five drops of the oil on a clean cotton cloth or handkerchief and hold it up to the person's nose to be inhaled.

The conventional consciousness-reviving substance is smelling salts. These are usually an aromatic mixture of carbonate of ammonium with some fragrant scent. Rosemary and other essential oils provide effective plant-based alternatives to revive an unconscious person. "You generally want to rouse an unconscious person," Hobbs says, "because bodily functions are depressed during unconsciousness and it's not a particularly desirable state."

Take a first-aid flower essence such as Bach Flower Rescue Remedy. The most well-known first-aid flower essence is Rescue Remedy, a liquid formula that comes in a tiny amber bottle with a fine glass dropper top. When a person is unconscious, administer it by rubbing a few drops into the lips, behind the ears, or on the wrists, or soaking a cotton cloth in a pint of water with five to six drops of Rescue Remedy and applying it as a compress to the wrists or behind the ears. After the person has revived, place three to four drops of the liquid concentrate directly from the bottle under the tongue. You can also dilute it by putting four drops in one-quarter glass of water, tea, or juice. This should be sipped every three to five minutes.

The first-aid combination flower essences have a stabilizing effect on many people. They are especially useful for any situation or emergency that causes dizziness, faintness, panic, or hysteria.

Following are additional natural remedies for specific causes of dizziness and fainting.

MILD VERTIGO

In addition to sitting or lying and closing the eyes or focusing on a nearby object, or any of the above-mentioned natural remedies, try some of the following steps to relieve mild dizziness spells.

For mild dizziness associated with motion sickness, take ginger. Ginger (*Zingiber officinale*) is widely available fresh or dried, in capsules, and as a liquid concentrate or extract. Take large quantities of ginger to treat or prevent motion sickness. Dried ginger seems to be more effective than fresh ginger. An adult dosage is six to eight capsules or one to two grams of powdered ginger root taken about forty-five minutes before departing. Or take one-half to one tablespoon with water. Ginger is usually the main component of combination herbal products for motion sickness that go by names such as Travel-Ease and Motion Ease. These can be found in most natural foods stores.

Kids can be given a smaller dose along with other sources of the herb, including ginger tea and nonartificially flavored ginger snap cookies or ginger ale (real ginger ales can have about 1,000 mg of ginger per eight ounces).

Ginger is the premier herb for preventing and relieving mild vertigo associated with motion sickness. In fact, one recent study published in the British medical journal *Lancet* showed that ginger is more effective at relieving these conditions than Dramamine, the conventional pharmaceutical remedy. (See "Chapter 22: Travel Problems" for further natural remedies for motion sickness.)

For chronic vertigo from various causes, take the herb ginkgo. "This is an especially good herbal treatment for elderly persons with mild vertigo, which is often due to poor blood supply to the brain," says Joseph Pizzorno, N.D. He notes that it does have to be taken regularly in continued daily dosages of three 40-mg capsules.

An herb that is currently taking off in popularity in the United States, ginkgo has long been popular in the Orient. An extract made from the leaves of this ancient tree species can boost overall circulation and brain function. One study found that almost half of the seventy subjects with chronic vertigo who were given ginkgo no longer felt dizzy after three months of treatment.

Try one of the homeopathic combination remedies. For instance, Boiron's product HBN (Homeopathy by the Numbers) 194 is formulated to relieve dizziness/vertigo. It contains the remedies *Conium 6X* (from hemlock) and *Granatum 3X* (pomegranate).

Take the flower essence Scleranthus. Flower therapists especially recommend Scleranthus for people who suffer from episodes of dizziness associated with a lack of poise and balance, or indecision. A first-aid flower essence combination such as Rescue Remedy also works well to counter mild vertigo.

POSTURAL HYPOTENSION

"The body has a mechanism," notes naturopath Joe Pizzorno, the founding president of Bastyr College in Seattle, one of the world's foremost accredited colleges of natural medicine, "so that it maintains proper blood pressure while you stand up from a lying or sitting position. If you can't maintain normal blood pressure under normal conditions, then something is wrong with one of the body's systems. It usually depends on the particular patient, but it is definitely worth diagnosing and dealing with."

Andrew Weil, M.D., the author of *Natural Health, Natural Medicine,* notes that on the other hand you don't want to go too far. "It's not so much that you want permanently to raise your blood pressure as you want to work on the reflex that changes blood pressure when you change position. Low blood pressure is generally healthful."

Natural treatments range from quick, symptomatic cures such as simply standing up more slowly and not changing posi-

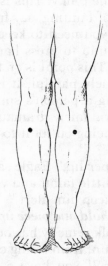

Illustration #15:

Pressing on the acupressure point below the knee can help a person recover from dizziness.

tion so suddenly, to a number of other techniques that can allow your body's blood pressure regulators to function more effectively.

Learn how to increase your blood pressure temporarily using physical or mental exercises done for a moment or two before standing. Researchers have proven that a few simple tasks can quickly provide a small boost in blood pressure. For instance, increase blood pressure before standing up by briefly clenching all the muscles of both arms. You can get a similar mild boost by doing some mental chore, such as saying the alphabet backward.

Apply a quick massage to the acupressure point four finger-widths below the kneecap, one finger-width outside of the shin-bone. This point (see illustration #15) on the stomach meridian "helps to ground and stabilize a person," notes Michael Reed Gach, an acupressure teacher and practitioner.

EMOTIONAL SHOCK AND NERVOUS EXHAUSTION

In addition to putting your head between your knees, or lying down with your feet elevated, try some of the following steps either as a faint comes on or afterward.

Press on an acupressure point that can prevent an imminent fainting episode. "The one that we use," says David Eagle, an acupuncturist and Oriental Medical Doctor, "is the point at the base of the fingernail of the pinky. This is the best one for when someone is on the verge of fainting, say from the sight of blood, and for whatever reason you need to keep him or her alert. Use the fingernail of your thumb to press hard into the base of the person's pinky fingernail. This point is on the heart meridian and pressing it can be extremely painful. It is traditionally used in Chinese medicine to bring a person's spirit back into the body suddenly. We've had several fairly dramatic experiences using it. The person will go from being out of it to going, 'Ow!' They may even get angry.

"The point on the upper lip," Eagle says, "is better for when a person is just feeling a little faint, and you don't really need to give him a jolt of pain to keep him alert."

Cut an onion in half, hold one piece up to your nose, and take a few deep whiffs. This folk remedy has been known to prevent a person on the verge of a faint from losing consciousness.

Try a flower essence. If you have a more extensive flower essence collection than Rescue Remedy, try either of two ingredients of this first-aid revival remedy: Rock Rose (for terror and panic) or Star of Bethlehem (for grief and emotional numbness). Follow dosage suggestions on the label.

Take the homeopathic remedy Aconite. This is the remedy for a person who is in a state of fear or emotional shock and looks pale, tense, and restless. If you have a more complete set of homeopathic remedies try the following:

- *Nux vomica,* for those who feel faint from the sight of blood
- *Ignatia,* for those who are faint from emotional upset or grief
- *Coffea,* for those who are faint from overexcitement

Repeat an affirmation that can instill a sense of power and strength in dealing with the situation. For instance, say to yourself: *I am sure of myself. I am emotionally strong and resilient. I can do what I need to do to cope with this situation. I feel secure and stable.*

Take some of the Chinese prepared medicine Ding Xin Wan. Ding Xin Wan is made up of nine herbs and other active ingredients, processed into brown pearl-like balls that come one hundred to a bottle. A standard dose is six pills two to three times daily.

Oriental healers have more than a dozen herbal preparations that they prescribe for various combinations of dizziness, weakness, agitation, and "neurasthenia," a condition of fatigue and anxiety thought to result from nervous exhaustion. Herbalists' selection will depend in part on which organ system (for instance, spleen, kidney, or heart) needs to be nourished. Ding Xin Wan ("stabilize heart pills"), one of the more popular choices, "is specially made for nourishing the general body, dispersing internal heat, and soothing nerves," according to its producer, Min-Kang Manufactory in Yichang, China. "It's great for dizziness accompanied by fatigue and anxiety," herbalist Christopher Hobbs says.

See "Resources" for mail-order sources of Oriental herbs.

STIFLING ATMOSPHERE/HEAT FAINT

Sometimes you get stuck in a place that desperately needs cool, fresh air, but for some reason you can't open the windows or otherwise increase the oxygen level. Here are some alternative steps that often help.

Rub ice cubes on the insides of the wrists or run cold tap water over them. The wrists contain many veins and arteries, and cold water on them has the effect of swiftly contracting them and thus increasing blood flow to the brain. Rubbing the wrists is a favorite massage technique among Chinese for restoring the flow of vital energy.

Massage an acupressure point on the sole of the foot that can help revitalize the body. Putting strong pressure on the first point along the kidney meridian can help restore consciousness. It is located on the bottom of the foot at the base of the ball between the two pads.

Take the homeopathic remedy **Pulsatilla.** This is the recommended remedy for the person who needs air in a stuffy atmosphere.

Take the flower essence Clematis. If you have a full complement of flower essences, try Clematis, which is one of the five essences that make up Rescue Remedy. It is used by itself for a faraway sensation that often precedes a faint. "Clematis is the remedy for fainting, coma, or for any form of unconsciousness, for all such conditions indicate a 'loss of interest,' whether enforced by circumstances or not, in present conditions," notes Dr. Philip M. Chancellor, author of *Bach Flower Remedies.*

◆ Prevention and Recovery

A variety of herbs, nutritional supplements, and other natural remedies can play important roles in the long-term treatment of dizziness and fainting from mild vertigo, postural hypotension, emotional shock and nervous exhaustion, and stifling atmosphere.

For mild dizziness or unhealthfully low blood pressure, begin an herbal treatment program using one of the adaptogen herbs. The adaptogens are a special class of herbs that perform the remarkable function of restoring balance to various bodily systems without regard to the direction of the imbalance. In other words, if your blood pressure is too high, these herbs lower it, and if it is too low, these herbs raise it. Many people take adaptogens regularly to adjust more easily to the rapidly changing conditions of their lives.

Hobbs says that it is necessary to distinguish between two major causes of mild vertigo. The first is dizziness due to what the Chinese refer to as "bodily depletion or deficiency," a condition of constant fatigue or low vital energy that may be due to such factors as malnourishment or too much stress. The second is dizziness due to an excess condition. He says, "If dizziness is from a deficiency condition, my advice would be for the person to avoid stimulants like caffeine, follow a more healthful diet, get plenty of rest, and take adaptogenic herbs like Siberian ginseng, reishi, and astragalus to restore balance, counter stress, and fight fatigue. Also take ginkgo, which works directly to improve circulation to the inner ear."

◆ Siberian ginseng is the queen of adaptogens, an extraordinarily versatile herb that has been used for over four thousand years by the Chinese as a revitalizing tonic to increase longevity and improve general health. Siberian ginseng *(Eleutherococcus senticosus,* sometimes referred to as eleuthero) is the root of a shrub widely grown in the Far East. Hobbs says that Siberian ginseng has even stronger adaptogenic qualities than Chinese ginseng *(Panax ginseng)* and is less expensive as well. Studies have shown that people with both hypotension and hypertension show normalization of blood pressure after being treated with an extract of Siberian ginseng.

"Eleuthero works especially well for postural hypotension that is associated with long-term stress and debility," says naturopath Joseph Pizzorno.

Siberian ginseng is widely available in tincture and capsules. It is often combined with other adaptogen herbs such as schizandra. Follow dosage directions on labels.

◆ Reishi, a healing mushroom, is an adaptogen and a "deep immune activator," says Hobbs. A harder more woodlike mushroom than shiitake, it is available in dried, powdered extract tablets or capsules. Take two 100-mg tablets or capsules daily.

◆ Astragalus is one of the traditional Chinese herbs used to strengthen (or "tonify") the body's overall vitality and support the spleen. Make a decoction from six to nine grams of the dried root, or purchase astragalus in concentrated extract form at your local natural foods store and take according to label instructions.

For mild dizziness related to an excess condition, take heart-boosting herbs. According to Hobbs, "Vertigo that's accompanied by a low-pitched sound in the ears is more often related to an excess condition like high blood pressure. In that case the person needs to consider meditation or other antistress measures, plus herbs like garlic and hawthorn that are good for the heart and circulation."

◆ Garlic is widely used in Mediterranean countries that have relatively low rates of heart disease. Scientists have recently begun to confirm that its use can prevent heart attacks by lowering both cholesterol levels and blood pressure. Garlic has many uses in cooking, and garlic supplements are now a major industry in the United States. Use fresh garlic, garlic juice, liquid garlic extracts, or "allicin-stabilized" tablets.

◆ Native American, Chinese, and European herbalists have long used preparations made from hawthorn flowers, leaves, and berries to remedy circulation problems. Hawthorn contains many bioflavonoids and other chemical compounds that affect heart function. A number of studies have confirmed the herb's positive effects on the heart and blood vessels. Hawthorn is best taken over a prolonged period. Hawthorn products are widely available in standardized extract form. Follow label directions for dosages.

Hobbs notes that low blood pressure can also be caused by a blood deficiency—an insufficient volume of circulating blood—or a weak heart. The body is thus not efficiently supplying the brain with oxygen. "Young women who are menstruating may benefit from taking dong quai, the number one herb for building more blood and blood that is rich in hemoglobin. A holistic program for building better blood might also include fresh greens, chlorophyll-rich foods, and natural, plant-based iron supplements."

◆ Dong quai *(Angelica sinensis)* is a species of angelica that is one of the most widely used Oriental herbs. Traditional Chinese healers use it as a blood tonic and to treat a variety of female conditions, including PMS and painful menstrual cramps. It's available in bulk as a powder or thin root slices, bottled in extract form, or encapsulated. Follow dosage instructions on the label. Dong quai shouldn't be taken during pregnancy or periods of heavy menstruation.

For mild vertigo, see a chiropractor, physical therapist, or other bodyworker. These specialists may be able to correct a misalignment in the head, neck, or spine that is causing dizziness, or they may suggest exercises that can help restore your sense of balance.

Correct any dietary imbalances that may be leading to excessively low or high blood pressure or nervous exhaustion. Salt's connection with high blood pressure is so well known that a few people have gone to the other extreme. They've decreased their salt intake so much that the resulting lower volume of blood contributes to postural hypotension. Your body needs some salt, and it needs even more if you're living in a hot climate and sweating a lot. Excessive salt intake, on the other hand, can lead to dizziness from high blood pressure and swelling in the inner ear.

Your condition may also benefit from eating smaller, more frequent meals, and getting enough nutrients, particularly the B complex vitamins, protein, and chromium, according to nutritionist Shari Lieberman, Ph.D., coauthor of *The Real Vitamin & Mineral Book.* "All of these help prevent dizziness by benefiting the circulation system or neurotransmitter flow," she says. "Most people are already eating enough salt, and in my experience blood sugar and other dietary factors are much more important factors."

Pizzorno says that he has seen some patients with excessively low blood pressure that resulted from being on an overly strict vegetarian diet, or on a fast. "Usually all I do is suggest a more balanced diet and the postural hypotension goes away."

Lieberman cautions that too much vitamin E may cause dizziness from postural hypotension or mild vertigo. "If you want to start taking vitamin E therapeutically, start with 200–400 IU daily and build up slowly to 800 IU or higher. I've experienced it myself, and a number of people I've talked to said that dizziness was a side effect when they started vitamin E supplementation by taking in excess of 800 IU daily."

People who suffer from nervous exhaustion often respond to an improved diet of whole, natural, nutrient-dense foods taken in regular meals. If low blood sugar is a factor, occasional high-protein snacks may be helpful.

Get some regular exercise. One of the effects of a long period of inactivity is postural hypotension. If that's a factor in your situation, undertake a program of walking, swimming, or some other activity to strengthen the circulatory system. Lieberman says, "I recommend to my patients that they start slowly with an aerobic program, maybe five minutes per day. They can add a minute per week to bring it up to twenty to thirty minutes per day."

Take an essential-oil bath. Aromatherpaists say that a long-term technique for relieving exhaustion is to take a warm bath to which you add two drops each of essential oil of Chamomile, Lavender, and Geranium.

For emotional shock and nervous exhaustion, start a program that includes taking one of the herbs that can have a stimulating effect on the circulatory and nervous systems. Herbalists have long prescribed remedies for boosting the physical energy of patients who are pallid and weak, while calming their chronically nervous or anxious mental state. Two of the most potent such whole-body tonifiers are rosemary and oats.

◆ Rosemary is a useful garden herb that has been the basis for a stimulating tonic wine that has been popular in Europe for almost eight hundred years. Rosemary is a shrublike plant whose leaves contain a volatile oil with camphorlike properties widely used by aromatherapists. According to the late herbal scientist Rudolf Fritz Weiss, M.D., author of *Herbal Medicine,* "Rosemary has in the main a general tonic effect on the nervous and circulatory systems, especially the vascular nerves. This makes it an excellent drug for all states of chronic circulatory weakness, including hypotension." Weiss notes that rosemary is also an ideal tonic for elderly people, and an appetite stimulator.

The crushed and dried herb can be used to make a tea. A number of herbal companies make tinctures, extracts, or concentrated herbal drops. Follow label instructions for use. A few drops of essential oil of Rosemary can be put in a bath (since the effect is invigorating, you may want to take such baths in the morning rather than before trying to sleep at night), combined with a few teaspoons of a vegetable oil for use as a massage oil, or added to a vaporizer or sprinkled on a cotton cloth and inhaled. (The undiluted oil should not be taken internally.)

◆ Oats *(Avena sativa)* serves as both a whole food and a healing herb. Oats contain an alkaloid that stimulates the central nervous systems. "The whole plant," says Richard Mabey, consultant editor of *The New Age Herbalist,* "in medicinal doses provides a range of therapeutic and nutritional substances that feed a debilitated nervous system, making this a valuable remedy for exhaustion, convalescence, and depression." You can eat oats as a porridge or take it in concentrated extract form.

Pizzorno says that he's seen patients suffering from emotional shock and nervous exhaustion improve by using Chinese ginseng and Siberian ginseng.

Though it doesn't usually happen in water, fainting is like drowning in one way: you lose consciousness from the effects of hypoxia, a fall in the body's oxygen level. Thus, recovering from a fainting episode is similar to (though much easier than) recovering from a drowning one. You want to revitalize the lungs and body and thereby reoxygenate the blood and brain. See the recovery section in "Chapter 14: Drowning" for suggestions on how to accomplish this using diet and supplements, herbs, essential oils, massage, yoga, and breathing exercises.

FOURTEEN

Drowning

THIS CHAPTER COVERS:

◆ *drowning*
◆ *near-drowning*

SEE "CHAPTER 3: BASIC EMERGENCY CARE" FOR:

◆ *unconsciousness*
◆ *how to do rescue breathing*
◆ *how to do chest compressions and CPR*
◆ *shock*
◆ *the recovery position*

Drowning is the second leading cause (after auto accidents) of accidental death in Americans under the age of forty-five, claiming some nine thousand lives each year. Almost ten times as many people experience near-drowning episodes, in which they are submersed in water but rescued. Thousands of near-drowning victims, however, suffer brain injuries.

Drowning is a form of suffocation in which water or some other liquid cuts off the supply of air to the lungs. In most cases, though not always, the suffocation is caused by inhaling water into the lungs. This in turn leads to asphyxia, the loss of consciousness from too little oxygen and too much carbon dioxide in the blood reaching the brain. When the brain is deprived of oxygen for four to five minutes, death follows.

Any body of water capable of covering a person's face is large enough to drown in. People have drowned in puddles, bathtubs, and even washbuckets. Attila the Hun drowned in his own blood from a nosebleed he suffered while sleeping. Typically, though, people drown in lakes, rivers, and backyard pools. Negligence (not keeping close enough watch on a toddler near water), boating accidents, and injuries (diving into unknown waters and hitting the bottom or a submerged object, for instance) are common causes. Drowning can also result from a sudden health problem while swimming, including abdominal cramps, fainting, seizures, and heart attacks.

Jumping or falling into extremely cold water is potentially life-threatening in a number of ways. It may cause sudden death, by slowing the heartbeat and inducing a heart attack or by making the victim gasp and inhale a lungful of water. It can also lead to death from hypothermia, in which the body's core temperature falls to dangerously low levels (see "Chapter 15: Exposure to Altitude and Cold"). In rare cases, however, cold water can actually increase a near-drowning victim's chances for survival.

A contributing factor in the drowning of many adult males is drinking. One Australian study showed that almost two of every three men who drowned had been consuming alcohol. Clearly, if you dive, don't drink.

In a typical drowning case, a victim who is within sight of a boat or shore suddenly tires and begins to panic. No longer able to keep his head above water, he holds his breath and then starts gasping for air. Sinking below the surface, he swallows water, blocking his airway and partially filling the stomach and lungs. The amount of oxygen getting filtered into the blood by the lungs drops, the brain begins to shut down, and the victim loses consciousness. He then breathes in more water. If not rescued and provided effective first aid, he soon dies.

A victim caught up in this deadly scenario may or may not be able to call for help. You can assume someone needs rescuing if he or she is thrashing about in the water, is in the water fully clothed, or is making clumsy attempts at swimming and seems to be able to keep only his or her head above water. Up close, the near-drowning victim is likely to appear blue in the face, lips, and ears. The skin may be cold and pale. The victim may be breathing faintly or not at all, be unconscious or semiconscious, and have a weak or absent pulse.

◆ Rescuing a Drowning Person

The two most immediate concerns in a drowning are to call for emergency help and to get the victim out of the water safely. If there are more people in the rescue party than are needed in the rescue effort, immediately dispatch one to summon professional help.

If you must make a solo rescue of a drowning victim, think first of self-preservation. This may sound callous, but remember that you won't save anyone from drowning if you die first. And faced with two near-drowning victims, a subsequent rescuer may have little chance of saving either victim. Clearly, any rescue attempt you make should not unreasonably endanger your own life.

The safest way to rescue a drowning victim is by staying out of the water and extending something for the victim to grab on to. Only as a last resort should anyone get in the water or onto ice to rescue someone. Swimming rescues in which the rescuer attempts to grab a drowning victim and pull him or her to shore should be undertaken only by lifeguards and others who have passed training courses in water rescue, such as those offered by Red Cross chapters. The danger is that the drowning victim, in a state of terror that is pumping massive doses of strength-enhancing adrenaline into the bloodstream, will overwhelm the rescuer. A panicked drowning victim is likely to have only one thought: grab on to and climb up and over anything he can touch. Drowning victims sometimes unwittingly drag a rescuer to a watery demise.

So consider first how you can reach a drowning victim indirectly. From dock, land, or boat, extend a board, stick, or pole, or throw a rope, sheet, or ring buoy. Even if you have to swim or wade part of the way, it is safer to extend or throw an object for the victim to grab than to grapple with the victim directly. If a rowboat is handy, use it to approach the victim rather than swimming to him or her.

If you are untrained and decide to risk your life by making a swimming rescue of a drowning person, bringing something to extend or throw is still a good idea. Swim out close enough to the person to extend the object, but not close enough for the person to grab on to your body. Pull the person to safety.

If you must grab the person, the safest way to perform a swimming rescue depends on the victim's state of mind. Stop out of reach of the person and reassure her. Sometimes that is enough to calm the person and induce her to start swimming. If the victim can't swim but seems collected enough to cooperate with the rescue effort, you can approach her from the front, have her put her hands on your shoulders, and use a breaststroke to return to shore.

Such simple swimming rescues are the exception rather than the rule. Much more frequently the victim is wild-eyed and flailing in sheer panic. In that case, tell him what you're doing and approach him from underwater or from behind. Lift him by the hips to poke his head out of the water. Level off the body, put the victim on his back with his head back and chin out of the water, and reach one arm around his chest, cupping the chin with one hand. Use a sidestroke to swim ashore while keeping his head out of the water.

If the near-drowning victim continues to panic and grabs at you as you try to approach him, stay away. The danger is that he will bear-hug you and use his panic-enhanced strength to drag you down with him. Wait for him to tire or calm down, and then reapproach. If you have a considerable strength advantage, you can grab him and try to keep his head out of the water while embracing him tightly with both arms. If this doesn't calm the person and he should grab you, especially by the throat or head, do whatever you can to escape. Forcefully push him away or dive underwater (in which case he'll almost assuredly let go to get his head above water again). Surface and try again to gain the person's confidence.

Remember that your life is in danger, and a direct swimming rescue is difficult even with proper training and in the best of circumstances. Training courses in water rescue cover a multitude of potential problems the rescuer may face and involve many hours of practice in the water and on land. If you're attempting a swimming rescue and the victim is about to drown you as well as himself, do whatever you have to do to save your life. Then consider other ways to rescue the victim. If the attempt ultimately fails, there is no dishonor in being unable to do what one is neither trained to nor capable of doing.

DEAD OR ALIVE?

A drowning victim who isn't breathing, is ice-cold, and has no pulse is not necessarily dead. Of course, he or she will soon be dead if not revived, but don't assume you can't help unless you're absolutely sure.

Small children have been revived after being totally submersed in cold water for up to an hour. The shock of the cold water apparently sometimes causes a small child's metabolism to slow down without shutting off. Even though the child is no longer breathing, the brain continues to get just enough oxygen to keep the body alive. Such cold-water survival does not occur in adults, however, since they have a lower ratio of skin surface to body mass and thus cool too slowly. It is possible for a conscious and breathing adult, on the other hand, to survive for an hour or so even in freezing water.

The important point is that near-drowning victims can sometimes be pulled back from the brink of death, even if they're not breathing and have no heartbeat. The rule of thumb is that a cold-water drowning victim is not dead until his body is warm.

◆ The Basic First-Aid Steps for Drowning

As soon as possible after rescuing a near-drowning victim, summon emergency help and check the ABCs: airway, breathing, and circulation (see "Chapter 3: Basic Emergency Care"). If the victim is not breathing or is breathing with great difficulty, getting his or her blood reoxygenated as quickly as possible is crucial. Ideally the rescuer should begin to do rescue breathing even as the victim is carried through the surf or pulled on board a boat.

If the drowning incident resulted from a dive into shallow water, check for head or neck injuries before unnecessarily moving the victim's body. If head or neck injuries are evident, take care to keep the victim's head and neck in line with the rest of the body.

If the victim is not breathing, you should also check the neck for a pulse. If there is no pulse, begin CPR (see Chapter 3) while continuing to do rescue breathing.

Don't bother to try to drain water from the victim's lungs before starting rescue breathing or CPR. Putting the victim in a jackknife position for this purpose, for instance, is a waste of precious time and potentially dangerous as well. First of all, about one in ten drowning victims does not inhale any water into the lungs, due to intense spasm of the vocal cords. They can, however, still fall unconscious and suffocate. Some other drowning victims inhale only small amounts of water. Even if a person has inhaled large quantities of water, if you do rescue breathing correctly, the air you blow into the person's lungs will get through the water in bubbles and enter the blood, but you may have to blow hard for this to occur.

If the lungs are not being inflated during hard rescue breathing, the victim may have something blocking his or her airway. It is also possible for a tight, water-filled stomach to prevent the lungs from expanding. In such cases keep the victim on his back and do the Heimlich maneuver (see Chapter 3).

Continue doing rescue breathing or CPR without even momentary interruption for up to an hour, or until rescue personnel arrive. Even if the heart is beating weakly, rescue breathing can keep the victim alive.

Once you've restored breathing and heartbeat to a near-drowning victim, the person is not yet out of danger. Drowning can cause death not only by asphyxiation but by inducing severe shock. Shock is common in near-drownings, and you need to take steps to treat or prevent it (see Chapter 3). If the victim hasn't suffered any head or neck injuries, place him or her in the recovery position (see Chapter 3). This will prevent choking on any water or bodily fluids that are vomited up.

Hypothermia is also a concern, particularly if the victim has been in water that is less than 70° F. Remove cold, wet clothes and cover the person with something warm.

Keep the victim quiet and calm. Don't allow the victim to get up and start walking around or exercising to warm up, for instance. It's not unheard of for a person to narrowly survive a drowning only to succumb to a heart attack shortly after being revived. Near-drowning victims may also develop immediate complications, including severe shortness of breath. Reassure the victim that medical help is on the way.

WHEN TO SEEK MEDICAL CARE

Any near-drowning victim, regardless of whether water has been inhaled into the lungs, should be checked out by a medical professional. Even near-drowning victims who are quickly revived at the scene are routinely hospitalized. This is because taking fluids into the lungs plays havoc not only with those organs' delicate inner membranes and the respiratory system in general, but with a number of the body's other systems and organs as well. Complications, both immediate and delayed, are common in near-drownings.

Flooding the lungs with water can harm, or wash away, an agent lining the organ's inner membranes. This substance helps maintain the structure of small air cells before the oxygen/carbon-dioxide exchange can be made. Inhaled water can also be absorbed from the lungs directly into the bloodstream, where it dilutes the blood, thereby destroying red blood cells and throwing out of kilter the fine balance of various chemicals and elements in the blood. These chemical imbalances can disturb the smooth beating of the heart and cause a heart attack.

To some extent the harmful consequences of inhaling water depend upon the type of water. For instance, salt water in the lungs tends not to be absorbed into the bloodstream. Rather, it can draw pints of blood out of the bloodstream into the lungs. This internal loss of blood can suffocate and kill the patient or lead to serious complications such as pulmonary edema (the accumulation of abnormally large amounts of watery fluid within the alveoli of the lungs) should he or she survive. Likewise, inhaling polluted water into the lungs can damage air cells and cause infections, inflammation, or pneumonia.

Complications from near-drowning may appear within a minute of rescue, or days later. A near-drowning episode is a near-death episode. Don't take it lightly.

WHAT TO EXPECT FROM EMERGENCY AND HOSPITAL PERSONNEL

At the scene of a near-drowning, rescue personnel may use special equipment to administer 100 percent oxygen if breathing is labored or to massage the heart if there's no pulse.

At the hospital, the patient may continue to be given 100 percent oxygen. Other treatment will depend on potential complications, including pulmonary edema and other lung disorders, metabolic and electrolyte imbalances, kidney failure, blood plasma deficiencies, and circulatory disturbances. Two of the most common dangers are hypoxia, caused by a decrease in the oxygen supplied to or utilized by body tissue, and hemolysis, a diluting of the blood and rupturing of red blood cells.

Hospitals will usually closely monitor the victim's heart and lung functions and repeatedly test the blood and urine, until the victim recovers. Many doctors will prescribe large doses of antibiotics to prevent pneumonia, corticosteroid drugs to reduce lung inflammation, and other pharmaceuticals.

◆ Natural First-Aid Remedies

Drowning is a major medical emergency that requires sophisticated first aid and close medical follow-up. There are a few natural remedies that can help during the initial crisis, but many more that can be of benefit during the recovery phase. Do the following only if they don't interfere with basic steps to restore breathing and circulation.

If the person is unconscious, press on the acupressure revival point on the upper lip. Locate the point two-thirds up the lip toward the base of the nose, and press on it gently but firmly with the end of your thumb.

Administer the homeopathic remedy Antimonium tartaricum. This is the best homeopathic remedy for near-drowning, recommended when a patient is cold and blue, covered with clammy sweat, and breathing with a rattling sound. Homeopathic companies produce it in pellets from a form of the nonmetallic element antimony. You can give *Antimony* pellets if the victim is conscious and ready to swallow something. Alternatively, crush the pellets into a powder, dissolve the powder in water, dip a clean cloth into the solution, and touch the cloth to the inner lining of the victim's cheek. The *Antimony* will be absorbed through the cheek's mucous membrances. Repeat every ten to fifteen minutes or until the victim improves.

If you don't have *Antimony*, the homeopathic shock remedies *Aconite* and *Arsenicum* may be helpful. Never give an unconscious victim anything to swallow, however.

Administer a flower essence first-aid combination such as Bach Flower Rescue Remedy. If a near-drowning victim is awake and breathing, you can place three to four drops of the liquid concentrate directly from the bottle under his or her tongue. You can also dilute it by putting four drops in one-quarter glass of water, tea, or juice. This should be sipped every three to five minutes. When a near-drowning victim is unconscious, administer full-strength Rescue Remedy by rubbing a few drops into the lips or gums, behind the ears, or on the wrists, or soak a cotton cloth in a pint of water with five to six drops of Rescue Remedy and apply it as a compress.

Bach first used Rescue Remedy in its original form (containing Rock Rose, Clematis, and Impatiens; he had not yet discovered the other two essences that make up today's Rescue Remedy) in 1930. He was at a seaside community when a storm wrecked a small boat offshore. Rescuers in a lifeboat fished the two boaters out of the surf, but the younger man was unconscious and blue in the face. As he was being carried ashore to a nearby hotel, Bach moistened the victim's lips with some drops of Rescue Remedy. Bach related that the young man quickly recovered consciousness.

Rub the person's hands, feet, and ears. The vigorous chafing action can help get circulation moving again and return oxygen to the brain. Practitioners of Chinese folk medicine say that touch and massage can also have an important spiritual benefit on the near-drowning victim. Holly and David Eagle, both of whom are Oriental Medical Doctors, recommend rubbing and pulling on the person's ears while calling or whispering the person's name. David Eagle says, "This is traditionally done to bring the spirit back solidly into the body. When a person has been unconscious or stopped breathing, he may 'lose his being' or get dislocated from his self. Often after he comes to, he'll be spaced-out. Kids in particular will be in a dreamy state, talking about angels and God. This is an indication that the soul is not yet rooted back in the body. Stimulating the hands, feet, and ears pulls the soul back into the body."

RECOVERY FROM NEAR DROWNING

A trained herbalist, naturopath, homeopath, or other health practitioner can work with physicians or other medical professionals to devise a program to help a near-drowning victim recover. Natural practitioners can also tailor a program to alleviate any complications that occur. What follows are some general suggestions for practices and remedies to strengthen the lungs and respiratory system and boost the immune system.

Supplement the daily diet with the following vitamins, minerals, and nutrients:

- two to five grams of vitamin C with bioflavonoids, to bowel tolerance, to promote healing, counter the effects of stress, prevent throat spasms, act as an antihistamine, and reduce sensitivity to toxins in the air
- 5,000 IU of vitamin A in the form of beta carotene, to repair tissue, heal mucous membranes, and offer protection from infection
- 50–150 mg of vitamin B complex, including B_6, to stimulate immunity
- 400 IU daily of vitamin E, to destroy free radicals
- 0.5–2 mg copper, to help restore healthy hemoglobin, which carries oxygen and carbon dioxide between lungs and tissues, and to help absorb iron
- 500–750 mg magnesium, to relax lung muscles
- 25–50 mg zinc for immune system and to promote healing
- 10–20 mg coenzyme Q10, a vitaminlike nutrient, and 30–150 mg Ge-132, a synthetic organic compound of the trace mineral germanium, to increase the body's supply of oxygen

Nutritionist Shari Lieberman also recommends that anyone on an antibiotic regimen take an acidophilus supplement, to help reestablish the proper balance of friendly bacteria in the intestines and protect the liver from toxins.

Acidophilus has become the generic term for various types of naturally occurring live bacteria that are increasingly popular as dietary supplements. It is available in the form of tablets, powders, capsules, and liquids sold in most natural foods stores. Look for acidophilus products that have labels providing information on how many live or "viable" bacteria each capsule or teaspoon provides, an expiration date with a guarantee of product viability until that date, and a listing of additional ingredients. Take doses of acidophilus that provide approximately 10 billion organisms per day.

To help clear the lungs, soothe mucous membranes, and boost the immune system, take advantage of healing herbs. Two of the best after a near-drowning episode are garlic and ginkgo.

- ◆ Garlic and other members of the allium family counter bacterial and viral infection, help remove from the body toxic chemicals such as lead and mercury, lower blood pressure, prevent asthma attacks, and reduce inflammation. Fresh garlic, garlic juice, "allicin-stabilized" tablets, and liquid garlic extracts have high levels of allicin, one of garlic's most important healing compounds. Fresh garlic that has lost its odor may have also lost its medicinal value. Proponents of "odor-controlled" tablets contend that these products release allicin during digestion and have significant health effects.

- ◆ Ginkgo, the world's most ancient tree species, has been used by the Chinese for thousands of years to prepare remedies for asthma, bronchitis, coughs, and other conditions. Scientists have isolated an active ingredient, ginkgolide B, that counteracts the effects of a substance in the body known as platelet activation factor (PAF). Ginkgolide B prevents PAF from constricting bronchial tubes and thus interfering with breathing. A standardized extract of ginkgo leaves has also been shown to benefit circulation, blood conditions, metabolism, and immune function, according to herbal researcher Steven Foster. The extract can also prevent damage from free radicals in the body after a near-drowning. Some studies indicate ginkgo counters hypoxia. Concentrated drops, standardized extracts, and other herbal preparations of ginkgo are widely available from natural foods stores. Follow label instructions on dosage and use.

Other herbs that may benefit respiratory and circulatory problems include licorice, mullein, and cayenne. Herbalist Christopher Hobbs says that ginger tea after the emergency can help treat nausea, and a cinnamon tea is one of the best for strengthening and warming the lungs.

Eat a healthful balance of natural and whole foods that promote lung function, including:

- dark green leafy vegetables such as mustard greens and turnip greens, legumes such as dried beans and peas, whole-grain cereals, sea vegetables, seafoods, and other foods high in iron, copper, and other nutrients
- concentrated chlorophyll supplements such as the algae-based green foods spirulina, chlorella, and blue-green algae, and products made from the young grasses of wheat and barley, to boost the immune system and scavenge free radicals in the body
- shiitake or reishi mushrooms, in fresh, dried, or concentrated supplement form, for their immune-boosting powers
- onions, which contain a compound that may aid free breathing
- warm grapefruit juice, which is a good lung tonic

Also supplement the diet with high levels of the omega-3s and omega-6s, the desirable essential fatty acids that have a natural anti-inflammatory effect. Sources of beneficial EFAs include:

- fatty, cold-water fish such as salmon, cod, mackerel, sardines, bluefish, herring, and tuna, and oil supplements made from these fish
- canola, flaxseed, and hemp oil
- evening primrose, borage, and black-currant oil

Lieberman notes that traumatic situations can affect diet. She says, "Near-drowning victims may feel nauseous, so they may want to eat smaller, more frequent meals."

Avoid the foods that may aggravate the lungs, including:

- highly refined sugars and carbohydrate products, high-fat cheese and other dairy products, and overly spicy and acidic foods, all of which can weaken the respiratory sys-

tem by contributing to hypoglycemia, or low blood sugar, and leading to the accumulation of mucus in the airways
- ◆ high amounts of (non-omega-3 or -6) fats and oils, which slow the healing process and weaken the lungs

Regularly perform a simple breathing exercise that can strengthen the respiratory system. In general you want to practice breathing more slowly, deeply, quietly, and regularly, while trying to extend exhalation. Natural health advocate Andrew Weil, M.D., recommends the following simple yogic breathing exercise, which Indian yogis have been doing for thousands of years. It is a natural tranquilizer for the nervous system and energizer of the respiratory system.

Practice it, he says, in any position, but start by sitting with your back straight. Place the tip of your tongue against the ridge of tissue just behind your upper front teeth, and keep it there during the entire exercise. To inhale, close the mouth and draw air in quietly through the nose to a mental count of four. Hold your breath for a count of seven. Now exhale completely through the mouth and around the tongue, making a whoosh sound and silently counting to eight. If the tongue position seems awkward, try pursing your lips slightly. Inhale again and repeat the cycle three more times for a total of four breaths.

Weil notes that the exhalation should always take twice as long as the inhalation, so the ratio of 4:7:8 is important. According to yoga theory, the position of the tongue on the ridge of the mouth is a factor in completing an energy circuit in the body.

Regularly practice a few basic yoga exercises that can relax the breathing muscles and open the airways. One of the best such positions, or asanas, is the cobra. Lie on your stomach with your forehead on the floor, palms down under the shoulders. Inhale deeply as you slowly use your back muscles to raise first your head and then your chest off the floor. Straighten your arms as you tilt your head back as far as possible within your comfort zone. Exhale as you slowly reverse the motion and come back to a prone position. Rest for a few breaths and then repeat.

Massage the acupressure points that can boost recovery from drowning. Two sets of points may be helpful: the lung points located in the outer portion of the upper chest, about two inches below the shoulder end of the collarbone; and a set of points four finger-widths below the kneecap toward the outside of the shinbone.

To locate the lung points, acupressurist Michael Reed Gach suggests using the thumbs to press on the muscles that run horizontally below the collarbone until you find a knot or sensitive spot. Maintain firm pressure with the thumbs while the person breathes deeply for two minutes. "These points are good for recovery; they stimulate and heal the lungs," he says.

For best results massaging the leg points, suggests Gach, "If the person is lying on her back, bring the knees up for better leverage. These points are strengthening, stabilizing, and reorienting."

Check your natural pharmacy shelves for respiratory and immune system boosters. You are likely to find a number of effective combination remedies, both herbal and homeopathic. An herbal combination remedy for improving the functioning of the lungs that comes highly recommended by Oriental Medical Doctor David Eagle is Dr. Esteban's Purifying Formula, made by the Latin American Naturopathic Clinic Program in Limón, Costa Rica. Eagle says, "It's helpful for increasing oxygen stimulation, stimulating lung tissue, and preventing infection." The formula combines the herbs chaparral, garlic, goldenseal, osha, and echinacea. The standard dose is two capsules every six hours.

Tap the chest to send healing vibrations throughout the rib cage and lungs. This unique "stimulus for fuller breathing" is suggested by the German-born "physical reeducation" teacher Carola Speads of New York City. She teaches a form of mind, body, and breath work that emphasizes "the role of breathing as an integral element of our bodily and emotional equilibrium."

To tap your chest, Speads says to sit or stand and form a cup with your hands, as you would to swim the crawl. Use the right hand to tap gently on the upper left part of the chest, and the left hand to do the other side. Tap a spot three or four times in succession and then move to a nearby spot, gradually covering the whole area. Breathe evenly and deeply while tapping. "Tapping stimulates not only breathing but circulation and muscle tone as well," Speads reports in her book, *Ways to Better Breathing.* See it for further techniques and exercises for better breathing.

Massage the upper back to aid the circulation of blood and lymph, relax respiratory muscles, and relieve stress and anxiety. A few simple Swedish-massage strokes can greatly benefit the near-drowning victim. In a quiet environment have the subject remove his shirt and lie on his stomach on the floor, or any surface that's firm yet comfortable for the subject and convenient for the bodyworker. Some bodyworkers suggest a cushion under the chest for working on the back and shoulders. The bodyworker applies a light vegetable or massage oil to her hands and spreads it evenly over the subject's upper back and shoulders. Effective massage strokes to use include gliding the hands up each side of the spine and circling back to the waist, kneading the upper back and shoulders, pressing and rotating the pad of the thumbs slowly into sore points for a few moments before gently releasing pressure, and lightly drumming on the subject's back with cupping or chopping movements.

Sing. Singing is a tremendous exercise to strengthen and heal the lungs and respiratory system.

Help promote better lung functioning by using any number of aromatherapy treatments involving the essential oils Eucalyptus, Peppermint, or Tea Tree. For instance:

♦ Place six to eight drops of oil on a tissue or clean cloth and inhale deeply.

♦ Put four to five drops of oil in a pan of water and heat to a simmer. Drape a towel over your head, lean over the pan, and inhale the aromatic steam. (Asthma sufferers should not use this method, as steam can sometimes result in choking.)

♦ Massage a few drops into the chest a few times a day. (Peppermint should be diluted four drops in 2 teaspoons of carrier oil before being applied directly to the skin to prevent itchiness.)

♦ Use an essential-oil vaporizer to evaporate one of these oils into the room, to enhance breathing exercises.

Aromatherapists also recommend the essential oils of Clove and Cinnamon for some respiratory problems. Like Peppermint, these should be diluted before applying to the skin.

Consider as well the emotional and psychological consequences of near-drowning and seek appropriate counseling as needed. The victim has had a tremendously frightening experience. Nightmares and phobias that result may be helped by some form of psychological counseling. See "Resources" for how to contact the Association for Humanistic Psychology and other counseling groups.

PREVENTION

Some simple steps could prevent the vast majority of drownings. Perhaps chief among these are to abstain from drinking alcohol when swimming or boating, to institute a buddy system for any water-related activity, and to recognize early signs of fatigue when in the water. Other general guidelines include:

Always take care to check out the unique characteristics of a swimming site. How deep is the water? Are there submerged hazards? What is the water temperature? Are there currents or tides? What about dangerous marine life, such as jellyfish or sharks? Informed answers to such questions can be especially crucial if the area is new to you and is not supervised by a lifeguard.

Check to see whether rescue devices are readily available. Making sure there is a boat, ring buoy and rope, or long pole can save the life of a drowning victim, and forgo the need for an untrained person to make a dangerous swimming rescue.

Don't swim alone long distances underwater. People who swim underwater sometimes take a series of deep breaths before diving into the water. This does oxygenate the blood in a way that allows the person to hold his breath longer. It also sometimes causes "shallow-water blackout," in which the victim loses consciousness without warning and is quickly in serious trouble.

Homeowners who have a pool should be especially conscious of safety measures, even if they have no children of their own. At a minimum any backyard pool should be enclosed on all four sides with at least a five-foot fence. If the pool is an above-ground one, remove the ladder when it is not in use. If there are doors or windows that exit directly into the pool enclosure from the house, these need to be monitored closely and kept locked if small children are around. This is especially important when children have been left with baby-sitters or elderly grandparents. Pool owners who have small children should consider installing an alarm in the water that goes off whenever a person jumps (or falls) in. Adults need to set and maintain firm ground rules for pool use regarding supervision and horseplay.

Keep a close eye on infants and never leave them unattended anywhere near water. A few inches of water are all it takes to make a tragedy. Many infants are among the some two hundred people who drown in bathtubs (and even toilets) each year. Also, don't rely on flotation devices to keep a child afloat in a pool. These can give watchers and infants alike a false sense of security. Infants sometimes fall out of devices or tip upside down in them. An estimated two out of three near-drownings among children occur during brief lapses in supervision.

Take a course in rescue breathing, CPR, and water safety and rescue. No book, this one included, can take the place of dedicated practice and lessons from an experienced teacher. If you spend a lot of time around water, being prepared for the worst is the best way to prevent it from ever happening.

FIFTEEN

Exposure to Altitude and Cold

THIS CHAPTER COVERS:

♦ *high-altitude sickness*
♦ *frostnip and frostbite*
♦ *hypothermia*

Mountain climbers know that the dangers of their sport are hardly limited to falling off a cliff. It is more likely that they will suffer injury or death from exposure to two of nature's extremes: high altitude and cold temperature. These situations can lead to such medical emergencies as high-altitude sickness, frostbite, and hypothermia, conditions that can be painful, disfiguring, or even fatal.

Yet you don't have to be a member of the twenty-thousand-foot club to be exposed to these risks. Hikers, trekkers, skiers, and winter-sports enthusiasts may face one or more of these hazards in seemingly unthreatening places. The tourist who flies from Boston to Santa Fe—from sea level to seven thousand feet—and immediately goes out for a strenuous run may develop the early symptoms of high-altitude illness. The young child whose mittens fall off while making a snowman may quickly develop frostnipped fingers. The inadequately dressed football fan who belts down a half dozen drinks while sitting in the stands for four hours on a cold, windy day may start down the slippery slide to hypothermia.

Exposure is "nature, red in tooth and claw," in Tennyson's words. It is the elements mercilessly weeding out the weak, the unprepared, and the foolhardy. Only by learning to respect nature's powers, and by taking some simple precautionary steps and recognizing early symptoms, can you lessen your chances of ever becoming a victim to exposure.

> *They had entered the so-called deathzone, where big mountains tend*
> *to wreck the delicate mechanisms of human physiology. Nothing*
> *lived up here for long except lichen and a rare breed of spider with*
> *antifreeze glycerine for blood.*
> —FROM *THE ASCENT* BY JEFF LONG

◆ High-Altitude Sickness

This condition perfectly fits the definition of insidious—operating
in a slow, not easily apparent manner, and more lethal than
seems evident. Some people can be affected at altitudes as low as
five thousand feet. Most people who quickly climb (and some who
transport themselves by plane, car, or ski lift) to above ten thousand feet develop headaches and sleeping problems, the first
indications of high-altitude sickness. A number of individuals
have died from altitude sickness without ever going higher than
that height, an altitude reached by millions of Americans each
year. Mountain peaks in the western United States range from
eight thousand to fourteen thousand feet, with much of the state
of Colorado being at such altitudes. Hike in the Swiss Alps or trek
in Nepal and you're likely to reach twelve to fifteen thousand feet.
If you're a serious mountain climber, of course, life begins at
fifteen thousand feet (and sometimes ends at 20,320 feet, the
height of Mt. McKinley in Alaska, the highest peak in North
America, or 29,028 feet, the height of Mt. Everest, the highest peak
in the world).

Some people assume they are immune to high-altitude sickness because they've driven to the top of New Hampshire's Mt.
Washington (6,288 feet), walked around a bit, motored away, and
"never felt a thing." Two factors prevented any ill effects: there
was little physical exertion, and the time spent at that altitude
was limited. The question, however, is not *whether* an individual
suffers from high-altitude sickness, but under what circumstances
and at what height. For instance, even the hardiest Sherpa would
quickly contract an acute case of altitude sickness and shortly
pass out and die above a certain altitude, probably about thirty
thousand feet.

The height at which the average person begins to feel the
symptoms of high-altitude sickness varies tremendously. Studies
indicate that perhaps a third of those climbing to six thousand to
ten thousand feet develop at least mild symptoms, as do over half
of those who climb above ten thousand feet. In addition to how
high you go, other factors include:

- ◆ the pace at which you climb or the degree to which you exert yourself
- ◆ how long you stay at a high altitude
- ◆ individual susceptibility (even well-conditioned athletes become victims)

Some 40 million people worldwide live year-round at altitudes over eight thousand feet, and scientists estimate that humans could settle permanently up to about seventeen thousand feet. Millions more people visit heights over eight thousand feet and never suffer any symptoms. Clearly, the body can adjust to and survive high altitudes. Knowing how can make the difference between life and death.

CAUSES

The direct cause of high-altitude sickness is thin air. All of the earth's air up to an altitude of about sixty miles is 21 percent oxygen. Why then does the body start to starve for oxygen at an altitude of one to two miles? Because air is compressed at sea level by the weight of all the air above it. As you increase your altitude from sea level, air pressure drops and the air's density decreases. The molecules of air are so spread out at eighteen thousand feet that you inhale about 50 percent less oxygen with each breath than you inhale at sea level.

With increasing altitude the gas molecules floating around in your intestines also thin out and expand, resulting in a condition called "high-altitude flatus expulsion" by scientists and "the mountain farts" by plain old folks. You may not want to climb high if you're constipated, and others in your party may not want you to lead if you've just eaten a big meal of beans.

The effects on the rest of your body aren't as innocuous. Since the lungs are taking in less oxygen, less is available to transfer to the blood and ultimately to tissues and organs. The body begins to develop a form of hypoxia, a lack of oxygen that can ultimately result in death.

In its wisdom the body makes a number of adjustments to forestall death from oxygen starvation. It increases the breathing and heart rates, thus pumping more blood through the system, and makes some chemical changes in the blood to allow more oxygen to be released to bodily tissues. Some of the other changes the body undergoes, however, are not as beneficial. Cells in some parts of the body accumulate fluids. This may cause, for instance, the hands, feet, and face to swell up from fluid retention. Of even greater concern is the accumulation of fluid in the lung spaces where the exchange of oxygen and carbon dioxide normally takes place. This leaky lung condition is known as high-altitude pulmonary edema, or HAPE, and usually develops within the first two to four days of rapid climbing over eight thousand feet. Another serious condition that may accompany acute altitude illness is high-altitude cerebral edema, or HACE, from an increase in fluid causing a swelling of the brain. Both HAPE and HACE are potentially life-threatening complications.

SYMPTOMS

High-altitude sickness develops along a continuum from mild to acute. Mild symptoms may take a day or two to show up, or they may be provoked within hours by a rapid unacclimatized climb. In its mild form high-altitude sickness is characterized by:

◆ hangoverlike feelings of fatigue, headache, nausea, and loss of appetite
◆ sleep disturbances, including frequent awakening, bizarre dreams, and insomnia
◆ breathing problems, including cycles of heavy and light breathing, shortness of breath, and difficult breathing
◆ a decreased ability to perform physical work or exercise
◆ mental problems, such as apathy, forgetfulness, or mental sluggishness

If steps are not taken to reverse the condition, oxygen levels in the blood continue to fall and the symptoms worsen. The victim experiences a rapid decay of physical and mental abilities and becomes progressively more lethargic, clumsy, and confused. He or she may start to hallucinate. Breathing problems may be accompanied by coughing and a gurgling sound in the chest. Vision blurs and the skin turns blue. In its acute stage, high-altitude sickness can lead to unconsciousness, coma, and death.

Acute high-altitude sickness may be accompanied by HAPE or HACE. HAPE may first show up as fatigue and a dry cough. (This latter condition may also merely be a symptom of "altitude throat," a sore throat from taking in dry, cold air through the mouth.) If HAPE is not reversed, the victim may develop more severe symptoms such as shortness of breath, blue lips and nails, and a gurgling sound in the chest. At its most severe the victim may cough blood and then collapse into a coma.

Symptoms of HACE include headache, nausea, loss of coordination, hallucinations, stupor, and finally coma.

ADJUSTING TO ALTITUDE

There are three important steps to keep in mind whenever you venture above about five thousand feet, whether by climbing, ski lift, driving, or flying.

Allow time for your body to acclimatize to the lower oxygen levels before going on to further heights. There are a number of ways to do this.

- ◆ Take a day or two to rest before beginning an ascent or undertaking strenuous activity at that height.
- ◆ Climb slowly. Mountaineers note that it is not so much height itself that presents the health risks, but the speed of ascent. There are various formulas for determining how fast you can safely climb. Conditions and individual susceptibility vary, but as a general guideline figure on taking two to four days getting used to an altitude over eight thousand feet before going any higher, and then taking at least one rest day for each two days of climbing, which should not exceed more than fifteen hundred feet per day. At altitudes over fourteen thousand feet, the rate of ascent should be cut to five hundred to a thousand feet per day and rest days should be even more frequent.
- ◆ Play high, sleep low. Especially if you're climbing or skiing at altitudes over ten thousand feet, you can avoid the worst effects of high altitudes by descending a thousand to two thousand feet to sleep. The benefits are most dramatic the first day over ten thousand feet.

Recognize and closely monitor the early warning signs of high-altitude sickness. Especially if you go above seven thousand to eight thousand feet (and you may not want to go at all if you have heart or lung diseases), you should closely monitor any early symptoms of high-altitude sickness. Further ascent should be postponed until symptoms subside.

Descend to a lower altitude if the condition worsens. If you don't feel any better after three or four days, or if you've allowed a mild case of altitude sickness to develop into an acute one, HAPE, or HACE, the best treatment is an immediate descent of two thousand to four thousand feet, preferably to below five thousand feet.

BASIC FIRST AID FOR HIGH-ALTITUDE SICKNESS

If symptoms of mild altitude sickness such as headache or insomnia do appear, don't panic. Minor symptoms are frequently harmless and short-lived. If you climb no higher and rest for two to four days, the body will often acclimatize to the thinner air and the symptoms will disappear. The symptoms will disappear even quicker if you descend, of course. As little as five hundred to a thousand feet of descent is enough to cure most cases of mild altitude sickness.

Victims of acute altitude sickness, HAPE, and HACE should be kept calm, still, and warm, if possible, and should descend to a lower altitude as quickly as possible. They may need to be carried and should never be allowed to descend alone, due to their serious physical condition and the likelihood that their judgment is impaired.

If bottled oxygen is available, it can help speed recovery. Restrict the victim's salt intake since salt can aggravate fluid retention problems. Offer the victim water or fluids, but not alcohol.

Emergency personnel may prescribe various drugs to treat acute altitude sickness, including anti-inflammatory cortisonelike steroid drugs (prednisone, dexamethasone), sedatives, and pain relievers. Doctors also sometimes prescribe drugs to prevent high-altitude sickness. For instance, physicians may suggest diuretics and the anticonvulsive drug acetazolamide (Ak-Zol, Diamox) to control fluids. Some researchers say that acetazolamide may also increase the lungs' ability to process oxygen, though this claim is not sufficiently substantiated by scientific studies for it to be made by any of the drug's manufacturers. Health-conscious climbers consider such preventive drug treatments dangerous, noting that drugs can mask the early signs of altitude sickness and lead to more serious cases. The side effects of taking acetazolamide include drowsiness, dehydration, weakness, and emotional depression, all of which may present special hazards to mountain climbers. Drug treatment should be considered only under medical supervision.

A recent innovation for treating acute altitude sickness is the Gamow bag, a device that resembles a sleeping bag but functions as a hyperbaric (high pressure) oxygen chamber. Small enough to be portable, it is inflated by a foot pump in emergency situations to, in effect, deliver a lower altitude to wherever it is taken. The victim of altitude sickness is put inside the bag to breathe the "richer" (actually, higher pressure) air. Even a few minutes inside the bag has been known to relieve some cases of altitude sickness.

NATURAL REMEDIES FOR HIGH-ALTITUDE SICKNESS

There is no substitute for the common sense measures of climbing slowly, monitoring early symptoms, and descending to a lower altitude for the prevention and treatment of altitude-related conditions. There are, though, a number of natural techniques that can complement these steps and possibly help prevent an episode or speed the body's ability to acclimatize to altitude.

To help counter mild symptoms of altitude sickness:

Take the stimulating herbs ginger or cayenne. "These are the two best and most readily available metabolic and respiratory stimulants," herbalist Christopher Hobbs notes. "They're good remedies both for mild altitude sickness and exposure to the cold."

◆ Oriental healers use ginger internally and externally for its warming and stimulating effects. The root is rich in volatile oils that boost the heart, lungs, and kidneys. For acute conditions put fifteen to twenty drops of the tincture, standardized extract, or concentrated drops in half a cup of warm water and drink. You can also make a tea from the dried powder by adding one and a half teaspoonfuls to a cup of water. Bring it to a boil, simmer for five to ten minutes, and drink.

◆ Cayenne is an herb ground from the dried fruit of various capsicum peppers, especially the long conical variety *Capsicum frutescens*. Cayenne is widely used as a spicy seasoning in Latin American and Oriental cuisines. One of cayenne's active ingredients is the phenol compound capsaicin. Scientific studies have established that capsaicin reduces inflammation and pain. In the Orient cayenne is a popular "crisis herb" for its heating and stimulating effects on the kidneys, lungs, stomach, and heart. Hobbs says, "For immediate effects put a half teaspoon in a small glass of warm water and drink. It activates the heart and circulation and thus helps in situations when you're not getting enough oxygen." Cayenne is also available in capsule and liquid forms.

(If high-altitude sickness is accompanied by hypothermia, internal use of cayenne should be avoided. That's because in high doses cayenne can open skin pores and cause sweating, which cools the body. Ginger, however, tends to heat the body's core and thus doesn't present this potential problem.)

Oriental Medical Doctor Holly Eagle agrees that herbs can help to treat the symptoms of high-altitude sickness, though she notes that sometimes nausea and vomiting prevent the person from ingesting anything. "The best thing is descent by five hundred feet or more first, and then herbs for nausea [such as ginger], circulation and respiration," she says.

Take the homeopathic remedy Argentum nitricum. Homeopaths recommend this remedy (made from silver nitrate) for dizziness or a sensation that the mountains are closing in on you.

RECOVERY AND PREVENTION

To prevent an episode of high-altitude sickness, or to help someone recover after he or she has descended, try some of the following steps.

Take additional amounts of the amino acid tyrosine. Tyrosine is one of the twenty amino acids that form the building blocks of proteins. It is considered an "unessential" amino acid because it is normally manufactured by the body. Tyrosine plays an important role in metabolism and proper functioning of the nervous system. Some nutritional therapists use tyrosine supplements to counter emotional stress and depression, since low blood levels have been tied to a deficiency of the brain neurotransmitters and mood hormones epinephrine and dopamine. Proponents also tout tyrosine as a treatment for chronic fatigue syndrome and premenstrual syndrome.

In the course of their research, scientists have also explored tyrosine's potential to prevent high-altitude sickness. In one study researchers gave subjects high doses (six grams daily) of tyrosine and put them through the equivalent of a rapid climb to over fifteen thousand feet. The tyrosine was tied to higher levels of performance and alertness, and its use resulted in fewer complaints about muscle soreness and headaches. The subjects who took tyrosine also seemed to be more resistant to the cold.

Though the subjects reported no adverse effects from the high doses of tyrosine, research on this amino acid is in its infancy, and the long-term effects of taking two to six grams daily are unknown. A more prudent approach would be to start with 500 mg of tyrosine three times daily before meals every day for a week before attaining high altitudes, gradually increasing the dosage if needed. A number of vitamin companies market tyrosine and amino acid supplements. Consult with a health practitioner before you take higher amounts and if you suffer from high blood pressure or take monoamine oxidase (MAO) inhibiting antidepressants.

Take extra vitamin C and E, and the vitaminlike coenzyme Q10. Each day for at least a week before attaining altitude, take two grams of vitamin C, 400 IU of vitamin E, and 30–50 mg of coenzyme Q10 (coQ10).

Studies indicate that taking high levels of these nutrients before and during a climb may help the body adjust to higher altitudes and improve physical endurance. Exercising at high altitudes also increases free radical activity, and vitamins C and E are powerful antioxidants that neutralize free radicals. CoQ10 may help the body's cells use oxygen.

Eat for high-altitude health. Start eating a diet high in complex carbohydrates at least two days before the climb, and continue to eat nutritious carbohydrate foods while climbing. Many mountain climbers have found that eating frequent small meals works better than having one or two large ones to keep a steady supply of energy available. A diet high in dark green leafy vegetables and other chlorophyll-rich foods such as wheat grass or barley grass will help build blood rich in hemoglobin, which carries oxygen from the lungs to the tissues.

Take herbs that can help you adapt to new conditions and better utilize oxygen. Two of the most promising ones to try are Siberian ginseng and ginkgo.

- Siberian ginseng has been used for over four thousand years by the Chinese as a revitalizing tonic to increase longevity and improve general health. Sometimes referred to as eleuthero, it is the root of a shrub widely grown in the Far East. Herbalists refer to it as an adaptogen, a special class of herbs that are able to restore balance to various bodily systems without regard to the direction of the imbalance. Adaptogens also increase the body's resistance to stress, fatigue, and disease. "Eleuthero strengthens the body against both high altitude and cold," Hobbs notes.

Siberian ginseng is widely available in tincture and capsules and is often combined with other adaptogenic herbs such as schizandra. Follow dosage directions on labels.

◆ Ginkgo has been used by the Chinese for thousands of years to treat respiratory problems, and studies have found that it improves circulation to the heart and brain. Take 40 mg three times per day of a standardized extract that contains at least 24 percent ginkgo heterosides.

While climbing or exercising at high altitudes, stop to take ten to twelve deep breaths every four to six minutes. This breathing technique can help you maintain optimum levels of oxygen in the blood.

Avoid drinking alcohol. Among alcohol's adverse effects are that it tends to dehydrate the body, a situation that can contribute to high-altitude sickness.

Do some mild but not strenuous exercising while you're waiting to get acclimatized to the high altitude. Reaching a high altitude is not the time to run a marathon, but neither is it couch-potato time. Walking is a beneficial exercise for speeding acclimatization.

Also refer to the suggestions for ways to strengthen the lungs and respiratory system and boost the immune system in the recovery section of "Chapter 14: Drowning." The near-drowning recovery steps could also be used to help prevent high-altitude sickness, since they increase the effectiveness and efficiency of respiration and circulation.

◆ Frostnip and Frostbite

Whenever you're exposed to a windchill below about 20° F, there's a danger that frostnip or frostbite may develop. At highest risk are your body's extremities—fingers and toes—and parts of the face, including the ears, cheeks, and nose. Not only are these parts most likely to be left exposed to the cold, they freeze faster because they have a high surface-to-volume ratio and the body's response to severe cold is to "sacrifice" these parts first. That is, to preserve warmth for important internal organs, the body first shuts down circulation to its extremities.

If you allow these parts of the body to stay cold for long enough, a number of unhealthy things happen. Blood vessels constrict and the blood itself thickens. Transmission of normal pain messages through the nerves is disrupted, making the area feel numb and possibly preventing you from realizing the damage under way. Fewer vital nutrients get to surrounding tissues, and ice crystals form in the fluids in and around cells. The freezing process damages and dehydrates cell tissues and membranes, sometimes irreparably. In extreme cases the freezing can affect deep nerves, muscles, and even bones, ultimately causing digits or an entire limb to become gangrenous and need to be amputated.

CAUSES

A variety of factors can combine with freezing temperatures to increase the risk of developing frostbite, including:

Wind. Above freezing, every mile per hour of wind lowers temperature by roughly one degree F. Below freezing, the effect is even more dramatic. For instance, a twenty-mile-per-hour wind on a 10° F day creates a windchill factor of − 25° F.

Circulation problems. People who suffer from conditions such as diabetes and atherosclerosis are at greater risk for developing frostbite.

Drug consumption. Recreational drugs including alcohol and tobacco can increase the risks of frostbite by restricting peripheral circulation, promoting dehydration, or clouding judgment. Certain prescription drugs also present potential problems. For instance, the beta blockers used to lower blood pressure can decrease the flow of blood to the skin.

High altitudes. Air temperature and windchill are likely to be lower. Some of the potential effects of high-altitude sickness, such as fatigue and poor judgment, can also lead to injury from cold.

Touching a substance considerably colder than air temperature. Skin cells can freeze almost instantaneously when they come in contact with a piece of extremely cold metal. Volatile liquids such as gasoline that freeze at temperatures much lower than does water (gasoline can still be in liquid form at a bone-chilling − 65° F) are also a frostbite hazard should they get spilled on exposed skin. (In a recent letter to *The New England Journal of Medicine,* a doctor related the unique emergency action an Eskimo father took when his five-year-old son licked a handrail in subzero weather "and was instantly frozen to the railing by his tongue and upper lip. His father attempted to free him but could not. Instead, the father helped his son by a novel and effective means— he urinated on the boy's tongue. . . . The father had acted pragmatically and swiftly in dispensing this unusual first aid. His efforts certainly averted more serious frostbite.")

Previous frostbite. Cells that have been frozen once are more likely to refreeze.

SYMPTOMS AND STAGES

In its earliest stages frostbite is called frostnip. It is characterized by skin that is tingling or numb. During and after treating a frostnip, usually all you feel is some mild pain and then perhaps some tenderness. The effects of the cold are not severe enough to cause blisters or peeling after the area has been thawed.

Mild frostbite affects only slightly deeper tissues. The skin takes on a harder texture sometimes accompanied by a yellow-and-white or blue-and-white mottled color. The body part may feel prickly or itchy. Rewarming causes noticeable pain or even a burning sensation. There may be some clear blistering and peeling in the days after the injury. Even mildly frostbitten tissue may henceforth always be sensitive to the cold.

Severe frostbite affects deep skin and other subsurface tissues, including in the worst cases bones. The affected area is cold and stiff to the touch. It usually swells and turns a deadly, pale shade of gray. Thawing causes excruciating, burning pain. The skin fails to recover its normal color and texture, remaining cold, blue, and swollen. If the tissue is completely dead, it will turn black and eventually mummify if not amputated.

BASIC FIRST AID FOR FROSTBITE

Along with putting butter on a burn, rubbing snow on a frostbite is one of the folk remedies that should be retired from circulation. Applying snow to relieve a frostbite is no more helpful than would be putting out a lit cigarette on a burn. Dry snow on a frostbite is bad enough; if the snow is wet, it will promote freezing of tissue even faster and more thoroughly. When your skin is frozen, you need to rewarm it, not freeze it further. (The one exception to this rule, discussed below, is that you shouldn't thaw a frostbitten body part if there is a possibility that it will refreeze.)

Even if you want to prevent a frostbitten body part from thawing, rubbing it, with snow or any other substance, is not recommended. That's because the pressure and friction can easily damage delicate cells and increase the chance of infection. A frostbitten body part should be handled like a DDT-weakened eggshell. So leave the snow on the ground and find some shelter and heat, the latter preferably in the form of warm water.

Sometimes all that is needed to treat frostnip or a superficial frostbite is a warm body or part thereof. Put chilled fingers, for instance, in the armpit or between the thighs, or have another person cover the fingers with two warm hands. Apply gentle pressure, but don't massage the area of frostnip.

For a more severe frostbite, warm water is the best heating agent. Ideally the water should be between 104 and 108° F. Anything hotter risks burning the skin (children's skin is more heat sensitive than adults'). Keep in mind that numbness may prevent the victim from being able to feel a burn. Remove any jewelry or constrictive clothing, including boots, socks, and gloves. Place the frostbitten extremity in the warm-water bath, which will have to be rewarmed frequently as the icy tissue cells thaw out in it. If it is not possible to submerge the part, apply repeated warm-water compresses.

It is rarely a good idea to thaw a frostbitten extremity with dry radiant heat. For instance, don't put a frozen hand in front of a fire, hold it over a hot stove, or torch it with a blow-dryer. All of these methods can cause severe burns. Water also has the advantage of conducting heat better than air.

Thaw a severe frostbite rapidly, since speed increases the chance of tissue recovery and diminishes the duration of pain. The skin is thawed when it regains its soft texture, flesh color, and sense of sensation. Except in the most advanced cases the frostbitten body part should regain normal color and sensation within twenty to thirty minutes of warm-water treatment. If it hasn't, call a medical professional. Remember to rewarm the rest of the person as well—hypothermia (see next section) is an even more serious exposure emergency. Offer blankets and warm fluids.

It is necessary to reemphasize that there is one circumstance in which you should not rewarm a frostbite injury: whenever there is a danger that the body part will refreeze. It is better to leave the tissue frozen than to start a freeze-thaw cycle, which can cause more severe tissue damage than a simple frostbite injury. For instance, let's say you hike through deep snow to an overnight campsite and find your toes frostbitten. If you know they will refreeze on the trek back out the next day, and that's the earliest you can leave, it is better to allow them to stay frostbitten overnight than to start a freeze-thaw-refreeze cycle. The frostbitten feet should be wrapped and padded the next day (in general you don't want to walk on or otherwise use a frostbitten extremity) and rewarmed as soon as possible.

Once you've thawed severe frostbite, gently dry the area with a towel. Put sterile gauze or clean cotton between fingers or toes to absorb moisture. Allow them to dry further in the open air, making sure there's no danger of refreezing. The bodily tissue is still extremely delicate and should be moved or used as little as possible. Also, do not massage the part.

During the first few days of recovery, you can bathe the frostbitten area in warm, soapy water twice a day. At this time, you can begin light massage and gentle range-of-motion exercises to help prevent stiffness.

WHAT TO EXPECT AT THE HOSPITAL

While you can treat frostnip yourself, frostbite should usually be evaluated by a medical professional. For instance, if a mild frostbite covers an extensive area of the body, it should be medically evaluated. Also any frostbite that has been warmed up but is still painful, blue, or swollen, or any that results in blisters the next day, should be looked at by a medical professional. These are indications that the freezing has affected deep tissues. In such cases keep the extremity elevated and transport the victim to the practitioner or to a hospital.

Emergency treatment of severe frostbite usually includes some type of painkiller and often a sedative, since the process is painful and the possible outcome (loss of fingers, toes, or more) frightening. Doctors may also recommend special drugs that dilate blood vessels in the extremities, and antibiotics to prevent infection. The natural herbal product aloe cream is widely used in hospitals to cover frostbite blisters that are left intact.

In most cases tissues heal by themselves and amputation can be avoided. New skin often develops in the place of any that turns black and falls off. Surgeons will usually monitor a frostbite injury for weeks or longer before deciding that tissues are permanently and irrevocably damaged.

NATURAL FIRST-AID REMEDIES FOR FROSTBITE

Most frostbite injuries beyond frostnip are potentially serious medical emergencies that call for basic first aid and quick medical treatment. Natural remedies can play a role when combined with the basic steps. Some of the natural remedies that follow can also help during the earliest stages to prevent a mild frostbite from becoming more severe.

Take advantage of the powerful local heating effects of yarrow or cayenne. Cayenne and yarrow are two of the best peripheral vasodilators—they increase circulation to the hands, feet, fingers, and toes. Yarrow will only work when taken internally. Cayenne can be taken orally or applied externally in any of the following ways:

◆ Gently rub the tincture, oil, or standardized extract into the frostbitten skin.
◆ Mix one teaspoon of the powdered herb with four ounces of olive or other vegetable oil and apply.
◆ Put five to ten drops of tincture or oil, or a half teaspoon of powder, in warm water and submerse the frostbitten area.

As was noted in the discussion of cayenne under high-altitude sickness, when there's the possibility that the person has hypothermia, avoid internal use of cayenne (and yarrow as well) since they can cause sweating and cool the body. When frostbite may be accompanied by hypothermia, ginger is a better herb to take internally than yarrow or cayenne since ginger has the effect of increasing heat production in the body's core.

For frostnipped fingers, apply acupressure to points on the body's energy pathway known as the Triple Warmer. This meridian runs from the tip of the ring finger on both hands up the arm and around the ears to the temple (see illustration #16). Massage the points on the back of the hand about a half inch from the outside base of the ring finger. Or try the points on the outside of the forearm, midway between the two bones, two and one-half finger-widths below the wrist crease. Acupressure authority Michael Reed Gach suggests pressing on these points by holding opposite sides of the wrists with fingers and thumbs. "Warm compresses on these points would also help," he says.

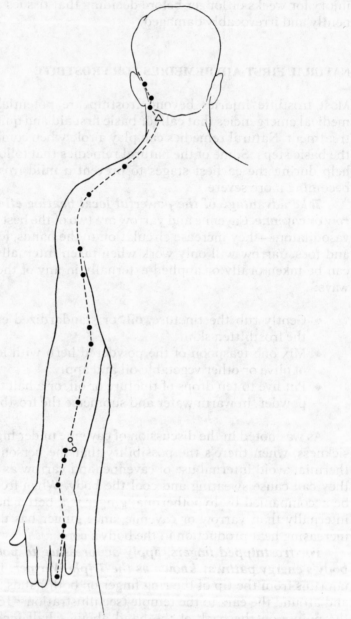

Illustration #16:

The energy channel or meridian known as the Triple Warmer, which runs from the fingers to the head, contains points on the back of the hand and on the outside of the forearm that can be pressed to help relieve frostnipped fingers.

Prepare a relieving herbal wash or bath. Make a tea out of one of the following herbs and add it to warm water to make a foot or hand bath to thaw the injury. Or pour a few cups of the tea in a warm bath to soak the whole body. You can also use these teas once a day after the frostbite to wash the injury and boost recovery.

- ginger root powder
- oatstraw (the green stalk, leaves, and grain of the oat plant)
- horsetail, whose beneficial effect on frostbite injuries may be due to its high silica content
- ginkgo leaves

Gingko is a popular remedy in the Orient for treating frostbite and chilblains. Chilblains is a painful swelling or sore caused by exposure to cold, usually affecting the fingers, toes, or ears.

If you're out in the wilderness, you might consider one of the few recorded Native American remedies for frostbite. Various tribes would soak frostbites in decoctions made from the leaves of the American or white beech (*Fagus grandifolia*), the winter buds of the balsam poplar (*Populus balsamifera*) tree, the leaves of broom sedge (*Andropogon virginicus*), or white pine (*Pinus strobus*) bark.

Take a megadose of niacin. This is the B vitamin that causes your face to get hot and flushed when you take 75–100 mg. "That's because niacin is a vasodilator," nutritionist Shari Lieberman notes. "It opens up veins and capillaries, allowing more blood and oxygen to get to extremities. For frostbite, you want to take five hundred milligrams of a special flush-free form of niacin called inositol hexaniacinate. You can also take this supplement to prevent frostbite. I've had outstanding success using it with patients suffering from Raynaud's disease, a circulatory disorder that makes people prone to frostbite." If you take over 75–100 mg of niacin at one time, make sure it is the flush-free form, Lieberman warns. "Take five hundred milligrams of the regular niacin and you'll think you're dying," she says.

Gently apply a warming herbal liniment to the affected part. Warming liniments dilate local blood vessels and increase circulation to surface skin areas. One of the most popular warming liniments available at most natural food stores is Tiger Balm, an ointment combination of camphor and menthol. Another popular product, also from the Orient, is White Flower Analgesic Balm, a combination of wintergreen, menthol, camphor, and oils of Lavender, Eucalyptus, and Peppermint.

Take a frostbite-relieving homeopathic remedy. Two that homeopath Jennifer Jacobs, M.D., recommends to be taken internally are:

- *Agaricus.* Made from the fly agaric mushroom, this is the remedy for frostbite characterized by cold, numbness, or tingling; or a sensation of being pierced by needles of ice.
- *Lachesis.* Made from snake venom, use this for a bluish or purplish appearance or icy cold feet.

More common homeopathic remedies that may be helpful include two that can be applied locally as ointments or sprays:

- *Hypericum.* This is good when surface nerves need to be calmed.
- *Apis.* This is good for the stinging and burning pain that occurs when warming a frostbite.

Gently apply essential oils that can help elevate local skin temperature. Lightly rub five drops of Eucalyptus, Geranium, or Ginger diluted in one teaspoon of vegetable oil into the area. Alternatively, you can safely apply two to three drops of the essential oil of Lavender directly to the skin.

Try one of the folk remedies traditionally used to treat frostnip. Exactly why any of the following would work is not clear, but many a kitchen doc has had success with them.

- Take a cucumber slice, dip it in warm water, and place it on the area of frostnip.
- Cut an onion in half and gently rub it over the injury.
- Crush a radish and apply its juice to the injury.
- Squeeze fresh lemon juice onto the skin.

For frostbitten toes or fingers that have been warmed up, apply a few drops of the natural antibiotic Tea Tree oil and then cover with aloe. These remedies will help prevent infection and speed healing.

Use healing herbs to treat frostbite blisters that form the day after the injury. Herbalist Christopher Hobbs recommends preparations of the all-purpose healer calendula, or poultices made from herbs containing the potent wound healer allantoin, such as comfrey and plantain. Allantoin promotes healing and prevents further tissue damage. You can use comfrey root powder to make a paste that is spread on the injury and covered. (Don't use comfrey, however, on an open wound or on blisters that have popped.)

Aloe also works well to speed the healing of a frostbite injury, as do almost all burn creams, according to Oriental Medical Doctor Holly Eagle (see "Chapter 9: Burns"). "Among our favorites is Sierra Sage Marigold Skin Creme produced by Simplers Botanical of Forestville, California. It's a soothing salve made from marigold, yarrow, and chamomile flowers, the essential oil of Lavender, vitamin E, and other ingredients. Marigold Skin Creme is wonderful on the aftereffects of frostbite injuries for taking the red and heat out." A number of herbal manufacturers produce burn creams; check your local natural foods store.

◆ Hypothermia

The surface temperature of your hands and feet can drop over seventy degrees, from 98.6° to 20°, without killing you. You may not even suffer permanent damage if the frozen tissue is rewarmed quickly enough. But if the temperature of your body's core—the site of vital organs such as the heart, lungs, and kidneys—drops a fraction of that seventy degrees, you're immediately faced with the life-threatening condition known as hypothermia. In fact, mild hypothermia begins with a core drop of only a few degrees, to below 95°.

Like fainting, which makes the body horizontal and brings blood to the brain, hypothermia is another case of the body's innate wisdom, enforcing a wise survival strategy during a time of crisis. When prolonged exposure to extreme cold causes the body's internal temperature to plunge, your brain's thermoregulatory center reacts. It begins to shut down nonessential bodily functions in a way that preserves internal heat and protects the brain and other vital organs, thus postponing death. Surface blood vessels constrict (increasing the risk of frostbite, as we've seen, but that's a lesser evil than hypothermia), sending more warm blood to heat the core. Energy metabolism increases dramatically, allowing the body to burn fuel faster and to produce more heat. Muscles shiver, the heart beats faster, and sweating stops, all in order to slow down heat loss and preserve what warmth the body has for the vital core.

This is all well and good as far as it goes, but the body cannot sustain this level of energy expenditure. Your body's engine is revving beyond the redline, and the fuel gauge is plunging toward empty. By the time the internal temperature reaches about 90°, exhausted heart muscles, if they don't fail completely in the form of a fatal attack, allow blood pressure to drop. As remaining calories get burned up, energy metabolism and brain function begin to slow and sputter. Let your body's core temperature sink to about 80° and your body will resemble a cold, stiff corpse. Only a trained or keen observer will realize that you may still be revivable. Below about 77°, your body's caloric reserve is likely to be totally depleted. The internal organs shut down, your heart stops beating, and you are dead.

CAUSES

Poor and homeless people trying to survive through cold winters are probably at greatest risk of dying from hypothermia. With their inadequate clothing and lack of central (or any other kind of) heating, they face death whenever the weather conspires to combine cold temperatures, high wind, and low humidity.

If other factors are present (such as wet clothes, illness, or alcohol), the temperature doesn't even have to be that cold—a number of people have died from hypothermia without the air temperature's dropping below 30–50° F.

Some other factors in the onset of hypothermia include:

Reduced home temperatures. A number of sick or elderly people die each year from setting their household thermostat at or below 55–60° F during the winter. Even this can be a fatally low temperature when combined with such factors as circulatory disease, lack of exercise, inactivity, and malnourishment. Gerontologists recommend that elderly people keep indoor temperatures during the winter at least 65°–70°F, and higher if over seventy-five years old.

Cold-water submersion. Water is a double-edged sword. While warm water is better than warm air for curing frostbite, cold water can almost instantly cause either frostbite or hypothermia. That's because water is an excellent conductor of both heat and cold. One estimate is that it is one hundred times easier to become hypothermic in 77° water (which is about as warm as continental water in the United States gets) than 77° air. Health authorities agree that it is best to assume that anyone pulled from cold water is suffering from hypothermia.

Winter sports and activities. Whether you're cross-country skiing or shoveling snow, hypothermia is a risk especially when combined with immobility (from breaking a bone while skiing alone, for instance) and inadequate clothing.

Auto breakdown. A car is a refrigerator on wheels once it runs out of fuel. It's always a good idea to be prepared for the worst, with extra clothing and blankets, if you're traveling in a cold and isolated area. If you do break down in a storm, it is usually best to bundle up and stay in the car, where at least you're protected from the wind and you will eventually be found.

Age and body type. The elderly (due to circulatory diseases and heat-regulating problems) and the young (due to immobility and lack of body fat) are more at risk for hypothermia than most people.

Drugs. Alcohol poses a triple whammy, since it dilates surface blood vessels, inhibits shivering, and contributes to dehydration. Barbiturates and other drugs can also lead to excessive loss of body heat.

SYMPTOMS OF HYPOTHERMIA

The first and most important sign of a slight drop in core temperature is shivering, as the muscles contract and expand in an attempt to generate heat. With some elderly victims, however, shivering may not occur, and you will have to rely either on a thermometer reading of 95° or below or on whether their skin is cold to the touch. As the core temperature continues to drop, metabolism, pulse, and heartbeat all slow down. The severely hypothermic person stops shivering and becomes lethargic, disoriented, or dizzy. He or she may slur words, appear confused, or make serious errors in judgment such as wanting to be left alone or not covering up from the cold. As the condition becomes more severe, muscles go stiff and the person loses consciousness. At this point the body is cold, rigid, and corpselike. Death from shock or cardiac arrest is imminent.

BASIC FIRST AID FOR HYPOTHERMIA

Treating hypothermia is somewhat like treating a whole-body frostbite. As quickly and safely as possible you want to remove the source of cold and rewarm the person. Hypothermia is a more serious medical emergency than is frostbite though, so it is important to determine immediately whether you're dealing with a mild or severe case.

If the hypothermia is severe, call for emergency help as soon as possible. Keep the victim calm. Don't allow him or her to panic or to exercise to "warm up the body." Both of these can increase sweating, which is a cooling mechanism that causes heat loss. These activities may also result in the person's inhaling large quantities of cold air.

There are some other things you should not do:

◆ Do not move the victim except to get him or her out of the cold.
◆ Do not massage or rub the victim's limbs.
◆ Do not put the victim in a hot bath.

Such actions can actually worsen hypothermia by drawing blood out of the body's core (which lowers the temperature there) or by flooding the heart with cold blood (which can cause a heart attack). "The skin gets very cold when a person is hypothermic," notes Joseph Pizzorno, N.D. "Putting a person in a hot bath dumps all that ice-cold blood and fluid from the skin directly into the core and can quickly drop the core temperature. The key is to heat the core from the inside out, and the best way to do that is to allow the body to warm itself."

Persons who are suffering from severe hypothermia after being immersed in cold water need to be handled with extreme care. Warming them too quickly can overstrain the heart or lead to death from a type of "rewarming shock."

If possible, get a severe hypothermia victim indoors and keep him lying down. Gently remove any wet clothes and dry the victim. Wrap him in blankets or put him in a sleeping bag. Or else put the victim unclothed into a sleeping bag along with another person who can act as a giant hot-water bottle. "Another body is the quickest, safest, and most profound treatment for hypothermia," Holly Eagle says, "not just because of the heat but because of the energy of another being."

You can also apply warm compresses or hot-water bottles (well-insulated, or filled with warm water) to the side of the victim's chest, or to the groin. No form of heat should be placed on the arms or legs, where it could draw blood away from the core.

If severe hypothermia strikes while you're in the wilderness, get the victim out of the wind, remove any wet clothes, and wrap him or her in blankets or a sleeping bag. Some 75 percent of the body's heat is lost through the head, so keep the victim's head and neck covered. Monitor the victim's ABCs (airway, breathing, and circulation; see Chapter 3). Have the victim carried to safety if possible. If he or she is conscious, you can offer regular sips of a warm, sweet, nonalcoholic drink such as apple cider.

Victims of severe hypothermia should be hospitalized and need to be treated cautiously, preferably by a medical professional. Not until after the hypothermia emergency has been dealt with should you focus on other injuries, including frostbite. Keep in mind that treatments for frostbite that return circulation to the body's extremities can draw blood from the body's core and thus worsen a case of hypothermia. Also remember that for several hours after being rewarmed the person faces further risk of hypothermia yet may seem almost normal.

The end stages of severe hypothermia can resemble death, with the victim cold, stiff, and glassy-eyed. The pulse may be so faint that you can't easily detect it. The victim may still, however, be alive, so you should take the necessary steps to revive him or her until death is confirmed.

For a mild case of hypothermia get the victim to warm shelter and immediately remove and replace any wet clothes. Wrap the victim in blankets and sit him or her by a fire or some other heat source. The victim can also get in a sleeping bag or take a warm but not hot bath. Warm water or other nonalcoholic drinks can help replenish fluids.

NATURAL FIRST-AID REMEDIES FOR MILD HYPOTHERMIA

There are fewer natural remedies for mild hypothermia than mild frostbite, but here are some worth trying that can complement conventional treatments.

Use natural remedies to prevent emotional shock. Two of the most popular are flower essence first-aid remedies, such as Bach Flower Rescue Remedy, and the homeopathic remedy *Aconite*.

- ◆ To take Rescue Remedy, place three to four drops of the liquid directly from the bottle under the tongue. You can also dilute it by putting four drops in one-quarter glass of water, tea, or juice. This should be sipped every three to five minutes. If the person is unconscious, administer full-strength Rescue Remedy by rubbing a few drops into the lips or gums, behind the ears, or on the wrists, or soak a cotton cloth in a pint of water with five to six drops of Rescue Remedy and apply it as a compress.

♦ Homeopaths use *Aconite* when the person is fearful and restless, cannot bear to be touched, and has pain that is followed by numbness and tingling sensations. He or she may also experience sudden nausea and vomiting.

Take the homeopathic remedy Cuprum metallicum. Made from copper, this is the remedy if hypothermia is accompanied by cramps.

Drink a warming ginger tea. Herbalists widely consider ginger *the* winter herb for people who live in cold climates. "Ginger tea is the hands-down best as an effective but mild circulatory stimulant," Oriental Medical Doctor David Eagle says. "Practitioners of Chinese medicine consider ginger tea to be warming to the central part of the body. It brings blood to the stomach. You don't want to drink it boiling hot, though, since if it's too hot, you can start to sweat and thus lose heat from the body's surface."

RECOVERY AND PREVENTION

If you're planning an adventure that will expose you to extended periods of cold, you can gain an edge on the chilly weather by using foods, herbs, massage, and other approaches to stoke your internal engine and support total body circulation. Even more importantly, take the common-sense precautions of wearing the right clothes and always staying with a companion in dangerously cold conditions. A buddy can not only notice frostbite on the face that you may not feel, he or she can save your life if a broken bone or other medical emergency incapacitates you. A cold-resistant wardrobe is also absolutely essential. No amount of natural circulation enhancement can overcome being clad in a T-shirt and a denim jacket in a blizzard. As Hal Weiss emphasizes in his useful book *Secrets of Warmth*, it is much easier to stay warm than to rewarm once you've become cold.

Dress for winter success by wearing a number of layers, water-repellent and windproof coat, waterproof boots, two pairs of socks, and mittens rather than gloves. Prevent rapid heat loss by covering the head and ears, and the face if necessary. Wool and down garments are warmer than cotton ones, which tend to get wet from sweat and then cool the body. If you plan an extended stay in a cold or icy place, it's a good idea to carry extra socks and mittens to replace any that get wet.

Going on a week-long trek in the Himalayas is not a good time to diet or start a fast. Rather, you want to provide plenty of high-energy fuel for the body to burn and convert to heat. Help protect your body from the cold by eating nutritious foods that are high in complex carbohydrates, protein, and calories, including legumes, nuts and seeds, root vegetables, chicken or fish, and whole grains. Frequent gorp snacks (mixtures of nuts, raisins, dried fruits, and chocolate that are popular with hikers for quick energy) during heavy exertion in the cold are a good idea. You should also drink plenty of fluids to prevent dehydration, which can increase the risk of injury from exposure to cold. (Caffeinated and alcoholic beverages, on the other hand, can cause dehydration.)

Some of the same herbs mentioned in the section on high-altitude sickness can also be used to help prevent frostbite or hypothermia by boosting circulation throughout the body and enhancing the body's ability to adapt to new conditions. Among these herbs are ginkgo and Siberian ginseng. Hobbs says rosemary tea can also be helpful.

Practitioners of traditional Chinese medicine often recommend foods as well as herbs for their potential healing effects. The food that they recommend above all others for combatting coldness in the internal body and numbness in the arms and legs is cherries. This fruit is said to have a warming energy and the ability to "expel cold and damp" and move blood circulation. Cherries' warming powers are tied to the fruit's effect on the spleen and the stomach, which are viewed by traditional Chinese healers not as isolated organs but interdependent parts of a broader energy system capable of regulating heat within the body. Other circulation-boosting foods to add to your diet for increased protection from the cold include garlic and onions.

Traditional Chinese healers also confirm the common sense conclusion that warm, cooked foods are better during cold weather than raw or cold foods such as salads, tropical fruits, ice cream, and iced drinks. On the other hand, you should avoid eating a lot of overly hot and spicy foods. While in the short run they have a heating effect on the body, ultimately they can cause sweating and thus cool it. That's why hot, spicy foods are popular among Mexicans and other inhabitants of tropical climates and not dwellers of the North.

If your fingers or toes seem to get frostnip easily, it may be because of an increased susceptibility from an episode earlier in life. It is also possible that chronic tingling and numbness or poor circulation in the extremities is tied to a nutrient deficiency, especially too little B₆ or iron. Try taking a B complex and balanced mineral supplement for a month to see whether the condition disappears. Vitamin B₆ may also help the body adapt to the cold. In one study, animals given B₆ supplements survived exposure to a cold climate at a much higher rate than did animals that were not given the supplements.

A set of useful acupressure points for improving overall circulation, according to acupressure authority Michael Reed Gach, are located on the shoulder. Gently but firmly massage the points midway between the base of the neck and the outside of the shoulder, about one-half inch below the top of the shoulders.

Keep your circulatory system in top shape by getting plenty of rest and doing frequent aerobic exercise. Regular skin brushing with a spongelike loofah or other coarse brush can help maintain active circulation. Some people find alternating hot and cold showers stimulates their circulation.

One trick to keeping your hands and feet warm in frigid weather is not washing them too frequently, since soap removes the thin layer of oil that serves as a natural blanket for the skin. Also leave rings and other jewelry at home since they can constrict circulation.

Another trick is to sprinkle a little cayenne powder in your gloves or socks. Cayenne has a few disadvantages, such as staining cloth and irritating some people's skin. Used in large quantities, or when you're active enough to cause the feet to sweat, it can also make the extremities too hot or even cause blisters to form. "Don't put it in the sock but put it in the shoe," suggests David Eagle. Ginger powder has a similar though more mild local warming effect. Some herbal hikers don't leave home without these. Try a little at first and see if they work for you.

Above all, try to stay warm and dry, and keep moving. High winds, wet or muddy ground, and deep snow are all worrisome conditions best confronted only by the prepared.

SIXTEEN

Eye and Ear Emergencies

THIS CHAPTER INCLUDES:

+ *foreign bodies in the eye*
+ *snow blindness and frozen cornea*
+ *chemical and thermal burns of the eyes*
+ *acute glaucoma*
+ *ruptured eardrum*
+ *acute ear infections*

SEE "CHAPTER 10: CONTUSIONS" FOR:

+ *black eye*

Eye problems can adversely affect not only vision but other important health functions relating to mood and metabolism. And healthy ears are necessary not only for hearing but balance and orienting the body in space. Thus, diseases or injuries affecting the eyes or ears should never be taken lightly. Permanent loss of sight or hearing is a major penalty to pay for ignoring the health of these sensitive, easily damaged external organs. Though professional care is often necessary, since hospitals and medical professionals have special tools to examine and treat the eyes and ears, anyone can benefit by gaining a working understanding of emergencies of the eyes and ears, natural remedies for them, and when to go beyond self-care first aid.

◆ Emergencies of the Eyes

With an estimated one billion working parts, the eye is one of the most complex organs of the body. It's also extremely sensitive, because of a preponderance of nerve endings. To oversimply, the eye is a two-chambered, liquid-filled camcorder. The eye's first chamber is bounded by the outermost layers of the eyeball and the inner lens. Light first penetrates the eye through the outermost layers, which include the conjunctiva (the delicate surface), the sclera (the tough "white of the eye" outer layer), and the cornea (the curved central membrane). Light then passes through the aqueous humor (the fluid in the first chamber), the iris (the circular curtain of muscle that colors the eye), the pupil (the central dark opening in the iris), and finally the lens.

Behind the lens is the second chamber, filled with the vitreous humor (a jellylike fluid) and bounded at the back by the retina (the thin inner layer of visual and nerve cells that transform light into nerve impulses). Also at the back of the eyeball is the optic nerve, which transmits visual data in the form of electrical impulses to the brain. The visual process is exceedingly fast—when awake, each eye sends the brain about one billion messages per second. The result is the miracle of vision.

◆ Foreign Bodies in the Eye

Your eyes are sensitive enough to register a single dead blood cell passing through the vitreous humor—that's what you're seeing when one of those mysterious "floaters" passes through your field of vision. When you get a piece of sand, which is thousands of times larger than a single blood cell, caught in your eye, it is no surprise that sharp pain and impaired vision can result.

Some of the most common foreign objects that get caught in the eyes are contact lenses (which should probably be called native objects rather than foreign objects), eyelashes, dirt or dust, and wood or metal flakes caused by working with a drill or other power tool. Sometimes the foreign body is so small it is invisible, though you know it is there from the pain. The eyes will often perform their own garbage removal: tears will form and wash the object away. If that doesn't happen, there's a danger that the object will get pushed across the cornea by the eyelids (or by rubbing the eye) and thus cause a corneal scratch or abrasion.

Under certain circumstances it is best to allow a medical professional to remove a foreign body from the eye. For instance, get medical help if:

- ◆ The person (particularly a child) cannot stay still and calm while you examine the eye and attempt to remove the object, and the eye does not naturally wash the object out.

- You cannot locate the foreign body.
- The object appears to be embedded in the cornea.
- The foreign body is on the iris or the pupil.

After the object has been removed, you should also contact a medical professional if the person:

- experiences sharp pain or pronounced swelling in the eye, or even mild pain after twenty-four hours
- is sensitive to light
- has blurry vision or some other lasting vision problem
- can't keep the eye open
- has a sensation of something still in the eye

A tiny foreign body that is allowed to remain in the eye can cause constant pain, an infection, and possibly irreversible visual damage. An object that scratches the cornea can lead to persistent pain, sensitivity to light, blurry vision, and a red or lusterless eye. In such cases tightly cover the eye with a patch and seek medical help.

A doctor or other medical professional will examine the eye and look for a foreign body using a small, high-powered magnifying lens and well-focused light. Obvious particles can usually be removed with a moistened cotton applicator, a magnet, or a saline solution. The doctor may also use a special fluorescent dye that, when applied to the eye and viewed under ultraviolet light, highlights tiny objects and scratches. In some cases doctors use pharmaceutical drops to relax eye muscles and relieve pain. The doctor may want to x-ray the eye to make sure no foreign bodies have gotten within the eye. If a foreign body is superficially embedded in the cornea, a doctor will often anesthetize the eye and then remove the object with the tip of a hypodermic needle. Surgeons remove deeply embedded objects in an operation performed under high magnification.

After removing an object, doctors usually prescribe an ophthalmic antibiotic ointment and patch the eye overnight. (If the cornea has been scratched, both eyes are covered to discourage eye movement.) Doctors may suggest a follow-up visit the next day to check for infection.

Some eye doctors may routinely use atropine for diagnosis or prescribe anti-inflammation drugs or ophthalmic painkillers for the patient to self-administer. Such recommendations are controversial, and you may want to obtain a second opinion. Atropine and corticosteroid preparations such as prednisolone can cause serious complications including glaucoma, and some topical analgesics can delay healing and cause allergic reactions.

HOW TO REMOVE FOREIGN OBJECTS FROM THE EYE

As Hippocrates said, first do no harm. Wash your hands to prevent an infection. Avoid pressing on or rubbing the eyeball. Finally, don't even think about using tweezers or some other sharp instrument for removing something from an eye. One false move, and you can puncture the cornea and cause irreversible damage.

Find a place where a steady and powerful light source can be focused on the eye. With the thumb and forefinger gently open the eye and look for the foreign body. Have the person look right and left, up and down as you examine the eye. Look first at the visible parts of the eyes and in the corners. If the person is wearing contact lenses and they're in the right position, leave them in.

If the object is not immediately visible, check under the eyelids, beginning with the lower one. Gently grasp the lower lid by the eyelashes and have the person look up as you pull down the lid. Check both the cornea and the inside of the eyelid. If the object is not there, have the person look down while you examine the upper lid. A slender stick, such as a cotton swab or a match stick, will help you look under the upper lid. Put the stick across the exterior of the upper eyelid, grasp the upper eyelashes, and pull them up and back to fold the eyelid back over the stick. "Everting" the eyelid in this manner allows a close look at the upper half of the cornea. Properly done, it shouldn't be painful.

If you see a foreign body on the eye, here are some safe ways to remove it:

Holding the eye open, flush the object off the cornea using a gentle stream of clean water. Pour water from a cup or use the spray nozzle next to the kitchen sink if it has a gentle setting. Another way to wash your eyes is to fill a sink or basin with water and put your face in. Holding the eye open, move your head from side to side to allow water to flow over the cornea.

Holding the eye open, remove the particle with the moistened corner of a piece of clean cloth or a moistened cotton swab. Don't use a tissue or a dry cotton swab, since loose fibers may come off and stick to the eye. A drop of lukewarm milk in the eye may help isolate the foreign object.

If the particle is under the eye's upper lid, pull the upper lid

down over the lower lid. Hold it there for a second and then gently release. This often causes tears to flush the foreign body out of the eye.

If the offending object is a contact lens, and the eye is rapidly swelling and you cannot get prompt medical help, remove the lens. Hold the upper eyelid open while the person looks toward his or her nose with the eye. Use your thumb to slide the contact toward the white area at the outside corner of the eye, pulling the skin there down and out. This should pop the lens off the eye. Though a contact lens can slide under a lid or even scratch the cornea, contrary to urban folk tales it cannot slide into the back of the eyeball. The way that the conjunctiva is folded back onto itself at the edge of the eye prevents such a calamity.

In the vast majority of cases an object has not scratched the cornea, and you don't need to do any further treatment.

NATURAL REMEDIES FOR FOREIGN BODIES IN THE EYES

The following natural remedies may help if you have removed a foreign body from the eye but it is still irritated, if you have a slight corneal abrasion, or if your eyes are irritated from wearing your contacts too long.

Treat the eye with a soothing herbal compress or eyewash. To make an eyewash, brew an infusion or decoction using one ounce of herb per pint of water, or eight to ten concentrated drops. Settle it out, strain through an unbleached coffee filter, and cool to room temperature. Put the liquid in a clean eyecup or other container and slowly pour over the open eye, blinking and rolling the eye.

The herb at the head of many herbalists' list of eye remedies is eyebright *(Euphrasia officinalis)*, long used as an herbal folk remedy for eye problems. Other herbs often used alone or with eyebright to relieve redness, swelling, and irritation of the eye include goldenseal, echinacea, and fennel seeds.

"A number of Native American tribes used goldenseal to soothe eyes irritated by prairie smoke, or accidentally scratched," herbalist Christopher Hobbs notes. "Goldenseal is a good antibacterial; it and eyebright are both anti-inflammatory. I've had such success using these two herbs for eye problems that I haven't had to look elsewhere for remedies."

Hobbs says that to make an eye compress, put one teaspoon each of goldenseal and eyebright in a half cup of water. Simmer for ten minutes and then steep for ten minutes. Filter the solution through an unbleached coffee filter and allow to cool to room temperature. Soak a clean cotton pad or piece of gauze about two inches in diameter in the solution, then place the cloth over the closed eye. Keep the eye closed, though the herbal solution will seep around the eyelid and bathe the eyeball.

"For an irritation or abrasion, resoak the cloth as it dries out and leave it on for an hour or longer," Hobbs says. "I've seen this eye compress clear up conjunctivitis, eye rashes, and sties when it is taped loosely and kept on overnight."

Holly Eagle and David Eagle, both acupuncturists and Oriental Medical Doctors, say that one of their favorite herbs for eye injuries is fennel seeds. "A fennel-seed decoction, applied with an eyedropper, is soothing to the eyes," David Eagle says. "My favorite instant eyewash product," adds Holly Eagle, "is Rue and Fennel Compound from Herb Pharm of Williams, Oregon. It includes concentrated drops of those two herbs plus eyebright, goldenseal, and mullein flower. It is quite nice for a range of eye problems." Rue and Fennel Compound is available in glass bottles ranging in size from one to thirty-two ounces from many natural food stores.

Take the homeopathic remedy Euphrasia, made from the eyebright plant. "You can either make a mild eyewash using *Euphrasia* mother tincture or take pellets orally," says homeopath Jennifer Jacobs, M.D. *"Euphrasia* is used by homeopaths for various injuries to the eyes, especially when there is profuse watering of the eyes with a burning pain, and swelling and redness of the eyelids."

Cover the eye for fifteen to twenty minutes with a slice of cucumber. Holly Eagle says that this folk remedy has a soothing, cooling effect on an eye that is irritated after a foreign body has been removed. It's also easier to prepare than another folk remedy for eye irritation, a poultice of grated apple wrapped in a clean, damp cotton cloth.

◆ Snow Blindness and Frozen Cornea

Just as your skin can get burned from too much sun, too much intense light can also burn your eyes. The most common form of "corneal sunburn" is snow blindness, resulting from the failure to wear eye protection while climbing snow- or ice-covered mountains or while skiing. A field of snow is like a giant mirror reflecting light up into the eyes. At high altitudes there's also less air to filter out incoming ultraviolet radiation, so without sunglasses (or even with low-quality ones) you can easily get an overdose of burning rays. Another way to burn the corneas is by sitting for too long, without appropriate eye protection, under a tanning lamp. A less common condition is welder's arc burn. If you do welding without tinted goggles or a slitted hood, the intense light generated can harm the delicate cornea.

These types of eye burns usually aren't apparent for six to twelve hours. Then the eyes begin to get red, tears form, the eyelids swell, and the cornea may turn hazy. The condition can be extremely painful.

The most severe cases may call for professional treatment. Physicians usually recommend eye drops and pain relievers, including a topical anesthetic and possibly aspirin or codeine.

Self-care at home is often all that's needed. With contacts removed, apply cold compresses to the closed eyelids. Used chamomile tea bags or a clean cotton cloth dipped in cold water work well. You can also help relieve pain by submerging your head in cold water to bathe the eyes. If you can, put patches over both eyes for twelve to twenty-four hours to keep them still and promote healing. Only the more severe cases take more than twenty-four hours or so to clear up.

If you're being exposed to extreme light conditions and have forgotten or lost your sunglasses, you can fashion primitive sunglasses by cutting slits to see through in cardboard strips that are worn like glasses.

Skiers and snowmobile riders who don't protect their eyes are also at risk of freezing their corneas. Frostbite of the cornea is rare, but can result from exposing the eyes to extremely low temperatures. As with other frostbites, often there is no pain until rewarming begins. The person may have blurry vision and be sensitive to light. Treat by applying warm compresses to the closed eyelids and then patching the eyes for a few hours. (See "Chapter 15: Exposure to Altitude and Cold" for frostbite recovery and prevention suggestions.)

◆ Chemical and Thermal Burns of the Eyes

Even mild chemicals, such as shampoo or swimming-pool chemicals, can cause excruciating pain when they get in your eyes. That's because the eyes are more sensitive to chemicals than the skin. Anytime a cleaning fluid or some other toxic chemical, whether wet or dry, gets in the eyes, you should treat it as an emergency.

Toxic chemicals in the eyes usually cause such symptoms as:

◆ swollen eyelids
◆ hazy cornea
◆ severe pain

The best first step for a chemical burn to the eyes is to call your local poison-control center. If you can, be ready to inform them of the type of chemical involved. Household powders that are strongly alkaline, such as many drain cleaners as well as lime, plaster, and cement, can result in especially dangerous chemical burns to the eyes. These powders are difficult to remove once they get into the eyes. Even continuous flushing may not be enough. Alkaline powders react with the moisture on the eyes' surface to form painful clumps. Tiny alkali particles also lodge in the eye and can continue to cause progressive damage for days. An alkali burn that's improperly treated can perforate the eyeball a week after the exposure, causing blindness.

Alkali burns to the eyes typically require immediate professional medical attention. Hospital personnel will apply a topical anesthesia to the eyes, flush them repeatedly, and carefully pick particles out of the eyes. The person may be offered morphine for the pain. Hospitalization is often required.

A chemical burn from an acid can also be harmful and painful to the eyes. In general acid burns cause damage more rapidly than alkali burns but end up being less serious, because the worst damage is over within the first few hours rather than progressive harm occurring for up to a week. Basic treatment for serious acid burns to the eyes includes flushing with a saline solution or water, applying a topical anesthetic, and taking painkillers. Hospitalization may be required.

If you suffer a chemical or thermal burn to the eyes, refrain from pressing on or rubbing them. Rubbing the eye can accelerate the damage. It can also get the chemical on your hand and thus provide a way for you to accidentally contaminate the unaffected eye.

It's a good idea to call the poison-control center and flush the eyes even if you're not sure the chemical is harmful. Flush them with water as rapidly and thoroughly as possible. (See "How to Flush the Eyes," below.) Do this even before taking out contact lenses (make sure the strainer is in the sink to prevent the lenses from being washed down the drain). Remove the contacts after flushing the eyes. Flushing will both remove the toxic substance from the surface of the eye and reduce the concentration of the chemical that's left behind.

Don't try to neutralize an acid burn by flushing the eye with an alkaline substance, or vice versa. Use water or a dilute saline solution. After flushing the eye, remove any large chemical particles with moistened sterile gauze.

Patch both eyes or cover them with cold compresses after the flushing, even if only one was contaminated, to help keep them still. Seek medical help for any chemical burn to the eyes.

Thermal burns on the eyes usually result from exposing them to an unexpected source of steam or hot air, such as from having the eyes too close to a microwaved popcorn bag as it is opened. Often the cornea will become hazy after a thermal burn, and the eye may swell considerably.

Treat a thermal burn to the eyes in a way similar to the treatment of other burns (see "Chapter 9: Burns"). Apply cold compresses, avoid rubbing the eyes, and don't put on butter, greasy ointments, or fluffy cotton bandages. Also don't contaminate the burned area by breathing on it or otherwise exposing it to potential sources of bacteria. If there's considerable swelling of the eyes or if the person has any difficulty seeing, seek professional care immediately. Doctors may treat corneal burns with special drops, a local anesthetic such as proparacaine, systemic painkillers such as morphine, and hospitalization.

HOW TO FLUSH THE EYES

A sterile saline solution is the preferred liquid for flushing the eyes. You can make your own by dissolving ½ teaspoon salt in a cup of boiled water. Or just use bottled or tap water. You can also prepare an herbal eyewash. Chamomile or eyebright tea works well. An eyewash needs to be cooled to body or room temperature, of course. Also, keep in mind the necessity to prepare an herbal solution in a way that will prevent bacterial contamination.

If a chemical has gotten into only one eye, make sure you flush by positioning the person's head with the contaminated eye down. That will prevent you from flushing the chemical from one eye into the other. Especially if the victim is a child, you may have to hold the eyes open. Flush with a steady but gentle stream of water for fifteen minutes or more. The longer the better. You can use any of the following techniques:

◆ Use an eyecup to direct a steady stream of water from the inside corner of the eye (next to the nose) to the outside corner. Funnel-shaped eyecups are available at most pharmacies and can be a valuable addition to the home medicine kit. If you don't have an eyecup, try a spouted measuring cup or whatever is clean and available.

◆ Use the spray nozzle from the kitchen-sink hose if you have one, and the pressure can be controlled so that the flow of water is slow and gentle.

◆ If both eyes or other parts of the face are contaminated, quickly take off your clothes, get in the shower, and flush the eyes there.

Depending on the severity of the contamination of the eye, you should persist with the flushing for fifteen to thirty minutes, or until medical help arrives. Remove contact lenses after flushing.

NATURAL REMEDIES FOR THERMAL BURNS TO THE EYES

In addition to a cold-water flush and cold compresses, try some of the following remedies to cool a mild thermal burn to the eyes.

Put cold chamomile tea bags or raw potato slices on the closed eyes for fifteen to twenty minutes. Wet and reapply every five minutes or so.

Take the homeopathic remedy Euphrasia. Homeopaths recommend *Euphrasia* for watery eyes accompanied by burning pain and swollen, red eyelids.

◆ Acute Glaucoma

Glaucoma is a serious eye disease that afflicts over 2 million people in the United States. About 10 percent of persons with glaucoma suffer from the acute, sudden-onset form, which is a medical emergency. Acute glaucoma typically strikes the elderly and affects only one eye at a time. If it's not treated immediately, acute glaucoma can damage the optic nerve, impair peripheral vision, and even cause blindness.

Glaucoma results when the aqueous humor, the reservoir of fluid held between the cornea and the lens, increases in volume. This causes too much pressure to develop within the eye. With acute glaucoma the cause of the fluid buildup is a blockage in the drainage system at the root of the iris. The obstructed outflow channel prevents normal runoff of the aqueous humor. (In a healthy eye the aqueous humor is replenished a number of times each day.) As pressure builds, the iris is pushed into the angle where it meets the cornea. Thus the medical term for this acute condition: closed-angle or angle-closure glaucoma.

The sudden increase in intraocular pressure causes the person to feel severe pain in the affected eye. Since the iris is pushed up toward the cornea, the pupil (the hole in the middle of the iris) remains fixed and often dilated. The person often experiences blurry vision and halos around light sources. These first symptoms may last an hour or two and then disappear, causing no permanent eye damage. When an attack is extended, the person may vomit and develop a hazy cornea.

Acute glaucoma attacks that are not treated are often followed up days or weeks later by more serious attacks that cause irreversible nerve damage at the back of the eye. Thus, a person with acute glaucoma should be taken to the emergency room as soon as possible. Treatment should start within twelve to forty-eight hours of an attack to avoid permanent vision loss within a few days. In the hospital, doctors are likely to administer sedatives and analgesics, reduce eye pressure with special eye drops, and then do surgery or laser therapy to open up the drainage channel in the iris.

NATURAL FIRST-AID REMEDIES FOR ACUTE GLAUCOMA

There are two natural treatments to offer the victim *on the way to the hospital.*

Take homeopathic **Belladonna** *30C.* Give a dose every fifteen minutes for up to an hour. *Belladonna* is specific for dilated pupils and pain in one eye that's made worse by bright light. Don't use a homeopathic *Belladonna* remedy less dilute than 24X or 12C (that is, don't use a 10X or 6C remedy), and don't use any herbal preparations of belladonna at all, for reasons discussed below.

Apply firm pressure to the acupressure point in the middle of the web between the thumb and index finger. This point has an energetic connection to the eyes according to traditional Oriental medicine.

Natural remedies play a limited role in first aid for acute glaucoma, and even chronic glaucoma should be treated by a conventional physician. Nevertheless there are a few alternatives worth exploring that may help persons with glaucoma maintain proper fluid pressure within the eye.

Naturopaths and herbalists say that the herb bilberry *(Vaccinium myrtillus)* may prevent acute glaucoma attacks or play a role in the treatment of chronic glaucoma. Ever since British RAF pilots during WWII swore that eating bilberry jam before night missions helped improve their vision, scientists have been studying the fruit of this plant for active ingredients with potential effects on the eye. Clinical evidence has accumulated that certain of bilberry's constituents, the anthocyanosides, can indeed markedly affect biochemical reactions in the eye and improve night vision, among other beneficial effects. Look for bilberry extract products with a 20–25 percent anthocyanoside content. Take 80–160 mg three times daily.

Some nutrient deficiencies have been linked with glaucoma. If you're at risk, consider increasing your intake of the following vitamins and minerals.

Vitamin B₆, 50–75 mg daily as part of B complex. Studies show that B₆ may help regulate eye pressure.

Vitamin C, two to five grams daily in mixed doses or to bowel tolerance, with rutin and other bioflavonoids. These nutrients may be used to both prevent and treat glaucoma. Researchers have found that people who consume low levels of C may have increased intraocular pressure, a precondition of glaucoma. In clinical studies people who have taken two grams of C daily for about a week have successfully reduced dangerous levels of eye pressure.

Vitamin D, 200–400 IU daily, and calcium, 800–1,200 mg daily. Ophthalmologist Arthur Knapp, M.D., of New York City has successfully treated some cases of glaucoma with this vitamin/ mineral combination. Calcium is a prime ingredient in collagen-bearing connective tissues, including the sclera, the eye's hard, opaque external layer. Vitamin D plays a major role in calcium assimilation.

Nutritionist Shari Lieberman notes that a few studies indicate that food sensitivities can increase pressure within the eye. She adds, "I've had glaucoma patients who've been weaned off of eye drops by using nutritional means, but someone with glaucoma should never just stop using the drops. Changes in therapy should be made gradually, and in consultation with a physician."

Anyone who is susceptible to developing acute glaucoma should avoid substances that dilate the pupils (such as the herb ephedra) or contain the alkaloid atropine. Common atropine-containing drugs include many antispasmodics as well as the anti-motion-sickness drug scopolamine. These agents increase internal eye pressure and can induce an acute glaucoma attack.

Another primary source for atropine is the herb belladonna. The suggestion above to take homeopathic *Belladonna* 30C, however, does not present a risk, since a 30C dilution is beyond the Avogadro limit. That is, the remedy is diluted well beyond the point where there would be any molecules of belladonna left.

◆ Preventing and Recovering from Eye Emergencies

Protect your eyes with goggles or special impact-resistant glasses whenever you use objects or chemicals that may injure the eyes. Working with power tools, playing racquetball, and swimming can harm the eyes if protective steps are not taken. One common cause of injuries to the eyes is the household use of bungee cords, the elasticized ropes people use to fasten packages, garbage tops, and the like. When the hook at the end of a tightened bungee cord slips off something, it can snap up into the eyes. Take extra care when you handle bungee cords.

A number of herbs and nutritional supplements can help the eyes recover from an injury or illness. The two premier herbs for the eyes are bilberry, a natural vision booster, and ginkgo, a potent free-radical scavenger that prevents damage to the retina. Look for bilberry extract products with a 20–25 percent anthocyanoside content (take 80–160 mg three times daily), and ginkgo-extract products with 24 percent ginkgo heteroside content (take 40 mg three times daily).

Vitamins and minerals of special benefit to the eyes include:

Vitamin A, 25,000 IU daily in the form of beta carotene, or extra green leafy vegetables or orange-colored fruits and vegetables such as carrots. Scientists have determined that the chemistry of vision is closely tied to vitamin A in the body.

Vitamin B complex, 50 mg twice daily. The B vitamins help maintain optimal health of eye cells.

Vitamin C, two to five grams in mixed doses daily or to bowel tolerance, for its antioxidant properties. The antioxidants protect the eye lens and can reduce the risk of cataracts and other eye diseases.

Vitamin E, 400–800 IU daily, for its antioxidant and immunity-boosting effects.

Selenium, 200 mcg daily, another antioxidant.

Zinc, 25–50 mg daily. A deficiency in this mineral has been linked to certain eye problems, and supplementation may halt progressive loss of vision.

Here's one of the best traditional Chinese acupressure massages for stimulating the eyes. Sitting, put your elbows on a table and make two fists. Bring your eyes to the fists and put the thumbs on the temples. Use the middle joint of the forefinger of each hand to rub points around the perimeter of the eye sockets. Gently rub each point four times counterclockwise and then four times clockwise (see illustration #17). This massage will help relax the eyes and increase local circulation.

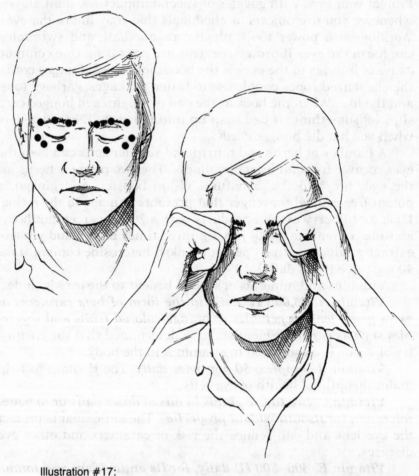

Illustration #17:

You can perform a traditional Chinese acupressure massage to stimulate your eyes by rubbing points around the perimeter of the eye sockets.

◆ Emergencies of the Ears

Like the eyes, the ears collect waves—sound waves rather than light waves—from the environment and convert them to nerve impulses that are sent to the brain for processing. This remarkable hearing process starts at the outer or external ear, with its uniquely varied and undulating folds of cartilage and skin. The inch-long outer-ear canal leads to the eardrum, the finely tuned, vibrating membrane that serves as a barrier to the middle and inner ear. The middle ear contains the hammer, anvil, and stirrup, the smallest bones in the human body. These transmit sound into the inner ear, site of the cochlea. This snail-shaped set of fluid- and membrane-filled tubes is the ear's retina: it converts sound into nerve impulses, which are then carried by the auditory nerve to the brain. The inner ear is also the site of the semicircular canals, which govern balance and orientation in space.

Another main part of the ear is the eustachian tube. Named after a sixteenth-century Italian anatomist, the eustachian tube is a slender canal, normally closed, running between the middle ear and the pharynx, the cavity at the back of the throat containing the mouth and nasal passages. The eustachian tube is an important link between ear, nose, and throat that serves to equalize air pressure on both sides of the eardrum.

Injuries to the outer ear usually don't require any special first-aid steps. A common injury is catching an earring on something and causing a laceration in the lobe. Use direct pressure, sterile dressings, cold compresses, and other basic methods to stop bleeding from the pinna (the top of the outer ear) or the lobe and to reduce pain and swelling. (See "Chapter 6: Bleeding.")

Any blood or clear fluid that is draining out of the middle or inner ear should be evaluated by a medical professional. In the meantime don't block the ear canal or try to clean the middle ear. Cover the outer ear with sterile gauze taped loosely to the head. Have the person lie down on his side with the injured ear facing down to promote drainage. Call for emergency help.

◆ Insects and Other Foreign Bodies in the Ears

Insects and other foreign bodies in the ear may cause pain and a decrease in hearing. There are a few risks involved in attempting to remove a small object from the ear, but a careful, calm approach can reduce these risks.

First, assess the situation. Keeping the person calm, use a flashlight or other strong light source to inspect the ear. If you can't see the object in the external ear canal, leave the removal job to a professional. Doctors have special tools that help them see and grasp objects stuck in the ear. If you poke around in the ear with tweezers trying to remove a small object you can't see, you are likely just to push the object farther in. This may perforate the eardrum and damage the person's hearing.

If you can clearly see what's stuck in the ear, and it's an insect, try to induce the insect to crawl out on its own accord. This lessens the chances that the bug will bite or sting the person in the ear. Here are a couple of suggestions, in the order to try them:

◆ Turn the person's head ear up to induce the insect to crawl out.

◆ Turn the ear toward the sun or a strong light source (at night shine a flashlight in the ear), since some bugs are attracted to lights and may decide to crawl out.

◆ As a last resort, when medical help is not readily available and the insect is causing the person pain, put a few drops of a lukewarm vegetable oil (olive oil works well) in the ear to drown the insect. The risk with putting oil in the ear is that it can make some objects expand, so make sure you're dealing with an insect before using this method.

If you can clearly see an inanimate object in a person's ear, tilt the head and try to shake it out. Use tweezers to remove it only if the person can stay calm and still. Don't risk perforating a squirming child's eardrum; take the child to a medical professional for removal. Turn the person's head so that the ear with the object in it points down. Carefully remove the foreign body with tweezers.

If you can't get the entire object out, seek professional help. Emergency room personnel may recommend local anesthesia (or even general anesthesia for small children) and then use forceps or a suction tool to remove the object. Unless the ear canal has been damaged, no further care is necessary.

The outer-ear canal sometimes gets clogged with a native rather than foreign substance: earwax. If this happens, don't reach for a cotton swab. Cleaning the ear canal with a swab is likely only to push wax in toward the eardrum. Rather irrigate the canal with warm water or a few drops of 3 percent hydrogen peroxide to loosen and remove the wax. You may have to use a bulb syringe and perform an earwash twice a day for a day or two for the wax to loosen and fall out.

◆ Ruptured Eardrum

The eardrum, or tympanic membrane, protects the inner ear from dirt and infection, among other functions. Anything that causes a sudden increase in pressure on the eardrum can rupture it. Slapping the ear, being too close to a sudden explosive noise, and diving into deep water are common causes of ruptured eardrums. It's also possible for a middle-ear infection to cause a rupture.

Ruptured eardrums cause severe pain and partial loss of hearing. First aid is limited to covering the outer ear with sterile gauze to protect against infection and obtaining professional medical evaluation. In most cases the eardrum repairs itself within a few weeks. It is necessary to keep the ear clean and dry in the meantime to prevent a middle-ear infection.

A Chinese medical journal reports that practitioners in China have had some success using slices of fresh garlic applied to the eardrum to treat ruptures. The researchers who performed one study found that garlic slices helped repair perforated eardrums in eighteen of nineteen persons. Consult with a knowledgeable alternative practitioner about this and other home remedies for ruptured eardrum, since preventing infections is crucial.

◆ Acute Ear Infections

The number of doctor visits for ear infections have soared since 1975, for mostly unknown reasons (some researchers suspect that the increase is related to the advent of widespread day care for young children, which exposes them to more germs). Pediatricians report that ear infections may be the single most frequently diagnosed medical condition affecting American children today. One recent estimate that forcefully dramatizes the problem: for every 100 babies and toddlers under the age of two in 1990, there were 102 trips taken to the doctor for ear infections. Another revealing statistic: infections of the outer, middle, or inner ear account for nearly a third of the trips children up to the age of five make to the doctor.

Outer-ear infections affecting the ear canal (otitis externa) or the lobe are the least serious type of ear infection. Almost all lobe infections are related to ear piercings, often when the hole is initially cut. Infections can also occur in the aftermath of an allergic reaction to an earring post that is made of nickel or some other common metal.

To clear up the infection, stop wearing earrings temporarily unless the ear has just been pierced. In the latter case, you want to keep a post in the hole or it will quickly close up. Oriental Medical Doctor Holly Eagle says, "I've found that if you switch to at least an eighteen-karat or higher gold post or loop, it won't cause allergic reactions as nickel posts do and it won't aggravate an infection. Eighteen-karat gold is better tolerated than either gold-coated or fourteen-karat gold posts. You can save your hole that way."

Also wash the infected area with soap and water, and two or three times a day put a few drops of echinacea concentrate or tincture, Tea Tree oil, 3 percent hydrogen peroxide, or other natural disinfectant on the inflamed area. Prevent the infection from getting too dry, since the local skin can crack and become more irritated. If the infection doesn't clear up within a few days, contact a health professional.

"I had my ear pierced last year," herbalist Christopher Hobbs says, "and it got infected. Tea Tree oil and echinacea took care of it readily."

Outer-ear-canal infections are sometimes called swimmer's ear, since getting water in the canal from frequent swimming is a common cause. Such infections can also result, however, from routine showering and shampooing. The culprit is bacterium such as *Pseudomonas aeruginosa*, which proliferates in the damp environment of the ear canal, especially if the protective, antibacterial earwax coating in the canal has been scratched or removed.

The initial symptoms of an outer-ear infection are usually an itching or tickling feeling in the ear canal. As the infection progresses a watery fluid may drain from the ear, and the ear may become painful. (When moving or wiggling the external ear increases the pain, that's a sign that you probably have an infection of the outer rather than middle ear.) Other symptoms include an inflamed and swollen ear canal, a slight fever, and temporary loss of hearing. If the condition is severe enough to be causing dizziness, ringing in ears, impaired hearing, or pain when applying eardrops, contact a health professional immediately since it is possible (though rare) for an external ear infection to rupture the eardrum.

It is important to try to keep the ear canal dry if it has become infected. Shield it from water even while you take a shower, with earplugs or a shower cap.

Middle-ear infections, what doctors call otitis media, are common in infants and children. Many middle-ear infections are due to swelling and blockage of the eustachian tube, which is smaller and more horizontal in infants and young children than it is in adults. This configuration allows fluid, bacteria, or viruses to travel more easily up the tube from the pharynx. Whenever the child's immunity has been compromised, the possibility of a middle-ear infection increases. Some common triggers include recent illnesses such as an upper-respiratory-tract infection, an allergy, and conditions that cause fluctuations in air pressure, such as flying and travel to high altitudes.

The most common organisms cultured from middle-ear fluid during acute infections include the pervasive *Streptococcus pneumoniae* and *Haemophilus influenzae*. Middle-ear infections have been known to harm the eardrum and lead to impaired hearing. There is a slight risk that the infection could spread beyond the ear to other head tissues or even the brain.

Common acute middle-ear infection symptoms include earache, redness or bulging of the eardrum, and a fever of 103° F or higher along with chills. There is also likely to be considerable sharp or throbbing pain and a sense of fullness from the pressure building up in the middle ear. A child with an acute middle-ear infection may be extremely agitated and irritable and will often pull at the ear to relieve pressure.

Conventional medical treatment often starts with eardrops and nose drops or a nasal spray to help open the eustachian tube. Virtually all doctors recommend a ten-day course of oral antibiotics, though these have no effect if the infection is viral in origin. The problem is that there's no easy way to tell whether the infection is viral or bacterial, so doctors prescribe antibiotics such as amoxicillin or ampicillin for them all. These drugs have become so widely used (critics say abused) that some bacteria are now becoming resistant to common antibacterial drugs. Other adverse effects from frequent consumption of pharmaceutical antibiotics include a weakened immune system, diarrhea, and the destruction of "friendly" bacteria in the intestine.

Middle-ear infections have become a chronic problem for many children. With antibiotics becoming less reliable, more and more doctors are turning to surgery for a cure. The recommended procedure is called a myringotomy. Doctors place a tiny plastic tube through the eardrum to make it easier for fluid to drain into the throat via the eustachian tube. Many alternative practitioners (and a small minority of conventional doctors) consider the surgical procedure controversial, contending that children with inserted tubes are more likely to suffer from further middle-ear infections. Naturopath Michael Murray notes that a number of studies have found that there is no difference in the outcome among children with middle-ear infections who are treated with surgery plus antibiotics, surgery alone, antibiotics alone, or neither surgery nor antibiotics. Furthermore, some studies indicate that children who are not given antibiotics experience fewer further infections compared to those who do take antibiotics.

In spite of the lack of agreement on routine care, it is a good idea to consult with a medical professional about treating a middle-ear infection. If a child's infection has progressed to the point where there is an ear discharge and the child has a fever of 103° or higher, a doctor may recommend a trip to the nearest emergency room.

Children shouldn't be given aspirin or other chemical relatives of salicylate acid for an ear infection that may be accompanied by a viral condition, because of the risk of causing Reye's syndrome. Recommended basic first-aid steps for a middle-ear infection are limited to acetaminophen and warm treatments. For instance, apply a hot-water bottle, hot pack, or a warm compress to the ear. Warmth helps to improve blood supply and decrease swelling.

An easy way to apply warm air to the ear is to use a hair dryer. Put it on the low setting, hold it eighteen to twenty inches from the ear, and shoot warm air into the affected ear. If the air warms the earlobe and outer ear to an uncomfortable degree, hold a straw up to the hair dryer and wrap a dry washcloth or small towel around the two to block all the air except that which is directed through the straw. Then hold the other end of the straw an inch or so outside the ear so that the warm air flows into the ear canal. Be extra careful using this method on a squirming child, since he could jerk his ear into the straw and endanger the eardrum.

NATURAL FIRST-AID REMEDIES FOR EAR INFECTIONS

A number of natural remedies offer promising alternatives to drugs and surgery for various types of ear infections.

For an outer-ear-canal infection, put a few drops of an equal mixture of white vinegar and 70 percent isopropyl alcohol in the ears several times a day. Apply the drops by tilting your head so that the liquid stays in the canal for thirty seconds or so. You can also try applying a few drops of full-strength echinacea concentrate or tincture, or gently flushing the ear with a 3 percent hydrogen peroxide solution.

When an infection or other condition has clogged the middle ear, take steps to open the eustachian tubes. For instance:

- Yawn. This action exercises the muscle that opens the tube at the back of the throat.
- Chew gum. This helps some people, and kids love gum, though chewing is not as effective as yawning.
- Drink plenty of warm teas (try chamomile or yarrow) and soups. Extra liquids can help thin ear secretions and promote drainage.
- Massage the area around the outer ear. Try pulling gently down on the earlobe, stroking the neck, and rubbing the temples. These actions can encourage drainage and increase blood flow. Increase the positive effects of the massage by using a massage oil made from three to five drops of essential oil of Eucalyptus or Lavender diluted in a teaspoon of olive or other vegetable oil.

Combat ear infections using topical applications of antibacterial herbs instead of pharmaceutical-strength oral antibiotics. The three herbs most strongly recommended by herbalists for relieving ear infections are mullein, echinacea, and garlic.

The ears respond better to warm drops of liquid than cold. An easy way to warm herbal concentrates, tinctures, and oils is to place the tightly closed herbal bottle in a glass of hot water for a few minutes. Test the oil on your wrist to make sure it is not overheated.

- Though scientific studies are lacking that demonstrate mullein flower oil's effects on ear infections, this is one of the most frequently recommended herbs for this condition. Mullein's active ingredients include mucilage and aucubin, which may explain its ability to soothe irritated mucous membranes. (It's also a popular herb for the lungs.) For earaches, use mullein oil made from infusing the plant's fresh flowers in olive or other oil. Put five to ten drops in the ear every two to three hours.

◆ Echinacea is an excellent all-purpose antibacterial herb. Put five to ten drops of the concentrate, extract, or tincture in the ear every two to three hours.

◆ Garlic is a common food/herb that can be used in an endless variety of ways to treat earaches. A folk method is to insert a fresh garlic clove, with the paperlike surface layer removed, into the outer ear canal (never far enough that it can't be easily removed, or you'll have two ear problems instead of just one). Cover the garlic clove with a hot wet cloth to make a type of warm compress. Reheat the cloth every few minutes to keep it warm.

A simpler garlic application is to put a few garlic oil drops directly in the ear every few hours. Plug the canal gently with a piece of cotton.

You can make garlic oil by mincing or crushing three cloves of garlic in two to three tablespoons of olive oil. Place the mixture in a clean wide-mouth glass jar, cover, and shake. Let it sit at room temperature for a few days and then strain through cheesecloth.

A number of herbal companies package garlic oil in small dropper bottles. You can also use as drops garlic extract in liquid form (Kyolic Aged Garlic Extract is one such product). Garlic supplements taken orally may help as well. Follow dosage suggestions on labels.

As with herbal drops for the eyes, keep in mind the necessity to prepare any herbal eardrops in such a way as to avoid bacterial contamination. Also, if you're using an oil such as mullein or garlic, it is best to thoroughly dry the ear first with a few drops of the vinegar/alcohol mixture. Drying the ear prevents the oil from sealing in excess moisture and making the problem worse.

The natural-pharmacy sections of large natural foods stores stock some natural eardrop products, which are often combinations of mullein, garlic, and other herbs.

Take an appropriate homeopathic remedy to relieve an ear infection. The remedies most commonly recommended by homeopaths include:

◆ *Pulsatilla.* This is effective for an earache that comes on after a cold. The child wants to be held and tends to be mild, weepy, or whiny rather than crying loudly. The *Pulsatilla* child has no thirst and experiences worse pain at night. The earache is made worse from warmth and relieved by cold applications.

- ◆ *Belladonna*. This remedy is useful for a throbbing or piercing ear pain that comes on suddenly and is accompanied by a high fever and dilated pupils. The ear canal or drum appears red. The child's face may be flushed and dry.
- ◆ *Chamomilla*. This is helpful for the child who is in great pain and seems oversensitive to touch. Unlike the gentle *Pulsatilla* child, the *Chamomilla* child is extremely irritable, impatient, and inconsolable and may cry loudly. One cheek may be red and the other pale. The *Chamomilla* child is made better by carrying and worse from warm applications.
- ◆ *Aconite*. This is used at the onset of an earache, when pain comes on after the child has gotten wet or chilled. The outer ear is hot and painful, and the child is thirsty, restless, and sensitive to noise. The pain is made better from warm applications.

A number of homeopathic producers have combination remedies to relieve the pain of ear infection. For instance, there's Earache Formula from Medicine from Nature. The ingredients in Earache Formula are *Aconitum* 3X, *Belladonna* 6X, *Chamomilla* 6X, and *Kali mur* 3X.

Apply healing acupressure massage to the two points behind and below the earlobes. Acupressure teacher Michael Reed Gach suggests pressing on these points in the hollow, sensitive area in back of the jawbone. "Use your index and middle fingers to press in on both sides gradually," he says. "The area is likely to be sore. If you find the right point, it will feel like the pain from the finger pressure is triggering right into the middle ear." He suggests complementing these point massages with gentle stroking of the neck and temple.

◆ Preventing and Recovering from Ear Emergencies

Parents of a newborn can take an important step in assuring the future health of their child's ears by making the choice of breast-feeding over bottle-feeding. A number of studies have found that bottle-feeding leads to recurrent ear infections. The reason may be partly mechanical (formula from a bottle easily drips out of the baby's mouth and into the ears when a child is fed while lying down) and partly nutritional. Breast milk is rich in nutrients, fatty acids, and antibodies that may be missing or improperly balanced in infant formula. Breast-fed infants also tend to suffer from fewer food allergies during the toddler years. Many alternative practitioners cite allergies to dairy, wheat, corn, and soybeans as a major cause of chronic middle-ear infections.

The following nutritional and herbal supplements can help protect against ear infections as well as speed recovery from them. (Depending on the child's size and age, you should reduce dosages by one-half or more for children. Check with a knowledgeable nutritionist or alternative practitioner.) Dosages are daily amounts.

- vitamin A in the form of beta carotene, 25,000 IU, to strengthen mucous membranes and help control the infection
- vitamin B complex plus B$_6$, 50–100 mg, to relieve ear pressure and promote proper functioning of the immune system
- vitamin C plus bioflavonoids, two to five grams in mixed dosages or to bowel tolerance, to help prevent infections, increase immunity, and scavenge free radicals
- zinc, 25–50 mg, to reduce infection
- manganese, 15–30 mg, since studies have linked a deficiency of this mineral to ear disorders
- ginkgo, 40 mg three times per day of standardized extract containing 24 percent ginkgo heterosides, to prevent hearing loss, increase blood flow to the brain, and improve the transmission of nerve impulses

Recurrent ear infections sometimes yield an almost nonexistent bacterial count when lab tests are done. Some practitioners of natural medicine contend that the root cause of such infections is not bacteria per se but a type of self-perpetuating inflammatory process that needs to be broken. Thus, the essential fatty acids such as the omega-6 GLA may be helpful for their anti-inflammatory effects. Sources of beneficial EFAs include fatty, cold-water fish such as salmon, cod, and mackerel (and oil supplements made from these fish); canola, flaxseed, and hemp oil; and evening primrose, borage, and black-currant oil.

Secondhand smoke may increase the frequency of ear infections, so help children avoid close association with smokers. Ear infections are also more likely to happen after a cold or the flu, so take extra care of the ears during this crucial time. For instance, you may want to avoid swimming then.

Earwax protects the ear canal from excess water. If you're repeatedly cleaning the wax out of a child's ears, you may be hindering this important protective function. Ears naturally clean themselves. Wax dries up and falls out or is washed out of the ear canal.

Swimmers can help prevent outer-ear infections by wearing earplugs or noseplugs, or tilting and shaking the head after swimming to allow water to drain out of the ear. If you suffer from recurrent swimmer's ear, try to keep the ears dry while showering, or after showering dry the canals with a hair dryer set on the low setting and held about a foot from the ear. Alternatively you can use a few drops of the fifty-fifty solution of white vinegar and isopropyl alcohol. "After you take a shower," notes Andrew Weil, M.D., "if you put a few drops of this mixture in your ears, the alcohol evaporates and helps to dry the ear." Apply by tilting the head to keep the drops in the canal for about thirty seconds.

If earaches become chronic in your child, consider reducing your child's consumption of dairy foods. Though studies are lacking, anecdotal evidence abounds that these foods are mucus forming and can promote ear infections. Some alternative practitioners also contend that highly refined and sweetened foods help create an internal environment that promotes the growth of bacteria and thus encourages infections. Foods that the Chinese and other traditional societies consider to be beneficial for the ears include azuki, kidney, and black beans; green leafy vegetables; and dark yellow vegetables such as squash. Practitioners of traditional Chinese medicine say that these foods are also good for the kidneys, which are the organs that are energetically tied to the ears.

If you do take a course of antibiotics to counter an ear infection, consider supplementing the treatment with acidophilus taken orally to help replenish the gut with friendly flora. *Acidophilus* has become the generic term for various types of naturally occurring live bacteria that are increasingly popular as dietary supplements. It is available in the form of tablets, powders, capsules, and liquids sold in most natural foods stores. Look for acidophilus products that have labels providing information on how many live or "viable" bacteria each capsule or teaspoon provides, an expiration date with a guarantee of product viability until that date, and a listing of additional ingredients. Take doses of acidophilus that provide approximately 10 billion organisms per day.

The yoga positions known as the plow and the shoulder stand can increase circulation to the ears and possibly benefit hearing. Lying on your back on the floor is the starting position for both "asanas." For the shoulder stand, bring your feet straight up in the air. Support your back with your hands, keeping the upper arms and elbows on the ground. For the plow, bring your thighs down over your head, keeping your legs straight, until your toes touch the floor. Both of these are somewhat advanced yoga positions that need many subtle refinements to be done correctly. It is best to learn them from an experienced yoga teacher or a detailed yoga book (see "Resources").

If your job or environment constantly exposes you to noise levels that may be harmful to your hearing, consider purchasing earplugs to protect your ear.

SEVENTEEN

Heat Illness

THIS CHAPTER COVERS:

◆ *heat cramps*
◆ *heat exhaustion*
◆ *heatstroke*

SEE "CHAPTER 9: BURNS" FOR:

◆ *sunburn*

SEE "CHAPTER 13: DIZZINESS AND FAINTING" FOR:

◆ *heat faint*

SEE "CHAPTER 18: HIGH FEVER" FOR:

◆ *how to reduce a fever*

Whenever a sudden heat wave strikes a temperate area, in the first few days it is likely that some people will suffer from heat-related disorders such as heat cramps, heat exhaustion, and heatstroke. Although the body can acclimatize to high temperatures and humidity after a week or so, even acclimatization does not offer blanket immunity. Any combination of hot weather with other factors such as fatigue, alcohol, dehydration, obesity, and malnourishment may prove harmful or even fatal in some cases. Scientists estimate that heat waves are responsible for 1,200 deaths during an average American summer.

The four most common types of heat illnesses are:

Heat faint. Standing or sitting for a long time in a hot place can cause blood to pool in the lower extremities, depriving the brain of blood and leading to a fainting episode. You can usually recover quickly by lying down in a cool place and drinking some liquids. (See "Chapter 13: Dizziness and Fainting" for further discussion and natural remedies.)

Heat cramps. These are painful muscle contractions that most often occur in the abdomen or legs after rigorous exertion in the heat. Rest and fluids usually provide immediate relief.

Heat exhaustion. The cause of this condition is usually some combination of heat, physical exertion, and dehydration. The person may experience rapid breathing, a racing heart, light-headedness, and nausea. The body's core temperature may rise only slightly. Heat exhaustion can usually be prevented by avoiding overexertion in the heat and drinking plenty of water or mineral-rich drinks.

Heatstroke. Also known as sunstroke, this is the most serious heat illness, an urgent medical emergency that has a 10–20 percent fatality rate even among those who were previously healthy, diagnosed early, and received proper care. Extreme environmental conditions cause the body's core temperature to rise to 106° or higher. At that point all of the body's systems begin to deteriorate rapidly. Without immediate treatment the victim falls into a coma and dies.

◆ When the Body Overheats

A rise in body temperature due to heat disorder is different from a rise in body temperature due to high fever. When invading bacteria, for instance, cause an infection, the body's natural thermostat, located in the hypothalamus at the base of the brain, raises its setting and thus increases the body's temperature. This fever both heals and protects (see "Chapter 18: High Fever"). A heat disorder, on the other hand, occurs as a result of conditions such as excessive exertion in hot weather, severe dehydration, or confinement of a child in an overheated car. In such cases the body's thermostatic setting remains normal, but the environmental conditions prevent the body from cooling itself.

The body responds in a number of ways to environmental heat and humidity. It pulls heat-holding blood from its internal core and sends it to the extremities and the surface of the skin, where blood vessels dilate and the heat is more easily released out of the body. The body also releases sweat from the skin, which has a cooling effect as the liquid evaporates off the body. When either of these mechanisms go on for too long, however, consequences start to ripple through the body. Too much blood drawn from the core causes a lack of oxygen in the brain, leading to dizziness, confusion, fainting, and ultimately coma. When the body loses too much fluid and becomes dehydrated, it shuts down sweating to conserve what is left. This impairs the body's ability to cool itself.

Fluid is arguably more important to the human body than is food, since you can survive for weeks or months without eating, but only three to four days without drinking. An adult's body weight is approximately 55–65 percent water and an infant's as much as 70 percent. Under certain conditions you can sweat a quart or more an hour of fluids—one study found that top swimmers can sweat three pints in an hour of swimming. Walking under a tropical sun without protective clothing can cause a loss of over twenty quarts in a single day. An illness or activity that results in as little as a 10 percent loss of body water may pose a significant health hazard, while a 20 percent loss can be fatal.

Body cells need regular replenishment of their fluid stores to function properly. Water is a major component of not only bodily fluids such as blood, lymph, and digestive fluids, but seemingly solid body parts such as bones (which are 20 percent water). When excessive sweating is combined with inadequate consumption of liquid, bodily fluid levels fall. This results in a number of significant changes in the body's functioning. Dehydration can cause an actual decrease in the volume of blood circulating in the body. The blood itself thickens and undergoes chemical changes as electrolytes are lost through the sweat.

Electrolytes are minerals such as potassium, sodium, calcium, and magnesium dissolved in the blood and other bodily fluids. In solution form, these minerals allow the conveyance of minute electrical currents crucial for the proper functioning of muscles and nerves. Without sufficient electrolytes, muscles get weak and lose coordination, the heart beats abnormally, and the body's heat regulator falters.

Athletes in the early stages of dehydration may suffer a drop in performance and endurance levels. If their fluid and electrolyte loss is extreme, however, the body can go into shock. Drillmaster-like high school coaches who hold back water from their players during sweltering practice sessions regularly kill a half dozen or so athletes each year.

Hot-weather exertion is not the only cause of dehydration. It is also possible to become dehydrated from prolonged bouts of constipation, diarrhea, vomiting, or fever. Substances that induce more urination—diuretics—can promote dehydration. Diuretics include pharmaceutical drugs such as Lasix as well as caffeine and herbs such as horsetail. Because of infants' faster metabolism and elderly people's less sensitive thirst mechanism, these groups face a greater risk of dehydration than do most adults. You can also become dehydrated during cold weather, when you can lose large amounts of moisture from the breath.

Symptoms of dehydration include dry lips and mouth, and skin that is dry, easily wrinkled, or old looking. The person may be able to urinate only small amounts of dark-colored urine. Pinch the skin on an infant's scalp, and if the skin stays raised, the child may be dehydrated.

WHAT TO DRINK

In most cases the cure for dehydration is simply to drink more water. Sometimes special steps or types of fluids are necessary to rehydrate a person. For instance, if a child vomits up everything she drinks, try to get her to take many frequent sips. If the condition is advanced and the person is taken to the hospital, a doctor may replace fluids and electrolytes intravenously, then attempt to treat the underlying condition.

Water will prevent most cases of dehydration and will help in the treatment of many cases as well. If fluid loss has been extreme, however, and the body's electrolyte stores are depleted, there are better liquids than water to restore proper functioning of the cells. These include:

Oral hydration solution. This is a standard formula recommended by health organizations worldwide. It involves two glasses. Glass One is filled with eight ounces of fruit juice. "Orange and apple juice are best, for their potassium content," notes naturopath Joseph Pizzorno, "but you can use other juices as well." Add one-half teaspoon honey (or sugar for an infant under one year old) for glucose and then a pinch of table salt for sodium. Glass Two is filled with eight ounces of water to which is added one-fourth teaspoon baking soda, for sodium bicarbonate to balance electrolytes. The person should take alternate sips, a few from Glass One and then a few from Glass Two.

A mineral-rich vegetable or soy bouillon. Herbalist Christopher Hobbs says, "The one I recommend is Dr. Bronner's Balanced-Mineral-Bouillon, which contains tremendous amounts of potassium salts and mineral ions. You just mix a tablespoon in a cup of water and drink. I think this is better than heavily sugar-sweetened drinks for treating dehydration or a heat disorder, because sugar is a stimulant and ultimately its effect is heating rather than cooling." One tablespoon of Dr. Bronner's Balanced-

Mineral-Bouillon provides 2,150 mg potassium as well as 750 mg sodium, 30 mg calcium, 25 mg phosphorus, and 9 mg magnesium. Made by All-One-God-Faith, Inc. of Escondido, California, the concentrate comes in eight-ounce bottles.

A natural mineral complex. One of the best for dehydration is Emergen-C, which is produced by the Alacer Corporation of Buena Park, California, in handy three-gram packets. Emergen-C is a powder that dissolves in a fizz when sprinkled in a glass of water or juice. Each packet provides 1,000 mg of vitamin C, 145 mg of potassium, and lesser amounts of sodium, calcium, magnesium, zinc, and manganese. "The combination of vitamin C and electrolyte-balancing minerals helps you to rehydrate," says Oriental Medical Doctor Holly Eagle.

Natural foods stores also carry a number of herbal/potassium liquid supplements that go by such names as Ultimate Herbal K and Vital K. These typically contain hundreds of milligrams of potassium per tablespoon, as well as other minerals and B vitamins. Look for brands that are unsweetened, or sweetened with fruit juice concentrate or honey rather than fructose or artificial sweeteners.

Fresh fruit and vegetable juices. Orange and grapefruit juice are good potassium sources and can be blended with a banana for even more potassium. Fresh carrot juice is another ready source of potassium.

Liquid-chlorophyll drinks. Concentrated sources of chlorophyll include the algae-based green foods spirulina, chlorella, and blue-green algae, and products made from the young grasses of wheat, barley, and alfalfa. The minerals in these supplements are easily digested and assimilated. Most chlorophyll supplements come in either a powder or liquid concentrate. Though labels will have suggested serving sizes, these products are concentrated foods and it is safe to drink as much as you want.

A homemade sport drink. You can make your own electrolyte drink by adding to one quart water two tablespoons of honey or sugar and one-half teaspoon salt. The danger with homemade drinks is mixing them improperly and adding too much salt. More is not necessarily better in this case. If you drink water that is too salty, you may vomit and become more dehydrated. Measure correctly and use the ratio of half a teaspoon salt per quart of water if you do make a homemade electrolyte drink.

An electrolyte-balanced sports drink. Gatorade is the most popular of these. It is a flavored, artificially colored sugar solution that contains 110 mg of sodium and 25 mg of potassium per eight ounces. A better choice is the natural product Recharge from

Knudsen and Sons of Chico, California. Like Gatorade, Recharge comes in a couple of flavors and readily quenches the thirst. Recharge, however, is 45 percent juice and has no added sugar or artificial colors. Per eight ounces it provides less sodium (20 mg) but more potassium (40 mg) than Gatorade.

Defenders of highly sweetened sports drinks such as Gatorade contend that sugar can increase your endurance and help the body absorb salt. Whether the body makes best use of mildly sweetened drinks (2–4 percent sugar) or heavily sweetened ones such as Gatorade and most soft drinks (10–12 percent sugar) is still being studied. Most nutritionists advise avoiding drinks that are sweetened by adding large amounts of refined sugars.

A person suffering from dehydration or a heat illness shouldn't drink fluids containing alcohol or caffeine, which can increase fluid loss.

◆ Heat Cramps

Even though they are the least serious of the three major heat disorders, heat cramps should not be ignored. It is possible for heat cramps to progress to heat exhaustion, and for heat exhaustion to lead to heatstroke. By learning to recognize the symptoms and to follow some simple treatment steps, you can stay cool and alive even under the most extreme conditions.

Heat cramps are painful muscle contractions that usually strike the abdomen, arms, or legs. Such cramps are more common among athletes and persons in top shape who have large muscle mass. When you overexert yourself on a hot day, the muscles generate a lot of heat, the body sweats profusely, and bodily salt reserves are quickly depleted. The lower sodium level in the blood induces cramping of the muscles.

In addition to heavy sweating, the warning signs for heat cramps include light-headedness and weakness. The body's core temperature often remains normal or only slightly elevated.

The basic treatment steps are:

Stop the exertion. The cramps themselves usually make further exertion impossible.

Find a cool place. Getting out of the sun will lessen electrolyte loss by slowing sweating.

Drink fluids. Water will help cool the body, but it doesn't do anything to replace lost electrolytes. Supplement water with one of the mineral-replacing drinks mentioned above in the section "What to Drink."

Gently but firmly massage the cramped muscles to help relax them. It may also be helpful to have the person sit and elevate his or her feet eight to twelve inches. Depending upon the severity of the cramps, the person may want to rest a day or longer before resuming physical exertion. Don't rub the body with alcohol or take aspirin.

NATURAL REMEDIES FOR HEAT CRAMPS

The following remedies can supplement the basic first-aid steps to bring speedy relief for heat cramps.

Massage the area of cramping with a muscle-relaxing essential oil. Apply a few drops of undiluted Lavender to the skin and massage into the cramped muscle.

***Take the homeopathic remedy* Cuprum metallicum.** Homeopaths use this remedy, made from copper, for cases of cramps that are accompanied by nausea and are made better by drinking cool water.

Drink a cooling herbal tea. "Certain teas can help cool the body," Hobbs says, "though they may need to be combined with an electrolyte source. The Chinese use honeysuckle flower or chrysanthemum flower to make cooling teas. Both are readily available here in the U.S." Other cooling herbal teas include peppermint, gotu kola, and hibiscus flower. Drink these teas cool or cold.

◆ Heat Exhaustion

Also called heat prostration or heat collapse, this form of heat illness usually occurs when excessive exertion and a lack of acclimatization combines with temperatures over 90° and humidity over 70 percent. The direct result is that the body loses large amounts of fluid through sweating. The loss of the fluid itself, or sometimes principally the loss of electrolytes, affects the heart and blood vessels and leads to mild forms of shock. Heat exhaustion differs from the more severe heatstroke in that the body's core temperature may be normal or only slightly high.

Heat exhaustion doesn't always announce itself with clear signs and symptoms. In some cases the person is not even sweating or complaining of thirst. If the main cause of the heat exhaustion is insufficient water, the person's early symptoms are likely to be intense thirst, weakness, and lack of muscle coordination. If the main cause is an electrolyte loss, he or she may first suffer from heat cramps, nausea, and diarrhea. Other early symptoms whatever the cause may include headache, tiredness, dizziness, and loss of appetite. If heat exhaustion is not treated, the person's condition may quickly worsen. Advanced symptoms include skin that's cold and clammy, a racing heart, dilated pupils, and irrational behavior.

Heat exhaustion that's untreated can lead to heatstroke. Suspect heatstroke if the person's skin turns from cold and clammy to hot and dry. Other signs that heat exhaustion has advanced to heatstroke are loss of body control (the person has trouble walking, for instance) and unconsciousness. (Fainting on a hot day, however, that's not preceded by other symptoms may be merely a case of heat faint.)

Heat exhaustion may strike anyone. At highest risk are people who are unacclimatized to the hot weather. They may not even realize they're being afflicted because heat exhaustion can develop over several days. It can also affect athletes who compete in hot weather, and anyone with inefficient circulation or sweating, including, for instance, obese people and the elderly.

BASIC FIRST AID FOR HEAT EXHAUSTION

Basic first aid for heat exhaustion is similar to that for heat cramps. Do the following steps as quickly as possible.

Get the person out of the heat to a cool, shaded place. Have the person lie down and rest.

Raise the person's feet eight to twelve inches and gently rub his or her legs. These steps will aid circulation.

Replace fluids and electrolytes. Have the person drink a little at a time to prevent nausea. Slightly salted cool water or one of the electrolyte-replacing drinks mentioned above in "What to Drink" are better than water in those cases in which the person is suffering from marked mineral loss.

Help cool the person. Since most people suffering from heat exhaustion do not have markedly elevated body temperatures, gentle cooling steps are usually sufficient. For instance, apply cold wet compresses to the head and neck, or fan the whole body. If the person's body temperature is over 102°, use any of the more quick-acting cooling suggestions outlined in the section on "How to Cool the Body" under heatstroke.

Monitor the person's condition to make sure it doesn't

worsen. Watch for signs of shock, increasing body temperature, convulsions, or heatstroke. When the immediate emergency is over, discourage any further activity or exposure to heat that may make the condition recur. People who have suffered from heat exhaustion tend to be sensitive to further episodes.

Call for emergency help or take the person to a medical practitioner if your treatment of the early symptoms of heat exhaustion is not working after half an hour, or whenever heat exhaustion has proceeded to the point where mental confusion or fainting occurs.

Emergency treatment of heat exhaustion may include diagnostic tests to monitor kidney function and electrolyte levels in the blood. If the person is unable to drink, he or she may be given fluids intravenously. Sometimes the person is hospitalized for observation.

NATURAL FIRST-AID REMEDIES FOR HEAT EXHAUSTION

Along with the basic steps of cooling and rehydrating the person suffering from heat exhaustion, use any of the following natural healing techniques.

Apply acupressure to points that can help restore a person's vital energy. "From the Chinese perspective," herbalist Christopher Hobbs says, "a person suffering from heat exhaustion or heatstroke is so hot that pores and everything else open right up. Vital energy flows out of the body, causing the person to collapse. Acupuncture and acupressure are used to contain vital energy, to close off pores and allow *qi*—the vital energy—to build up again." Two sets of points to accomplish this are the point in the webbing of each hand between the thumb and index finger, and a point on each wrist.

Acupressure teacher Michael Reed Gach says, "The point on the hand is located on the outside of the hand on the highest spot of the muscle when the thumb and index finger are brought close together. Manipulating this point gets the energy going down, stabilizing and grounding the person." Gach warns against using this point on pregnant women, since doing so can cause premature labor contractions.

The point on the wrist is located in the middle of the inner side of the forearm, two and one-half finger-widths from the wrist crease. Press the point firmly, holding for at least two minutes.

Take an appropriate Chinese prepared medicine to "clear

summerheat." Traditional Chinese healers also treat or prevent heat disorders (which they term summerheat conditions) with combinations of herbs that are strongly cooling and refreshing. These include Huo Xian Zheng Qi Pian, Red Dan, and Liu Shen Shui.

♦ Huo Xian Zheng Qi Pian is also known as Huo Xian Zheng Qi Wan and Lophanthus. These "Agastaches Qi-Correcting" pills are typically used in the aftermath of summerheat diseases to promote recovery.
♦ Red Dan is the "People's Elixir" or "Benevolence Pills." It is a commonly used preventive medicine during the summer for any prolonged activity in sunshine.
♦ Liu Shen Shui, or "Six Spirits Fluid," is the most potent of the summerheat medicines. It is a liquid formula for emergency conditions often used to treat the symptoms of heatstroke.

See "Resources" for mail-order sources of Chinese herbs.

Take the homeopathic remedy Veratrum album *to relieve heat exhaustion.* Homeopaths recommend this remedy in most cases of heat exhaustion, particularly when the person is nauseous, weak, and has pale, clammy skin.

Take advantage of the gentle cooling effects of certain essential oils. Any cold-water treatment, whether applied by soaking a cloth to make a compress or simply pouring or sponging the water over parts of body, can be supplemented by adding ten to fifteen drops of the following essential oils to each quart of cool water:

♦ Eucalyptus
♦ Lavender
♦ Peppermint

Apply traditional folk remedies to the forehead, wrists, and back of the neck in the form of cold compresses. These include:

♦ cold water and vinegar
♦ the scrapings of a raw potato
♦ fresh violet leaves or infusion

◆ Heatstroke

Heatstroke is the opposite of hypothermia and is sometimes even referred to by scientists as hyperthermia. As with other heat disorders, a number of factors may singly or in combination lead to heatstroke, including strenuous activity, hot and humid weather, poor ventilation, dark and heavy clothes, and dehydration or electrolyte loss. These conditions conspire to rob the body of its ability to cool itself by sweating. The rising core temperature starts to toast internal organs. Left unchecked, the damage can quickly become irreversible.

Hospitals report that the most common victims of heatstroke are middle-aged alcoholic males. Heatstroke also occurs among children and the elderly, those who take sedatives or antidepressants, and people suffering from heart disease, diabetes, or obesity. It strikes teens and young adults relatively rarely, though no one who works out or plays for too long in extremely hot weather is immune.

Heatstroke often comes on gradually. The early symptoms are similar to those for heat exhaustion: weakness, dizziness, and nausea. There may be cramps and headache. Usually the person has an extremely dry mouth and is very thirsty. Except when the victim is a well-conditioned young athlete, the heatstroke victim stops sweating. The skin is flushed, dry and hot, and sometimes blue from lack of oxygen. Though the person's core temperature is over 106°, he or she may feel cold. The person's urine is dark, the pulse is rapid and strong, and the rate of breathing is increased. Mental problems such as confusion and drowsiness become more pronounced as the person's condition worsens. If the temperature reaches 108° or higher, the person may suffer from seizures, coma, or worse—heatstroke kills some five thousand Americans each year.

HOW TO COOL THE BODY

A person suffering from heatstroke should be cooled as quickly as possible. This means getting them out of the sun and into a cool, shaded place, preferably air-conditioned. Remove all or most of the person's clothing and then cool the person with one or more of the following methods, listed from those that act most rapidly to lower body temperature to those that offer slower cooling effects.

Put the person in a cold shower, spray him with water from a garden hose, or splash or pour water over him. Don't splash or spray the person in the face, though, and advise the person of your intentions beforehand so the treatment is not a shock. Constant spraying with cold water cools the body more quickly than immersing it in a tub, since the water can more readily evaporate from the skin and thus add to the cooling effect. Splashing methods must be maintained to be effective. Just throwing a bucket of water over someone will lower the person's body temperature a mere .01° F.

Immerse the person in a cold-water bath, stirring the water frequently. If you're in the wilderness, you can immerse the person's trunk in a cold stream. You should closely monitor the person's airway, breathing, and circulation while doing this.

Cover the person with a cold, wet sheet and continuously fan him or her. Wrapping the sheet around the victim's entire body would add to the cooling effect.

Apply ice packs or cool towels to the body, particularly to circulation-rich areas such as the wrists, underarms, groin, and neck. You can also do prolonged sponging of the skin with ice-cold water (don't use alcohol since the vapors can be inhaled).

BASIC FIRST AID FOR HEATSTROKE

Heatstroke is a major medical emergency that calls for immediate and dramatic treatment.

Cool the person as quickly as possible. Use the most effective and readily available of the steps listed above.

Gently rub the extremities to stimulate circulation. Massage can accompany most of the cooling steps. Cool blood near the surface of the skin flows to the body's core and cools the organs there, while warm internal blood flows to the skin, where it is more easily cooled.

Summon emergency personnel as soon as possible. If you have to transport the person to the hospital yourself, during the trip keep him wrapped in a cold, wet sheet, with the head elevated. Don't offer aspirin, acetaminophen, or other fever-reducing "antipyretics" that act by lowering the body's thermostat setting. Remember, in a heat disorder the thermostat remains set at a normal temperature—it is environmental conditions that have conspired to rob the body of its ability to cool itself.

Offer liquids only with caution. Fluids are less important than cooling the body in heatstroke first aid. If the person is alert and thirsty, you can offer sips of cool water. Be careful, however, when you give heatstroke victims anything to be taken orally, since choking is a danger.

Take the person's temperature every ten minutes or so. You want to cool a heatstroke victim until her temperature reaches 101–102°, but not below that point. If you can get the temperature to that level, dry the person and take her to the hospital. If transportation to a hospital is not possible, keep the person in a cool place.

Watch the victim closely for signs of shock and check the body temperature every half hour. It's possible for the person's temperature to start rising again over the next two to four hours. (See Chapter 18 for a discussion of how to determine bodily temperature.)

HOSPITAL TREATMENT

Heatstroke is always a serious emergency. If you recognize the early signs, summon medical personnel as soon as possible. Without treatment, a person suffering from heatstroke will almost certainly die. Even with proper treatment, as many as one in five victims may not survive.

Emergency room doctors will first check a heatstroke victim's breathing. Often they will administer supplemental oxygen through a mask. To reduce the patient's body temperature as quickly as possible, doctors may strip the patient, place ice packs on the body, and direct a fan onto him or her. Some hospitals are equipped to suspend the nude patient in a mesh net and spray the entire body with cool water and air.

When further treatment of severe cases is called for, emergency personnel may perform an internal "abdominal wash" with a special cooling solution. They may also insert a urinary catheter to monitor urine output and administer intravenous solutions to maintain blood pressure and urine output. Victims of heatstroke whose core temperature exceeded 106° are routinely hospitalized. Such elevated temperatures can damage vital internal organs including the heart, kidney, and liver. It's not unheard of for persons to survive the initial heatstroke episode but subsequently to die from complications.

NATURAL FIRST-AID REMEDIES FOR HEATSTROKE

The following natural remedies and techniques should be considered only as adjuncts, not substitutes, for the basic steps outlined above.

Apply acupressure to a point at the top and back of the head that is traditionally used in China to treat heatstroke. To find it, place the left fingers behind the left ear and the right fingers behind the right ear, suggests Michael Reed Gach, author of numerous books on acupressure. Move the fingertips up to the top of the head, feeling for the hollow toward the back of the top, center of the head. Hold the point in an indentation (the "soft spot" on an infant) for three minutes as you breathe deeply and slowly.

Administer an appropriate homeopathic remedy. Give the following every fifteen to thirty minutes until the patient improves:

- *Glonoine.* Use this remedy, made from trinitroglycerine, if the person has some sweat on the skin, a throbbing headache and red face, and seems to be in a stupor.
- *Belladonna.* This is the right remedy for heatstroke characterized by burning, hot, and dry skin, dilated pupils, and a strong pulse. The person shows signs of delirium rather than stupor.

Homeopath Jennifer Jacobs, M.D., notes that long-term, "constitutional" treatment can help reduce sensitivity to heat.

Try one of the following traditional folk remedies for heatstroke.

- Put distilled witch hazel extract in the cold water being applied to the body.
- Drink watermelon juice, or a decoction of the stems and leaves of the Chinese cucumber plant *T. kirilowii*, a type of gourd that is the source for the underground AIDS medicine known as Compound Q. Both of these are traditional Chinese folk remedies for heatstroke. (Keep in mind that you should administer *with caution* anything that is to be swallowed by persons suffering from heatstroke.)

◆ Recovering from Heat Illness

Anyone who has just suffered a heat disorder should take extra steps to recover from the effects of exhaustion and dehydration. The following simple steps can be part of a program worked out with your medical practitioner for restoring full health to the heart, lungs, and other major organs.

Rehydrate your body by drinking large amounts of fluids. After a heat illness you need large amounts of water to replace the fluids lost through sweat. (You may also need minerals to replace electrolytes in the blood, in which case drink mineral-rich vegetable broths and fruit juices instead of water.) Fruits and other juicy foods contain significant amounts of water but not enough to rehydrate after an emergency.

Eat foods that will help replenish your blood's chemical balance. Studies have found that half of all heatstroke victims have seriously low potassium levels and that muscle magnesium levels of men who exercised vigorously on a hot day fell 12 percent. Other minerals may also be deficient in people who have suffered heat disorders. "After a heat illness it's a good idea to rebuild your electrolyte levels as quickly as possible," herbalist Christopher Hobbs says.

A variety of common grains, legumes, and fresh fruits and vegetables are high in potassium, including winter squash, bananas, cantaloupes, lentils, potatoes, and split peas. Foods high in magnesium include kidney beans and soybeans.

Replace lost electrolytes by drinking balanced-mineral fluids or taking multimineral supplements. Combination mineral products such as Emergen-C and Dr. Bronner's Balanced-Mineral-Bouillon (see "What to Drink" above) or multimineral supplements are more widely available and easier to take than individual mineral supplements. For instance, you can buy potassium supplements at the natural foods store, but the tab size is limited by law to 99 mg (higher dosages are available by prescription only), about what you get in one large bite of a banana. Sodium, potassium, and phosphorus are all widely available in a broad variety of foods.

Nutritionist Shari Lieberman, R.D., recommends the following optimum daily allowances for other common minerals:

- ◆ 500 mg of magnesium
- ◆ 1,000–1,500 mg calcium
- ◆ 15–30 mg manganese

◆ Preventing Heat Illness

A person who has suffered from heat exhaustion or heatstroke is more likely than the average person to fall victim to it in the future. Such people should take extra precautions, such as the following simple preventive steps.

Keep your body hydrated by drinking lots of fluid before, during, and after exertion. The key is to drink something every twenty minutes or so during heavy exercise, regardless of whether you feel thirsty. The special cells in your brain that stimulate the sensation of thirst are unreliable for preventing dehydration. They don't kick into action until after you've lost a lot of fluid from sweating. By then your electrolytes could be falling and your body temperature rising, a dangerous combination.

Water will meet the needs of the vast majority of people who exercise or otherwise exert themselves, as will fruit or vegetable juices. (Beer and other alcoholic beverages don't count as fluids since they can have an adverse effect on the body's heat-regulating mechanism.) One study that compared the benefits of water to electrolyte-added sports drinks found that the only advantage to the latter was that people tended to drink slightly more of them. Rarely will a person experience a mineral shortage unless he or she exercises for three to four hours (somewhat less if the exertion and the weather are extreme). For instance, marathon runners who drink only water during a marathon have been known to experience dizziness and other electrolyte-loss symptoms by the end of the race. In such cases drinking water (as a treatment) is actually counterproductive, since it further dilutes the blood. So if you're planning on heavy levels of exertion and massive sweating during hot weather, consider replacing lost minerals at regular intervals during your activity.

You can usually prevent heat cramps by drinking a full glass of water about thirty minutes before any heavy exercise, along with small amounts every fifteen to twenty minutes.

Stay out of the sun and heat during midday summer hours when the temperatures are highest. Seek a shaded, well-ventilated place (or take a dip in a cold-water stream) during the hours of twelve to two P.M. This is the traditional siesta time in the tropics, where the people have firsthand knowledge of the hazards of working when the sun is at its highest. Don't take a nap in the heat, however, if you're getting dizzy from the hot sun. Unless you start to cool off, it may be a nap from which you never awaken.

Pace yourself at outdoor activities when it's hot and humid. Temperature and humidity combine to increase dramatically your rate of sweating and raise the odds of overheating the body. So cut back during hot weather. This is particularly important at the beginning of the summer when you're not yet acclimated to the heat. If the temperature is over 90° F and the humidity over 85 percent, outdoor exertion should be almost completely curtailed to prevent heat disorders. If you do exercise during hot weather and begin to feel dizzy or faint, stop immediately.

Wear cooling clothes. When it is hot and humid, the best clothes are lightweight and light colored, to reflect the heat rather than absorb it. Hot-weather clothes are also loose fitting, to allow cooling as the wind passes through, and clean (a shirt that has been sweat-drenched won't breathe well because of the dried salt). Cotton garments breathe better than synthetics, while wool holds heat in and is inappropriate for hot weather. A light-colored, ventilated hat that shades the neck can also help prevent heat buildup in the body. That's because the head and neck contain an abundance of blood vessels that are close to the skin. These blood vessels allow the body to gain or lose heat there quickly.

Avoid substances that can make you sweat more than usual or otherwise interfere with the body's heat-regulating mechanisms. These include alcohol, caffeine, cigarette smoke, aspirin, and over-the-counter fever medications.

Eat cooling foods. During the hottest days of summer it's a good idea to eat light, easily digested foods high in carbohydrates and water content. Summer salads and fresh fruit make great sense; that huge barbecued steak does not. Two fluid-laden foods that practitioners of traditional Chinese medicine say are particularly cooling to the body are watermelon and cucumber. Juicing these can allow you to consume large quantities.

Fatty foods such as meat tend to produce heat in the body, as the native peoples of the arctic can confirm. High-protein foods also increase urination, which can contribute to dehydration. Nutritionist Shari Lieberman also suggests that on a hot day you should eat smaller, more frequent meals to keep too much blood from being diverted to the body's core for digestion. For the same reason it's advisable to allow the body a few hours to digest solid foods before engaging in strenuous exercise.

Don't take salt tablets. Salt tablets used to be a common preventive recommendation for athletes or others who sweat profusely, but no longer. Researchers have determined that taking salt tablets poses a number of health risks. Salt tablets can irritate the stomach and cause vomiting, hastening dehydration. They can raise the salt concentration in the blood and increase the possibility of harmful blood clots developing. Salt tablets can also hold fluids in the stomach longer, leaving less fluid available for necessary sweat production. If salt is needed during treatment for heat exhaustion or heatstroke, it should be dissolved in water.

EIGHTEEN

High Fever

THIS CHAPTER COVERS:

◆ *when and how to reduce a fever*

SEE "CHAPTER 11: CONVULSIONS AND SEIZURES" FOR:

◆ *febrile convulsions*

SEE "CHAPTER 17: HEAT ILLNESS" FOR:

◆ *heat cramps*
◆ *heat exhaustion*
◆ *heatstroke*

SEE "CHAPTER 21: SKIN INJURIES" FOR:

◆ *local infections*

Give me fever and I will cure all disease.
—HIPPOCRATES

Humanity has but three great enemies: Fever, Famine, and War. Of these, by far the greatest, by far the most terrible, is fever.
—SIR WILLIAM OSLER

Judging from the above quotes, the pioneering fourth-century B.C. Greek physician and the noted nineteenth-century Canadian physician have violently divergent opinions about fever. Which is fever, friend or foe? Modern research is increasingly coming down on the side of Hippocrates, that fever is a basically beneficial bodily response. At its extreme, of course—an exceedingly high fever that persists for many days—fever can be a killer. Even so, few today would agree with Osler that fever is a scourge, much less that it deserves to rank ahead of famine and war.

Also known as pyrexia, fever is an elevated body temperature that may be due to a systemic (body-wide) infection, an underlying disease, or even a normal bodily process such as ovulation. Like dizziness and fainting, fever is a symptom rather than a disease in itself. Fever is also a defense mechanism. "The best definition for fever is not a morbid or pathological disease state, but rather a state of hyperfunctional repair," naturopath Ross Trattler says. He adds, "Fever is not the problem to be cured, but the *result* of the problem and *part* of the cure."

Though both fever and heat disorders are characterized by an increase in body temperature, the underlying causes and mechanisms are different. A fever occurs when invading bacteria, for instance, cause an infection. The body's natural thermostat, located in the hypothalamus at the base of the brain, responds by raising its set-point and thus increasing the body's temperature. A heat disorder, on the other hand, occurs as a result of conditions such as excessive exertion in hot weather, severe dehydration, or confinement in a closed space (for example, locking a child in an overheated car). In such cases the body's thermostat setting remains normal, but conditions prevent the body from cooling itself (see "Chapter 17: Heat Illness").

FEVER PHOBIA

The average person's temperature is 98.6° F, measured orally. This fluctuates on a daily or even hourly basis, and some people's average may be anywhere from 96° to 100°. In general a temperature of 101–102° is considered a mild fever, 102–104° moderate, and over 104° high. Anything over 106° is rare and cause for immediate emergency care. Scientists say that 106° is the point at which temperature itself becomes dangerous. In other words, you can suffer ill effects with a fever below 106°, but the ill effects are from underlying conditions, not the fever per se. If you had to and were in good health, you could probably tolerate a temperature of 107° for eight to ten hours. Many human cells can't survive temperatures above 110°, and the body's upper limit is an estimated 113°.

One of the most common reasons people go to the doctor's office is for treatment of a mild to a moderate fever. Many of these visits could be avoided if people recognized fever as one of the body's most effective ways for healing itself. Fever is a normal and even desirable response to illness or injury. It constitutes evidence that the body is attempting to repel an invasion by foreign substances or counter a toxic condition. Thus, using drugs or other means to eliminate a fever and lower the body's temperature can be counterproductive for long-term health.

New York Times health writer Jane Brody recently noted, " 'Fever phobia' has become a frequent topic of concern in the pediatric literature. Experts say that undue attention to a child's temperature and mishandling of fevers generate a great deal of unwarranted parental anxiety, avoidable medical complications, and countless calls and costly visits to doctors, clinics, and emergency rooms." Despite the increased recognition in the medical profession about the extent of fever phobia, most parents and even most doctors are loath to let a sleeping fever lie. A recent questionnaire found that 60 percent of pediatric residents would characterize fever as a defense mechanism, but almost all would promptly attempt to reduce a fever when treating a patient.

In most cases it is better to address a fever by treating the underlying cause. Nevertheless there are times when a high fever itself presents a danger to a person and effective first-aid measures are necessary. As J. F. Donaldson said, treat fever "as a friend but one whose visit had best be fitting and short."

◆ The Mechanism of Fever

When minute organisms such as various types of bacteria and viruses invade your body, incubate, and then rapidly multiply, you have what doctors call an infectious disease. One of the symptoms will often be a fever. Here's why.

The body's immune system reacts in a number of ways to counter infectious agents. It increases breathing and heart rates, sending additional oxygen throughout the body. In the bloodstream, it activates the white blood cells to fight the invading organisms. Researchers have found that an internal bodily temperature rise to 102° is associated with an increase in immune-boosting T-cell production by as much as twenty times. Some white blood cells engulf the foreign substances, while other white blood cells increase their production of specialized antibodies to disarm or destroy the newcomers. White blood cells, as well as specialized cells in other parts of the body, also release into the bloodstream certain hormonelike peptides that are known as interleukin-1.

Interleukin-1 provides a further boost to the immune system, increasing the invader-fighting power of white blood cells and helping to produce new ones. Interleukin-1 also affects the body's internal thermostat, in effect kicking up the set-point. The body begins to create more heat, perspiration (a natural cooling mechanism) increases, and appetite decreases. You have a fever.

Recent studies indicate that fever helps to reduce the growth of or to destroy harmful viruses and bacteria, which usually have a narrow optimum temperature range. Fever-induced high temperatures increase the production and strengthen the effect of interferon, a cellular protein that slows the rate of viral reproduction. This allows white blood cells and antibodies to destroy the viruses or bacteria faster than they can reproduce. In time the body cures itself.

Research indicates that fever may also increase the body's levels of prostaglandins, hormonelike fatty acids found throughout the body that affect body temperature, inflammation, and other bodily processes. Aspirin suppresses prostaglandin production, which is why it is effective at lowering fever.

Recent research supports this view of fever as a special defense mechanism to reestablish health and balance. Studies of animals with fever have found that reducing a fever can at times interfere with immune response enough to allow pathogens to attack the body's organs and cause death. A more likely potential disadvantage of routinely reducing all fevers is that it can give a false sense of security. You may have made the person temporarily more comfortable, but you haven't addressed the underlying condition, except possibly to exacerbate it. Finally, diseases such as typhoid fever and Colorado tick fever have distinctive fever patterns. When you intervene with the fever unnecessarily early on, you can make it more difficult to correctly diagnose the underlying condition.

THE HEALTH BENEFITS OF FEVERS

New studies have begun to lend definitive support to the traditional wisdom that fever is a healing mechanism, a welcome sign that the immune system is doing its job. Researchers say that among fever's beneficial effects are its abilities to do the following:

Shorten illness. Scientists have reported that when humans are routinely given fever-reducing drugs, the illness lasts longer and does more damage to the body.

Make infection less contagious. Studies have found that patients with fever are less contagious than those with the same infection but who have suppressed their fever with medication.

Aid in eliminating toxins. In the days before antibiotics, some practitioners used fever for its cleansing effects on the body. It was even used as a therapy in the treatment of syphilis, gonorrhea, and other conditions. Recent animal research confirms that artificially induced fevers can reduce the death rate from infection. In Europe, so-called hyperthermia techniques are being used to treat cancer, with promising results.

Therapeutic use of fever is still controversial. Critics of fever claim that fever is nonessential to the healing process, and that some conditions, such as herpes simplex eruptions, are activated by a rise in body temperature.

Despite the reservations, fever is increasingly being recognized as one of the body's most effective defense mechanisms, says Andrew Weil, a medical doctor as well as advocate of natural healing. "Fevers may be dramatic and productive of discomfort, but it is important not to mistake them for primary symptoms of disease," he says.

CAUSES AND SYMPTOMS ASSOCIATED WITH FEVER

The three major infectious agents capable of inducing a fever are:

- ◆ viruses, including those that cause some types of influenza, mononucleosis, rabies, Epstein-Barr, and AIDS
- ◆ bacteria, including *Haemophilus influenzae*, certain *Streptococcus* bacteria such as *Streptococcus pneumoniae*, *Salmonella*, and the bacteria that lead to diseases including tuberculosis, typhoid fever, and scarlet fever
- ◆ fungi, including those that cause histoplasmosis, a fungal infection of the lungs

A fever can also result when certain parasites or toxic agents get into the blood or lymph systems. For instance, you can get a fever from *Plasmodium*, single-celled parasites that enter your bloodstream from certain mosquitoes and cause malaria. Fever may also be a symptom of or be associated with:

- ◆ infections or diseases of the abdomen and intestinal tract, including appendicitis, peritonitis, and viral gastro-enteritis
- ◆ ear infection
- ◆ pelvic infection
- ◆ meningitis (which can be caused by a virus or bacterium) or encephalitis (usually viral)

There are also many causes of fever other than infection. Fever is a prominent component of many inflammatory and auto-immune diseases, including arthritis, allergies, inflammatory bowel disease, and a host of others. Fever may accompany certain malignant tumors, as well. Other, sometimes overlooked, under-lying causes of fever include:

♦ drug abuse, or allergic or hypersensitive reactions to drugs including over-the-counter laxatives and antihistamines, antibiotics including penicillin, anticonvulsants, and vaccines
♦ bites or stings, as from a scorpion
♦ poisoning, as from DDT
♦ long-distance running

WHEN TO CALL FOR HELP

Recognizing the symptoms that accompany fever can be as important as determining how high the body's temperature is. In some cases (a mild viral infection, for instance) a fever of 104–105° is of little concern. In other cases (appendicitis, for instance) a fever of 101° can be an indication of a serious disease. Pay attention to factors such as how long the fever is lasting, how the person is responding, and whether he or she is listless, sweating, and so forth. When a person with a fever looks severely ill or shows any of the following potential signs of a serious illness, contact your medical professional. (Possible underlying conditions are in parenthesis after the symptom.)

♦ bluish skin
♦ coughing up dark mucus, shortness of breath (pneumonia)
♦ headache, diarrhea, vomiting (gastroenteritis)
♦ fever upon returning from a hot climate (rare tropical illness), or recurrent fevers (malaria)
♦ sore throat (tonsillitis)
♦ pain on urinating, urinating more frequently (urinary-tract infection)
♦ severe thirst, dry mouth, little or no urine, refusing to drink for several days (dehydration)

Contact a health professional if a child's fever is accompanied by any of the following symptoms. (Possible underlying conditions are in parenthesis.)

- severe headache, nausea, sensitivity to bright lights, drowsiness, and a stiff neck characterized by head and spine pain when the chin is tucked to the chest or held up in the air as the neck is extended backward (meningitis)
- convulsive movements or a seizure (underlying central nervous system infection, epilepsy; see "Chapter 11: Convulsions and Seizures")
- a rash or red dots under the skin (German measles, chickenpox, meningitis, measles)
- hearing impairment (congenital rubella)
- pulling at the ear (ear infection; see "Chapter 16: Eye and Ear Emergencies")
- abnormal breathing (bronchitis, pneumonia, croup; see "Chapter 8: Breathing Problems")
- swelling between the ear and jaw (mumps)
- lack of reaction, listlessness (pneumonia, meningitis)

Since a mild to moderate fever is actually beneficial to healing, it's important to know how to get accurate body-temperature readings. You also need to know when a fever is too high, and how the danger point differs among people of different ages and states of health.

HOW TO DETERMINE BODY TEMPERATURE

To take a person's temperature, first shake a medical thermometer, then attempt to get an oral, rectal, or armpit reading.

Oral. Thermometers to be put in the mouth have a long and slender bulb. Put the bulb end under the tongue, close the mouth, and don't talk for three minutes. Getting children under age four to cooperate can be tough, and they've been known to bite the bulb, so usually it's better to get a rectal reading from them. An oral reading averages one degree or so lower than rectal readings. Average normal is 98.6°.

Rectal. Rectal thermometers have a larger, rounder bulb. Typically they're used only on infants up to age four. Lubricate, insert the end into the rectum, and leave it there for a minute. If the child is uncooperative, you can get a reading accurate to within a degree after only twenty to thirty seconds. Rectal temperatures average about one degree higher than oral temperatures. Thus, normal is 99.6°.

Armpit. Use any type of thermometer to get an armpit (axillary) reading. This is often the easiest way to take a child's temperature. Raise the arm, wedge the thermometer into the armpit, lower the arm, and hold the thermometer there for three to five minutes. The longer the better—quick armpit measurements can be unreliable. Unless it's left under the arm for ten minutes or so, temperatures are likely to average about one degree lower than oral.

New to the market are plastic thermometer strips that you stick on a child's forehead. They're quick and easy to use but provide only a ballpark estimate of body temperature. A high-tech instrument some practitioners are using is an instant "thermoscan" that gives an accurate reading after merely touching it to the ear; at $100 or so it's expensive for home use.

In addition to determining the body's temperature, you may find it helpful to know whether the temperature is rising or falling. When a fever is rising, the body raises its internal temperature by reducing sweating and increasing metabolic and muscle activity. Thus the skin tends to be hot and dry. The pulse is often rapid and the person may experience chills, shivering, and body aches. The person's appetite is diminished and he or she feels weak. Fever convulsions in children are more likely to occur when the victim's temperature is rising.

When body temperature is falling, sweating—the body's cooling mechanism—increases. This is usually a sign that, unless the temperature is dangerously high or there are other worrisome symptoms, the fever is breaking and you can let it run its course. The person may be thirsty and tired from the effects of the fever episode, but is usually no longer feeling chills or muscle aches.

Once you have determined a person's temperature, consider whether other factors may be responsible before assuming that the cause is a fever. A number of factors other than illness can cause your temperature to rise, including:

Daily variations. A fever, like a normal body temperature, may vary by two degrees or so depending upon normal daily rhythms. Your body temperature is at its height from eight to eleven P.M. and will usually drop to its low point by four to six A.M. Fevers also typically rise in the evening and fall by the next morning, sometimes repeating the cycle for several days.

Ovulation. Until women reach menopause, they experience a temperature increase of one-half to three-quarters of a degree at ovulation that lasts until the next menses.

Environmental heat. Hot, humid weather, being overbundled with clothing, drinking hot liquids, and vigorous exertion can all cause noticeable rises in body temperature that may be confused with a fever.

WHEN IS A FEVER TOO HIGH?

All medical practitioners agree that a fever in people of a certain age and health status should be watched more carefully. The safe upper limit and duration of a fever for an otherwise healthy adult is much different from what is safe for infants, children, pregnant women, and the elderly or infirm.

Keep in mind that every individual is unique. A thermometer reading that represents a mild fever for most people may make some people extremely uncomfortable. A fever of 102° may be high enough to cause febrile seizures in one child, while another child easily tolerates 104°. If you have young children, make a point to observe them closely when they have a fever. Use this information to guide future treatment decisions. Always remember that although fevers can be beneficial to healing, it is not necessary to become a fever martyr.

Here are some high-fever guidelines for various groups of people:

Otherwise healthy adults. Health authorities differ on what constitutes a dangerously high fever for an adult and how long you can safely experience it before you should use cooling treatments. The most conservative recommendations, such as those by the authors of *The American Red Cross First Aid & Safety Handbook*, are to seek immediate medical attention for any fever over 103°, or one that is over 101° if it persists for more than one to two days. Some conventional and most alternative practitioners suggest more lenient guidelines. They say that in general a fever can go to 104–105° during a simple acute illness in a normal individual, or persist at 103° for three to five days, before you should contact a practitioner or take cooling steps. There is widespread agreement that a body temperature in the 104–106° range increases the risk of dehydration and needs to be closely monitored. There is also agreement that anything above 106° requires immediate cooling treatments.

Infants under six months old. Fevers that affect infants need to be closely monitored because young children's temperature-regulating mechanisms are not yet fully functional. In babies under three months, local infections often become systemic ones. Thus, fevers in infants can reach the danger point much more rapidly than fevers in adults. One estimate is that as many as 30–40 percent of infants under three months with a temperature over 104° may have a serious disease.

The consensus among both conventional and alternative practitioners is that parents should seek medical attention for an infant under three months old who has a temperature over 100° measured rectally, or for a baby who is three to six months old with a temperature over 101°. Also check with a medical professional whenever a fever lasts longer than twenty-four hours in an infant under six months old.

Children older than six months. A rule of thumb is to consult a practitioner when a child has a temperature over 103° for more than twelve hours. Children's temperatures can rise rapidly, sometimes not from a fever but from overdressing or continuous exercise. Fever can provoke seizures in children experiencing a rapid rise in temperature (see "High Fever (Febrile) Convulsions" in Chapter 11). On the other hand, the risk of a high fever causing brain damage in children is often overstated. Some studies indicate that it is the underlying condition, such as meningitis or encephalitis, that in rare cases causes brain damage rather than the effects of the fever per se.

Pregnant women. Health authorities suggest that the upper limit for fevers in pregnant women is 102°. Higher temperatures may be harmful to the fetus, especially during the first three months of pregnancy. Researchers have determined that women who suffer high fevers during pregnancy have an increased likelihood of giving birth to infants with birth defects.

The elderly or infirm. People who suffer from chronic illnesses such as heart or lung disease may experience difficulties tolerating prolonged high fevers. The high energy costs of a fever have been known to exhaust people who are weak or thin, leaving them defenseless against the invading disease. Fever can accelerate weight loss in cancer patients or lead to confusion or delirium in the elderly.

In general the elderly have lower average body temperatures than younger people. A fever that is prolonged for more than one to four days should be closely monitored.

HOW EMERGENCY PERSONNEL TREAT HIGH FEVER

Doctors or hospital workers will use measures similar to those you can use at home to reduce a dangerously high fever. They have some special equipment (in cases of heatstroke they may hang a person in a mesh net and spray the body with cold water) but will usually rely on cold compresses, cool sponge baths, or tepid-water immersion (see next section, "Basic First Aid for a High Fever"), depending on the severity of the fever. They may also recommend fever-reducing drugs such as acetaminophen (Tylenol, Datril).

If the body temperature is at a safe level, medical personnel will focus on determining the cause of the fever. Depending on the patient and other symptoms, doctors may order a range of diagnostic lab tests including a complete blood count, a urine culture, and a chest X ray. Infants and children with high fevers will be closely examined for other symptoms (a rash, enlargements of liver or spleen) that may indicate a more serious infectious disease. Children or adults who are suspected of having meningitis may be given a lumbar puncture to withdraw cerebrospinal fluid for analysis. (This diagnostic procedure itself presents risks. One study found that the odds of bacterial meningitis developing in a child who had undergone lumbar puncture at the initial visit was over twice that for children who had not undergone a lumbar puncture.)

Many fevers are caused by a viral disorder that will go away without invasive treatment. Perhaps as few as one in five fevers are caused by bacteria such as *Streptococcus pneumoniae* that can be killed by antibiotics. (Viruses are not affected by antibiotics.) Bacterial infections, however, can be serious, so some pediatricians routinely treat fevers with antibiotics even before lab results come back confirming the presence of a bacterial infection. A recent study in the *New England Journal of Medicine* raised doubts about this practice. It said, "Researchers concluded that the routine treatment of high fever with standard oral doses of [the antibiotic] amoxicillin in small children is unwarranted, except when actual laboratory evidence of a bacterial infection justifies it." Another recent study found that the duration of fevers in children treated with antibiotics was about thirty-six hours longer than fevers in children not given antibiotics.

Other treatments will depend on the diagnosis of the underlying condition. A person with a benign viral infection will be sent home and advised to rest in bed and drink plenty of fluids. A person with a more serious invasive disease may need intensive measures including hospitalization.

◆ Basic First Aid for a High Fever

Researchers who have studied fever in animals say that they typically stop eating and seek out a warm place to take an extended rest. Human animals should do likewise. People should also drink plenty of fluids to prevent dehydration. When necessary, you should take steps to lower the fever, including the following:

Rest. The best place to be when you have a fever is in bed. A calm, quiet environment allows you to recuperate and listen to your body. Being in bed also allows you to easily regulate your warmth levels. The room should have good air circulation. Clothing and blankets should be only heavy enough to prevent chills. If you become overheated and are sweating, remove blankets or take off clothes. (Heatstroke is a major medical emergency that should be prevented at all cost.)

Fast. One of the ways that the body conserves energy that is needed to fight off an illness is to reduce the appetite for food. Fasting for twelve to twenty-four hours prevents the body from sending a lot of its resources (blood, heat) to the gut to do the work of digestion. Temporary fasting also helps the body eliminate toxic wastes. Medical researchers have found that the decrease in gastric acid secretion associated with fever and fasting helps prevent the body temperature from rising too high. A feverish adult who eats minimally will rarely have a fever exceed 104°; a fasting child, 105°.

If you do experience hunger during a fever, eat light, easily digested foods such as vegetable soup or fresh fruits. They can provide nutrients and help slake your thirst without requiring a lot of energy to digest. The same kinds of foods help promote recovery when a fever is over.

If you have a fever, check with a medical professional before fasting for longer than one day.

Drink fluids. Whether or not you stop eating, continue to drink plenty of liquid. Since sweating often accompanies a fever, it's possible to lose a lot of fluid and become dehydrated. This weakens the body, increases the risk of heat disorders, and makes it more difficult to heal the illness causing the fever.

You can drink water, herbal teas, or fruit or vegetable juices. Try lemon juice with honey, or grape, carrot, or grapefruit juice. Dilute them if they're too filling. Drinks that are 100 percent fruit juice are preferable to those that are sweetened with refined sugar. Commercial sports drinks such as Gatorade are rarely necessary to replace minerals lost by sweating. In any case there are a number of much more nutritious alternatives (see "What to Drink" in Chapter 17). Also avoid drinks with caffeine or alcohol, since these can have a weakening and dehydrating effect on the body.

Most people prefer drinks that are cool to lukewarm. Hot teas can either heat the body or increase sweating and thus cool the body. You can encourage children to take in fluids by letting them suck on frozen fruit juice, ice cubes, or a clean, wet sponge or cotton cloth.

Take steps to cool the body when appropriate. As we've emphasized in the first half of this chapter, most of the time it is best to let a fever run its course without intervening. There are few hard and fast rules for when you should step in and attempt to reduce a fever. In general, reduce a fever:

- that has continued without lowering itself for three to five days
- that is over 105–106° in a healthy adult

Refer to the discussion of causes and symptoms for details relating to complicating conditions, and to the section on special considerations for children, pregnant women, and the elderly or infirm. Fever has many faces. Patients and treatment decisions are unique.

When you do decide to treat a fever, "you don't want to reduce the temperature too much," notes Joseph Pizzorno, N.D. "If you do reduce it too far, the body will waste metabolic energy trying to generate heat. You also have to allow time for the body to respond to the cooling treatment. The oral temperature will lag behind the treatment, since the treatment cools the outside of the body and it takes time for the cooling effects to reach the core. If you overcool the outside of the body, you'll cause the core to drop much further than expected. A sign that you've gone too far is when the person starts to shiver."

To reduce the core temperature to 102–103°, stop the cooling treatment when the oral temperature registers 103–104°. The body will continue to cool an additional one to two degrees.

At the same time you want to be careful not to do anything that may start the temperature on its way back up. For instance, don't overdress the feverish person in heavy clothing or cover him or her with too many layers of blankets. And don't suggest a break for that two-hour aerobics class—rigorous exercise increases heat production in the body.

The following cooling treatments are ordered from the mildest and most slow-acting to the strongest and quickest-acting. Keep in mind that water will feel cooler to a feverish person than it does to a person with a lower body temperature. Always stop a cooling treatment if the person starts to shiver. You can complement any of these cooling treatments with a light-friction massage or brisk towel rub.

- ◆ Drink cold water.
- ◆ Soak the feet in a basin of cool water.
- ◆ Apply cool or cold compresses. These can be wet or dry. For instance, soak and wring slightly a cotton cloth and put it on the person's forehead or behind the neck. Other areas of the body that generate a lot of heat and thus are good places to apply cooling compresses are the armpits, groin, and wrists. Keep the rest of the body covered with clothes or blankets.
- ◆ Sponge the body with tepid (81–92°) or neutral (93–96°) water. The person can remain in bed or get in a bath. Use a wet sponge or cotton cloth. In bed, start with the face and forehead. Then sponge one limb at a time before drying it slightly (leaving the skin damp allows evaporation to have its cooling effects) and going on to the next. In the bath, sit in waist-deep water and sponge the face and upper body. Protect the person from drafts.

Naturopath Joe Pizzorno notes that the following three techniques are more intense cooling methods that generally should be used only after consulting with your medical professional.

- ◆ Take a whole-body bath in neutral water. This helps both to cool the body and to remove toxins (and odor) from the skin.
- ◆ Apply an ice bag or cold compress to the area of the chest over the heart. Don't put ice directly on the skin.
- ◆ Take a whole-body bath in water that is gradually made tepid. The person should enter the bath when the water is warm. Gradually add more cold water until the water temperature is lowered to about 85–87°.

Don't attempt to cool the body with an alcohol sponge bath. In some cases this can be deadly. Although little alcohol is absorbed directly through the skin, it is easy to inhale dangerous amounts, quickly causing dizziness, headache, and fainting. Even when it's not deadly, alcohol gives off an odor unpleasant to many people, and it can overcool the skin by evaporating too quickly. This can cause shivering, which in turn reheats the body, since shivering is a method for generating heat.

Some parents will attempt to reduce a fever with aspirin or acetaminophen. There are good reasons to avoid both such fever treatments. One is that scientists have discovered that antibiotics are more effective when a fever has not been suppressed by aspirin. A more important reason is that when children who have certain viral illnesses such as chickenpox are given aspirin (acetylsalicylic acid) to lower a fever and relieve pain, there's a risk that they'll develop Reye's syndrome. This is an acute, often fatal neurological disorder that is still considered "rare" by some physicians, though it is now one of the top ten killers of children in the United States. Not only children but teens (who often have their own aspirin supply) and even adults (according to a 1987 article in the *Archives of Internal Medicine*) are at risk for dying from aspirin-induced Reye's syndrome. Many health-conscious parents never give their children aspirin for a fever and certainly not if the cause of the fever may be a viral illness such as chickenpox or the flu. In such cases, also don't use any other products that contain aspirin or any form of salicylate, including Pepto-Bismol. It is interesting to note that Hippocrates' pro-fever view was still prominent until the turn of the century, when aspirin was introduced. Aspirin manufacturers heavily promoted aspirin for its fever-reducing powers, possibly fanning the fires of fever phobia in the public.

Acetaminophen is preferable to aspirin, though a recent study of children with chickenpox treated with acetaminophen suggests this practice may also be unwise. Researchers found that taking acetaminophen lengthened the course of the disease. They concluded that the "data suggests the effects of fever were actually beneficial in fighting off the virus, and that fever should be allowed to run its course."

◆ Natural First-Aid Fever Remedies

Alternative practitioners in general may be more willing to let a fever run its course than conventional medical professionals. That's not always the case, however. And while natural fever reducers such as herbal white-willow-bark preparations are milder acting than conventional drugs such as aspirin, any agent that reduces a fever when it is not necessary to do so can interfere with the body's best efforts to heal itself. That said, the following are some natural techniques that can be used along with the basic steps to help reduce a dangerously high fever.

First, a word about herbs for fever. A few herbs, such as quinine from cinchona bark to relieve malarial fever, are especially effective against specific types of fevers. So many other herbs have traditionally been used to regulate a fever that the

Peterson Field Guide to Eastern/Central Medicinal Plants by Foster and Duke, in the index entry for "fever," says simply: *throughout.* A short list of fever herbs prominently used by herbalists includes licorice, lobelia, catnip, peppermint, thyme, rose hips, stinging nettles, feverfew, linden flowers, chamomile, bayberry, lemon balm, sweet basil, ginger, cayenne, white willow bark, meadowsweet, echinacea, elder flower, boneset, red clover tea, goldenseal, calendula, and dandelion.

All of these herbs don't work in the same way, of course. To help determine which herb is best for various types of fever, herbalists categorize herbs according to how they affect the body. Three useful categories of fever-reducing herbs include painkilling antipyretics; circulatory stimulants and diaphoretics; and tonics, adaptogens, and alteratives.

- Painkilling antipyretics include white willow bark and meadowsweet, both natural sources of salicin, a chemical relative of salicylic acid and aspirin. Herbalist Christopher Hobbs says, "If the person with the fever has hot, red skin, these herbs can help lower body temperature. They also tend to be faster acting in their effects on body temperature than sweat-inducing herbs like boneset. When a fever is too high, though, you shouldn't rely on herbs. Cool sponge baths and other external applications work faster than anything that is taken orally to lower body temperature."
- Circulatory stimulants and diaphoretics (agents that induce sweating) include some herbs that are warming and stimulating, such as ginger and cayenne, in which case they may actually cause the body temperature to rise slightly before sweating has its cooling effect. When the body temperature is not dangerously high, and you want to take advantage of "sweat therapy," these herbs are helpful. Because they do at least initially increase the fever, many herbalists recommend that they be used for this purpose with the guidance of a knowledgeable herbalist.

  More popular for home use to lower a fever are diaphoretic herbs that are cooling and stimulating, such as yarrow, elder, and boneset. Even these, however, should not be used if the fever is dangerously high. Hobbs says, "Diaphoretic herbs are usually taken as a warm or hot tea to induce sweating. Yarrow, elder, and boneset are good for when a fever seems to be 'stuck inside' the body, when the outside of the body feels cool or room temperature, but not burning hot."

◆ Tonics, adaptogens, and alteratives are all agents that through various mechanisms help restore overall bodily health by boosting immunity and fighting bacterial infections. Antiviral and detoxifying herbs that can be used this way in conjunction with others to fend off a fever include echinacea, barberry, and garlic.

Add some helpful natural substances to the water used for compresses, sponging, or bathing. Try any of the following for a subtle boost in the water's cooling and healing properties:

◆ mint or sage tea
◆ lemon juice
◆ vinegar
◆ two to three drops of the essential oils of Eucalyptus, Peppermint, or Lavender per cup of water (mix thoroughly) for a compress, or ten to fifteen drops in a bath
◆ a tea made from the herbs yarrow or elder

Adding an herbal tea to a bath can be a gentle way to administer an herb to an infant.

To reduce pain and lower the body's thermostat setting, turn to herbal forms of "natural aspirin." The two most prominent herbal aspirins are white willow bark and meadowsweet.

◆ Natural pharmacies carry a number of willow-based remedies. The fresh or dried herb can be used to make a somewhat unpleasant-tasting tea. Many herbalists instead recommend products that are marketed as willow-based aspirin substitutes, some of which are standardized for the salicin content. Follow dosage directions on the label.

The bark of various willow species has long been used for its pain-relieving and fever-reducing properties. The Greeks used willow bark remedies two thousand years ago, and willow was a popular herb for fever among Colonial Americans. It's not clear whether Native Americans knew of it in advance of Europeans, but many tribes were using it by the seventeenth century.

White willow *(Salix alba)* bark, as well as the bark of white or silver poplar, is rich in the glucoside salicin, which in the late nineteenth century was listed in the *U.S. Pharmacopoeia*. The entry was removed in 1926 because natural sources of salicin were quickly being replaced by aspirin, a synthetic compound derived from the chemically related salicylic acid. Natural willow preparations have made something of a comeback in recent years. They act like aspirin to reduce inflammation and fever.

◆ The herb meadowsweet *(Filipendula ulmaria)* is another source of natural salicin. In fact, it was an extract of meadowsweet flower buds that was used by German scientists in the early 1850s to synthesize acetylsalicylic acid (aspirin). The new drug was ignored for fifty years until the folks at the German Bayer company decided it had potential as an arthritis remedy. In the early decades of this century aspirin skyrocketed in popularity.

The dried leaves and flowers of meadowsweet are used to make various herbal preparations, including teas, tinctures, and concentrated drops.

Though herbal meadowsweet and white-willow-bark products have never been linked to Reye's syndrome, these herbs do contain natural salicin, a close chemical relative of the aspirin precursor salicylic acid. Therefore it is best to err on the side of safety and avoid these herbs when children have a fever that may be due to certain viral illnesses, because of the risk of Reye's syndrome.

Take a sweat-inducing herb when a fever is in the safe range but you want to bring it down even more. Some of the more popular fever-reducing diaphoretics include yarrow, elder, and boneset.

◆ Yarrow's wound-healing properties when used externally are more well-known among Western herbalists, but taken as a tea, yarrow is a classic fever remedy especially among the traditional "ayurvedic" medical practitioners of India. Yarrow is often used in combination with elder flower to reduce a fever. Take it in the form of a tea, tincture, or concentrated drops.

◆ Herbalists from the time of ancient Greece onward have made use of the therapeutic properties of the flowers and berries of the elder shrub or tree *(Sambucus canadensis, S. nigra)*. The small, white flowers are rich in bioflavonoids and tannins and, as an infusion, make an excellent diaphoretic. Elder flower is often combined with yarrow to treat fevers, colds, and the flu. The leaves, root, unripe berries, and bark of the elder plant should not be used internally.

◆ Boneset *(Eupatorium perfoliatum)* got its colorful name

because early herbalists used boneset leaf tea to relieve an infectious tropical disease called breakbone fever (dengue). Boneset was also widely used, with some success, during flu epidemics in nineteenth-century America. The herb remains a popular home remedy for relieving colds and the flu and for lowering a fever. Some studies performed by German plant scientists indicate that boneset can boost the body's immunity. Boneset, however, may contain the same kind of liver-damaging pyrrolizidine alkaloids found in comfrey and thus shouldn't be taken internally for an extended period of time.

Oriental Medical Doctor David Eagle warns that diaphoretic herbs should not be used to lower a fever if you are already sweating. Also, discontinue taking a diaphoretic if your body temperature is not coming down. Eagle says, "In such cases you increase the risk of dehydration. Sweating as a mechanism to bring down a fever often works, but if it's obviously not working, quit!

"Also, if you do sweat, it is best to keep yourself warm or stay in bed. You want to avoid feeling chilled while sweating."

Take an herb to boost the immune system and fight the underlying infection. A fever associated with what practitioners of traditional Chinese medicine call a "surface condition," such as a cold or the flu, is often helped by taking immune-boosting herbs. Echinacea, barberry, and garlic are classic immune boosters for such conditions. Hobbs notes that these herbs can be used by themselves or in conjunction with other immune-boosting herbs, such as astragalus, ligustrum, and reishi, that are often better for conditions associated with long-term or profound deficiencies, such as cancer or chronic fatigue syndrome.

◆ Echinacea helps stabilize body temperature by stimulating white blood cells that fight infection and enhancing the body's ability to dispose of bacteria and harmful chemicals.
◆ Along with goldenseal, barberry *(Berberis vulgaris)* and its close relative Oregon grape *(Berberis aquifolium)* are prominent berberine-containing plants. Berberine is a potent antibiotic. Animal studies have shown that berberine also has a fever-reducing effect that is three times as potent as aspirin's. The mechanism may be an increased activation of the white blood cells.

Barberry root bark preparations are potentially toxic when taken in large quantities or for long periods of time; children under two years old and pregnant women should not use barberry.

◆ Garlic is another favorite folk remedy for treating colds and the flu and for boosting the body's infection-fighting powers. Some scientific studies suggest that the sulfides in garlic work in a way that is similar to penicillin and the sulfa drugs to counter the growth of bacteria.

Wrap cool, wet compresses around the person's calves. Some practitioners of hydrotherapy (water therapy) say that this technique is more effective than sponging down the entire body. Soak two cotton cloths or dish towels in cold water and wring slightly. Apply the cloths over and around the person's calves, covering the area between the ankle and knee. Do both legs at the same time. Leave on for about twenty minutes and repeat the procedure.

Naturopaths warn that this technique is appropriate to use only if the person's feet are warm before the treatment begins. As a general rule cold water should not be applied to parts of the body that are already cold.

Use homeopathic remedies to assist the body's natural healing powers. Many homeopaths will refrain from prescribing a homeopathic remedy at the start of a fever. That's because the fever itself is a remedy of sorts and because an early prescription "may confuse the remedy picture." When reducing a fever is appropriate, however, homeopath Jennifer Jacobs, M.D., notes that homeopathic remedies can play an important medical role. Here are the principal ones to choose from:

◆ *Belladonna.* This is the most common homeopathic remedy for reducing a simple fever that is fairly high, often 103–104°. The candidate for *Belladonna* has a flushed, hot face, red lips, dilated pupils, dry skin, and cold extremities.

Though skeptical about homeopathy, a Massachusetts counselor and mother was recently convinced of that system's effectiveness after administering *Belladonna* to her three-year-old son. She says, "My boy was into the second day of a virulent flu going around the neighborhood. He had the classic symptoms of the *Belladonna* patient: extremely hot to the touch, red in the face, and an uncomfortably high fever. He was alternately listless and agitated and seemed to be on the verge of febrile convulsions. After checking with a homeopathic physician, I gave my son five pellets of *Belladonna* 30X. Within a matter of minutes he stopped crying, became more calm, and wanted to play. The fever had peaked, and by the nexxt day he was back to his normal rambunctious self."

◆ *Aconite*. This is helpful for mild fevers (101–102°) triggered by exposure to cold and extreme stress, and in the early stages of a condition that comes on suddenly and intensely. The person is often thirsty and may be anxious, restless, and fearful.

◆ *Pulsatilla*. Use this for the tearful, clinging child who seems to crave affection. The fever is mild, but rises at night, and the person feels worse in warm rooms. The person is not usually thirsty.

◆ *Ferrum phos*. Try this for fevers that have come on slowly. The person's symptoms are less intense than those that would call for *Aconite* or *Belladonna*. The condition is made better by cold applications.

Check out your natural foods pharmacy section for combination homeopathic fever remedies such as Natra-Bio Fever Tincture.

Apply healing acupressure massage to a point just above the tip of the shoulder blade. Acupressure Institute founder Michael Reed Gach says, "For self-care, take your left hand and reach around to your right shoulder. Find and press on the knotted area about midway between the base of the neck and the outside of the shoulders. With your right hand use your thumb to press against the fingers of the same hand, thus stimulating the base of the nail of each finger. Working on the shoulder and the hands like this combines to lower body temperature."

To help reduce a fever, some practitioners of traditional Chinese medicine also advise manipulating a point on the bladder meridian at the base of the small toe, or a point on the kidney meridian three finger-widths above the ankle bone on the inside of the leg.

Take nutritional supplements that can improve the body's infection-fighting powers and thus remove the underlying cause of the fever. A good choice is an "insurance level" multivitamin and mineral program that includes the eleven vitamins, four minerals, and three trace elements for which the federal government has determined there are recommended dietary allowances (RDAs). Many supplement companies offer insurance-level, "one-a-day" formulas, though in most cases the pills or capsules are meant to be taken up to six times per day. Such supplementation often exceeds the RDAs, thus providing greater protection against marginal nutrient deficiencies.

If you're not taking an insurance level of vitamins and minerals, consider adding some of the following:

- vitamin A in the form of beta carotene, 15,000–25,000 IU daily, to fight infection and strengthen the immune system
- vitamin B complex, 50–100 mg daily
- riboflavin, 50–300 mg daily (fevers and other illnesses can increase the need for this B vitamin)
- niacin, 25–300 mg daily (prolonged fever can lead to a niacin deficiency)
- vitamin C plus mixed bioflavonoids, 250–1,000 mg per hour, up to five grams daily or to bowel tolerance (pregnant women should avoid megadoses of vitamin C)

During a fever caused by an infection you should avoid taking supplements that contain iron. The extra iron gets released into the tissues as the body attempts to lower the fever. Many bacteria actually need iron to grow in the body, so you want to limit their supply.

Take the Chinese prepared-medicine Chuan Xin Lian Antiphlogistic Pills. Produced by the United Pharmaceutical Manufactory of Guangzhou, China, this medicine is sold thirty-six or one hundred tablets to the bottle, and the recommended dosage to lower a fever is two to three pills three times daily.

Chuan Xin Lian Antiphlogistic Pills is a traditional remedy used to "clear heat" and reduce inflammation such as that which accompanies common colds and the flu. Antiphlogistic (which means acting against inflammation or fever) Pills are a combination of three Chinese herbs, primarily the febrifuge andrographis. Chinese researchers have found that this formula has pronounced cooling and antibacterial effects. Oriental Medical Doctor Holly Eagle says, "This is a wonderful and readily available over-the-counter fever remedy."

Chinese prepared medicines are available at Oriental pharmacies and by mail order from herbal distributors (see "Resources").

Eat fresh star fruit twice a day. Star fruit is the food that comes highly recommended by practitioners of traditional Chinese medicine. They say that the fruit has "cold qualities" that help it to reduce a fever, relieve the cough of a common cold, and promote urination. Other foods used by the Chinese to reduce a fever include cucumbers, muskmelon, and water chestnut.

Finally, here are a few fever-lowering folk remedies and suggestions.

- ◆ Apply compresses of onion and vinegar combined, or peeled garlic cloves, on the stomach or bind them to the bottoms of the feet.
- ◆ Visualize being frozen solid in the middle of a giant ice cube, being caught outside naked in a raging snowstorm, or other chilling ideas.
- ◆ Clear the bowels. Constipation can sometimes be a factor in keeping the body's temperature up.

RECOVERY FROM HIGH FEVER

High fever is similar to heat illness in its effects on the body. After an episode of either it is important to rehydrate and reestablish optimal nutrient levels in the body's blood and cells (many people find that they crave raw fruits and vegetables). See the suggestions under "Recovering from Heat Illnesses" in Chapter 17.

NINETEEN

Muscle and Joint Injuries

THIS CHAPTER COVERS:

♦ *cramps*
♦ *strains, ruptures, and sprains*

SEE "CHAPTER 7: BONE INJURIES" FOR:

♦ *dislocations*

SEE "CHAPTER 10: CONTUSIONS" FOR:

♦ *bruise*

SEE "CHAPTER 17: HEAT ILLNESS" FOR:

♦ *heat cramps*

The body's intricate system of interconnecting bones is held together—and moved—by durable tissues including the muscles, tendons, and ligaments. The muscles are made up of long fibers containing special elongated cells that, through a series of complex biochemical reactions, can expand and contract to produce movement. The tapered end of a muscle where it is attached to a bone is the tendon. Ligaments are the tough, fibrous tissue that connects bone to bone, thus holding joints together. Overuse or the sudden twisting or stretching of a muscle, tendon, or ligament may cause the many separate fibers of these tissues to tear or snap. The resulting injury benefits from immediate treatment.

Injuries to the muscles and joints range from those that are relatively easily treated, such as stiff, aching muscles and tendinitis (in which a tendon becomes inflamed, often from repeated use, as with "tennis elbow") to much more serious traumas. Joint dislocations, for instance, require professional medical response in almost all cases (see "Chapter 7: Bone Injuries"). The most common muscle and ligament injuries include:

- cramps, a sudden, involuntary, and painful tightening of a muscle
- muscle strains (also known as pulled muscles), an over-stretching and partial tearing of a muscle or tendon
- ruptured muscles, a complete tearing of a muscle
- ruptured or severed tendons, in which a tendon is ripped away from a bone, or the muscle away from the tendon, either from a deep cut or a sudden force
- sprains, an overstretching, or partial or complete tearing of the fibers, of the ligaments around a joint

We'll consider the strains, ruptures, and sprains together in this chapter, as the first-aid response is similar for all three.

◆ Cramps

The muscles need just the right combination of bodily chemicals, oxygen, and blood to work strongly and efficiently. After strenuous exercise or after a huge meal that pulls a large amount of blood to the gut to do the work of digestion, muscles may be denied proper nutrients or waste disposal. Two possible results are cramps, in which the muscles contract involuntarily and don't immediately respond to your mental command of "Relax!" and spasms, in which the muscles undergo a series of relatively brief contractions alternating with relaxations.

Almost everybody experiences muscle cramps or spasms occasionally in the abdomen, arms, neck, back, or other areas of the body. Cramps frequently strike at night after you've performed some kind of strenuous exertion during the day. The legs are a favorite target, with muscles in the calves or feet suddenly knotting up into a tight, painful ball. Muscle contractions are also common as a result of sitting or standing in an uncomfortable position for an extended period (meditators new to the cross-legged position are likely to get cramps). Muscles that are cold or tired are more likely to develop cramps.

Cramps during the day that are not associated with overexertion may be from exercising soon after eating. Just jumping into frigid water may be enough to cause cramps. Abdominal cramps may be a sign of bowel disease, poor digestion, or food poisoning.

Cramps are sometimes an indication of a cardiovascular or circulatory problem. In addition cramps can be a symptom of a variety of conditions, including:

- dehydration or heat exhaustion (see "Chapter 17: Heat Illness")
- a reaction to certain medications, including diuretic drugs used for high blood pressure
- nutritional imbalances, including a deficiency of potassium, vitamin E, or zinc; an excess of protein intake, which can cause the blood to become overly acid; and an improper ratio of calcium/magnesium intake
- alcoholism
- anemia
- arthritis
- a thyroid condition
- certain rare muscle diseases

The vast majority of cramps (especially those that strike the legs) are temporarily painful but otherwise not harmful to your health. Most cramps clear up naturally within five minutes. Even at their most benign, however, muscle cramps are a signal that you should make changes to promote better circulation and feeding of oxygen and nutrients to the muscles, establish more balanced exercise patterns, and avoid fatigue or stress.

Many elderly people suffer from frequent muscle cramps. Contact a medical professional if your cramps appear regularly, cause severe pain, or last for longer than thirty minutes or so.

BASIC FIRST AID FOR CRAMPS

If you get a cramp while performing some kind of physical activity, the first step in treating it is to stop running or swimming, for instance. Slowing to a walk for five to ten minutes will often allow the cramp to disappear on its own.

Stretching and massaging the muscle are also likely to speed the loosening up of the cramped area. Stretching needs to be done with a degree of caution, since it's possible for a cramped muscle to more easily get strained if it is stretched too forcefully. Toes can usually be uncramped by pulling up on them and pointing them toward the knee. For a side stitch that occurs while running, try bending over slightly while pressing your fingers into the area of the cramp, inhaling deeply, and exhaling through pursed lips. Then raise your hand over your head on the affected side to stretch the abdomen.

Massage can encourage blood flow and help to relax a cramped muscle. Use firm, steady strokes both on the cramp itself and over the length of the affected muscle or group of muscles. For a cramp in the foot, massage the entire leg. Start with stretching, gliding, and kneading strokes and then use the side of the palms to make chopping strokes as the muscle begins to relax. For a cramped calf muscle, sit down and take ahold of your foot with one hand, pulling the toes toward the knee. Bend the cramped leg at the knee so that you can massage the calf muscle with the other hand.

In almost all cases, rest, stretching, and massage will alleviate a cramp. For persistent or recurrent cramps, you can take the further step of applying heat. Warm, wet compresses, a heating pad, or a hot-water bottle applied to the area of cramping can help you to restore blood flow and circulation to the area. Heat relaxes muscles and lowers the sensitivity of nerves. Heat, along with massage, is an effective preventive step if you have frequent cramps in one area of your body.

Make a hot wet compress by soaking a cotton towel in hot water or soaking a towel and then heating it in a microwave; wring slightly before applying. Cover the compress with a piece of plastic and a dry towel to retain heat.

To use a hot-water bottle, fill it halfway with hot or boiling water. Lay it flat to put the cap on so that it doesn't hold a lot of air. Cover it with a towel if it is too hot for the skin. A child's skin is more sensitive to heat than an adult's, so be careful with children. Heat treatments in general need to be closely monitored to prevent burns.

Over-the-counter warming liniments work for some people, though in many cases the cramp is too deep to benefit. Liniments include mentholated creams such as Ben-Gay, as well as natural products such as Tiger Balm and White Flower Analgesic Balm, the Chinese prepared medicine Zheng Gu Shui, and Breezy Balms Warm Up Rub (see "Natural First-Aid Remedies for Contusions" in Chapter 10). These shouldn't be applied along with a heating pad, or covered with a wrapping, since that could result in a burn. Heating ointments should also be patch-tested to prevent skin irritations.

If you get a cramp while swimming, take a deep breath and roll to a facedown position in the water. Grasp and knead the cramp firmly with one or both hands, applying vigorous pressure if necessary to relax the muscle.

NATURAL FIRST-AID REMEDIES FOR CRAMPS

Here are some techniques to try along with the basic steps to help alleviate persistent cramps.

Apply acupressure to the point on the upper lip, two-thirds of the way up from the upper lip to the nose. "This first-aid revival point has traditionally been used for cramps," acupressure authority Michael Reed Gach says. "You can also hold the cramping muscle. First just lightly knead it with a light finger pressure. Slowly the muscle will release and you can go in deeper. Once the muscle has completely relaxed, hold points at different depths to prevent a further spasm."

Do deep breathing to help relieve a cramp in the diaphragm. Purse the lips, take a deep breath, and exhale with force. Repeat this cycle until the cramping stops. This breathing exercise can also help to prevent cramps by warming up the diaphragm before exercising.

Apply the herb arnica, in any of its many forms, to the site of the cramp. Herbal concentrates and tinctures of arnica are more widely available than either the whole fresh plant or dried flowers. Apply five to ten drops of the concentrate directly to the cramp. Dilute the tincture before applying to the skin by mixing approximately one tablespoon of tincture per pint of cold water.

A small minority of individuals may experience an allergic reaction to arnica, so test it first on a small patch of skin. Also, don't apply it to broken skin, which increases the chance of irritation.

This premier bruise herb, long recommended by herbalists and homeopaths to alleviate the effects of shock and trauma on the muscles, can also help relax a cramped muscle.

Homeopathic manufacturers use arnica to make both ointments, lotions, and tinctures for external application and pills for internal consumption. Though the least-diluted topical homeopathic *Arnica* remedy is usually 1X (a ten percent solution), the same external warning applies as for the herbal preparation: don't use *Arnica* tincture on broken skin; the alcohol in the base material may be irritating to a cut or abrasion. Spread some of the ointment or lotion on a cramp. Dilute a tincture in water as you would an herbal preparation, and apply with a cold compress.

Take the homeopathic remedy Cuprum metallicum *to help relieve cramps of the calves, legs, and feet.* Made from copper, this is one of the most commonly recommended homeopathic remedies for cramps. The *Cuprum metallicum* person often has cold extremities, looks pale and drawn, and may suffer from mental exhaustion. The cramps sometimes follow a period of heavy work.

Homeopathic manufacturers produce a number of combination remedies for relief of minor muscular cramps.

Try a traditional cramp-relieving folk remedy. Here are a few of our favorites:

◆ Relieve a leg cramp by applying a metal spoon to it.
◆ Relieve a foot cramp by pressing on the front and back of the nail of the big toe.
◆ Apply an onion poultice to a cramp. Chop up an onion, add some salt, and place the mixture onto the skin. If that's too messy for you, put the onion between two layers of cheesecloth or a light cotton cloth, tape or secure to the body, and cover with plastic to keep moist. Folk healers praise onions for their ability to remove toxins and congestion under the skin.
◆ Use an Epsom salts pack. To relieve a muscle cramp, dissolve an ounce of Epsom salts in a quart of hot water, soak a hand towel, wring slightly, and apply to the cramp.

Epsom salts is a white, crystalline product (purified magnesium sulfate) named after the town in England where it was first identified some five hundred years ago. Epsom salts has been a popular folk remedy ever since, externally for stiff joints and aching muscles, and (less common today) internally as a laxative. It is widely available in pharmacies.

◆ Strains, Ruptures, and Sprains

Athletes are frequent victims of strains, ruptures, and sprains. The twisting, jumping, and sudden starts and turns of sports are tailor-made to cause injuries to the muscles and joints.

All of these injuries can cause pain, swelling, bruising, and some loss of function, so differentiating among them can sometimes be difficult. The extent of swelling, in addition, is not a reliable indicator of an injury's severity. Swelling is often more a function of how rapidly an injury was treated with ice than how badly torn a muscle or ligament is.

Keep in mind that strains and ruptures affect muscles and tendons. The cause may be overuse or an excessive stretch, resulting in pain, swelling, bruising, and gradual stiffening of the area. A strained (or pulled) muscle usually still functions, though with pain. If a tendon is ruptured, expect that there will be some loss of ability to make a characteristic motion.

Sprains affect ligaments, so the pain, swelling, and bruising is around a joint area. A sprain usually follows a forceful fall, sudden wrenching movement, or other trauma. In some cases a trauma may cause a muscle strain in addition to a sprain. A sprained joint often still works somewhat, though it is tender to the touch and movement causes considerable pain. Except in the most severe cases of complete tearing of ligament fibers, the joint does not appear deformed or misshapen. A sprain loosens a joint, so there's often excessive motion associated with the joint when it is stretched or manipulated.

Even trained medical professionals can have difficulty telling the difference between some sprains and fractures. A sprained wrist, for example, usually needs to be x-rayed to determine whether it is broken. It is always best to treat a sprain as if it is a break if you're not sure. You can sometimes tell by gently pressing on the bones around the injured joint, listening and feeling for the sound of broken bones rubbing together. Also, a fractured or dislocated body part is sometimes visibly deformed or out of place. A fractured foot in most cases will be too painful to walk on, while a sprained ankle or foot can bear some weight, with pain. If you can hold a cup of tea in your hand after an injury, your wrist may be sprained, but it's probably not broken. (See Chapter 7 for first aid for fractures and dislocations.)

Whenever a severe strain or sprain seems unimproved after twenty-four hours, consult with a medical professional. Call for emergency help if:

- ◆ the person is in tremendous pain
- ◆ a body part or joint is not working properly
- ◆ the injury area is misshapen
- ◆ there is numbness, tingling, or some other sign of impaired circulation beyond the injured area
- ◆ a fracture or dislocation is suspected

Emergency room treatment of strains, ruptures, and sprains usually focuses on the physical exam to determine the exact extent of tearing or rupturing. X rays are common, and the person is often given analgesics for pain. Further treatment may include casts or splints to immobilize the area, and physical therapy. Surgery is required to reconnect the two ends of a ruptured tendon and may be suggested to repair ruptured muscles or badly torn ligaments.

RICE: THE BASIC TREATMENT FOR STRAINS, RUPTURES, AND SPRAINS

Tearing and twisting injuries to the muscles, tendons, and ligaments are treated in a similar fashion. The principal steps are summarized by the acronym RICE, for rest, ice, compression, and elevation. The RICE treatment will help limit the immediate pain, swelling, and internal bleeding.

Rest. Immobilizing an injured muscle or ligament helps to control bleeding. If possible, surround the injury with pillows, towels, or rolled-up blankets and keep it still for the first day. Depending upon the severity of a sprain, it may benefit from an extended period of rest. Immobilize a sprained finger or toe by taping it to the digit next to it. If necessary, you can immobilize a sprained shoulder, ankle, or elbow using a sling. (See Chapter 7 for instructions on how to make basic slings.)

Ice. Applying cold immediately to a muscle or joint injury is the most important of the RICE steps. Cold is an effective pain-killer, numbing the area and preventing nerves from sending pain messages to the brain. Cold also constricts local blood vessels, stems internal bleeding, and reduces the release of histamines, thus further limiting inflammation. By keeping swelling in check, cold overcomes a major impediment to quick healing, since inflammation tends to restrict movement in the injured area, allowing muscles and joints to become stiff.

Remove clothing or jewelry from around an injured joint and apply ice to the injury as quickly as possible, preferably within minutes of the trauma.

You can safely apply ice in a variety of forms. The easiest way is to immerse the injury in ice water. You can also make an ice pack by putting some crushed ice in a plastic bag and wrapping it in a towel or cloth. A bag of frozen corn from the freezer makes a handy instant ice pack. Health product companies offer a number of flexible cold packs that are cooled in a freezer and are reusable. For a portable first-aid kit, you can include instant cold packs such as 3M's Cold Comfort. These are activated by breaking open chemical packets inside a plastic covering. They last fifteen to twenty minutes and are used only once.

Apply ice to the injury for fifteen to twenty minutes, then take the cold off for the same length of time. Reapply for another twenty minutes every three to four hours for the first twenty-four hours, or until there are no further signs of inflammation.

Be careful not to overdo cold, since there's always the possibility of causing frostbite or tissue damage. Never put ice directly on the skin. You want the area to become slightly numb and reddish, but not white, a sign that circulation has been too severely restricted. Cold also shouldn't be used on victims who have impaired circulation, cardiovascular disease, or diabetes.

Compression. Wrapping a strain or sprain with an elastic bandage offers support to the injury and prevents further bleeding and swelling. You can use strips of cloth, the well-known Ace brand bandage, or others such as the Coban Action Wrap. To avoid cutting off circulation, don't wrap the injury too tightly. If the sprain is to the wrist or ankle, leave the fingers or toes exposed and check periodically for tingling, numbness, loss of motion, or blue skin, all signs of inadequate circulation. Use a figure-eight pattern to compress an ankle sprain (see illustration #18). If the bandage is too tight, take it off for fifteen minutes and reapply. Keep the area wrapped for three to four days.

Elevation. For an arm or leg with a strain or sprain, lie down and elevate the injured part above heart level. This helps to drain blood and fluids from the muscle or joint and thus reduce swelling.

Recovery. The RICE technique will usually limit pain and swelling such that the injury is improving after twenty-four hours. If not, check with your medical professional. Even if the initial treatment has worked well, for the next few days you should avoid walking on a sprained ankle, for instance, if it causes even minor pain.

If the pain and swelling have begun to subside after the first twenty-four to forty-eight hours, you can switch from cold to warm applications. (See heating suggestions under the section on "Basic First Aid for Cramps.") Apply heat to the injury for twenty minutes every three to four hours, or as often as possible for the next few days.

Pain and swelling are usually reduced enough after twenty-four to forty-eight hours to allow gentle movement of the injured part. You can help ease the first movements by placing the injury in a bath or basin filled with warm water, or by applying hot

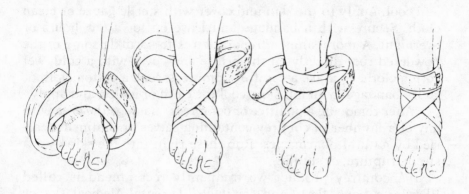

Illustration #18:

Apply an Ace-type bandage in a figure-eight pattern to compress an ankle sprain and prevent swelling.

compresses, and then doing gentle, range-of-motion exercises. Move the part up to the point it causes pain, but no farther. Do this three times a day until normal movement has returned. If the injury starts to swell again, go back to ice, elevation, and compression.

Once the pain has subsided enough to allow normal movement, you still have to be careful not to reinjure the muscle or ligament. Strains and sprains can cause tissue fibers to become loose or stretched, making the muscle or joint unstable. Refrain from overexerting an injured muscle or joint as long as pain remains. Make your return to activity gradual. Even minor muscle strains can take two weeks to heal. You may not want to run on a severely sprained ankle for three weeks or longer. It can take up to six months for a badly torn ligament to regain its normal strength.

NATURAL FIRST-AID REMEDIES FOR STRAINS, RUPTURES, AND SPRAINS

Natural remedies can boost the healing process by preventing inflammation, increasing circulation, and reducing pain at the site of muscle and joint injuries.

Apply a comfrey poultice or compress to the injured muscle or joint. To make a comfrey poultice, mix three tablespoons of powdered root with three ounces of hot water. Stir into a paste and cool. Apply to the skin and cover with sterile gauze or clean cloth. Secure with a bandage and leave on for a few hours or overnight. A more simple preparation is to sprinkle some of the powdered root directly on the bruise and cover with a cold, wet cotton cloth. To make a comfrey compress, soak a cotton cloth or gauze bandage in an infusion, cool the cloth or gauze, and apply.

After removing a poultice or compress, massage the area with any of a number of comfrey-containing salves or ointments carried by natural pharmacies. Rub these right into the skin over a strain, rupture, or sprain.

"A comfrey product we frequently recommend is called BF&C, for bone, flesh, and cartilage," Oriental Medical Doctor David Eagle says. "It's based on a formula by the herbal and naturopathic pioneer Dr. John R. Christopher. Nature's Way of Springville, Utah, makes it in ointment and capsule form." The ointment formula combines comfrey with olive oil, beeswax, and Peppermint oil. In capsules BF&C contains slippery elm, calendula, white oak bark, and other herbs. The comfrey is left out of the capsule product because of the concern that the pyrrolizidine alkaloids in comfrey are potentially harmful when taken internally.

Allantoin, an active ingredient in comfrey, promotes the growth of new cells and reduces inflammation. Allantoin is easily absorbed through the skin and penetrates deeply, where it particularly promotes the activity of cells that produce connective tissue.

Apply herbal or homeopathic arnica externally to the injury three to four times per day. Arnica's deep-seated action on the muscles is helpful for strains and sprains. (See the section "Natural First-Aid Remedies for Cramps.")

Take oral doses of an appropriate homeopathic remedy. Homeopaths recommend:

◆ *Arnica.* This is the best first remedy for a strain or sprain, especially if the injury was accompanied by much bruising or shock.
◆ *Rhus tox.* This is a popular sprain remedy, often used after *Arnica. Rhus tox* is the rusty-gate remedy: the injury is still painful, especially on initial movement, but feels better after the joint is warmed up. *Rhus tox* is also helpful for relieving the pain of muscle strains due to overexertion.

Use acupressure to relieve the pain of a sprained wrist, hand, or ankle. For a wrist or hand sprain, acupressure expert Michael

Reed Gach says to feel around the wrist crease for hollow areas between the bones and tendons. "When you find a hollow area, press firmly. The point that will be the most effective when pressed will connect with the pain from the sprain."

Use the same approach for a sprained ankle, Gach suggests. "Feel for the hollow in the ankle and then press on the spot firmly." Gach notes that another point that works especially well right after an ankle sprain is in the large hollow directly in front of the large outer ankle bone. He says, "Pressing on this point works like a charm to relieve pain and swelling and strengthen the joint."

To help speed recovery from a strain or sprain, take brome-lain. Take 200–300 mg at the time of the injury, and 500–700 mg per day, between meals, for three to four days afterward.

Bromelain is a natural enzyme derived from the pineapple plant. In addition to assisting digestion, bromelain is now being used for a variety of conditions, including sports injuries. Clinical studies have demonstrated that bromelain has anti-inflammatory and wound-healing properties. One hypothesis is that bromelain helps break down fibrin, a blood protein central to the clotting process. This allows for better tissue drainage and reduces localized pain and swelling.

Bromelain is available in 100-mg tablets from a number of supplement manufacturers. The product Quercetin Plus with Bromelain, available from Doctor's Best of San Clemente, California, combines the anti-inflammatory powers of bromelain with those of the bioflavonoid quercetin. Follow dosage directions on the label.

"If you really want to boost the healing powers of bromelain," Joseph Pizzorno, N.D., suggests, "along with it take some curcumin, the yellow pigment from the spice turmeric. By adding curcumin you get a much better anti-inflammatory response than when using bromelain by itself."

An East Indian plant of the ginger family, turmeric (*Curcuma longa*) has long been used by practitioners of ayurveda (the traditional healing system of India) and traditional Chinese medicine internally as a digestive aid and topically as a wound healer and anti-inflammatory remedy. Herbalists say it is especially effective for treating sprains, cramps, and muscle pain. In ancient times a potent household remedy was to make a poultice from turmeric mixed with slaked lime (calcium hydroxide).

Plant researchers have determined that an alcoholic extract of the turmeric root is as effective as cortisone for acute inflammation, though somewhat less so for chronic inflammation. A number of herbal companies offer tablets or concentrated herbal drops of turmeric that are high in curcumin. Pizzorno recommends taking with bromelain 250–500 mg of curcumin from turmeric between meals.

Take an immediate megadose of vitamin C plus bioflavonoids. To help recover from a serious muscle or joint injury, immediately take three to four grams of C plus 300–1,000 mg of bioflavonoids. An optimal ongoing daily dose is two to five grams of C plus bioflavonoids, in mixed doses, or to bowel tolerance.

Vitamin C helps form collagen, a fibrous protein found in connective tissue, bone, and the walls of blood vessels. Collagen helps hold the body's cells together. Without it, blood vessels become weak and fragile, making it much easier for blood to leak into the surrounding tissues and cause bruises. The bioflavonoids have an anti-inflammatory effect. They also play an important role in wound healing, tissue repair, and bleeding control. Like vitamin C the bioflavonoids are valuable antioxidants as well, helping to control harmful free radicals after an injury.

Use essential fatty acids to help keep inflammation to a minimum. Sources of beneficial EFAs include:

◆ fatty, cold-water fish such as salmon, cod, mackerel, sardines, bluefish, herring, and tuna, and oil supplements made from these fish
◆ canola, flaxseed, and hemp oil
◆ evening primrose, borage, and black-currant oil

"The omega-3 and omega-6 essential fatty acids are particularly good to take after any joint injury," says nutritionist Shari Lieberman. "They work very much like the pharmaceutical drugs prednisone or cortisone to prevent swelling and decrease inflammation. EFAs may even help prevent arthritis from eventually developing in the joint."

Apply the Chinese prepared medicine Wan Hua, a circulatory booster. Herbalist Christopher Hobbs says, "This is an oil that's good for any type of strains or sprains." It's also a popular contusion remedy (see "Chapter 10: Contusions"). Wan Hua contains ginseng, calamus, and other herbs; it does not provide as much local heat as Tiger Balm and other liniments. Wan Hua is sold in 15-ml bottles as Die Da Wan Hua You ("myriad flowers impact trauma oil") by the United Pharmaceutical Manufactory in Guangzhou, China.

Try one of the following strain- and sprain-relieving folk remedies. These may work for you.

- ◆ Peel an orange, apply the white side of the peel to the injury, and tape or hold it in place with a bandage to help reduce swelling.
- ◆ Apply equal amounts of ginger juice and sesame oil.
- ◆ Pack some slices of onion around a sprained ankle or finger to prevent or reduce swelling.
- ◆ Beat together a tablespoon of honey, a tablespoon of salt, and the white of one egg, apply to a sprain, and cover.
- ◆ Apply to the injury a mix of one tablespoon of olive oil and five to ten drops of the essential oil of Wintergreen, and cover.
- ◆ Mix the common spice turmeric with water or some egg white and apply it to the skin. This is an effective poultice but does have the drawback of staining lighter skin yellow.
- ◆ Massage a paste of cider vinegar and sea salt into a muscle or joint injury.
- ◆ Turn to tofu. Leah Fineberg, an acupuncturist and athlete from Santa Fe, says, "I treat a lot of sports injuries. For any minor sprain, bump, or bruise, apply cool, fresh tofu. As it warms or turns yellow, apply a fresh slice. The tofu draws out the heat and is much more effective than ice. My softball team always keeps tofu in the cooler."
- ◆ Massage a paste that is two parts aloe gel and one part each goldenseal, comfrey root, and slippery elm into the injury.
- ◆ Apply wheat germ oil to the injury.

PREVENTING AND RECOVERING FROM MUSCLE AND JOINT INJURIES

Cramps and strains that occur during exercise or sports activities can often be prevented by warming up and stretching the muscles before strenuous exertion. Stiff, inactive muscles register a temperature of 98° or so. Just five minutes of stretching and moving gently can raise the muscles' temperature to 101°, increasing circulation and helping to relax them. Heat applications, whether from vigorous rubbing, a whirlpool bath, or hot compresses, can have a similar beneficial effect. Warming up and stretching are especially important to prevent reinjuring a previously sprained ankle or strained muscle, for instance.

Avoiding extremely cold substances, whether applied to the skin or taken internally, after exercising can also help prevent cramps. Oriental Medical Doctor Holly Eagle says, "If you're still hot from exertion, don't take a liquid right out of the refrigerator and drink it or drink something with a lot of ice in it or eat ice cream. From the Chinese perspective, cold causes constriction and sluggish circulation of blood and energy in the body and thus can lead to cramps."

Since sprains tend to be more accidental in nature, it may be worthwhile to take some time after an accident to consider how inadequate training, poor technique, or lousy equipment may have contributed to the injury.

Muscles benefit from healthy circulation, so anything that improves overall circulation can play a preventive role, while heavy smoking or other activities that adversely affect circulation may contribute to muscle injuries.

Help prevent muscle cramps by drinking sufficient water while exercising, and by not working a muscle to the point of exhaustion. If you have frequent cramps in the legs at night, raising the foot of the bed a few inches may help prevent cramps by discouraging blood from pooling in the legs.

A growing number of European runners, bikers, and other athletes recommend the homeopathic combination-remedy Sportenine, produced by Boiron, to help prevent exercise-related cramps and muscle aches. Fans of Sportenine, which is widely available in natural foods stores in the United States, say that the remedy helps eliminate lactic acid buildup in the muscles. Lactic acid is a byproduct of muscle metabolism that contributes to fatigue. Sportenine comes in tablets that contain the homeopathic remedies *Arnica* 9C, *Sarcolacticum* 6X, and *Zincum* 6X.

There are a wide variety of herbs that can be part of a program to prevent cramps and to help a person recover from injuries to the muscles, tendons, and ligaments. Herbalists knowledgeable about sports medicine frequently recommend the following as oral remedies that can help boost recovery, strengthen ligaments, and regenerate connective tissues:

◆ Siberian ginseng or eleuthero, the noted adaptogen, can be used to counter lactic acid buildup in the muscles, to increase oxygen use, and to improve energy storage in the muscles. Taken internally it reestablishes balance in the body. (Follow dosage directions on labels.)

◆ Ginkgo, the ancient tree species whose leaves and fruits have medicinal properties, can be taken to improve circulation. Take 40 mg three times daily of the standardized extract containing 24 percent ginkgo heterosides.

- Horsetail, a traditional European remedy that is one of the best herbal sources for collagen-building silicon and other trace minerals, can be used to relieve joint pain. A popular horsetail extract is Alta Sil•X Silica, produced by Alta Health Products in Pasadena, California; suggested use is one to three 500-mg tablets daily with meals.
- Nettles, a plant that in the field has stiff stinging hairs that some people touch to relieve their arthritis, can be used to reduce inflammation. Herbal companies offer a variety of powdered and liquid nettle remedies; follow dosage directions on labels.

A valuable general practice to prevent muscle and ligament injuries, suggests naturopath Joe Pizzorno, is to eat a lot of cherries, blueberries, raspberries, and blackberries. Scientists have found that the compounds that give these berries their deep blue-red color can improve the strength and integrity of muscles, blood vessels, and bones.

You can also prevent cramps and help sprains and strains heal by taking the following nutrients:

- Calcium and magnesium in balance (for instance, 1,500 mg calcium and 750 mg magnesium) help repair bone and connective tissue and prevent cramps that usually occur at night. Joe Pizzorno, N.D., says, "Magnesium deficiency is a common and often unrecognized cause of muscle cramps. Magnesium is lost through the sweat, and many peoples' diets contain inadequate amounts of magnesium. One reason is that those who exercise a lot tend to be afraid of fat, and the richest source of magnesium is nuts and seeds, which some people avoid because of the high fat content. If a person is having a lot of cramps, I may recommend about four ounces of nuts and seeds, or about four hundred milligrams of supplemental magnesium, per day. Magnesium is especially helpful for men over the age of forty who exercise because a lack of magnesium has been tied to cardiac failure from a spasm of the coronary artery." Other reliable food sources of magnesium include soybeans, avocados, and black-eyed peas. There have been no known cases of magnesium toxicity caused by a supplement.
- Vitamin E, 400–800 IU daily (increase dosage gradually), relieves cramps in legs. One medical study found that vitamin E provided almost complete relief for 103 out of 105 patients with nighttime leg and foot cramps.

◆ Potassium (250–500 mg) and magnesium (400 mg) after an intensive workout prevent muscle cramps later on. Some vitamin companies offer these minerals together in potassium magnesium aspartate tablets. "I've used these to prevent muscle cramps with excellent results," says registered dietitian Shari Lieberman. "I particularly recommend it for people who exercise."

◆ Silicon, 2 mg daily, assists in collagen formation and tissue regrowth.

◆ Vitamin D (400–600 IU) and zinc (25–50 mg) stimulate calcium uptake and tissue repair.

◆ Vitamin B complex (50–100 mg) improves circulation.

◆ Vitamin B$_6$ (25–50 mg) helps repair and strengthen tendons and ligaments.

◆ Vitamin C plus bioflavonoids, two to five grams daily in mixed doses or to bowel tolerance, help rebuild collagen, the fibrous protein found in connective tissue.

Many of the above herbs (such as ginkgo) and nutrients (such as vitamins C and E) are effective antioxidants. "Athletes and others who are physically active require a lot of antioxidants, because muscle injuries cause free radicals to form in the body," says Lieberman. Antioxidants combine with and neutralize the free radicals to help reduce swelling and speed recovery. Athletes should take antioxidants before and after heavy exertion.

TWENTY

Poisoning

THIS CHAPTER COVERS:

◆ *chemicals and other toxic substances*
◆ *food poisoning*

SEE "CHAPTER 5: BITES AND STINGS" FOR:

◆ *venomous bites and stings*

SEE "CHAPTER 16: EYE AND EAR EMERGENCIES" FOR:

◆ *chemical and thermal burns of the eyes*

SEE "CHAPTER 21: SKIN EMERGENCIES" FOR:

◆ *poison ivy, oak, and sumac*

Accidental poisonings from drugs, toxic chemicals, contaminated food, and a host of other sources account for an estimated 5 million medical emergencies in the United States annually. Most of the victims are infants and toddlers, and accidental poisoning is a leading cause of childhood death. The good news is that an estimated 80–90 percent of poisoning accidents can be treated successfully at home using a few essential self-care remedies. By being prepared and responding rapidly to an accidental poisoning, you can improve the odds that first-aid treatment will resolve the crisis.

◆ Chemicals and Other Toxic Substances

Ingesting a poisonous substance can have adverse effects on various tissues of the body. Some poisons may do the most damage to the nervous system, while others may burn the esophagus, harm

443

the blood's ability to carry oxygen to tissues, damage the digestive system and the liver, or threaten the immune system.

The main ways that poisons enter the body are:

Through the skin. The bite or sting from a venomous animal injects a poisonous substance into the body (see "Chapter 5: Bites and Stings"). A toxin also enters the body through the skin when a person is sprayed by a poisonous insecticide or pesticide.

Through the lungs. Using toxic cleansers in an enclosed or poorly ventilated place can lead to inhaling poisonous fumes. Some common poisonous fumes include chlorine, ammonia, and natural gas. Symptoms include dizziness, headache, difficulty breathing, nausea, fainting, and pale or bluish skin color.

Carbon monoxide, a natural byproduct of combustion, is an especially dangerous gas because it has no smell or color. It can build up in a house from a poorly maintained heating system, or from using a gas oven for heating purposes. The early symptoms of carbon monoxide poisoning are headache and dizziness, which are followed by shortness of breath, weakness, and possibly coma and death.

Through the digestive tract. Ingesting a toxic substance orally is the most common route a poison takes into the body. The list of potentially poisonous substances is almost endless (one estimate is that there are over 250,000 household products that may be toxic), but about half of all accidental poisonings result from taking one of the following substances:

◆ over-the-counter drugs such as aspirin, acetaminophen, and laxatives
◆ cosmetics and perfumes
◆ household soaps, detergents, disinfectants, and cleansers, including bleach and furniture polish
◆ corrosives, such as oven cleaner and drain cleaner
◆ insecticides, pesticides, and weed killers
◆ vitamins

Colored, candylike vitamins are among the most common agents of childhood poisoning. The fat-soluble vitamins, especially vitamin A, are more toxic than the water-soluble vitamins, such as B complex and C. (Unlike preformed vitamin A from animal sources, the vitamin A precursor beta carotene derived from plants is nontoxic.) The micronutrient responsible for most childhood poisonings, however, is iron. Iron overdose is responsible for about a dozen deaths per year in the United States, usually from children eating their mother's prenatal iron supplements. The iron in multivitamins can also be poisonous to young children who get ahold of a bottle and consume more than a few tablets. Iron ingested in multivitamins accounts for about twenty thousand (nonfatal) poisoning cases annually, according to the federal Centers for Disease Control.

Other common sources of accidental poisoning include alcohol, cigarettes, paints and varnishes, poisonous plants (including philodendron, dieffenbachia, and wisteria) or mushrooms, and automotive products. According to a recent issue of the herb journal *HerbalGram*, although poison control centers nationwide record numerous incidents of plant poisonings, none have ever reported an accidental poisoning due to ingestion of a commercial herbal product.

Accidental poisoning can result from taking legal drugs (amphetamines, depressants, and narcotics) or illegal (cocaine). Drug poisonings are difficult to diagnose since the symptoms vary depending on the drug, how much was taken, and the individual. The person may experience hallucinations, sweating, drowsiness, nausea, seizures, and unconsciousness.

Heavy metals such as lead, mercury, and cadmium are extremely toxic, but only rarely are they responsible for an acute poisoning episode. Much more frequently they are ingested in minute amounts over a long period of time, from polluted air, water, or food. Heavy metals accumulate in brain and other body tissues, eventually compromising the nervous, immune, and other systems.

Most substances that are potentially poisonous carry warnings on the label or package, but not all. Poisoning accidents are more likely to happen in the kitchen or bathroom than in any other room of the house. The "witching hour" of four to six P.M., when parents are distracted with making dinner, and kids are grouchy and overtired, is when most poisonings occur.

The signs of poisoning may be dramatic—an open container and a child with a suspicious liquid or powder on his mouth, skin, or clothing. Often the immediate signs are less clear, and symptoms may take some time to develop. The person may begin to act queerly, become depressed, or suddenly start to vomit. Symptoms vary widely and may be limited to a skin rash or stomach pains. Other possible signs of poisoning include headache, fever, dizziness, nausea, chest pain, seizures, blurred vision, vomiting, and paralysis.

BASIC FIRST AID FOR CHEMICAL POISONING

Here are the most important steps to take to rescue a victim of poisoning. Follow these guidelines regardless of the instructions on a product label. Label information may be wrong or outdated.

When a poison is absorbed through the skin:
Remove the person's clothes and use lots of water to wash any parts of the body exposed to the toxin. Wear rubber gloves to protect yourself from being contaminated by the toxin. Wash affected areas with water for ten minutes or more, positioning the person so that the toxic substance washes off the body rather than onto other areas of the body. (See Chapter 16 for how to flush a toxic substance from the eyes.)

Call for emergency medical help. Keep the person calm and warm while waiting for assistance. Check and monitor airway, breathing, and circulation. See "Chapter 9: Burns" for further treatments of chemical burns to the skin.

When a poison is inhaled:
Rescuing a person who has been overcome by smoke or poisonous fumes is best accomplished by more than one person. The danger, of course, is that the same gas will overcome the rescuer as well. Here are the basic rescue steps:

Call for emergency medical help. When the person may be difficult to reach, you should place the call before you enter the area with the fumes. Alert rescue personnel to the possible need for oxygen. If you can't phone emergency personnel, at least notify others at the scene of the emergency.

Protect your lungs during the rescue. If protective breathing equipment is not available, wet a cloth, wring it slightly, and put it over your nose and mouth. Take several deep breaths before you enter the area with fumes. Try to stay below any visible smoke or fumes. Don't do anything that could ignite a gas, such as striking a match.

Get the person out of the area with fumes as quickly as possible. Supplying fresh air for the poison victim is the top priority, more important even than basic first aid. Carry or drag the person to the nearest exit (see "Chapter 3: Basic Emergency Care" for how to safely transport an injured person). If possible, open windows and doors to disperse poisonous fumes, or cut off fumes from a gas stove or an automobile at the source. This is of secondary importance to removing the victim, however.

When in fresh air, provide basic first aid. Depending on the person's condition, you should loosen any tight clothing on the victim, check the ABCs (airway, breathing, and circulation; see Chapter 3), or put the person in the recovery position. Protect a convulsing person from harming himself (see "Chapter 11: Convulsions and Seizures"). Keep the person warm and calm, and don't offer liquid or food.

Notify a medical professional. Someone who has been overcome by smoke or poisonous fumes should be medically evaluated even if she seems fine. If you haven't yet called for emergency help, do it now.

When a poison is ingested:

Stop the ingestion of poison. If the victim is a child, grab the poisonous substance from him or her and place it out of reach. If necessary, any poison still in a child's mouth should be rinsed out with water. If the poisonous substance is a gas, physically remove the person and cut off the poison at the source if possible.

Check and monitor the ABCs: airway, breathing, and circulation. (See "Chapter 3: Basic Emergency Care.") If the victim is unconscious and not breathing, do CPR (see Chapter 3). If the person is having a seizure, take the necessary protective steps. For instance, loosen the person's clothing and remove dangerous objects from the immediate vicinity (see Chapter 11). If the person is unconscious but breathing, or conscious but drowsy, put him or her in the recovery position and drape with a blanket to keep warm (see Chapter 3).

If the person is unconscious or having seizures, call emergency personnel. If you need to go to the emergency room, bring the container of the poisonous substance (or a sample of what has been vomited up), if possible.

Call your local poison control center even if you only suspect poisoning. The number is in the emergency number section at the front of all phone books. Keep it posted along with other emergency numbers next to your phone. Parents should make sure that baby-sitters know where the number is posted and how to respond to a poisoning emergency.

Be prepared to tell the poison control center staff person the details of the poisoning. What is the substance involved? How much has been ingested? Over what period of time? How old is the victim? What is his health status? Has he vomited? How close is medical help?

Follow the instructions of the poison control center or your medical professional. When possible, you want to remove the poison from the body before it is absorbed. How and when you do that will depend on the answers to the questions just listed. If the person is conscious and not convulsing, you may be advised to do one of the following:

◆ Dilute the poison. This is almost universally helpful. Give the poisoned person one to two glasses of water or milk to be drunk immediately in small sips. The person shouldn't drink it so quickly that he just vomits it back up, since vomiting may be harmful (see below). In certain instances, water may be preferable to milk (such as when the person has swallowed a petroleum product). Never give fluids or anything else orally to an unconscious or convulsing person.

◆ Induce vomiting. For anyone over one year old, the best way to induce vomiting is to give the person one tablespoon of syrup of ipecac (see natural remedies, below) followed by one to two glasses of water. Repeat the dosage in twenty minutes if vomiting does not occur.

Syrup of ipecac is better and more reliable than folk remedies such as eating raw eggs (which does not always induce vomiting and may put the individual at risk for food poisoning) or drinking saltwater. If you don't have syrup of ipecac, induce vomiting physically by placing the person facedown and sticking your fingers down the back of the person's throat. (Holding a child upside down or bent over may help.) Drinking some milk or a few tablespoons of olive oil may help coat the esophagus and make vomiting less unpleasant.

Induce vomiting only if instructed to do so by a knowledgeable person. Vomiting certain poisons, such as strychnine, can do more physical harm than allowing them to pass through the body. It's even possible to do permanent damage to the esophagus by vomiting up a caustic substance. Here are a few general guidelines:

• Poisons that burn the throat as they're swallowed shouldn't be vomited back up. Don't induce vomiting if the poison is a corrosive liquid, including ammonia, bleach, or strong detergents, acids, and alkalies. Check container label information. Also suspect corrosive poisoning if there are burns on the person's mouth or lips.

• Don't induce vomiting for oily substances and petroleum distillates such as gasoline, kerosene, cleaning fluids, or paint thinners. On their way up the esophagus, these may form droplets that get drawn into the lungs. There they can wreak more havoc than if they were to go through the digestive tract. Suspect petroleum distillate poisoning if the person's breath smells like gasoline, kerosene, or turpentine.

- Most drugs and poisonous plants are not corrosive and it is all right to induce vomiting when they're consumed.
- If you're not sure of the poisonous substance, don't induce vomiting.
- Don't induce vomiting if the person is unconscious.

These are just general guidelines for inducing vomiting. Check with a poison control center for specific instructions.

◆ Neutralize the poison. Strong acids are uncommon household items, though they can be found in home darkrooms for developing photos. An alkaline substance such as baking soda dissolved in warm water can help neutralize acids. Strong alkalis are more common around the home. Potentially poisonous alkalis include drain cleaners such as Drāno and oven cleaners. An acidic solution such as vinegar or lemon juice mixed with water can neutralize an alkali.

◆ Take large amounts of activated charcoal to absorb the poison in the digestive tract. Activated charcoal is available over the counter at natural foods stores and pharmacies. It comes in a powder, liquid, tablets, and capsules (Charcoal Plus, Charcocaps). Activated charcoal can absorb syrup of ipecac, so generally you don't give activated charcoal until after the person has vomited. A typical dosage to remove poisons from the body is five to seven teaspoons of activated charcoal in a glass of water. Follow the dosage advice of the poison control center.

Calm and reassure the person. If emergency personnel have been summoned, tell the person that help is on the way. Continue to monitor the ABCs and take any necessary steps to prevent or treat seizures, choking, and shock. Don't leave the person alone until you're sure the danger has passed. Loosen the person's clothing. Keep him or her warm and seated with a pillow behind the head and shoulders.

NATURAL FIRST-AID REMEDIES FOR CHEMICAL POISONING

The two principal natural remedies are ipecac, to induce vomiting, and activated charcoal, to absorb the poisonous substance as it passes through the digestive tract. Both of these remedies are widely used by doctors and hospitals as well as naturopaths and other natural practitioners.

Use syrup of ipecac to induce vomiting, when safe and necessary. The dried roots of this tropical South American shrub contain the alkaloid emetine, a substance that induces vomiting. Conventional pharmaceutical companies worldwide market inexpensive, sweet-tasting syrup of ipecac made with tiny amounts of emetine, and the medicine has saved many lives by quickly emptying the stomachs of poison victims.

Substances in ipecac irritate stomach walls and increase the secretion of gastric enzymes. This stimulates the "vomiting center" in the medulla of the brain, and within about fifteen to twenty minutes, in most cases, the person throws up. Ipecac empties about one-third of the stomach's contents. This may or may not be enough to avoid further harm—check with your poison control center.

One or two doses of the syrup preparations are safe even if not vomited. Some pharmaceutical companies, however, also sell the concentrated fluid extract of ipecac. These are much more toxic than the syrup preparations and need to be diluted before taking. Stick to concentrated sugar solutions. Homeopaths use extremely dilute preparations of ipecac to treat persistent and extreme nausea and some types of poisoning. Homeopathic preparations are completely nontoxic.

Syrup of ipecac should be in all first-aid kits, but you should always check with a poison control center or medical professional before using it.

Take activated charcoal to help excrete poisons. Activated charcoal is a stiff, black, spongelike mass of pure carbon. It glides through the stomach and the intestines without being absorbed. On its way, however, it binds with toxins, wastes, and other substances (including pharmaceutical drugs and nutritional supplements).

Pharmaceutical companies process pure carbon in a special way to make activated charcoal. Particles of activated charcoal have many small chambers and cavities that add up to an extensive surface area. These are perfect for catching and trapping the large molecules of most toxic substances, which is why charcoal is also used in air and water filters. Charcoal works by *adsorption;* it collects substances in a condensed form on its surfaces, as distinct from *absorption,* which is to take in and incorporate or assimilate a substance. Activated charcoal adsorbs poisons and drugs in the stomach and intestines and then is excreted along with them by the body. It further prevents toxins from being absorbed into the bloodstream by coating intestinal walls.

Activated charcoal is quickly gaining a reputation as an effective antigas remedy. Recent studies indicate it may also reduce harmful cholesterol levels in the blood. For over 150 years, ever since a French pharmacist shocked a group of medical colleagues by gulping down some charcoal along with a hefty dose of strychnine, activated charcoal's most dramatic use has been as an antipoison first-aid remedy.

Charcoal is used for most types of poisonings. It is neither, however, a poison panacea nor a universal antidote. It won't adsorb cyanide, nor certain acids or bases with small molecular structures. Though charcoal saved the French pharmacist's life, it would be foolhardy or even fatal to test it like that. Nor should you use activated charcoal for all poisons. Check with a poison control center or medical professional.

Take an appropriate homeopathic remedy. Homeopath Jennifer Jacobs, M.D., usually recommends one of the following:

Arsenicum. This is helpful if there is severe vomiting, and exhaustion accompanied by anxiety and restlessness.

Veratrum album. Persons with severe vomiting accompanied by cold sweat on the brow may benefit from taking *Veratrum album.*

Aconite. This is useful to help relieve a poisoning accompanied by fear, agitation, and restless tossing.

Nux vomica. This remedy is good for treating persistent nausea after a poisoning episode.

Apply acupressure to the point four finger-widths below the kneecap toward the outside of the shinbone. This will help relieve the symptoms of nausea and stomach disorder. According to acupressure authority Michael Reed Gach, "Pressing on this point helps to stabilize the stomach. To help neutralize the toxic substance, you can also hold the second toe at the base of the nail. This is where the stomach meridian ends."

For cases of mild poisoning, some of the following natural remedies may complement the basic steps.

Take some extra pectin. A water-soluble fiber, pectin is found in the outer skin of apples, oranges, carrots, potatoes, and other fruits and vegetables. Herbalist Christopher Hobbs notes, "Pectin is popular in Russia and elsewhere as a poison remedy because it contains highly charged molecules that attract and bind with heavy metals and water-soluble toxins, allowing the body to better excrete them. Put a tablespoon of pectin in a glass of water or juice and swallow with another cup of tea or water. It's great for pulling poisons out of the body."

Pectin fiber supplements are widely available at natural foods stores.

Try some natural substances that can help soothe and coat the respiratory and digestive tracts. Mucilaginous substances such as slippery elm preparations and oatmeal may help protect the sensitive lining of the digestive tract from irritation by the poisonous substance.

Take any of the following folk remedies said to be mild poison antidotes:

◆ milk of magnesia
◆ burnt toast
◆ strong tea

PREVENTING CHEMICAL POISONING

The vast majority of accidental poisonings could be prevented if more people took some basic precautions. Four out of five poisonings occur in homes, and most of these occur to children when the parents are either at home or nearby. Small children are the most frequent victims of accidental poisonings because they put virtually anything in their mouths, regardless of taste. Children between the ages of one to three make up the majority of poisoning fatalities. Child-resistant caps on containers of drugs, vitamins, and other potentially toxic substances have had immense success in preventing poisonings, but thousands are still poisoned every day in the United States (in part because child-resistant caps themselves are effective only about half the time because they're not properly tightened, are defective to begin with, or kids figure them out).

The best way to prevent skin exposure to toxic chemicals in the home or garden is to use nontoxic, natural alternatives. A minor industry has sprung up in the past decade offering nontoxic alternatives to everything from cleansers to cosmetics to paints (see "Resources" for mail-order firms).

If you do use a spray insecticide or other product with potentially toxic fumes, protect your skin with gloves and long sleeves, your eyes with goggles, and your lungs with a mask. Thoroughly wash or shower immediately afterward. If you work indoors using a product with toxic fumes, open windows to allow fresh air to come in. Prevent carbon monoxide poisoning by regular checks of your heating system.

Caustic products such as oven cleaners, bleaches, drain cleaners, and dishwashing soap that are often kept under the kitchen sink should be removed from the kitchen. Toxic substances should be kept out of the reach of children by putting the poisons in cabinets or closets that can be locked. If cabinets can't easily be locked, install childproof latches and handles. Poisons kept in the garden shed or laundry room also need to be secured. Relying solely on height from the floor to keep a toddler from a toxic substance is effective only temporarily. By age three to four, most kids can use chairs and tables to reach anywhere an adult can.

Alcohol, vitamins, drugs, and even natural remedies should be kept in locked or securely childproofed places. Drugs and vitamins, which account for about two in every five childhood poisonings, should be explicitly labeled and kept in their original containers. Children need to be more closely supervised when visiting other homes, especially if the new home has no young children. As many as one in three childhood drug poisonings result from a child taking a grandparent's prescription drug. Children are sometimes poisoned when they retrieve a toxic substance or a prescription drug out of the household garbage.

Many accidents occur when a parent of a small child is interrupted while using an oven cleaner or other toxic substance. A mother leaves the cleaner behind to answer the phone or doorbell, and the child takes a taste. Always take the substance with you, or put it where it can't be reached.

Never transfer a poisonous substance to a new container that once held food. Putting cleaning fluid, for instance, into a former juice bottle is an accident waiting to happen. Most poisonings of adults result from storing a poison in a drinking container. The inverse—making a drinking-water container out of a container that formerly held a toxic substance—should also never be done. "I've heard of such instances," Oriental Medical Doctor Holly Eagle says, "in which a person drank a few gulps of pure bleach before he realized that the container he had picked up and drunk from was not the one he had turned into a water jug."

One of the most important preventive steps parents can take is to teach small children respect for drugs, remedies, and vitamins, natural and otherwise. Don't take medicines in front of children. Children should not be encouraged to take any of these by telling them "it tastes like candy," or even worse, that it is candy. Sweet, fruit-flavored vitamins can be thought of as candy by children even without parental help.

The hazards of children's vitamins were demonstrated to one father of two young children in an all-too-typical way: "My wife and I came into the kitchen early one morning to find that our two-year-old son and four-year-old daughter had found a container of children's vitamins that we'd been keeping on top of the refrigerator. The kids opened the vitamin bottle and between the two of them quickly polished off the contents, about twenty tablets or so total. My wife immediately called the local poison control center and told the staff person about the contents of the vitamins, and the age and size of the children. It turned out that the dosages involved were almost assuredly not toxic, but the center staff person suggested that we induce vomiting and then closely watch the kids just in case.

"We gave the children syrup of ipecac and then a couple of cups of water. About ten minutes later, after we swirled the children around in circles for a minute, they both erupted like volcanoes. After that the kids were fine, and we didn't need to go to the emergency room. Even so, it was an unenjoyable morning for all involved. Everyone learned some important lessons. The children never again wanted to eat more than one vitamin at a time, and my wife and I made sure they never had the opportunity in any case. We now buy vitamins with child-resistant caps and keep the pills well out of the children's reach."

◆ Food Poisoning

Of the estimated 100–300 million cases of diarrhea in the United States each year, one-third are suspected to be caused by contaminated food. In addition, according to the FDA, some nine thousand Americans die each year from food poisoning. Public health authorities agree that bacterial or viral contamination of food that occurs during shipping, preparation, or handling poses a risk to increasing numbers of people. Contaminated or mishandled poultry, meat, and fish are among the most common causes of food poisoning, while another type of food poisoning results from eating toxic foods such as certain exotic mushrooms.

An enormous range of viruses, bacteria, and other microorganisms represent a threat to safe food. Typically these toxins are present in small amounts in foods, but multiply to dangerous levels when food is not thoroughly cooked or is left out at room temperature for more than an hour or two, as often happens at parties, company picnics, and the like. The most common microorganisms that cause food poisoning include:

- *Salmonella.* This is the most common food-poisoning bacteria, usually causing a problem in poultry, eggs, milk, or fish that is left out at room temperature for an hour or longer or is improperly cooked. The food poisoning known as salmonellosis afflicts an estimated 2–4 million Americans annually.

   Many public health authorities say that *Salmonella* contamination of poultry has risen dramatically in the past decade, as chicken processing plants have stepped up line speeds and switched to mechanical eviscerators. At the same time, budget cuts and changes in federal inspection procedures have hampered effective regulation. Estimates of the percentage of chicken carcasses that are contaminated with *Salmonella* by the time they reach supermarkets go as high as 35–75 percent. Food scientists say that another bacterium, *Campylobacter,* is also commonly found on processed chickens and may be responsible for as many cases of food-borne illness as *Salmonella.*
- *Staphylococcus.* Certain strains of this organism typically contaminate food when a food preparer sneezes or coughs in a way that allows the bacteria to travel from body to food. The bacteria create a toxin, and it is this toxin, rather than the bacteria themselves, that leads to diarrhea, vomiting, and abdominal cramps. The toxin is not killed by normal cooking, so preventing transmission of the bacteria to food is crucial.
- *Clostridium botulinum.* This bacterium can cause botulism, a rare but potentially fatal type of food poisoning. Botulism most frequently results from eating low-acid vegetables or meats that haven't been canned properly, often by a home canner. Some twelve to thirty-six hours after eating food contaminated by *C. botulinum* the person may experience dizziness, slurred speech, difficulty breathing and swallowing, nausea, vomiting, diarrhea, fever, and swelling of the stomach or abdominal pain.
- *E. coli.* It was a virulent strain of the bacterium *E. coli* that

caused the food poisoning outbreaks that affected over five hundred residents of the Pacific Northwest in early 1993. In the worst case, a two-year-old boy died, over two dozen people experienced kidney failure, and more than one hundred people were hospitalized after eating undercooked, bacteria-contaminated hamburgers at Jack in the Box fast-food restaurants in Washington State. Federal officials estimate that at least twenty thousand cases of *E. coli* infection occur each year nationwide, though the figure may be substantially higher since thirty-nine states don't require doctors to report cases to authorities.

    E. coli bacteria are commonly found by the billions in the human gut as well as the intestines of cattle. The variant (*E. coli* 0157:H7) responsible for the recent food poisoning episodes is thought to contaminate meat at the time of slaughter. Unsanitary processing and food preparation can allow these bacteria to multiply even to the point that proper cooking won't kill all of them.

Bacterial contamination of steaks is less common than hamburgers because bacteria on the surface of meat are usually killed by cooking. Hamburger, which is ground and mixed, provides a larger surface area for bacterial growth, and the bacteria can survive in the rare inside of a cooked burger. Bacterial contamination of poultry, however, is much more common than the contamination of red meat because the most contaminated part of an animal is usually its skin, which isn't removed from chickens and turkeys destined for the dinner table.

    Food poisoning from these or other microorganisms should be suspected if the ill person recalls eating a food that on reflection didn't taste right or seemed to have been left out at room temperature for some time. Food poisoning is probably the culprit when several people who eat together become ill within a day or two of each other.

    Most cases of food poisoning are limited to mild symptoms resembling gastroenteritis: diarrhea, vomiting, and stomach pains. Depending on the infecting agent, symptoms may appear as quickly as thirty minutes after eating a contaminated food or as long as forty-eight hours later. Mild cases often clear up on their own within one to two days. The main risk is dehydration from vomiting and diarrhea. Rarely, a food poisoning episode will last a week or longer and develop into a severe case of blood poisoning.

Most food poisoning episodes respond to simple treatments including bed rest and plenty of fluids. Further food usually makes things worse until the stomach settles. Light, nutritious, easily digested foods, such as vegetable soups, are best to break the fast. Conventional physicians may recommend drugs to control diarrhea and vomiting. If a stool culture identifies the bacterial culprit, doctors may prescribe antibiotics such as ampicillin.

You should contact a medical professional if:

- ◆ the food poisoning doesn't clear up within a week or leaves the person dehydrated
- ◆ the victim is very young, elderly, or immune-compromised
- ◆ he or she is having difficulty in breathing, severe abdominal pain, or a fever over 100°
- ◆ vomiting or diarrhea are severe for more than a day or two

BASIC FIRST AID FOR FOOD POISONING

First aid for food poisoning is important when symptoms strike suddenly and severely, causing physical problems such as difficulty breathing and acute abdominal pain.

Call your medical professional or local poison control center. Respond as best as you can to the questions about the victim and the possible causes. Don't use any "universal antidote" or neutralizing substance unless told to do so by center or physician. In most cases of food poisoning it is not necessary to induce vomiting, though it often helps the person feel better and isn't harmful.

Try to identify the cause of the food poisoning. If it is a food in your kitchen, save the container for possible later testing. If the person vomits, save some of the vomitus for evaluation.

Provide basic emergency care. In cases of acute food poisoning such as botulism, as well as acute allergic reactions to food, be prepared for potentially life-threatening symptoms. Check the ABCs (airway, breathing, and circulation; see "Chapter 3: Basic Emergency Care"), put the victim in the recovery position if he or she is unconscious, and protect him or her from harm by seizures if they occur (see Chapter 11). Calm and reassure the person.

Keep the person hydrated. If the person is breathing easily, is conscious, and has not vomited, provide milk, water, or herbal tea. Sipping liquids slowly can help the person avoid vomiting. Replace lost electrolytes if necessary (see "What to Drink" in "Chapter 17: Heat Illness").

NATURAL FIRST AID FOR FOOD POISONING

Natural remedies are preferable to over-the-counter drugs such as antacids or antidiarrhea products, which can interfere with the body's attempts to flush toxins.

Take activated charcoal or food-grade clay to adsorb toxins and remove them through the digestive tract. Take three to five grams of activated charcoal every fifteen minutes for one hour.

Clay such as bentonite, or montmorillonite, is a finely powdered mineral product that is often used externally for its "drawing" and drying powers. Clay can also be taken internally if it is produced to meet special formulating standards. Clay for internal consumption comes in both powder and liquid form. Carefully check labels before taking clay internally. In the digestive tract clay acts much like activated charcoal to absorb toxins in the intestines and carry them out of the body.

In natural foods stores powdered bentonite clay is often available in one-pound bags. A popular liquid, colloidal bentonite product is Sonne's #7, made by Sonne's Organic Foods of Kansas City, Missouri, and sold in quart jars. Follow dosage recommendations on the label.

Take a milk-thistle-seed product to aid the liver in its processing of toxins. Herbalist Christopher Hobbs recommends taking three to four capsules per day after a poisoning episode. In tincture form, take two dropperfuls every three to four hours the first day, then a dropperful three times a day for the next three to four days.

Herbal companies use milk thistle seeds *(Silybum marianum)* to make silymarin, a standardized extract of a complex compound. Milk thistle has been used as a liver remedy for thousands of years, and recent research done mainly in Germany confirms that the plant can protect the liver. Silymarin helps liver cells regenerate and boosts the organ's ability to filter blood and break down toxins. Silymarin prevents liver damage from toxins including solvents, alcohol, and drugs.

According to Hobbs, author of *Milk Thistle: The Liver Herb,* "Milk-thistle-seed extract is especially crucial after ingesting any fat-soluble poison, including most pesticides and herbicides, or a bacterial compound like from food poisoning. The body won't be able to get rid of these until the liver has a crack at them. Silymarin stabilizes liver cell membranes and prevents toxins from disrupting the liver's function. The liver then transforms the poison into a water-soluble substance that can be excreted from the body."

Milk-thistle-seed products are helpful both taken regularly as a preventive measure and taken after exposure to a toxin. Concentrated herbal drops and capsulated extract products of milk thistle seed are widely available from various herbal companies. Probably the most well-known such product is Thisilyn, a patented milk thistle extract that over the past twenty years has been used widely in scientific studies on silymarin. Thisilyn was developed by the German herbal company Madaus AG and is available in the United States from Madaus Murdock/Nature's Way of Springville, Utah. Each Thisilyn capsule contains 200 mg of milk thistle extract, standardized for a flavonoid content of 70 percent silymarin (140 mg). It's relatively expensive as compared to many herbal supplements.

Other herbal preparations that may help the liver and alleviate the symptoms of food poisoning include:

- ◆ garlic tablets or extracts
- ◆ ginger or turmeric extract or concentrated drops
- ◆ a tea brewed from plantain or skullcap
- ◆ dandelion-root tablets

Hobbs suggests as well taking lots of echinacea or black walnut tincture or concentrate after a case of food poisoning to kill and inhibit the contaminating pathogen in the body.

Take a megadose of vitamin C with bioflavonoids. Large amounts of vitamin C can help flush toxins from the body. Take 1,000 mg per hour for two to three hours, or to bowel tolerance. Megadoses of vitamin C should be avoided during pregnancy.

Have a soothing whole-body massage. Practitioners of Chinese massage suggest the following for symptoms of food poisoning or acute gastroenteritis. Have the person lie facedown. Massage down the middle and along both sides of the vertebrae. Have the patient turn over. Then use the flat of the thumb to massage along the sides of the midline of the abdomen above the navel. Next move to the head and use the thumbs to apply acupressure thirty to forty times on the midpoint between the inner ends of the eyebrows. End the massage by pressing on the point in the depression at one fingerwidth outside the end of the eyebrow.

Use an appropriate homeopathic treatment. The most commonly recommended ones include:

Arsenicum. This is the homeopathic remedy most frequently used to treat food poisoning. It helps relieve vomiting, diarrhea, and burning abdominal pain. The patient is often anxious, restless, chilly, and thirsty for sips of water.

Ipecac. This is the remedy for persistent and extreme nausea, even after vomiting. The person typically doesn't feel as awful as the *Arsenicum* patient and isn't anxious or chilly. He or she usually has little thirst and may feel better when exposed to fresh air.

Belladonna. This remedy is helpful in the earliest stages of food poisoning, especially when symptoms come on suddenly. The person is typically feverish and flushed.

Nux vomica. This is useful when symptoms include diarrhea and cramps or a bloated feeling in the abdomen, as from gas. The person usually gets some relief by defecating. He or she feels irritable and chilly and is better after vomiting.

Take some of the Chinese prepared medicine known as Lophanthus pills. Called Huo Xian Zheng Qi Wan ("Agastaches Qi-Correcting Pills") by the Chinese, this remedy is used to treat "summerheat diseases" as well as acute gastric upsets such as those from food poisoning. It contains agastaches, a member of the mint family, and other herbs. According to Holly Eagle, "Three of the herbs in the Lophanthus formula act specifically against the major bacteria that cause food poisoning, during both the acute phase and recovery. I've had patients who were still not feeling right a week after suffering from food poisoning. One dosage of Lophanthus and the person is feeling well again. This remedy is in my precious category."

Lophanthus comes in small pills or vials of tablets. Purchase them from an Oriental pharmacy or a mail-order distributor of Oriental prepared medicines (see "Resources").

Try one of the following folk medicine remedies for food poisoning.

♦ Dissolve one to two tablespoons of castor oil in a glass of water with lemon juice and sip.
♦ Help neutralize the toxins in the body by drinking black tea, milk of magnesia, or lemon water, or eating burnt toast, onions, or garlic.
♦ Sit in a low-heat sauna for a while to sweat out toxins.
♦ Rub and massage the tender point in the crease under the middle toe.

PREVENTING FOOD POISONING

Simple precautions can prevent most cases of food poisoning. Even poultry that is contaminated with *Salmonella* bacteria can be safe to eat if it is prepared under sanitary conditions and properly cooked. Here are some of the most important considerations.

◆ When handling and preparing foods, keep your hands clean. Let someone else cook meals for others when you're sick.

◆ Keep countertops, cutting boards, and cooking utensils clean. After using, wash or scrub with soap and water everything a piece of meat or chicken has touched, including can openers, sponges, and the like.

   Until recently it was universally accepted as self-evident that plastic cutting boards were preferable to wooden ones for cutting meat. Being nonporous, plastic was presumed to be easier to keep free of food-poisoning bacteria. No longer. A pair of microbiologists at the University of Wisconsin's Food Research Institute recently tossed this conventional wisdom out the window. The researchers were testing wooden cutting boards to find out if they could somehow be made more inhospitable to bacteria, when lo and behold it turned out that all wooden cutting boards, regardless of the type of wood, are dramatically more antibacterial environments than are plastic boards. The researchers found that within three minutes of spreading bacteria over a wooden board, 99.9 percent of the bacteria were unrecoverable and presumed dead. On plastic boards, the bacteria not only didn't disappear, they multiplied. The researchers cautioned against interpreting their findings as a license to become sloppy about kitchen safety.

◆ Throw out bulging cans, cracked eggs, and any food that tastes or smells spoiled. Leave home canning to those who know what they're doing, or boil all home-canned foods for at least ten minutes before tasting.

◆ Refrigerate meat and poultry and don't let it warm up to room temperature after cooking. A general guideline is to avoid letting meat, poultry, and other high-protein foods sit in an environment where the temperature is between 40° and 150° for over two hours. Thaw foods in the refrigerator or use a microwave, rather than letting them sit on a counter at room temperature. Serve small quantities and keep the rest refrigerated.

◆ Cook foods thoroughly enough for the pink to disappear in red meat and for fish to flake. Thoroughly cooked chicken has clear juices, with no red in the joints or pink in the flesh. After the 1993 food poisoning incident in the Pacific Northwest, the FDA revised its recommendation for the minimum safe internal temperature that should be reached while cooking hamburger, raising it from 140° to 155°. If you eat hamburger, cook it thoroughly at home and don't order it rare at a restaurant. Microwave ovens can have cold spots, so foods need to be turned and closely checked for thorough cooking. Precooked foods purchased from delis and gourmet shops for consumption a few hours later are safer to eat if they're reheated thoroughly.

◆ Eat in restaurants that have a reputation for serving fresh foods in a clean environment.

◆ Foods served at picnics, parties, and the like should be kept in a cooler, especially any poultry, meat, fish, or eggs. Potato and tuna salads are common causes of food poisoning when they're allowed to sit out and warm up.

If your upcoming weekend schedule involves a lot of partying and picnicking, fortify your body to prevent food poisoning by taking supplements starting a few days before. Take acidophilus (approximately 10 billion organisms per day), 25,000 IU daily of beta carotene, vitamins C (two to five grams in mixed doses daily, or to bowel tolerance) and E (400–800 IU), and selenium (50–200 mcg).

Acidophilus has become the generic term for various types of naturally occurring live bacteria that are increasingly popular as dietary supplements. It is available in the form of tablets, powders, capsules, and liquids sold in most natural foods stores. Look for acidophilus products that have labels providing information on how many live or "viable" bacteria each capsule or teaspoon provides, an expiration date with a guarantee of product viability until that date, and a listing of additional ingredients.

◆ Recovery from Acute Poisoning

The following steps may be helpful to speed recovery after you've suffered an episode of chemical or food poisoning.

Go on a temporary fresh-juice fast. Immediately after an acute poisoning, you want to help cleanse the digestive system and prevent reabsorption of the toxin. If you can, stop solid foods for a day or two; continue to drink fresh vegetable broths or fruit juices. Afterward slowly reintroduce light, easily digested foods high in water and fiber content.

Fasting for longer than three days should be done only under the guidance of a medical professional.

If you don't want to fast, at least eat lightly. For a week or so after the poisoning, avoid fatty, spicy, or sugary foods that could irritate the stomach and slow the work of the intestines. White rice that is boiled into a porridge is simple to make and easy on the digestive system. Another good choice is a slippery-elm gruel, both to help soothe your throat and digestive tract and to take in important nutrients. A gruel is a thin, easily digested porridge. Use about one ounce of finely powdered inner bark of slippery elm per ounce of water or milk. Slowly mix the powder and liquid into a thick paste. Flavor with cinnamon or nutmeg.

Drink extra water and fluids. This helps speed the elimination of the toxin from the body.

Take acidophilus to help repopulate your intestines with friendly bacteria. Two tablespoons or more per day of live acidophilus can help to restore the microclimate of your intestines.

Prevent free-radical damage. Antioxidant supplements such as the following can help reduce free-radical damage from chemical poisoning:

- ◆ vitamin C plus bioflavonoids (two to five grams in mixed doses daily, or to bowel tolerance)
- ◆ coenzyme Q10, a vitaminlike nutrient (10–20 mg)
- ◆ vitamin E (400–800 IU)
- ◆ selenium (50–200 mcg)

Protect the liver. Supplements to help promote the formation of the liver enzymes that detoxify most poisons include:

- ◆ silymarin (follow label directions)
- ◆ extracts of the healing mushrooms reishi or shiitake (follow label directions)
- ◆ vitamins B complex (50–100 mg daily) and C

Detoxify the blood. Supplements to help lessen the effects of food poisoning include:

- microalgae and other green foods
- astragalus
- garlic (also has liver-protective effects)
- Siberian ginseng (eleuthero)

TWENTY-ONE

Skin Emergencies

THIS CHAPTER COVERS:

- *eruptions from poison ivy, oak, and sumac*
- *local skin infections*
- *splinters and fishhook removal*

SEE "CHAPTER 4: ALLERGIC REACTIONS" FOR:

- *acute reactions (anaphylactic shock)*
- *allergic reactions to pollen, metal, etc.*

SEE "CHAPTER 5: BITES AND STINGS" FOR:

- *human, animal, and insect bites and stings*
- *puncture wounds*

SEE "CHAPTER 6: BLEEDING" FOR:

- *cuts and scrapes*

SEE "CHAPTER 9: BURNS" FOR:

- *minor first- and second-degree burns*
- *sunburn*
- *chemical burns*

SEE "CHAPTER 15: EXPOSURE TO ALTITUDE AND COLD" FOR:

- *frostnip and frostbite*

The skin is the largest and most visible of the body's organs, so it's usually no secret when it suffers one of its frequent injuries or infections. Allergic reactions, germs, or traumas may cause the soft, supple surface of the skin to redden, inflame, blister, tear, or bleed. The skin is a complex organ that plays a central role in many bodily functions, from regulating temperature and conserving moisture to protecting other organs from injury and infection. Keeping the skin performing optimally is vital to overall health.

The top part of the skin's tough outer layer, or epidermis, provides the body's first line of defense against bacteria, viruses, and fungi. Dead and dying skin cells are shed at the skin's surface, and new cells are continuously being generated and pushed up from below. All of the epidermis's important biological supplies are provided by the skin's thicker dermis layer. The dermis contains one-third of the body's supply of blood, a rich network of nerves to transmit pain and pleasure, sweat glands to cool the body, and sebaceous glands to provide the oily, waxy substance that keeps the skin supple.

Many natural healers contend that biochemical imbalances in general tend to move from the inside out. From this perspective, skin symptoms are often a healthy sign that the body is working to heal an internal imbalance, which may be due to stress, poor diet, or other factors. Suppressing the symptom on the skin, whether a rash or inflammation, therefore is not as important as boosting the body's ability to heal itself.

◆ Eruptions From Poison Ivy, Oak, and Sumac

The skin can react to various types of allergy-causing substances it comes in contact with. Such allergic reactions are known as contact dermatitis, a condition that causes an inflammatory skin rash. In "Chapter 4: Allergic Reactions," we talked about nickel, cosmetics, and some other substances that can cause contact dermatitis. In this chapter we're focusing on contact dermatitis from plants. Some five dozen varieties of poisonous plants in the United States can cause contact dermatitis, including goldenrod, hollyhock, nettle, ragweed, and daisies. But the main culprits by far are poison ivy, poison oak, and poison sumac, which together are responsible for over 350,000 cases of skin poisoning in the United States each year.

Poison ivy. This is a wicked warlock of a plant, a shape-shifting poisoner. (To humans, that is. To some wild animals and dozens of types of birds, its berries or leaves are a source of food.) Poison ivy can grow as a shrub, a single-stemmed ground cover, or a trailing or climbing vine. It's found throughout the continental United States, mostly east of the Rockies. It is adaptable, capable of growing in shady areas around cool streams and lakeshores, or on sunny hillsides up to about four thousand feet. It is easiest to identify by its leaves, which always come in leaflets of three to a stem. Thus the adage, "Leaves of three, let it be." The leaves vary widely in color, shape, size, and texture, from hairy and saw-toothed to heart-shaped and smooth-edged. In New England the leaves often turn a striking scarlet in the fall. Poison ivy may have small whitish green flowers in spring, and white berries in the fall (see illustration #19).

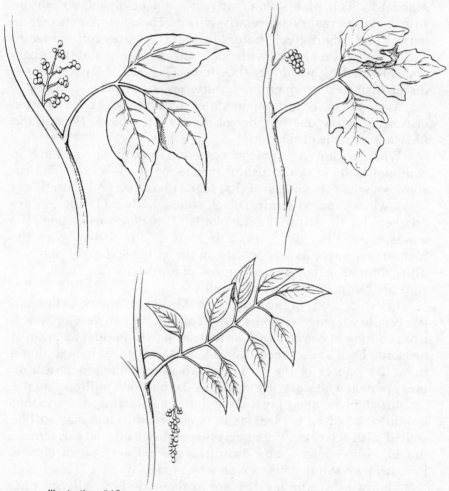

Illustration #19:

Poison ivy (top left) and poison oak (top right) can be identified by their leaflets of three, while poison sumac plants (bottom) have a row of six to ten leaflets opposite each other with a single leaflet at the end of the stem.

Poison oak. Poison oak may also be a shrub, ground plant, or vine. It grows predominantly in California and Oregon, though plants may be found throughout the West and Southwest. Its leaves sometimes have the distinctive shape of all oak leaves but may take many forms. Like poison ivy, poison oak comes in many shapes and colors, but the leaves always come in leaflets of three connected at the end of a stem that comes off the larger stalk.

Poison sumac. A tall shrub or small tree, this toxic plant favors swamps, bogs, and other wet places along the Southeastern seaboard. Such places don't attract a lot of hikers, so poison-sumac-caused rashes are relatively rare. Poison sumac has white berries and bright green, pointy leaves. The leaves come seven to eleven leaflets on a stem, with one leaflet at the tip and the others opposite each other down the stem. The leaves' smooth edges distinguish them from nontoxic varieties of sumac.

All of the lower forty-eight states, with the possible exception of Nevada, grow one of more of these three plants. Hawaii and Alaska have none of the three.

What poison ivy, poison oak, and poison sumac have in common is their sap, urushiol (pronounced *oo-roo-she-ol*). Urushiol is a sticky, colorless oil that tends to oxidize and stain things black when exposed to air. (Black stains on dying fall leaves are another clue to identifying the plants.) Urushiol runs through the leaves, stems, berries, bark, and roots of the plants, with the highest concentrations appearing in the spring and early summer. Thus, human exposures are most common in the spring and summer but may occur year-round.

Urushiol is one of the most toxic skin agents known to humanity. People who are very sensitive to poison ivy can develop a rash from coming in contact with as little as one-billionth of a gram of urushiol. Even at average rash-causing doses, it's estimated that a mere five ounces of the oil is enough to have caused a rash on every person who's ever lived within the past one million years.

Urushiol is not only potent but long lasting. Gloves that crumbled a poison ivy leaf six to twelve months ago may still be coated with active oil. Under certain conditions the oil can remain potent even longer—some centuries-old poison ivy specimens have been known to cause a rash when touched.

The rash-causing mechanism in the body is an allergic one, so the first time urushiol gets onto your skin and into your bloodstream, you often have no immediate reaction. The circulating urushiol causes the immune system to set in process a series of biochemical events (see "Chapter 4: Allergic Reactions") that will allow the body, during subsequent exposures, to recognize urushiol as a foreign invader and to repel it. In some people, this primary exposure to urushiol results in a rash about a week or so later.

After this initial exposure to poison ivy, if you've become allergic to urushiol and you again come in contact with it, within two to four days your body will mount its defense, rushing histamines and various antibodies to the skin tissues. On the surface of the skin, the result is an inflamed red rash. In more severe cases, which may break out in as few as four to twelve hours, there may eventually be large, oozing blisters, fever, and puffiness around the face or genitals. The eyes may swell shut or breathing may be impaired. Such severe symptoms constitute a medical emergency, which physicians usually treat by injecting corticosteroid drugs to reduce the swelling.

Poison ivy, oak, and sumac rashes are extremely itchy. It's best to resist the urge if possible. If you scratch persistently enough, you can infect the blisters with bacteria and complicate the condition.

Note that the rash itself is not contagious. When the rash spreads from one part of the body to another, or from one person to another, it's because there's oil being transferred by hands, fingers, or clothing. It's a good idea to wash your hands after touching the rash to avoid spreading urushiol, especially during the early stages when there's still likely to be some oil there.

THE MYTH OF IMMUNITY

Some 18–20 million Americans are highly sensitive to poison ivy, poison oak, and poison sumac. These plants cause the most common allergy in the country, affecting about half the population. Unfortunately, that doesn't mean that the other half of the population is immune to the effects of urushiol.

About one-third of all people seem to have childhood immunity to the effects of urushiol. These persons may think that they have lifetime immunity, only to come down with their first poison ivy rash sometime in middle age. Not only can sensitivity to the oil develop at any time, sensitivity may come and go. The previously immune can develop a rash. Those who have experienced bad rashes in the past can at least temporarily become immune. And repeat exposures may either diminish or increase the intensity over time.

The truth is that fewer than one person in twenty probably has a lifelong immunity to poison ivy, poison oak, and poison sumac. Assume you're not that rare person. Avoid urushiol oil as you would an open flame.

BASIC FIRST AID FOR POISON IVY, OAK, AND SUMAC

It's crucial to wash the skin as quickly as possible after getting urushiol on it. Mild soap and running water help to remove the oil before it has a chance to get beneath the skin's surface. Don't take a bath to wash the oil off, since it will get transferred to other parts of the body through the bathwater.

For mild cases of contact dermatitis from plants, conventional physicians usually recommend calamine lotion. The main ingredients in this liquid are oxides of iron (which gives calamine its pink color) and zinc (which has a cooling effect on the skin). Calamine also dries the rash somewhat but otherwise has little direct effect on it. Symptomatic relief of itching is calamine's main attraction.

In addition to calamine, some physicians may recommend over-the-counter cortisone creams to relieve itching. These rarely do much good. More effective for symptomatic relief is a shot of cortisone, if it is given within the first twenty-four hours. After that doctors may recommend oral corticosteroids such as prednisone to reduce inflammation. The potential side effects of cortisone-class drugs are numerous, ranging from allergic reactions when applied topically to changes in mood and personality when taken orally.

Another potent class of drugs physicians sometimes recommend is antihistamines, which can reduce the intensity of the allergic response. Some calamine lotions, such as Caladryl, have added antihistamines, though there is little evidence that antihistamines applied topically have any effect at all. Oral antihistamines, such as Benadryl, have side effects including drowsiness. Even topical applications are capable of causing further allergic reactions.

In the majority of cases, poison ivy reactions disappear on their own within a week or two.

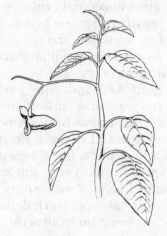

Illustration #20:

Hikers often use the delicate jewelweed plant as a poison ivy remedy.

NATURAL FIRST-AID REMEDIES

A number of herbs, homeopathic remedies, and other natural medicines can be used to help the body reverse a reaction to poisonous plants such as poison ivy, oak, and sumac.

Apply to the rash one of the premier anti-poison-ivy herbs. Two of the most popular plant remedies for poison ivy, oak, and sumac are jewelweed *(Impatiens biflora)* and grindelia *(Grindelia squarrosa, G. camporum)*.

◆ In the wilderness, jewelweed often grows near poison ivy. Jewelweed's tiny, orange-yellow, cornucopia-shaped flowers with reddish or white spots make it easy to recognize in the summer (see illustration #20). Pick the leaves and the juicy stems and crush them in your hands. Put the plant and the juice directly on the rash. If you've brushed against a poison ivy plant but haven't yet developed a rash, a jewelweed poultice can also help prevent a reaction.

"I consider jewelweed to be a lifesaver," says a nature-lover from New York State. "I pick the stems, leaves, and flowers, place them in boiling water for about five minutes, let them steep, and strain. I freeze this tea into ice cubes and apply it to poison ivy rashes. It relieves the itch and reduces the inflammation."

There's abundant anecdotal evidence like this supporting jewelweed's positive effect on poison ivy rashes. Scientific evidence is less available, though one study indicated jewelweed was as effective as pharmaceutical cortisone creams in treating poison ivy rash.

◆ Also known as gumweed and gum plant, grindelia has significant pain-relieving and anti-inflammatory qualities. As a leaf poultice it's a famous Native American remedy for poison ivy, insect bites, and wounds. Herbalist Christopher Hobbs notes, "You can put a few drops of the tincture on the lesions and spread it with your finger. The drops actually form a bandagelike, resinous, shiny coating over the top of the rash. You can apply grindelia before going to bed, and it helps prevent you from scratching and spreading the rash."

Grindelia is common in parts of California and the Pacific Northwest. In the wild, pound the sappy leaves and flowers and apply. Concentrated herbal drops and fluid extracts of grindelia are available from a number of herbal producers.

In addition to jewelweed and grindelia, herbalists today draw upon a range of effective poison ivy remedies. Among the most common are:

◆ plantain
◆ myrrh
◆ goldenseal
◆ witch hazel
◆ calendula
◆ slippery elm
◆ aloe
◆ comfrey

You can also try any of the above herbs, as well as yellow dock *(Rumex crispus)* to relieve a rash resulting from exposure to the stinging-nettle plant.

Hobbs notes that it is worthwhile to take echinacea tincture orally to boost the immune system if you get a severe case of contact plant dermatitis. In the same vein, for rashes that recur over weeks or months, Holly Eagle, an Oriental Medical Doctor, recommends taking astragalus or other herbs that boost your immunity. If you take cortisone for a severe case of poison ivy, also consider taking Siberian ginseng, a potent adaptogenic herb that helps to restabilize the adrenal gland.

Take advantage of the drying powers of clay. Hobbs says that his favorite poison ivy and oak remedy is only partly herbal: "Make a heavy salt solution by dissolving one tablespoon of salt in half a cup of water." Mix into this solution enough cosmetic clay to make a spreadable paste and then blend in five to seven drops of essential oil of Peppermint. The menthol in the Peppermint cools to give some immediate relief, while the salt and clay work to dry the rash. The paste will dry after an hour or so on the skin. You can wash it off and reapply or leave it on overnight.

"I have a lot of experience with poison ivy and poison oak, since I'm susceptible to it and I spend a lot of time in the woods. I've tried all kinds of remedies and never found one that works as well."

Apply a clay and goldenseal paste for poison ivy or oak rash. Holly Eagle and David Eagle, O.M.D., highly recommend this remedy. David Eagle says, "We've found that the most effective paste is one made from a fifty-fifty mix of green clay and goldenseal-root powder. It seems to draw out any oil that is left on the skin and reduce any burning and itching. Put on a thin coat and let it dry. In the early stages when you're miserable and the rash is causing a stinging pain, you may want to apply it, let it dry, and wash it off two to three times within an hour, and then reapply and leave it on."

Cosmetic or green clay is a fine clay powder often available in the beauty-care section of most natural foods stores. Hobbs notes that bentonite, a type of clay applied externally and sometimes taken internally (to absorb toxins in the intestines; see "Natural First Aid for Food Poisoning" in "Chapter 20: Poisoning") is slightly more coarse than cosmetic clay but also works well in this formula.

Take the homeopathic remedy Rhus tox, made from (what else?) the poison ivy plant. Many people have found that homeopathic *Rhus tox* works to heal poison ivy blisters quickly and to keep the rash from spreading.

Along with the much less common remedy *Rhus diversiloba*, from poison oak, *Rhus tox* is used for skin eruptions that match the symptoms of plant rashes: itching, burning, blisters, and scratching. The *Rhus tox* patient is worse at night and made better by warm applications.

Two other popular poison ivy remedies include:

♦ *Ledum.* This is often used immediately after an exposure, as a preventive measure. It may be helpful when itching is relieved by cold water.

♦ *Sulphur.* Use this for a burning itch made worse by warm bathing, or when the itching is so severe the person scratches the rash until the blisters start to bleed. The itching is usually worse at night.

Homeopathic manufacturers offer a number of combination remedies for poison ivy. Hyland's Poison Oak/Poison Ivy tabs, for instance, are a homeopathic combination-remedy containing *Rhus tox, Croton* (croton oil from seeds), and *Xerophyllum* (basket-grass flower), all in tablets of 6X strength.

Massage the essential oil of Tea Tree onto the rash. Put six to eight drops of Tea Tree in a tablespoon of olive or other vegetable oil and apply to the site of the rash. See the section on natural remedies for skin infections, following, for other suggestions on how to apply Tea Tree oil.

A woman from Dover, New Hampshire, confirms Tea Tree's effectiveness against poison ivy. She says, "Last week a friend visited with an annoying case of poison ivy on her arm. She had been using a prescription cortisone cream, which had not relieved the itching at all. I gave her some Tea Tree oil to put on, and within a few minutes she was no longer itching and scratching."

Apply healing acupressure massage to points above and below the skin injury. Michael Reed Gach, author of *Acupressure's Potent Points,* says that applying firm pressure above and below the rash can help relieve the pain and increase circulation. "You can also press on the point in the middle of the web between the thumb and index finger to reduce the inflammation and itching of poison ivy," he says.

Increase your daily intake of nutritional supplements that can help heal skin tissues and boost immunity. Some of the most important dietary considerations include daily doses of:

♦ vitamin C plus bioflavonoids, two to five grams in mixed dosages or to bowel tolerance (poison ivy rash is basically an allergic response, and high levels of vitamin C and bioflavonoids, especially hesperidin and quercetin, act as a natural antihistamine and anti-inflammatory)
♦ vitamin A in the form of beta carotene, 25,000 IU
♦ zinc, 25–50 mg (for skin repair)
♦ vitamin B complex, 50–100 mg
♦ vitamin E, 400–800 IU (to prevent scarring)

Supplement your diet with high levels of the omega-3s and omega-6s, the desirable essential fatty acids that have a natural anti-inflammatory effect. Sources of beneficial EFAs include:

- fatty, cold-water fish such as salmon, cod, mackerel, sardines, bluefish, herring, and tuna, and oil supplements made from these fish
- canola, flaxseed, and hemp oil
- evening primrose, borage, and black-currant oil

Try one of the many natural products on the market for soothing skin irritations. A number of herbal combination remedies can help relieve a skin rash from poison ivy or other causes. A popular one is Breezy Balms Oak Away, which comes in a two-ounce spray bottle. This is a topical, fine-mist herbal spray for poison ivy, oak, and sumac. The main ingredients are ocean water, jewelweed, mugwort, manzanita, comfrey, plantain, witch hazel, other herbs, and isopropyl alcohol. The product is made by Breezy Balms of Davenport, California.

Try one or more of the many folk remedies for rash from poison ivy, oak, or sumac. As is the case with insect stings, burns, and bruises, there's no lack of suggestions for easy-to-use home remedies for poison ivy sufferers.

- Take advantage of baking soda's soothing properties. This is a popular kitchen remedy. One way to apply it is to dissolve a teaspoon of baking soda in a glass of water, dip a clean cloth into the solution, and drape the cloth over the affected area for fifteen to twenty minutes. You can also make a thick paste of baking soda, using a powder-to-liquid (try water or witch hazel) ratio of 3:1. Another method is to dissolve one-half to one cup of baking soda in your bath.
- Try colloidal oatmeal. Colloidal oatmeal is finely ground powdered oatmeal. It turns into a slippery mass when mixed with water. Added to a bath, it disperses throughout the water and forms a thin gel that coats your skin, holding moisture in and providing relief from itching. Oatmeal-type cereals are too coarsely ground to bind with water and have this soothing effect. Either grind your own oats down to a flourlike powder or look for the popular commercial colloidal oatmeal product Aveeno in your local pharmacy. Add one to two cups of colloidal oatmeal to the bathwater.

- Apply cider vinegar. Bathe the rash area in cider vinegar diluted 1:10 with water. Or apply cooling compresses made from soaking a clean cloth in a vinegar-and-water solution.
- Take a hot shower. People who have tried this say that at first it makes the pain and itching worse, but then quickly provides some relief.
- Apply a healing layer of clay paste. Clay can help by pulling toxins to the skin's surface.
- Hang out at a beach and go swimming in saltwater. Sun and saltwater seem to quickly dry out poison ivy rashes.
- Apply pieces of cold, fresh tofu to the rash. Use a cool, wet cloth to bind them in place for fifteen to twenty minutes.
- Rub the fruit, juice, and rind of cold, fresh watermelon all over the rash. Allow the skin to dry naturally. If watermelons are out of season, try a lemon.
- Mix pure honey with goldenseal-root powder and apply to the poison ivy. Bandage the area lightly for a few days.
- Break open a few capsules of vitamin E oil and rub it onto the rash.
- Apply fresh mud to the area, leave it on till it dries, and shower it off. To prevent bacterial contamination, use this one only in the early stages of a rash, when the skin is unbroken.

PREVENTING POISON IVY AND OTHER TYPES OF PLANT CONTACT DERMATITIS

The first and most important preventive step is learning to identify hazardous plants. In addition to the simple "leaves of three" guideline for poison ivy and poison oak, take some time to learn about the potentially toxic plants and their typical variations in leaf size, shape, and texture in your area.

Physical barriers to the urushiol oil are effective at preventing rashes, and mandatory if you know you'll be working or walking in an infested area. Gloves, boots, and long-sleeved clothes prevent direct contact, but themselves become secondary carriers of the oil if not thoroughly washed. Some outdoorspeople have had success using a coating of soap on the skin as a barrier. There are also some commercial barrier products that go by such names as Ivy Shield, Oak-N-Ivy Armor, and Ivy Block. Look for them at outdoor-equipment stores. Two drawbacks to barriers applied directly to the skin are that when you wash the blocking substance off your skin, you also wash off the skin's own protective oil coating. Also, whenever you apply an impenetrable covering to the skin you impair its ability to perform its functions, such as regulating temperature and removing toxins. So skin barriers are better as occasional measures rather than everyday steps.

If you do get urushiol oil on your skin, wash it off with soap and plenty of running water as quickly as possible, preferably within an hour of contact. Even if washing doesn't completely prevent a rash, it will often lessen an eruption's severity. Applying rapidly flowing water to the site of the contact is more effective than rubbing the area with a wet towel, since the latter may just spread the oil around rather than remove it. Be careful not to wash the urushiol off your body in a way (for instance, in the shower) that allows the oil to drip onto another part of your body.

Some campers who are far from running water have started to pack disposable alcohol wipes to use when they've touched poison ivy. A much more effective product than alcohol wipes is Tecnu Poison Oak-N-Ivy Cleanser made by Tec Laboratories of Albany, Oregon. It is a liquid mixture of mineral spirits, propylene glycol, and other chemicals that was developed in the early 1960s to remove radioactive fallout from the skin without using water. Thankfully, it has never had to catch on for that purpose. Within the past twenty years it has been widely used to cleanse urushiol from the skin of lumberjacks, telephone line workers, and others with frequent occupational exposure to poison ivy, oak, or sumac. Laboratory tests have confirmed its effectiveness at preventing and reducing rashes when applied either before or soon after a reaction has developed. Tecnu Poison Oak-N-Ivy Cleanser can also be used to decontaminate clothing and tools.

"Tecnu works better than anything I've ever seen at removing the oil and preventing rashes," says Andrew Weil, M.D. "I've used it after contacting poison oak, and you just don't get a rash."

Pet owners have to be wary of coming in contact with urushiol oil that has gotten onto a cat or dog. Animals' thick fur prevents rashes on their skin, but animals can act as a carrier of the oil to humans. Children who experience repeated rashes may be getting them from contact with a pet.

If you need to rid your property of some poison ivy or oak, don't even bother if all you intend to do is attack it with a weed cutter and then burn it. It'll just grow back, and setting it on fire sends tiny droplets of the urushiol oil wafting through the air in the smoke. You, or anybody within miles, can inhale the oil and get a harmful lung reaction. Rather, put on some heavy gloves and some old clothes you don't need and uproot the plants. Leave the plants on the ground to dry out and then bury them. Wash your tools with a solvent. Throw out the gloves and clothes.

If you insist on keeping the clothes, multiple washings in hot water and strong detergents are necessary to get rid of the oil residues. Medical practitioners have found that whenever a rash stubbornly persists despite continued treatment, it is almost always because the person is constantly repoisoning him- or herself by wearing contaminated clothing.

One bad idea is the following folk remedy for preventing allergic reactions to poison ivy: chewing or eating the leaves. In theory this could work—exposing the body to small amounts of an allergy-causing agent is how conventional allergists induce immunity in some patients. But in practice, eating the leaves is more likely to give you a nasty, even fatal, case of poison ivy of the digestive tract. If you want to go with the like-cures-like theory of healing, use safe and nontoxic homeopathic dilutions.

Finally, you can help prevent allergic reactions by changing your belief in your own susceptibility. In other words, decide you are immune to poison ivy, and you become more immune. Japanese scientists proved this by hypnotizing subjects and rubbing their skin with leaves from various plants. Some subjects who were normally allergic to a toxin experienced little or no skin reaction when told that a poisonous substance was harmless, yet did develop a rash when rubbed with a harmless leaf that they were told was toxic! "The power of belief was greater than the power of the toxin," clinical psychologist Ted Grossbart, Ph.D., noted about this study.

◆ Local Skin Infections

With its large surface area and position as the body's first-line defense against invading bodies, it is not surprising that the skin frequently suffers from superficial infections. A bite, cut, or a scrape can open up a channel for bacteria to wander in and multiply. Scabies is a type of skin infection caused by a tiny mite that burrows into the skin and lays eggs. If the skin's surface is kept too wet, various types of fungi can be nurtured and lead to athlete's foot, ringworm, and other infectious conditions.

Such infections are generally limited to the skin's upper layers, resulting in bothersome if not exceedingly painful symptoms such as redness, swelling, and itching. In some instances an infection can become so widespread that bacteria get into deeper tissues. If germs enter the bloodstream, they present a more serious health risk.

Superficial skin infections such as impetigo, cellulitis, and ringworm are rarely life-and-death emergencies but may nonetheless be dangerous. Some types are highly contagious and may spread rapidly. As general guidelines, you want to contact your medical professional when:

 ◆ an infection is accompanied by high fever, muscle aches, or stiffness in the neck
 ◆ there are red streaks extending away from the site of an infection
 ◆ the pain or swelling is severe, or lesions are rapidly spreading
 ◆ the infection is located on the head, face, or hands
 ◆ the person has diabetes, a circulation problem, an immune deficiency, leukemia, or AIDS
 ◆ home treatment doesn't improve the condition after three to seven days
 ◆ a pregnant woman develops an infection that may be from the herpes virus

The microorganisms most likely to infect the skin are bacteria, viruses, and fungi.

Bacterial infections. When the common *Staphylococcus* or *Streptococcus* bacteria break below the surface of the skin, they can cause various types of skin infections.

 ◆ Impetigo is a highly contagious skin condition often caught by children. It is characterized by blisters that pop and develop into yellowish brown crusts on the skin. Impetigo presents an added danger when it affects infants and toddlers.
 ◆ Boils and carbuncles start as infections of hair follicles. If a follicle becomes plugged from something, such as a deodorant or antiperspirant, debris backs up and traps bacteria. When the bacteria multiply and the body responds to the infection with increased blood and infection-fighting cells, boils take on their red and swollen look. Carbuncles are large, severe boils or groups of boils joined by a network of small tunnels.
 ◆ Bacterial nail infections are most common among dish-

washers who keep their hands immersed in dirty water. The bacteria get under the nailbed, eventually causing pain, redness, and swelling.

♦ Cellulitis is an acute, spreading (that is, not walled off, as a boil is) skin infection caused most often by *Streptococcus* bacteria that enter the skin through a lesion, small cut, sore, or surface infection. For unknown reasons, skin problems on the face and lower leg seem to become infected more easily than those located elsewhere on the body. A sign of cellulitis is red lines running away from the infection. The lymph glands may swell, and the person may come down with a fever, signs that bacteria have entered the bloodstream. When an infection is that advanced, see a medical professional immediately.

Viral infections. Certain viruses may be to blame for infectious diseases, such as measles, chickenpox, and shingles, that cause blisters or rashlike eruptions on the skin. The following are the most common local skin infections caused by viruses.

♦ Cold sores are also known as herpes simplex 1. This condition is characterized by groups of small blisters followed by a painful, itchy ulcer. Cold sores usually appear around the mouth and lips. (The herpes simplex 2 virus results in outbreaks around the genitals.) The affliction can be spread by contact with saliva and is most contagious just after the blisters have popped. The first infection is often the most severe, with the blisters sometimes accompanied by fever and fatigue. After the first episode the virus stays in the body and may be reactivated at any time, though many people never experience further outbreaks. Some health authorities estimate that nine out of ten Americans harbor the virus in the body. A secondary outbreak may be triggered by a variety of conditions, from fever to stress to sexual activity.

♦ Warts are caused by viruses that invade the skin and make skin cells multiply rapidly, leading to the hard, little, cauliflowerlike bumps that afflict many people. There are a number of types of warts, including the common skin warts often found on hands, plantar warts on the bottom of the feet, and genital warts, the most serious wart infection, found around the crotch.

Fungal infections. The microorganisms responsible for the greatest number of skin infections are fungi. A variety of fungi, prominently *Trichophyton*, can cause any of various skin diseases doctors refer to as tinea or ringworm. In popular usage, ringworm refers to the infection when it's on the scalp, and other terms are used for related fungal infections of certain areas of the body: athlete's foot, jock itch, and fingernail and toenail infections. The *Trichophyton* fungi live on the outer layers of the skin, preferring a warm, moist, dark environment with dead skin cells handy to feed on. Such conditions are common inside bodily folds, or in a sweaty sock. Fungal infections can be hard to get rid of when the person is susceptible or in any way immune compromised. The most common fungal skin infections include athlete's foot, ringworm, and nail fungus.

- ◆ Over 10 million Americans (mostly men; rarely children) suffer from athlete's foot at any point in time. It tends to develop first between third to fifth toes, as a result of fungal exposure of feet that are overdamp and sweaty. The symptoms may be white, peeling, and moist skin around the toes, or skin that is dry, red, burning, and itchy. In advanced cases the skin can crack or develop fissures, possibly allowing bacteria to invade.

  The condition is often routine, though it is possible for it to lead to a bacterial infection. You should consult a medical professional if inflammation becomes incapacitating, there's noted swelling in the leg, or you develop a fever.
- ◆ Ringworm is a fungal infection that is more common in children than adults. Scaly, round, itchy patches appear in a ring shape on the scalp. As the condition spreads, the harmful fungi expand at the outer edges of the circle and the inner rings start to heal. The process can briefly rob the scalp of small patches of hair. Ringworm is highly contagious. Small children often catch it from each other, or from dogs or cats.
- ◆ Nail fungus is usually first observed as a darkening in the tips of the fingernail or toenail. The discoloration then spreads toward the cuticle, eventually making the nail thick and rough-edged. The nail becomes unsightly but may not hurt.

BASIC TREATMENT FOR LOCAL SKIN INFECTIONS

Doctors rely on a range of over-the-counter topical medications to counter skin infections. Some of the most common drugs include clotrimazole, miconazole (Micatin), and tolnaftate (Tinactin).

These will often relieve the itching in a day or two and the rash within a week or two. Topical corticosteroid drugs sometimes relieve the itching, but worsen the eruption itself.

If the infection is persistent, doctors turn to more potent prescription medications, both topical and oral. Ringworm on the scalp can be made less contagious with creams, but a course of oral drugs is often used to cure it. For a nail fungus, six months to a year of conventional treatment with oral antifungals or medicated nail polishes may be required. The treatment is so protracted that many people with nail infections just give up and live with the condition indefinitely.

Penicillin injections are used for impetigo. To treat boils, doctors prescribe oral antibiotics. Medical personnel may also open the boil with a scalpel to drain it. For athlete's foot, in addition to antifungals doctors may prescribe a powerful antiperspirant to help keep the feet dry. Warts may be treated with topical applications or removed by dissolving, electrifying, or freezing agents.

There is a lot of crossover drug use. Bacterial nail infections sometimes respond to antifungal creams, while fungal nail infections may improve by taking oral antibiotics such as griseofulvin.

The usual treatment routine is to dry the infected area thoroughly, using a hair dryer if necessary. A cream is then applied to kill the bacteria, virus, or fungus. This is repeated twice a day. The infection often seems to clear in a week or two, though doctors recommend that the treatment continue for a month to prevent an immediate recurrence. A consultation with a medical professional is needed if the infection does not respond to the first week of treatment. Laboratory tests can help determine whether an allergy, dermatitis, or other skin condition is responsible for the symptoms.

NATURAL FIRST-AID REMEDIES FOR LOCAL SKIN INFECTIONS

The best natural treatments should be complemented by the common sense guidelines of allowing the body time to rest and keeping the area cool and dry.

Use the essential oil of Tea Tree to help reverse almost all types of skin infections. Tea Tree's powerful antiviral and antifungal properties and its mild effect when used straight on the skin make it an excellent first choice for a natural remedy against athlete's foot, fungal nail infections, and ringworm. There are a number of ways you can apply it, once or more daily:

- Soak your nail or feet for ten to fifteen minutes in a bowl of warm water to which you've added ten to fifteen drops of Tea Tree oil. Dry thoroughly after the soaking.
- Apply a warm compress made by soaking a cotton cloth in a cup of warm water with six to eight drops of Tea Tree. Wring, apply, cover with a dry towel or plastic, let the compress sit till it cools, and reapply.
- Put six to eight drops of Tea Tree in a tablespoon of olive or other vegetable oil and apply to the site of infection.
- Make a powder by mixing eight to ten drops of Tea Tree into a cup of dry green clay. Apply to the infection.
- Apply one undiluted drop over the infected area. This works well on infections that cover a tiny area, such as cold sores, warts, and boils.
- For hard-to-cure nail infections, Cynthia Olsen, author of *Australian Tea Tree Oil Guide*, recommends soaking the fingernail or toenail in pure Tea Tree oil for five minutes twice daily until the infection clears.
- Apply one of the various commercial Tea Tree creams and salves found on the shelves of natural foods stores. Follow label directions.

Tea Tree is a minor ingredient in the natural athlete's-foot remedy NutriBiotic Skin Spray, which contains water, a standardized extract of citrus, alcohol, and the essential oils of Tea Tree and Chamomile. It is made by NutriBiotic of Lakeport, California, and is packaged in a four-ounce spray bottle. The cooling, antibacterial action works well on cuts and scrapes, too.

Other essential oils that can be used successfully to counter skin infections include:

- Lavender
- Eucalyptus
- Garlic
- Chamomile

Dilute fifteen drops of any of these oils in a tablespoon of olive or other vegetable oil and apply to the site of infection.

Apply a goldenseal-root powder pack to treat a simple bacterial skin infection. Joseph Pizzorno, N.D., says that "a goldenseal pack virtually always drains a mild bacterial infection within twelve hours. Mix goldenseal-root powder with water or, if you have it, calendula succus, which is the juice of the calendula flower. Pack the paste over the infection and leave it on for twelve hours. Calendula succus works well by itself if you don't have goldenseal. Put it over the area and cover with something that is nonporous for twelve hours."

Goldenseal-root powder is widely available in capsules from herbal companies. Well-stocked natural foods stores may carry goldenseal root in the form of a boxed loose powder. Calendula succus is available from Herb Pharm of Williams, Oregon, in bottle sizes ranging from one to thirty-two ounces, and from other herbal companies.

Spread echinacea cream, liquid extract, or salve on boils and other skin infections. This immunity-stimulating herb helps the body defend against viral infections.

Take advantage of the powerful infection-clearing properties of garlic. Garlic can be used to treat athlete's foot and other skin infections. Apply it in any number of ways, a few times per day:

◆ Make a poultice of minced garlic and put it directly onto the skin, or wrap the garlic in a piece of cheesecloth and tape it to the skin. Leave on for fifteen to twenty minutes.

◆ Take three to five garlic tablets or capsules orally every day.

◆ Add powdered garlic to honey and apply to the skin as a poultice.

◆ Open garlic capsules and dust the feet and toes with the powder.

◆ Put minced garlic into your shoes to treat athlete's foot.

Apply a tincture of myrrh to fungal infections of the nails and skin. Myrrh makes an excellent topical application when mixed with calendula cream or lotion, goldenseal powder, or green clay.

Other herbal preparations that can be used to help reduce bacterial, viral, or fungal skin infections include:

◆ witch hazel extract, which has antiviral tannins; like myrrh and goldenseal it can help dry cold-sore lesions and relieve itching

◆ aloe gel, which can be especially useful to alternate with drying agents such as witch hazel

◆ pau d'arco (for athlete's foot, make a strong decoction and soak your feet in it, or drink it)

◆ black-walnut tincture, which has potent antifungal compounds (it will stain the skin and nails a dark, blackish purple color)

Herbal companies market various types of salves and lotions for minor skin infections. For instance, WiseWays Herbals produces a Black Walnut Tea Tree Salve that also contains calendula, nettles, slippery elm, and other herbs. Such products often work exceptionally well on fungal infections, skin rashes, and the like.

For athlete's foot, rub the feet with a stiff-bristled brush while showering. When you remove the flakes of dead skin always found on the body's surface, you scrape off fungi as well. Brush the entire foot lightly but vigorously.

Take a homeopathic remedy. Homeopaths treat shingles, warts, athlete's foot, and ringworm with any of a dozen or more remedies, depending on the symptoms. "The person is better off getting constitutional treatment for most types of viral skin infections," homeopath Jennifer Jacobs, M.D., says. Among the most common remedies to use if you do want to try to self-treat a skin infection are:

- for boils, *Belladonna* in the early stages when there is redness and heat around the area, and *Hepar sulphur* if the boil is especially painful and sensitive to pressure
- for impetigo, *Antimonium crudum* (from black sulfide of antimony) for the usual symptoms, or *Rhus tox* if there is excessive itchiness
- for cold sores, oral *Rhus tox* during an acute outbreak, plus topical *Calendula* applications

Give oral doses of 6X or 12X potency every three to four hours during acute stages of a skin infection, then two to three times daily as symptoms clear up.

Will your warts away. Warts are particularly amenable to psychological and placebo effects. If you have a prayer, affirmation, ritual, or any other mind/body technique that you know works well for you, it may help remove your wart. "Compared to the clear and lasting success of belief, placebo, and folk remedies for warts, the scientific approach of conventional medicine is pitiful," notes Andrew Weil, M.D., author of *Health and Healing*.

Try one of the following traditional home remedies. Most of these will work for athlete's foot and other fungal infections. Do these applications for five to ten minutes once or twice a day.

- Apply vinegar to increase the level of acidity on the skin's surface and discourage fungal growth. For athlete's foot, you can soak your feet in a vinegar solution (dilute it 1:4 in water), or wash between the toes or elsewhere with dilute or straight vinegar.

A wart-removing technique some people have found helpful is to saturate a cotton ball in cider vinegar, wring it out, and tape it on the wart overnight. It may take two weeks or so of treatment before the wart blackens and falls off.

♦ Apply a 3 percent hydrogen peroxide solution to the affected area.

♦ For athlete's foot, give your feet a salt-water soak. Use four teaspoons salt per quart warm water.

♦ Rub a baking soda paste onto the site of a fungal infection. Rinse and dry thoroughly.

♦ Pour some vitamin E oil onto a bandage and apply the bandage to a wart. Replace the bandage each day for several days.

♦ Apply hot compresses to a boil to draw more blood and boost the healing process.

PREVENTING SKIN INFECTIONS

Skin infections vary in degrees of contagion. For instance, common warts are somewhat contagious and venereal warts are quite contagious. Authorities also disagree on how contagious specific skin infections are—some say athlete's foot is highly contagious while others say that the fungus is not easily transmitted from person to person. Despite the variations, it makes sense to follow some basic preventive guidelines, both to inhibit the development of an infection on your own skin and to discourage passing infections between people.

If someone in your family suffers from a skin infection, particularly a viral or fungal one, avoid touching the area or wash your hands afterward. Don't share personal and hygiene items such as towels, clothing, combs, toothbrushes, and eating utensils. Herpes in particular is highly contagious and easily spread by kissing or touching, both to other people and to other parts of the body, especially the eyes.

The fungus responsible for athlete's foot and most other skin infections grows best when given a moist, dark environment. So it is important to dry the skin thoroughly after washing or swimming, particularly between the toes. If you're prone to athlete's foot, change your socks frequently, wearing light, white cotton socks in summer and wool in the winter. Natural fibers are better at wicking perspiration away from the skin than synthetic fibers such as nylon. Wear well-ventilated leather or canvas shoes; these breathe better than plastic or rubber shoes. Don't wear boots all day, and avoid overly tight shoes altogether. Rotate wearing two pairs of shoes, allowing them to dry, in the sun if possible, between wearings. Try to expose the feet to fresh air and natural sunlight frequently (wear sandals in the summer). Wear rubber clogs around pools and gym showers.

Similarly, help prevent jock itch by keeping the crotch area cool and dry: wear cotton underwear and dry well after bathing.

Cold sores can sometimes be averted by applying ice for ten minutes per hour at the first sign of an outbreak. Also apply cream or tincture of echinacea topically, and take one to two dropperfuls of echinacea tincture orally every two hours for up to eight hours, or until the tingling or itching sensation subsides. Effective long-term protection from cold sores is sometimes available by consuming foods high in the amino acid L-lysine, including fish and yogurt. L-lysine is also available as a dietary supplement.

It's impossible to live in a sterile environment, so maintaining healthy skin and a strong immune system is just as important as preventing the conditions that encourage microbial growth. For instance, the outer layer of the skin maintains a slightly acidic pH. This helps to prevent microorganisms on the skin from multiplying out of control.

On the negative side are all those unhealthful habits that tend to undermine skin and immune function, including smoking, excessive drinking, regular consumption of broad-spectrum antibiotics and other potent pharmaceutical drugs, exposure to radiation, and a high-fat, high-sugar diet.

On the positive side, consider taking the following nutrients on a daily basis to help replenish friendly bacteria, inhibit fungal growth, and stimulate immune response:

- an acidophilus supplement
- B complex, 50–100 mg
- vitamin C plus bioflavonoids, two to five grams in mixed dosages or to bowel tolerance (avoid megadoses of C if pregnant)
- zinc, 25–50 mg
- vitamin A in the form of beta carotene, 25,000 IU

◆ Splinters and Fishhook Removal

Objects that get stuck in the skin present special first-aid challenges. When the object is small, such as a splinter of wood, metal, or glass, or a fishhook, it should be removed as quickly as possible. With small puncture wounds, there is always the possibility that dirt or bacteria can get trapped beneath the skin, leading to infection.

When an object larger than a splinter, such as a pencil, or larger than a fishhook but also barbed, such as an arrow, punctures the body, it is best *not* to remove it. Pulling a large object out of an injury may cause extensive tissue damage and may increase bleeding. In some cases, such as pulling out an object that has punctured the lungs, it can quickly be fatal. Leave a large penetrating object in the body and don't touch it. Try to cover it, using a paper cup and tape or loose bandages, in a way that immobilizes it while the person is transferred to the hospital or while emergency personnel are summoned.

BASIC FIRST AID FOR SPLINTERS AND FISHHOOKS

Even splinters and fishhooks should at times be removed only by medical professionals. Call for medical help if:

◆ a splinter or fishhook is embedded near an eye or an artery
◆ a splinter is large and deep, broken up, or made of glass
◆ a wooden splinter gets wet, since this can cause it to swell and become more difficult to remove
◆ you can't get all of the object out from under the skin
◆ the injury becomes red, swollen, and painful, or starts to bleed

Splinters. Splinters are usually no more than bothersome. It is important to remove them, however, because left in, they can lead to a local or even systemic infection.

The simplest method for removing splinters is to attach a piece of tape to the splinter and give it a quick yank in the direction from which it went in. If this doesn't work, you need to grab the splinter or poke it out using other tools.

Start with bright light, a needle, and a good set of tweezers. Wash your hands and sterilize the needle and the tweezers (put them in boiling water for two to three minutes, hold them over an open flame for fifteen to twenty seconds, or pour antiseptic solution over them). Allow the tools to cool naturally if they've been sterilized with heat.

Examine the splinter closely to determine how it went under the skin. Press down with a finger on the point of the splinter that is embedded in the skin, pushing it toward the entrance wound as you grab at the exposed end with the tweezers. Pull it out at the same angle that it went in. Try to grab the splinter with your first effort, since poking a splinter often starts to break it up into fragments that are harder to remove. If the splinter is totally embedded and you can't grab the end with the tweezers, use the sharp tip of the needle to try to lift the splinter out. Don't dig deeply if it's not working.

Afterward wash the injury area with antiseptic solution, apply antibiotic ointment, bandage, and discuss with your medical professional the need for a tetanus shot.

Fishhooks. Removing a fishhook that has penetrated the skin is easy if the barb has not sunk beneath the surface of the skin. Gently pull the tip out in the same direction it went in.

When the fishhook has penetrated deeply enough for the barb to be embedded, simply pulling it out may cause extensive tearing and cutting of tissue as the barb rips up toward the skin's surface. Rather, if medical help is not available, you need wire cutters to remove an embedded fishhook. Wash your hands and clean the area around the wound first.

The wire cutter method works best when the barb has penetrated so deeply that it has curved back up toward the surface of the skin or has actually come through the surface. If the barb hasn't broken through, you need to push it through. First, if possible, numb the surface of the skin where the barb is to break through, using ice or a few drops of Clove oil. Use needle-nose pliers or your fingers to grasp the straight end of the fishhook and to give a quick twist to the fishhook until the barb comes through the surface of the skin. Use the wire cutters to cut off the barb. Then back out the rest of the fishhook through the entry wound.

Treat the wound as you would a puncture wound (see "Chapter 5: Bites and Stings"). Wash thoroughly in soap and running water. Soak the injury in or irrigate it with an antiseptic solution for a few minutes and bandage lightly and loosely with sterile gauze since closing off the injury increases the risk of infection. Have a medical professional check it out. The person may need a tetanus shot.

NATURAL FIRST-AID REMEDIES FOR SPLINTERS

For splinters that balk at mechanical removal, here are a few natural methods for drawing the splinter up toward the surface of the skin, where it is more easily grabbed. Drawing methods take a day or longer to work, so it is better to remove a splinter mechanically if at all possible.

Apply an herbal poultice over the splinter. A number of herbs, when applied as a paste, help to draw foreign matter out of tissue. The simplest way to make a paste is to add hot water to the powdered herb. Apply the paste over the splinter, either directly to the skin or over a piece of gauze. Wrap with gauze and renew it every four hours. Or leave it on overnight, and in some cases, in the morning the splinter will have been drawn to the surface of the skin. Make the paste out of powdered herb of:

◆ slippery elm bark
◆ comfrey root
◆ fenugreek seeds

Fenugreek *(Trigonella foenumgraecum)* is one of the oldest medicinal plants, with herbal applications of the seeds dating back to the ancient Egyptians. In addition to its use as a drawing poultice, it has been taken internally for reproductive disorders and as an aphrodisiac. The seeds are high in mucilage, protein, and vitamins.

Oriental Medical Doctor Holly Eagle also recommends black ointment for its powerful drawing properties. She says, "We've seen a whole range of case histories in which it worked to draw out not only splinters but toxins from bites and such. Black ointment works well on boils, too."

Though a number of herbal companies make forms of black ointment, Eagle says that she's had the best success using the product formulated by Nature's Way, which contains ten herbal ingredients (including allantoin from comfrey root, juniper tar, plantain, and goldenseal root) and activated charcoal in a base of wheat-germ and olive oils, pine tar, pine gum, beeswax, and lanolin.

After the splinter has been removed, a calendula or echinacea salve applied to the area can help prevent an infection.

Take a homeopathic remedy for splinters. When a splinter can't easily be removed by tweezers, homeopaths recommend a couple of remedies to aid the body's efforts to expel it.

♦ *Silicea*. Made from flint, this is the most common splinter remedy. It is taken orally to promote expulsion of foreign bodies from tissue. Homeopath Jennifer Jacobs, M.D., says, "*Silicea* works so well sometimes it will even expel a splinter that has been embedded for years."

♦ *Hepar sulphur*. If *Silicea* doesn't work, or for a splinter that is especially sore and tender to the touch, try this oral remedy, made from calcium sulfide.

Try one of the following traditional folk remedies for helping to expel a splinter. Leave any of these topical applications on overnight or renew every few hours until the splinter surfaces.

♦ Apply a kaolin poultice. Kaolin is a fine white clay that's been used since ancient times in the treatment of diarrhea (and still was, until 1989, in the over-the-counter product Kaopectate). You can find kaolin in some well-stocked natural foods stores.

♦ Tape a slice of raw onion around the splinter.

♦ Apply pine resin to the splinter.

♦ Wrap the splinter area with a fresh plantain leaf.

♦ Grate a potato or the core of a cabbage, macerate it, and apply it as a poultice to the splinter.

♦ Recovering from Skin Emergencies

You can take a number of positive steps after an injury or infection to restore skin to its best condition. Proper diet and nutrients can nourish the skin; exercise, rest, and relaxation can lessen the adverse effects of stress; and such techniques as sauna and massage can improve circulation and the elimination of toxins.

Some of the unhealthful habits that should be avoided all of the time but especially during recovery from a skin emergency include smoking, applying harsh chemicals or cosmetics to the skin, and exposing the skin to levels of ultraviolet light capable of causing a burn.

With its large reservoirs of blood, oils, and other fluids, the skin is one of the first tissues to suffer from dehydration. Thus, drinking adequate fluids is essential for optimal skin health. Depending upon such individual factors as body size, weather, and activity level, most people should be drinking at least one to two quarts of water, herbal teas, and fruit juices every day. Foods that are high in water content, such as fresh fruits and vegetables, are some of the best for skin health as well.

Consider taking the following nutrients on a daily basis to boost skin function and help it recover from skin emergencies. All of the following are either antioxidants that scavenge harmful free radicals or cell builders critical for growth and repair of tissue:

- vitamin A in the form of beta carotene, 25,000 IU
- vitamin C plus bioflavonoids, two to five grams in mixed doses or to bowel tolerance (avoid megadoses of C if pregnant)
- zinc, 25–50 mg
- selenium, 100–200 mcg
- vitamin B complex, 50–100 mg
- folic acid, 400–800 mcg
- vitamin B$_{12}$, 25–300 mcg
- silicon, 1–2 mg

A vigorous massage has the dual benefit of increasing circulation and vitality of skin tissues and alleviating harmful mental stress that can lead to premature aging of the skin.

TWENTY-TWO

Travel Problems

THIS CHAPTER COVERS:

- *motion sickness*
- *jet lag*

Travel problems such as motion sickness and jet lag are minor emergencies compared to fractures, allergic reactions, and many of the other first-aid problems covered in previous chapters. By definition, though, travel problems occur away from home, and sometimes in a foreign country where the language and customs—to say nothing of the over-the-counter drugs and natural remedies—may be unknown. Travel problems thus present unique challenges and opportunities for friends of natural first aid.

◆ Motion Sickness

Marcus Cato said that he had never repented but three times in his whole life, once when he had paid a ship's fare to a place instead of walking.
—PLUTARCH, CIRCA A.D. 110

Also known as seasickness and car sickness, motion sickness is the nausea and vomiting brought on by riding in a boat, car, plane, or roller coaster. As the above quote from the famous Greek biographer and historian indicates, motion sickness has probably afflicted humanity ever since the first horse or boat ride. (It's no accident that the word *nausea*, like *nautical*, has as its root the Greek *naus*, for ship.) Motion or seasickness can strike anyone, including at times the most sea-encrusted sailor. Studies and anecdotal reports indicate that even animals are not immune to motion sickness's adverse effects.

493

Researchers trace the root cause of motion sickness to a problem in how the body's nervous system deals with conflicting information supplied to it by the sense organs. Normally the eyes gather visual data that tell the nervous system something about where the body is and in which direction it is moving. Nerve cells in the skin and muscles also report on how the body is moving. Finally, the semicircular canals and other parts of the inner ear gather and relay data relating to bodily balance, gravitational effects, spinning motion, and orientation in space.

Motion sickness results when environmental conditions conspire to confuse the nervous system about the data it is getting from these sense organs. In a pitching boat, the eyes tell the brain that the body is standing still on the deck, while the touch sense organs and the ear relay a jumble of reports indicating movement. The brain and nervous system tell the gastrointestinal system to deal with the problem, which it does by unloading the contents of the stomach.

The early symptoms of motion sickness include sleepiness, dizziness, feeling cold and clammy, rapid breathing, sweating, and nausea. All of these symptoms are common and can possibly be related to other, more serious conditions, though if they're occurring together while you're traveling in a car, plane, or boat, you can be pretty sure motion sickness is the cause.

Conventional doctors typically recommend drugs to prevent and treat motion sickness. The two most popular motion-sickness drugs are the antihistamines Dramamine and Bonine, which are most effective when taken thirty minutes before embarking on a boat or plane. Both drugs have the unwanted side effect of causing considerable drowsiness. An up-and-coming alternative on the pharmaceutical scene is the prescription drug scopolamine, which can be administered through a dime-sized patch attached behind the ear (Transderm Scop). The patch delivers minute doses through the skin for up to three days. Side effects other than dry mouth are rare, though they can include drowsiness and blurred vision. Scopolamine should not be used by people with glaucoma. A final drawback is that it's expensive.

NATURAL REMEDIES FOR MOTION SICKNESS

Motion sickness is one of the conditions for which there are a number of remedies that are not only demonstrably safer, but in the case of ginger, have also proven to be more effective than conventional drug therapy.

***Take the herb ginger, the premier natural motion-sickness
remedy.*** Take large quantities of ginger to prevent motion sickness. Dried ginger seems to be more effective than fresh ginger.
An adult dosage is six to eight capsules or one to two grams of
powdered ginger root taken about forty-five minutes before departing. Or take one-half to one tablespoon with water. Ginger is
widely available in capsules, concentrated extracts, and the like.
It is usually the main component of combination herbal products
for motion sickness that go by such names as Travel-Ease and
Motion Ease. These can be found in most natural foods stores.

Kids can be given a smaller dose along with other sources of
the herb, including ginger tea and nonartifically flavored ginger-
snap cookies or ginger ale.

The Chinese and others have used ginger for thousands of
years, both as a flavoring and as an herbal folk remedy. Ginger
helps expel gas from the intestines and relaxes and soothes the
intestinal tract. Sailors have long known of its ability to counter
seasickness. A number of studies in the past decade have confirmed ginger's effectiveness against seasickness, including a famous (among herbalists, anyway) 1982 report in the British medical journal *Lancet*. The authors of the *Lancet* study concluded
that powdered ginger was an even more effective motion-sickness
remedy than Dramamine.

Ginger is also still taken by pregnant women to prevent
stomach distress and morning sickness. Scientists think that
ginger acts on both the nervous and digestive systems to prevent
nausea and vomiting.

***Press on the acupressure point located in the middle of the
inner side of the forearm two and one-half finger widths above
the wrist crease.*** "This is the most famous point for relieving
nausea, motion sickness, and even the morning sickness of early
pregnancy," notes Michael Reed Gach, author of *Acupressure's
Potent Points*. Known as P6 for its location on the pericardium (or
"heart governor") meridian, or energy pathway, this point has
even attracted the attention of scientists and health-product producers. Gach notes that studies have confirmed the antinausea
effects of manipulating the point. A number of manufacturers
now make cloth wristbands with a slightly protruding knob that
stimulates the P6 point as the band is worn on the wrist (see
illustration #21). The Sea Band and other wristbands are available from mail-order catalogs (see "Resources").

***Take a few doses of the common homeopathic remedy* Nux
vomica.** This is the most widely prescribed antinausea homeopathic remedy, especially for persistent nausea. If you suffer from

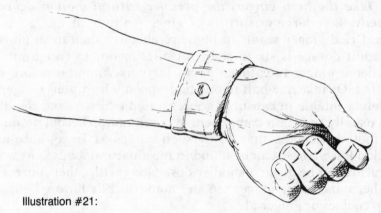

Illustration #21:

Special cloth bands stimulate an acupressure point in the wrist to help prevent nausea from motion sickness.

motion sickness frequently or have a varied homeopathic kit, consider the lesser-known motion-sickness remedies *Cocculus* or *Tabacum* before or during an episode.

◆ *Cocculus* (from Indian cockle seeds) is for the person who feels dizzy and exhausted, experiences extreme nausea from the smell of food, and wants to lie down.

◆ *Tabacum* (from tobacco) is better for the person who is pale, faint, or cold and sweaty. He or she has a characteristic sinking feeling in the stomach. Symptoms improve when the person is exposed to fresh air.

Do deep-breathing exercises. Breathing teacher Carola Speads, author of *Ways to Better Breathing*, contends that you can avoid motion sickness if you "concentrate on your exhalation, making sure they are not stifled. Keeping your breaths flowing out and in rhythmically makes it impossible to pull your stomach up and hold it and yourself in a cramped position—one of the main causes of nausea." She suggests humming forcefully as a good way to use the breath as a motion-sickness prevention and cure.

Take the flower essence remedy Scleranthus. This is the essence that promotes stability in a person, in the sense that it helps a person suffering from indecision and uncertainty regain poise and emotional balance. Flower essence practitioners say that it reduces mood swings and has a positive effect on motion sickness.

Try the Oriental prepared medicine widely known as Pill Curing. It comes packaged in ten small vials and a typical dose is one to two vials. Those who suffer from motion sickness take it thirty to sixty minutes before departure.

Pill Curing is a popular and versatile combination of more than a dozen herbal and other substances, used to relieve indigestion and summer colds as well as nausea resulting from motion sickness. The Chinese term for the formula is Kang Ning Wan, which translates roughly as "Healthy and Quiet Pills," and it is sold as Pill Curing by the United Pharmaceutical Manufactory of China.

Pill Curing is available from Oriental pharmacies and mail-order herbal catalogs (see "Resources").

Try one of the many folk remedies for motion sickness. All of the following are time-tested steps that have worked for sailors and others.

♦ Eat cold stewed tomatoes with saltine crackers before and during the trip. Dry soda crackers may help by absorbing excess fluid in the stomach.
♦ Suck on a lemon (rinse the teeth afterward to prevent tooth decay) or drink fresh lemon juice.
♦ Drink a cup of peppermint tea.

PREVENTING MOTION SICKNESS

General guidelines for preventing motion sickness are to get sufficient rest and sleep, drink plenty of fluids to prevent dehydration, and avoid alcohol and large, fatty meals before and during the journey. While traveling, sit in the part of a vehicle where there is the least movement and keep your head still. Situate yourself so that you can see the horizon. If you get queasy, fix your eyes on the horizon or some stationary object in the distance.

Before embarking, eat a healthful diet that leads to a settled stomach. Many veteran travelers recommend eating light, easily digested meals at frequent intervals. Others suggest a liquid diet before traveling, or crackers and ice water. You may also benefit by taking extra vitamin B_6 (50 mg daily; motion sickness may at times be an actual symptom of a B_6 deficiency). Some practitioners say that motion sickness may be prevented by taking B complex (50–100 mg daily), three to four teaspoons of brewer's yeast, or two to three activated-charcoal tablets to soak up acids. Another tip: each day for two to three days before departure, take three 40-mg capsules of the herb ginkgo, for better inner ear function.

Here are some practical guidelines, organized by mode of travel.

In a car or bus. Ride in the front seat, where it is easiest to look out the front window. Children are frequent victims of car sickness until they reach adolescence, and a main factor may be that this is when they become tall enough to easily look out a window. Roll down a window to increase the supply of fresh air. Suggest to children that they not read or play games that require looking down at pages or a game board.

On a boat. Sit in the middle of a boat, preferably up on deck. Unless you have something better than hand-holding to offer, ignore other people who are throwing up; you can't help them at that point, and they're likely to make you sick.

In a plane. Sit in the middle rather than in the tail, since the latter is where a plane moves the most. Choose a seat over the right wing because the prevailing turning patterns of the aircraft will cause fewer disorienting opportunities. Also fly at night, when you can't see the many bouncing movements of the plane against the clouds and ground.

When astronauts suffer from motion sickness (which they do, frequently) it can be a major problem. Vomiting while wearing a helmet could asphyxiate an astronaut. Thus, NASA has in recent years developed an abiding interest in finding side-effect-free alternatives to the conventional drug therapies for motion sickness. NASA's search has led them to successfully explore biofeedback and relaxation-training programs to prevent motion sickness. Such treatments could be the wave of the future for motion sickness, to use an apt metaphor.

◆ Jet Lag

The human body is a machine, declared seventeenth-century scientists. No, it's a computer, decided mid-twentieth-century scientists. Recent advances in understanding may well lead scientists of the next century to describe the body as a clock. And one of the main ways we experience malfunctions of the body-as-clock is through jet lag.

Flying across just two time zones disrupts the body's internal biological clock, causing changes in body temperature, blood pressure, breathing and heart rate, and sleeping and waking patterns. All of these vital functions ebb and flow in a daily, or circadian, rhythm. Jet travel throws the body out of sync with this rhythm, leading to the common symptoms of fatigue, disorientation, insomnia, and irritability.

Jet travel is but one way to fool with your internal clock. Switching back and forth between a day and a night shift can also disrupt normal bodily rhythms. When such practices cause some of the more serious effects, such as lapses in reasoning, accidents happen. The late hour and changing work-shift schedules were cited as contributing to the disastrous *Exxon Valdez* oil spill in Alaska in March 1989.

The body's main clock is located in a small section of the brain connected by the optic nerve to the retina at the back of the eye. The brain cells receive information about light and dark from the retina. Light is thus crucial to setting the body's clock. (Blind people can suffer from a type of perpetual jet lag.) Along with temperature and other factors, light also regulates the secretion of the hormone melatonin, which is produced by the tiny pineal gland in the center of the brain. Melatonin affects mood, performance, and fatigue. Researchers say that melatonin plays an important role in maintaining regular sleep patterns and biological rhythms.

Conventional treatment of jet lag is mainly limited to sleeping pills, though doctors are paying increasing attention to therapies employing either diet or light. Some of the latest research explores how to use pills containing minute doses of melatonin to counter the effects of jet lag. One recent study by an endocrinologist in England found that melatonin pills significantly decreased the symptoms of jet lag among sixty-one persons tested. Another double-blind, placebo-controlled study of seventeen persons who flew from London to San Francisco found that none of those who took five milligrams of melatonin a day had symptoms of jet lag, while six of nine persons who took a placebo had significant symptoms.

NATURAL REMEDIES FOR PREVENTING AND TREATING JET LAG

Some of the most effective treatments for jet lag, natural or otherwise, are spread out over a few days—before departure, during the trip, and afterward. As with motion sickness, it is best to combine the elements of prevention and treatment for treating jet lag.

Take melatonin hormone supplements. A prominent melatonin supplement is Melatone, made by Cardiovascular Research,

Ltd. of Concord, California. Melatone comes in 3-mg capsules, sixty to a jar. To help prevent jet lag, take one capsule when you arrive in a new time zone approximately an hour before you go to sleep.

Small amounts of the hormone melatonin can help jet-lag sufferers to reset their biological clocks. Andrew Weil, M.D., author of *Natural Health, Natural Medicine,* says, "I've tried melatonin and given it to others, and it works. I travel a lot, and I've found that melatonin is much simpler and more effective than other jet lag remedies." Melatonin supplements are classified as food supplements. A new product, it is increasingly available in natural foods stores, pharmacies, or through health professionals.

Taken orally, melatonin is rapidly absorbed into the bloodstream, metabolized, and eliminated from the body. Studies indicate that side effects from taking melatonin are negligible.

Use adjustments in your exposure to bright light as a way to speed adaptation to your new environment. Sunlight at the right time of day can have a powerful anti-jet-lag effect, notes light researcher Dr. Alfred J. Lewy of the Oregon Health Science Center in Portland. If you're traveling through six or fewer time zones, he suggests the following steps:

- If you're flying east to west, leave your sunglasses off when you arrive and try to get a few hours of sunshine at the end of the day. This will help reset your body's clock to a later bedtime.
- If you're flying west to east, try to get some bright sun on arrival early in the day to aid the shift to an earlier schedule. If you're due to arrive at night, while on the plane pull your window shade down, turn off your reading light, or better yet put on eyeshades during what would be nighttime at your destination. In effect this tricks your body into thinking it is in its new time zone already, thus reducing symptoms of jet lag.

Beginning a few days before departure, start to take Siberian ginseng, a powerful adaptogenic herb. Siberian ginseng is widely available in tincture and capsules and is often combined with other adaptogenic herbs such as schizandra. Follow dosage directions on labels.

Siberian ginseng has been used for over four thousand years by the Chinese as a revitalizing tonic to increase longevity and improve general health. Sometimes referred to as eleuthero, it is the root of a shrub widely grown in the Far East. Herbalists refer to it as an adaptogen, a special class of herbs that are able to restore balance to various bodily systems without regard to the direction of the imbalance. Adaptogens also increase the body's resistance to stress, fatigue, and disease.

An adaptogenic herbal product that works well is Yerba Prima Adaptoplex, which combines eleuthero, schizandra berry, shiitake, and American ginseng. These herbs can help normalize the body's stress response and eliminate fatigue, says Richard Israel, author of *The Natural Pharmacy Product Guide*. He reports, "I use [Adaptoplex] to combat the effects of jet lag whenever I fly long distances. A couple of tablets before and after a flight are enough to keep me from experiencing any jet-lag symptoms on a three-to-five-hour flight. Longer flights may need additional doses."

Korean or Chinese ginseng *(Panax ginseng)* may also benefit jet-lag sufferers because of its adaptogenic and antistress effects. Ginseng improves the functioning of the adrenal gland and protects the body against mental and physical fatigue. The Chinese prepared medicine Pill Curing, mentioned as a natural motion-sickness remedy, can also help prevent jet lag when taken before departure.

Take oral doses of homeopathic Arnica for jet lag. The feelings of jet lag are similar to the soreness and tiredness you get from overexertion. *Arnica* can relieve such symptoms. If you can't sleep because your body clock is a few hours behind local time, you can also try taking the homeopathic combination remedy Hyland's Calms Forté, made by Standard Homeopathic. Calms Forté is a popular sleep aid that combines nine homeopathic remedies, including *Chamomilla* 2X and *Passiflora* 1X (from passionflower). Take one to three tablets thirty to sixty minutes before retiring.

Use an aromatherapy treatment to counter jet lag. Aromatherapy's positive effects on jet lag have recently been recognized by airlines such as Air New Zealand, which includes in their "afterflight regulator kit" a three-day supply of two essential-oil formulas, one labeled "Awake" and one "Asleep." The airline adopted the formulas after testing the aromatherpy kits on two thousand frequent-flying volunteers. Some 73 percent of the subjects said that the oils, used in the bath or shower, improved the subject's ability to overcome jet lag, according to a spokesperson for the formula producer, Daniele Ryman Ltd. of London (see "Resources"). Almost half of the people given placebos were also helped; if you think it will help, do it! It probably will.

Eat an anti-jet-lag diet. In recent years Dr. Charles Ehret of the U.S. Department of Energy's Argonne National Laboratory in Illinois developed an effective plan, with extensive dietary recommendations, for countering the effects of jet lag. His anti-jet-lag diet takes advantage of the differing effects of proteins, carbohydrates, and fats on the brain's biochemistry. By alternating heavy and light eating days, you can speed up the body's ability to shift its internal clock.

The complete dietary plan starts three days before departure day and is somewhat complicated, with varying instructions depending upon direction of travel (east- or westbound) and number of time zones crossed. A simplified plan follows:

On day one eat a breakfast and lunch high in protein, and dinner and evening snacks high in carbohydrates. On day two, eat nothing but salads, soups, and other light, easily digested foods. Day three is a repeat of day one. On day four, departure day, set your watch to the time zone of your destination and then eat a high-protein breakfast at that time zone's breakfast time. If this sounds intriguing and you want the full set of recommendations (including when it's best to drink caffeinated beverages, and a host of suggestions relating to exercise and other nondietary steps), see "Resources."

Use a quick acupressure massage to alleviate jet lag. "I travel a lot and have found acupressure is all I need for jet lag," Michael Reed Gach, author of *Acupressure's Potent Points,* says. "There are four points to press, what the Chinese call 'the four gates,' two on each side of the body. The points are in the middle of the webbing between the thumb and index finger, and on the top of the foot in the valley between the big toe and second toe.

"For jet lag I also work on the middle back, pressing on and flexing it. Standing up, I make fists and place them in my lower back on either side. Then I exhale as I lean back and apply some firm pressure with the fists. You can also try rocking on the middle of your back on a carpeted floor."

Consume higher amounts of the essential amino acid tryptophan to help reduce the effects of jet lag and get enough sleep at your destination. Tryptophan is a natural sleeping aid found in a variety of foods, including turkey, milk, corn, legumes, cereal grains, and some nuts and seeds. In the body tryptophan plays an important role in production of the brain neurotransmitter serotonin. A lack of serotonin has been tied to depression and sleep-related problems in some people, and some scientists say that increased serotonin levels may help prevent jet lag. A number of studies done prior to 1989 using tryptophan supplements substantiate anti-jet-lag effects for tryptophan. In one study performed at the University of California San Diego School of Medicine, fifty-one Marines were flown across eight time zones. Those subjects given tryptophan supplements slept more during flight and upon arrival and performed some tests better than the subjects given a placebo.

Tryptophan in supplement form was removed from U.S. markets by the FDA in November 1989, when over six hundred people taking it regularly developed a rare blood abnormality known as eosinophilia. As of mid-1993, tryptophan is not yet back on natural foods store shelves. A number of nutritional authorities believe, however, that the ill effects suffered by those who took tryptophan supplements were caused by contamination due to faulty production techniques. That is, correctly produced tryptophan supplements may not cause the harmful side effects that led to the product's banning. So it is possible that tryptophan supplements will someday be back on the market.

If and when the health issue has been resolved, you can try 500–1,000 mg of tryptophan thirty minutes before going to bed to help induce sleep. Including 600 mg calcium and 300 mg magnesium and a cup of chamomile tea may provide further slumber power. If tryptophan supplements remain banned, try some turkey or a glass of warm milk.

Take extra nutrients to counter the effects of travel. Air travel has adverse effects beyond monkeying with the body's clock. Flying may expose the body to higher levels of radiation, stress, and pollution. Some of the antioxidant and stress-protecting vitamins and minerals that can help include:

- vitamin A in the form of beta carotene, 25,000 IU daily
- vitamin C plus bioflavonoids, two to five grams in mixed doses daily, or to bowel tolerance (particularly important to support the adrenals)
- vitamin E, 400–800 IU daily, in gradually increased dosages
- vitamin B_6, 100–300 mg daily
- selenium, 200 mcg daily
- zinc, 25–50 mg daily

Try any of the following quick hits. Though none should be considered a magic bullet, these suggestions have helped many people.

- Before you depart, for each time zone you'll be crossing count back the same number of days. For the number of days that is equivalent to the number of time zones you will cross, go to sleep and get up one hour earlier than normal if you plan to fly east, one hour later if west. As a result, on departure day your body is already operating on the basis of your new time zone. "I've found this technique to be effective," says frequent flyer Dr. Andrew Weil.

◆ Exercise upon arrival at your destination. Elson M. Haas, M.D., author of *Staying Healthy with Nutrition*, offers the following tip: "Doing some exercise and stretching after landing, followed by a warm bath or sauna, a massage, and a light meal, is a great way to recharge in a new city and does wonders for jet lag."

◆ If you're on a short trip (for example, one to two time zones away), remain on your home schedule for meals and sleeping. Before departure it might be helpful to organize your home schedule so you're on a rational plan.

◆ Upon arriving at a new area, acupuncturist and Oriental Medical Doctor Holly Eagle suggests, eat some local wild plants. "Choose an edible native weed, herb, or food that is hardy and grows well in the area, not one that is endangered or just hanging on. Each bioregion has such indigenous plants. We've found that eating them seems to have a grounding and reorienting effect on the body," Eagle says.

◆ Wear earplugs while flying. Many people find that the loud, high-pitched whine of nearby jet engines for hours on end is disruptive to the nervous system. Holly Eagle notes that the sounds are often above the average hearing range of humans and can be extremely irritating. She says, "I know a musician who had a terrible jet-lag problem and flew quite frequently because of his career. Finally he was told to wear earplugs or ear-covering headphones to protect his ears while flying. He's told us that since using a heavy set of headphones he's had absolutely no jet lag. None." Eagle adds that you may reap some minor benefit merely by listening to the airplane Muzak over the earphones supplied by the airline.

◆ Fly during the day and arrive in the evening to avoid disrupting normal sleep patterns.

◆ Take steps to avoid dehydration. Drink plenty of fluids before and during the flight, but abstain from alcohol. Pressurized cabins, alcohol, and caffeine combine to increase the risk of dehydration.

◆ Avoid extensive napping on arrival. This just delays adjustment to your new schedule.

RESOURCES

Resources

◆ **Organizations, Books, and Products**

The following resource guide is organized by subject: basic health and first aid, natural health, herbalism, homeopathy, and so forth. The books and magazines included here are those that were prominent resources for researching *The Natural Health First-Aid Guide*. The organizations and member associations can provide background information in their fields. Some also offer lists of practitioners or can refer you to state organizations that maintain practitioner lists. Almost all of the products mentioned in this book are commonly available at natural foods stores. Companies and mail-order sources are provided for uncommon and hard-to-find products.

BASIC HEALTH AND FIRST AID

Books

The American Medical Association Handbook of First Aid and Emergency Care developed by the AMA (New York: Random House, rev. ed., 1990)

The American Red Cross First Aid & Safety Handbook by the American Red Cross and Kathleen A. Handal, M.D. (Boston: Little, Brown and Company, 1992)

Before You Call the Doctor by Anne Simons, M.D., Bobbie Hasselbring, and Michael Castleman (New York: Fawcett Columbine, 1992)

Current Emergency Diagnosis & Treatment edited by Charles E. Saunders, M.D., and Mary T. Ho, M.D. (Norwalk, Conn.: Appleton & Lange, 1992)

Emergency Medical Procedures: For the Home, Auto, and Workplace edited by Patricia B. Hill (New York: Prentice Hall Press, rev. ed., 1990)

First Aid for Kids: An Emergency Guidebook for Parents by Martin J. Cooper (Deerfield Beach, Fla.: Health Communications, 1991)

Where There Is No Doctor: A Village Health Care Handbook by David Werner with Carol Thuman and Jane Maxwell (Palo Alto, Calif.: The Hesperian Foundation, rev. ed., 1992)

For Further Information and to Find a Practitioner

American Academy of Physical Medicine and Rehabilitation
122 S. Michigan Ave., #1300
Chicago, IL 60603
(312) 922-9366

American College of Emergency Physicians
P.O. Box 61911
Dallas, TX 75261

American Red Cross
National Headquarters
Washington, D.C. 20006
(check your phone book to find a local chapter)

National Safety Council
1121 Spring Lake Drive
Itasca, IL 60143
(800) 621-7619

U.S. Consumer Product Safety Commission
Washington, D.C. 20207
(800) 638-2772

Products

National Child Care Company
84 Business Park Dr.
Armonk, NY 10504
(800) 777-8215
(914) 273-9303
The company's Emergency Child Care division offers a lunch-box-sized Infant & Child Emergency Care Kit with two dozen types of dressings, (conventional) medicines, and tools; $29.95. Natural Child Care makes a number of natural child-care products for teething and first-aid problems, though these natural products are not included in the Emergency Care Kit.

Perfectly Safe
7245 Whipple Ave., N.W.
North Canton, OH 44720
(800) 837-5437
Offers a variety of tools to childproof the home, including over forty-five products in a Comprehensive Home Safety Kit ($79.95). Also safe toys, child-safe medicine boxes, first-aid kits, and the book *The Perfectly Safe Home* by company president Jeanne Miller.

Sawyer Products
P.O. Box 188
Safety Harbor, FL 34695
Sells the Extractor Pump venom-suctioning device for bites from snakes, spiders, and bees; a half dozen variously sized first-aid kits; and over-the-counter products for treating poison ivy and other conditions.

The SelfCare Catalog
5850 Shellmound Ave.

Emeryville, CA 94662
(800) 345-3371
Sells a variety of innovative self-care tools, such as the acupressure wrist-band for motion sickness, tweezers with a magnifying lens attached, and the Ear-Ease warming cup to relieve pain from ear infections.

WILDERNESS AND TRAVEL FIRST AID AND MEDICINE

Books

Hypothermia, Frostbite and Other Cold Injuries edited by James A. Wilkerson, M.D. (Seattle, Wash.: The Mountaineers, 1986)
Jet Smart by Diana Fairechild (Maui, Hawaii: Flyana Rhyme, 1992)
Mountaineering First Aid by Martha J. Lentz, Steven C. Macdonald, and Jan Carline (Seattle, Wash.: The Mountaineers, 1990)
Overcoming Jet Lag by Dr. Charles F. Ehret and Lynne Waller Scanlon (New York: Berkley Books, 1983)
The Pocket Doctor: Your Ticket to Good Health While Traveling by Stephen Bezruchka, M.D. (Seattle, Wash.: The Mountaineers, 2nd ed., 1992)
Secrets of Warmth by Hal Weiss (Seattle, Wash.: Cloudcap, 1992)
Simon & Schuster's Pocket Guide to Wilderness Medicine by Paul G. Gill, Jr., M.D. (New York: Fireside, 1991)

Products

Tec Laboratories, Inc.
615 Water Ave., S.E.
P.O. Box 1958
Albany, OR 97321
(503) 926-4577
(800) ITCHING
Produces the Sting-x-tractor for removing insect venom, Tecnu Poison Oak-N-Ivy Cleanser, and Poison Oak-N-Ivy Armor.

REI
P.O. Box 1700
Sumner, WA 98352
(800) 426-4840
Offers a pocket-size tick removal and storage kit.

Argonne National Laboratory
Office of Public Affairs
9700 S. Cass Ave.
Argonne, IL 60439
Send a stamped, self-addressed envelope to receive a free pocket-size card describing an abbreviated version of Dr. Charles Ehret's anti-jet-lag diet.

PRESCRIPTION AND OTC DRUGS

Books

The Essential Guide to Prescription Drugs 1992 by James W. Long, M.D. (New York: Harper Perennial, 1992)

Graedons' Best Medicine: From Herbal Remedies to High-Tech Rx Breakthroughs
by Joe Graedon and Teresa Graedon (New York: Bantam Books, 1991)
The Informed Consumer's Pharmacy by Ellen Hodgson Brown and Lynne
Paige Walker, D.Ph. (New York: Carroll & Graf Publishers, 1990)
The People's Pharmacy by Joe Graedon (New York: St. Martin's Press, 1985)
Physicians' Desk Reference (Montvale, N.J.: Medical Economics Data, 46th
ed., 1992)

NATURAL HEALTH AND MEDICINE

Books

Better Health Through Natural Healing by Dr. Ross Trattler (New York: Mc-
Graw-Hill, 1988)
Childhood Ear Infections by Michael Schmidt, D.C. (Berkeley, Calif.: North
Atlantic Books/Homeopathic Educational Services, 1990)
The Encyclopedia of Alternative Health Care by Kristin Gottschalk Olsen (New
York: Pocket Books, 1989)
Encyclopedia of Natural Medicine by Michael Murray, N.D., and Joseph Piz-
zorno, N.D. (Rocklin, Calif.: Prima Publishing, 1991)
Health and Healing: Understanding Conventional and Alternative Medicine by
Andrew Weil, M.D. (Boston: Houghton Mifflin, 1983)
The Natural Family Doctor by Dr. Andrew Stanway with Richard Grossman
(New York: Fireside, 1987)
Natural Health, Natural Medicine by Andrew Weil, M.D. (Boston: Houghton
Mifflin, 1990)
Natural Healthcare for Your Child by Phyllis Austin, Agatha Thrash, M.D., and
Calvin Thrash, M.D. (Sunfield, Mich.: Family Health Publications, 1990)
The Natural Pharmacy Product Guide by Richard Israel (Garden City Park,
N.Y.: Avery Publishing Group, 1991)
The Natural Remedy Bible by John Lust, N.D., and Michael Tierra, C.A., O.M.D.
(New York: Pocket Books, 1990)
A Textbook of Natural Medicine by Joseph E. Pizzorno, N.D., and Michael T.
Murray, N.D. (Seattle, Wash.: John Bastyr College Publications, 1989)
World Medicine: The East West Guide to Healing Your Body by the editors of
Natural Health (Los Angeles: Jeremy P. Tarcher, Inc., 1993)
Your Healthy Child: A Guide to Natural Health Care for Children by Alice
Likowski Duncan, D.C. (Los Angeles: Jeremy P. Tarcher, Inc., 1991)

Magazines

Natural Health: The Guide to Well-Being
17 Station St., P.O. Box 1200
Brookline Village, MA 02147
(617) 232-1000

For Further Information and to Find a Practitioner

American Academy of Osteopathy
3500 DePauw Blvd., #1080
Indianapolis, IN 46268
(614) 366-7911

American Association of Acupuncture and Oriental Medicine
4101 Lake Boone Trail, #201
Raleigh, NC 27606
(919) 787-5181

American Association of Naturopathic Physicians
P.O. Box 20386
Seattle, WA 98102
(206) 323-7610

American Chiropractic Association
1701 Clarendon Blvd.
Arlington, VA 22209
(703) 276-8800

American Holistic Health Association
P.O. Box 17400
Anaheim, CA 92817
(714) 779-6152

American Holistic Medical Association
American Holistic Nursing Association
4101 Lake Boone Trail, #201
Raleigh, NC 27607
(919) 787-5146

American Osteopathic Association
142 E. Ontario St.
Chicago, IL 60611
(312) 280-5800
(800) 621-1773

American Society of Clinical Hypnosis
2200 E. Devon Ave., #291
Des Plaines, IL 60018
(708) 297-3317

Association for Applied Psychophysiology and Biofeedback
10200 West 44th Ave., #304
Wheat Ridge, CO 80033

John Bastyr College of Naturopathic Medicine
144 N.E. 54th St.
Seattle, WA 98105
(206) 523-9585

National College of Naturopathic Medicine
11231 S.E. Market St.
Portland, OR 97216
(503) 255-4860

Products

Enviro-Tech Products
17171 S.E. 29th St.
Choctaw, OK 73020

(800) 445-1962
(405) 390-3499
Sells biomagnetic products.

Safe and nontoxic paints, cleansers, and body-care products are available from a variety of mail-order companies. Here are a few that offer a range of useful products.

Ecco Bella
6 Provost Square, Suite 602
Caldwell, NJ 07006
(201) 226-5799
(800) 322-9366

Seventh Generation
Colchester, VT 05446
(800) 456-1197
(802) 655-3116

The Natural Choice
Eco Design Co.
1365 Rufina Circle
Santa Fe, NM 87501
(800) 621-2591
(505) 438-3448

HERBS AND HERBALISM

Books

Clinical Handbook of Chinese Prepared Medicines by Chun-Han Zhu (Brookline, Mass.: Paradigm Publications, 1989)

Earth Medicine, Earth Food by Michael A. Weiner (New York: Fawcett Columbine, 1972)

Echinacea: Nature's Immune Enhancer by Steven Foster (Rochester, Vt.: Healing Arts Press, 1991)

Echinacea: The Immune Herb! by Christopher Hobbs (Capitola, Calif.: Botanica Press, 1990)

Edible Wild Plants: A North American Field Guide by Thomas S. Elias and Peter A. Dykeman (New York: Sterling Publishing Company, 1990)

The Family Herbal by Barbara and Peter Theiss (Rochester, Vt.: Healing Arts Press, 1989)

A Field Guide to Medicinal Plants: Eastern and Central North America by Steven Foster and James A. Duke (Boston: Houghton Mifflin, 1990)

Garlic: Nature's Original Remedy by Stephen Fulder and John Blackwood (Rochester, Vt.: Healing Arts Press, 1991)

Gingko: Elixir of Youth by Christopher Hobbs (Capitola, Calif.: Botanica Press, 1991)

Guide to Medicinal Plants by Paul Schauenberg and Ferdinand Paris (New Canaan, Conn.: Keats Publishing, 1977)

A Handbook of Native American Herbs by Alma R. Hutchens (Boston: Shambhala Publications, 1992)

The Healing Herbs by Michael Castleman (Emmaus, Pa.: Rodale Press, 1991)

The Healing Power of Herbs by Michael T. Murray, N.D. (Rocklin, Calif.: Prima Publishing, 1991)

Herbal Emissaries: Bringing Chinese Herbs to the West by Steven Foster and Yue Chongxi (Rochester, Vt.: Healing Arts Press, 1992)

Herbal Medicine by Rudolf Fritz Weiss, M.D. (Beaconsfield, England: Beaconsfield Publishers, 1988)

The Herbs of Life by Lesley Tierra, L.Ac. (Freedom, Calif.: The Crossing Press, 1992)

Jeanne Rose's Modern Herbal by Jeanne Rose (New York: Perigee Books, 1987)

Milk Thistle: The Liver Herb by Christopher Hobbs (Capitola, Calif.: Botanica Press, 1984)

The New Age Herbalist, consultant editor Richard Mabey (New York: Macmillan Publishing Company, 1988)

The New Holistic Herbal by David Hoffman (Rockport, Mass.: Element Books, rev. ed., 1991)

Out of the Earth: The Essential Book of Herbal Medicine by Simon Y. Mills (New York: Viking Arkana, 1991)

Outline Guide to Chinese Herbal Patent Medicines in Pill Form by Margaret A. Naeser, Ph.D. (Boston: Boston Chinese Medicine, 1990)

Planetary Herbology by Michael Tierra, C.A., N.D. (Santa Fe, N.M.: Lotus Press, 1988)

Ten Essential Herbs by Lalitha Thomas (Prescott, Ariz.: Hohm Press, 1992)

Magazines

HerbalGram
American Botanical Council
P.O. Box 201660
Austin, TX 78720
(512) 331-8868
(800) 373-7105

For Further Information and to Find a Practitioner

American Botanical Council
P.O. Box 201660
Austin, TX 78720
(512) 331-8868
(800) 373-7105

Herb Research Foundation
1007 Pearl St., #200 F
Boulder, CO 80302
(303) 449-2265

Botanica Press
Box 742
Capitola, CA 95010
(408) 429-6373

Products

The following companies are mail-order sources of traditional Chinese prepared medicines, books on Chinese herbs, and bulk Chinese herbs.

East Earth Trade Winds
P.O. Box 493151
Redding, CA 96049
(916) 241-6878
(800) 258-6878

Meridian Traditional Herbal Products
44 Linden St.
Brookline, MA 02146
(617) 739-2636
(800) 356-6003

HOMEOPATHY AND FLOWER ESSENCES

Books on Homeopathy

Boericke's Materia Medica with Repertory by William Boericke, M.D., and
   Oscar E. Boericke, M.D. (New Dehli, India: B. Jain Publishers, rev. ed.,
   1991)
The Complete Homeopathy Handbook by Miranda Castro (New York: St.
   Martin's Press, 1990)
Everybody's Guide to Homeopathic Medicines by Stephen Cummings, M.D.,
   and Dana Ullman, M.P.H. (Los Angeles: Jeremy P. Tarcher, Inc., rev. ed.,
   1991)
The Family Guide to Homeopathy by Dr. Andrew Lockie (New York: Prentice
   Hall Press, 1989)
The Homeopathic Emergency Guide by Thomas Kruzel, N.D. (Berkeley, Calif.:
   North Atlantic Books/Homeopathic Educational Services, 1992)
Homeopathic Medicine at Home by Maesimund B. Panos, M.D., and Jane
   Heimlich (Los Angeles: Jeremy P. Tarcher, Inc., 1980)
Homeopathic Medicine for Children and Infants by Dana Ullman, M.P.H. (New
   York: Jeremy P. Tarcher/Perigee Books, 1992)
Sports & Exercise Injuries: Conventional, Homeopathic & Alternative Treatments
   by Steven Subotnick (Berkeley, Calif.: North Atlantic Books, 1991)

Books on Flower Essences

Flower Remedies by Christine Wildwood (Rockport, Mass.: Element Books,
   1992)
*Harmony is the Healer: The Combined Handbook to Healing Flowers, Color
   Therapy, Schüssler Tissue-salts, Emergency Homeopathy and Other Forms
   of Vibrational Medicine* by Ingrid S. von Rohr (Rockport, Mass.: Element
   Books, 1992)

For Further Information or to Find a Practitioner: Homeopathy

International Foundation for Homeopathy
2366 Eastlake Ave. E., #329
Seattle, WA 98102
(206) 324-8230

National Center for Homeopathy
801 N. Fairfax St., #306
Alexandria, VA 22314
(703) 548-7790

For Further Information or to Find a Practitioner: Flower Essences

Ellon Bach USA, Inc.
644 Merrick Rd.
Lynbrook, NY 11563
(800) 433-7523
(516) 593-2206

Flower Essence Society
P.O. Box 459
Nevada City, CA 95959
(916) 265-9163
(800) 548-0075

Products

Ellon Bach USA, Inc.
644 Merrick Rd.
Lynbrook, NY 11563
(800) 433-7523
(516) 593-2206

Flower Essence Services
P.O. Box 1769
Nevada City, CA 95959
(916) 265-0258
(800) 548-0075

ACUPRESSURE, MASSAGE, YOGA, AND BODYWORK

Books

Acupressure for Everybody by Cathryn Bauer (New York: Henry Holt and Company, 1991)
Acupressure's Potent Points by Michael Reed Gach (New York: Bantam Books, 1990)
Chinese Massage: A Handbook of Therapeutic Massage from the Anhui Medical School, China (Point Roberts, Wash.: Hartley & Marks, rev. ed., 1987)
The Sivananda Companion to Yoga by Lucy Lidell (New York: Fireside, 1983)
Yoga for the West: A Manual for Designing Your Own Practice by Ian Rawlinson (Sebastopol, Calif.: CRCS Publications, 1987)

For Further Information or to Find a Practitioner

Acupressure Institute
1533 Shattuck Ave.
Berkeley, CA 94709
(510) 845-1059

American Massage Therapy Association
820 Davis St., #100
Evanston, IL 60201
(708) 864-0123

Feldenkrais Guild
706 Ellsworth St., Box 489

Albany, OR 97321
(800) 775-2118
(503) 926-0981

Feldenkrais Resource Catalog
P.O. Box 2067
Berkeley, CA 94702
(800) 765-1907

Iyengar Yoga Institute
2404 27th Ave.
San Francisco, CA 94116
(415) 753-0909

North American Society of Teachers of the Alexander Technique
P.O. Box 3992
Champaign, IL 61826
(217) 359-3529

Rolf Institute of Structural Integration
302 Pearl St.
P.O. Box 1868
Boulder, CO 80306
(800) 530-8875
(303) 449-5903

AROMATHERAPY AND ESSENTIAL OILS

Books

Aromatherapy for Common Ailments by Shirley Price (New York: Fireside, 1991)

Aromatherapy: Massage with Essential Oils by Christine Wildwood (Rockport, Mass.: Element Books, 1991)

Aromatherapy: The Encyclopedia of Plants and Oils and How They Help You by Daniele Ryman (New York: Bantam Books, 1993)

The Art of Aromatherapy by Robert Tisserand (Rochester, Vt.: Healing Arts Press, 1977)

Australian Tea Tree Oil Guide by Cynthia B. Olsen (Fountain Hills, Ariz.: Kali Press, 2nd ed., 1991)

Complete Aromatherapy Handbook by Susanne Fischer-Rizzi (New York: Sterling Publishing Company, 1990)

The Complete Book of Essential Oils & Aromatherapy by Valerie Ann Worwood (San Rafael, Calif.: New World Library, 1991)

The Complete Home Guide to Aromatherapy by Erich Keller (Tiburon, Calif.: H J Kramer, Inc., 1991)

The Encyclopedia of Essential Oils by Julia Lawless (Rockport, Mass.: Element Books, 1992)

The Practice of Aromatherapy by Jean Valnet (Rochester, Vt.: Healing Arts Press, 1990)

For Further Information or to Find a Practitioner

American Aromatherapy Association
P.O. Box 3679
Pasadena, CA 91031
(818) 457-1742

Products

The following companies are mail-order sources of essential oils.

Aroma Vera
5901 Rodeo Rd.
Los Angeles, CA 90016
(800) 669-9514

Aura Cacia
P.O. Box 399
Weaverville, CA 96093
(800) 437-3301

Daniele Ryman, Ltd.
Park Lane Hotel, #101
Piccadilly, London
England W1Y 8BX

Simplers Botanical
Box 39, Forestville, CA 95436
(707) 887-2012

NUTRITION AND SUPPLEMENTS

Books

The Doctors' Vitamin and Mineral Encyclopedia by Sheldon Saul Hendler,
  M.D., Ph.D. (New York: Fireside, 1990)
Healing Nutrients by Patrick Quillin, Ph.D., R.D. (Chicago: Contemporary
  Books, 1987)
Prescription for Nutritional Healing by James F. Balch, M.D., and Phyllis A.
  Balch, C.N.C. (Garden City Park, N.Y.: Avery Publishing Group, 1990)
The Real Vitamin & Mineral Book by Shari Lieberman and Nancy Bruning
  (Garden City Park, N.Y.: Avery Publishing Group, 1990)
The Right Dose: How to Take Vitamins & Minerals Safely by Patricia Hausman,
  M.S. (Emmaus, Pa.: Rodale Press, 1987)
Staying Healthy with Nutrition by Elson M. Haas, M.D. (Berkeley, Calif.:
  Celestial Arts, 1992)

For Further Information or to Find a Practitioner

Academy of Orthomolecular Medicine/Huxley Institute
P.O. Box 1731
Boca Raton, FL 33429

American Nutrition Society
9337 Shoslane Ave.
Northridge, CA 91324
(818) 345-4365

518 *Resources*

Products

Ohio Hempery
14 North Court St., #340
Athens, OH 45701
(614) 593-5826
(800) 289-4367
Produces hemp oil, high in beneficial essential fatty acids, and other hemp products.

TRADITIONAL FOLK REMEDIES

Books

Chicken Soup & Other Folk Remedies by Joan Wilen and Lydia Wilen (New York: Fawcett Columbine, 1984)

Chinese System of Food Cures: Prevention and Remedies by Henry C. Lu (New York: Sterling Publishing Company, 1986)

The Doctors Book of Home Remedies by the editors of Prevention Magazine Health Books (Emmaus, Pa.: Rodale Press, 1990)

Folk Medicine by D. C. Jarvis, M.D. (New York: Fawcett Crest, 1958)

Gypsy Folk Medicine by Wanja von Hausen (New York: Sterling Publishing Company, 1992)

Jude's Herbal Home Remedies by Jude C. Williams (St. Paul, Minn.: Llewellyn Publications, 1992)

Live and Be Well: New Age and Age-Old Folk Remedies by Joan Wilen and Lydia Wilen (New York: Harper Perennial, 1992)

More Chicken Soup & Other Folk Remedies by Joan Wilen and Lydia Wilen (New York: Fawcett Columbine, 1986)

The Old Herb Doctor: An Old Catalogue of Traditional Folk Remedies (North Hollywood, Calif.: Newcastle Publishing Company, 1981)

Traditional Home & Herbal Remedies by Jan de Vries (Edinburgh, Scotland: Mainstream Publishing Company, 1986)

MISCELLANEOUS

Books

Common-Sense Pest Control by William Olkowski, Sheila Daar, and Helga Olkowski (Newtown, Conn.: The Taunton Press, 1991)

Cross Currents by Robert O. Becker, M.D. (Los Angeles: Jeremy P. Tarcher, Inc., 1990)

Furtive Fauna: A Field Guide to the Creatures Who Live on You by Roger M. Knutson (New York: Penguin Books, 1992)

Hyperventilation Syndrome: A Handbook for Bad Breathers by Dinah Bradley (Berkeley, Calif.: Celestial Arts, 1992)

The Immunization Decision by Randall Neustaedter, O.M.D., L.Ac. (Berkeley, Calif.: North Atlantic Books, 1990)

Natural Insect Repellents: For Pets, People, and Plants by Janette Grainger and Connie Moore (Austin, Tx.: The Herb Bar, 1991)

The Perfectly Safe Home by Jeanne Miller (New York: Fireside, 1991).

Toxicology: The Basic Science of Poisons edited by Louis J. Casarett, Ph.D., and John Doull, M.D., Ph.D. (New York: Macmillan Publishing Company, 1975)

Ways to Better Breathing by Carola Speads (Rochester, Vt.: Healing Arts Press, 1992)

For Further Information and to Find a Practitioner: Specific Medical Conditions

Andrews/Reiter Epilepsy Treatment Program
550 Doyle Park Dr.
Santa Rosa, CA 95405
(707) 578-8985

Asthma and Allergy Foundation of America
1125 15th St. N.W., #502
Washington, D.C. 20005
(800) 727-8462
(202) 466-7643

Epilepsy Foundation of America
4351 Garden City Drive
Landover, MD 20785
(800) EFA-1000
(301) 459-3700

National Jewish Center for Immunology and Respiratory Medicine
1400 Jackson Ave.
Denver, CO 80206
(303) 388-4461
(800) 222-LUNG

For Further Information and to Find a Practitioner: Emotional and Spiritual Issues

Association for Humanistic Psychology
1772 Vallejo St.
San Francisco, CA 94123
(415) 346-7929

Association for Transpersonal Psychology
P.O. Box 3049
Stanford, CA 94309
(415) 327-2066

◆ Natural First-Aid Kits

HERBAL KITS

The Rocky Mountain herbal company **Nature's Apothecary** markets a number of small herbal kits, including the Dental Poultice Pac for toothaches and abscesses ($5) and the Clear Eyes Eyewash Kit (including eyebright extract, an eyecup, and a filter; $8). Nature's Apothecary is currently reformulating their extensive Home Herbal Medicine Kit to make it more affordable and compact.

Nature's Apothecary
997 Dixon Rd.
Boulder, CO 80302
(800) 999-7422

The Herbal Pack from **Herbal Products and Development** of Aptos, California, is one of the most handy and comprehensive natural first-aid kits we've seen. Over a dozen herbal remedies, plus bandages, earplugs, and scissors come in a folding canvas pack with four large pouches to keep it all organized. The total weight of pack and medicines is only thirteen ounces. Included are remedies for bleeding and swelling, motion sickness, skin conditions, food poisoning, and more. A booklet lists full ingredients and indications for all remedies. Some of the remedies are common ones from herbal producers, while a few are Chinese-prepared medicines or remedies prepared by the kit's producer, Paul Gaylon. He says, "I choose the remedies based on reasonable cost, effectiveness, easy refills, and versatility." The Herbal Pack Natural First Aid Kid is available by mail order and carries a suggested retail price of $39.95. A somewhat smaller version called the Com Pack Natural First Aid Kit sells for $19.95.

In addition HPD sells a three-item Natural Traveler Sun Protection Kit which retails for $11.95, as well as other herbal products.

Herbal Products and Development
P.O. Box 1084
Aptos, CA 95001
(408) 688-8706

HOMEOPATHIC KITS

Boiron, one of the largest homeopathic companies, offers a number of common-ailment and first-aid kits. The Natural Home Health Care LeKit is one of the most popular kits on the market. It contains thirty-six single-remedy medicines in their distinctive blue tubes, including the flu remedy *Oscillococcinum* (os-ceel-o-kok-si-num). The kit also contains four external remedies: tinctures of *Calendula* and *Hypericum*, and ointments of *Arnica* and *Calendula*. Easy-to-follow instructions and a sturdy storage case are included. Suggested retail price is $64.95. Boiron's Travel LeKit is a more compact collection of single remedies (twenty-two multidose and sixteen unit-dose tubes) and the flu remedy. The Travel LeKit retails for $59.95.

Boiron also markets three Mini-Kits, for sports and traumas, childhood disorders, and first aid. Each has six single-remedy medicines in tubes, along with instructions. Suggested retail price is $17.50 each.

Boiron sells the kits to homeopathic pharmacies and does not mail-order the kits directly to consumers. Contact them for the dealer closest to you.

Boiron
1208 Amosland Rd., Box 54
Norwood, PA 19074
(800) 258-8823

Dolisos America, a homeopathic producer based in Las Vegas, offers two extensive medical kits in carrying cases. The Single Remedy Family Kit holds forty-eight single remedies, a Flu-Solution remedy, *Calendula* ointment and tincture, and *Arnica* cream. The Family Kit is available in two potencies and carries a suggested retail price of $70. The Energy Medicine Kit provides forty-eight combination remedies, including a dozen or so for minor emergencies such as bruises, insect bites, and poison ivy. It also has *Calendula* ointment and tincture, and *Arnica* ointment. The more expensive combination remedies raise its price to $150. Dolisos sells primarily to homeopathic pharmacies but will take mail and phone orders.

Dolisos America
3014 Rigel Ave.
Las Vegas, NV 89102
(702) 871-7153
(800) 365-4767

Historical Remedies Medicines Company offers a number of single-remedy homeopathic kits. The Medicine Case for Home and Travel has eight common remedies, while the Woman's Medicine Chest and the Medicine Box for Children offer ten remedies. The kits contain some of the most popular emergency remedies, such as *Aconite, Arnica, Apis, Rhus tox,* and *Chamomilla.* The kits have a suggested retail price of $50 and are available by mail-order from Historical or in homeopathic pharmacies and some beauty salons and spas. Historical also sells Without Body Hurts (containing *Arnica, Rhus tox,* and *Byronia*) and two other three-remedy packets for $15.50.

Historical Remedies Medicines Company
122 So. Wabasha St.
St. Paul, MN 55107
(612) 224-9344
(800) 676-6654

Homeopathic Educational Services is not a producer but a homeopathic resource company, with both a mail-order business and a store. HES carries an extensive line of products relating to homeopathy, including video and audiotapes, over one hundred books, posters, and T-shirts, and individual remedies. It also sells most of the medicine and first-aid kits produced by Standard and Boiron, a homeopathic first-aid wall chart for $11.95, and a set of sixteen illustrated remedy cards for first-aid use ($17.95).

Homeopathic Educational Services
2124 Kittredge St.
Berkeley, CA 94704
(800) 359-9051
(510) 649-0294

Store address:
2036 Blake St.
Berkeley, CA 94704

New Mexico–based **Nova Homeopathic Therapeutics** markets bottles of combination remedies for skin rash, burn, and injury/trauma in a trial-sized first-aid package that retails for $8.

Nova Homeopathic Therapeutics
5600 McLeod N.E., Suite F
Albuquerque, NM 87109
(800) 225-8094

The Standard Homeopathic Household Kit from **Standard Homeopathic Company** contains twenty-nine single-remedy medicines in small plastic bottles. Two versions are available, with remedies in either 6X or 30X potencies. Instructions and a compact case are included. Suggested retail price is $47.95–54.95. Standard also sells the seven-remedy Hyland's Kids' Kit for $15.95. Available from pharmacies and mail-order direct.

Standard Homeopathic Company
210 West 131st St.
Box 61067
Los Angeles, CA 90061
(800) 624-9659

Luyties Pharmacal Company offers a thirty-one-remedy homeopathic kit, available in 3X or 6X potencies ($50) and 12X or 30X potencies ($60).

Luyties Pharmacal Company
4200 Laclede Ave.
St. Louis, MO 63108
(800) 325-8080
(314) 533-9600

Washington Homeopathic Products is a manufacturer and retailer that produces two economical and highly compact single-remedy kits: the Medicine Box, a fifty-vial kit of mostly 6–12C potency remedies, and the twenty-remedy Urgent Care Kit. The kits retail for $55 and $30, respectively. Washington sells these kits, and those of a few other homeopathic producers, to natural foods stores and homeopathic pharmacies as well as mail-order to consumers. Washington also maintains a store at the address below.

Washington Homeopathic Products
4914 Del Ray Ave.
Bethesda, MD 20814
(800) 336-1695
(301) 656-1695

◆ Natural First-Aid Videos

In conjunction with **Morningstar Publications,** well-known herbalist Debra Nuzzi has created an informative and well-produced double-video set called "Herbal Preparations and Natural Therapies: Creating and Using a Home Herbal Medicine Chest." Four hours long and accompanied by a 140-page reference manual, the video can serve as a complete home course in how to collect, prepare, and administer or apply herbal remedies. Cost is $95.

Morningstar Publications
997 Dixon Rd.
Boulder, CO 80302
(800) 288-7610

Video Remedies has produced "Homeopathic First-Aid for the Family," a thirty-eight-minute instructional video that focuses on how to treat emergencies, sports injuries, and common illnesses with homeopathic remedies. The video is $39.95; a matching fourteen-remedy (twelve oral; two ointments) homeopathic first-aid kit is available for an additional $30. Video Remedies also sells a "Homeopathic First-Aid for Pets" video for $19.95.

Video Remedies
P.O. Box 290866
Davie, FL 33329
(305) 452-1129
(800) 733-4874

Index

ABCs (airway, breathing, circulation), 78, 79, 80–81, 87–88, 91, 96, 104, 130, 181, 186, 207, 230, 232, 267, 305, 324, 355, 457
in poisonings, 446, 447, 449
Abscesses, 247, 291–96
Absorption, 64, 451
Accidents, 201, 264, 296, 304
Acetaminophen, 413, 416–17
Acetylcholine, 12, 274, 275
Acidophilus, 122–23, 163, 244–45, 295–96, 327, 383, 487
and poisoning, 462, 463
Aconite, 50, 174, 182, 220, 223, 240, 290, 325, 451
for convulsions, 272, 277
with dizziness/fainting, 311
for ear infections, 381
for fever, 423
for hypothermia, 355, 356
Activated charcoal, 63–64, 111, 161, 497
for poisoning, 449, 450–51, 458
for stings, 150
Acupressure, 6, 16–20
for black eye, 250–51
first-aid revival point, 96, 97*f*
for spider bites, 144
for toothache, 283
Acupressure points, 111, 112*f*, 242, 250–51, 325
for alleviation of jet lag, 502
for asthma, 211
bleeding-control, 174–75
for circulation, 358
for contusions, 255
for convulsions, 272
with cramps, 430
for dizziness, 306
for ear infections, 381
for eyes, 372, 372*f*
for fainting, 310
for fever, 423
for frostbite, 347, 348*f*
for glaucoma, 369
for heatstroke, 398
for hyperventilation, 224
kidney meridian, 312

for motion sickness, 495, 496*f*
for muscle/joint injuries, 436–37
for nosebleed, 177
for poisonings, 451
recovery from drowning, 329–30
for seizures, 277
for skin problems, 474
for tooth trauma, 289
vital energy restoration, 393
Acupuncture, 6, 276–77, 393
Acu-yoga, 17
Adaptogens, 312–13, 341–42, 419, 500–01
Adolph's (meat tenderizer), 61, 111, 150
Adrenaline. *See* Epinephrine
Adsorption, 64, 451
Agaricus, 350
Airway, 80, 93, 306
opening, 81, 82*f*
see also ABCs
Alcohol use, 319, 342, 353, 395
Alexander Technique trainers, 218
Alfalfa-leaf extracts, 198
Allantoin, 45, 184, 194, 254, 345–51, 436
Allergic reactions, 90, 99–114, 130, 168, 229, 237, 257, 293, 362, 430
acute, 87, 100, 103–08
in animal bites, 119
to arnica, 252
to bee stings, 146, 147–48, 155
causes of, 100–03
and dizziness, 301
to essential oils, 22
first aid for mild, 108–11
and garlic, 67
recovery and prevention, 111–14
skin, 465, 466, 468–69, 478
to spider bites, 143
Allergies
and asthma, 205–06, 215–16
Allergy-relief medication, 105
Allopathy, 10, 11
Aloe, 35–36, 161, 178, 282, 293, 346, 472, 484
for bites/stings, 162
for burns, 237–38
for frostbite, 350, 351

Alteratives, 418, 419
Alternative philosophy, 5
Altitude, 343
    adjusting to, 337–38
    exposure to, 333–58
    see also High-altitude sickness
Amino acids, 244, 273
Analgesics, 69, 149
    topical, 362
Anaphylactic shock, 87, 100, 106, 146
Anesthetics, 69
Animal bites, 115–26
    first aid for, 118–20
    natural remedies for, 120–22
    prevention of, 125–26
    recovery from, 122–25
Animal dander, 101, 112
Ant stings, 146–55
Antibacterials, 69, 120–21, 172
Antibiotics, 42, 66, 69, 122–23, 138, 140,
        141, 259, 292, 295–96, 324, 327,
        413, 416–17, 482
    for ear infections, 377, 378, 379, 383
Anticonvulsants, 269, 271, 273, 274, 277,
        338
Antifungals, 69, 482
Antihistamines, 107, 149, 470, 494
Anti-inflammatories, 69, 161, 209, 260
Antimonium crudum, 485
Antimoniun tartaricum, 325
Antioxidants, 69, 114, 260, 261, 371, 438,
        442, 492, 503
Antiseptics, 70
Antispasmodics, 70, 370
Antivenom, 132, 133, 137, 138
Antivirals, 70
Anxiety, 222, 223, 224, 302
Apis, 50–51, 53, 121, 144, 161, 290, 350
    for allergic reactions, 106
    for stings, 151–52, 156
Arachnids, 101, 135–46
Argentum nitricum, 340
Arnica, 251, 430
    for contusions, 251, 252, 253
Arnica, 51, 96, 240
    for bleeding, 174, 177, 182
    for bone injuries, 193
    for contusions, 252–53
    for jet lag, 501
    for muscle/joint injuries, 436
    for snakebite, 133
    for tooth trauma, 290
Aromatherapy, 6, 20–22, 177–78, 215,
        224, 241–42, 277, 315
    for dizziness, 307
    for jet lag, 501
    for lung function, 331
Arsenicum, 52, 210, 223, 325, 451, 460

Artificial respiration. *See* Rescue breath-
    ing
Asphyxia, 318
Aspirin, 101, 206, 250, 259, 272, 280, 284,
        396, 406
    in fever reduction, 416–17
    natural, 419–20
Asthma
    long-term treatment of, 212–15
    prevention of, 215–18
Asthma attacks, 104, 204–18
    first aid for, 207
    natural remedies for, 209–12
    symptoms of, 206–07
Astragalus, 123, 124, 294, 313, 421, 464,
        472
Astringents, 70, 120–21, 182–83
Athlete's foot, 481, 482, 483, 485, 486
    prevention of, 480–81
Atropine, 361–62, 370
Ayurveda, 213, 437

Back-slap technique, 92
Bacteria, 291, 406, 407, 413
    resistant, 377
Bacterial infections (skin), 479–80, 484
Baking soda, 64–65, 110, 161, 295
    in bath, 241
    for skin problems, 475, 486
    for stings, 152
Barberry, 419, 421–22
Baths, bathing, 412, 419
    essential oil, 315
    herbal, 35, 349
    whole-body, 241, 416
Bee stings, 104, 113, 146–55, 161–62
Behavior therapy, 277
Belladonna, 272, 294
    for ear infections, 381
    in eye emergencies, 369
    for fever, 422–23
    for heat illness, 398
    for poisoning, 460
    for seizures, 277
    for skin infections, 485
    for teething, 286, 287
    for toothache, 283, 290
Bentonite, 150, 458
Berberine, 421
Beta-boosting bronchodilators, 208
Beta carotene, 114, 260, 261, 462
    see also Vitamin A/beta carotene
Bilberry, 370, 371
Biofeedback, 5, 214, 277, 498
Bioflavonoids, 183, 259–60, 314
    see also Vitamin C/bioflavonoids
Biological clock, 498–99, 500
Biomagnetism, 194–95

Bites, 24, 115–63, 408, 444
Black currant, 199–200
Black eye, 250–51
Black ointment, 145, 293, 490
Black-walnut tincture, 484
Black widow, 135, 136–37, 143
Bleeding, 119, 130, 164–84
    from ears, 373
    under the nails, 178–79
    from rectum, 179–80
    severe, 27, 76
Bleeding-control points, 174–75
Bleeding episodes, 183–84
Blood
    chemical balance of, 399
    detoxifying, 464
Blood pressure, 309, 310
    low/high, 312–13, 314–15
Blood purifiers, 70
Body
    cooling, 395–96
    overheated, 386–90
Body temperature, 404, 415
    and convulsions, 272
    determining, 409–10
    see also Heat illness; Hypothermia;
        Fever
Bodywork, 16, 200, 217, 314
Boils, 479, 482, 485, 486
Bone injuries, 185–203
    natural remedies for, 192–95
    preventing, 201–03
    recovery from, 195–201
    treatment of, 200–01
Bones
    broken, 27, 93
    immobilizing, 187–89
Boneset, 31
    see also Comfrey
Borage, 199–200
Boron, 196, 297
Breast-feeding, 114, 218, 274, 381–82
Breath-holding, 221–25
Breathing, 80, 82, 84, 182, 275, 305
    deep, 216, 430, 496
    pursed-lip, 210
    see also ABCs
Breathing exercises, 329, 496
Breathing problems, 90, 204–25
    in allergic reactions, 103, 104, 106
Bromelain, 60–61, 161, 255, 291, 437–38
Bronchial spasms, 209–10
Brown recluse, 135, 137–38, 144
Bruises, 180, 246–50, 291
    natural remedies for, 251–59
    see also Contusions
Bruisewort. *See* Comfrey
Burn creams, 351

Burns, 24, 36, 226–45
    first aid for, 234–36
    first-, second-, third-degree, 226–27,
        233, 234, 235, 236
    natural remedies for, 236–43
    preventing, 245
    recovery, 244–45

Caffeinated beverages, 211
Calcarea phos, 286, 287
Calcium, 23, 196, 197, 198, 261, 273, 297,
        370, 399
    and brain metabolism, 273–74
    and cramps, 441
    and teeth, 298
Calendula, 52, 172, 295
    for burns, 241
    for skin infections, 485
Calendula, 31, 37, 49, 110, 133, 293, 350,
        472, 474, 484
    for burns, 239–40, 241
    for cuts and scrapes, 171
    for insect bites, 161
    for rectal bleeding, 179
    tincture of, 120, 121, 142
Camphor, 257
Camphor oil, 97, 98, 277, 307
Canker sores, 291, 295, 297
Cantharis, 240
Capsaicin, 283–84, 339
Carbon monoxide, 444, 453
Carbuncles, 479
Cardiopulmonary resuscitation (CPR),
        27, 80, 84–86, 232–33, 267, 322,
        323, 332
Castor oil, 258, 295
Cat scratch fever, 118
Catnip, 276, 285
Catnip tea, 221, 286
Cayenne, 210, 283–84, 328, 339–40, 347,
        359, 418
Cellulitis, 479, 480
Chamomile, 37–38, 56, 110, 224, 239,
        282, 285, 289
Chamomile cream, 229
Chamomile oil, 254–55, 277, 315, 483
Chamomile tea, 221, 286
Chamomilla, 224, 283, 286, 287, 381
Charcoal, 111
    see also Activated charcoal
Chemical burns, 230, 234
    of the eyes, 365–68
Chemical poisoning, 442–54
    first aid, 446–49
    natural remedies for, 450–52
    prevention of, 452–54
Chest compressions, 80, 84–86, 85f, 88
Chest tap, 330

Chest tie, 189
Chilblains, 349
Children, 114, 198
  asthma attacks, 212
  body temperature, 410
  breath-holding, 221, 224
  breathing problems, 211
  bruises, 247
  burns, 233
  choking, 89, 91–93
  CPR, 84–86
  croup, 218–21
  cuts and scrapes, 169
  dosages, 32
  drowning, 321–22, 332
  ear infections, 375–81
  fever, 408, 411–12, 422
  motion sickness, 498
  nosebleeds, 175, 178
  poisoning, 443, 444–45, 452, 453, 454
  rescue breathing, 84
  seizures in, 263, 265, 270–72, 277
  spider bites, 143
Chinese ginseng, 313, 316
Chiropractic, 4, 6, 218, 277, 314
Chlorophyll supplements, 162–63, 184, 261, 328, 389
Choking, 76, 78, 89–93, 96
  first aid for, 90–93
Chuan Xin Lian Antiphlogistic Pills, 424
Cider vinegar, 476, 486
Cinnamon oil, 282, 331
Circulation, 80–81, 82, 83, 88, 93
  see also ABCs
Circulatory stimulants, 418
Clay, 458, 473, 476
Clematis, 312
Clostridium botulinum, 455
Clove, 56–57
Clove oil, 281–82, 286, 287, 292, 331
Cocculus, 496
Coenzyme Q10, 298, 326, 341, 463
Coffea, 283, 311
Cold, exposure to, 333–58
Cold air, 219
  and asthma, 206, 218
Cold compresses, 177, 412, 416, 422
Cold-milk compress, 151, 229–30
Cold sores, 480, 487
Cold treatments, 248–49, 250, 251
  in muscle injuries, 433–34
  for toothache, 280–81, 289
Cold-water therapy, 65, 237
  with burns, 235, 236
Collagen, 259, 438, 442
Colloidal oatmeal, 110, 241, 475
Coltsfoot, 213–14
Coma, 133, 154, 306, 386, 395

Comfrey, 38–40, 178, 184, 193–94, 282, 418, 420–21, 472, 490
Comfrey poultice, 144, 239–40, 253–54, 435–36
Compresses, 419
  for burns, 237, 240
  cold, 177, 412, 416, 422
  for cuts and scrapes, 170–72
  herbal, 34f, 35, 282
  hot, 486
  for stings, 151
Compression, 434, 435f
Constricting band, 105, 130–31, 143
Contact dermatitis, 466, 470
Contact lenses, 360, 363, 365, 366–67, 368
Contusions, 246–61, 273
  first aid for, 248–50
  natural remedies for, 251–59
  prevention and recovery, 259–61
Conventional medicine, 5, 6–8
Convulsions, 262–78, 393
  in fever, 410
  first aid for, 265–68
  prevention and recovery, 272–78
Cooling treatments
  with fever, 415–17
Copper, 261, 326
Copperheads, 126
Coral snake, 126, 127–28, 131
Cortisonelike drugs, 107, 149, 208–09, 338
Cottonmouth snakes, 126, 127
Counseling, 277, 331
Cramps, 427–31
  preventing, 439, 440, 441–42
Croup, 218–21
Cryotherapy, 248
Cucumber, 364
Cuprum metallicum, 356, 391, 431
Cuts and scrapes, 24, 169–75
  natural remedies, 170–75

Decoctions, 32–33, 124, 240, 349
Decongestants, 71
Deep breathing technique, 223, 496
Deet, 155, 158
Dehydration, 272, 353, 357, 387–88, 395, 399, 401, 402, 404, 504
  with fever, 413, 414
  fluids to cure, 388–90, 400
  skin, 491
Demulcents, 71
Dental emergencies, 279–98
  prevention and recovery, 296–97
Desensitization, 108, 155, 160, 222
Detoxifiers
  blood, 70
  digestive, 71

Diabetic coma/shock, 88–89, 299
Diaphoretics, 418, 420–21
Dietary imbalances, 314–15
    see also Nutrition/diet
Digestive detoxifiers, 71
Digestive tract
    poison ivy of, 478
    poisons entering through, 444–45,
        447–49
Ding Xin Wan, 311
Dislocations (bones), 189–91, 193–94,
        203, 426–27
    first aid for, 191
    when to self-heal, 192
Diuretics, 338, 387
Dizziness, 299–317, 386, 395, 416
    causes of, 301–02
    first aid, for, 303
    natural remedies for, 306–12
    prevention and recovery, 312–17
Do-in, 17
Dong quai, 314
Drag transport, 94–95
Drowning, 318–32
    first aid for, 322–24
    natural remedies for, 324–26
    prevention of, 331–32
Drowning victim(s), 321–22
    rescuing, 319–21
Drugs, 7, 343, 408
    and allergic reactions, 101–02, 107
    for anxiety, 222
    and hypothermia, 353
    and poisoning, 445, 453
    and seizures, 264
Dust, 101
Dust mites, 101, 108, 112

E. coli, 455–56
Ear emergencies, 372–84
    prevention and recovery, 381–84
Ear infections
    acute, 375–81
    natural remedies for, 378–81
Eardrum, ruptured, 375
Ears
    foreign bodies in, 373–75
Earwax, 374–75, 382–83
Echinacea, 40–41, 114, 119, 123, 244,
        282, 285, 419, 459
    for ear infections, 376, 379, 380
    in eye emergencies, 363
    for fever, 421
    for mouth and gum infections, 292–93
    for skin infections, 484
    for snakebite, 132–33, 134
    for toxic bites/stings, 162
Echinacea tincture, 120, 142, 150, 172,
        472, 487

Elastic bandages, 434, 435*f*
Elder, 418, 420
Electric shock, 231–32, 234, 264
Electrical stimulation, 195
Electroacupuncture, 277
Electrolytes, 225, 387, 388, 391, 392, 393,
        395, 399
Eleuthero. *See* Siberian ginseng
Elevation, 251, 434
Emergen-C, 389, 399
Emergency(ies)
    assessing, 76–77
    first-aid remedies for, 96–98
Emergency care, basic, 75–98
Emergency medical personnel, 78, 79,
        87, 104, 105, 181, 187, 230, 232,
        248, 299, 305, 319, 324, 354, 393,
        396, 408–09, 411–12, 432–33, 457,
        479, 488
    in poisoning, 446, 447–48
    in high-altitude sickness, 338
    see also Medical professionals/treatment
Emergency medicine, 6–7, 12, 15
Emergency response guidelines, 26–27
Emetics, 71
Emotional shock, 304, 306, 310–11, 312,
        316–17
    natural remedies for, 355–56
Energy points, key, 17–19
Enokidake, 125
Enzymes, 60–63, 109
Ephedra, 41–42, 106, 107, 209–10, 370
Ephedrine, 41–42, 106, 107, 209, 210
Epiglottitis, 218–21
Epilepsy, 262, 263–69, 270, 274, 276–77,
        278
Epinephrine (adrenaline), 105, 208
Epsom salts, 110, 431
Essential fatty acids (EFAs), 198–99,
        212–13, 328, 382, 438, 475
Essential oils, 6, 20–22
    in baths, 315
    for contusions, 254–55
    for dizziness, 307
    first-aid, 30, 31, 55–60, 97–98
    for frostbite, 350
    for heat illness, 391, 394
    herbs, 33–34
    for lung function, 331
    for mouth infections, 293–94
    for poison ivy, 474
    for seizures, 277
    for skin infections, 482–83
    for teething/toothache, 281–82, 286
Eucalyptus, 57–58
Eucalyptus oil, 172, 215, 221, 282, 331,
        350, 394, 483
Euphrasia, 364, 368
Evening primrose, 199–200

Exercise, 202, 315, 342, 504
  aerobic, 358
  and asthma, 206, 216
Exposure, 27, 304, 333–58
Extracts (herbs), 33
Eye(s)
  flushing, 367–68
  foreign bodies in, 360–64
Eye burns, 365–68
Eye emergencies, 359–72
  black eye, 250–51
  prevention and recovery, 371–72
Eyebright, 363–64

Fainting, 303–06, 386, 392, 416
  causes of, 303–05
  first aid for, 305–06
  natural remedies for, 306–12
  recovery from, 312–17
Fasts, 414, 463
Febrile convulsions, 263, 268, 270–72
Feldenkrais practitioners, 217
Fennel seeds, 363, 364
Fenugreek, 490
Ferrum phos, 177, 423
Fever
  causes and symptoms, 407–08
  as defense mechanism, 404, 406, 407
  first aid for high, 413–17
  health benefits of, 406–07
  high, 263, 270–72, 403–25
  mechanism of, 405–13
  natural remedies for, 417–25
  recovery from, 425
Fever phobia, 404–05
Field horsetail, 197–98
Finger sweep, 82, 91–92
Fingernails, blood under, 251
Fingers, 188, 251
First aid
  for allergic reactions, 104–05, 108–11
  for animal bites, 118–20
  for asthma, 207
  for burns, 234–36
  for chemical poisoning, 446–49
  for choking, 90–93
  for contusions, 248–50
  for convulsions, 272
  for cramps, 428–30
  for croup, 219
  for dislocations, 191
  for dizziness, 303
  for drowning, 322–24
  for ear emergencies, 375
  elements of natural, 29–30
  for fainting, 305–06
  for food poisoning, 457
  for fractures, 186–87
  for frostbite, 344–46

  for heat exhaustion, 392–93
  for heatstroke, 396–97
  for high-altitude sickness, 338–39
  for high fever, 413–17
  for hyperventilation, 223
  for hypothermia, 353–55
  for internal bleeding, 181–82
  introduction to natural, 3–27
  for neck and spinal injuries, 79–80
  for poison ivy, oak, sumac, 470
  for seizures, 265–68
  in shock, 88
  for snakebites, 129–31
  for spider bites, 143
  for splinters and fishhooks, 488–89
  for stings, 149
  for toothache, 280–81
  for unconsciousness, 77–78
First-aid kit
  natural, 28–72
  prescription-only, 105
First-aid remedies
  for basic emergencies, 96–98
  homeopathic, 48–54
  natural, 30–32
Fishhooks, 488–91
Flax, 199
Fleas, 159–60
Flies, 159
Flower essences, 14–16, 287, 307, 308–
    09, 355–56
  for dizziness and fainting, 310–11
  first-aid, 30, 54–55
  in motion sickness, 496
  in treatment of drowning, 325
Flower remedies, 6, 96–97, 152
Fluid replacement, 388–90, 392, 393,
    399, 400
Fluids
  with dehydration, 388–90, 400
  with fever, 413, 414–15
Folic acid, 183, 274, 492
Folk remedies, 5, 6, 24–26, 310
  for bruises, 258–59
  for burns, 242–43
  for cramps, 431
  for fever, 425
  for frostbites, 344
  for frostnip, 350
  for heat illness, 394, 398
  for hemorrhoids, 180
  for motion sickness, 497
  for muscle/joint injuries, 438–39
  for nosebleed, 177
  for poison ivy, oak, sumac, 475–76
  for poisonings, 452, 460
  for skin infections, 485–86
  for splinters, 491
  for toothache, 283–84

Food poisoning, 454–62
    first aid for, 457
    natural remedies for, 458–60
    prevention of, 461–62
Foods
    causing allergies, 102–03, 113–14, 276
    first-aid, 31, 63–68
    see also Nutrition/diet
Fractures, 185–89, 193–94, 195, 201, 432
    first aid for, 186–87
Free radicals, 62, 260, 261, 326, 438, 463, 492
Fresh or dried plant (herbs), 32
Frostbite, 236, 249, 333, 342–51, 355, 434
    causes of, 343–44
    first aid for, 344–46
    hospital treatment for, 346–47
    natural remedies for, 347–51
    symptoms/stages of, 344
Frostnip, 342–51
Frozen cornea, 364–65
Fungal infections (skin), 480–81, 484–85, 486
Fungi, 407

Garlic, 65–67, 122, 159, 180, 260, 284, 313, 314, 375, 419, 459, 464
    antiseizure herbs, 276
    for ear infections, 379, 380
    for fever, 421, 422
    for mouth infections, 293–94
    for near-drowning victims, 327
    for skin infections, 484
    for spider bites, 144
Garlic supplements, 244
Geranium oil, 255, 315, 350
Ginger, 239, 257, 282, 308, 347, 418, 459
    for high-altitude sickness, 339
    for motion sickness, 495
Ginger oil, 350
Ginger powder, 349, 358
Ginger tea, 328, 356
Ginkgo, 213, 260, 497
    for ear infections, 328
    for exposure, 342
    for eye emergencies, 371
    for frostbite, 349
    for muscle/joint injuries, 440
    for near-drowning victims, 327–28
    for vertigo, 308
Ginkgolide B, 213, 327
Glaucoma, acute, 368–71
Glonoine, 398
Goldenseal, 42–43, 123, 292, 472
    for eye emergencies, 363–64
    for fever, 421
    for poison ivy/oak, 472, 473
Goldenseal-root powder, 121, 483–84

Grand mal (tonic-clonic seizures), 264–65, 266–68, 269
Grindelia, 471, 472
Guided imagery, 214, 215
Gum disease, 292, 296, 298
Gum healers, 293–94
Gums, 279, 280, 289, 297, 298

Hammock carry, 95
Hawthorn, 260, 313, 314
Heart attack, 90, 104, 299, 319, 323
Heat cramps, 385, 386, 390–92, 400
Heat exhaustion, 385, 386, 390, 391–94
Heat faint, 385–86
Heat illness, 385–402, 404
Heat treatments, 249, 251, 429
Heatstroke, 385, 386, 390, 391–92, 393, 395–98
Heimlich maneuver, 77, 90–93, 322
Hemorrhoids, 179–80
Hemp, 199
Hepar sulphur, 294, 485, 491
Herbal compress/eyewash, 363–64
Herbal liniments, 257, 349–50
Herbal poultices, 34, 282, 490
Herbal products, 33, 475
    finding, 35–48
Herbal teas, 224, 391, 414, 419
Herbs/herbalism, 4, 6, 8–10, 123
    antibacterial, 379–80
    antiviral/detoxifying, 419
    for asthma, 213–14
    astringent, 291
    for burns, 237, 244
    for contusions, 252–54
    for convulsions, 276
    for cuts and scrapes, 170–71
    for dizziness/fainting, 312–13
    for emotional shock, 316–17
    for exposure, 341–42
    external application of, 34–35
    for eye emergencies, 371
    for fever, 417–19
    first-aid, 30, 31, 32–34, 97–98
    for food poisoning, 459
    for frostbite, 350–51
    heart-boosting, 313–14
    for heat illness, 394
    for hemorrhoids, 179–80
    for high-altitude sickness, 339–40
    for hypothermia, 357
    for immune system, 114, 421–22
    for internal bleeding, 182–83
    for joint injuries, 440–41
    for mouth infections, 293–94
    for near-drowning victims, 327–28
    for poison ivy, 471–73
    for skin infections, 484–85
    for snakebite, 133–34

Herbs/herbalism *(cont.)*
  sweat-inducing, 420–21
  for toothache, 282
High-altitude cerebral edema (HACE),
    336–37, 338
High-altitude pulmonary edema (HAPE),
    336–37, 338
High-altitude sickness, 333, 334–42
  causes of, 335–36
  first aid for, 338–39
  natural remedies for, 339–40
  recovery and prevention, 340–42
  symptoms of, 336–37
Histamine, 100, 109, 128
Holism, 5
Home-remedy pastes, 110–11
Homeopathic remedies, 22, 48–54, 232
  for allergic reactions, 113
  for asthma, 210
  for bite wounds, 121
  for bleeding, 174
  for bone injuries, 193, 194
  for burns, 240–41
  for contusions, 251, 252–53
  for convulsions, 272, 277
  for cramps, 431
  for croup, 220
  for dizziness/fainting, 308, 311, 312
  in drowning, 325
  for ear infections, 380–81
  for eye emergencies, 364, 368
  for fever, 422–23
  first-aid, 30, 31
  for frostbite, 350
  for heat cramps, 391
  for heat illness, 398
  for high-altitude sickness, 340
  for hyperventilation, 223–24
  for hypothermia, 355, 356
  for internal bleeding, 182
  for jet lag, 501
  for motion sickness, 495–96
  for mouth infections, 294
  for muscle/joint injuries, 436, 440
  for nosebleed, 177
  for poison ivy/oak, 473–74
  in poisonings, 451, 459–60
  potency, 48–49
  for skin infections, 485
  for splinters, 490–91
  for stings, 151–52
  for teething, 286–87
  for toothache, 282–83, 290
Homeopathic suppositories, 179
Homeopathy, 5, 6, 10–16
Honey, 243, 476
Horsetail, 349, 441
Hospital treatment
  of allergic reactions, 107–08
  of animal bites, 120
  of asthma attacks, 208–09
  of burns, 233–34
  of croup, 220
  of drowning victims, 324
  of fractures, 189
  of frostbite, 346–47
  of heatstroke, 397
  of snakebite, 132
Household items, first-aid, 31, 63–68,
    150–51
Household products
  causing allergies, 102
Human bites, 115–26
Huo Xian Zheng Qi Pian, 394
Hydration, 400, 457
Hydrogen peroxide, 67–68, 120, 172, 259,
    284, 295, 298, 486
  for ear infections, 374–75, 376
Hydrotherapy, 237, 422
Hypericum, 52–53, 121, 143, 172, 241,
    251, 252, 290, 295, 350
Hyperthermia, 395, 407
Hyperventilation, 221–25
Hypothermia, 304, 319, 323, 333, 340,
    345, 347, 351–58
  causes of, 352–53
  natural remedies for, 355–56
  recovery and prevention, 356–58
  symptoms of, 353–55
Hypoxia, 317, 335

Ice, 433–34
Immobilization, 79, 187–89
Immune system, 123–24, 405–06, 487
  and allergies, 99–100, 114
  herbs for, 421–22
Immune system boosters, 71, 329
Immunotherapy, 108
Impetigo, 479, 482, 485
Infectious disease, 405
Infusions, 32, 240
Insect bites, 157–63
Insect repellents, 155, 158
Insect stings, 108, 146–55
  preventing, 154–55
Insect venom, 101, 111
Insulin shock, 87, 88–89
Internal bleeding, 164, 180–83, 247
Ipecac, 43–44, 210, 450, 460
Iron, 183, 198, 261, 424, 444–45
Iron supplements, 183–84

Jellyfish stings, 161–62
Jet lag, 498–504
Jewelweed
  for poison ivy, 471–72, 471f
Jing Wan Hong, 240

Jock itch, 487
Joint injuries, 426–42
　natural remedies for, 435–39
　prevention and recovery, 439–42
Joints, immobilizing, 187–89
Juices, 389, 400, 414

Kelp, 198, 242–43, 274
Kidney meridian, 312, 423
Kissing bugs, 160
Knitbone. *See* Comfrey

L-Lysine, 487
Lachesis, 350
Lavender oil, 21–22, 58, 111, 120, 121,
　172, 224, 315, 391, 394, 483
　for burns, 241–42
　for contusions, 254
　for convulsions, 277
　for stings, 152
Lecithin, 274–75
Ledum, 53, 119, 121, 251, 253, 290
　for bleeding, 174
　for poison ivy, 474
　for spider bites, 144
　for stings, 151–52
Lemon juice, 161, 172
Life energy, 17–19
Ligaments, 426, 432, 440
Lightning strike, 232–33
Ligustrum, 123, 124, 421
Liniments, 33, 429
Liquid-chlorophyll drinks, 389
Liu Shen Shui, 394
Liver enzymes, 463
Lobelia, 210
Lophantuus pills, 460
Lung function, 330, 331
　diet and, 328–29
Lungs
　poisons entering through, 444, 446–47
Lyme disease, 139, 140–41

Magnesia phos, 283
Magnesium, 23, 196, 197, 198, 212, 225,
　244, 261, 273, 274, 297, 326, 399
　and brain metabolism, 273–74
　and cramps, 441, 442
Magnesium sulfate, 212
Magnetic resonance imaging (MRI), 195,
　302
Magnets, healing, 194–95
Maitake, 125
Manganese, 196, 197, 297, 382
Massage, 6, 16–20, 325–26
　acupressure: eyes, 372, 372f
　for asthma, 211
　for bone injuries, 200
　for cramps, 391, 428–29

in recovery from drowning, 330–31
for skin, 492
whole-body, 459
see also Acupressure points
Materia medica, 11, 49
Meadowsweet, 420
Medical alert tag, 111, 267
Medical professionals/treatment
　with croup, 219–20
　with convulsions and seizures, 269
　in drowning, 323–24
　in eye emergencies, 360–61, 367
　treating fevers, 412–13
　see also Emergency medical personnel;
　　Hospital treatment
Medications, blood-thinning, 247
Melatonin, 499, 500
Melatonin hormone supplements, 499–
　500
Menthol, 257
Mercurius, 294
Meridians, 17, 18f, 312, 423
Metals, 110, 113
Milk, cold compresses with, 229–30
Milk thistle, 113, 458–59
Mind/body techniques, 277, 485
Minerals, 23, 24, 114, 163, 198, 387
　and asthma, 212–13
　and contusions, 261
　and croup, 221
　in dehydration, 388–89
　and eye emergencies, 371–72
　and fever, 423–24
　and heat illness, 399
　for near-drowning victims, 326–27
　and seizure disorders, 276
　see also Trace minerals
Mold spores, 101
Monosodium glutamate (MSG), 103, 216
Mormon tea, 41, 210
Mosquitoes, 157–59
Mother tincture(s), 16, 48
Motion sickness, 301, 308, 493–98
Mouth infections/abscesses, 291–96
　natural remedies for, 292–96
Mouth-to-mouth resuscitation. *See*
　　Rescue breathing
Mucilage, 154, 214, 243, 379, 452, 490
Mud, mudpacks, 153, 476
Mullein, 214, 328, 379–80
Muscle injuries, 253, 426–42
　natural remedies for, 435–39
　prevention and recovery, 439–42
　RICE treatment for, 433–35
Mushrooms, healing, 114, 123, 124–25,
　163, 313, 328, 463
Myringotomy, 377–78
Myrrh, 282, 290–91, 292–93, 472
　for skin infections, 484–85

Nail fungus, 481, 482
Nail infections, bacterial, 479–80, 482
Nails, bleeding under, 178–79
Natural remedies, 6
    action of, 68–72
    for allergic reactions, 106–07, 108–111
    for animal bites, 120–22
    for asthma, 209–15
    for bone injuries, 192–95
    for burns, 236–43
    for chemical poisoning, 450–52
    for contusions, 251–59
    for cramps, 430–31
    for croup, 220–21
    for cuts and scrapes, 170–75
    for dizziness/fainting, 306–12
    in drowning, 324–26
    for ear infections, 378–81
    for eye emergencies, 368
    with fever, 417–25
    for food poisoning, 458–60
    for foreign bodies in the eyes, 363–64
    for frostbite, 347–51
    for glaucoma, 369–71
    for heat cramps, 391
    for heat exhaustion, 393–94
    for heatstroke, 398
    for high-altitude sickness, 339–40
    for hypothermia, 355–56
    for insect bites, 161
    for internal bleeding, 182–83
    for jet lag, 499–504
    for motion sickness, 494–97
    for mouth infections/abscesses, 292–96
    for muscle and joint injuries, 435–39
    for nosebleed, 176–77
    for poison ivy, oak, sumac, 471–76
    for postural hypotension, 309–10
    for skin infection, 482–86
    for snakebite, 132–34
    for spider bites, 143–45
    for splinters, 490–91
    for stings, 149–54
    for teething, 285–87
    for tooth traumas, 289–91
    for toothache, 281–84
Naturopaths, 201
Neck and spinal injuries, 78–80, 86, 93, 94, 95, 186
Nervines, 71
Nervous exhaustion, 310–11, 312, 314–15, 316–17
Nettles, 244, 441
Niacin, 297, 349, 424
Nosebleeds, 175–78
Nutrition/diet, 6, 264
    and allergic reactions, 114
    and animal bites, 122–23

    and asthma, 215
    and bleeding, 183–84
    and bone injuries, 195–200, 202
    and breathing problems, 213
    and burn recovery, 244–45
    circulation-building, 357–58
    and contusions, 259–61
    and dizziness, 301
    and ear emergencies, 382, 383
    and exposure, 341
    and eye emergencies, 371–72
    and glaucoma, 371–72
    and heat illness, 399, 401
    and hemorrhoids, 180
    and insect bites, 158–59
    and jet lag, 502
    and muscle/joint injuries, 441–42
    and near-drowning, 326–27, 328–29
    and nosebleed, 177
    and seizure disorders, 275–76
    and skin problems, 475
    and teeth, 296–98
Nutritional deficiencies, 247, 263–64, 298
Nutritional supplements, 23–25
    antiseizure, 273–76
    for asthma, 212
    for fever, 423–24
    first-aid, 31, 60–63
    for jet lag, 503
    with poison ivy/oak, 474
    for skin, 492
Nux Vomica, 311, 451, 460, 495–96

Oak bark, 290–91
Oats, 316
One-person back carry, 95
Onion, 65–67, 150, 258, 310, 328
Oral Rehydration Solution, 272
Oregon grape, 421
Orthomolecular medicine, 5
Osteopathy, 200–201, 217, 277
Osteoporosis, 202, 298
Otitis media, 377
Oxygen therapy, 67, 68

Painkilling antipyretics, 418
Pancreatin, 109
Panic attack, 221–25
Papain, 61, 110–11, 156, 161
    for stings, 149–50
Para-aminobenzoic acid (PABA), 229
Partial seizures, 265
Pau d'arco, 44, 123, 133, 244, 484
Pectin, 451–52
Penicillin, 12, 482
Peppermint, 58–59
Peppermint oil, 98, 152, 229, 242, 282, 286, 307, 331, 394, 473

Periodontal disease, 298
Pertussis vaccine, 102, 113
Pesticides, 444
Petit mal (absence seizures), 265, 268, 269
Phosphorus, 174, 200, 232, 240
Photosensitivity, 22, 228–29
Physical therapist, 314
Pill Curing, 496–97, 501
Placebo, 211–12
Plaintain, 44–46, 133, 171, 183, 184, 244, 472
  for mouth infections, 294
Plaintain leaves, 153–54, 161, 250, 289–90
  for bite wounds, 121–22, 122*f*
Platelet activation factor (PAF), 213, 327
Poison control center, 366, 447, 450, 451, 457
Poison ivy, oak, sumac, 466–78
  first aid for, 470
  myth of immunity to, 469–70
  natural remedies for, 471–76
  prevention of, 476–78
Poisoning, 27, 264, 408, 443–64
  recovery from, 462–64
Polio vaccine, 102
Pollen, 100–01, 108, 112
Postural hypotension, 301–02, 306, 309–10, 312, 315
Potassium, 198, 225, 273, 274, 399
  and cramps, 442
Poultices
  for burns, 237, 239–40
  for cuts and scrapes, 170–72
  herbal, 34, 282, 490
  for snakebite, 133–34
Pregnancy, 10, 22, 24, 39, 55, 109, 268, 314, 487
Pregnant women, 198, 214, 393, 479
  fevers in, 412, 422, 424
  ginger for, 495
Pressure
  in treatment of deep wounds, 165–66
Pressure bandage, 166
Pressure point control, 166–68, 167*f*
Prevention, 5
  of allergic reactions, 111–14
  of animal bites, 125–26
  of asthma, 215–18
  of bone injuries, 201–03
  of burns, 245
  of chemical poisoning, 452–54
  of choking, 93
  of contusions, 259–61
  of convulsions and seizures, 272–78
  of croup, 221
  of dental emergencies, 296–98

of dizziness and fainting, 312–17
of drowning, 331–32
of ear emergencies, 381–84
of eye emergencies, 371–72
of food poisoning, 461–62
of heat illness, 400–02
of hemorrhoids, 180
of high-altitude sickness, 340–42
of hyperventilation, 225
of hypothermia, 356–58
of insect stings, 154–55
of jet lag, 499–504
of motion sickness, 497–98
of muscle/joint injuries, 439–42
of nosebleeds, 177–78
of poison ivy/oak, 476–78
of skin infections, 486–87
of snakebite, 134–35
of spider bites, 145–46
Propolis, 243, 293
Prostaglandins, 406
Pseudoephedrine, 42, 106
Pseudoginseng, 173–74
Psychoneuroimmunology, 15
Pulmonary edema, 324, 336–37
Pulsatilla, 312, 380, 423
Pulse, 80, 84, 182, 305
  neck, 81*f*
Puncture wounds, 119, 121, 166–68, 488, 489
Pyrexia. *See* Fever
Pyridoxine (B₆) antagonists, 274
Pyrrolizidine alkaloids, 39

Qi Li San, 256

Rabies, 116–17, 120, 125–26
Rape (seed/oil), 199
Rattlesnakes, 126, 127
Recommended daily allowances (RDAs), 23, 163, 197, 213, 276, 423–24
Recovery
  from acute poisoning, 462–64
  from allergic reactions, 111–14
  from animal bites, 122–25
  from bleeding episodes, 183–84
  from bone injuries, 195–201
  from burns, 244–45
  from contusions, 259–61
  from convulsions and seizures, 272–78
  from croup, 221
  from dental emergencies, 296–98
  from dizziness and fainting, 312–17
  from ear emergencies, 381–84
  from eye emergencies, 371–72
  from heat illness, 399
  from high-altitude sickness, 340–42

Recovery *(cont.)*
  from high fever, 425
  from hypothermia, 356–58
  from muscle/joint injuries, 434, 439–42
  from near-drowning, 326–31
  from nosebleed, 177–78
  from skin emergencies, 491–92
  from toxic bites/stings, 161–63
Recovery position, 82, 88, 93–94, 323, 447
Rectal bleeding, 179–80
Red Dan, 394
Reflexology, 17
Rehydration, 399, 425
Reishi, 114, 123, 124–25, 163, 313, 328, 421, 463
Relaxation, 214, 277, 498
Rescue, swimming, 320–21
Rescue breathing, 79, 80, 81–84, 83*f*, 86, 88, 92, 322, 323, 332
Rescue Remedy, 54–55, 96–97, 107, 272, 312
  for bone injuries, 193
  for dizziness, 307, 310
  for drowning, 325
  for hyperventilation, 224
  for hypothermia, 355–56
  for strings, 152
  for tooth trauma, 290
  for vertigo, 309
Respiratory boosters, 330
Rest, 249, 251
  with fever, 414
  for muscle injuries, 433
Reye's syndrome, 378, 417, 420
Rhus tox, 53, 253, 436, 473–74, 485
Riboflavin, 424
RICE (REST, ICE, COMPRESSION, ELEVATION)
  treatment for strains, ruptures, sprains, 433–35
Ringworm, 479, 481, 482, 485
Rock Rose, 224, 310–11
Rocky Mountain spotted fever, 139–40
Rolfers, 217
Rosemary, 316
Rosemary oil, 97, 98, 255, 307
Ruptures, 427, 431–42
Ruta, 53–54, 253

Sage oil, 277
St.-John's-wort, 244, 252
  oil of, 239
Salicin, 420
Salmonella, 455, 461
Salt tablets, 401–02
Salves/ointments
  herbs, 33

Schizandra, 313, 500
Scleranthus, 308–09, 496
Scopolamine, 371, 494
Scorpion bites, 135–46
Scorpions, 138–39, 144
Scrapes. *See* Cuts and scrapes
Sea creatures, stings from, 156
Sea vegetables, 198
Seat carry, 95
Seaweeds, 274
Sedatives, 71
Sensory triggers, 264
Seizures, 395
  with fever in children, 421
  in poisonings, 447
  types of, 263, 264–65
  see also Convulsions and seizures
Selenium, 244, 371, 492, 503
  and poisoning, 462, 463
Self-hypnosis, 5
Septic shock, 87, 292
Shepherd's purse, 170–71, 182–83
Shiatsu, 17
Shiitake, 114, 123, 124, 163, 328, 463
Shock, 27, 76, 84, 86–89, 96, 97, 105, 130, 147, 182, 187, 191, 230, 232, 301, 393
  basic treatment of, 87–89
  with burns, 235
  in heatstroke, 396
  in hypothermia, 351
  in near-drownings, 323
Shock position, 79, 88, 88*f*
Siberian ginseng, 313, 316, 440, 464, 473
  with exposure, 341–42
  for jet lag, 500–501
Side effects, 22, 101–02, 107
Silica, 261
Silica (Silicea), 294, 491
Silicon, 196–07, 297, 442, 492
Silymarin, 113, 463
Skin
  color of, 304
  freezing, 343–44, 345
  healthy, 487, 491
  poisons entering through, 444, 446
Skin emergencies, 465–92
  recovery from, 491–92
Skin infections, 478–87
  basic treatment for, 481–82
  natural remedies for, 482–86
  prevention of, 486–87
Skin irritation remedies, 475
Skin patch tests, 22, 55, 252, 430
Skin rash, 110
Skull cap, 276
Sling(s), 188–89
Slippery elm, 46, 472, 490

Smelling salts, 98, 307
Smoke, secondhand, 382
Snake oil, 25
Snake venom, 128–29, 130, 131
Snakebite, 126–35, 161–62
    first aid for, 129–31
    hospital treatment for, 132
    natural remedies for, 132–34
    preventing, 134–35
    severity of, 129
Snow blindness, 364–65
Sodium, 273, 274, 390
Spider bites, 135–46, 161–62
    first aid for, 143
    natural remedies for, 143–45
    preventing, 145–46
Spiders, 135–38
Spinal injuries. *See* Neck and spinal
        injuries
Spiritual healing, 5, 12
Splinters, 488–91
Splinting, 187–88
Spongia, 210, 220
Sports drinks, 389–90, 400, 414
Sprains, 427, 431–42, 440
    preventing, 441–42
Staphylococcus, 455, 479
Star fruit, 424–25
Star of Bethlehem, 311
Steroids, 107
Stifling atmosphere, 304, 311–12
Stimulants, 71, 225, 278
Sting-x-tractor, 148–49
Stinger, removing, 148–49
Stinging nettles, 109–10, 183, 198
Stings, 24, 110–11, 115–63, 408, 444
    first aid for, 149
    natural remedies for, 149–54
    recovery from, 161–63
    of sea creatures, 156
Stoneroot, 179–80
Strains, 427, 431–42
    preventing, 441–42
Streptococcus, 479, 480
Stress, 206, 225, 278
Stretcher, 96
Styptics, 170–72
Sulphur, 474
Sunburn, 228–30
    corneal, 364–65
Sunlight, 202, 500
Sunscreens, 229
Sunstroke. *See* Heatstroke
Sweat therapy, 418, 420–21
Sweating, 386, 387, 390, 391, 395, 400,
        401, 410
Swedish Bitters, 151
Swimmer's ear, 376

Symphytum, 194, 200

Tabacum, 496
Tablets, capsules, lozenges, 33
Tarantulas, 136, 138
Taurine, 273
Tea bags, 230, 289, 295, 368
Tea tree, 59–60
Tea Tree oil, 120, 121, 142, 242, 286, 293,
        298, 331
    for ear infections, 376
    for frostbite, 350
    for insect bites/stings, 161
    for poisoning, 474
    for skin infections, 482–83
    for spider bites, 144
Teas, 32, 221, 237
Teeth, loose, cracked, 287–91
Teething, 284–87
Temporomandibular joint (TMJ) syn-
        drome, 280, 301
Tendons, 426, 432, 440
Tepid-water immersion, 412, 416
Tetanus, 117–18, 120, 137
Tetanus, vaccine, 102
Thermal burns
    of the eyes, 365–68
Therapeutic massage, 5
Thiamin, 158–59
Tick bites, 135–46
Tick paralysis, 139, 140
Ticks, 139–42, 146
    removing, 141–42
Tiger Balm, 257, 349, 429
Tinctures
    herbal, 33
Toes
    broken, 188
    crushed, 251
Tonics, 418, 419
Tooth trauma
    natural remedies for, 289–91
Toothache, 279–84, 294
    first aid for, 280–81
    natural remedies for, 281–84
Toothpaste, 298
Topical medications
    for skin infections, 481–82
Touch, 325–26
Tourniquets, 130, 131, 165
Toxic substances, 52, 443–54
Toxins, 407
Trace elements, 163
    and fever, 423–24
    and seizure disorders, 276
Trace-mineral supplement, 163
Trace minerals, 11–12, 196–97, 198, 213,
        297

Traditional wisdom, 5
Transporting injured person, 94–96
Trauma, 93
  to teeth, 279, 280
Travel problems, 493–504
Trichophyton, 481
Triple Warmer, 347, 348f
Tryptophan, 502–03
Tui-na, 17
Tumeric, 437–38, 459
Tyrosine, 340–41

Ultrasound, 201
Ultraviolet light, 228, 229
Unconsciousness, 77–78, 79, 84, 88, 147,
    186, 299, 303
  in convulsions/seizures, 262, 265
  in drowning, 325
  first aid for, 97–98
  in poisonings, 447, 449
Urtica, (Urtica urens), 110, 240
Urushiol, 468–69, 470, 477
Usnea, 172

Vaccines, vaccinations, 264
  allergic reactions to, 101–02, 113
  rabies, 117
  tetanus toxoid, 117
Valerian, 224, 276, 285
Vasodilators, 347, 349
Venom
  bee, 146, 147, 148, 155
  snake, 128–29, 130, 131
Venomous snakes, 126–28, 127f
Venomous spiders, 136–38, 143
Veratrum (Veratrum album), 182, 394, 451
Vertigo, 300, 306, 308–09, 312, 314
  chronic, 308
Vinegar, 68, 161, 177, 229, 485
Viral infections, 480, 484, 486
Viruses, 406, 407
Vital energy, 394
Vitamin A, 24, 62, 63, 113
  and brain function, 275
  toxicity, 444
Vitamin A/beta carotene, 23, 122, 196,
    212, 221, 244, 297, 326, 371, 382,
    424, 474, 487, 492, 503
Vitamin B complex, 113, 122, 159, 212,
    244, 315, 326, 358, 370, 371,
    382, 424, 442, 474, 487, 492
  and contusions, 260
  and poisonings, 463
Vitamin B_6, 358, 370, 442, 497, 503
  and convulsions/seizures, 274
Vitamin B_{12}, 183, 492
Vitamin C, 23, 24, 25, 61–62, 63, 161,
    196, 216, 221, 247, 297, 371

for bites/stings, 162
for burns, 237, 239
and exposure, 341
and poisoning, 462, 463
Vitamin C/bioflavonoids, 113, 114, 177,
    183, 212, 244, 326, 370, 382,
    424, 442, 487, 492, 503
  and brain function, 275–76
  and contusions, 259–60
  for mild allergic reactions, 109
  for muscle/joint injuries, 438
  for poisoning, 459
  for skin problems, 474
  for snakebite, 133
Vitamin D, 23, 24, 196, 202, 228, 297,
    370, 442
Vitamin E, 23–24, 62–63, 113, 114, 122,
    212, 221, 224, 260, 326, 371, 503
  for burns, 237, 238–39
  and convulsions/seizures, 274
  and cramps, 441
  and dizziness, 315
  and exposure, 341
  and poisoning, 462, 463
  for skin problems, 474
Vitamin E oil, 143, 161, 178, 184, 239,
    240, 295, 298, 476
  for bites/stings, 162
  for skin infections, 486
Vitamin K, 177, 183, 247, 252, 259
Vitamins, 23–24, 114, 163, 198
  and asthma, 212–13
  in childhood poisonings, 444–45, 453,
    454
  and croup, 221
  and eye emergencies, 371
  and fever, 423–24
  first-aid, 60–63
  for near drowning victims, 326–27
  and seizure disorders, 274–76
Vomiting, 77, 87
  inducing, 448–49, 450

Walking assist, 95
Walnut, 287
Wan Hua, 257–58, 438
Warm treatment
  for toothache, 281
Warts, 480, 482, 485, 486
Wasp stings, 146–55
Watermelon, 398, 476
Watermelon Frost formula, 294–95
White Flower Analgesic Balm, 257, 282,
    349–50, 429
Wildcrafting, 32, 35
Willow, 419–20
Witch hazel, 46–47, 171, 179, 183, 252,
    398, 472, 484

Wound healers, 72, 170–72
Wounds, deep, 164, 165–68

Xanthine preparations, 208
Yarrow, 47–48, 170, 183, 244, 282, 418
  and fever, 420
  for frostbite, 347
  for tooth trauma, 289–90
Yellow dock, 154, 472
Ylang-ylang, 224
Yoga, 214, 216–17, 278, 329, 383–84
Yunnan Paiyao, 173–74, 256

Zarontin, 269
Zheng Gu Shui, 255–56
Zhu ling, 125
Zinc, 12, 114, 158, 183, 196, 244, 261,
    273, 297, 326, 371–72, 382, 442,
    487, 492, 503
  for skin problems, 474
Zinc lozenges, 221
Zinc oxide, 229
Zoopharmacognosy, 8

About the Advisory Panel

David and **Holly Eagle,** both of whom are Doctors of Oriental Medicine and licensed acupuncturists, have been working with Oriental medicine for over twenty years. They incorporate Chinese and Western herbology, acupuncture, conventional medicine, homeotherapeutics, and nutrition into their clinical practice. They are professional consultants for the K'an Herb company and lecture and teach widely on Chinese medicine. With Kiiko Matsumoto they have coauthored a professional text on acupuncture techniques for trauma. The Eagles practice at Ancient Roots Medical in Santa Cruz, California, where they specialize in the treatment of advanced chronic diseases, difficult pregnancies, and childhood illnesses.

Michael Reed Gach is the founder and director of the Acupressure Institute in Berkeley, California. He has been studying and developing acupressure techniques for common ailments for twenty years. Gach is the author of *Acupressure's Potent Points, Acu-Yoga, Arthritis Relief at Your Fingertips, The Bum Back Book*, and other books, as well as audio and videotapes on acupressure self-help techniques. He teaches at Kaiser Permanente Medical Center and conducts acupressure practitioner trainings throughout the United States.

Christopher Hobbs is a fourth-generation herbalist and botanist with more than twenty years' experience with herbs. Founder of Native Herb Custom Extracts (now Rainbow Light Custom Extracts) and the Institute for Natural Products Research, Hobbs writes and lectures internationally on herbal medicine. He is a consultant to the herb industry and practices in Santa Cruz, California. He is the author of numerous monographs and books on herbs, including *Ginkgo: Elixir of Youth, Medicinal Mushrooms*, and *Foundations of Health: The Liver and Digestive Herbal*.

Jennifer Jacobs, M.D., M.P.H., is a homeopathic family physician who practices in Edmonds, Washington. She is a past president of the International Foundation for Homeopathy and for the past ten years has been an instructor in its year-long course for health professionals. Dr. Jacobs is a research fellow in epidemiology at the University of Washington, where she has done work on the homeopathic treatment of childhood diarrhea. She was recently appointed to represent homeopathy on the National Institutes of Health Panel on Alternative Medicine.

Shari Lieberman, Ph.D., R.D., C.N.S., is a clinical nutritionist with a private practice in New York City. She holds a doctorate in clinical nutrition and exercise physiology and is a registered dietitian and certified nutrition specialist. She is the nutritional consultant for the nationally syndicated "Home Shopping Network" show as well as for several companies. She writes frequently on diet and health for national publications and is the coauthor of *The Real Vitamin & Mineral Book.*

Joseph Pizzorno, N.D. (Doctor of Naturopathy), is the founding president of Bastyr College in Seattle, one of the world's foremost accredited colleges of natural medicine. He is the coauthor of the definitive *Encyclopedia of Natural Medicine* and *A Textbook of Natural Medicine.*

Andrew Weil, M.D., is a graduate of Harvard Medical School, a medical and botanical researcher, and a practicing physician. He is a regular columnist for *Natural Health* magazine and an internationally known lecturer on topics relating to wellness and self-care, conventional and alternative medicine, and mind-active drugs. He is the author of *Natural Health, Natural Medicine; Health and Healing; The Natural Mind; The Marriage of the Sun and Moon;* and (with Winifred Rosen) *From Chocolate to Morphine.* Dr. Weil teaches at the University of Arizona College of Medicine and lives in Tucson.

About the Authors

Mark Mayell worked at *Natural Health* for twelve years, including seven years as editor of the magazine and two years as editor of *Natural Health*'s book publishing division. He has also served as the editor of *Nutrition Action*, the monthly newsletter of the Washington, D.C., nutrition advocacy group Center for Science in the Public Interest. He has written extensively on alternative approaches to health for *Natural Health, Utne Reader,* and other magazines and is on the Board of Advisors of the American Holistic Health Association. Mark has a master's degree in philosophy and social policy from George Washington University. He currently lives with his wife and two children in the Boston area, where he is working on another book for *Natural Health,* to be titled *52 Steps to Natural Health.*

About *Natural Health* Magazine

Natural Health: The Guide to Well-Being (formerly *East West Journal*) has been the leading national magazine on alternative health, herbalism, bodywork, personal growth, and natural foods for over two decades. *Natural Health* provides more than half a million readers in the United States and around the world with practical information on health and longevity. As a recent magazine review by *USA Today* noted, *Natural Health* "is far too splendid to be confined to a health-food store shelf."

Among the magazine's awards for coverage of issues relating to natural health is the 1989 Alternative Press Award for Service Journalism. *Natural Health* is one of only three magazines listed under the Health and Nutrition Magazines category in *The New York Public Library's Desk Reference: The Ultimate One-Volume Collection of the Most Frequently Sought Information.*

The editors of *Natural Health* have written numerous books on natural healing and whole-foods cooking, including *World Medicine; Quick and Natural Rice Dishes; Meetings with Remarkable Men and Women: Interviews with Leading Thinkers on Health, Medicine, Ecology, Culture, Society, and Spirit; Sweet and Natural Desserts; Shopper's Guide to Natural Foods;* and *Natural Childcare.*

Natural Health is produced bimonthly in Brookline, Massachusetts, by a staff of twenty-five. For subscription information write or call Natural Health, 17 Station St., P.O. Box 1200, Brookline Village, MA 02147; (617) 232-1000.

EMERGENCY PHONE NUMBERS

Poison Control Center _____

Fire Department _____

Police Department _____